small arms survey
2005

---

weapons at war

HEI

A Project
of the Graduate Institute
of International Studies,
Geneva

OXFORD

UNIVERSITY PRESS

Great Clarendon Street, Oxford OX2 6DP

Oxford University Press is a department of the University of Oxford.
It furthers the University's objective of excellence in research, scholarship,
and education by publishing worldwide in

Oxford New York

Auckland Cape Town Dar es Salaam Hong Kong Karachi
Kuala Lumpur Madrid Melbourne Mexico City Nairobi
New Dehli Shanghai Taipei Toronto

With offices in

Argentina Austria Brazil Chile Czech Republic France Greece
Guatemala Hungary Italy Japan Poland Portugal Singapore
South Korea Switzerland Thailand Turkey Ukraine Vietnam

Oxford is a registered trade mark of Oxford University Press
in the UK and in certain other countries

Published in the United States
by Oxford University Press Inc., New York

British Library Cataloguing in Publication Data

Data available

Library of Congress Cataloging in Publication Data

Data available

Typeset in Garamond Light by Latitudesign
Printed in Great Britain
on acid-free paper
by Ashford Colour Press Limited
Gosport, Hampshire

ISBN 0-19-928085-1   978-0-19-928085-8

1 3 5 7 9 10 8 6 4 2

FOREWORD

The twentieth century was the most violent in human history, killing more than 200 million people in hundreds of conflicts: wars of aggression, ideological wars, and genocidal massacres prominent among them. How will the new century compare? There has been an encouraging decline in the number of conflicts, but at the beginning of 2005 there were still at least 23 armed conflicts under way around the world, many of them long-standing, and with almost a dozen recently ended conflicts at particular risk of returning to open warfare.

In the new century, armed conflict is a particularly complex phenomenon. It is often fought between parties within a single nation, or across many states between non-state armed groups that share ideological, ethnic, or religious goals. Combatants are rarely enlisted soldiers beholden to international humanitarian law. We witness the frequent targeting of civilians—including women and children—and the use of terror against whole communities for strategic goals.

Despite their complexities, the vast majority of today's conflicts share at least one important feature: they are fought primarily with small arms and light weapons. Small arms are responsible for the majority of deaths inflicted in combat. They also facilitate the forced displacement that leads to even more death from disease and malnutrition.

The international community has made slow but steady progress in preventing the outbreak, escalation, and recurrence of conflict around the world. But informed policy responses are urgently needed and, in this context, a solid understanding of the role of small arms and light weapons is indispensable. Obtaining an accurate picture of the use, impact, sourcing, and trade—both legal and illicit—of these weapons is essential to our ability to understand and resolve current conflicts and prevent future ones from erupting.

The *Small Arms Survey 2005: Weapons at War* provides a detailed account of small arms in conflicts, including their production, transfer to war zones, use in conflicts, and efforts to reduce stockpiles and civilian possession when peace seems within reach. It is an invaluable resource for states and international organizations working to prevent suffering, encourage development, and improve human security.

Gareth Evans
President and CEO
International Crisis Group
April 2005

Contents

ABOUT THE SMALL ARMS SURVEY

The Small Arms Survey is an independent research project located at the Graduate Institute of International Studies in Geneva, Switzerland. Established in 1999 with the generous financial support of the Swiss Federal Department of Foreign Affairs, it currently receives additional funding from Australia, Canada, Denmark, Finland, France, the Netherlands, New Zealand, Norway, Sweden, and the United Kingdom.

The objectives of the Small Arms Survey are: to be the principal source of public information on all aspects of small arms; to serve as a resource centre for governments, policy-makers, researchers, and activists; to monitor national and international initiatives (governmental and non-governmental) on small arms; and to act as a clearing house for the sharing of information and the dissemination of best practices. The Survey also sponsors field research and information-gathering efforts, especially in affected states and regions. The project has an international staff with expertise in security studies, political science, law, economics, development studies, and sociology. It collaborates with a worldwide network of researchers, partner institutions, non-governmental organizations, and governments.

Notes to readers

Abbreviations: Topic-specific lists of abbreviations are placed at the end of each chapter.

Chapter cross-referencing: Chapter cross-references appear capitalized in brackets throughout the text. For example, in Chapter 9: 'Small arms proliferation and misuse also continues to be a significant cause of direct deaths in post-conflict settings, where violence levels can linger at elevated levels after the fighting has stopped (POST-CONFLICT).'

Exchange rates: All monetary values are expressed in current US dollars (USD). When other currencies are additionally cited, unless otherwise indicated, they are converted to USD using the 365-day average exchange rate for the period 1 September 2003 to 31 August 2004.

Small Arms Survey: The plain text—Small Arms Survey—is used to indicate the overall project and its activities, while the italicized version—*Small Arms Survey*—refers to the publication itself. The *Survey,* appearing italicized, refers generally to past and future editions of the yearbook.

Web site: For more detailed information and current developments on small arms issues, readers are invited to visit the Small Arms Survey Web site at: <http://www.smallarmssurvey.org>

Small Arms Survey

Graduate Institute of International Studies

47, Avenue Blanc

1202 Geneva, Switzerland

Tel.: +41 22 908 57 77

Fax: +41 22 732 27 38

Email: smallarm@hei.unige.ch

Web site: www.smallarmssurvey.org

ACKNOWLEDGEMENTS

This is the fifth edition of the *Small Arms Survey*. It is a collective product of the staff of the Small Arms Survey project, based at the Graduate Institute of International Studies in Geneva, Switzerland. A large number of researchers in Geneva and elsewhere have contributed to this volume, and it has benefited from the input and advice of a number of government officials, activists, experts, and colleagues from around the world who form part of the growing small arms research community.

The principal chapter authors were assisted by a large number of in-house and external contributors who are acknowledged in the relevant chapters.

In addition, detailed comments on the chapters were provided by: Jurgen Brauer, David Capie, David DeClerq, Louise Doswald-Beck, Anna Di Lellio, Jeremy Ginifer, William Godnick, Iain Hall, Macartan Humphreys, Neil MacFarlane, Colin Mathers, Caroline Moser, Carol Nelson, Ryan Nichols, Wolf-Christian Paes, Pablo Policzer, Michael Pugh, Les Roberts, Christiana Solomon, Reinhilde Weidacher, Jeremy Weinstein, Siemon Wezeman, and Adrian Wilkinson.

Eric G. Berman, Keith Krause, and David Mutimer were responsible for the overall planning and organization of this volume. Emile LeBrun and Glenn McDonald provided valuable editorial inputs during the in-house review process. Tania Inowlocki managed the editing and production of the *Survey*; she, Michael James, and Richard Jones copy-edited the book. Nicoletta Forni provided the layout and design; Donald Strachan proofread the *Survey*; and Lisa Kenwright of Indexing Specialists (UK) compiled the index.

Dominic Byatt and Claire Croft of Oxford University Press provided support and encouragement throughout the production of the Survey. Anne-Kathrin Glatz, Sahar Hasan, Stéphanie Pézard, and Ruxandra Stoicescu assisted with research. Delphine Zinner, Fridrich Štrba, and Carole Touraine provided administrative support.

The project also benefited from the support of personnel of the Graduate Institute of International Studies, in particular Philippe Burrin, Jasmine Champenois, Andrew Clapham, Wilfred Gander, Oliver Jütersonke, and Nicole Mouthon.

We are extremely grateful to the Swiss Government for its generous financial and overall support of the Small Arms Survey project, in particular Heidi Grau, Thomas Greminger, Laurent Masmejean, Peter Maurer, Marc Stritt, Anton Thalmann, and Stefano Vescovi. Financial support for the project was also provided by the Governments of Australia, Canada, Denmark, Finland, France, the Netherlands, New Zealand, Norway, Sweden, and the United Kingdom. The project has also received financial support for various research projects from the Geneva International Academic Network (GIAN), the Organisation Internationale de la Francophonie, the United Nations Development Programme (UNDP), and the South Eastern Europe Clearinghouse for the Control of Small Arms and Light Weapons (SEESAC). The project further benefits from the assistance and support of a number of governmental and international agencies, including the International Committee of the Red Cross, the UN Department for Disarmament Affairs, the UN Institute for Disarmament Research, and the World Health Organization.

In Geneva, the project has received support and expert advice from: David Atwood, Prosper Bani, Peter Batchelor, Cate Buchanan, Christophe Carle, Martin Griffiths, Randall Harbour, Magnus Hellgren, Peter Herby, Yann Hwang, Yudit Kiss, Elli Kytömäki, Patricia Lewis, Bennie Lombard, Merete Lundemo, Harri Mäki-Reinikka, Patrick McCarthy, David Meddings, Jennifer Milliken, Johan Nordenfelt, Geraldine O'Callaghan, Ann Pollack, Daniël Prins, Fred Tanner, Peter Truswell, and Camilla Waszink.

Beyond Geneva, we also received support from a number of colleagues. In addition to those mentioned above, and in specific chapters, we would like to thank: Pete Abel, Lina Abu Nuwar, Philip Alpers, Antonio Rangel Bandeira, Ilhan Berkol, Michael Brzoska, Peter Croll, Spyros Demetriou, Pablo Dreyfus, Paul Eavis, Kristine Eck, Sami Faltas, Rubem César Fernandes, William Godnick, Björn Hagelin, Roy Isbister, Kaste Joseph, Joakim Kreutz, Guy Lamb, Christopher Langton, Edward Laurance, Patricia Leidl, Andrew Mack, Nicolas Marsh, Sarah Meek, Lisa Misol, Colleen Mone, Yeshua Moser-Puangsuwan, Pasi Patokallio, Rebecca Peters, Jorge Restrepo, Stina Torjesen, Hanna Ucko, Peter Whelan, and Brian Wood.

Our sincere thanks go out to many other individuals (who remain unnamed) for their continuing support of the project. We also express our apologies to anyone we have forgotten to mention.

Keith Krause
Programme Director

Eric G. Berman
Managing Director

Principal Chapter Authors

Introduction
Keith Krause with David Mutimer
Chapter 1
Stéphanie Pézard
Chapter 2
James Bevan
Chapter 3
Aaron Karp
Chapter 4
Anna Khakee
Chapter 5
Glenn McDonald
'Shooting Gallery'
Katie Kennedy
Chapter 6
Anna Khakee with
Nicolas Florquin
Chapter 7
James Bevan
Chapter 8
Stephanie Schwandner-Sievers
with Silvia Cattaneo
Chapter 9
Christina Wille with Keith Krause
Chapter 10
Robert Muggah
Chapter 11
Eric G. Berman

Small Arms Survey 2005

Editors
Eric G. Berman and Keith Krause
Yearbook Coordinators
Glenn McDonald
and David Mutimer
Publications Manager
Tania Inowlocki
Editorial Consultant
Emile LeBrun
Layout and Design
Latitudesign
Copy-editors
Tania Inowlocki, Michael James,
and Richard Jones

Sudan People's Liberation Army
troops pass by the skulls of
government soldiers on the
road near Kapoeta
(© Martin Adler/Panos Pictures)

Introduction

One of the core motivating factors behind the creation of the Small Arms Survey in 1999 was the need for a better understanding of the use and impacts of small arms—including in armed conflict. In the first four editions of the annual *Small Arms Survey,* as well as in numerous other publications, the Survey has pursued this mandate by exploring many facets of small arms, from their production, trade, regulation, and misuse to their particular roles in different states and regions.

The fifth edition of the *Small Arms Survey* focuses on the direct and indirect role of small arms in contemporary violent conflicts. As such, this volume develops in depth one important strand of work begun at the project's inception. It describes the many ways in which small arms and light weapons threaten human life and well-being in collective violence, while also focusing how these weapons are implicated in the origins, exacerbation, and aftermath of violent conflict. The *Small Arms Survey: Weapons at War* explores these themes in places such as the Democratic Republic of the Congo (DRC), Indonesia, Rwanda, Sierra Leone, Sudan, and the former Yugoslavia—where armed conflicts have formed the backdrop against which efforts to combat the proliferation and misuse of weapons have unfolded.

The connections between small arms availability and violent conflicts are complex and multifaceted. Chapters in this *Small Arms Survey* show that there is no clear-cut relationship between the supply of weapons and the outbreak of conflict, no easy way to assess the number of deaths caused by small arms in conflict, and no simple solution to coping with weapons in the aftermath of conflict. But as various chapters point out, practical and cost-effective control measures can be designed to curb the misuse of weapons at different points in the chain that leads from the production of a weapon to its use in conflict.

Before any consideration of armed conflict—and the roles small arms play in conflict—can take place, three important issues must be addressed:

- What should count as armed conflict?
- What types of deaths should count as 'caused' by armed conflict?
- What are the ways in which small arms cause conflict deaths?

Contemporary conflict dynamics

The dynamics of modern conflicts are complex, and often do not feature any of the traditional 'markers' of war. In many cases there are 'no fronts, no campaigns, no bases, no uniforms, no publicly displayed honors, no *points d'appui,* and no respect for the territorial limits of states' (Holsti, 1999, p. 36). Another feature of modern war is the preponderance of civilian casualties. From the Thirty Years War of the 17th century—which is estimated to have caused the deaths of one-third of the population of Central Europe (Limm, 1984)—to the two World Wars as well as numerous civil wars and humanitarian catastrophes throughout the 20th century, the civilian population has suffered mightily from violent conflict.

1

'War' is also a politically fraught term—is the political violence in places such as Colombia or the Philippines a 'war,' a 'violent conflict', a 'rebel movement', or something else? Is the 'war on terror' a war? These distinctions have political nuances and legal consequences (concerning the applicability of international humanitarian law and state responsibility, for example). The difficulty in capturing the shifting nature of contemporary war should not, however, prevent analysts from being precise about what is (or is not) being studied.

Although there are competing definitions of what constitutes 'war' or 'violent conflict' (CONFLICT DEATHS), the *Small Arms Survey* defines violent conflict as widely as possible, without regard for precise legal or political distinctions, for two reasons. First, because it is important to study differences or similarities in the ways small arms and light weapons are used in both large- and small-scale conflicts. Small arms are, of course, used in the most intense and violent conflicts, but they may be relatively more important (in terms of death, injury, and insecurity) in smaller or less intense violent conflicts. Indeed, from the point of view of small arms misuse, a clear delineation between 'violent conflict' and other forms of violence (large-scale criminal activity, for example) may not be possible.

Further, the human suffering caused by small arms and light weapons should not be disregarded because it fails to meet an arbitrary body-count threshold, or because one or more of the parties is not a state. Indeed, it is important to include low-level violence (such as in Nigeria), conflicts in which the state does not play a direct role (such as in Papua New Guinea), and those in which the state preys on its citizens without declaring war (such as in Guatemala between 1960 and 1996).

The *Small Arms Survey* thus follows the World Health Organization's definition of collective violence, amending it only to add the word 'armed'. Collective violence thus is:

> the instrumental use of [armed] violence by people who identify themselves as members of a group—whether this group is transitory or has a more permanent identity—against another group or set of individuals, in order to achieve political, economic or social objectives (Krug et al., 2002, p. 215).

This definition takes armed conflict not as *sui generis*, but as a category of collective violence. In this way, the *Small Arms Survey* situates armed conflict within the context of a range of violent practices—armed and unarmed, collective and individual—all of which result in the loss of life.

Measuring armed conflict deaths

Quantifying the human costs of conflict is one of the most important—and challenging—tasks for the researcher studying armed violence. At first glance, data abounds. But a clear understanding of what is being counted is essential to an accurate evaluation of data and sound policy recommendations. Recent reports have publicized figures such as 3.8 million deaths in DRC since 1998, 100,000 estimated excess deaths in Iraq since 2003, and 345,000–385,000 possible deaths in Darfur, Sudan, since February 2003. These numbers recognize that the human cost of violent conflict cannot merely reflect the number of people who are directly killed in fighting, but must include *indirect* mortality caused by conflict. Other, much lower, estimates, such as the 27,000–51,000 people who are estimated to have died in wars worlwide in 2002 and 2003, are based on tracking only *direct* victims of armed violence.

These numbers do not contradict each other, but they do count different things. As the chapter on death in conflict shows, indirect deaths make up the vast majority of victims in recent wars in such places as DRC and Sudan—

potentially up to 80 per cent (CONFLICT DEATHS). These people die from dysentery, malaria, or other preventable causes when they lose access to basic health care and essential services as they flee their towns and villages, and as violent conflict grinds down or eliminates the infrastructure of basic services. The failure to distinguish between direct and indirect conflict deaths sows confusion in many debates about the impacts and implications of current conflicts.

The distinction between direct and indirect deaths is, however, ultimately an academic one. To the people affected by violent conflict, it matters little whether the death of a child or partner was caused by a bullet, or by disease or starvation because the family was forced to flee its home. It is important—as epidemiological studies of conflict zones show—to count all deaths from violent conflict, and not simply to focus on those caused by the use of violent means, on combatants or civilians.

Capturing the role of small arms

Small arms have been a feature of modern warfare for hundreds of years, but their role in modern conflict mortality has been difficult to measure. The *Small Arms Survey 2005* estimates that between 60 and 90 per cent of direct deaths in violent conflicts are caused by small arms. It is not possible to develop a more precise, or average, figure, since the variation depends on the nature and scope of the particular conflict. Conflicts in which civilians are directly targeted, or in which small arms and light weapons are more widely available than other arms, or in which the tactics of the combatants impose their use, are more likely to have a higher proportion of direct deaths from small arms (CONFLICT USE). Other major causes of direct conflict deaths include bombing, the use of informal explosive devices, and major conventional weapons systems.

The role of small arms in conflict deaths is not limited to direct deaths, however. A full assessment of the use of small arms in conflict finds that they are implicated in even more indirect deaths. While small arms cause direct conflict deaths in a straightforward way—through fatal wounds and injuries caused by bullets or other projectiles—they cause indirect conflict deaths in a different way. Just as a heat wave kills indirectly through heart failure, dehydration, or other factors (but seldom as a direct result of 'heat'), small arms conflict contributes to deaths indirectly through disease, starvation, and the destruction of health infrastructure. Though people may not die from bullet wounds, weapons are ultimately responsible for their deaths.

In the case of small arms, it is practically impossible to test the counterfactual: 'If the small arms were not present (or were present in lower numbers) but the conflict still occurred, how many people would have died?' But the availability of weapons encourages some individuals and groups to resort to violence instead of relying on non-violent means of resolving conflicts or achieving their goals. As the quantity and quality of small arms diminish, the intensity and levels of violence associated with armed conflict is also reduced. Furthermore, it appears that the availability of ammunition, the lethality of the available weapons, and the possibilities for resupply can also affect violence levels, though this has yet to be demonstrated systematically. These points are discussed in various chapters of the *Small Arms Survey 2005*, and although it may not be possible to quantify the exact magnitude of the human tragedy caused by the proliferation and misuse of small arms and light weapons, it is possible to outline more precisely their role in contemporary armed conflicts.

Chapter highlights

The *Small Arms Survey 2005* departs from the format of previous editions by being divided into two sections. The first consists of chapters that (as in previous years) provide new or updated information on global small arms production, stockpiles, transfers, and international measures. This year, the *Survey* includes an introductory overview of small arms ammunition, an issue receiving growing international attention.

The second section is dedicated to issues surrounding armed conflict and its aftermath, including the sourcing of weapons to violent conflicts, weapons use, small arms and conflict deaths, and post-conflict disarmament, demobilization, and reintegration. This section is rounded out with two case studies: one exploring the concept of 'gun culture' in the illustrative case of Kosovo, and another focusing on the Central African Republic. Between the update and conflict sections is a survey of contemporary artistic representations of arms and armed violence.

Update chapters

Chapter 1 (Ammunition): Small arms ammunition presents a range of problems of proliferation and misuse analogous to those of the arms themselves. There are legal and illicit users of ammunition, and diversion to conflict zones is common. Despite its critical role in violence in both conflict and armed crime, however, ammunition has been neglected in measures to address small arms proliferation and misuse. This chapter surveys the state of knowledge on a range of small arms ammunition issues, including production, trade, regulations, stockpiling, and disposal.

The chapter also explores the impact of ammunition availability on small arms use, particularly in conflict areas, and highlights the arguments for enhanced control measures. It finds that although ammunition is occasionally included in small arms measures, real control strategies have yet to be developed at the national, regional, and international levels.

Chapter 2 (Production): Unlike previous *Survey* chapters, this year's products and producers chapter investigates what constitutes the 'small arms industry', a label that covers a wide range of firms, some of which dedicate only a small part of their operations to weapons-related production. Based on information obtained from 349 firms, this study divides the industry into sectors based on product type, production method, capacity, target markets, and other factors. This sectoral approach is illustrated with descriptions of specific firms in the United States and elsewhere. It parallels studies of other industries and is a first step to more thorough analysis, policy-making, and research on the subject.

Chapter 3 (Stockpiles): Increasing international momentum to counter small arms proliferation and misuse helped bring to the fore state efforts to manage small arms stockpiles in 2004. The reductions from weapon collections and destruction, however, were overshadowed by new acquisitions, and some regions were only marginally engaged in reduction efforts.

Completing the *Small Arms Survey's* region-by-region analysis of national stockpiles begun in 2001, the chapter also estimates weapons holdings in two regions that have so far not been closely scrutinized: the Middle East and north-east Asia. The Middle East is thought to be home to 58 to 107 million small arms, the majority of which (45 million to 90 million) are owned by civilians. A preliminary assessment finds that military and police forces in north-east Asia have access to about 22 to 42 million small arms and light weapons, while numbers of civilian small arms in the region remain an enigma. Lack of transparency about holdings in countries in both regions means these estimates are only tentative.

Chapter 4 (Transfers): Poor state transparency in arms transfers continues to preclude a full understanding of the international authorized trade in small arms. This chapter updates the analysis of the global authorized small arms trade through UN Comtrade data, with a particular focus on major exporters and importers, types of small arms traded, and total values for the year 2002. The global trade in 2002 closely resembles the picture previously provided, with the United States, Italy, Brazil, Germany, the Russian Federation, and China the most significant exporters, and the United States, Cyprus, Saudi Arabia, and South Korea topping the list of importers.

An analysis of available customs seizure data suggests that most illicit small arms trafficking takes the form of small-scale transfers. The spottiness of seizure information is surprising, however, given the international community's focus on the illicit trade. Finally, the chapter updates the Small Arms Trade Transparency Barometer, this year identifying the United States, Germany, and the United Kingdom as the most transparent exporters, and Israel as the least transparent. Two aspects of the small arms trade call out in particular for better transparency: government-to-government transactions and the identification of end users for exports.

Chapter 5 (Measures): Although most policy attention is focused on small arms, global and international measures also tend to cover light weapons, either explicitly or implicitly. One category of light weapons, man-portable air defence systems (MANPADS), has received considerable attention, and the Wassenaar Arrangement and Organization for Security and Co-operation in Europe have recently taken bold steps to curb MANPADS proliferation through the development of stringent control measures.

The emerging strong international framework to deal with MANPADS still requires national implementation of standards. The transfer control systems of key exporting states can readily support the implementation of these new measures and, encouragingly, these same systems can also be used to control strictly the transfer of a broader range of small arms and light weapons.

Contemporary art section ('Shooting Gallery'): This year the *Small Arms Survey* delves into the visual arts for the first time. Showcasing 17 recent works from a diverse group of artists—from the legendary Andy Warhol to today's emerging performance artists—'Shooting Gallery' explores how contemporary artists respond to the issue of small arms. Using a variety of media—from paint, photography, and sculpture to video and performance pieces—the artists scrutinize the gun itself, its components, the evidence of its presence, and the symbolism behind it. They consider how arms appear—or fail to be noticed—in the news media and film footage; the role of small arms in 'shoot'em-up' video games; how arms are employed by states and powerful actors; and the loss of life and ensuing grief due to routine armed violence. This section's exploration of the role of the gun in themes as diverse as murder, loss, militarization, empowerment, protection, insecurity, and the numbing of society to violence adds a cultural dimension to research on the impact of small arms on society.

Armed conflict chapters

Chapter 6 (Conflict Sourcing): Because of its likelihood to contribute to death and suffering, conflict sourcing is a major concern for the international community. Examining selected recent and current internal conflicts in Africa, the Americas, Central Asia, and the Caucasus, this chapter identifies routine sourcing patterns. Through corruption, theft, and seizure, government stockpiles constitute an important source of arms in virtually all conflict zones; sometimes they represent the dominant source for all combatants. Conflict weapons are also commonly sourced by a steady cross-border trickle of weapons (the 'ant trade') that can generate large stocks over time. While less common, local production can also be a source of supply. Small arms procurement patterns often become more sophisticated and diversified over the course of a conflict. The chapter highlights the need to add issues such as border control and corruption to the international agenda.

Chapter 7 (Conflict Use): How exactly are small arms and light weapons used in armed conflicts? What factors affect combatants' choices of weapons and targets? While the use of small arms in conflict encompasses a broad range of social phenomena—from group dynamics to masculine identities—this chapter focuses in particular on factors that facilitate or inhibit the most indiscriminate forms of armed violence. Factors affecting weapons use include material controls on where weapons can be used and for what purpose; availability factors, such as size, weight, and capacity of the weapons; and organizational factors, such as social constraints and shared understandings of acceptable limits to armed violence.

A better understanding of the primary factors affecting the use of weapons in conflict can aid efforts to prevent the worst forms of armed violence. Promising options include targeting the most destructive weapons first in disarmament, demobilization, and reintegration (DDR) programmes; limiting the production and transfer of particularly destructive light weapons; and enhancing stockpile and trafficking controls to cut off the sources of the most destructive weapons available to combatants.

Chapter 8 (Gun Culture): Permissive 'gun cultures' are sometimes assumed to contribute inexorably to armed violence. This chapter challenges this assumption through a case study of Kosovo in the 1990s, and brief studies of conflicts in El Salvador, Georgia, Kyrgyzstan, and Tajikistan. The term 'gun culture' is often used to denote different behaviours and activities, and unpacking this term in each of the cases examined is important for understanding the dynamics of each conflict.

The relationship between 'gun cultures' and conflict cannot be reduced to a direct contribution or cause. Social attitudes to the presence of guns interact with economic, political, and historical factors to shape how armed conflict erupts. In the Kosovo case, both militant and pacifist groups mobilized the same Albanian traditions of customary law and social attitudes to generate solidarity among fellow ethnic Albanians.

Chapter 9 (Conflict Deaths): One of the most important—but often unobtainable—indicators of armed conflict is the number of people killed. Since deaths during violent conflict are rarely systematically recorded, researchers rely on a variety of information sources and estimation techniques. This chapter examines how current conflict death estimates are generated, what they include and exclude, and how they likely underestimate the real number of deaths.

It finds that most recent estimates of direct conflict deaths underreport the magnitude of the death toll, mainly because they depend on media reports, which are inherently incomplete. The total number of direct conflict deaths is probably two to four times higher than currently reported, and direct deaths were probably between 80,000 and 108,000 in 2003. A complete assessment of the human toll must not only include *direct* deaths from armed violence, but also the *indirect* deaths arising from the consequences of armed violence. The number of indirect victims in recent violent conflicts (such as in Darfur or DRC) has been several times greater than the number of *direct* conflict deaths.

Small arms and light weapons are responsible for the majority—between 60 and 90 per cent, depending on the conflict—of *direct* conflict deaths. They also play a clear, but unquantifiable, role in causing indirect conflict deaths.

Chapter 10 (Post-conflict): The period that follows the declared end of fighting is often designated 'post-conflict', but this does not necessarily imply an end to violence or a return of stability and security. Post-conflict environments are commonly marked by ongoing social unrest, and the crucial early steps towards peace, if not properly administered, can tip back into violent conflict. Indeed, almost half of all countries emerging from conflict suffer a relapse within five years of signing a peace agreement. Even if open conflict does not resume, armed violence can remain above pre-conflict levels. In the light of this, and in recognition of the tenuous nature of many ceasefires, there is increasing focus on reducing weapons stockpiles as part of overall peace processes, and DDR programmes are proliferating in post-conflict settings. Yet available evaluations show widely different levels of success.

Current approaches to DDR and weapons reduction suffer from several weaknesses, including the lack of political will, confusion over objectives, a disproportionate focus on disarmament selection bias, inadequate financing, and coordination gaps. DDR and weapons reduction programmes also continue to substitute for political solutions, the reform of governance and judicial sectors, and sustainable development. Many of the initiatives instituted after a conflict ends fail to address the demand for firearms—an essential factor underlying persistent armed violence.

Chapter 11 (Central African Republic): Often overlooked in examinations of armed violence in Africa, the experiences of the Central African Republic (CAR) have relevance far beyond its borders, especially with regard to widely held assumptions about security-sector reform. This chapter focuses on the massive influx of arms in to CAR between 1996 and 2003, which has affected the state's ability to regulate weapons among civilians. The lack of effective regulation, coupled with increasing stockpiles, has created a clear threat to security. Evidence suggests that non-state actors in CAR are better armed than government forces (with the exception of the presidential guard). The government, which claims that 50,000 small arms are circulating nationally beyond its control, may also be underestimating the scale of the problem. While firearms-related death and injury levels in CAR are low, the country suffers from the economic and psychological effects of small arms use and availability. Arms recovery programmes in CAR have been poorly designed and badly implemented, have been less successful than claimed, and arguably have undermined rather than enhanced security.

Towards 2006

The year 2004 witnessed an acceleration of international activity on small arms. Negotiations on an international instrument on the marking and tracing of weapons began, and a number of programmes for stockpile management, the destruction of surplus stocks, and post-conflict DDR were launched. Although progress on regulating arms brokering was slower, a UN expert group on this issue will probably be established in 2005 or 2006. And states are already gearing up for the 2006 UN review conference, perhaps the most important upcoming event on the small arms calendar. The next edition of the *Small Arms Survey* will focus on the key themes that will be on the agenda in 2006, including understanding the demand for arms, counting the cost of armed violence, providing victim assistance, regulating civilian weapons possession, as well as case studies drawn from ongoing research in Afghanistan, Brazil, Cambodia, Colombia, Haiti, Papua New Guinea, Tajikistan, and elsewhere.

BIBLIOGRAPHY

Holsti, K. J. 1996. *The State, War and the State of War*. Cambridge: Cambridge University Press.
Limm, Peter. 1984. *The Thirty Years War*. London: Longman.
Krug, Etienne et al., eds. 2002. *World Report on Violence and Health*. Geneva: World Health Organization.

ACKNOWLEDGEMENTS

Principal authors
Keith Krause with David Mutimer

Bearing a bandolier filled
with hundreds of bullets,
an Iraqi Kurdish soldier
stands at a checkpoint
along a road to Kirkuk,
northern Iraq, in March 2003.
(© Abdullah Zaheeruddin/Getty Images)

Rounding out the Gun:
AMMUNITION

INTRODUCTION

In 1996–97, mutinous soldiers from the Central African Republic (CAR) supplemented their arsenal by seizing weapons from members of the armed forces, gendarmerie, and police of Zaire as they crossed the border. Many of the armaments seized, such as Galil and M-16 automatic rifles, proved to be of little value, though, because the corresponding ammunition, 5.56 mm cartridges, was almost impossible to obtain in CAR. Having no use for these otherwise perfectly functioning weapons, the soldiers threw them into the Ubangi River (Berman, 2005).

This example underscores the crucial point that, without ammunition, small arms and light weapons are useless. Weapons and ammunition are complementary goods: an increase in the demand for weapons results in an increase in demand for ammunition, and their prices shift accordingly. In many instances, the procurement of ammunition can be more problematic than that of weapons: while weapons are durable goods, which can be used for many years in several areas of conflict, ammunition is quickly depleted and stocks must be replenished.

Despite its critical role in conflict, ammunition has so far been neglected in the arms control debate. In 1999, the UN Group of Experts on the problem of ammunition and explosives acknowledged this fact and stated that 'attempts to address small arms and light weapons would be incomplete if they did not include due regard for ammunition and explosives. Ammunition and explosives controls cannot be the sole remedy, but left unaddressed, they could represent a serious flaw and a missed opportunity' (UNGA, 1999, sec. 11, pp. 4–5).

The sheer scale of ammunition stocks underscores this observation. In the Russian Federation, 140 million rounds of ammunition have reportedly been designated for destruction between 2002 and 2005, and this is only the tip of the iceberg (Faltas and Chrobok, 2004, p. 109). Ukraine estimates it stocks around 2.5 million tonnes of ammunition, Belarus some 97,000 tonnes, and Kazakhstan and Uzbekistan a further 90,000 tonnes. The case is similar in southeastern Europe. Albania, Bosnia and Herzegovina, and Bulgaria alone are believed to stock some 400,000 tonnes of ammunition (Greene, Holt, and Wilkinson, 2005, p. 14).[1] This is to say nothing of the rest of the world.

'Ammunition' encapsulates numerous items, ranging from small-calibre cartridges to mortar rounds or rocket-propelled grenades. For the purpose of this short chapter, we will focus on small arms ammunition. The UN definition of small arms includes revolvers and self-loading pistols, rifles and carbines, assault rifles, and sub-machine and light machine guns (UNGA, 1997, p. 11). Small arms ammunition encompasses cartridges for handguns and rifles, shotgun shells,[2] and their components.

Because they are complementary, small arms and ammunition present a number of similar problems. Ammunition regulation is a complex matter because, as with small arms, there are legal and illicit users; ammunition produced for legitimate purposes may end up being transferred to conflict zones or misused by some individuals.

Ammunition also raises a host of specific questions, including:

- How widespread is ammunition production, and what technological developments are associated with it?
- What impact does ammunition availability have on conflict?

- How have issues regarding the production, supply, and control of ammunition been addressed at the national, regional, and international levels?
- Can the regulation of ammunition have an effect on the misuse of small arms?

The main findings of this chapter are as follows:
- Although less copious than their small arms counterparts, ammunition producers are present in all regions of the world; many countries want to be self-reliant and develop their own production facilities.
- The military ammunition cottage industry is less widespread than that of firearms. In some cases, guns are craft-produced to fit the type of ammunition that can be found on the market.
- The type and quantity of ammunition available to an armed group influences its choice of weaponry to a great extent.
- Ammunition issues are not adequately addressed in regional aor global agreements, nor through legal instruments.
- Improved ammunition controls can help identify illicit cases of shipping and stockpiling, smuggling routes, and individuals or groups engaging in acts of weapons misuse.

CHARACTERISTICS OF CARTRIDGES AND SHOTGUN SHELLS

As noted above, small arms ammunition comprises cartridges for handguns and rifles, and shells for shotguns. Cartridges and shells consist of four main components: the primer (explosive); the propellant (powder); the projectile; and the case (see Figure 1.1).

- **Primer.** Primers are initiating explosives and belong in the high-explosive category (like dynamite and TNT); they are very sensitive to shock or heat and can detonate if subjected to either.
- **Propellant (powder).** At the end of the 19th century, black powder (a mixture of nitrate, charcoal, and sulphur) was replaced by smokeless powder, still in use today. Smokeless powder can be single-base (when nitrocellulose is the only explosive) or double-base (if it also contains nitroglycerin in addition to nitrocellulose) (Saferstein, 1995, p. 334; FAS, 2004).
- **Projectile.** Depending on the intended use, different types of bullets can be manufactured: ball (the most common); armour-piercing (with a harder core); tracer (containing a chemical in the base that leaves a trace of light along the bullet's trajectory); incendiary (containing a chemical that ignites on striking); and ranging or spotter (containing a chemical that produces a flash on striking). Bullets can be ogival or cylindrical in shape, and the nose of the bullet can be round, half-flattened ('semi-wadcutter'), or flattened ('wadcutter'). A bullet can be either fully jacketed (that is, entirely covered in a harder metal) or not.
- **Case.** The cartridge casing contains the primer, the propellant, and the projectile; it is the only component that can be reused. Cases have a heat-absorbing property that protects the bore of the gun during shooting.

Shotgun shells have a plastic body ('tube') that holds the primer, powder, and shot. Shot pellets held in a wad serve as projectiles for shotguns, although other types of projectiles can also be used, such as flechette rounds.

Figure 1.1   Schematic representations of a cartridge and a shotgun shell

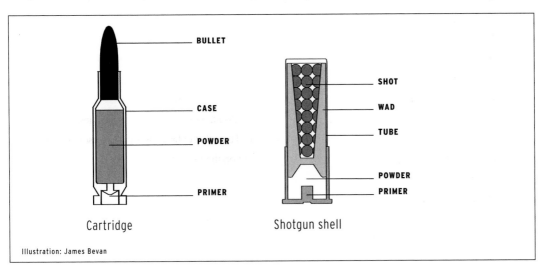

BULLET

CASE

POWDER

PRIMER

SHOT

WAD

TUBE

POWDER

PRIMER

Cartridge

Shotgun shell

Illustration: James Bevan

Box 1.1   Counting cartridges

An Antioquia Police officer stands guard before ammunition seized during a raid on the Revolutionary Armed Forces of Colombia (FARC) in January 2004 in Medellín, Colombia.

© Fredy Amariles/AFP/Getty Images

With regard to stockpiles, an estimated All Up Weight (that is, the weight of ammunition and packaging) is the most relevant variable for planners assessing transportation needs and the best means of disposal. For regular stockpiles, the quantity of cartridges can be deduced from their overall weight: since sealed boxes are assumed to be full, the packaging statistics (dimensions, weight when full, and the number of rounds in a box) can be used to calculate the total number of rounds stored.

When ammunition is seized, the quantity is generally expressed in terms of the number of cartridges. Production figures are expressed in terms of the number of cartridges produced per day. An average eight-ton truckload can contain close to 750,000 5.45 x 39 mm ball cartridges, which weigh approximately 10.75 grams per round (Cutshaw and Ness, 2004, p. 4). The calibre and the type of metal or alloy of which ammunition is made help to determine its weight, which can vary considerably.

Ammunition is defined in terms of calibre. The calibre measures the diameter of the gun's barrel and is expressed in hundredths or thousandths of an inch (for instance, .22 or .357) or in millimetres (for example, 9 mm). Cartridges with the same calibre can differ according to the length of the case (such as 7.62 x 39 mm, 7.62 x 51 mm, or 7.62 x 63 mm). One explanation for the large number of cartridge types currently in existence is that many countries used to set their own standards for their military weapons (including 7.5 mm French, 7.5 mm Swiss, and .303 British round). In recent years, many of the new weapons that have been produced have been manufactured to

Table 1.1   An overview of some common types of cartridges

Calibre in millimetres and inches	Other names	Types of weapon	Examples of weapon
5.45 x 39 mm	5.45 mm Kalashnikov/ Russian; 5.45 x 39 mm Soviet	Sub-carbines, assault rifles, light machine guns	AK-74 (Russian Federation)
5.56 x 45 mm 0.223	5.56 mm NATO; 0.223 Armalite/Remington	Rifles, machine guns, carbines	FN FNC, FN Minimi (Belgium), Heckler & Koch G41 and G-36 (Germany), Galil (Israel), Beretta AS 70/90 (Italy), Vektor R4 (South Africa), Enfield L85A1 (UK), AR15/M16 (US)
7.62 x 39 mm	7.62 mm M43/Kalashnikov/ Obr 43 g; 7.62 x 39 mm Soviet	Carbines, rifles, light machine guns, machine guns	Chinese Type 56 carbine and, assault rifle and Chinese Type 68 rifle (China); Kalashnikov AK-47 and AKM and Simonov SKS (Russian Federation), Zastava M70B1 (former Yugoslavia)
7.62 x 51 mm 0.308 Winchester	7.62 mm NATO	Rifles, machine guns	FN FAL (Belgium), Heckler & Koch G3, PSG1, and MSG90 (Germany), M14 Rifle (US)
7.62 x 63 mm 0.30-06 Springfield	0.30 US Service/Browning	Bolt action rifles, semi-automatic rifles, machine guns	Browning M1919A4 (US)
9 x 17 mm 0.380 auto	9 mm Browning short/ Kurz/Corto; 0.380 ACP	Mainly pistols	Taurus PT 52 S (Brazil)
9 x 18 mm Makarov	9 x 18 mm Soviet; 9 mm PM Stechkin/Type 59	Pistols, sub-machine guns	Makarov and Stechkin pistols (Russian Federation)
9 x 19 mm Parabellum	9 mm Luger/Patrone '08	Pistols, revolvers, semi-automatic carbines (it is the world's predominant sub-machine gun cartridge)	Glock 17 (Austria), Browning High Power Model 1935 (Belgium), Uzi (Israel), Beretta Models 92 and 93R (Italy), some SIG pistols (Switzerland)
0.357 Magnum	0.357 Smith & Wesson Magnum	Revolvers	Manurhin MR73 (France), Desert Eagle (Israel), Colt Python, Colt King Cobra, and Ruger GP100 (US)
0.45 ACP	0.45 Auto Colt/ Automatic; 11.43 x 23 mm Norwegian Colt	Pistols, revolvers, carbines, sub-machine guns	Colt M1911/M1911A1 and Smith & Wesson 625 (US)
12.7 x 99 mm 0.50 Browning		Machine guns, anti-matériel rifles	Barrett 0.50 models and Browning M2HB .50 (US)
12.7 x 108 mm	12.7 x 107 mm; 12.7 Russian Federation machine gun; 12.7 mm DShK/Type 54	Machine guns, heavy machine guns, and anti-matériel rifles	Type 77 (China), 12.7 mm Gepard M2 and MA1 (Hungary)

Note: Bold text signifies the most commonly used names.
Sources: Hogg (2002); Cutshaw and Ness (2004); Jones and Cutshaw (2004)

North Atlantic Treaty Organisation (NATO) standards (5.56 x 45 mm and 7.62 x 51 mm). All weapons produced in the former Soviet bloc, as well as in countries such as China and North Korea, however, continue to apply their own standards (see Table 1.1).

The diameter of a shotgun barrel is expressed in terms of gauge. The higher the value of the gauge, the smaller the diameter of the barrel; for instance, a 12-gauge shotgun has a larger bore diameter than a 16-gauge shotgun (0.730 versus 0.670 inches) (Saferstein, 1995, p. 446).

PRODUCTION

Industrial production

Most ammunition manufacturers could be more accurately described as assembly plants, producing only a few components themselves and subcontracting the manufacture of the rest of the cartridge or shell to other companies (see Box 1.2). Ammunition manufacturers then assemble the complete round. On a worldwide scale, there are more bullet producers than case producers, more case producers than powder producers, and more powder producers than primer producers (Stohl, 1998, p. 9).

Box 1.2   Rationalizing ammunition production

RUAG Ammotec (Germany and Switzerland) is equipped to manufacture all necessary components except propellant; yet, for certain types of ammunition, the company subcontracts work to other firms, especially when only small quantities are needed. RUAG Ammotec itself produces high-quality, leaded and unleaded (that is, environmentally friendly) primers. The company produces most of its bullets and casings in-house, except when small quantities are needed (fewer than 10,000 units per year) or specific types for which it is not worthwhile investing in relevant equipment.[3]

The companies that produce weapons are generally not the same ones that make ammunition (PRODUCTION). The two processes need different raw materials and machinery, and utilize different marketing techniques (UNGA, 1999, sec. 24, p. 6). Most ammunition producers specialize in certain types of products: a number of South African companies, for instance, focus on 'big game' hunting. Ammunition plants also have very different equipment requirements; some still use machinery that dates back to the Second World War, while others use new Computer Numeric Control (CNC) methods to mass produce high-quality ammunition. The latter allow the manufacturer to switch quickly from one type and calibre of ammunition to another (UNGA, 1999, sec. 19, p. 6).

Many countries have sought to develop their own production capacity in order to be self-reliant. Some, such as Iran, Pakistan, and South Africa, started producing ammunition in response to the imposition of embargoes, before looking for export markets (DeClerq, 1998). Small-calibre (no larger than 12.7 mm) ammunition production is widespread (encompassing 76 countries), but uneven (Omega Foundation, 2003). Major differences exist between regions, and the geographical distribution of ammunition producers is quite similar to that of small arms producers (see Figure 1.2).

The UN Group of Experts on the problem of ammunition and explosives noted that a number of countries are reluctant to provide information on the amount of ammunition that they produce annually or the number of plants that they have on their territory (UNGA, 1999, sec. 22, p. 6). Developing countries willing to undertake local production often work under licence from major companies; in a number of instances, these technology transfers have raised concerns about who the final end-users are, especially when the recipients are located near conflict zones (see Box 1.3). This is the case with the Eldoret ammunition factory in Kenya, the construction of which was completed in 1996 by FN-Herstal (Belgium) and which produces 20,000–60,000 cartridges per day (Kamenju, 2001; Kwayera, 2003) for the armed forces, police, and wildlife services of Kenya. Concerns about the possible dissemination of Kenya-made cartridges to surrounding conflict areas are mitigated by the fact that Eldoret does not produce the 7.62 x 39 mm cartridges that would fit an AK-47, the most common conflict gun in the region (Kamenju, 2001).

Figure 1.2   Distribution of total ammunition and small arms producers by region

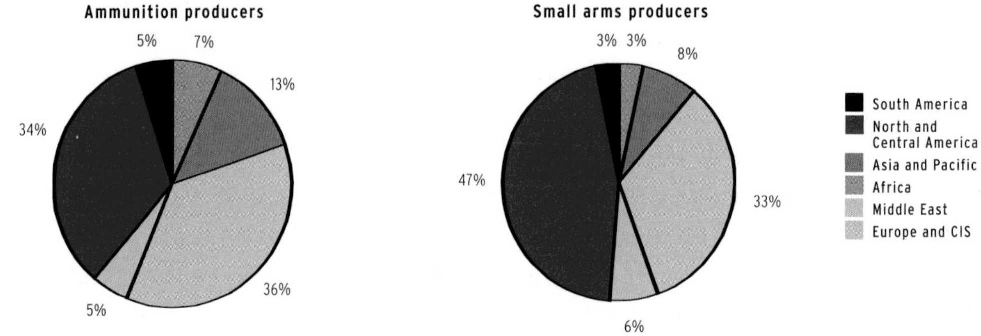

Note: Small arms comprise pistols, revolvers, rifles, carbines, sub-machine guns, and light and heavy machine guns, while ammunition consists of all calibres equal to or less than 12.7 mm.

Source: Omega Foundation (2003)

Box 1.3   Licensed production: New Lachaussée in Tanzania

In 2003, New Lachaussée—which is part of the Forrest Group run by George Forrest, whose activities in the mining sector of the Democratic Republic of Congo (DRC) elicited concern in 2002 from a UN Group of Experts (UNSC, 2002)—was scheduled to build an ammunition production facility in Mwanza, Tanzania, close to Lake Victoria. The company, based in Liège, Belgium, would deliver and supervise an ammunition production line, as well as provide local training and technical assistance (Chambre des Représentants de Belgique, 2004). Belgium's national export credit agency, Ducroire, supported the project by awarding New Lachaussée with insurance cover worth USD 10.6 million for a total investment value of EUR 11 million (approximately USD 13.3 million) (Africa Confidential, 2004).

A number of NGOs launched a campaign to protest the sale of military material to Tanzania by New Lachaussée. The purpose was to block the transaction and licence. The Belgian project was attacked on three main grounds. First, it allegedly contravened the fourth and seventh criteria of the 1998 *European Union (EU) Code of Conduct on Arms Exports* (now part of Belgian law), according to which arms should not be exported to countries where they could threaten regional stability, and where there is a risk of diversion (GRIP, 2004). On several occasions, Tanzania has reportedly served as a country of transit for weapons bound for conflicts in the region (HRW, 1999; GRIP, 2004).

Second, it breached international guidelines for export credit agencies, according to which countries should avoid 'unproductive expenditures' towards Heavily Indebted Poor Countries (HIPCs), which include Tanzania. Such expenditures are defined as 'transactions that are not consistent with these countries' poverty reduction and debt sustainability strategies and do not contribute to their social and/or economic development' (OECD, 2001).

Third, it blatantly contradicted Belgium's proclaimed commitment to restoring peace in the Great Lakes Region, especially in Burundi and the Democratic Republic of Congo (GRIP, 2004). The Belgian Law of 26 March 2003 states that exports must be consistent with Belgium's foreign policy interests and objectives (Chambre des Représentants de Belgique, 2004; GRIP, 2004).

The case sparked an important debate in Belgium, particularly in the lower house of parliament in early 2004 (Chambre des Représentants de Belgique, 2004), and before the Minister-President of the Walloon Government, Jean-Claude Van Cauwenberghe. On 11 February 2004, the licence was denied on the grounds that an export licence for ammunition production risked exacerbating the problem of small arms proliferation and disrupting the peace process in the region (Bayet, 2004).

A reversal occurred on 17 Feburary 2005, when the foreign relations minister for the Walloon government, Marie-Dominique Simonet, decided to grant the export licence to New Lachaussée because of what she deemed a gradually improving situation in Tanzania. She nevertheless attached a number of conditions to the authorization. Notably, the old Tanzanian chain of production is to be dismantled, and the new one is to produce ammunition with a distinctive marking that should enable its tracing—and hopefully prevent diversion to conflict zones. Despite these reassurances, the granting of this licence to New Lachaussée is still feeding a heated debate, both at the Walloon and the federal governing levels (*Le Soir*, 2005; RTBF, 2005).

Handloading and craft production

Ammunition can also be produced on a small scale. Some people make their own ammunition by assembling the different components themselves (see Box 1.4). Known as handloading or reloading (because the same case can be used several times), this activity is considered a hobby with its aficionados, dedicated Web sites and training manuals, and monthly columns in gun magazines. In the United States, most of the different ammunition components (including powder and primer) can be easily bought at local stores,[4] and companies that produce reloading equipment, parts, and accessories have formed a National Reloading Manufacturers Association. While this mode of production is usually cheaper, it is also likely to be less reliable, due to the lack of quality control and varying skill levels among craftsmen. The volume of ammunition produced through handloading is extremely low compared to industrial production (UNGA, 1999, sec. 18, p. 5). Only simple lead-based projectiles can be manufactured at home with the proper materials and skills: jacketed and other complex projectiles have to be purchased new (Gebhardt, 2004). Consequently, most handloaders in the United States and in other developed countries do not routinely handload common military rounds (Gebhardt, 2004).

In addition to the different components of a cartridge (case, primer, propellant, and projectile), the basic elements needed for handloading are proper tools and data. Tools include a 'press' and a selection of dies that are specific to the calibre of the cartridge being reloaded. Data handbooks, sometimes published by the manufacturers themselves, specify how much of a particular type of propellant should be used in order to ensure optimum and safe performance of the finished product. All of these elements can be purchased in most gun stores. The cases can be simply picked up off the ground and cleaned for reuse, rather than purchased new (Gebhardt, 2004).

Box 1.4   A handloader comments on his hobby

I begin reloading by first cleaning the used case in a tumbler, using a mixture of crushed walnut shells and a chemical substance. Then I process each case through a die that resizes it for shape and diameter, while at the same time punching out the used primer. A new primer is installed in each case, using a hand-held tool. One must be careful to install the proper size and type of primer for the cartridge being reloaded. There are small- and large-calibre pistol primers and small- and large-calibre rifle primers.

Using a calibrated device called a powder measure, I pour and weigh several measures of powder to ensure that I have calibrated the device for the correct amount (weight) of propellant. I then charge each empty, reprimed case with this amount of propellant. It is important to ensure that one never 'double charges' an empty case.

The final step is to seat a new projectile to a measured depth and crimp the mouth of the case around the projectile so that it will neither fall out nor be seated deeper when cycled through the action of the firearm. When I have completed this step, I use a micrometer to measure the finished cartridge. I know from my data the minimum and maximum length allowed for the finished cartridge.

Now all that is left is to place the loaded cartridges into an appropriate plastic or paper storage container, labelled as to type and amount of propellant used, projectile calibre and weight, and date of loading.

Author: James Gebhardt

The extent of ammunition craft production outside of developed countries is difficult to assess. According to the International Committee of the Red Cross (ICRC), 'non-state entities may be reluctant to accept the risk to life and weapons systems which "home-made" production of munitions and ammunition would entail' (ICRC, 1999); but this assertion is contradicted by numerous accounts of ammunition craft production worldwide. In 2004, the Nigerian police made several arrests of illegal arms manufacturers and seized 5.56 mm, 7.65 mm, and 9 mm home-made cartridges (AllAfrica, 2004a; 2004b).

Although production of one's own ammunition does not require complex skills, and the ammunition made in this manner is reliable enough to be used confidently by the handloaders themselves, what may prove challenging in certain areas is finding the different components. The quality of the powder and primer must be of sufficient quality for the ammunition to be usable—but it is still possible to produce one's own powder, provided the ingredients are available. Brass casings, too, are difficult to craft produce (DeClerq, 1998), but this may not be a problem, since old cases can be reused a number of times (while all other components can be used only once). Projectiles, meanwhile, are relatively easy to manufacture: one only needs a cutting machine, which can mould anything in metal (DeClerq, 1998).

Technological developments

Small arms ammunition technology is relatively stable: 'Ammunition technology in all its permutations is best described as a mature technology; that is to say, there can be few revolutionary breakthroughs expected in the immediate future' (Cutshaw and Ness, 2003, p. 15). One noticeable change, however, is the development of non-lethal weapons (see Box 1.5), providing law enforcement and military forces with the opportunity to graduate their response.

Box 1.5   Ammunition in non-lethal weapons

'Non-lethal' weapons, such as rubber bullets, are more accurately termed 'less-than lethal' or 'sub-lethal' weapons. Rubber bullets are mostly employed in crowd control operations; they are made of either plain rubber or rubber-coated steel. They are shot from a canister mounted on the muzzle of an ordinary rifle (an M-16 for instance). Although not designed to kill, rubber bullets can cause permanent damage or even death. Because of their very low ballistic coefficient, they are erratic in flight and can generate unintended casualties if they hit soft tissue (eyes, for instance). Rubber bullets have been used in a number of contexts, most notably in Northern Ireland and the Palestinian Territories, where, at times, they have been responsible for loss of life and permanent injuries. A medical report on the use of rubber bullets by the Israeli Defense Forces concluded, in October 2002, that 'this type of ammunition should therefore not be considered a safe method of crowd control' (Mahajna et al., 2002, p. 1795). The Israeli Defense Forces have consequently issued new regulations to counter improper use of rubber bullets and to limit accidental casualties. Since the 1970s, the British Army has been using plastic baton rounds (PBRs) instead of rubber bullets, although these have caused fatalities as well; so, too, have beanbags, which are small nylon pockets containing birdshot.

Sources: Blue Line (1997); Di Maio (1999, pp. 304-05); Krausz and Mahajna (2002); Mahajna et al. (2002); Small Arms Survey (2004, pp. 221-24)

Each year a number of new products stand out as developments in ammunition production. For instance, pre-fragmented bullets driven at hyper-velocity have recently been developed (under the trade name of 'Quik-Shok') for the 0.22 calibre long rifle. On impact, these pre-fragmented bullets dissociate into three components that create larger wounds (Cutshaw and Ness, 2003, p. 5). Also, caseless cartridges that weigh 50 per cent less than classic ammunition have been developed; they are made of a block of propellant in which a bullet is embedded (DeClerq, 1999b). Use of these new cartridges is limited, though, mostly to the German Heckler & Koch G11 automatic rifle.

The shift towards lighter ammunition is a logical consequence of the process by which personal automatic rifles have progressively replaced, in military forces, high-powered rifles; the former have an increased ammunition capacity and rate of fire (Hogg and Weeks, 2000, p. 221).

Another innovation in ammunition, which is rendered even more necessary by increased magazine capacity, is the development of 'green' ammunition. Lead, which is currently present in most types of bullets and primers, is toxic if inhaled or ingested, and can cause neurological damage. This issue is of particular concern for shooting ranges where discharged bullets, shotgun pellets, and primers after firing, leave high concentrations of lead in the immediate environment. In the case of outdoor ranges, certain physical conditions, such as acidic soil, are particularly conducive to ground pollution: bullets and shots slowly dissolve into the soil and groundwater, endangering wildlife and drinking water supplies (Kennedy, 2004; AP, 2004d). The cost of lead cleaning is considerable: the US Army Environmental Center (USAEC) estimates it at USD 130–400 per cubic metre (USAEC, 1999).

Such concerns have led to the development of cartridges with lead-free bullets and primers. These new, non-polluting cartridges are designed mainly for range use. In 1995, the US Army launched a 'green bullet' programme (USAEC, 1999), and after technical tests proved that these bullets were as accurate as lead-core ones, they went into production, in March 1999, at the Lake City Army Ammunition Plant in Missouri. The latter is currently developing 5.56 mm bullets with a tungsten–tin or tungsten–nylon core, and aims to manufacture 7.62 mm, 9 mm, and .50 calibres in the medium term (USAEC, 1999). The Federal Law Enforcement Training Center (FLETC), which trains the employees of 76 federal agencies, uses these non-polluting bullets in 75 per cent of its activities that involve ammunition consumption. This switch from lead to unleaded ammunition is estimated to have eliminated more than 30 tons of lead waste from the FLETC's three campuses (CNN, 2004). Unleaded ammunition is being produced worldwide, and national armies, such as the Danish Armed Forces (Nordic Business Report, 2004), are increasingly choosing to utilize it.

THE IMPACT OF AMMUNITION AVAILABILITY ON WEAPONS USE

Storage and shelf life

Ammunition longevity is expressed in terms of shelf life and service life. Shelf life could be viewed as the ammunition's 'expiry date' and is defined by the Pentagon as: 'the total period of time [...] that an item may remain in the combined wholesale (including manufacturer's) and retail storage systems and still remain suitable for issue to and/or consumption by the end user' (US Department of Defense, 1997). Service life, meanwhile, is the length of time that an item is expected to be in working order.

In practice, ammunition can be, and often is, used well beyond its shelf life. Also called 'stability', the service life of ammunition is determined by how long it takes for the propellant to decompose. If the propellant is well made and stored, it will remain serviceable for many decades. Ammunition, however, can be quickly degraded by moisture and heat, and must be stored in a dry and cool place, preferably in the producer's original packaging; excessive and frequent variations of temperature are particularly damaging to powder: 'under good storage conditions (i.e. stable temperature and low humidity combined with properly sealed packaging), small arms ammunition can last 50 years or more without significant deterioration' (UNGA, 1999, p. 20). Handloaded ammunition is seldom as robust as factory-produced ammunition made to military specifications.

As the propellant decomposes (that is, the stabilizer within it becomes depleted), its burning properties change and it will generate more pressure on firing. Since military small arms are designed to withstand significantly high pressure, the shooter faces little danger in using old ammunition. Decomposed primer or propellant, however, may also cause it to misfire, that is, the primer will either not ignite, or it will ignite but fail to ignite the powder; in both cases the faulty cartridge can simply be ejected. A third possibility is that the primer will ignite enough powder to dislodge the bullet from the case, but not enough to allow it to travel all the way through the barrel; if a bullet that is blocked in the barrel goes unnoticed, and another cartridge is loaded and fired, this may, in some instances, severely damage or rupture the barrel or breech, with a risk of injury to the shooter.[5]

Military small arms ammunition is generally made to withstand greater temperatures and amounts of moisture than civilian ammunition. In the Pacific region, for instance, some armed groups have been using old .303 and .50 Browning Machine Gun (BMG) cartridges that date back to the Second World War. Such cartridges were still usable thanks to their thick brass casings; also, the Allies had stored them in their original containers, which were designed to repel tropical moisture. Despite these precautions, however, a number suffered water damage over the years, leading to the primer and/or the powder failing to fire.[6] Ammunition is also likely to become unusable with age as a result of it being deformed by external corrosion and thus no longer fitting the weapon for which it was designed.

Ammunition availability and conflict

A common notion is that it is the weapon that determines the choice of ammunition, not the other way round. In practice, though, the availability of ammunition often proves decisive in the selection of weapons, and influences the value that combatants place on a given model. In Ghana, weapons are craft produced depending on the type of ammunition that can be procured on the market (Aning, 2005); and in the conflicts in Bougainville and the Solomon Islands, some guns were handmade specifically to suit ammunition stocks inherited from the Second World War (Alpers, 2005).

> The availability of ammunition often proves decisive in the selection of weapons by combatants.

Although weapons and ammunition are complementary, they have different production structures, and it can happen that one is widely available while the other is scarce. Non-state armed groups, in particular, often have irregular supply lines that result in occasional (sometimes endemic) shortages of ammunition (Small Arms Survey and CECORE, 2004).[7] In the 1990s, the Tajik opposition, for instance, initiated attacks and engaged in kidnapping to solve their ammunition problem (Torjesen, Wille, and MacFarlane, 2005, p. 12). A similar example comes from Cambodia, where the Khmer Rouge experienced a severe lack of ammunition in the last years of the war (after the withdrawal of Chinese support)—although it was still possible to find weapons in sufficient quantities.[8]

Weapons for which the corresponding ammunition cannot be found are, at least temporarily, useless. As noted above, in CAR, in the late 1990s, 5.56 mm cartridges were in extremely short supply,

Palestinian children look at bullets donated to Hamas activists during a campaign in the Gaza Strip in April 2004.

meaning that many Western-produced rifles, machine guns, and carbines could not be used (Berman, 2005). A similar example can be drawn from the rebellion that took place in the early 1990s in northern Mali, where any weapon for which it was too difficult to find ammunition was considered almost useless.[9] When rebels bought weapons abroad, their choice was constrained by the fact that they needed those whose ammunition could later be obtained from the arsenals of the Malian Armed Forces—their main source of supply. According to one Malian ex-combatant, the FN-CAL (Belgian) assault rifles that could be imported from Mauritania were of limited utility because they use 5.56 mm ammunition, and Malian troops possess, for the most part, Chinese and Russian-type cartridges (7.62 x 39 mm).[10] In Papua New Guinea (PNG), weapons like AK-47 assault rifles are of little value, since only NATO-calibre ammunition is available; although Soviet-type weapons are easy to obtain in nearby Asia, they are, therefore, unlikely to end up in PNG (Alpers, 2005).

During a conflict, ammunition is needed in great quantities. Assault rifles, which are widely used, consume a large number of cartridges, and the lack of training and discipline in certain armed groups leads to excessive expenditure of cartridges (UNGA, 1999, sec. 48, p. 9). The amount of ammunition needed also depends on the intensity (planned or actual) of the conflict. For this reason, there may be a high demand for ammunition, even though the quantity of firearms used may be low. Because ammunition stocks are rapidly depleted, there is often a risk of shortage, and hence ammunition is considered an extremely valuable commodity. In Malian rebel groups, an ordnance officer would distribute ammunition to combatants before each mission. The type and quantity of ammunition supplied would depend on: the amount of ammunition remaining in the arsenal (if ammunition was scarce, only the best shooters would be dispatched, tasked with acquiring more for the group); the kind of weapon needed by the combatant; and the strength of the combatant (due to the weight of ammunition).[11] In Cambodia, Khmer Rouge combatants involved in attacks would only carry 60 cartridges each; ammunition was strictly rationed.[12]

> During conflict, ammunition is needed in great quantities and stocks can be rapidly depleted.

The high value accorded to ammunition is illustrated by the fact that many armed groups consider ammunition wastage to be a grave offence. Among Malian armed groups, sanctions for shooting in the air included having one's head shaved as a symbol of shame or being confined to barracks for a week.[13] Using ammunition to shoot birds or other animals was also prohibited in the former rebel Uganda National Rescue Front II (UNRF II) (Small Arms Survey and CECORE, 2004). An impending shortage of ammunition can compel a group or a country, whenever possible, to diversify its means of supply (see Box 1.6).

As with any commodity, the price of ammunition is dependent on supply and demand. When ammunition is scarce and demand is high, its price will increase. A sudden peak in demand for ammunition occurs when there is a conflict, or when trade routes are cut (due to an arms embargo, for instance).

The availability of ammunition in a given conflict depends on many variables. One critical factor is whether the combatants enjoy the support of foreign states or groups. Rebel groups in Burundi and the Democratic Republic of Congo (DRC), for example, receive important quantities of ammunition from Rwanda and Uganda.[14] For those groups that do not have external backing, other key sources of supply are domestic procurement: raids on military and police arsenals, and in some cases direct purchase from government forces themselves.[15] Another source of supply is, to a much lesser extent, craft production (Capie, 2004; Small Arms Survey and CECORE, 2004).

The availability of ammunition has direct consequences for how firearms are used in a conflict. During the Rwandan genocide of 1994, it even had an impact on the categories of people killed, and on the kinds of weapons used to kill them. Those who were shot (rather than butchered with machetes) were mostly young adults (Verwimp,

> **Box 1.6   Ammunition shortage in the United States: diversifying supply**
>
> In May–June 2004, the US military experienced a major shortage in small-calibre ammunition, related to the wars in Afghanistan and Iraq, as well as to increased training—since the terrorist attacks of 11 September 2001, soldiers have been required to undergo live-fire training twice a year instead of once (Manufacturing and Technology News, 2004; Merle, 2004). In June 2004, the chief executive of the Lake City Army Ammunition Plant in Missouri, which manufactures small-calibre ammunition for the US military, reported that his facility had experienced its fastest production increase since the Vietnam War (AP, 2004a). Yet, in spite of the 1.2 billion cartridges already produced annually by Lake City, the armed services are still short of 300-500 million cartridges (Wingfield, 2004), and there is some indication that soldiers in Iraq have not been able to obtain all the ordnance that they have needed (AP, 2004c). It is estimated that the US Army will require 1.5 billion cartridges annually from 2004, three times the quantity used in 2001 (Merle, 2004).
>
> To avoid tapping into its strategic reserves, the Pentagon imported 130 million cartridges from the United Kingdom in June 2004, and awarded contracts to Israeli Military Industries and Winchester Ammunition, commissioning each to produce 70 million more 5.56 mm and 7.62 mm cartridges (Leser, 2004; Merle, 2004). In January 2005, a news report suggested that the United States intended to purchase 300 million 5.56 mm cartridges, for around USD 62.5 million, from Taiwan (AFP, 2005). Private contractors have been approached about supplementing supply from Lake City on a regular basis (Wingfield, 2004); more than a dozen ammunition manufacturers responded, in September 2004, to the US Army's draft request for proposals, involving 500 million cartridges per year (5.56 mm rifle cartridges as well as 7.62 mm and .50 calibre machine-gun cartridges) (Scully, 2004). The shortage has raised concerns that the US military may become dependent on foreign suppliers (Merle, 2004).

The availability of ammunition has direct consequences for how firearms are used in a conflict.

2005). The reason is that ammunition stocks were limited, forcing the perpetrators to save supplies and to select their targets carefully. Firearms, then, were used against those who were considered most threatening, that is, 'young to middle-aged men with a respected status in the commune' (Verwimp, 2005).

The amount of ammunition available affects potential weapons misuse; if ammunition is scarce, armed groups will enforce, if their authority structure permits it, a 'shooting discipline' so as to avoid wasting a single round. In such circumstances, military targets of strategic value are likely to be preferred to civilian ones. Also, when ammunition is scarce, only the best shooters are tasked with conducting attacks, reducing the risk of collateral damage. When ammunition is easily available, by contrast, there is likely to be less restraint in the employment of firearms. A shortage of ammunition can also induce a change in military objectives: interviews with former rebels in Mali and Uganda revealed that the usual response to a lack of ammunition is to launch an assault on state arsenals in order to regain a sufficient number of cartridges, before pursuing other goals.[16]

It should be noted, however, that the consequences of a shortage of ammunition depend to a large extent on the type of war being fought. If the civilian population is the main target, as in Rwanda, it is likely that such a shortage will lead to weapon substitution, that is, to the use of bladed weapons and probably the targeting of the most vulnerable sections of the population.

Limiting the availability of ammunition

Because ammunition availability shapes, to a certain extent, the use of weapons, many countries have laws limiting the type and/or quantity of ammunition that can be legally purchased, used, or stored by civilians.

Individual access to ammunition

In most countries, the sale of ammunition is, like that of firearms, prohibited with respect to certain categories of the population, such as minors, mentally disabled persons, or repeat offenders. Retail services must comply with these national regulations (see Box 1.7). In most Pacific states, for instance, people can purchase ammunition only if they have a licence for the corresponding type of firearm (Alpers and Twyford, 2003, p. 62). In the United Kingdom, a shotgun certificate is required for anyone wanting to buy corresponding cartridges (United Kingdom Home Office, 2004, p. 17).

A limit is sometimes placed on the quantity of cartridges or shells that one is allowed to purchase. In most Pacific states, there is a ceiling on the amount of ammunition that can be bought for a given licence (Alpers and Twyford, 2003, p. 62). In South Africa, special authorization is needed for anyone wishing to possess more than 2,400 primers, or 200 cartridges per licensed firearm (Government of South Africa, 2004, ch. 8, art. 74).

Another way to limit the quantity of ammunition available is to impose restrictions on the size of magazines for semi-automatic weapons. The assault weapons ban that was in force in the United States from 1994–2004 prohibited high-capacity magazines for a number of weapons (Butterfield, 2004; AP, 2004b; see also PRODUCERS).

Civilian storage of ammunition is regulated in many countries; a UN survey that collated the responses of 69 states on national firearms regulations found out that 'the majority of responding States place restrictions on the storage of firearms and ammunition, and firearms must usually be stored in such a way as to preclude immediate use (that is, unloaded or otherwise disabled; or secured in a safe or locked cabinet)' (UN, 1998, p. 57).

Restrictions on the type of ammunition

States also regulate the sale or use of certain types of ammunition that are considered to be particularly dangerous. Armour-piercing bullets, for instance, have been at the centre of a long debate in the United States. Dubbed 'cop-killer bullets' because of their capacity to penetrate standard bullet-proof vests, they were, ironically, invented in the 1960s for law enforcement purposes, and were designed to pierce obstacles made out of metal (particularly vehicles) or glass. Although most high-powered rifle bullets can also go through body armour, the United States has specifically restricted the manufacture and importation of armour-piercing ammunition since 1986. It can be used only by

---

Box 1.7   Gun control advocates versus Kmart

One outstanding scene in Michael Moore's 2002 film *Bowling for Columbine* is when two students who were severely wounded in the Columbine High School massacre of 20 April 1999 ask the management of Kmart to provide a refund for the 17-cent bullets bought in one of their stores and now lodged in their bodies. To emphasize their point, one of the students (aged 18) went to the local Kmart and purchased easily 1,000 cartridges of 9 mm and .38 special ammunition. Twenty-four hours after their first visit to Kmart's headquarters in Troy, Michigan, a company spokesperson told Moore and the students that Kmart would phase out the sale of its handgun ammunition within the next 90 days in its 2,100 stores nationwide (Klein, 2001). Everyone's astonishment, including Moore's, was visible: no one expected such a quick victory.

Since then, however, the company has denied that it capitulated before the film-maker. According to a company spokesperson, this decision was based solely on 'marketing concerns', since handgun ammunition was quite insignificant for Kmart in terms of quantities sold (AP, 2001a).

This was not the first time that Kmart had found itself in the spotlight with regard to gun control. In 1997, the company was found liable for selling a rifle to an intoxicated man who used it to shoot his ex-girlfriend (Center to Prevent Handgun Violence, 1997). In November 1999, US television celebrity Rosie O'Donnell resigned from her position as a Kmart spokesperson because of her pro-gun control stance. One month later, Kmart decided, under pressure from demonstrators, not to sell rifles and shotguns at a New York store that it had just opened (AP, 2001b).

federal, state, or local authorities, exported, and employed in tests and experiments (United States Code, 2003, title 18, part I, ch. 44, sec. 922). This type of ammunition is also subjected to strict record-keeping and must be clearly marked as armour-piercing (Legal Community Against Violence, 2004).

Box 1.8   Origins of the prohibition on the use in war of expanding bullets

In the 1890s, a new type of bullet with lead exposed at the tip was developed for military use. These 'dum-dum' bullets, which are not fully jacketed, expand on impact. The name 'dum-dum' comes from the location of the British factory in India where they were manufactured, mainly for use in colonial wars.

Delegates present at the First Hague Peace Conference declared, on 29 July 1899, that: 'The Contracting Parties agree to abstain from the use of bullets which expand or flatten easily in the human body, such as bullets with a hard envelope which does not entirely cover the core or is pierced with incisions' (*Hague Declaration* (IV, 3) *concerning Expanding Bullets*). To this day, the ban on the use of expanding bullets (also known as soft-nosed, soft-point, hollow-point, open-tip, or semi-jacket bullets) in armed conflicts still holds: all bullets for military use must be covered by a full-metal jacket (FMJ).

In Brazil, the use of certain calibres[17] is restricted to the armed forces, the police, small arms collectors, and registered sport shooters. Such ammunition, which is not sold in gun shops, can only be purchased direct from the factory and must be authorized by the Brazilian Army's Directorate of Controlled Products (DFPC) (Dreyfus, 2004).

The ban on expanding ('dum-dum') bullets is another example of a restriction that applies to the type of ammunition used (see Box 1.8). Adopted at the Hague Conference of 1899 (*Hague Declaration 3 concerning Expanding Bullets,* a treaty which entered into force in September 1900), this prohibition now has the status of customary law (Coupland and Loye, 2003, p. 135; ICRC, 2005, Rule 77, p. 268), and the use of such bullets has been recognized as a war crime in the 1998 Rome Statute of the International Criminal Court (art. 8(2)(b)(xix)). A recent study by the International Committee of the Red Cross (ICRC) found that it is also prohibited under customary international law in cases of non-international armed conflicts (ICRC, 2005, Rule 77, p. 268).

The use of expanding bullets against civilians has nevertheless been signalled in several instances, including in Papua New Guinea (Bougainville) (Amnesty

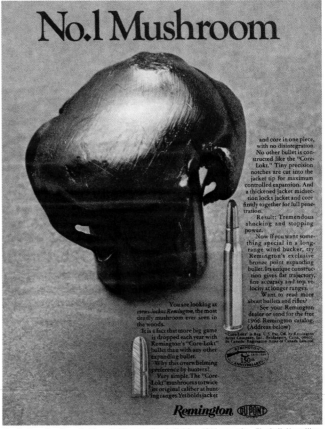

Remington advertises its 'Core-Lokt' expanding bullet in a 1966 magazine. The bullet's selling point: it 'mushrooms to twice its original caliber ... yet holds jacket and core in one piece'.

© Remington, 1966

Box 1.9   Terminal ballistics

Terminal or 'wound' ballistics describes the trajectory of a projectile and its effects once it has hit its target.

One common misperception is that a bullet makes a straight hole in the body; in reality, the hole created is much larger than the bullet itself. This so-called temporary cavity puts a great deal of pressure on surrounding organs and tissue, damaging them, even though they never came into contact with the bullet. This cavity is also made bigger as a result of the movement of the bullet, which becomes unstable and starts wobbling or even tumbling end-over-end as it moves along its path. The size and location of the temporary cavity determines the overall damage done. Small, low-velocity missiles like pistol bullets will produce only a small temporary cavity, while high-velocity rifle bullets will create a large one. Beyond a certain threshold, the temporary cavity may be too large to be contained in the organ or tissue hit (if it does not have sufficient elasticity), and may cause it to 'burst'.

The extent of the wound also depends on the design of the bullet: bullets that expand on impact create a larger temporary cavity than non-expanding ones.
> Hollow-point bullets have a hole at the top, and sometimes incisions to ensure additional expansion on hitting the target; their expansion creates sharp edges (and, in case of high velocity, fragmentation). They are mostly used for hunting, because they increase the likelihood that the animal will be killed and not just wounded.
> Soft-point bullets expand as well, but typically they do not fragment (they assume a 'mushroom' shape on impact).
> Entirely-jacketed bullets do not expand, but they still cause significant tissue damage at high velocity.

Sources: Coupland (1999); Di Maio (1999); DeClerq (1999b); Gebhardt (2004)

International, 1997, p. 13) and the Palestinian Territories (UN ECOSOC, 2000). In the context of law enforcement, the use of such ammunition is authorized because it ricochets less, and the fact that it flattens on impact means that there is less chance that it will pass through the intended target and wound innocent bystanders—it is thus considered 'safer' for use in urban surroundings. Lastly, these bullets have very strong stopping power when shot at close range, making them particularly attractive to self-defence users. This is why law enforcement officers, as well as units that specialize in anti-terrorist or hostage release operations, use expanding bullets.

New types of expanding bullets have little in common, though, with the original 'dum-dum'. Their energy when fired from a handgun is about one-sixth of that produced by bullets fired from 19th century military rifles (Coupland and Loye, 2003, pp. 140–41) (see Box 1.9).

MEASURES

International and regional measures to control small arms ammunition

Ammunition is mentioned in a number of international and regional instruments that focus on small arms control. In order to assess to what extent current regulations on small arms also apply to ammunition, one must examine two questions:

- Does the instrument, in principle, cover ammunition, as reflected in its definitions section?
- If ammunition does appear in the instrument's definitions section, is this accompanied by concrete and specific provisions relating to it?

Although most international instruments cover ammunition in their definitions, their operational provisions often ignore ammunition, concentrating solely on small arms (McDonald, 2005); this is often true for regional instruments as well (see Table 1.2).

At the international level, the 2001 *UN Protocol against the Illicit Manufacturing of and Trafficking in Firearms, Their Parts and Components and Ammunition ('Firearms Protocol')* includes a definition of ammunition in Article 3, which does not apply to ammunition components (such as the case and primer) if these are not already regulated by the relevant state (UNGA, 2001a, p. 3). A closer look reveals, however, that many of this instrument's provisions do

Table 1.2   Regional small arms instruments

Instrument	Date of adoption	Is small arms ammunition covered in the definitions?	Specific provisions on small arms ammunition
ECOWAS Moratorium and *Code of Conduct* (ECOWAS, 1998; 1999)	31 October 1998 and 10 December 1999	Yes (Art. 3 of the Code of Conduct)	The whole text covers small arms ammunition and components
European Union Code of Conduct on Arms Exports (EU, 1998)	8 June 1998	Yes. See Common Military List: ML3 referring to ML1 (EU, 2003b)	The whole text covers small arms ammunition
Council Common Position on the control of arms brokering (EU, 2003a)	25 June 2003	Yes	The whole text covers small arms ammunition
Nairobi Protocol (Nairobi Protocol, 2004)	21 April 2004	Yes	None. Ammunition is only mentioned in the definitions
Inter-American Convention against the Illicit Manufacturing of and Trafficking in Firearms, Ammunition, Explosives, and Other Related Materials (OAS, 1997)	14 November 1997	Yes	The whole text covers small arms ammunition, except for Art. VI on marking and Art. XI on record-keeping, which deal with firearms only
OAS Model Regulations (OAS, 1998)	2 June 1998	Yes	Contains detailed procedures for the import, export, and in-transit shipment of ammunition
Bamako Declaration on an African Common Position on the Illicit Proliferation, Circulation and Trafficking of Small Arms and Light Weapons (OAU, 2000)	1 December 2000	Unclear	Says that states should establish as criminal offences the illicit manufacturing of, trafficking in, and illegal possession and use of, ammunition (V. 3. A. iii). States should encourage the codification and harmonization of legislation governing the manufacture, trading, brokering, possession, and use of ammunition (V. 3. B. ii)
OSCE Document on Small Arms and Light Weapons (OSCE, 2000)	24 November 2000	No	Mentions ammunition only in relation to post-conflict disarmament, demobilization, and reintegration (DDR) programmes, for instance the 'disposal and destruction of surrendered or seized small arms and ammunition' (V. D. 5)
SADC Protocol (SADC, 2001)	14 August 2001	Yes (Art. 1, para. 2)	The whole text covers small arms ammunition

not pertain to ammunition. Article 8 on marking and Article 9 on deactivation, for instance, apply only to firearms, not to ammunition (UNGA, 2001a, pp. 5–6).

The *UN Programme of Action* of 2001 is the only global instrument that covers most issues pertaining to small arms, from manufacture to stockpile management. Although ammunition was included in the definition of small arms and light weapons the UN Panel of Experts put forward in 1997 (UNSG, 1997, III.26(c)), the *Programme* has no definition of small arms and light weapons. Nor do its provisions use the word 'ammunition' (McDonald, 2005). Nevertheless, several states have supplied information on ammunition when reporting on their implementation of the *Programme*. They have referred to ammunition mainly in relation to changes in national legislation and regulations, and in connection with assistance provided or received for stockpile destruction. Many countries have also provided precise figures on ammunition collected or destroyed (Kytömäki, 2004).

There seems to be widespread understanding that ammunition is part of the arms proliferation problem, and should, therefore, be regulated at the regional and international levels. This understanding is often reflected in the titles, introductions, and definitions of the international and regional texts that address the issue of small arms and light weapons. Recognizing the importance of ammunition, the UN General Assembly recommended in 1997 that a study be conducted to assess all aspects of the problem of ammunition and explosives (UNGA, 1999, p. 1). Few, if any, subsequent steps have been taken, however, to address the ammunition issue at the international level.

Marking and tracing

The simplest way to trace ammunition is by lot number. If cartridges have been taken out of their original packaging, their origin can still be determined to a certain extent using their headstamp. Marking, however, could be improved by adding the lot number to the headstamp, or by engraving the bullet itself.

Lot numbers

If the ammunition is still in its original packaging, identification is facilitated by the fact that the name, calibre, type, and producer, as well as the year and lot of manufacture, are printed on the box (UNGA, 1999, para. 77, p. 12). The lot of manufacture, in particular, is used to trace ammunition during transportation (UNIDIR and Small Arms Survey, 2003, p. 59) (see Box 1.10).

Los HP-86/I
RP
50 Patronen 9 mm x 19 Parabellum
Weichkern

© George G. Kass, Forensic Ammunition Service

Marking of an ammunition box to be used by the German police. Indicated are: the producer (HP for the Austrian manufacturer Hirtenberg Pat); the year of production (86 for 1986); the lot number (1); the recipient (RP for police forces of Rhineland-Palatine); and the number, calibre, and type of cartridges (50 soft-core cartridges, calibre 9 x 19mm Parabellum).

Although the lot number lacks precision (there are usually between 250,000 and one million cartridges in a single batch), it nevertheless allows the source of manufacture to be identified, as well as a particular production run, which is useful in the event of malfunctioning (UNGA, 1999, sec. 21, p. 6). For similar reasons of quality control, all ammunition components are given their own lot number prior to assembly. The lot number also helps trace the provenance of stolen boxes of ammunition when or if they are recovered (see Box 1.11).

Box 1.10   Regulating the transport of ammunition

As it consists, in part, of explosives, ammunition for small arms (and light weapons) is classified as a 'dangerous good' by the UN and is thus subject to a series of rules governing various aspects of its transport.

In 1953, the UN Economic and Social Council (ECOSOC) set up a Committee of Experts on the Transport of Dangerous Goods and tasked it with developing and harmonizing regulations in this area for all modes of transport. The committee published an initial set of recommendations in 1956, which has been updated regularly and has been referred to as 'Model Regulations' since 1996. The fourteenth revised edition is scheduled for publication in late 2005.

An expansion of the original committee's mandate resulted in the creation of a Sub-Committee of Experts on the Transport of Dangerous Goods (TDG Sub-Committee), which continues to carry out technical work on this issue. The TDG Sub-Committee consists of 27 'expert countries', together with non-voting observers, representing various states, international organizations, NGOs, and industry bodies.

The Model Regulations are not legally binding. Nevertheless, they form part of national legislation in many, perhaps most, states around the world, often as a result of their incorporation into legally binding multilateral instruments (Kervella, 2003, sec. 4). European agreements governing the transport of dangerous goods by road, rail, and inland waterway have made the Model Regulations the basis of their own legally binding rules. At the international level, they have been applied—again in legally binding form—to rules developed for maritime and air transport.

The Model Regulations provide a detailed, item-by-item classification for such goods, based on the type of risk involved. Small arms ammunition falls under Class 1, dealing with explosives. Among other things, the Model Regulations set out standards for transport packaging, including its testing and certification. General packing provisions for small arms cartridges (UN classification no. 0012) mandate the use of 'good quality packagings ... which shall be strong enough to withstand the shocks and loadings normally encountered during transport'. More detailed instructions prescribe the kinds of materials to be used in the construction of outer packaging (UN, 2003, part 4, pp. 5, 27).

The Model Regulations also establish rules for labelling, marking, and documentation designed to ensure that dangerous goods can be identified as such by all those involved in their transport (UN, 2003). But they do not address the question of responsibility or penalties for non-compliance. In general, it is for each state to decide how to monitor and enforce implementation of the Model Regulations, in accordance with national legislation.

Author: Glenn McDonald
Sources: Kervella (2003); UN (2003); Berkol (2004)[18]

Box 1.11   Ammunition smuggled from Paraguay to Brazil

On 2 August 2002, Brazilian Federal Police agents seized 50,000 rounds of ammunition in different parts of Rio de Janeiro. According to police sources, the ammunition was bound for several criminal groups based in the city's slums (*favelas*). The items seized were 5.56 mm, 7.62 mm, 9 mm, .306, and .40 cartridges manufactured by Companhia Brasileira de Cartuchos (CBC) in Brazil and by the Czech Republic. Since the CBC bullets were still in their original boxes, the police could tell that these cartridges belonged to lot number LT 547.4-Trim/POL K N-135 L 479/81, which the company had exported to Paraguay. Identification of the lot number was, therefore, vital to tracing the trafficking route back to Paraguay, whose law allowing foreign tourists to buy small arms and ammunition was being intensively taken advantage of by Brazilian criminals. After Brazilian government and civil society representatives applied heavy pressure, this law was eventually overturned by Paraguay.

Author: Pablo Dreyfus

Cartridge marking and headstamps

In some instances, the lot or batch number is not just printed on the box, but also engraved on the base of the cartridge. This is one of the measures recently adopted in Brazil to counter ammunition proliferation (see Box 1.12). Once ammunition is taken from its packaging, only the headstamp can be used for identification.

A headstamp is a distinctive mark printed on the bottom of the case. It identifies the manufacturer and the country of origin, and is still readable after the cartridge has been fired. Headstamps sometimes also include the date of manufacture (mostly for military ammunition), the calibre, and the army unit that placed the order (in the case of military ammunition) (International Ammunition Association, 2003; UNGA, 1999, sec. 75, p. 12).

Although generally reliable, headstamps do not provide a full guarantee of the origin of the ammunition: on several occasions, deceitful headstamps have been used to conceal the actual source (International Ammunition Association, 2003). Some ammunition used in covert military operations bears no marking at all, or employs markings with a secret meaning. Some dealers also put their own trade mark on the ammunition, which is designed especially for them (UNGA, 1999, sec. 75, p. 12). Another problem is the complexity of the current headstamping classification system, which is due to the very large (and constantly changing) number of ammunition producers and the necessity to use cryptic symbols and codes because of a lack of space on the bottom of the casing.

Box 1.12   Improving police accountability through ammunition marking: the new Brazilian Statute of Disarmament

On 22 December 2003, Federal Law No. 10,826—the Statute of Disarmament—was finally passed. It was the product of a decade of campaigning for a federal law that would establish tight controls over the circulation and use of small arms. Besides forbidding the carrying of small arms by civilians and calling for a referendum on a ban on small arms and ammunition sales to civilians (scheduled for October 2005), it incorporates provisions targeted at the small arms and ammunition industries. Measures include a mandatory electronic link between the databases of the army (which controls production, imports, and exports) and the Brazilian Federal Police (which, under the new law, is tasked with centralizing registration data and information on seized weapons and ammunition). In the past, lack of communication and failure to exchange information between the two institutions has prevented an efficient struggle against diversion and trafficking. The law also establishes a centralized ballistic information system, managed by the Brazilian Federal Police, which will contain samples of bullets fired by every small arms item manufactured in Brazil. This should allow for small arms used in crimes to be identified.

As for ammunition, the new law stipulates that the headstamps on 5.56 mm, .30, 7.62 mm, 9 mm, .357, .380, .38, .40, .45, and .50 calibre cartridges and 12-gauge shotgun shells produced in Brazil for the police and armed forces must include the lot number. This should enhance the security of military and police stockpiles, as police will be able to identify patterns of leakage (of ammunition) from either institution to organized criminal entities.

The sanctions set out in the law should be deterrent enough: trafficking in ammunition and diverting, stealing, and illegally stockpiling ammunition fall under Articles 17 ('Illegal trade in firearms') and 18 ('International arms trafficking'), which specify prison terms of between 8 and 16 years.

The law could also help in identifying those responsible for unjust killings through analysis of the lot numbers engraved on empty casings found at shoot-out scenes. Hopefully, this could lead to the emergence of a virtuous circle whereby police units feel compelled to increase their level of training and to use firearms only when absolutely necessary.

Author: Pablo Dreyfus

Marking cartridges with the lot number is already common practice in a number of countries. Since 1985, Industria Militar (INDUMIL), which has a monopoly on small arms ammunition production in Colombia, has marked cartridges with a lot number that identifies the army purchaser. Similar procedures exist in Austria and Germany (Dreyfus, 2004).

The advantage of headstamps is that they cannot be tampered with; someone trying to erase this marking would cause the primer to fire, rendering the cartridge unusable. The downside is that if one disposes of the spent case, there is no way of identifying the projectile anymore. The same problem arises when a case is employed several times, as with reloading, or in the rare instances when caseless cartridges are used.

© George C. Kass, Forensic Ammunition Service

Headstamp of a cartridge manufactured by Dynamit Nobel AG Troisdorf (DAG) of Germany for the country's military, as indicated by the NATO symbol at the top. The lot number is 75-28.

Bullet marking

A potential solution to the problem highlighted above is to engrave the base of the bullet, rather than the case, with a serial number or code (UNIDIR and Small Arms Survey, 2003, pp. 59–60). This method of marking is currently under review in California, United States, where all handgun bullets may soon have to be laser-marked (Reuters, 2004). The Ammunition Coding System (ACS) that is being tested would engrave a code on both the bullet and the case. This code would be unique for each box of bullets sold, and would be entered into a database, along with personal information about the purchaser of the ammunition, creating a general record of all ammunition sales in the state (Ammunition Coding System, 2004). It would represent a major improvement on classical forensic tests, whereby one needs to recover the firearm (often a difficult task) to see if it matches a given bullet. This initiative is, however, likely to spark debate on the additional cost to manufacturers, especially the smallest ones, since the price of a laser-engraving machine is quite high (Ammunition Coding System, 2004). Such technology may be beyond the reach of most developing country producers. Another concern relates to ensuring the confidentiality of the information collected (which only authorized law enforcement personnel should be able to access). It also remains to be seen whether this method will work with military ammunition, the base of which can be damaged during firing, which may result in the engraved number becoming unreadable.

In cases where the primer is manufactured by the same company as the finished cartridge, such as CBC in Brazil, it is possible to mark the cup containing the priming mixture. Original CBC cartridge primers are marked with a 'V' on the external side, allowing forensic experts to distinguish between newly produced cartridges and those that have been reloaded; the latter would have the CBC headstamp but no 'V' on the primer cup.

International and regional marking and tracing initiatives

At the international level, the Group of Governmental Experts on Tracing Illicit Small Arms and Light Weapons stated in its 2003 report that '[a]mmunition and explosives … are generally regarded as a part of the problem of small arms and light weapons', and acknowledged the work done in 1999 by the Group of Experts on the problem of ammunition and explosives (UNGA, 2003, para. 33). Nevertheless, little progress has been made to date in translating such awareness into concrete international action.

In December 2003, the UN General Assembly, pursuant to the recommendation of the same group of governmental experts, established an Open-Ended Working Group to negotiate an international instrument for identifying and tracing illicit small arms and light weapons. It soon emerged, though, that there was no consensus within the group on whether its mandate covered ammunition. As of 15 February 2005, it appeared unlikely that the international tracing instrument, when finalized in June 2005, would contain firm commitments in relation to ammunition, although it seems possible that there will be some acknowledgement in the instrument of the need for follow-up work.

Other international instruments address ammunition only partially, if at all. The record-keeping provisions of the legally binding *UN Firearms Protocol* apply to ammunition only 'where appropriate and feasible' (Art. 7). Article 8 of the protocol, on marking, deals only with firearms (UNGA, 2001a). The *Programme of Action* underlines the importance of marking and tracing for small arms and light weapons, but does not mention ammunition (UNGA, 2001b).

Almost all of the regional instruments that cover marking, record-keeping, and tracing, such as the *Inter-American Convention* (OAS, 1997), the *SADC Protocol* (SADC, 2001), the *OSCE Document on Small Arms and Light Weapons* (OSCE, 2004), or the recent *Nairobi Protocol* (2004), limit themselves to firearms, ignoring ammunition. The *Bamako*

Declaration (OAU, 2000) is the only exception. It encourages the development of common standards for marking and record-keeping for both small arms and ammunition (OAU, 2000, sec. V. 3. B. ii).

Management and destruction of ammunition stockpiles

Maintaining and securing existing military stockpiles are matters of the utmost importance. Ammunition that has expired or become obsolete, unserviceable, or redundant is routinely removed from military stockpiles. When ammunition is still in usable condition, excess stocks are sometimes given to other countries (DeClerq, 1999a). At other times, however, such ammunition is simply kept, leading to excessive accumulation and storage problems. A 1996 report by the United States General Accounting Office (GAO) pointed out, for instance, that the Marine Corps was storing approximately three million .50 calibre cartridges for a machine gun (the M85) that was not in use anymore; but this ammunition could not be used with any other weapon (US GAO, 1996, p. 4). In the past decade, ammunition stockpiles have increased as a result of the reduction of the size of the armed forces in many countries (UNGA, 1999, sec. 60, p. 10).

Stockpile mismanagement can represent a serious threat to life and the environment, in addition to the risks of diversion. In November 2003, the OSCE adopted a *Document on Stockpiles of Conventional Ammunition* that seeks to help participating states to identify their surplus stocks, and to request assistance with their management if needed (OSCE, 2003).

Destruction of small arms ammunition is not particularly difficult or expensive, at least for small quantities (DeClerq, 1999a). Unlike grenades and mortar bombs, small arms ammunition contains very little explosive material that can be used for its own destruction (UNDDA, 2001, p. 25). Consequently, it is usually burnt, or simply fired, using different methods (see Table 1.3). Large quantities of ammunition, meanwhile, are more difficult to dispose of, since burning may result in the emission of toxic particulates into the air.

> Stockpile mismanagement can represent a serious threat to life and the environment, in addition to the risks of diversion.

Table 1.3   Ammunition destruction methods

	Most suitable depending on the:		Advantages	Disadvantages
	quantity of ammunition	condition of the ammunition		
Firing	Small	Good	Leaves only empty cases	Creates projectile debris, need for a safety area
Burning using an improvised incinerator	Small to medium	Poor	Mobile, requires little equipment	Needs a long cooling-down period, creates smoke
Large-scale burning using improvised means	Large	Poor	Ceremonial destruction	Needs a significant amount of preparation time and a long cooling-down period, creates smoke
Burning using a mobile incinerator	Small	Poor	Reusable, mobile, easy	Only small quantities can be handled at a time
Burning using a fixed incinerator	Any	Any	Little or no air and noise pollution	Not mobile, requires constant fuel supply
Rotary kiln incineration	Large	Any	Efficient, little or no air pollution	Very high cost (purchase and maintenance), lack of mobility, requires fuel supply

Source: Adapted from UNDDA (2001, pp. 26–39)

A number of private companies, mainly located in North America and Western Europe, specialize in ammunition and explosives destruction, be it excess state stockpiles or remnants from theatres of conflict. A few ammunition manufacturers provide similar demilitarization services, such as Nammo AS of Norway or SNC Technologies of Canada (Nammo, 2005; SNC Technologies, 2005).

Ammunition is sometimes included in post-conflict weapons collection programmes. The Small Arms Reduction Project of the United Nations Development Programme (UNDP) assists the Government of Bosnia and Herzegovina in destroying its surplus and obsolete ammunition (UNDP, 2005). In Albania, weapons in exchange for development (WED) programmes implemented in three districts allowed 13 million rounds of ammunition to be collected (UNDP, 2004, p. 6)—although it should be remembered that, when Albanians raided military depots in March 1997, they seized between 900 million and 1.6 billion cartridges (Van der Graaf and Faltas, 2001, p. 165; UNDP, 2004, p. 6). The disarmament, demobilization, and reintegration (DDR) programme in Liberia (1996–99) was also particularly successful in reducing ammunition stockpiles: more than five million rounds of small arms ammunition were collected (BASIC, 2004; AllAfrica, 2004c; AllAfrica, 2004d). Following some tense discussions with the Liberian government over the fate of the weapons and ammunition, all of the items were destroyed in October 1999 (BICC, 2005).

Some programmes specifically target ammunition. In 2002, for example, Canada took the lead in a NATO Maintenance and Supply Agency (NAMSA) ammunition destruction project in Albania, established to reduce the country's surplus stocks of ammunition (OSCE, 2002, pp. 16–17). This programme aims to destroy a total of 11,665 tons of ammunition (Republic of Albania, 2004).

One recurrent problem with ammunition collection is that, as with weapons, the items handed in are often old and unusable, while the population retains ammunition that is still in good condition. This seems to have been the case, for instance, with the ammunition recently collected in the Solomon Islands (Alpers and Twyford, 2003, pp. 94–95). Attempts to find ammunition caches may prove more fruitful than efforts to unearth firearms, since ammunition contains explosives and powder that trained dogs, for example, may detect more easily (SEESAC, 2003, p. 19).

It is also worth noting that, despite the obvious complementary roles played by weapons and ammunition in perpetrating conflict, ammunition is often forgotten in weapons collection and destruction programmes. In Mali, for example, a public bonfire of weapons ('Flame of Peace') was organized in March 1996 as part of the reconciliation process. An estimated 2,600–3,000 rifles, machine guns, grenade launchers, and pistols were destroyed (Poulton and Ag Youssouf, 1998, p. 120; DeClerq, 1999a, p. 8), but very little ammunition was collected. The weapons that were handed over to the Malian authorities apparently contained one cartridge each, yet most were destroyed without ammunition—and no ammunition was placed in the Flame of Peace for fear that it may represent a hazard to the people watching (Poulton and Ag Youssouf, 1998, p. 120). Hence, major stockpiles of cartridges and shotgun shells remained unaccounted for, and soon people started acquiring new weapons in order to be able to use this leftover ammunition, or they sold it to those who still had weapons.[19]

> Ammunition is often forgotten in weapons collection and destruction programmes.

Ammunition and the small arms control agenda

Ammunition production sources are easier to map than those of weapons, because there are fewer ammunition producers than small arms producers in the world, and the former are more easily identified (ICRC, 1999). A relatively small number of companies produce primers, whose manufacture involves complex techniques and whose manipulation is risky (they are ultra-sensitive to heat, shock, and friction, which can result in a violent detonation) (Saferstein, 1995, p. 335; SAAMI, 2005). Producers of ammunition components could therefore be a good target for ammunition control.

One argument for targeting ammunition centres on the fact that weapons are a durable good while ammunition is not: three of its four components (projectile, powder, and primer) can be used only once. Although ammunition's longevity can extend well beyond its official shelf life, 'small arms and light weapons used in conflict require frequent re-supply of ammunition and therefore enhanced controls on ammunition and its explosive components and on the manufacturing technology to produce them could be of particular value in dealing with the existing dissemination of small arms and light weapons and reducing the incidence of their use in conflict or post-conflict situations' (UNGA, 1999, sec. 104, p. 16). The fact that the shelf life can be very long only matters if the ammunition does not need to be used for a long time. In conflict settings, by contrast, ammunition stocks are depleted very rapidly, fuelling a need for constant resupply. Because high expenditure of ammunition often signifies severe conflict or intense waste (through 'spraying' rather than aiming at targets), it serves as a good indicator of potential weapons misuse. Limiting ammunition proliferation and keeping supplies under control could help in preventing some of this misuse.

High expenditure of ammunition often serves as a good indicator of potential misuse.

Marking military and police ammunition, as in Brazil, or all bullets, as in the project currently under review in California, could represent a major improvement by making purchasers more accountable and limiting the risk of abusive use of firearms. In regions where there is a danger of ammunition being diverted to armed or criminal groups, marking ammunition could even be more useful than marking the weapons themselves, since it is quickly depleted. If one started marking all sold ammunition today, it would probably take just ten years to mark most of the ammunition transferred worldwide—while guns already in circulation are likely to remain so for decades.

Another instrument that has proved effective in the past is export control, or, more specifically, the restriction of ammunition exports to countries that may resell the imported products, or where they are likely to be misused. Australia, the major exporter of ammunition to PNG, decided in 2002 to limit drastically its sales to the country, for fear that they might accentuate existing proliferation and fuel violence; New Zealand has taken a similar stand (Alpers, 2005).

CONCLUSION

Ammunition, it seems, has long been considered nothing more than a subsidiary of weapons. In 1999, the Group of Experts on the problem of ammunition and explosives highlighted the 'insufficiency and unavailability of existing information on matters related to ammunition for small arms and light weapons and explosives in all their aspects' (UNGA, 1999, sec. 9, p. 4). This chapter has introduced a number of issues pertaining to small arms ammunition, but much more remains to be done on a subject that has been neglected to date. A closer look at light weapons ammunition, for instance, would raise significantly different questions regarding international transfers, stockpile management, and detection of caches, as it contains much more explosive material than its small arms counterpart, and is used almost exclusively in military settings.

Looking at the problem of firearms misuse through the ammunition lens leads to consideration of new control strategies. Up to now, however, international instruments have covered ammunition very imperfectly, leaving it mostly to individual governments to decide on whether they should report on ammunition-related matters. The ammunition issue is often left aside because it is considered either too complex, or of secondary importance. In practice, though, measures that target ammunition can be easier to implement than those that focus on firearms. Headstamping, for example, is a marking that can not be tampered with—unlike the marking of firearms.

Widening the scope of small arms research to include all aspects of ammunition will facilitate understanding of larger patterns of weapons proliferation and misuse, particularly in conflict regions. Knowing more about how ammunition is produced, stored, sold, used, and ultimately destroyed will provide a clearer idea of ammunition availability, and what steps can be taken to control its spread. Effective post-conflict ammunition collection programmes and improved security of existing stockpiles are measures in need of further development and more effective implementation. This, in turn, will affect small arms use and misuse.

Additionally, it should be noted that, as with small arms, most proposed or existing initiatives concentrate on controlling supply; yet the demand side should not be neglected. Efforts to control production and transfers will prove useless if demand is high enough to encourage a diffusion of technology and craft production; improved and efficient stockpile destruction methods will be of little use if the populations involved mistrust the process and thus keep their ammunition. Further research is thus needed on the determinants of the demand for weapons and ammunition, and how the two are interrelated.

LIST OF ABBREVIATIONS

ACS	Ammunition Coding System
BMG	Browning Machine Gun
CAR	Central African Republic
CBC	Companhia Brasileira de Cartuchos (Brazil)
CIS	Commonwealth of Independent States
CNC	Computer numeric control
DDR	Disarmament, demobilization, and reintegration
DFPC	Directorate of Controlled Products (Brazil)
DRC	Democratic Republic of Congo
ECOSOC	Economic and Social Council (UN)
ECOWAS	Economic Community of West African States
EU	European Union
FLETC	Federal Law Enforcement Training Center (United States)
FMJ	Full-metal jacket
GAO	General Accounting Office (United States)
HIPCs	Heavily Indebted Poor Countries
ICRC	International Committee of the Red Cross
INDUMIL	Industria Militar (Colombia)
NAMSA	NATO Maintenance and Supply Agency
NATO	North Atlantic Treaty Organisation
NGO	Non-governmental organization

OAS	Organization of American States
OAU	Organization of African Unity
OSCE	Organization for Security and Co-operation in Europe
PBRs	Plastic baton rounds
PNG	Papua New Guinea
SADC	Southern African Development Community
UN	United Nations
UNDP	United Nations Development Programme
UNRF II	Uganda National Rescue Front II
USAEC	US Army Environmental Center
WED	Weapons in exchange for development

ENDNOTES

1. These figures, however, include small arms as well as non-small arms ammunition. This chapter also addresses ammunition designed for heavy machine guns and anti-matériel rifles because, in basic terms, it differs from small arms ammunition only in size.
2. Shotguns are not specifically mentioned in the UN definition of small arms (UNGA, 1997, sec. 26, pp. 11–12).
3. Interview with a representative of RUAG Ammotec, September 2004.
4. Correspondence with James Gebhardt, American firearms hobbyist, 27 September 2004.
5. Correspondence with James Gebhardt, American firearms hobbyist, 10 December 2004.
6. Correspondence with Philip Alpers, gunpolicy.org, 24 January 2005.
7. Interview with Malian ex-combatants, Bamako, Mali, 2–3 September 2004.
8. Interview between Christina Wille, senior researcher at the Small Arms Survey, and a former Khmer Rouge commander, Pailin, Cambodia, 1 February 2005.
9. Interview with Malian ex-combatants, Bamako, Mali, 2–3 September 2004.
10. Interview with Malian ex-combatants, Bamako, Mali, 2–3 September 2004.
11. Interview with Malian ex-combatants, Bamako, Mali, 2–3 September 2004.
12. Interview between Christina Wille, senior researcher at the Small Arms Survey, and a former Khmer Rouge commander, Pailin, Cambodia, 1 February 2005.
13. Interview with Malian ex-combatants, Bamako, Mali, 2–3 September 2004.
14. Interview with Henry Boschoff, military analyst at the ISS (Institute for Security Studies, Pretoria), Geneva, 8 October 2004.
15. Interview between Christina Wille, senior researcher at the Small Arms Survey, and a former Khmer Rouge commander, Pailin, Cambodia, 1 February 2005.
16. Interview with Malian ex-combatants, Bamako, Mali, 2–3 September 2004; Small Arms Survey and CECORE (2004).
17. 5.56 x 45mm, .22-250, .243 Winchester, .270 Winchester, .308 Winchester, .375 Winchester, 7mm Mauser, 7.62 x 39mm, 7.62 x 51mm, .30-06, 9mm, .357 Magnum, .38 Super Auto, .40 Smith & Wesson, .44 Magnum, .44 Special, .45 Colt, .45 Auto, .50, 12-gauge.
18. Additional source: interview with Sergio Benassai, Head of Italian Delegation to the Sub-Committee of Experts on the Transport of Dangerous Goods, Geneva, 9 December 2004.
19. Interview with Malian ex-combatants, Bamako, Mali, 2–3 September 2004.

BIBLIOGRAPHY

AFP (Agence France Presse). 2005. 'U.S. Seeks To Buy Ammunition From Taiwan: Report.' Accessed 6 January.
 <http://www.defensenews.com/story.php?F=586112&C=america&P=true>

Africa Confidential. 2004. 'Belgium/Tanzania: Gun law.' Vol. 45, No. 2, 23 January, p. 8.

AllAfrica. 2004a. 'Nigeria: Police Nab Illegal Arms Manufacturer.' 31 March.

—. 2004b. 'Nigeria: Police Sack Arms Factory.' 8 April.

—. 2004c. 'UN Mission Disarms Over 18,000 Ex-Rebels in Liberia.' 5 May.

—. 2004d. 'Factions Yet to Surrender Heavy Weapons—UN Report On Liberia.' 16 September.

Alpers, Philip. 2005. *Gunrunning in Papua New Guinea: from arrows to assault weapons in the Southern Highlands.* Geneva: Small Arms Survey. Forthcoming

Alpers, Philip and Conor Twyford. 2003. *Small Arms in the Pacific.* Occasional Paper No. 8. Geneva: Small Arms Survey. March.

Ammunition Coding System Web site. 2004. Accessed 13 October 2004. <http://www.ammocoding.com>

Amnesty International. 1997. 'Papua New Guinea—Bougainville: The Forgotten Human Rights Tragedy.' Accessed 8 February 2005.
 <http://web.amnesty.org/library/pdf/ASA340011997ENGLISH/$File/ASA3400197.pdf>

Aning, Emmanuel Kwesi. 2005. 'The Anatomy of Ghana's Secret Arms Industry.' In Eric Berman and Nicolas Florquin, eds. *Armed Groups and Small Arms in the ECOWAS Region*. Geneva: Small Arms Survey. Forthcoming.

AP (Associated Press). 2001a. 'Kmart to Phase Out Sale of Handgun Ammunition.' 28 June.

—. 2001b. 'Kmart kills ammunition sales.' 29 June.

—. 2004a. 'Producers struggle to keep U.S. soldiers in Iraq supplied.' 7 June.

—. 2004b. 'The Expiration Monday of a 10-year federal ban on assault weapons means firearms like AK-47s, Uzis and TEC-9s can now be legally bought—a development that has critics upset and gun owners pleased.' 13 September.

—. 2004c. '3rd Army Commanders felt ammunition was short before Iraq invasion, internal report says.' 27 November.

—. 2004d. 'California Activists Call For Lead Ammunition Ban to Aid Condors.' 18 December.

BASIC (British American Security Information Council). 2004. 'Removing Surplus Small Arms and Light Weapons from Russian Society: Lessons from Weapons Collection and Destruction Programmes in Other Countries and Regions.' Accessed 15 October 2004. <http://www.basicint.org/WT/smallarms/removing_surplus-IDpres-1201-tables.htm>

Bayet, Hugues. 2004. 'Communique de presse.' Namur, Belgium, 12 February. Accessed 17 February 2005. <http://www.eca-watch.org/problems/arms/documents/BelgianMinisterVanCauwenberghePressRelease.doc>

Berkol, Ilhan. 2004. *Transport des matières dangereuses dans le contexte des armes légères*. Background paper (unpublished). Geneva: Small Arms Survey.

Berman, Eric. 2005. *Small Arms and Light Weapons in Central African Republic*. Geneva: Small Arms Survey. Forthcoming.

BICC (Bonn International Conversion Center). 2005. 'Help Desk for Practical Disarmament: Liberia.' Accessed 27 January 2005. <http://www.bicc.de/helpdesk/stories/liberia.html>

Blue Line: Canada's National Law Enforcement Magazine. 1997. 'Force agrees to stop using weapon.' April.

Butterfield, Fox. 2004. 'With Ban Lifted, Some Gun Shoppers Find Lower Prices.' *The New York Times*. 16 September.

Capie, David. 2004. *Armed Groups, Weapons Availability and Misuse: An Overview of the Issues and Options for Action*. Background paper for a meeting organized by the Centre for Humanitarian Dialogue, in advance of the Sixth Meeting of the Human Security Network in Bamako, Mali. 25 May. Accessed 23 February 2005. <http://www.hdcentre.org/datastore/Armed_groups_briefing.pdf>

Center to Prevent Handgun Violence. 1997. 'Florida Supreme Court Upholds Verdict Against K-Mart for Selling Gun to Intoxicated Customer Who Shot Estranged Girlfriend.' News Release. 17 July. Accessed 8 October 2004. <http://www.bradycampaign.org/press/release.php?release=73>

Chambre des Représentants de Belgique. 2004. Commission des relations extérieures, CRIV 51 COM 130 of 20 January.

CNN (Cable News Network). 2004. 'Feds Take Shot at Unleaded Ammo.' 27 July.

Coupland, Robin. 1999. 'Clinical and legal significance of fragmentation bullets in relation to size of wounds: retrospective analysis.' *British Medical Journal,* Vol. 319. 14 August, pp. 403–406.

Coupland, Robin and Dominique Loye. 2003. 'The 1899 Hague Declaration concerning Expanding Bullets: A treaty effective for more than 100 years faces complex contemporary issues.' *International Review of the Red Cross*, No. 849. 31 March, pp. 135–42. Accessed 22 February 2005. <http://www.icrc.org/Web/eng/siteeng0.nsf/htmlall/irrc_849_Coupland_et_Loye/$File/irrc_849_Coupland_et_Loye.pdf>

Cutshaw, Charles Q. and Leland Ness. 2003. *Jane's Ammunition Handbook 2003–2004*. Coulsdon: Jane's Information Group.

—. 2004. *Jane's Ammunition Handbook 2004–2005*. Coulsdon: Jane's Information Group.

DeClerq, David. 1998. *The Role of Ammunition Controls in Addressing Excessive and Destabilizing Accumulations of Small Arms*. Ottawa: Department of Foreign Affairs and International Trade.

—. 1999a. *Destroying Small Arms and Light Weapons: Survey of Methods and Practical Guide*. Report 13. Bonn: BICC. April. Accessed 23 February 2005. <http://www.bicc.de/publications/reports/report13/report13.pdf>

—. 1999b. *Trends in Small Arms and Light Weapons (SALW) Development: Non-Proliferation and Arms Control Dimensions*. Ottawa: Department of Foreign Affairs and International Trade.

Di Maio, Vincent J.M. 1999. *Gunshot Wounds: Practical Aspects of Firearms, Ballistics, and Forensic Techniques,* 2nd ed. Boca Raton, FL: CRC Press.

Dreyfus, Pablo. 2004. *Tracking bullets in a violent place: the Statute of Disarmament and ammunition marking regulations in Brazil*. Background paper. Geneva: Small Arms Survey. November.

ECOWAS (Economic Community of West African States). 1998. *Declaration of a Moratorium on the Importation, Exportation and Manufacture of Small Arms and Light Weapons in West Africa*. Adopted in Abuja, Nigeria, on 31 October.

—. 1999. *Code of Conduct for the Implementation of the Moratorium on the Importation, Exportation and Manufacture of Small Arms and Light Weapons in West Africa*. Adopted in Lomé, Togo, on 10 December.

EU (European Union). 1998. *European Union Code of Conduct on Arms Exports*. 8 June. Accessed 23 February 2005. <http://www.smallarmssurvey.org/source_documents/Regional%20fora/European%20Union/EUCodeofConduct.pdf>

—. 2003a. *Council Common Position 2003/468/CFSP of 23 June 2003 on the control of arms brokering*. Reproduced in Official Journal of the European Union, No. 2003/L 156/79-L 156/80, 25 June. Accessed 9 February 2005. <http://europa.eu.int/comm/external_relations/cfsp/sanctions/468.pdf>

—. 2003b. *Common Military List of the European Union*. Reproduced in Official Journal of the European Union, No. 2003/C 314/01-C 314/26, 23 December. Accessed 9 February 2005. <http://europa.eu.int/eur-lex/pri/en/oj/dat/2003/c_314/c_31420031223en00010026.pdf>

Faltas, Sami and Joseph Di Chiaro III, eds. 2001. *Managing the Remnants of War. Micro-Disarmament as an Element of Peace-building*. BICC Disarmament and Conversion Studies No. 5. Baden-Baden: Nomos Verlagsgesellschaft.

Faltas, Sami and Vera Chrobok. 2004. 'Disposal of surplus small arms: A survey of policies and practices in OSCE countries.' Bonn: Bonn International Center for Conversion, British American Security Information Council, Saferworld and Small Arms Survey. January.

FAS (Federation of American Scientists) Web site (Military Analysis Network). 2004. Accessed 7 September 2004. <http://www.fas.org/man/dod-101/sys/land/bullets.htm>

Gebhardt, James. 2004. *Handloading*. Background paper (unpublished). Geneva: Small Arms Survey. 16 September.

Government of South Africa, Department for Safety and Security. 2004. *Firearms Control Regulations, relating to Firearms Control Act, 2000*. Accessed 23 February 2005. <http://www.pmg.org.za/docs/2004/appendices/040218firearmregulations.htm>

Greene, Owen, Sally Holt, and Adrian Wilkinson. 2005. 'Ammunition Stocks: Promoting Safe and Secure Storage and Disposal.' Biting the Bullet Briefing 18. London: International Alert, Saferworld, University of Bradford, and SEESAC. February.

GRIP (Groupe de Recherche et d'Information sur la Paix et la Sécurité). 2004. *Exportation de matériel militaire vers la Tanzanie*. Note d'analyse. 13 February. Reference G4526. Accessed 8 February 2005. <http://www.grip.org/bdg/g4526.html >

Hogg, Ian V. 2002. *Jane's Guns Recognition Guide*. Glasgow: HarperCollins.

—. and John S. Weeks. 2000. *Military Small Arms of the 20th Century: Expanded, Updated Illustrated Encyclopedia of the World's Small Caliber Firearms*, 7th ed. Iola, WI: Krause Publications.

HRW (Human Rights Watch). 1999. 'World Report 1999: Arms transfers to abusive end-users.' Accessed 12 October 2004. <http://www.hrw.org/worldreport99/arms/arms4.html>

ICRC (International Committee of the Red Cross). 1999. 'Arms availability and the situation of civilians in armed conflict: a study presented by the ICRC.' Accessed 17 February 2005. <http://www.icrc.org/WEB/ENG/siteeng0.nsf/htmlall/p0734?OpenDocument&style=Custo_Final.4&View=defaultBody2>

—. 2005. *Customary International Humanitarian Law*. Volume I: Rules (edited by Jean-Marie Henckaerts and Louise Doswald-Beck). Cambridge: Cambridge University Press.

International Ammunition Association. 2003. 'Headstamp Codes on Small Arms Ammunition Identifying Makers.' Compiled by Lew Curtis and John Moss. Accessed 8 October 2004. <http://cartridgecollectors.org/headstampcodes_bottom.htm>

Jones, Richard and Charles Cutshaw. 2004. *Jane's Infantry Weapons 2004–2005*. Coulsdon: Jane's Information Group.

Kamenju, Jan. 2001. *The Eldoret factory*. Background paper (unpublished). Geneva: Small Arms Survey. December.

Kennedy, J. Michael. 2004. 'Unfriendly fire: Lead in bullets fired at ranges pose a danger to soil, groundwater and wildlife.' *Los Angeles Times*. 22 June. Accessed 9 February 2005. <http://www.latimes.com/features/outdoors/la-os-lead22jun22,1,4661318.story?ctrack=1&cset=true>

Kervella, Olivier. 2003. *United Nations Mechanisms for the Development and Harmonization of Transport of Dangerous Goods Regulations*. Paper presented at the AEGPL 2003 Congress, Geneva. 4–6 June.

Klein, Amy. 2001. 'Kmart ends standoff, drops handgun ammo.' *Detroit Free Press*. 29 June. Accessed 9 February 2005. <http://www.freep.com/money/business/kmart29_20010629.htm>

Krausz, Michael M. and Ahmad Mahajna. 2002. 'Traumatic effects of rubber bullets.' *The Lancet*, Vol. 360. 16 November, p. 1607.

Kwayera, Juma. 2003. 'Kenya will not close Eldoret bullet factory, says Murungaru.' *The East African*. 20 October.

Kytömäki, Elli. 2004. *Ammunition in the UN Programme of Action Reporting Process*. Background paper (unpublished). Geneva: Small Arms Survey. 20 October.

Legal Community Against Violence. 2004. 'Federal Law Summary.' Accessed 9 February 2005. < http://www.lcav.org/content/Federallawsummary.asp#regulationoftypes >

Leser, Eric. 2004. 'L'armée américaine souffre d'une pénurie de balles.' *Le Monde*. 27 July.

Le Soir. 2005. 'La Wallonie arme la Tanzanie.' 17 February. Accessed 23 February 2005. <http://www.regions.be/Rubriques/Wallonie/page_5590_303306.shtml>

Mahajna, Ahmad et al. 2002. 'Blunt and penetrating injuries caused by rubber bullets during the Israeli-Arab conflict in October, 2000: a retrospective study.' *The Lancet*, Vol. 359. 25 May, pp. 1795–800.

Manufacturing and Technology News. 2004. 'Production Capacity will Increase to Two Billion Rounds: Bullet Industry is on the Rise due to Wars and Increased Training Needs.' 7 July.

McDonald, Glenn. 2005. *Small Arms Instruments of a General Nature: Applicability to small arms, light weapons, and their ammunition*. Background paper (unpublished). Geneva: Small Arms Survey.

Merle, Renae. 2004. 'Running Low on Ammo: Military Turns to Overseas Suppliers to Cover Shortages.' *The Washington Post*. 22 July, p. E01.

Nairobi Protocol for the Prevention, Control and Reduction of Small Arms and Light Weapons in the Great Lakes Region and the Horn of Africa ('Nairobi Protocol'). 2004. Adopted in Nairobi, Kenya, on 21 April. Accessed 9 February 2005. <http://www.saferafrica.org/DocumentsCentre/NAIROBI-Protocol.asp>

Nammo AS, Norway. 2005. 'Demil Division.' Accessed 23 February 2005. <http://www.nammo.com/rdp/index.html>

Nordic Business Report. 2004. 'Nammo AS signs licence and cooperation agreement with Danish defence forces.' 14 June.

NRMA (National Reloading Manufacturers Association). 2005. Accessed 17 February 2005. <http://www.reload-nrma.com/>

OAS (Organization of American States). 1997. *Inter-American Convention against the Illicit Manufacturing of and Trafficking in Firearms, Ammunition, Explosives, and Other Related Materials ('Inter-American Convention')*. Adopted in Washington, DC, on 14 November (entered into force on 1 July 1998). Reproduced in UN document A/53/78 of 9 March 1998. Accessed 23 February 2005. <http://www.oas.org/juridico/english/treaties/a-63.html>

—. 1998. *Model Regulations for the Control of the International Movement of Firearms, Their Parts and Components and Ammunition ('Model Regulations').* AG/RES. 1543 (XXVIII – O/98) of 2 June. Accessed 23 February 2005.
<http://www.cicad.oas.org/Desarrollo_Juridico/ENG/Resources/REGLAMENTO%20ARMAS%20ING.pdf >

OAU (Organization of African Unity). 2000. *Bamako Declaration on an African Common Position on the Illicit Proliferation, Circulation and Trafficking of Small Arms and Light Weapons.* Adopted in Bamako, Mali, on 1 December. Accessed 23 February 2005.
<http://www.smallarmssurvey.org/source_documents/Regional%20fora/Africa/Bamakodecl011201.pdf>

OECD (Organization for Economic Co-operation and Development). 2001. 'Official Export Credit Support to Heavily Indebted Poor Countries (HIPCs)—Statement of Principles.' 19 July. Accessed 21 March 2005.
<http://www.oecd.org/document/43/0,2340,en_2649_34179_2348715_1_1_1_1,00.html>

Omega Foundation. 2003. 'Global Survey of Small Arms and Light Weapons Companies.' Background paper (unpublished). Geneva: Small Arms Survey.

OSCE (Organization for Security and Co-operation in Europe). 2000. *OSCE Document on Small Arms and Light Weapons.* FSC.DOC/1/00 of 24 November. Accessed 23 February 2005. <http://www.osce.org/docs/english/fsc/2000/decisions/fscew231.htm>

—. 2002. *Workshop on the Implementation of the OSCE Document on Small Arms and Light Weapons.* Vienna, Austria. 4–5 February 2002. FSC.GAL/21/02 of 20 February. Accessed 23 February 2005. <http://www.grip.org/bdg/pdf/g1904.pdf>

—. 2003. *OSCE Document on Stockpiles of Conventional Ammunition.* FSC.DOC/1/03 of 19 November. Accessed 23 February 2005.
<http://www.osce.org/documents/fsc/2003/11/1379_en.pdf>

Poulton, Robin-Edward and Ibrahim ag Youssouf. 1998. *A Peace of Timbuktu: Democratic Governance, Development and African Peacemaking.* New York and Geneva: United Nations Institute for Disarmament Research (UNIDIR). March 1998.

Republic of Albania, Ministry of Defence. 2004. 'The Activity of the Armed Forces for the Disposal and Destruction of Weapons, Military Technology and Ammunitions.' Accessed 15 October 2004. <http://www.mod.gov.al/eng/industria/may2004.asp>

Reuters. 2004. 'Calif. Proposal Would Laser-Brand ID Number on Bullets.' 6 October.

RTBF (Radio Télévision Belge Francophone). 2005. 'Des armes pour la Tanzanie.' Accessed 23 February 2005.
<http://www.la1.be/rtbf_2000/bin/view_something.cgi?type=article&id=0172631_article&menu=default&pub=RTBF.LAUNE%2FLAUNE.FR.la_taille.HOME>

SAAMI (Sporting Arms and Ammunition Manufacturers Institute). 2005. 'Characteristics and Properties of Sporting Ammunition Primers.' Accessed 9 February 2005. <http://www.saami.org>

SADC (Southern African Development Community). 2001. *Protocol on the Control of Firearms, Ammunition and Other Related Materials in the Southern African Development Community (SADC) Region ('SADC Firearms Protocol').* Adopted in Blantyre, Malawi, on 14 August. Accessed 23 February 2005.
<http://www.smallarmssurvey.org/source_documents/Regional%20fora/Africa/SADC%20Protocol%20august%202001.pdf>

Saferstein, Richard. 1995. *Criminalistics: An Introduction to Forensic Science,* 5th ed. Englewood Cliffs, NJ: Prentice Hall.

Scully, Megan. 2004. 'US Army Looks to Private Sector for Long-Term Supplier of Bullets.' *Defense News.* 4 October, p. 20.

SEESAC (South Eastern Europe Clearinghouse for the Control of Small Arms and Light Weapons). 2003. *SALW Ammunition Detection Study.* Belgrade: SEESAC. 30 September.

Small Arms Survey. *2004. Small Arms Survey 2004: Rights at Risk.* Oxford: Oxford University Press.

—. and CECORE (Centre for Conflict Resolution). 2004. *Weapon use by former UNRF II combatants in Uganda.* Background paper (unpublished). Geneva: Small Arms Survey. December.

SNC Technologies, Inc. 2005. 'Services/Others.' Accessed 23 February 2005.
<http://www.snctec.com/index.php?section_id=25&master_section=25&superMaster_section=2>

Spencer, Jane. 2001. 'An Armed Society is a Polite Society.' Newsweek. 8 November. Accessed 9 February 2005.
<http://msnbc.msn.com/id/3067468/>.

Stohl, Rachel. 1998. *Deadly Rounds: Ammunition and Armed Conflict.* Project on Light Weapons Report 98.4. Washington, DC: Project on Light Weapons, British American Security Information Council (BASIC). May.

Torjesen, Stina, Christina Wille, and Neil MacFarlane. 2005. 'Tajikistan's Road to Stability: Reduction in Small Arms and Light Weapons Proliferation and Remaining Challenges.' Geneva: Small Arms Survey. Forthcoming.

UN (United Nations). 1998. *United Nations International Study on Firearm Regulation.* New York: United Nations.

—. 2003. *UN Recommendations on the Transport of Dangerous Goods. Model Regulations,* 13th ed. New York and Geneva: United Nations.

UNDDA (United Nations Department for Disarmament Affairs). 2001. *A Destruction Handbook: Small Arms, Light Weapons, Ammunition and Explosives.* New York: United Nations.

UNDP (United Nations Development Programme). 2004. *Support to Security Sector Reform Programme.* ALB/01/003. Quarterly Report No. 3. July–September. Accessed 8 February 2005. <http://www.salwc.undp.org.al/download/reports/qr/2004/3.pdf>

—. 2005. Small Arms (reduction) Project (SAP). Accessed 23 February 2005. <http://www.undp.ba/index.aspx?PID=21&RID=18>

UN ECOSOC (United Nations Economic and Social Council). 2000. 'Question of the violation of human rights in the occupied Arab territories, including Palestine: Letter dated 2 October 2000 from the Permanent Observer for Palestine to the United Nations Office at Geneva addressed to the United Nations High Commissioner for Human Rights.' Commission of Human Rights. 57th session. E/CN.4/2001/109 of 21 November.

UNGA (United Nations General Assembly). 1997. *Report of the Panel of Governmental Experts on Small Arms.* A/52/298 of 27 August, para. 29. Accessed 23 February 2005. <http://www.un.org/Docs/sc/committees/sanctions/a52298.pdf>

—. 1999. *Report of the Group of Experts on the problem of ammunition and explosives.* A/54/155 of 29 June. Accessed 23 February 2005. <http://www.smallarmssurvey.org/source_documents/UN%20Documents/Other%20UN%20Documents/A_54_155.pdf>

—. 2001a. *Protocol against the Illicit Manufacturing of and Trafficking in Firearms, Their Parts and Components and Ammunition, Supplementing the United Nations Convention against Transnational Organized Crime ('UN Firearms Protocol').* Adopted on 31 May. Reproduced in UN document A/RES/55/255 of 8 June. Accessed 23 February 2005. <http://www.undcp.org/pdf/crime/a_res_55/255e.pdf>

—. 2001b. *Programme of Action to Prevent, Combat and Eradicate the Illicit Trade in Small Arms and Light Weapons in All Its Aspects ('UN Programme of Action').* 20 July. Reproduced in UN document A/CONF.192/15 of 9–20 July 2001. Accessed 23 February 2005. <http://www.smallarmssurvey.org/source_documents/UN%20Documents/UN%202001%20Conference/A_CONF.192_15.pdf>

—. 2003. *Report of the Group of Governmental Experts established pursuant to General Assembly resolution 56/24 V of 24 December 2001, entitled 'The illicit trade in small arms and light weapons in all its aspects'.* A/58/138 of 11 July.

—. 2004. *Resolution on the Illicit Trade in Small Arms and Light Weapons in All its Aspects.* 9 January. Reproduced in UN document A/RES/58/241 of 9 January 2004. Accessed 23 February 2005. <http://daccessdds.un.org/doc/UNDOC/GEN/N03/508/98/PDF/N0350898.pdf?OpenElement>

UNIDIR (United Nations Institute for Disarmament Research) and Small Arms Survey. 2003. *The Scope and Implications of a Tracing Mechanism for Small Arms and Light Weapons.* Geneva: United Nations.

United Kingdom Home Office. 2004. *Controls on Firearms: A Consultation Paper.* May. Accessed 9 February 2005. <http://www.homeoffice.gov.uk/docs3/controls_on_firearms.pdf>

United States Code. 2003. Title 18 ('Crimes and criminal procedure'), part 1 ('Crimes'), ch. 44 ('Firearms'), sec. 922 ('Unlawful acts'). Accessed 21 February 2005. <http://www.access.gpo.gov/uscode/uscmain.html>

UNSC (United Nations Security Council). 2002. *Final Report of the Panel of Experts on the Illegal Exploitation of Natural Resources and Other Forms of Wealth of DR Congo.* S/2002/1146 of 16 October.

UNSG (United Nations Secretary-General). 1997. *Note by the Secretary-General: General and Complete Disarmament: Small Arms.* A/52/298 of 27 August. Accessed 22 February 2005. <http://www.un.org/Docs/sc/committees/sanctions/a52298.pdf>

US Department of Defense. 1997. *Shelf-Life Item Management Manual.* DoD 4140.27, MMLX of 26 September. Accessed 9 February 2005. <http://www.dlaps.hq.dla.mil/dodm4140.27.htm>

US GAO (United States General Accounting Office). 1996. *Defense Ammunition: Significant Problems Left Unattended Will Get Worse.* GAO/NSIAD-96-129 of June. Accessed 23 February 2005. <http://www.gao.gov/archive/1996/ns96129.pdf>

USAEC (US Army Environmental Center). 1999. *Greening Service Ammunition for Individual and Crew Served Weapons: Eliminating Lead Hazards on Firing Ranges.* Accessed 27 September 2004. <http://aec.army.mil/usaec/technology/rangexxi00a01.html>

Van der Graaf, Henny J. and Sami Faltas. 2001. 'Weapons in Exchange for Development: An Innovative Approach to the Collection of Weapons in Albania.' In Sami Faltas and Joseph Di Chiaro III, eds. 2001. *Managing the Remnants of War. Micro-Disarmament as an Element of Peace-building.* BICC Disarmament and Conversion Studies No. 5. Baden-Baden: Nomos Verlagsgesellschaft, pp. 159–82.

Verwimp, Philip. 2005. 'Traditional Weapons, Firearms and the Organisation of Massacres in Kibuye Prefecture, Rwanda.' *Journal of Peace Research.* Forthcoming.

Wingfield, Brian. 2004. 'With 2 Wars, U.S. Need of Munitions is Soaring.' *The New York Times.* 29 May, p. 10.

ACKNOWLEDGEMENTS

Principal author
Stéphanie Pézard

Other contributors
James Bevan, Pablo Dreyfus, James Gebhardt, and Glenn McDonald

SPG-9 73 mm recoilless
anti-tank gun rounds,
abandoned by the Libyan Army
in Chad in 1994.
(© Sven Torfinn/Panos Pictures)

Unpacking Production:
THE SMALL ARMS INDUSTRY

2

INTRODUCTION

The inaugural edition of the *Small Arms Survey* notes that 'the small arms industry is the most widely distributed sector of the global defence industry' (Small Arms Survey, 2001, p. 7). It determines that the number of firms producing small arms and light weapons has increased since the end of the cold war. The three subsequent editions of the *Survey* assess the overall size of the industry by listing companies known to engage in production; considering trends in production across regions; and demonstrating how market changes affect the entire industry (Small Arms Survey, 2002; 2003; 2004).

Yet research to date indicates that 'global trends' have diverse impacts on firms that comprise the small arms industry. The production chapter in the *Small Arms Survey 2004* is a case in point. Entitled 'Continuity and Change', it describes both great shifts affecting the industry and, concurrently, continuity in the production and use of a number of basic weapons across the globe. It makes reference to growth among certain high-tech weapons producers, to the enormous increase in ammunition production in some countries following the US-led intervention in Iraq in March 2003, and to the decline in production elsewhere. These trends were not applicable to the industry as a whole; rather, they were specific to certain products and firms. They raise questions that call for a new approach to the study of production. Such questions include:

- Do broad changes in defence procurement affect all manufacturers of small arms and light weapons similarly?
- Are there great differences between companies that principally manufacture small arms as opposed to light weapons?
- What are the linkages between small arms and non-small arms-related production?
- How does the capacity to manufacture small arms vary qualitatively between countries?

It has become clear, furthermore, that researchers and policy-makers need to be able to: discriminate between types of manufacturing that produce different products and hence behave differently; situate these types of manufacturing within a country's overall manufacturing capacity; and outline how different firms (and host nations) contribute differently to the problems of illicit proliferation.

What is the small arms industry? In response to this question, this chapter offers an initial answer: although it is frequently treated as a single entity, the industry is in fact highly differentiated. The chapter aims to demonstrate this and provides one set of foundations for future evaluations of small arms and light weapons production. It disaggregates the 'industry' into segments or sectors of like products and production practices and orients them in relation to all types of manufacturing industry, as opposed to simply arms production.

The chapter follows three broad lines of inquiry, which complement earlier explorations of companies and their production, financial, and workforce data:

1) the degree to which production technologies and processes differ from one variety of small arm and light weapon to the next;

2) the extent to which companies that produce various small arms and light weapons differ in terms of their size and manufacturing activities; and

3) the global distribution of companies operating in different sectors of small arms and light weapons manufacturing and its implications for the illicit trade in these armaments.

Many of the observations in this chapter are derived from a study of small arms and light weapons producers in the United States, largely because the country is the most diverse and data-rich case with which to develop a broad framework for assessing various forms of production. To illustrate the utility of the framework, as well as the limits of its application, the chapter contrasts and augments the findings derived from the US case with production patterns observable elsewhere.

It concludes that:

- There is a great deal of differentiation in the types of firms in the small arms industry and their products.
- Global trends thought to affect the industry as a whole often influence sectors within the industry very differently.
- The illicit proliferation of various types of weaponry has distinct implications for individual sectors of the industry.
- A number of these sectors and the products they manufacture have escaped even modest research and policy attention to date.
- Measures must be targeted at specific sectors and the countries and regions that host them.

WHY PURSUE A DIFFERENT APPROACH TO PRODUCTION?

Why approach production differently? The answer lies in one of this field's most important foundations: the 1997 United Nations definition of small arms and light weapons. Constituting a touchstone for both researchers and policy-makers, the definition is intentionally effects-driven. The UN Panel of Experts responsible for the definition produced a 'pragmatic and results-oriented report' in which small arms and light weapons that 'were of main concern' were defined according to a key characteristic: portability. In practice, the definition aggregates a number of very disparate weapon types because they comprise a broad category 'responsible for large numbers of deaths and the displacement of citizens around the world' (UN, 1997, para. 13). Importantly, therefore, the Panel of Experts defined a field of concern, not a unit of analysis. Distinctions between very different—albeit equally portable—weapons are thus often masked by general discussion of the 'small arms and light weapons industry'.

Measures must target specific sectors and the countries and regions that host them.

Indeed, this umbrella term suggests that firms share a number of qualities. It is typical, and often useful, to refer to similar manufacturers producing similar products as an industry—as the aerospace and automobile industries illustrate. As is the case in these enterprises, the small arms industry reveals fewer qualitative similarities as the focus of analysis narrows. Consequently, to arrive at a more differentiated view of small arms production, it is important to break down the industry into its constituent parts, thereby avoiding a number of limitations inherent in the industry-wide approach.

Box 2.1   Definition of small arms and light weapons

The *Small Arms Survey* uses the term 'small arms and light weapons' broadly to cover small arms intended for both civilian and military use, as well as light weapons intended for military use. When possible, it follows the definition used in the United Nations *Report of the Panel of Governmental Experts on Small Arms* (UNGA, 1997):

Small arms: revolvers and self-loading pistols, rifles and carbines, sub-machine guns, assault rifles, and light machine guns.

Light weapons: heavy machine guns, hand-held under-barrel and mounted grenade launchers, portable anti-aircraft guns, portable anti-tank guns, recoilless rifles, portable launchers of anti-tank missile and rocket systems, portable launchers of anti-aircraft missile systems, and mortars of calibres of less than 100 mm.

The *Survey* uses the term 'firearm' to mean civilian and military hand-held weapons that expel a projectile from a barrel by the action of an explosive. Unless the context dictates otherwise, the term 'small arms' is used in the *Survey* to refer to both small arms and light weapons, whereas the term 'light weapons' refers specifically to this category of weapons.

First, a uniform conception of the small arms industry masks a range of factors that distinguish companies. Firms make products that range from simple plastic mouldings and weapon components to complex integrated optical accessories and finished firearms. The differences are not unlike those between one company making brake pads, and another assembling satellite navigation systems in the automobile industry.

Second, although the linkages between manufacturers producing similar or complementary goods are often strong—as complete weapon systems often require joint ventures or contract work—manufacturers contributing to one type of finished weapon will rarely collaborate with manufacturers specializing in the production of a qualitatively different weapon. An extreme example is the absence of collaboration between most handgun manufacturers and producers of guided missile systems.

Third, given that ties between manufacturers are often weak, market forces are likely to affect sectors of the industry very differently. In fact, diversity of production—with producers specializing in such varied fields as metal machining, the fabrication of precision lenses, or electronic systems engineering—ensures that many producers do not limit themselves to defence-related products. Consequently, they are likely to be affected by market forces influencing the manufacture and sale of these non-arms-related items independently of forces thought to affect small arms and light weapons production and sales as a whole.

While some analysts have noted a high degree of differentiation in the industry, others have rightly suggested that research has not sufficiently emphasized this aspect (Lock, 2003). This chapter enters accumulated findings into a model of small arms and light weapons production that captures the significant differences in types of manufacturing.

INFERRING CATEGORIES

Recent discussions of small arms and light weapons production describe some very broad modes of manufacture. Examples include such categories as 'craft' production, which is used to denote often illicit, small-scale manufacturing and repairs that take place outside of recognized factories (Alpers and Twyford, 2003, pp. 16, 20; BASIC, 1996; Small Arms Survey, 2003, pp. 26–36). In addition, some research has drawn distinctions between private civilian market-destined production and state-owned military production (Dreyfus and Lessing, 2003) and between high- and low-tech manufacturing techniques (Bevan and Wezeman, 2004).

While these categories remain loosely defined, they demonstrate that simple methods of classification improve our understanding of small arms production by allowing researchers to distinguish between broadly recognizable forms of production.

The common means of discriminating between different products involves segmenting industries and markets. It is important to note that specific types of producers manufacture broad categories of weapons, and that these find niches in markets that are often distinct. As a result, many issues concerning the qualities of a product, the technology needed to produce it, and the eventual user are closely related.

A basic model can combine these supply- and demand-side factors to create, in simple theoretical terms, 'bundles of characteristics' (Lancaster, 1971; Berry, Levinsohn, and Pakes, 2003, p. 1). Such bundles of characteristics may be derived by combining the qualities of the particular type of weapon produced, the technology and production processes needed to produce it, and the type of user for whom it is produced (see Table 2.1).

Table 2.1   Characteristics differentiating products, production processes, and markets

Factor	Characteristics	Examples
Product type	Finished product or service	Accessory, pistol, rifle, repair
Production process	Technology required	Operator or computer machining, single item or mass production
	Product variety	Capacity to produce only rifles or rifles, pistols, and accessories
	Linkages and parallel production	Firms producing components for small arms as well as for the automobile industry
Market characteristics	Weapon effects	Single-shot weapons, explosive rounds
	Intended users	Civilian, law enforcement, military

These bundles of characteristics may be used to define sectors of industry according to their relative mixture of factor characteristics.

Product type is the simplest means of differentiating between manufacturers. As past analysis has demonstrated, small arms and light weapons may be divided into broad groups, based, for example, on the distinction between small arms and explosive-firing light weapons, or between guided and unguided weapons. Such differentiations are generally illustrative of variations in production techniques and between potential users.

Production processes are very similar for a wide range of small arms, but they differ in several respects. *Technology* differentiates various manufacturing methods, from the simple repair and fabrication of new parts using hand tools, to manually controlled machinery, to the latest computer-controlled machines. *Product variety* is another broad indicator, not only of the size and development of a firm, but also of the type of markets to which it sells. For instance, the specialist rifle producer is clearly distinguishable from a firm that mass-produces a wide range of pistols, rifles, and accessories. *Linkages* between arms- and non-arms-related production and *parallel production* further aid in classifying firms, as they help in identifying the particular place that a firm occupies within a country's overall industry.

Market characteristics are largely determined by the effects that a weapon is capable of producing—for instance, the single shot of a muzzle-loading rifle or the explosive impact of a rocket-propelled grenade (RPG) round are features that place limits on the expected utility of weapons for certain users. *Users,* defined as 'intended users', comprise an additional, if loose-fitting, means of differentiating weapon types.[1]

Such bundles of characteristics can (a) define products with very similar technical characteristics, (b) distinguish those firms, or branches of firms, specializing in the production of particular products of similar qualities, both arms- and non-arms-related, and (c) relate these factors to broad categories of potential users in the market.

To a large extent, these characteristics establish parameters for the type of firm—and often the sector or stage of industrial development—that can engage in various forms of small arms production. Moreover, the division of products and manufacturing processes involved in non-arms-related production enables us to reverse our analysis and to examine, albeit roughly, which countries or regions, given certain levels of general industrial development, may be able to participate in certain types of arms production, or acquire the technology to do so in the near future.

The rationale for including repairs and the production of accessories in the analysis is simple. Repairs contribute to the 'production' of serviceable weapons from unserviceable weapons, while accessories contribute to the more effective functioning of weapons. Whether from an industrial, consumer, or effects perspective, these are key considerations. Furthermore, repairs and accessories comprise much of the activity covered in this study (see Table 2.2).

Table 2.2   Production of complete weapon systems in contrast to other productive activity in a selection of 349 US firms

Product	Firms	Percentage of total firms (rounded)
Complete weapon systems	179	51
Repair	86	24
Ammunition	56	16
Accessories	28	8
Total	349	100

Source: Hoover's Inc. (2004)

SMALL ARMS PRODUCTION SECTORS

This section develops a framework for analysing small arms production worldwide. Based primarily on US firms and a comparison of these companies with firms elsewhere, this framework differentiates between product, production, and limited market characteristics to assess production and to pinpoint a number of relatively exclusive manufacturing sectors.

The initial step in the study was to identify the product, production, and market characteristics (see Table 2.3) of 511 known US producers and repairers of small arms and light weapons.[2] Annual sales and employment figures were available for 349 of the 511 companies, and only those firms were retained for investigation (Hoover's Inc., 2004).[3] Among the 349 firms in this study, there was a marked decline in available information for single-employee repairers and manufacturers in contrast to other forms of activity; it is consequently very likely that most of the excluded firms are single-employee operations.

One explanation for this discrepancy is that repair is very often a sideline activity. Repairers may register a company name, yet that name may represent a second business with a very low turnover. With the exception of the smaller firms engaged in repairs, however, product descriptions and, in most cases, catalogues were available for selected companies. Intended markets could easily be discerned by the way firms described their products to potential users.

Among the 349 firms evaluated, the most prominent activity is manufacturing, a feature of 75 per cent of the sample. As shown in Figure 2.1, repairs make up a large segment of other activities, yet it is likely that they represent a higher proportion of total activity, as many repairs are extremely small in scale and may go undeclared. Indeed, the vast majority (more than 70 per cent) of firms engaged in repairs employ only one person.[4]

While manufacturing is the most common mode of activity in the sample, the production of finished weapon systems—such as a complete pistol, rifle, or grenade launcher—does not constitute the bulk of activity. This finding underscores the importance of analysing repairs and the manufacturing of components and accessories, rather than focusing on the production of guns or complete systems. It is likely, moreover, that many manufacturers of small components are not included in the study; reasons for this are cited below.

This study does not include ammunition production. As the chapter on ammunition illustrates, little is known about the degree of difference among firms engaged in producing ammunition and components for ammunition. Until more information becomes available, categorizing products, production processes, and market characteristics will remain difficult (AMMUNITION). Nonetheless, preliminary investigations suggest that ammunition products, production, and markets are as differentiated as those of complete systems and components, and it is likely that ammunition production can be examined using the broad model outlined below.

Figure 2.1   Number of firms engaged in selected production activities (from a total of 349 US manufacturers)

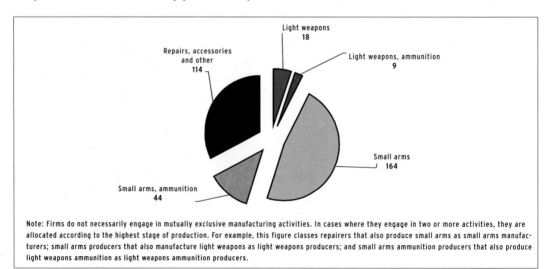

Note: Firms do not necessarily engage in mutually exclusive manufacturing activities. In cases where they engage in two or more activities, they are allocated according to the highest stage of production. For example, this figure classes repairers that also produce small arms as small arms manufacturers; small arms producers that also manufacture light weapons as light weapons producers; and small arms ammunition producers that also produce light weapons ammunition as light weapons ammunition producers.

Table 2.3 lists a select number of characteristics that indicate key differences between products, the manufacturing processes needed to produce them, the range of goods made by firms, and the potential users of such items. When bundled together, they suggest clear differences between firms engaged in the production of small arms and light weapons. As the table illustrates, in some cases, one factor, such as the level of technology or the range of products, is the primary means of distinguishing between firms. In others, several variables combine to make firms qualitatively different.

Table 2.3   Manufacturing sectors by product, users, process, range, and firm type, with distinctive features highlighted

Sector	Name	Product type	Users	Production process	Range	Firm type
1	Repairs and sporadic production	Repairs and sporadic production	Potentially all, although primarily civilian	Hand machining of replacement parts, assembly, modification, or amalgamation of existing weapon components	Various types of activity, but usually very similar basic operations	Usually small with a localized market
2	Components and accessories	Grips, stocks, and other plastic accessories	Potentially all, with the exception of suppressors for security forces	Processes range from simple, hand-operated machining to Computer Numeric Control (CNC) machining processes	Producers usually specialize in one type of component or a limited range of items that are simple to manufacture	Usually a large contract engineering firm producing many types of non-small arms components
		Scope mounts, suppressors, and other machined metal accessories				
3	Specialized	Single-shot rifles and handguns	Civilian	Limited production using hand-operated and sometimes CNC machining processes or even Electrical Discharge Machining (EDM) processes	Frequently single product types, such as a grenade launcher, a single-shot rifle, or a sniper rifle	Smaller firms dedicated to producing for a limited niche market, either civilian or security-related
		Revolvers	Civilian, law enforcement, military			
		Bolt- and lever-action rifles				
		Semi-automatic pistols				
		Single-shot grenade launchers, heavy machine guns, sniper rifles	Military			
4	Household name	Revolvers	Civilian, law enforcement, military	Mass production using hand-operated and often CNC or even EDM machining processes	Very limited range of product types—for example, an assortment of similar pistols or rifles—although sometimes many configurations of the same basic type	Larger firms mass-producing for a broad range of consumers; production primarily aimed at civilians
		Bolt- and lever-action rifles				
		Semi-automatic pistols				
5	Extensive-range	Pistols, rifles, sub-machine guns	Law-enforcement, military	Mass production using hand-operated and often CNC or even EDM machining processes	Broad range of products—for instance, the manufacture of pistols, assault rifles, and sometimes non-electronic light weapons	Large firms with a great number of machines, producing or having produced almost exclusively for the military market; often state-owned
		Semi- and fully automatic rifles	Military			
		Light and medium machine guns				
		Heavy machine guns				
		Single-shot grenade launchers				
		Automatic grenade launchers				
		Rocket launchers				

Table 2.3 **Manufacturing sectors by product, users, process, range, and firm type,**
(cont.) **with distinctive features highlighted (continued)**

Sector	Name	Product type	Users	Production process	Range	Firm type
6	High-tech	High-grade optics and fire-control systems	Civilian, law enforcement, military	Advanced computer-controlled grinding and milling of glass and metals; electronics engineering	Usually concentrate on one type of weapon or accessory	Firms produce primarily for the non-small arms field
		Guided weapon systems, night-vision sights	Military	State-of-the-art electronics engineering, metallurgy, and optical fabrication	Vast assortment of electronic products, including complete systems, but also components	Firms are very large and branch into many different types of production, from large defence systems to aerospace products

The following sections assess each of the six sectors highlighted in Table 2.3, which are derived from production trends observed in the study of the United States. Each section applies these US-derived sectors to a selection of cases from the rest of the world, compares the two, and concludes with a brief discussion on the implications for the small arms industry as a whole, as well as future directions for research.

Sector 1: Repairs and sporadic production

Product and service range:	Repair, assembly, minor fabrication
Examples:	Gunsmith shops, craft production, contract repairs
Principal markets:	Mainly local civilian

Producers in this sector differ from all other types of productive activity in the small arms and light weapons industry in that most do not manufacture complete systems. The majority of producers listed here specialize in repairs and only the larger enterprises engage in limited production. Even in these cases, production usually entails the assembly of parts made elsewhere, rather than on site.

Map 2.1 illustrates the 'tip of the iceberg' with respect to those countries known to host Sector 1 production. Even in well-documented cases, such as that of the United States, the extent to which actors are engaged in this activity remains unclear due to low technological barriers to entry. While some Sector 1 producers employ advanced machinery, most rely on hand-operated lathes and milling machinery common to all forms of basic metal product fabrication.

Two factors appear to relate to the stage of production achieved: the lower the level of development in a country or the lower the level of weapons proliferation, the greater the likelihood that enterprises will produce parts or even complete weapon systems. This is a simple function of, on the one hand, the availability of capital or supply networks for acquiring parts and, on the other, the availability of existing weapons as a source of parts. The following three groups of states in which repair and production occur are illustrative of how stages of production differ.

1) In developed countries, such as Australia, Germany, or the United States, parts for lawfully held weapons are plentiful and the purchasing power of consumers is relatively strong. In most cases, repairers may simply purchase and replace part of a weapon, rather than make it. If the weapon is beyond repair, the consumer is easily able to buy another—often from the repairer. The reverse of this phenomenon is equally illustrative. In the United Kingdom, following the 1997 ban on civilian handgun ownership—and hence a reduction in

Map 2.1   The six sectors of production worldwide

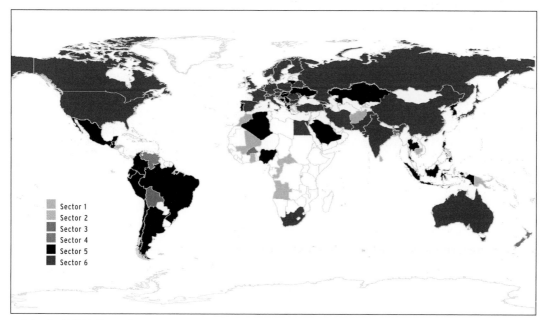

Notes: Map 2.1 highlights countries that are known to host the six sectors of small arms and light weapons manufacturing. Colour coding reflects the highest sector of production hosted for each country.

Sources: Dreyfus and Lessing (2003); Kante (2002; 2004); Godnick, Muggah, and Waszink (2002); Jones and Cutshaw (2004); Kiss (2004); NISAT (2005); Omega Foundation (2003); Small Arms Survey (2001; 2003; 2004); Weidacher (2005, forthcoming)

the availability of parts and weapons—the illicit fabrication of complete weapons, albeit on a very small scale, appears to have increased (House of Commons, 2000; NCIS, 2002).

2) In countries and areas where large numbers of illicit weapons are available, such as northern Pakistan or the Philippines, repair and assembly is also far more common than production, but the construction of complete weapons does appear to be more widespread in this sector than in more developed countries (BASIC, 1996; Capie, 2002). Like their counterparts in the United States, the very best gunsmiths produce complete weapons, but production rates remain low, and the reassembly of weapons from original factory components appears to be the norm (Small Arms Survey, 2003, p. 33).

3) In countries such as Ghana or Mali, where purchasing power is weak and factory-produced weapons are not particularly plentiful, complete weapons manufacture is more common (Small Arms Survey, 2003, pp. 29–30; Kante, 2004). Taking this argument further—and discounting cases such as Bougainville and the Solomon Islands, where construction of weapons has been crude in the extreme—perhaps the most striking examples of manufacture in the case of limited supply are those of Colombia and Sri Lanka. In both countries, the logistical skills of two large non-state armed groups—the Revolutionary Armed Forces of Colombia (Fuerzas Armadas Revolucionarias de Colombia, FARC) and the Liberation Tigers of Tamil Eelam (LTTE), respectively—have yielded large-scale repair and production of small arms and light weapons. Nevertheless, the majority of these weapon producers still utilize factory components when available (Dreyfus and Lessing, 2003).

Discounting non-state armed groups, repair and sporadic production appear to differ little across countries in terms of both size and structure of enterprise. Very often the basic setup of a shop in a developed country, such as Switzerland or the United Kingdom, differs little from one that might be found in Darra, Pakistan, or Danao City in the Philippines. Guns are sold in the front and the business will carry out limited repairs in the back using hand-operated machines (Capie, 2002; Small Arms Survey, 2003, pp. 26–36).

A Filipino gunsmith welds a crude sub-machine gun in a Sector 1 gun factory in Danao City, central Philippines, November 2003.

© Erik de Castro/Reuters

The vast majority of repair firms employ no more than one or two persons, and the analysis of US firms found none employing more than 25. In contrast, firms in the small arms manufacturing sector may employ hundreds of workers. Compared to producers as a whole, US firms specializing in the repair of weapons tend to constitute the lowest earners. Single-employee repair firms have an average turnover of approximately USD 40,000 per year, whereas single-employee small arms manufacturers (Sector 3) average around USD 70,000 per year (Hoover's Inc., 2004).

In the United States, most companies appear to specialize solely in the repair and production of small arms and light weapons. In less developed countries, however, enterprises have often moved into weapons manufacturing from related productive areas, with workers active as blacksmiths or locksmiths. In Ghana, for example, larger operations produce simple non-arms items, such as handcuffs, metal parts for automobiles, and bed frames.[5] Markets appear to be localized, or, in the case of larger firms, repairs may be conducted under contract for other companies. Firms may also serve a wider market because they are concentrated in an area that attracts many customers, such as Brescia, Italy, or Darra, Pakistan. On a smaller scale, this is true of hunting clubs in the Russian Federation and the United States, which act as centres for repair and production activity.[6]

The cases examined suggest that the skills needed to engage in repairs and sporadic production are widely available in a number of fields of industrial activity common to most, if not all, countries. Consequently, repair and sporadic production have become widespread, very difficult to assess in terms of likely scale and distribution, and hence hard to regulate. This review shows that very little is known about the extent to which these activities are performed in regions such as the Commonwealth of Independent States (CIS), or indeed in many of the nations not highlighted on Map 2.1. Yet, it does appear likely that, given a demand for weapons, small arms repairs and sporadic production would occur in localities with high concentrations of production activity in similar, non-arms-related fields, such as blacksmithing and other forms of metalwork. These factors, combined with appraisals of the level of weapons ownership in the locality, should suggest potential areas for future research, given that much activity appears to be driven by local demand.

As implied above, one point of concern is the extent to which weapon parts are available. The fact that most repair and sporadic production enterprises rely on factory-produced parts suggests that the production, exchange, and general availability of parts may be as relevant to small arms policy-making as the availability of complete weapons. As the following section illustrates, however, little is known about the global trade in weapons components.

Sector 2: Components and accessories

Components, defined here as parts essential for the functioning of a weapon, are diverse. In this sector, the emphasis is on machined metal parts and wooden or composite furnishings, which are components of

Product and service range:	Mass production of parts
Examples:	Barrels, grips, slides, stocks
Principal markets:	Civilian and military

a finished weapon. This chapter defines accessories as items that may be added to an existing weapon in order to improve its performance or adapt it to suit the user. Firms included in this sector manufacture simple accessories and do not produce such items as precision optical equipment and fire control systems. The latter are qualitatively different with respect to both composition and manufacture and are addressed in the commentary on Sector 6 producers. Examples of accessories include scope mounts, sound suppressors, and mounting rails, while components may encompass objects such as grips, slides, springs, and barrels. There is often little to distinguish the two, since most weapons may be enhanced beyond their original factory state, which can make components and accessories synonymous.

Several US companies produce accessories exclusively for target and sport shooting or expressly for security forces (Bravo, 2004; Mountain State, 2004; Sinclair, 2004). Others specialize in the production of a particular component, such as the grip or trigger, and produce for a variety of consumers (Pearce, 2004; Timney, 2004). Of particular note are so-called tactical weapon systems, which have mirrored the practice of customizing standard-issue weapons for Special Forces.

In contrast to their more sophisticated counterparts, most of these accessories are machined out of single pieces of aluminium or are injection-moulded using polymers, as reflected in the type of manufacturing machinery employed. Computer Numeric Control (CNC) machines are the norm in the United States, although a number of firms utilize more sophisticated equipment, including Electrical Discharge Machining (EDM) for more complex components (MGW, 2004; Dillon, 2004). The technologies involved elsewhere in the world do not differ markedly from those used by US firms. Producers in China and Taiwan, for example, manufacture a variety of products, ranging from magazines to scope mounts, for a wide assortment of pistols, sub-machine guns, and rifles, using the latest in CNC machines (Xianfeng, 2004).

Component manufacturers frequently make other products, such as precision hand and machine tools, or they perform specialized tasks such as deep-hole drilling (a core aspect of barrel-making) in fields as diverse as the aerospace, computer, optical, and oil sectors (Armatt, 2004; Lilja, 2004). Companies machining high-quality aluminium parts, including rails for weapons, also produce such goods as precision hose connectors and gas turbine rings for use in the transport industry (Yankee Hill, 2005). For many of these firms, components and accessories for small arms and light weapons represent only a small fraction of manufacturing output.

In the United States, component manufactures are usually larger than repairers, with numbers of employees ranging between 3 and 20 and annual turnovers varying between USD 175,000 and USD 600,000 (Hoover's Inc., 2004).

Countries hosting Sector 2 producers appear to be those where select firms produce very high-quality and expensive products for a select market, such as the United Kingdom and the United States (LEI, 2004). Yet, although the United States appears to host more firms dedicated to producing only small arms-specific components and accessories, it is

Little is known about the global trade in weapons components.

Box 2.2 Assault weapons, the US Assault Weapon Ban, and the emergence of personalized tactical weapon systems

Whether and how the expiry of the Federal Violent Crime Control and Law Enforcement Act of 1994 (Assault Weapon Ban) on 13 September 2004 will affect producers has been the subject of much debate.

While some observers expect the expiry of the ban to lead to an increase in the production and sale of assault-style weapons and related accessories, this study finds that the ban was primarily cosmetic as assault-style weapons were not necessarily covered by it. Moreover, it encouraged some new production and, consequently, the lifting of the ban may hurt some Sector 2 producers rather than aid them.

In brief, the Act prohibited the manufacture and sale in the United States of 19 different semi-automatic weapons:

- Norinco, Mitchell, and Poly Technologies Avtomat Kalashnikovs (all models)
- Action Arms Israeli Military Industries UZI and Galil
- Beretta Ar70 (SC-70)
- Colt AR-15
- Fabrique Nationale FN/FAL, FN/LAR, and FNC
- SWD M-10, M-11, M-11/9, and M-12
- Steyr AUG
- INTRATEC TEC-9, TEC-DC9, and TEC-22
- Revolving cylinder shotguns, such as (or similar to) the Street Sweeper and Striker 12. (Brady Campaign, 2002)

Nevertheless, the Act did not outlaw all semi-automatic weapons, but only those with multiple 'assault-weapon' features. It thus targeted only semi-automatic rifles that had detachable magazines and two or more of the following characteristics: a folding or telescoping stock; a pistol grip; a bayonet mount; a flash suppressor, or threads to attach one; or a grenade launcher (Brady Campaign, 2002). With the exception of a grenade launcher (assuming grenades were available), the removal of any such configuration of features would not have curtailed a weapon's firepower or destructive potential. Between 1994 and 2004, moreover, producers continued to manufacture and market weapons that differed only slightly from those banned outright (J&T, 2003).

During those ten years, Sector 2 producers designed, manufactured, and marketed new components and accessories designed to give ban-era weapons the *appearance* of their banned counterparts (Kuehl, 2003). In short, the Act spurred some Sector 2 production.

A Heckler & Koch MP5 9 mm sub-machine gun modified with accessories, including extra magazines, a magazine coupler, and under-barrel flashlight.

Furthermore, the Act seems to have done little to reduce public interest in assault weapons. Entire publications have since been dedicated to advertising such products as 'security force', 'tactical', or 'military' accessories (*Small Arms Review*, various dates; Springfield Armory, 2005).

Now that the Act has expired, a significant portion of Sector 2 firms remain devoted to producing items designed for tactical purposes, which may well enjoy increased sales in future. Firms specializing in pre-expiry modifications seem to have lost the market for their products. This brief study thus reveals how barriers to trade can have distinct, and often unintended, effects on firms producing different products.

difficult to determine the point of original manufacture of components of smaller weapons. Not unlike the components of many finished products, such as the switch on a table lamp or the handle of a saucepan, these parts remain anonymous to consumers.

To date, very little research has focused on the production of components and accessories, perhaps for the simple reason that this area of activity is extremely difficult to examine. As most of the items manufactured are not weapons in their own right, they are unlikely to be classified as weapons when traded. The manufacture of and trade in components and accessories—which may well serve to enhance the capacity of a weapon to cause loss of life or damage to infrastructure—are little regulated and have remained well out of the spotlight in small arms research and policy-making. As with repairs and sporadic production, the expertise and technology needed to produce components and accessories are widespread.

The findings presented here suggest at least two avenues for further research. The first should be to determine to what extent certain types of components and accessories augment the operational capacity of weapons—or to what extent they contribute to the prospect of individuals misusing them. A second valuable avenue of study would be to analyse the linkages between seemingly peripheral producers of components and accessories and 'mainstream' small arms manufacturers. This research could investigate to what extent major small arms producers outsource production of parts of complete weapons to manufacturers of components and accessories. For the most part, the items assessed here have been those targeted at users who wish to improve weapons already in their possession, rather than components purchased by major small arms manufacturers. The inter-firm trade in accessories and components may be considerable, yet it remains obscure and demands further attention.

Sector 3: Specialist production

In contrast to producers of components and accessories, the firms in this sector manufacture complete weapon systems. They remain distinct from household-name producers (Sector 4) in that they make a relatively limited set of product types, usually in few configurations, and typically of a quantity short of mass production.

Product and service range:	Labour-intensive small arms and light weapons production
Examples:	Sniper rifles, competition pistols and rifles, non-lethal weapons
Principal markets:	Some military, mainly civilian

Products vary widely, from single-shot muzzle-loading rifles to specialist high-precision competition pistols. In the United States, a small number of companies produce light weapons for the security forces and manufacture limited numbers of items, such as simple teargas and grenade launchers (Penn Arms, 2004). Some US firms manufacture specialist assault rifles—so-called tactical rifles—for law enforcement marksmen and military users (Hatcher Gun Company, 2004). Both inside and outside of the United States, the production of sniper rifles is a common activity (Truvelo, 2004),[7] as is the manufacture of some sub-machine guns (Jones and Cutshaw, 2004, pp. 224–27) and light weapons, including heavy machine guns (Manroy, 2004). Some firms produce for both the military and a small group of civilian users; their products include a very large number of .50 calibre rifles (Action Gun Works, 2004; Spider Firearms, 2004).

Products made specifically for civilian use include target rifles, custom-made to the owner's requirements, and a variety of shotguns (Cole Arms, 2004). In Western Europe, many of these shotgun-producing firms are well established, sometimes dating from the 18th and 19th centuries and serving the sporting market, where traditional craftsmanship is highly valued.[8]

Box 2.3   The micro business of .50 calibre rifles

Sniper rifles or anti-*matériel* rifles utilizing .50 calibre (12.7 mm) or larger ammunition are common products among small businesses. They are primarily employed against lightly armoured vehicles and communication installations, yet may be used to devastating effect against human beings (Small Arms Survey, 2004, pp. 27, 29).

Because they differ little in basic design from most bolt-action (sometimes semi-automatic) rifles but are labour-intensive to manufacture, these rifles are frequently made by specialist producers. Such is the case in the United States, where relatively small firms have supplied the military market for a number of years. Barrett Firearms Manufacturing, Inc., for instance, was created in 1983 and has since equipped the US Army, the US Marine Corps, and Special Forces in many countries (Barrett, 2004). Other US firms, such as Robar Companies Inc. and McMillan Bros. Rifles, also produce .50 rifles. These are primarily military weapons, but they are used by many civilians across the United States; the notable exception is the State of California, which banned the sale of .50 calibre rifles and above in September 2004 (California, 2005).

A number of firms producing .50 rifles in other countries are similar to those found in the United States, such as in Australia (PRS, 2004), South Africa (Truvelo, 2004), and the United Kingdom (Accuracy International, 2004; Jones and Cutshaw, 2004, pp. 125–39). Of 26 .50 calibre rifle models produced worldwide and listed in *Jane's Infantry Weapons,* however, only three—the British Accuracy International, the South African Truvelo, and the US Barrett—are known to be in service in nations other than where they were manufactured (Jones and Cutshaw, 2004, pp. 125–39). General trends in the transfer of small arms and light weapons suggest such a low number is unlikely and that trade in these specialist armaments is probably considerably higher than previously thought. The opaque nature of this sector of the small arms industry calls for more research.

© Fox Photos and Getty Images

A gunsmith at London's Holland and Holland gun manufacturing company aligns a telescopic sight on the bore of a .244 magnum rifle, December 1962. Holland and Holland has handcrafted firearms since 1835.

All Sector 3 firms are distinct in that they produce perhaps only a single type of weapon—for instance, shotguns, machine guns, or muzzle-loaders—at low output volume, yet they differ globally with respect to their markets. For example, there appear to be few firms producing military-style or military-specific weapons outside of the United States.

The size of the firm is generally small. US companies have between 1 and 50 employees and have annual turnovers not exceeding USD 7 million. Firms in Western Europe are of similar size, with few staffs exceeding 70 persons; turnovers vary but do not appear to be greater than USD 10 million (Hoover's Inc., 2004).

Computer-aided design (CAD) and computer-aided machining (CAM) are common among larger firms. Those producing at lower volumes for the specialist market may also utilize computer-controlled equipment, although, for the most part, they rely on sophisticated hand-operated machinery (Famars, 2004).

Many specialist producers have strong links to the non-arms-related industries, as is apparent in the historical development of some of the firms under review. Many were set up by individuals who had an interest in firearms and were formerly employed in engineering. Their areas of expertise range from testing racing engines to transport engineering (Action Gun Works, 2004; Knight Rifles, 2004; Spider Firearms, 2004). One consequence is that many of these enterprises offer innovative products beyond the scope of Sector 4 firms. The skills and manufacturing processes are very much akin to those of non-arms-related firms; in addition to weapons, many companies produce a range of machined products and offer machining services.

Specialist production pertains to a number of very different weapon types, most of which are relatively simple to manufacture, albeit labour-intensive. While the production of muzzle-loading weapons, for example, may not be of great importance to global trends in the misuse of small arms, what is of considerable significance is that small enterprises are manufacturing a number of highly destructive armaments of largely military origin. A case in point is the production of .50 calibre sniper rifles (see Box 2.3). From a policy perspective, as researchers in the United States are beginning to recognize, the proliferation of weapons produced by such firms is worrying, particularly with regard to civil aviation and critical infrastructure, such as oil refineries and chemical plants (VPC, 2002; 2003). Indeed, for firms with some experience of firearms manufacturing, a switch to producing high-value, high-velocity .50 calibre sniper rifles will prove relatively unproblematic, largely because of the widespread availability of .50 calibre ammunition (AMMUNITION).

Specialist producers may illustrate future trends in weapons manufacture.

Of particular importance is the degree to which specialist companies supply the military market, and which militaries they supply. One related aspect is whether trends in the use of specialized tactical weapons—displayed most notably by the US Armed Forces—have encouraged other states and non-state armed groups to follow suit. Furthermore, specialist producers also manufacture teargas launchers, rubber baton launchers, and similar weapons—so-called less-than-lethal munitions—for security forces. The use of these weapons against protesters in Thailand in October 2004, and by Sudanese police forces to perpetrate human rights abuses in Darfur in November 2004, suggests that the trade in such armaments with security forces is of pressing relevance for today's research and policy agendas (BBC, 2004a; 2004b).

In short, so little is known about specialist producers and their role in global production, save perhaps for the United States, that it is essential to investigate these firms further. With an emphasis on innovation, moreover, many of these companies may illustrate future trends in the types of products that will be in service tomorrow.

Sector 4: Household-name producers

Household-name producers manufacture complete weapon systems yet produce a relatively limited array of products (see Table 2.4), which are almost exclusively small arms. These firms differ from spe-

Product and service range:	Mass-produced small arms
Examples:	Pistols, revolvers, rifles, shotguns
Principal markets:	Mainly civilian

cialist producers in that they mass-produce weapons. To draw an analogy with the automobile industry, these companies appear to inhabit the kind of broad space occupied by manufacturers such as Ford or Renault. They tend to have long operating histories, sometimes of more than 100 years, and are distinct from extensive-range (Sector 5) producers in that most of their goods are destined for civilian use. Firms described as 'household names' are most common in the United States and either appear in states with extensive civilian small arms markets or produce primarily for such markets.

Table 2.4   A selection of Sector 4 firms worldwide

Firm	Weapons produced	Country of origin
Amadeo Rossi	Handguns, rifles, and shotguns	Brazil
J.G. Anschütz	Handguns and rifles	Germany
ArmaLite	Rifles	United States
Bersa	Handguns	Argentina
Henry Repeating Arm Co.	Rifles	United States
HS Product	Handguns	Croatia
Kahr Arms	Handguns and rifles	United States
The Marlin Firearms Co.	Shotguns and rifles	United States
O.F. Mossberg & Sons, Inc.	Shotguns	United States
Remington	Shotguns and rifles	United States
Savage Arms, Inc.	Rifles	United States
Smith & Wesson	Handguns	United States
Sturm, Ruger & Co., Inc.	Handguns, rifles, and shotguns	United States
Taurus International MFG, Inc.	Handguns, rifles, and shotguns	Brazil

Sources: Anschütz (2004); ArmaLite (2004); Bersa (2004); Henry (2005); Kahr Arms (2004); Kiss (2004); Marlin (2004); Mossberg (2004); Remington (2004); Rossi USA (2004); Ruger (2004); Savage Arms (2004); Smith & Wesson (2004b); Taurus (2004a)

In most countries, mass production for a principally civilian market follows the lead of US household-name producers; moreover, these firms often make goods extensively for the US market. One such firm is Taurus of Brazil, which, having purchased a former Beretta factory in Sao Paulo, successfully entered the US pistols market and later created an affiliated company in Miami, Florida (Taurus, 2004a). Likewise, Brazil's Amadeo Rossi and Argentina's Bersa sell well in the United States, but on a smaller scale (Bersa, 2004; Dreyfus and Lessing, 2003; Rossi USA, 2004). Croatia's HS Product is similar in having created a series of highly rated pistols and then having entered the US market, selling its products through Springfield Armory (Kiss, 2004, p. 28). A few exceptions are companies such as Germany's Anschütz, which began by supplying the German market with precision small-calibre sports weapons before turning to the US handgun and rifle market (Anschütz, 2004).

Manufacturing processes differ from those of specialist producers with respect to production runs rather than the range of technologies employed. Since these firms cater to the mass market, mass production is the norm. Technology is sophisticated: companies employ numerous CNC machines and engage in extensive research and development (R&D) as well as CAD and CAM work.

In the United States, firms tend to employ between 100 and 3,000 employees, with the majority employing between 200 and 500. Annual turnovers range from around USD 10 million to USD 150 million, although most companies report between USD 15 million and USD 50 million (Hoover's Inc., 2004). Firms in Western Europe appear to be similar to smaller household-name producers in the United States, with staff sizes of between 100 and 450 employees, and annual turnovers of between USD 30 million and USD 100 million (Anschütz, 2004; Walther, 2004; Weidacher, 2005, forthcoming). Italy's Berretta is something of an anomaly in that it produces for the military and civilian markets. The company employs some 2,300 workers and has annual sales of approximately USD 420 million, of which around 90 per cent is generated from civilian markets (Weidacher, 2005, forthcoming).

Household-name producers not only make very few types of small arms and light weapons, but also rarely devote much of their productive capacities to manufacturing non-arms-related products. Nevertheless, non-arms production is probably more of a factor among household-name producers than it is among specialist producers. In 2003, for example, sales of non-arms castings made up around 12 per cent (USD 17.3 million) of the annual trade of Sturm, Ruger & Co., while approximately 4 per cent (USD 4.7 million) of Smith & Wesson's annual sales came from metal processing and finishing, with a total of 13.2 per cent (USD 15.5 million) derived from non-firearm products (Ruger, 2003, p. 3; Smith & Wesson, 2004b, p. 4).

Similar to Sector 3 producers, a number of Sector 4 firms developed expertise in the non-arms industry before they became involved in weapons production (Kahr Arms, 2004). In the case of GLOCK, expertise in the field of metallurgy—or composites—provided it with the opportunity to move into the business of small arms production. Similar examples include Taurus of Brazil and HS Product of Croatia. Nonetheless, this pattern does not apply to the largest producers, which appear to have started out as small-time arms producers and only later branched out into non-arms-related production (Remington, 2004; Smith & Wesson, 2004b).

Household-name producers are typically associated with the civilian market for firearms, particularly in the United States, and have thus been the focus of considerable domestic research and frequent legal policy attention. As a result, their role in small arms and light weapons production is fairly well understood.

While Sector 4 products are not generally associated with violence in some of the world's armed conflict zones, weapons collection programmes in places as diverse as the Central African Republic and Kosovo have taken receipt of significant numbers of armaments manufactured by household-name producers (KPIS, 2003). As the Small Arms Survey's findings on transfers continue to reveal, weapons produced anywhere in the world have the potential to be used far and wide (TRANSFERS, CENTRAL AFRICAN REPUBLIC). This knowledge, together with the fact that these weapons have considerable military utility, underlines the need for close monitoring of the sector.

Sector 5: Extensive-range (primarily military) production

Extensive-range producers differ from household-name producers in that they manufacture a greater variety of qualitatively different products. These items are either targeted at the military market or are based on military-oriented products. Furthermore,

Product and service range:	Mass production of small arms and light weapons (and larger weapon systems)
Examples:	Assault rifles, light and heavy machine guns, rocket launchers
Principal markets:	Mainly military

these Sector 5 producers often manufacture explosive weaponry—often alongside large conventional weapons such as artillery—that are normally intended exclusively for the military. They are, however, distinct from Sector 6 producers in that the vast majority of products are characterized by relatively low technology and that the manufacture of electronics or optical equipment is rare.

Firms range from (1) independent, primarily military-destined producers that diversified into civilian production some time ago, to (2) producers that are predominantly under state control, yet are beginning to focus on civilian markets, to (3) suppliers to state armed forces that continue to produce solely for the military market. While these enterprises differ greatly in terms of ownership structures, they are comparable in that they often manufacture a similar array of products for military markets *and* have to respond to market forces differently from primarily civilian-oriented Sector 4 producers.

The first set of firms has long manufactured an assortment of civilian-destined armaments but produces primarily for the security and military markets.

Colt and Springfield Armory, for example, have long histories of providing weapons to US security forces (Colt, 2004). The latter continues to supply Special Forces with rifles and has also received a contract to supply the US Federal Bureau of Investigation. Much of the civilian-destined product range reflects this history and is based on military-issue weapons, including the M1911 pistol, the M14 rifle, and the M6 carbine (Springfield Armory, 2004).

A number of European firms are very similar in that they moved into civilian-destined production after having produced for state security forces (Sauer, 2004; Swiss Arms, 2004). Turkey's Sarsilmaz was founded in 1888 and, although it has long been a supplier to the Turkish Armed Forces, it also produces a range of pistols and shotguns aimed at the civilian market (Sarsilmaz, 2004). Like their US counterparts, these firms manufacture a wide variety of weapons, from pistols and rifles to sub-machine guns, assault rifles, and single-shot grenade launchers (HK, 2004; Swiss Arms, 2004; 2005). Some traditional producers of military weapons, such as Germany's Heckler & Koch, have added civilian production under a separate subsidiary, but they remain primarily military suppliers (HK, 2004; HKJS, 2004; Weidacher, 2005, forthcoming).

The second set of firms includes enterprises that remain under state control or have inherited large-scale manufacturing plants from the state. These companies have only recently diversified into civilian-destined manufacturing.

Some of them produce a wide assortment of ordnance, such as Romania's RomArm and Serbia and Montenegro's Žastava Oruje. These two enterprises recently diversified production and now produce weapons targeted at the sport, hunting, and personal defence markets (RomArm, 2004; Zastava, 2004). Zastava recently signed a contract to export approximately USD 7.5 million worth of goods to the US civilian market (SEESAC, 2004). In the Russian Federation, firms offer a similar line of products. Izhevsky Oruzheiny Zavod, Izhevsky Mekhanichesky Zavod, and Tulsky Oruzheiny Zavod all produce hunting and sporting firearms in addition to weapons for the military market (Pyadushkin, 2004a). Ukraine's Fort Association and the Metallist Uralsk Plant of Kazakhstan have likewise begun to diversify into manufacturing civilian-destined weapons (Pyadushkin, 2004b).

The third and last set comprises companies that produce weapons almost exclusively for the military and have not diversified into civilian production, except in a few minor cases. Products range from light and heavy machine guns to shoulder-launched multi-purpose assault weapons, such as the M72 Law (US Ordnance, 2004; Talley, 2004).

A Marine reservist holds his baby while his wife aims a shoulder-launched multi-purpose assault weapon produced by the Sector 5 manufacturer Talley Defense Systems. Camp Pendleton Marine Base, February 2003.

Companies including Industria de Material Bélico de Brasil (IMBEL) and Fábricas y Maestranzas del Ejército (FAMAE) of Chile manufacture assault rifles, some simple light weapons, and, in the case of IMBEL, pistols, but they do not produce for the civilian market (Dreyfus and Lessing, 2003). The situation is similar for European producers such as FN Herstal, which manufactures pistols, assault rifles, and machine guns for the law enforcement and military markets only (FN, 2004; FN Herstal, 2004). Larger firms, comparable to US companies such as Talley Defense Systems, produce a number of light weapons alongside larger conventional systems. They include: GIAT Industries of France, which produces the FAMAS assault rifle; the Hellenic Arms Industry, which produces various small arms and light weapons; Austria's Hirtenberger Group, which produces mortars and mortar ammunition; and Pakistan Ordnance Factories, which produces various small arms, light weapons, and ammunition.[9]

Most firms manufacture many different products and hence plants tend to be large and to utilize diverse equipment. In the more industrially developed countries, computer-controlled equipment is similar to that of firms in the United States and Western Europe. Less-developed countries engage in more labour-intensive production processes.

Less-developed countries engage in more labour-intensive production processes.

The size of firms varies according to the levels of technology employed. Some of the smallest European producers, such as Steyr Mannlicher, employ only around 100 employees, and annual turnover hovers around USD 20 million (Weidacher, 2005, forthcoming). Companies that are arguably less efficient, including Arcus of Bulgaria, employ as many as 3,000 workers but have an annual turnover of around USD 40 million (Kiss, 2004, p. 29). Similarly, Russian firms including Izhevsk Arms Plant and Tulsky Oruzheiny Zavod employ between 3,000 and 13,000 people and have annual turnovers of between USD 15 million and USD 50 million (Pyadushkin, 2004a). By contrast, the most advanced producers, such as Heckler & Koch, employ around 700 workers and have annual turnovers of about USD 120 million (Weidacher, 2005, forthcoming). Meanwhile, US companies employ as many as 500 people and have annual turnovers of somewhere between USD 2 million and USD 50 million (Hoover's Inc., 2004).

One observable trend in extensive-range production is that firms in the United States and Western Europe tend to be highly specialized and make few, if any, non-arms-related products.[10] In these countries, company ties with non-arms industries stem largely from their R&D capacities and extensive experience of product testing.[11] State-owned firms often offer a range of R&D-oriented services, such as engineering management, assistance in establishing maintenance programmes, ballistic analysis, and systems testing (FN Herstal, 2004; GIAT, 2004; POF, 2004). In less-developed countries, firms, particularly those with reduced markets and financial troubles, often produce a greater variety of non-arms-related items. RomArm and Arcus, for example, have diversified into non-arms-related manufacturing, including of such diverse goods as wooden and metal furniture, vehicle parts, washing-machine components, bicycles, and back-massaging equipment (RomArm, 2004; Arcus, 2004).

The likelihood is high that extensive-range producers manufactured the weapons most commonly used in any instance of armed violence during any protracted conflict throughout the world. The reason is that, by and large, companies operating under government control or contract constitute the sector most heavily involved in supplying overseas militaries, which, in turn, often endure stockpile losses. Colt's M-16 series of rifles, FN's FAL, and the Kalashnikov AK series are examples of the most widely proliferated weapons. Nevertheless, Sector 5 producers also make larger, more destructive systems, such as mortars and RPG launchers.

Sector 5 weapons are still transferred in abundance to countries in conflict and states with poor stockpile security records. In 2002, for instance, Indonesia purchased some 10,000 Kalashnikov assault rifles from an undisclosed Russian firm (Jane's, 2003), and the United States recently transferred M-16 rifles to Nepal (Jane's, 2004b).

Sector 6: High-tech electronics and optics systems manufacturing

Product and service range:	High-tech mass-produced accessories and systems
Examples:	Optics, thermal sights, fire control systems, man-portable air defence systems (MANPADS), anti-tank guided weapons (ATGWs)
Principal markets:	Some civilian, mainly military

High-tech producers manufacture high-precision components and systems, which, in many cases, parallel production processes in the aerospace, medical, and optical sectors. Among these producers are global giants of the defence industry, but also far smaller firms specializing in the production of technology-intensive electronics and optical equipment.

These firms differ considerably from most other small arms-related industrial enterprises. Instead of manufacturing products based on designs that have changed little in decades, they employ some of the most advanced production methods possible.

Smaller high-tech optics and components manufacturers

The smaller companies in this sector display very similar characteristics worldwide, although they differ somewhat in terms of their reliance on automated machinery. While they may be sophisticated, many of the items produced by less technologically advanced plants tend to be based on older, tried-and-tested designs. In the most advanced firms, production practices range from computer-controlled grinding of lenses to biometric standards, to the machining of titanium and aircraft-grade aluminium alloys, and electronics engineering (ATN, 2005). Companies that manufacture electronic components, such as laser sights, are typically specialists in vision and sighting equipment or otherwise are suppliers—so-called original equipment manufacturers (OEMs)—of components to such firms. In China, Taiwan, and the United States, for example, a number of companies that specialize in laser modules for all purposes also make complete sight systems for small arms and light weapons (LaserMax, 2004; Poe Lang, 2004).

Part of the Zeiss Lens Factory in Jena, Germany, circa 1909. The Zeiss Company was founded in 1846 and manufactures, among other things, a wide range of rifle scopes.

© Hulton Archive and Getty Images

Company size varies greatly, as does the degree to which firms engage in small arms-specific manufacturing. For instance, while Swarovski Optik—a maker of rifle scopes—employs a staff of around 550, the Swarovski Group, which manufactures a wide variety of non-small arms-related items, employs more than 14,000 people globally. The company as a whole produces an assortment of products, from telescopes and stone-dressing equipment, to crystal items for jewellery, to rifle scopes and rifle-mounted night-vision equipment (Swarovski Optik, 2004; Swarovski, 2004a). Many of the major scope manufacturers make telescopes and binoculars in addition to rifle scopes.[12]

Manufacturers of electronic components may employ between a few hundred and 5,000 or more persons and devote only a tiny fraction of their productive capacity to small arms-specific production (Coherent, 2004b; Furukawa, 2004). Night-vision manufacturers frequently produce electronic sensors for civilian surveillance purposes, including such devices as parking sensors, speed guns, and cameras (ATN, 2005; Bushnell, 2004). Companies producing OEM laser modules cater to all types of laser use, from machine alignment and process control, to medical technology, audio and visual applications, and telecommunications (Laser Devices, 2004; Surefire, 2004; WSTech, 2004).

The distribution of companies worldwide depends very much on the type of productive activity and the technology involved. Firms are located in countries and regions with reputable research establishments, such as China, the CIS, the United States, and Western Europe. Those selling on the optics market appear to be established businesses, and a large number, including Swarovski and Schmidt & Bender, hail from Germany and Austria, the early market leaders in the field (Swarovski, 2004a; Schmidt & Bender, 2004). Some more recently industrially developed countries, such as Japan, also manufacture precision optical accessories. Electronics companies, including those producing light-intensifying and laser equipment, tend to be located in areas with a high concentration of technology manufacturers, such as California (Rolyn, 2004; Lasermate, 2004; Coherent, 2004a), the south-east of England (Laser 2000; 2004; Lambda, 2004), and metropolitan Tokyo (NEC, 2004; Furukawa, 2004).

Global giants of the arms and aerospace industries

Countries hosting manufacturers of complete high-tech weapon systems, such as anti-tank guided weapons (ATGWs) and man-portable air defence systems (MANPADS), are states with a high density of high-tech production in most industrial fields. Nevertheless, countries differ in their level of high-tech development, and the firms they host differ in size, areas of productive activity, and the technology of weapons produced.

The most developed firms are typically in Japan, the United States, and Western Europe; they make the most sophisticated and, consequently, most expensive weapons currently available. The Raytheon Company of the United States, for example, produces the FIM-92 'Stinger' MANPADS, the Javelin ATGW, and thermal weapon sights (Raytheon, 2004a). Similarly, in Western Europe, companies such as Thales produce MANPADS, night-vision equipment, and thermal sights (Thales, 2004). The European Aeronautic Defence and Space Company (EADS), the largest producer in Europe, manufactures the Eryx and Milan ATGWs and the Mistral MANPADS, and is part of the European Stinger Project Group (EADS, 2004).

As Figure 2.2 illustrates, small arms and light weapons production occurs only in a few subsidiaries of most Sector 6 firms, with companies producing for areas as diverse as printing and medicine, although they may be dependent on defence sales (Raytheon, 2004b). Alliant Techsystems, Inc. (ATK) of the United States, for instance, manufactures parts for the space shuttle, ballistic missiles, and commercial aircraft, while General Dynamics makes nuclear submarines and executive jets (ATK, 2004a; 2005; GD, 2004a).

These firms differ in their focus on small arms and light weapons systems and components, to which they generally devote a tiny proportion of their total productive capacity. Around 30 per cent of activity at ATK, for example, centres on small and medium ammunition manufacturing, of which small arms and light weapons ammunition is but a part (ATK, 2004a). In the same way, small arms production only constitutes a minor portion of European Sector 6 activity. In the case of EADS, ATGW and MANPADS production comprises a fraction of the workload of its Defence and Security Systems division, which is responsible for generating only about 17 per cent of the company's total sales (EADS, 2003).

Most firms offer extensive R&D and testing facilities under contract, as well as consultancy services for a wide array of fields, including personnel management, air traffic control, and information technology. R&D expenditures in all areas of activity are high, ranging between around one and more than ten per cent of annual turnover (between roughly USD 30 million and more than USD 900 million).[13]

> Most giant high-tech producers offer extensive R&D and testing facilities.

Figure 2.2   Corporate map of Raytheon Company (shading indicates small arms-related production)

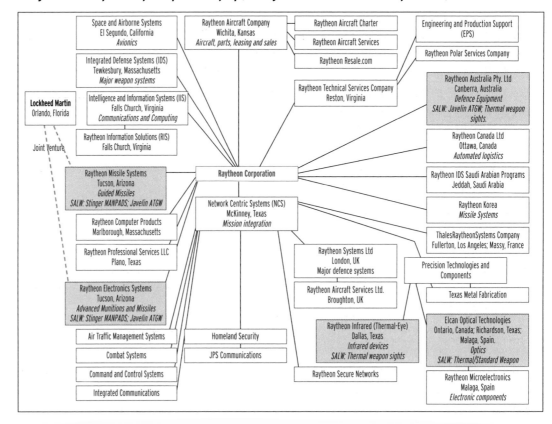

Sector 6 firms are often concomitant with high-tech development in the civil industrial sector, and indicators of such development, as Table 2.5 illustrates, provide insight into the distribution of high-tech small arms and light weapons production. In a number of states, however, this relationship does not hold.

While products and production processes in these nations are similar to those of US and Western European producers, they are usually at a lower level of technological advancement. Smaller producers, such as A.Q. Khan Laboratories of Pakistan and the Sakr Factory for Developed Industry of Egypt, make older models of guided ATGWs and MANPADS, as well as laser range finders (FAS, 2000; Jane's, 2004a). Larger manufacturers produce ATGWs as well as a variety of small arms; this group includes Israeli Military Industries (IMI), whose range of goods is comparable to that of Russian producers including the V.A. Degtyarev Plant and the KBP Instrument Design Bureau (IMI, 2004; Pyadushkin, 2004a). Similarly, Denel of South Africa offers a wide assortment of small arms and light weapons and accessories. These products range from rifles and machine guns produced by Denel's subsidiary Vektor, to range-finders and fire control systems for small arms manufactured by another subsidiary, Eloptro (Denel, 2004a; Eloptro, 2004).

Like their US and Western European counterparts, these firms are often heavily engaged in non-arms-related activity and frequently produce less technologically sophisticated civilian products. Denel, for instance, owns property, engineering, aviation, and personnel companies, and most of its high-tech production remains arms-related (Denel, 2004a). In the Russian Federation, the trend is towards manufacturing concerns, such as automobile production and basic medical technology (Degtyarev, 2004; KPB, 2004).

Table 2.5   Countries hosting Sector 6 producers (in red) and the top global R&D spenders *in all areas* **of industrial activity**

1	Sweden		Slovenia
2	Finland	24	Ireland
3	Iceland	25	China
4	Japan		Italy
5	South Korea		New Zealand
6	Israel	28	Spain
	United States	29	Brazil
8	Switzerland		Hungary
9	Germany		Romania
10	France	32	India
	Taiwan	33	Greece
12	Denmark		Poland
	Singapore		Portugal
14	Belgium		Slovakia
	Netherlands		South Africa
16	Austria	38	Chile
	Canada		Hong Kong
18	United Kingdom		Turkey
19	Norway	41	Argentina
20	Australia		Malaysia
21	Russian Federation		Venezuela
22	Czech Republic		

Sources: *Economist* (2004); Jones and Cutshaw (2004); NISAT (2005); Small Arms Survey (2004)

To sustain production and services in a wide variety of fields, and often in a multitude of subsidiaries, companies are usually far larger than those in any other production sector. In the United States, the size of firms ranges between 13,500 and more than 130,000 employees at giants like the Lockheed Martin Corporation. Annual turnovers range between about USD 2 billion and USD 39 billion.[14] In Western Europe, companies such as Thales report annual turnovers of around USD 13 billion and employ some 60,000 workers (Thales, 2003), while EADS has an annual turnover of USD 35–40 billion (EADS, 2003). Outside of the United States and Western Europe, firms tend to be much smaller, with Russian producers employing around 3,000–16,000 workers and companies such as IMI employing approximately 4,000 personnel. Turnovers range between USD 150 million and up to USD 250 million for Russian producers, with more successful companies like Denel and IMI turning over between USD 550 million and USD 700 million (Denel, 2004b; IMI, 2004; Pyadushkin, 2004a).

It is clear that there are gaps in current knowledge regarding production of and trade in high-tech small arms and light weapons. Complete systems, such as ATGWs or MANPADS, which are produced by the largest firms, are often the subject of costly government procurement programmes and are frequently well-publicized in trade publications; however, lower-value products, including optics and laser devices, remain largely beyond the scope of current research. While larger systems obviously constitute cutting-edge technology, a focus simply on firearms in the small arms and light weapons research field often obscures the symbiosis between high-tech accessories and low-tech firearms.

The direction of current research supports these observations. The debate over MANPADS suggests that these weapons are likely to remain on the policy agenda because they threaten the state-of-the-art armies of the most powerful nations (Small Arms Survey, 2004, p. 90). Although researchers have stressed the importance of ATGWs, the topic is only now beginning to attract the attention of policy-makers, and only states that are directly affected, such as Israel, appear to be expressing sufficient concern. The more obscure types of high-tech weaponry, particularly those items designed to be retrofitted onto existing weapons, remain even further from the spotlight.

As this chapter illustrates, Sector 6 products differ qualitatively from those of other sectors in the industry. Nevertheless, the field exhibits a great deal of synergy with producers of high-tech accessories, such as night-vision systems, laser sights, and scopes, and the less complex small arms and light weapons they are designed to complement. Like the production and trade in components and accessories (Sector 2), more research needs to be conducted on this sector to help determine the capacity of these products to change the shape and destructive effects of armed conflict. Recent events, such as the use of night-vision equipment by US troops in Fallujah, Iraq, in November 2004, underscore the degree to which high-tech accessories can enhance the effectiveness of weapons. There is thus a need to improve the monitoring of trade in such items, as their popularity is only likely to grow.

There is a need to improve the monitoring of trade in high-tech accessories.

CONCLUSIONS REGARDING THE FRAMEWORK EMPLOYED AND RECOMMENDATIONS FOR FURTHER RESEARCH

The findings presented in this chapter have clear policy relevance. A systematic analysis of the various sectors of production can help to fill gaps in knowledge and present a more detailed picture of the industry. It will also serve to identify more accurately the point of manufacture of the small arms and light weapons of main concern.

The chapter highlights the very high degree of differentiation among types of firms, the goods they produce, and their markets. This differentiation alone warrants continued sector-oriented approaches to further research on small arms and light weapons production.

The findings presented here also demonstrate how production sectors are distributed differently across countries and regions with various levels of industrial development. This observation is a prerequisite to a qualitative understanding of the kinds of weapons that are, or are likely to be, manufactured in certain parts of the world. Focusing on the varied distribution of firms and sectors can locate parties responsible for irresponsible production, and enable the formulation of better-targeted measures to control the illicit proliferation of small arms and light weapons.

This method can also yield a better picture of the parameters of the industry, such as the size and scope of manufacturing. This approach can help produce generalizations regarding firm types and sizes, which can then be applied to cases for which little data is available. Countries with similar aggregations of firms and sectors can be compared and contrasted more easily, and reasons for irresponsible production understood more fully.

The implications of a highly differentiated industry

Given the limited time and resources at the disposal of researchers and policy-makers, it is important to target problem weapons, and hence problem production, efficiently. The framework outlined here goes at least some way in facilitating research specific to some crucial producers, yet it discounts production that is peripheral or even unconnected to particular matters of concern.

Current debates, such as those over the proliferation of MANPADS or the expiry of the US Assault Weapon Ban, illustrate how concerns over different types of small arms and light weapons implicate different sectors of the industry

(Small Arms Survey, 2004, ch. 3). The case of MANPADS clearly relates to high-tech producers, while the Assault Weapon Ban implicates specialist (Sector 3) and components and accessories (Sector 2) producers.

A differentiated approach also offers insight into sectors of the industry that are likely to be affected by changes in markets as well as government policies. For example, in the case of a sector that serves primarily military clients, the expansion of an infantry procurement programme in one country is likely to boost extensive-range production of small arms and light weapons (Sector 5) in that state or in supplier nations. Crucially, it is less likely to affect household producers (Sector 4). Along these lines, US action in Iraq may have increased demand for components and accessories (Sector 2) for the enhancement of existing rifles, in addition to heightening Sector 5 production, but US repair and sporadic production (Sector 1) is not likely to be have been affected.

A high degree of differentiation is also observable in the degree to which sectors of the industry devote varying amounts of resources to small arms and light weapons production in relation to non-arms-related manufacturing. This chapter demonstrates that the firms that specialize most in small arms production—and are most dependent on small arms sales—are generally household-name producers (Sector 4), followed by extensive-range producers (Sector 5). Specialist producers (Sector 3) of small arms probably rank third. Yet components and accessories producers (Sector 2) and high-tech (Sector 5) manufacturers differ considerably; for them, small arms production is often a sideline activity with respect to overall industrial production and services. With regard to repairs and sporadic production (Sector 1), trends seem similar to the latter cases, although establishing the degree of specialization is often problematic.

These observations are of considerable importance for determining the effects of large-scale changes in markets for all products, both arms- and non-arms-related, and their effect on small arms and light weapons production in particular. Moreover, they are a prerequisite to any attempt to generalize about the size of the industry. With manufacturers, and indeed sectors, devoting different percentages of resources to the production of small arms and light weapons, better conclusions can be drawn concerning the role of a firm or sector in the overall industry. This might involve assessing the typical number of employees in firms in one sector, or the average revenue a firm in a particular sector is likely to generate from small arms sales. It might involve calculating the relative frequency of firms in a sector as a proportion of a country's overall industry. These figures can then be aggregated to create a better picture of the global small arms industry.

The implications of varied distribution of qualitatively different firms

By monitoring the varying volumes and values of small arms and light weapons exports around the world, researchers have been able to speculate as to which countries are the main suppliers and which states and regions are the most dependent on such products. These quantitative research tools can only be reinforced by a qualitative understanding of production as presented in this chapter, and their policy-relevant findings made more accurate.

The research offered here suggests that the distribution of firms is to a large extent dependent on a state's level of industrial development and its consumption patterns. Thus, the most advanced forms of Sector 6 production are largely the preserve of countries with well-developed high-tech industries in both the civil and defence spheres and modern, sophisticated military customers. Household-name production (Sector 4) usually requires strong domestic demand for civilian firearms, while Sectors 2 and above need a reasonable level of industrial capacity. These considerations help in determining the likelihood that production occurs in states where information concerning the extent of manufacture is scarce; they also aid in projecting the future distribution of the small arms and light weapons industry globally.

For instance, in recent decades, high overall growth in the manufacturing industries of states such as Singapore has been accompanied by concurrent developments in extensive-range and high-tech small arms and light weapons production. In contrast, Brazil's small arms and light weapons production is significant but not high-tech. Nonetheless, the country has a relatively advanced space programme and produces large conventional weapons. Given the trends observable among current Sector 6 producers, one should expect Brazil to move into high-tech production if there is sufficient political will.

From a policy perspective, focusing on the distribution of qualitatively different sectors—rather than on a country's overall contribution to the volume of small arms produced—yields important insight into the trade. The findings of this chapter suggest that certain states may contribute more to the small arms trade than previously assumed, while others may behave in more complex ways than hitherto acknowledged.

Nowhere is this more apparent than in the trade in components and accessories. Japan, for example, is not considered an actor in the global trade in small arms and light weapons, yet its Sector 6 production of optics is well advanced and it exports to countries and regions including the United States and Western Europe.

Trade patterns in all components and accessories shed light on trade patterns in small arms-specific products.

While knowledge of the components and accessories sector is limited, this review suggests that trade patterns in all components and accessories (be they arms-related or not) can help inform conclusions about trade patterns in small arms-specific products. The automobile and watch industries demonstrate that, while assembly of finished products often takes place in designated centres, such as Geneva or Detroit, components are often manufactured in regions with low labour costs, including South-east Asia. Sector 2 production may well follow this trend. Future research will be able to fill gaps with respect to crucial areas of manufacturing that have considerable input into the use and abuse of small arms and light weapons. In turn, these important findings will be able to inform the decisions of policy-makers.

Final note

This chapter is intended to lay a foundation for a better exploration of the dynamics at work in the small arms and light weapons industry. While noting a relative absence of linkages between certain sectors,[15] it seeks to emphasize that the 'global trends' often assumed to impact on the small arms and light weapons industry as a whole actually influence its individual sectors in distinct ways. Not only are sectors often extremely different in composition, in the items that they manufacture, and in terms of their markets, but the products traded also take on differing political significance and are affected by different government regulations. Indeed:

> The flow of defense hardware and software across national boundaries is not 'free', 'unrestricted', or 'unfettered'. Instead, it is subject to a wide array of nontariff barriers to trade such as 'export controls', the 'not invented here' syndrome, and, most importantly, the economically irrational but still widespread desire for national, and in one instance regional, defense industrial independence. (Ross, 2002, p. 35)

Importantly, such barriers to trade and integration differ greatly depending on the production sector. As a result, some goods may be subject to strict regulation, while others may be treated like any civil commodity. By presenting findings that underline such differences within the small arms and light weapons industry, this chapter suggests that, in future, researchers may find it useful to focus on the effects of market and policy trends on individual production sectors. Policy-makers stand to be better informed about the specific origins of the illicit small arms trade and how regulation affects it.

LIST OF ABBREVIATIONS

ATGW	Anti-tank guided weapon
ATK	Alliant Techsystems, Inc.
CAD	Computer-aided design
CAM	Computer-aided machining
CIS	Commonwealth of Independent States
CNC	Computer Numeric Control
EDM	Electrical Discharge Machining
IMI	Israeli Military Industries
MANPADS	Man-portable air defence systems
OEM	Original equipment manufacturer
R&D	Research and development
RPG	Rocket-propelled grenade

ENDNOTES

[1] The terms 'civilian' and 'military-style' weapons are common and have some utility. For instance, a Kalashnikov AK-74 is clearly designed as a weapon meant for military use. The fact that it is not uncommon in the hands of civilians throughout the world is indicative of how weapons circulate outside from state arsenals when the lines of demarcation between military and civilian become blurred.

[2] These firms appear in a 2003 list compiled by the Omega Foundation for the Small Arms Survey, which has been updated via product category searches on Hoover's online database (Omega Foundation, 2003; Hoover's Inc., 2004).

[3] All figures, with the exception of Leupold & Stevens, Inc. (2004) and Leitner–Wise Rifle Co. (2004), are from Hoover's Inc. (2004), which compiles a wide variety of data on firms of all sizes. Data and market analyses were provided by Hoover's Inc. and included data from Dun and Bradstreet (D&B) Corporation (2004). For copyright reasons, a company-by-company breakdown of figures cannot be provided. Instead, trends in company size and turnover are aggregated and presented.

[4] The sample as a whole can be depicted as an inverted pyramid—a Zipf or Pareto distribution—revealing very few large producers and many smaller manufacturers. This feature is common to the US industry generally (Axtell, 2001) and has been noted with respect to the US firearms industry (Diaz, 1999, p. 23).

[5] Author interview with Dr. Kwesi Aning of African Security Dialogue and Research, Accra, Ghana. 8 October 2004. Geneva, Switzerland.

[6] Author interview with Maxim Pyadushkin, Specialist in Russian defence industry production, Moscow, Russian Federation. 7 October 2004. Geneva, Switzerland.

[7] Author interview with F. J. Gebert, Managing Director, Truvelo, 14 June 2004. Paris-Nord, Villepinte: Eurosatory 2004.

[8] See Cogswell & Harrison, 2004; Piotti Fratelli, 2004; Poli, 2004; James Purdey & Sons, 2004; and J. Roberts & Son, 2004.

[9] See GIAT, 2004; HRMND, 2004; Hirtenberger, 2005; POF, 2004; 2005.

[10] A few companies, including Austria's Hirtenberger, produce items such as metal stamping parts and seat-belt pretensioners (Hirtenberger, 2005).

[11] See Colt, 2004; Picatinny, 2004; Springfield Armory, 2004; Talley, 2004; US Ordnance, 2004.

[12] See Burris, 2004; Bushnell, 2004; Leupold & Stevens, 2004; Zeiss, 2004.

[13] See ATK, 2004a; GD, 2004b; EADS, 2003; ITT, 2004b; Raytheon, 2004b; Thales, 2003.

[14] See ATK, 2004b; GD, 2004b; ITT, 2004b; Lockheed, 2004b; Raytheon, 2004b.

[15] Such events as a joint venture between handgun-maker Taurus of Brazil and the Australian high-tech manufacturer Metal Storm have been rare to date and are thus excluded from this analysis (Taurus, 2004b). They may, however, become more common in future.

BIBLIOGRAPHY

Action Gun Works. 2004. Company Web site. Sparks, NV: Dierks Industries. Accessed 10 September 2004. <http://www.dierksind.com>

Accuracy International. 2004. Company Web site. Crawley, United Kingdom: Accuracy International Ltd. Accessed 5 October 2004. <http://www.accuracyinternational.com>

Alpers, Philip and Conor Twyford. 2003. *Small Arms in the Pacific*. Occasional Paper No. 8. Geneva: Small Arms Survey. March.

Anschütz. 2004. Company Web site. Ulm, Germany: J.G. Anschütz GmbH & Co. KG. Accessed 3 October 2004. <http://jga.anschuetz-sport.com>

Arcus. 2004. Company Web site. Lyaskovets, Bulgaria: Arcus Co. Accessed 3 October 2004. <http://www.arcus-bg.com>

ArmaLite. 2004. Company Web site. Geneseo, IL: ArmaLite, Inc. Accessed 23 September 2004. <http://www.armalite.com>

Armatt. 2004. Company Web site. Zebulon, NC: Armatt G.S., Inc. Accessed 20 September 2004. <http://www.cyberfieds.com/armatt.html>

ATK (Alliant Techsystems). 2004a. 'Annual Report 2004: ATK on the Move.' Accessed 10 February 2005. <http://www.atk.com/Downloads/annualreport_ATK_2004.pdf>

—. 2004b. Form 10K: Annual Report Pursuant to Section 13 or 15(d) of the Securities Exchange Act of 1934. Submitted by for the fiscal year ended 31 December 2003; Commission file number: 1-3671. Washington, DC: United States Securities and Exchange Commission. Accessed 10 February 2005. <http://www.generaldynamics.com/ir/AnnualReport2003/PageF2.htm>

—. 2005. Corporation Web site. Edina, MN: Alliant Techsystems Inc. Accessed 10 February 2005. <http://www.atk.com>

ATN (American Technologies Network Corporation). 2005. Company Web site. San Francisco, CA: ATN. Accessed 10 February 2005. <http://www.atncorp.com>

Axtell, Robert. 2001. 'U.S. Firms are Zipf Distributed.' Washington, DC: The Brookings Institution. February. <www.brookings.org/ES/dynamics/papers/zipf/zipf.PDF>

Barrett. 2004. Company Web site. Murfreesboro, TN: Barrett Firearms Manufacturing, Inc. Accessed 5 October 2004. <http://www.barrettrifles.com>

BASIC (British American Security Information Council). 1996. 'Light Weapons Manufacture in the Public and Private Sectors: A View From Pakistan.' Project on Light Weapons Working Paper No. 2. London: BASIC. February.

BBC (British Broadcasting Corporation). 2004a. Report by the BBC's Fergal Keane from Darfur. 10 November. London: BBC.

—. 2004b. 'Thai protesters die in custody.' BBC News UK edition. 26 October. London: BBC. Accessed 24 January 2005. <http://news.bbc.co.uk/1/hi/world/asia-pacific/3954587.stm>

Beretta. 2004. Company Web site. Gardone Val Trompia, Brescia, Italy: Fabbrica d'armi Pietro Beretta S.p.A. Accessed 30 September 2004. <http://www.beretta.com>

Berry, Steven, James Levinsohn, and Ariel Pakes. 2003. 'Differentiated Products Demand Systems from a Combination of Micro and Macro Data: The New Car Market.' Cambridge, MA: Harvard University. 22 February. Accessed 29 October 2004. <http://post.economics.harvard.edu/faculty/pakes/papers/nmicroblp1.pdf>

Bersa. 2004. Company Web site. Ramos Mejía, Buenos Aires, Argentina. Accessed 3 October 2004. <http://www.bersa-sa.com.ar>

Bevan, James and Siemon Wezeman. 2004. 'Light weapons: a definitional paper.' Background paper (unpublished). Geneva: Small Arms Survey and Stockholm: Stockholm International Peace Research Institute.

Brady Campaign. 2002. 'The Assault Weapons Ban: Frequently Asked Questions.' Washington, DC: Brady Campaign to Prevent Gun Violence. Accessed 10 February 2005. <http://www.bradycampaign.org/facts/faqs/?page=awb>

Bravo. 2004. Company Web site. Hartland, WI: Bravo Company USA, Inc. Accessed 6 October 2004. <http://www.bravocompanyusa.com>

Burris. 2004. Company Web site. Greeley, CO: Burris Company. Accessed 29 September 2004. <http://www.burrisoptics.com>

Bushnell. 2004. Company Web site. Overland Park, KS: Bushnell Corporation. Accessed 29 September 2004. <http://www.bushnell.com>

California. 2005. An act to amend Sections 245, 12011, 12022, 12022.5, 12275, 12275.5, 12280, 12285, 12286, 12287, 12288, 12288.5, 12289, and 12290 of, and to add Section 12278 to, the Penal Code, relating to firearms. Assembly Bill No. 50. Chapter 494. Approved and filed 13 September 2004; due into force 1 January 2005. Sacramento, CA: California State Senate. Accessed 11 February 2005. <http://info.sen.ca.gov/pub/03-04/bill/asm/ab_0001-0050/ab_50_bill_20040913_chaptered.pdf>

Capie, David. 2002. *Small Arms Production and Transfers in Southeast Asia*. Canberra: Australia National University.

Chamberlain, E.H. 1933. *The Theory of Monopolistic Competition*. Cambridge, MA: Harvard University Press.

Cogswell & Harrison. 2004. Company Web site. Slough, United Kingdom: Cogswell & Harrison (Gunmakers) Ltd. Accessed 30 September 2004. <http://www.cogswell.co.uk>

Coherent. 2004a. Company Web site. Santa Clara, CA: Coherent Inc. Accessed 3 October 2004. <http://www.coherent.com>

—. 2004b. Form 10K: Annual Report Pursuant to Section 13 or 15(d) of the Securities Exchange Act of 1934. Submitted by for the fiscal year ended 27 September 2003; Commission file number: 0-5255. Washington, DC: United States Securities and Exchange Commission. Accessed 3 October 2004. <http://ccbn.mobular.net/ccbn/7/405/452>

Cole Arms. 2004. Company Web site. McMinnville, OR: Cole Arms Inc. Accessed 18 September 2004. <http://www.sites.onlinemac.com/colearms>

Colt. 2004. Company Web site. Hartford, CT: Colt's Manufacturing Company LLC. Accessed 23 September 2004. <http://www.colt.com>

Curran, J.G.M. and J.H. Goodfellow. 1990. 'Theoretical and Practical Issues in the Determination of Market Boundaries.' *European Journal of Marketing*. 24:1. January, pp. 16–28.

Degtyarev. 2004. Company Web site. Kovrov, Russia: V.A. Degtyarev Plant. Accessed 8 October 2004. <http://www.zid.ru>

Denel. 2004a. Company Web site. Pretoria: Denel (Pty) Ltd. Accessed 1 October 2004. <http://www.denel.co.za>

—. 2004b. Annual Report 2004. Pretoria: Denel (Pty) Ltd. Accessed 11 February 2005. <http://www.denel.co.za/Resources/AnnualReport2004.pdf>

Diaz, Tom. 1999. *Making a Killing: The Business of Guns in America*. New York: The New Press.

Dillon. 2004. Company Website. Scottsdale, AZ: Dillon Precision Products, Inc. Accessed 3 February 2005. <http://dillonprecision.com>

D&B Corporation. 2004. Data reported in Hoover's Inc. 2004. Hoover's Online Pro Plus Subscription Database. Austin, TX: Hoover's Inc. <http://premium.hoovers.com/subscribeuk>

Dreyfus, Pablo and Benjamin Lessing. 2003. 'Production and Exports of Small Arms and Light Weapons and Ammunition in South America and Mexico.' Background paper (unpublished). Geneva: Small Arms Survey.

EADS (European Aeronautic Defence and Space Company). 2003. 'To New Levels: Financial Statements and Corporate Governance 2003.' European Aeronautic Defence and Space Company EADS N.V. Accessed 7 October 2004. <http://www.eads.net/xml/content/OF00000000400004/3/00/29655003.pdf>

—. 2004. Company Web site. Schiphol Rijk, Netherlands: European Aeronautic Defence and Space Company. Accessed 7 October 2004. <http://www.eads.net>

Economist. 2004. *Pocket World in Figures 2004.* London: Profile Books Ltd.

Elcan. 2004. Company Web site. Midland, Ontario: Elcan Optical Technologies. Accessed 1 October 2004. <http://www.elcan.com>

Eloptro. 2004. Company Web site. Kempton Park, South Africa: Eloptro. Accessed 1 October 2004. <http://www.eloptro.co.za>

Evolution Gun Works. 2004. Company Web site. Quakertown, PA: EGW Inc. Accessed 20 September 2004. <http://www.egw-guns.com>

Famars. 2004. Company Web site. Brescia, Italy: Famars di Abbiatico & Salvinelli SRL. Accessed 3 February 2005. <http://www.famars.com/famars_today.htm>

FAS (Federation of American Scientists). 2000. 'Kahuta, Khan Research Laboratories, A.Q. Khan Laboratories, Engineering Research Laboratories.' Washington, DC: Federation of American Scientists. Accessed 7 October 2004. <http://www.fas.org/nuke/guide/pakistan/facility/kahuta.htm>

FN. 2004. Company Web site. Columbia, SC: FN Manufacturing LLC. Accessed 6 October 2004. <http://www.fnmfg.com>

FN Herstal. Company Web site. Herstal, Belgium: FN Herstal SA. Accessed 6 October 2004. <http://www.fnherstal.com>

Furukawa. 2004. Company Web site. Tokyo: The Furukawa Electric Company, Ltd. Accessed 3 October 2004. <http://www.furukawa.co.jp>

GAGC (Great American Gunstocks Company). 2004. Company Web site. Yuba City, CA: Great American Gunstocks Company. Accessed 20 September 2004. <http://www.gunstocks.com>

GD (General Dynamics). 2003. Annual Report 2003. Accessed 11 February 2005. <http://www.generaldynamics.com/ir/pdf/gd2003part1.pdf>

—. 2004a. Corporation Web site. Falls Church, VA: General Dynamics. Accessed 7 October 2004. <http://www.generaldynamics.com>

—. 2004b. Form 10K: Annual Report Pursuant to Section 13 or 15(d) of the Securities Exchange Act of 1934. Submitted for the fiscal year ended 31 December 2003; Commission file number: 1-3671. Washington, DC: United States Securities and Exchange Commission.

GIAT (Groupement des industries de l'armement terrestre). 2004. Organizational Web site. Saint-Etienne/Saint-Chamond, France: Groupement des industries de l'armement terrestre. Accessed 6 October 2004. <http://www.giat-industries.fr>

GLOCK, 2004. Company Web site. Deutsch-Wagram, Austria: GLOCK Ges.m.b.H. Accessed 3 October 2004. <http://www.glock.com>

Godnick, William, Robert Muggah, and Camilla Waszink. 2002. *Stray Bullets: The Impact of Small Arms Misuse in Central America.* Occasional Paper No. 5. Geneva: Small Arms Survey. October.

Hatcher Gun Company. 2004. Company Web site. Elsie, NE: Hatcher Gun Company. Accessed 18 September 2004. <http://www.hatchergun.com>

Henry. 2005. Company Web site. New York: Henry Repeating Arms Company. Accessed 11 February 2005. <http://www.henryrepeating.com>

Hicks, John. 1932. *The Theory of Wages.* 1963 edition. London: Macmillan.

Hirtenberger. 2005. Company Web site. Hirtenberg, Austria: Hirtenberger AG. Accessed 7 February 2005. <http://www.hirtenberger.at>

HK (Heckler & Koch). 2004. Company Web site. Oberndorf, Germany: Heckler & Koch GmbH. Accessed 30 September 2004. <http://www.heckler-koch.de>

HKJS (Heckler & Koch Jagd- und Sportwaffen). 2004. Company Web site. Oberndorf, Germany: Heckler & Koch Jagd- und Sportwaffen GmbH. Accessed 30 September 2004. <http://www.heckler-kochjs.de>

Hoover's Inc. 2004. Hoover's Online Pro Plus Subscription Database. Austin, TX: Hoover's Inc. <http://premium.hoovers.com/subscribeuk>

House of Commons. 2000. 'Illegal Firearms. Session 1999–2000.' Memoranda submitted by the Home Office. London: Home Affairs Committee Publications. Accessed 6 October 2004. <http://www.publications.parliament.uk/pa/cm199900/cmselect/cmhaff/uc95/uc9508.htm>

HRMND (Hellenic Republic: Ministry of National Defence). 2001. 'White Paper for the Armed Forces.' Chapter 5, section 2: The Hellenic Defence Industry. 27 January. Athens: HRMND. Accessed 6 October 2004. <http://www.hri.org/mod/fylladia/bible/e_toc.htm>

IMI (Israeli Military Industries). 2004. Company Web site. Ramat Hasharon, Israel: Israeli Military Industries. Accessed 7 October 2004. <http://www.imi-israel.com>

ITT. 2003. Form 10K: Annual Report Pursuant to Section 13 or 15(d) of the Securities Exchange Act of 1934. Submitted for the fiscal year ended 31 December 2003; Commission file number: 1-5627. Washington, DC: United States Securities and Exchange Commission. Accessed 10 February 2005. <http://www.itt.com/ir/downloads/10k_sec_itt_ar_03.pdf>

—. 2004. Corporation Web site. White Plains, NY: ITT Industries, Inc. Accessed 7 October 2004. <http://www.itt.com>

J&T. 2003. 'Complete AR-15 Weapon Kits.' Advertisement in *Small Arms Review.* Vol. 6:9. June, p. 19.

Jane's. 2003. 'Indonesia Expands Arms Purchasing.' *Jane's Intelligence Review.* Coulsdon, Jane's Information Group. 1 December.

—. 2004a. 'Fast Track to the Defence Industry.' Coulsdon: Jane's Information Group. Accessed 7 October 2004. <http://fasttrack.janes.com>

—. 2004b. 'Work This One Out.' Foreign report. Coulsdon: Jane's Information Group. 26 February.

Jones, Richard and Charles Cutshaw. 2004. *Jane's Infantry Weapons 2004–2005.* Coulsdon: Jane's Information Group.

Kahr Arms. 2004. Company Web site. Blauvelt, NY: Kahr Arms. Accessed 23 September 2004. <http://www.kahr.com>

Kante, Mamadou Sekouba. 2004. *De la fabrication locale d'armes au Mali: A travers la prolifération des armes légères.* FOSDA Monograph No. 8. Accra: La Fondation Pour la Sécurité et le Développement en Afrique. January.

Kiss, Yudit. 2004. *Small arms and light weapons production in Eastern, Central and Southeast Europe.* Occasional Paper No. 13. Geneva: Small Arms Survey. October.

Knight Rifles. 2004. Company Web site. Centerville, IA: Knight Rifles. Accessed 18 September 2004. <http://www.knightrifles.com>

KPB. 2004. Company Web site. Tula, Russia: KBP Instrument Design Bureau. Accessed 8 October 2004. <http://www.shipunov.com>

KPIS (Kosovo Police Information Systems). 2003. Database on reported and committed crimes. (No online access.) Data downloaded: January.

Kuehl. 2003. 'The mil. spec. 14.5" M-4 look you want with a civilian legal 16.1" barrel length.' Labadie, MO: Kuehl Precision Firearms. Advertisement in *Small Arms Review.* Vol. 6:9. June, p. 22.

Lambda. 2004. Company Web site. Harpenden, United Kingdom: Lambda Photometrics Limited. Accessed 3 October 2004. <http://www.lambdaphoto.co.uk>

Lancaster, Kelvin. 1971. *Consumer Demand: A New Approach.* New York: Columbia University Press.

Laser 2000. 2004. Company Web site. Kettering, United Kingdom: Laser 2000 (UK) Ltd. Accessed 3 October 2004. <http://www.laser2000.co.uk>

Laser Devices. 2004. Company Web site. Monterey, CA: Laser Devices, Inc. Accessed 18 September 2004. <http://www.laserdevices.com>

Lasermate. 2004. Company Web site. Pomona, CA: Lasermate Group, Inc. Accessed 3 October 2004. <http://www.lasermate.com>

LaserMax. 2004. Company Web site. Rochester, NY: LaserMax, Inc. Accessed 3 October 2004. <http://www.oemlasers.com>

LEI (Law Enforcement International). 2004. Company brochure. St Albans, United Kingdom: Law Enforcement International Ltd.

Leitner–Wise Rifle Co. 2004. Company Web site. Alexandria, VA: Leitner–Wise Rifle Co. Inc. <http://www.leitner-wise.com>

Leupold & Stevens, Inc. 2004. Company Web site. Beaverton, OR: Leupold & Stevens, Inc. Accessed 29 September 2004. <http://www.leupold.com>

Lilja. 2004. Company Web site. Plains, MT: Lilja Precision Rifle Barrels, Inc. Accessed 20 September 2004. <http://www.riflebarrels.com>
Lock, Peter. 2003. 'Review of the *Small Arms Surveys:* Emerging Paradigms of the Survey.' Hamburg: European Association for Research on Transformation e.V./Peter Lock. Accessed 18 September 2004. <http://www.peter-lock.de/txt/smallarms2003.html>
Lockheed. 2004a. Company Web site. Bethesda, MD: Lockheed Martin Corporation. Accessed 7 October 2004. <http://www.lockheedmartin.com>
—. 2004b. Form 10K: Annual Report Pursuant to Section 13 or 15(d) of the Securities Exchange Act of 1934. Submitted for the fiscal year ended 31 December 2003; Commission file number: 1-11437. Washington, DC: United States Securities and Exchange Commission. Accessed 7 October 2003. <http://www.lockheedmartin.com>
McInnes, Ross. 2004. '2003 Annual Results.' Neuilly-sur-Seine, France: Thales. 15 March. Accessed 8 October 2004. <http://www.thalesgroup.com/all/pdf/Analystes_web_engl.pdf>
McMillan. 2004. Company Web site. Phoenix, AZ: McMillan Bros. Accessed 5 October 2004. <http://www.mcbrosrifles.com>
Manroy. 2004. Company Web site. Beckley, United Kingdom: Manroy Engineering Ltd. Accessed 3 October 2004. <http://www.manroy.co.uk>
Marlin. 2004. Company Web site. North Haven, CT: Marlin Firearms. Accessed 22 September 2004. <http://www.marlinfirearms.com>
MGW. 2005. Company Web site. Augusta, GA: MGW Precision Inc. Accessed 3 February 2005. <http://www.mgwltd.com/firearms.html>
Mossberg. 2004. Company Web site. North Haven, CT: O.F. Mossberg & Sons, Inc. Accessed 22 September 2004. <http://www.mossberg.com>
Mountain State. 2004. Company Web site. Williamstown, WV: Mountain State Manufacturing. Accessed 1 October 2004. <http://www.msmfg.com>
NCIS (National Criminal Intelligence Services). 2002. 'United Kingdom Threat Assessment of Serious and Organised Crime 2002.' Chapter 7: Firearms. London: NCIS. Accessed 6 October 2002. <http://www.ncis.co.uk/ukta/2002/threat07.asp>
NEC. 2004. Company Web site. Kanagawa, Japan: NEC Compound Semiconductor Devices. Accessed 3 October 2004. <http://www.ncsd.necel.com>
NISAT (Norwegian Initiative on Small Arms Transfers). Database of small arms production, policy, and legislation. Oslo: NISAT. Accessed 22 February 2005. <http://www.nisat.org>
Omega Foundation. 2003. 'Global Survey of Small Arms and Light Weapons Companies.' Background paper (unpublished). Geneva: Small Arms Survey.
Pearce. 2004. Company Web site. Fort Worth, TX: Pearce Grip, Inc. Accessed 1 October 2004. <http://www.pearcegrip.com>
Penn Arms. 2004. Company Web site. Punxsutawney, PA: Penn Arms. Accessed 23 September 2004. <http://www.pennarms.com>
Picatinny. 2004. Organization Web site. Picatinny Arsenal, NJ: Picatinny. Accessed 5 October 2004. <http://www.pica.army.mil>
Piotti Fratelli. 2004. Company Web site. Gardone Val Trompia, Brescia: Piotti Fratelli s.n.c. Accessed 30 September 2004. <http://www.piotti.com>
Poe Lang. 2004. Company Web site. Taichung, Taiwan: Poe Lang Enterprise Co., Ltd. Accessed 3 October 2004. <http://www.laser-poelang.com.tw>
POF (Pakistan Ordnance Factories). 2004. Company Web site. Wah Cantt, Pakistan: Pakistan Ordnance Factories. Accessed 7 October 2004. <http://www.pofwah.com.pk>
POF (Pakistan Ordnance Factories). 2005. Defence Export Promotion Organisation (DEPO). Accessed 7 February 2005. <http://www.depo.org.pk/products/pof>
Poli. 2004. Company Web site. Gardone Val Trompia, Brescia, Italy: Armi F.lli Poli. Accessed 30 September 2004. <http://www.intred.it/poli>
PRS. 2004. Company Web site. Bundaberg, Australia: Precision Rifle Systems. <http://www.users.bigpond.com/pdunnprs> Accessed 5 October 2004.
Purdey & Sons. 2004. Company Web site. London: James Purdey & Sons Ltd. <http://www.purdey.com> Accessed 30 September 2004.
Pyadushkin, Maxim. 2004a. 'An Analysis of the Production of Small Arms and Light Weapons in Russia.' Background paper (unpublished). Geneva: Small Arms Survey.
—. 2004b. 'An Analysis of the Production of Small Arms and Light Weapons in the Commonwealth of Independent States.' Background paper (unpublished). Geneva: Small Arms Survey.
Raytheon. 2004a. Company Web site. Waltham, MA: Raytheon Company. Accessed 7 October 2004. <http://www.raytheon.com>
—. 2004b. Form 10K: Annual Report Pursuant to Section 13 or 15(d) of the Securities Exchange Act of 1934. Submitted for the fiscal year ended 31 December 2003; Commission file number 1-31552. Washington, DC: United States Securities and Exchange Commission. Accessed 7 October 2004. <http://www.raytheon.com/finance/static/node2640.html>
Remington. 2003. Form 10K: Annual Report Pursuant to Section 13 or 15(d) of the Securities Exchange Act of 1934. Submitted for the fiscal year ended 31 December 2003; Commission file number: 333-104141. Washington, DC: United States Securities and Exchange Commission. Accessed 23 September 2004. <http://www.sec.gov/Archives/edgar/data/916504/000119312504053255/d10k.htm>
—. 2004. Company Web site. Madison, NC: Remington Arms Company, Inc. Accessed 23 September 2004. <http://www.remington.com>
Robar. 2004. Company Web site. Phoenix, AZ: The Robar Companies, Inc. Accessed 5 October 2004. <http://www.robarguns.com>
Roberts & Son. 2004. Company Web site. London: J. Roberts & Son (Gunmakers) Ltd. Accessed 30 September 2004. <http://www.jroberts-gunmakers.co.uk>
Rolyn. 2004. Company Web site. Covina, CA: Rolyn Optics Co. Accessed 3 October 2004. <http://www.rolyn.com>
RomArm. 2004. Company Web site. Bucharest, Romania: RomArm. Accessed 30 September 2004. <http://www.romarm.ro>
Ross, Andrew. 2002. 'Defense Industry Globalization: Contrarian Observations.' In *Defense Industry Globalization: A Compendium of Papers.* Presented at a conference on 'Defense Industry Globalization', 16 November 2001. Washington, DC: The Atlantic Council of the United States.
Rossi USA. 2004. Company Web site. Miami, FL: Amadeo Rossi, SA. Accessed 3 October 2004. <http://www.rossiusa.com>
Ruger. 2003. Annual Report 2003. Southport, CT: Sturm, Ruger & Co., Inc. Accessed 22 September 2004. <http://www.ruger-firearms.com/Corporate/PDF/Annual%20Report%202003.pdf>
—. 2004. *Catalogue of Fine Firearms*. Southport, CT: Sturm, Ruger & Co., Inc. Accessed 20 September 2004. <http://ruger.com/Firearms/PDF/Ruger2003Catalog.pdf>
Sarsilmaz. 2004. Company Web site. Istanbul: Sarsilmaz. Accessed 30 September 2004. <http://www.sarsilmaz.com>
Sauer. 2004. Company Web site. Eckernförde, Germany: J. P. Sauer & Sohn GmbH. Accessed 3 October 2004. <http://www.sauer-waffen.de>
Savage Arms. 2004. Company Web site. Westfield, MA: Savage Arms, Inc. Accessed 28 September 2004. <http://www.savagearms.com>
Schmidt & Bender. 2004. Company Web site. Biebertal, Germany: Schmidt & Bender GmbH & Co. Kg. Accessed 3 October 2004. <http://www.schmidtbender.com>
SEESAC (South Eastern Europe Clearinghouse for the Control of Small Arms and Light Weapons). 2004. SEESAC Daily SALW Media Monitoring. Citing VIP News Service. Belgrade: SEESAC. 18 March.
Serbu. 2005. Company Web site. Tampa, FL: Serbu Firearms, Inc. Accessed 3 February 2005. <http://www.serbu.com>
Sinclair. 2004. Company Web site. Fort Wayne, IN: Sinclair International. Accessed 1 October 2004. <http://www.sinclairintl.com>
Small Arms Review. Various dates. Harmony, ME: Moose Lake Publishing.
Small Arms Survey. 2001. *Small Arms Survey 2001: Profiling the Problem.* Oxford: Oxford University Press.

—. 2002. *Small Arms Survey 2002: Counting the Human Cost*. Oxford: Oxford University Press.

—. 2003. *Small Arms Survey 2003: Development Denied*. Oxford: Oxford University Press.

—. 2004. *Small Arms Survey 2004: Rights at Risk*. Oxford: Oxford University Press.

Smith & Wesson. 2004a. Handgun Catalogue. Springfield, MA: Smith & Wesson. Accessed 20 September 2004.
<http://swcustomersupport.vista.com/userimages/2004_SW_Handgun.pdf>

—. 2004b. Form 10K: Annual Report Pursuant to Section 13 or 15(d) of the Securities Exchange Act of 1934. Submitted for the fiscal year ended 30 April 2004; Commission file number 1-31552. Washington, DC: United States Securities and Exchange Commission. Accessed 22 September 2004. <http://ccbn.10kwizard.com/xml/download.php?repo=tenk&ipage=2892689&format=PDF>

Spider Firearms. 2004. Company Web site. St. Cloud, FL: Spider Firearms. Accessed 18 September 2004. <http://ferret50.com>

Springfield. 2004. Company Web site. Geneseo, IL: Springfield Armory. Accessed 23 September 2004. <http://www.springfield-armory.com>

—. 2005. 'Fear No Evil: Any Mission, Any Conditions, Any Foe at Any Range. M1A SOCOM 16.' Geneseo, IL: Springfield Armory. Advertisement in *Guns & Ammo*. Vol. 49:1. New York: Primedia, Inc. January, p. 21.

SureFire. 2004. Company Web site. Fountain Valley, CA: SureFire, LLC. Accessed 1 October 2004. <http://www.surefire.com>

Swarovski. 2004a. Company Web site. Wattens, Austria: D. Swarovski & Co. Accessed 29 September 2004. <http://www.swarovski.com>

—. 2004b. 'The World of Crystal.' Company fact sheet. Wattens, Austria: D. Swarovski & Co. Accessed 3 October 2004.
<http://www.swarovski.com/SVK_Relaunch/GLOBAL/globalShowBinary/0,3210,15515,00.pdf>

Swarovski Optic. 2004. Company Web site. Absam, Austria: Swarovski Optik KG. Accessed 29 September 2004. <http://www.swarovskioptik.at>

Swiss Arms. 2004. Company Web site. Neuhausen am Rheinfall: SAN Swiss Arms AG. Accessed 30 September 2004. <http://www.sigarms.ch>

—. 2005. *When It Counts: Law Enforcement and Defense Products*. Neuhausen am Rheinfall: SAN Swiss Arms AG. Accessed 14 February 2005. <http://swissarms2.ath.cx/fileadmin/img/ext/sicherheit/downloads/SAN_LE_Katalog_E.pdf>

Talley. 2004. Company Web site. Mesa, AZ: Talley Defense Systems. Accessed 5 October 2004. <http://www.talleyds.com>

Taurus. 2004a. Company Web site. Miami, FL: Taurus International MFG, Inc. USA Accessed 20 September 2004. <http://www.taurususa.com>

—. 2004b. 'Authorized User Firearm Partnership.' Taurus News Release. Miami, FL: Taurus International MFG, Inc. USA. 25 November 2003. Accessed 11 November 2004. <http://www.taurususa.com/newsreviews/pr1103.cfm>

TDI Arms. 2004. Product catalogue. London: TDI Arms Ltd.

Thales. 2003. Consolidated financial statements of 31 December 2001, 2002, and 2003. Neuilly-sur-Seine, France: Thales. Accessed 7 October 2004. <http://www.thalesgroup.com/all/pdf/plaquette_GB_15_mars.pdf>

—. 2004. Company Web site. Neuilly-sur-Seine, France: Thales. Accessed 7 October 2004. <http://www.thalesgroup.com>

Timney. 2004. Company Web site. Phoenix, AZ: Timney Manufacturing, Inc. Accessed 1 October 2004. <http://www.timneytriggers.com>

Truvelo. 2004. Company Web site. Lyttelton, South Africa: Truvelo (Pty) Ltd. Accessed 3 October 2004. <http://www.truvelo.co.za>

UN (United Nations). 1997. *Report of the Panel of Experts on Small Arms*. A/52/298 of 27 August. Accessed 14 February 2005.
<http://www.un.org/Docs/sc/committees/sanctions/a52298.pdf>

UNGA (United Nations General Assembly). 1997. *Report of the Panel of Governmental Experts on Small Arms*. A/52/298 of 27 August.

USDOD (United States Department of Defense). 1995. 'Military Standard: Dimensioning of Accessory Mounting Rail for Small Arms Weapons.' MIL-STD-1913 (AR). Washington, DC: USDOD. 3 February. Accessed 20 September 2004.
<http://www.biggerhammer.net/picatinny/1913_specs.pdf>

US Ordnance. 2004. Company Web site. Reno, NV: U.S. Ordnance, Inc. Accessed 28 September 2004. <http://www.usord.com>

UWS (Ultimate Weapons Systems). 2004. Company Web site. Accessed 20 September 2004. <http://www.uws.com>

VPC (Violence Policy Center). 2002. 'Sitting Ducks: The Threat to Chemical and Refinery Industry from 50-Caliber Sniper Rifles.' Washington, DC: Violence Policy Center.

—. 2003. 'Just Like Bird Hunting: The Threat to Civil Aviation from 50-Caliber Sniper Rifles.' Washington: Violence Policy Center.

Walther. 2004. Company Web site. Amsberg, Germany: Carl Walther GmbH Sportwaffen. Accessed 3 October 2004. <http://www.carl-walther.de>

Weidacher, Reinhilde. 2005. *Military Small Arms and Light Weapons Production in Western Europe* (working title). Occasional Paper. Geneva: Small Arms Survey. Forthcoming.

Wisner's. 2004. Company Web site. Adna, WA: Wisner's Inc. Accessed 20 September 2004. <http://www.wisnersinc.com>

WSTech. 2004. Company Web site. Toronto: World Star Tech. Accessed 3 October 2004. <http://www.worldstartech.com>

Xianfeng. 2004. Company Web site. Zhejiang, China: Zhejiang Xianfeng Machinery Factory. Accessed 1 October 2004.
<http://www.gate-operators.com>

Yankee Hill. 2005. Company Web site. Florence, MA: Yankee Hill Machine Company Inc. Accessed 3 February 2005. <http://www.yhm.net>

Zastava. 2004. Company Web site. Kragujevac, Serbia and Montenegro: Žastava Oruje D.P. Accessed 3 October 2004.
<http://www.zastava-arms.co.yu>

Zeiss. 2004. Company Web site. Oberkochen, Germany: Carl Zeiss. Accessed 3 October 2004. <http://www.zeiss.de>

ACKNOWLEDGEMENTS

Principal author
James Bevan

Other contributors
Kwesi Anings, Eric Berman, Anne-Kathrin Glatz, Keith Krause, Emile LeBrun, and Maxim Pyadushkin

Anti-terrorist
commandos stand at
attention at Tokyo's
Narita International
Airport, April 2004.
(© Shizuo Kambayashi/AP Photo)

The Count Continues:
STOCKPILES

3

INTRODUCTION

The year 2004 saw powerful states struggling with unrestrained small arms proliferation. In Iraq and Afghanistan, in particular, armed individuals and groups continue to present a great obstacle to human security, coalition forces, and reconstruction efforts. Yet elsewhere, with far less firepower and attracting far less public attention, governments and civil society have quietly pressed on with a number of initiatives to address civilian small arms possession and armed violence.

The aspect of small arms stockpiles most prominent in 2004 was internationally sponsored disarmament. Efforts in Afghanistan, Cote d'Ivoire, Haiti, Iraq, Liberia, and Sudan attracted the most attention, but many more were tried or debated. At the domestic level, 2004 also represented a turning point in a number of states' efforts to control armed violence through enhanced domestic controls. All of these initiatives have hinted at strong national and international will to further the small arms control agenda.

The will to act has not been uniform. North-east Asia and the Middle East[1] are among the most prominent regions only beginning to assert a strong presence in small arms processes. They are addressed in depth in this chapter, which continues the regional review of past editions of the *Small Arms Survey*. This chapter's major conclusions include the following:

- Small arms disarmament has emerged as a prominent element of international, multilateral, and domestic efforts to control armed violence.
- Major initiatives may reduce local stockpiles, but disarmament reductions are outweighed by increases in global small arms stocks elsewhere.
- Arms reduction, both post-conflict and in societies not at war, is most successful when pursued as part of an integrated system of violence reduction initiatives.
- Middle Eastern militaries and police forces stockpile some 13 million–17 million firearms.
- North-east Asian militaries and police forces hold an estimated 22 million–42 million firearms.
- The Middle East has anywhere from 45 million to 90 million firearms in the hands of civilians.

The year was characterized by the continued working out of processes that began earlier. Ideas and approaches set in motion previously could be seen progressing and gaining broader support, as well-known dangers grew more troubling and incremental progress gradually made their effects more visible.

The cumulative effect was to confirm the steady globalization of the small arms agenda. No longer is small arms proliferation an issue exclusively for particular countries or regions. By examining the Middle East and north-east Asia, this chapter completes the region-by-region survey of small arms stockpiles initiated in the first edition of this yearbook.

While this undertaking remains general and open to revision and better information, it offers a sense of the scale of firearms inventories and their world distribution.

Since the small arms issue came on to the international agenda in the early 1990s, a few regions have remained aloof. Most of the governments of the Middle East and north-east Asia, regions that together contain one-quarter the world's population, were able to avoid small arms transparency and to keep the dimensions of their stockpiles secret, while debate focused on other parts of the world. This chapter shows that even in these regions, seemingly immune to global trends, small arms stockpile issues are beginning to demand attention. Although gaps and weaknesses still complicate global stockpile management, greater responsibility for small arms is gradually becoming more universally accepted.

2004: OLD PROBLEMS, NEW INITIATIVES

A number of initiatives in 2004 raised the profile of stockpile management. Some of these were the legacies of earlier years only now coming into full effect; others were designed and implemented in 2004. Most involve ongoing efforts. This reflects the fact that control initiatives, whether as part of formal, internationally-sponsored disarmament, demobilization, and reintegration (DDR), more ad hoc multilateral initiatives, or changes in national policy and implementation, are long-term endeavours.

It is a sign of the transformation that small arms disarmament has spread from the domain of specialists to become an increasingly routine element of global policy-making. Not just the international community, but affected states, former combatants, and their leaders have made small arms disarmament an accepted instrument for addressing a diverse spectrum of problems. Where the misuse of small arms has emerged as a vector of human suffering, disarmament wins rapid recognition as an essential part of the solution. Disarmament is a formal element in conflict resolution in countries as diverse as Afghanistan, Colombia, Iraq, Haiti, Liberia, and Northern Ireland. In addition, formal small arms disarmament was discussed in 2004 as part of conflict resolution in India, Lebanon, Nigeria, Spain, and Sudan, among others. The results of such efforts have been uneven and in some cases contradictory.

United States initiatives to control the estimated 7 million–8 million small arms loose in society in Iraq (Small Arms Survey, 2004, p. 49) have been of the trial-and-error variety, focusing primarily on light weapons such as machine guns, rocket-propelled grenades, and heavier ordnance (Centcom, 2003; BBC, 2004). Nonetheless, events in Sadr City, Baghdad, illustrate how initiatives aimed at local communities can bear fruit. Although figures have not been released, in October 2004 successes in collecting small arms and light weapons in the city prompted the Interim Government to extend an amnesty throughout the country (BBC, 2004; CNN, 2004). The collection effort appears to have targeted militias indirectly and to have been instrumental in offering them a dignified transition to a more political role (Schwartz, 2005). It demonstrates that adopting a community perspective can often be more successful in arms control than targeting any one set of armed actors.

Elsewhere, prominent international weapons reduction initiatives continue in states such as Liberia and Haiti, with mixed success yet clear indications of the necessity for multifaceted approaches to reducing demand for small arms (POST-CONFLICT).

With regard to stockpile management, a number of states, notably the United States, have been heavily involved in promoting the destruction of military small arms and light weapons. Initiated in 2005, the NATO Partnership for Peace Trust Fund has pledged to help Ukraine destroy an estimated 1.5 million military small arms and light weapons

Box 3.1   Iraq: Disarmament through trial and error

American-led initiatives to control the small arms loose in society in Iraq have been of the trial-and error-variety. 'Even before the war', notes the *Small Arms Survey* (2004, p. 47), 'Iraq's combined civilian and military small arms stockpile can be conservatively estimated at between 7 and 8 million firearms, with the potential to be considerably higher'. A lively cross-border weapons trade has made the situation more dynamic (Hider, 2003). An accurate tally probably must wait until the Iraqi conflict abates enough to permit systematic field research and public polling.

Campaigns against Iraqi small arms have been a staple of American operations since the early weeks of Operation Iraqi Freedom. These efforts have evolved over time. In the early days of the occupation, the Coalition Provisional Authority called for the confiscation of all civilian firearms.[2] On 24 May 2003 the Authority announced a 14-day amnesty to permit Iraqis to turn in light weapons (Centcom, 2003; BBC, 2004). In subsequent weeks this amnesty was diluted to permit Iraqis to keep a single automatic rifle or pistol, so long as it was not brandished publicly. The Authority and its successor, the Interim Government created on 30 June 2004, tried to absorb some of the surplus with cash incentives. In Iraq such efforts rapidly exhausted any amount of cash allocated, without making a palpable impact on insurgent attacks or civil violence (Hauser, 2004; Walt, 2004).

Originally aimed at all small arms in the hands of the general Iraqi public, these efforts gradually become more narrowly focused. As conflict with militias intensified, the Coalition shifted its emphasis from small arms in general to those of the militias in particular. This revised approach was part of a more focused strategy of trying to separate insurgents from civilian society.[3] A subsequent deal, brokered by Interim Prime Minister Iyad Allawi, sought agreement from 12 militias to disarm. Their

members were to demobilize and join the new Iraqi security services at a cost of roughly USD 200 million (Filkins, 2004). This plan collapsed because of practical problems of implementation, such as who would make the first move. Even so, it demonstrated the promise of a comprehensive disarmament combined with demobilization and reintegration.

The leading disarmament target became the Mahdi Army of Shiite leader Moktada al-Sadr. During the April 2004 battle of Fallujah, civil leaders appeared to have secured a commitment from the rebels to surrender their light weapons, but this later disintegrated (Fisher, 2004). The Mahdi Army was allowed to evacuate the shrines it had occupied without giving up its weapons. A less ambitious programme was aimed exclusively at Baghdad's Sadr City, a centre of support for al-Sadr's Mahdi Army. Although the number of weapons recovered has not been made public, officers involved express satisfaction with the undertaking.

An Iraqi National Guardsman drives a truck loaded with weapons collected in Sadr City, Baghdad, in October 2004.

© Wathiq Khuzaie/Getty Images

A major dispute over the future of Iraq has arisen over exactly this point. One school of thought has emphasized the importance of systematic DDR since before the war even began, stressing the need to keep armed men from becoming a disruptive force. Advocates continue to stress systematic disarmament through amnesties for insurgent militiamen and former police and soldiers (Barton and Crocker, 2003, pp. 8-9; 2004, pp. 79-80). Coalition insiders like senior adviser Larry Diamond stressed the need to combine disarmament with merging former combatants into the country's new police and armed forces (Diamond, 2004a). More recent proposals have recommended that disarmament become a prerequisite for participation in electoral politics (Diamond, 2004b). Other observers focus on the imperative for political solutions, implicitly obviating the need to deal directly with small arms issues (ICG, 2004).

The outcome of the debate is impossible to evaluate as of this writing, but there can be little doubt that small arms issues will continue to play a crucial role in debates over the future of Iraq. So long as small arms are the most prominent symbol of Iraqi instability, they will be the natural focus of efforts to bring peace and stability to that troubled country.

and 133,000 tons of ammunition. The project, which is likely to cost in the region of USD 27 million, is predicted to span 12 years (USDOS, 2005).

Also of note are ongoing efforts of the Small Arms and Light Weapons programme of the United States Defense Threat Reduction Agency (DTRA). The DTRA provides technical expertise and support to the Department of State, and as of January 2005 had conducted operations in Europe, Latin America, Asia, and Africa. The operations included assessments of the physical security of stockpiles, destruction assessments, and destruction assistance. The project's annual budget has increased from USD 1 million to USD 10 million and is expected to continue to grow (DTRA, 2005).

The year 2004 also saw some clear successes on the domestic front. This was true both of societies with high rates of armed violence, such as Brazil, South Africa, and Venezuela, and of countries, such as Australia, with comparatively low levels of armed violence.

A Venezuelan soldier stands on illegal firearms during the destruction of more than 10,000 illegal weapons confiscated by the National Guard, Caracas, May 2004.

© Jorge Silva/Reuters

In Brazil a national campaign is underway to persuade citizens to give up firearms. Following the enactment of the Disarmament Statute in December 2003, the high rates of public violence have become a fundamental political issue. The current campaign is centred on the government buying back any firearm—whether legally owned or not—for USD 40 to USD 120. These rates of compensation often are far below the commercial value of a firearm, suggesting that success has been the result of changes in perceptions of firearms ownership (Instituto Sou da Paz, 2005).

By March 2005 the campaign had recovered over 300,000 firearms from private hands (Instituto Sou da Paz, 2005). The Statute also provides for a referendum in October 2005 on whether to prohibit trade in arms and ammunition in Brazil. Civil society groups continue to mobilize support for a prohibition. Efforts to tackle armed violence in Brazil are centred firmly on the theme of disarmament (Instituto Sou da Paz, 2005).[4]

In 2004 Australia launched another round of its buy-back programme, which collected 68,727 weapons (Hudson, 2004). This figure was in addition to more than 700,000 weapons collected in earlier rounds (Australia, 2002). As in Brazil, the sheer number of weapons collected was not the most important aspect of the initiative. The continued receipt of large numbers of weapons suggests widespread changes in public perceptions of gun ownership (Bourgois, 2005). As happened in the United Kingdom, public perceptions were affected mostly by outrage at a massacre (in Port Arthur in 1996). The support of potentially affected communities is a core component of the decision to relinquish weapons.

Inspired by the reduction of firearms deaths after the first buy-back, the new campaign further tightened regulations by banning public possession of most types of handguns, including revolvers and semi-automatic handguns. In addition to reducing gun deaths and injuries, it was also expected to cut gun crime in general by draining the civilian stockpile from which most illegal guns were stolen (Australia, 2003).

In South Africa the Firearms Control Act of 2000 began to come into full effect in 2004. The Act has introduced controls on supply, possession, safe storage, transfer, and use of weapons (South Africa, 2001). Of greatest importance to typical gun owners, the act requires owners to apply for renewal of their existing firearms licences. To facilitate cooperation, the law also became the basis for an amnesty that ran from January to March 2005. By March 2005 12,100 firearms had been handed in (Kirsten, 2005). While the numbers of firearms received are not particularly high, other aspects of the Act are expected to do more to alter future small arms possession in South Africa and enhance the importance of domestic firearm controls.

However, in some instances, disarmament campaigns have faltered or simply failed to materialize. In Nigeria, efforts by President Olusegun Obasanjo to bring an end to violence between the two strongest warring militias in the oil-producing Niger Delta region led to a limited weapons buy-back programme with the aim of disarming both militias. The government offered USD 1,800 for the return of each assault rifle; 1,100 were reportedly turned in by mid-December 2004. The figure is, however, thought to be only a fraction of those held by the two groups. In terms of reducing stockpiles and violence, the initiative was not a success, although as an exercise in crisis management it clearly offered value in averting a potentially dramatic escalation in hostilities (HRW, 2005).

In the United States the theme for 2004 was clearly one of relaxed restrictions. This was manifested most spectacularly on 13 September 2004, when a ten-year-old ban on the sale of 19 types of semi-automatic firearms (the so-called Assault Weapon Ban) was allowed to lapse (PRODUCTION). The ban retained strong public support—71 per cent in one recent poll, 73 per cent in another—although American opinion on all matters related to gun control policy varies greatly according to the exact wording of the question (Annenberg Center, 2004; Schulman, 2004). Of greater political salience was the adamant opposition of the National Rifle Association.

The original law was far from ideal. Compromises in the legislation, inserted at the insistence of gun rights advocates, made it easy for manufacturers to circumvent the narrowly written provisions by modifying their products (Page, 2004). Nor was there much evidence of an effect on crime or gun injuries (Koper, 2004). Tellingly, there were few reports of significantly accelerated sales of banned weapons after the law expired (Eisenstadt, 2004). Even if the effects of the ban were debatable, though, the symbolic importance of its end was widely acknowledged by both its supporters and its adversaries.

Although it attracted less attention, actual firearms practice was affected more by a trend in state legislatures, where new laws have been passed making it easier for Americans to carry concealed guns in public (NRA-ILA, 2005). In practice, several states report that there has been less demand for the new licences than originally anticipated: half as many in the first year as predicted in Colorado (10,444 applicants) and one-quarter in Missouri (15,442), for example (*Columbia Daily Tribune*, 2005; Fong, 2004; Jones, 2004).

The year 2004 illustrates that far-reaching changes to firearm ownership patterns require concerted effort at the international, national, and community levels. It is at least as important to change the norms of firearm ownership—demand reduction—as it is to enact national legislation and launch international initiatives. As the Australian and US cases illustrate, societies differ in their perceptions of firearm ownership, but those perceptions are not necessarily fixed. The Australian, Brazilian, and UK cases present clear evidence that public opinion on the possession of weapons can change.

By March 2005, the Brazilian disarmament campaign had recovered over 300,000 firearms from private hands.

Nevertheless, taking a global view of small arms stocks can lead only to the conclusion that stockpiles are growing rather than shrinking. Production in regions such as the United States and the Russian Federation alone, estimated at around 4 million units for 2001, suggests that growth in stockpiles far outweighs the impact of known arms-reduction initiatives (Small Arms Survey, 2004, pp. 13, 16). Even NATO's initiative in Ukraine, probably the largest envisaged international stockpile reduction effort to date at 1.5 million arms, appears small in relation to potential global stocks.

ESTIMATING TOWARDS REALITY

Civilian ownership

Ascertaining the number of privately owned firearms in a society remains the toughest challenge for stockpiles research. In the absence of official registration reports, reliable public polling, or expert assessment, the scale of civilian gun ownership can be established only through indirect indicators. The most important indirect statistical insights come from:

- comparison with better documented but comparable societies;
- population size and per capita wealth;
- official gun crime rates (especially gun homicide, which presumably is the most reliably reported gun crime);
- the number of shooting deaths among on-duty police officers; and
- the number of confiscated or voluntarily collected illegal guns and collected unwanted guns.

None of this data is independently conclusive; it always must be interpreted through a skein of qualitative indicators as well. Population and wealth, for example, are useful only in light of the intensity of the local gun culture. For example, the Netherlands and Canada, two well-understood countries, have similar income levels but dramatically different gun cultures, with fundamental implications for the scale of public ownership. Other data like crime rates and gun confiscation must be interpreted with an appreciation of important local nuances.

None of these indicators in and of themselves allow an accurate sense of civilian ownership. The easiest check is by way of comparison with other countries in the same region with similar public gun cultures. This is the approach applied usefully on South America and Mexico in the *Small Arms Survey* (2004, pp. 50–54) and for the Middle East, in this chapter. Another check is to test estimated totals against accurate figures when they are available. This is the approach used in the case of Turkey.

This approach allows for a broad sense of the scale of private gun ownership in countries with inferior data. Consequently, such civilian estimates are given exclusively in terms of a range of likely stockpiles size.

Military inventories

Small arms policy is heavily influenced by the quality of data. In the absence of a sense of how many weapons there were to begin with, disarmament programmes such as those examined above can produce only inconclusive results. How well did disarmament work in places such as Afghanistan, Iraq, or Liberia? We may never know, because it was impossible to be certain of the original number of guns. Even in countries at peace national stockpile estimates tend to be controversial, vulnerable to being suppressed, or inflated for political purposes.

To evaluate global stockpiles and promote effective policy-making, the Small Arms Survey uses several kinds of data. Official national figures are preferred, but this is not consistently available and is rarely comprehensive. It is most firmly buttressed by public polling, but this must be done carefully to generate reliable results, and in practice is rarely done at all. Field research is easier to undertake but less conclusive. International trade data can convey a partial sense of total stockpile size. Expert estimates can be helpful but must be used cautiously. Too often there is no alternative to estimation by comparing national situations, establishing priorities, and identifying urgent problems and worrying trends.

Faced with an absence of official data in most cases, military stockpile estimates in the Small Arms Survey yearbooks are based on troop strength reported in various sources, most notably the International Institute of Strategic Studies' *Military Balance* series.

The scale of military small arms inventories in any country depends largely on doctrine, both past and present. While there are clearly disparities in weapon-holding trends in armed forces (Table 3.1), a working assumption is that a 'multiplier' derived from a reasonable ratio of small arms to persons in any given military force can be applied to yield small arms stockpile estimates. At present, the Small Arms Survey's multiplier of choice is 2.25 small arms for every serving member of the armed forces (Small Arms Survey, 2001, pp. 76–77).

As Table 3.1 illustrates, actual armament levels can be significantly higher. This is clearest for countries that historically relied on massed infantry doctrine or mass mobilization, especially the Maoist 'People's War'. One of the better-understood examples—the former Yugoslavia (Table 3.1)—maintained roughly 4.5 firearms per uniformed personnel to allow for sudden expansion. Other examples in Table 3.1 show how these doctrinal choices can push armament inventories much higher still. Field research suggests that nationalism and the lingering shadow of the national security state also leads some Latin American countries—such as Argentina and Brazil—to accumulate very large inventories. As personnel declined and weapons procurement continued, hording created ever-greater national multipliers, equal to at least three modern firearms per soldier, sailor, and airman.[5]

> Often, there is no alternative to estimation for comparing national situations, establishing priorities, and identifying urgent problems and worrying trends.

Table 3.1   Known military firearm inventories and multipliers

Country	Year	Armed forces personnel*	Military firearms	Firearms per person
Canada	2000	103,900	233,949	2.25
Central African Republic**	1996	3,000	3,300	1.10
Finland	2003	462,000	531,000	1.15
Macedonia***	2003	11,650	85,446	7.33
Russia	2003	3,360,000	15,000,000–45,000,000	4.6–13.4
Togo	2000	6,950	12,850	1.85
Yugoslavia	1989	705,000	3,115,000	4.42

*Active duty and reserves in all armed services.
**Excludes Presidential Guard.
***Personnel and firearms are for Macedonian army only.
Sources: Canada: Small Arms Survey (2001, p. 73); Central African Republic: Telephone interview by Nicolas Florquin, Small Arms Survey researcher, with a former senior Central African Republic government official, 23 March 2005; Finland: Small Arms Survey (2004, p. 46); Macedonia: Grillot et al. (2004, p. 16); IISS (2003, p. 76); Russia: Pyadushkin (2003, p. 29); IISS (2003, p. 89); Togo: Small Arms Survey (2002, p. 82); IISS (2000, p. 285); Yugoslavia: Gorjanc (2000); IISS (1989, p. 91)

Current force levels, therefore, are not generally treated as a reliable indicator of arms stocks. Regardless of downsizing, state armed forces often continue to hold numbers of weapons commensurate with previous personnel totals (Small Arms Survey, 2001, p. 71). In other countries, changes in doctrine may not be accompanied by concomitant

Military estimates
in the *Small Arms
Survey* refer
exclusively to
firearms; there still
is not enough
data to estimate
inventories of other
kinds of small arms
and light weapons.

reductions in stockpiled weapons. As an element of national security, stockpiled small arms are frequently maintained as 'insurance' for potential national emergencies.

Estimates of stockpiles must take this factor into account, whether or not it actually holds true. Thus, with regard to north-east Asia and the Middle East two sets of calculations are made: one using a country's estimated current force levels and the other employing the country's highest known force levels since the mid-1970s. The 2.25 multiplier is applied in each calculation to generate broad upper and lower parameters for military small arms stockpiles.

Estimating police inventories

In contrast to military figures, it is difficult to comment on the reliability of police figures in north-east Asia and the Middle East. This is simply because of the lack of transparency in both regions. Nonetheless, it is clear that broad assessments of military numbers are more readily available than those of police forces, due to a general preponderance of international security issues in research.

As a result, police estimates in this chapter are based, not on regularly updated lists of force levels, but on often solitary, anecdotal reports in the press and elsewhere. Without trends against which to estimate the relative validity of these figures, the Small Arms Survey can offer only tentative estimates of police force levels in north-east Asia and the Middle East.

Table 3.2   Multipliers derived from various police forces

Country	Year	Personnel	Firearms	Firearms per person
Belgium	2000	17,767	23,870	1.3
Japan	2004	240,000	250,000	1.0
Norway	2000	7,500	9,000	1.2
United States	2000	641,000	831,000	1.3

Sources: Belgium, Norway, United States: Small Arms Survey (2001, p. 70-71); Japan: Answers to the questions of the Small Arms Survey National Stockpiles Questionnaire by the Conventional Weapons Division of the Japanese Ministry of Foreign Affairs, August 2004.

As the figures in Table 3.2 illustrate, when the majority of serving police officers are armed, police forces tend to stock in the region of 1.2 firearms per person. The Small Arms Survey uses this multiplier to calculate weapons holdings based on the strength of armed police forces around the world. Despite the potential to overestimate police forces holdings in countries such as the United Kingdom, where the majority of police officers are unarmed, the multiplier is a useful means of gauging lower parameters of police small arms stocks.

REGIONAL REALITIES: IN THE SHADOWS

Progress on small arms policy-making requires an ever-improving sense of where the weapons are, who has them, and which pose the greatest dangers. In the absence of reliable and comprehensive national statistics, this process will continue to rely on a mix of official data, as well as expert estimates. So far this approach has created portraits of small arms possession in Africa (Small Arms Survey, 2003, pp. 80–86), Europe (2003, pp. 62–72), Latin America (2004, pp. 50–54), and South Asia (2002, pp. 99–102), in addition to a number of country-specific estimates such as Albania,

Iraq, and the United States, to name but a few (Small Arms Survey, 2002, pp. 68–69; 2003, p. 60; 2004, pp. 44–50). The process is an ongoing one; there will always be a need for better figures.

Two additional regions are examined systematically in this chapter. Although the Middle East and north-east Asia have an undeniable and often overwhelming presence in small arms debates—whether the topic is production, transfers, use, or consequences—they have escaped the most intense consideration of stockpile scale and management seen elsewhere in the world. The reasons for this oversight are not elusive. Many regional governments, including some of the very largest ones, are only beginning to acknowledge the importance of small arms availability in domestic security. Regional secrecy, well-known in innumerable other fields, is all too pervasive on these issues as well. Non-governmental organizations, which have pioneered small arms deliberations in much of the world, remain a nascent presence in these regions also.

Rather than aiming for the last word on Middle Eastern and north-east Asian small arms inventories, this edition of the *Small Arms Survey* provides a foundation for further investigation. Some of the figures presented here lack the scientific certainty required for reliable comparative analysis. Only concrete national insights from official data and carefully designed and administered public surveys can do that. General and uncertain as the figures presented here are, however, they allow better appreciation of the broad realities of small arms proliferation and priorities for action.

Previous estimates have catalysed international and domestic debate and action. Not only does a reasonable estimate of a country's or region's small arms stockpiles give some indication of how problematic its weapons are—the numbers–effects relationship—but it helps spark debate by presenting figures for comment, agreement, or refutation. This is particularly important with respect to the governments of the states and regions concerned. One of the best results the Small Arms Survey's stockpile analysis could elicit would be the release of reliable information and the encouragement of detailed public polling to improve the estimates presented in this chapter.

NORTH-EAST ASIA: THE WORLD'S LARGEST REGIONAL SMALL ARMS STOCKPILES?

Public officials throughout north-east Asia concede that firearms use is becoming an unprecedented source of public insecurity in the region. As described below, most countries in the region have seen government initiatives to reassure the public and restore government authority. Indeed, the state continues to dominate small arms issues to a degree largely unmatched elsewhere. Missing from this activity are regional proposals similar to those that have become commonplace in virtually every other part of the world.

This section looks at the scale and distribution of small arms in five countries of north-east Asia—China, Japan, North Korea, South Korea, and Taiwan. For most of the region, small arms inventories remain elusive. The dominance of the sovereign state, still the foundation of the region's security culture, is extremely relevant to small arms. The most obvious result is the lack of transparency and fundamental data.

State dominance is the result of large military establishments (IISS, 2004, pp. 152–72). China, for instance, while in the process of downsizing its armed forces by a planned 20 per cent, continues to field an estimated 2.25 million active personnel. This is in contrast to some 1.43 million in the United States (IISS, 2004, pp. 18, 146, 152). Another characteristic of the region is the relatively small size of police and internal security services in most of these countries. Although crime appears to be rising throughout the region, the societies remain largely peaceful. Several still rely more on alternative forms of social authority and law enforcement, such as local party sentinels in China. It is the size of the armed forces, rather, which characterizes small arms distribution in north-east Asia.

The countries of north-east Asia had some of the world's largest armed forces and reserve systems during the cold war; several still do. The axiomatic result was exceptional military small arms inventories. In the absence of official data, this finding relies on conventional multipliers for estimating military small arms inventories, based on the largest contemporary personnel strength of the armed forces and parameters based on national military doctrines.

Major lacunas remain. Civilian ownership, which predominates in the rest of world, cannot be estimated for much of north-east Asia, with the notable exception of Japan (Box 3.2), which provides official data on civilian gun ownership. The lack of indirect indicators of widespread gun ownership, such as those noted above, suggests that civilian ownership is not high elsewhere. The most likely exception is China, where qualitative (and largely unquantifiable) indicators suggest that private gun ownership could be substantial.

Box 3.2   Civilian small arms in Japan

Japan is believed to have one of the world's lowest known firearms homicide rates: fewer than 30 deaths a year between 1996 and 2000 (JNPA, 2000). Although small arms in Japan are a comparatively minor issue compared to other countries, the country is exceptionally sensitive to firearms problems. Japan is at the forefront of international efforts to deal with small arms issues. Of the northeast Asian countries in this study, Japan alone provides relatively easy access to information on civilian firearm stocks.

In 2004 the Japanese Ministry of Foreign Affairs provided the Small Arms Survey with information suggesting that, as of December 2003, civilian firearms 'subject to licensing' totalled 413,096 (Table 3.3). Under the Firearms and Swords Control Law, Japanese citizens must obtain a licence from the Public Safety Commission to own a firearm. There are no limits on the numbers of weapons any one individual can stock. As of December 2003, for instance, 192,820 citizens were licensed to possess hunting rifles and shotguns. This might suggest that Japanese firearms owners stock more than one small arm, but numbers of licensed citizens also include those licensed to own air rifles. This may distort assumptions about firearm ownership. The Ministry of Foreign Affairs was unable to provide information on unlicensed or unregistered firearms in civilian hands.

If these figures are accurate, they suggest that licensed gun ownership rates are around one firearm per 310 citizens. Table 3.3 illustrates just how low this rate of ownership is in comparison with certain European countries.

Despite the fact that small arms in Japan are a comparatively small problem, the country is exceptionally sensitive to firearms problems.

Table 3.3   Registered firearm ownership rates in Japan and selected European countries

Country	Year	Population	Year*	Firearms	Firearm/number of citizens
France	2002	59,278,000	2000	2,802,057	1/21
Japan	2004	128,085,000	2005	413,096	1/310
Sweden	2002	8,877,000	2000	2,096,798	1/4
United Kingdom**	2000-01	56,984,733	2000	1,793,712	1/32

*Year of population data.
** Figures for Scotland are combined with those of England and Wales for 2000 and 2001, respectively. Excludes Northern Ireland. Population figures for Northern Ireland (2001) subtracted from figures for remainder of the United Kingdom (2000).
Firearm sources: France, Sweden, United Kingdom: Small Arms Survey (2003, p. 69); Japan: Answers to the questions of the Small Arms Survey National Stockpiles Questionnaire by the Conventional Weapons Division of the Japanese Ministry of Foreign Affairs, August 2004. Population sources: UNESA (2005); NISRA (2001)

China

While firearms were invented in China (Chase, 2003), there is, ironically, more information available about the country's ancient guns than its current stockpiles. Despite wrenching social changes, China remains a peaceful place; guns are seldom seen. Police in most major cities patrol unarmed. But, as anyone who has witnessed a minor traffic accident in China can attest, armed authority usually is close by. China may be a relatively lightly-armed society, but its enormity appears to conceal arsenals of large absolute dimensions.

The People's Liberation Army (PLA) is the predominant owner of small arms in China. The PLA is undergoing extensive transformation as it sheds the guerrilla and large-formation doctrines inherited from its formative experiences in the Communist revolution and the Korean War (Scobell, 2003). Most of its equipment is the legacy of past doctrinal assumptions. Military factories produced small arms on a scale required to arm not only PLA regulars and reserve units but also politically reliable groups like Communist Party members, trusted classes, and students. Chinese production of better-known weapons like the Type-56 (AK-47) rifle is harder to estimate. Millions of these weapons were exported to allies and clients abroad. The number stored in China appears to reach the tens of millions (Small Arms Survey, 2002, p. 96).

While total armed forces today are estimated to number some 2,255,000 active personnel, this figure does not include reserve forces, which are estimated at around 800,000 (IISS, 2004, p. 170). With these force levels, a multiplier of 2.25 small arms per individual suggests the PLA could stockpile nearly 7 million small arms and light weapons.

A brief assessment of China's armed forces reveals that personnel levels have declined considerably since the cold war, and continue to do so (IISS, 1980, p. 62; 1985, p. 113; 2000, p. 194; PLA, 2004). In 1979 the PLA was probably at its largest in terms of personnel, with some 4.3 million active troops and around 7 million reserves[6] (IISS, 1979, pp. 60–61). The 2.25 multiplier applied to these figures would suggest holdings of over 25 million small arms, many of which could now be held in reserve.

If we assume that the 2.25 multiplier has some validity in the case in question, stocks are thus likely to number between 7 million and 25 million small arms. If the estimation techniques are reliable, the true figure would fall somewhere between these, admittedly very wide, parameters. It would do so as a function of, on the one hand, the service life of stockpiled weapons and, on the other, China's particular policies on weapons retention. We know little of either factor, so the parameters must remain wide.

Police forces in China are far smaller in number than the PLA, and consist of the People's Police (PP) and a subbranch, the People's Armed Police (PAP). The PAP clearly carry weapons, although it is unclear how many police officers in the PP do so. In addition, a number of other police forces, including the Prison Police and the Judicial Police, may carry firearms (IRBC, 2004).

The PP constitutes perhaps 86 per cent of China's combined police forces (Xiancui, 1998). The Small Arms Survey (2002, p. 95) estimated that the PP numbered some 3.4 million and suggested that perhaps half could be armed, but the estimate is not sufficient to generate even the broadest stockpile numbers. The PAP was estimated at 659,000 in 1991, at 960,000 in 2000, and between 1.1 million and 1.5 million in 2004 (IISS, 2004, p. 173; SolPo, 2000; USDOJ, 1993a).

Since estimates of the PP are uncertain, a figure of around 1.3 million firearms is derived from PAP numbers alone. This figure uses the conservative 2004 estimate of 1.1 million personnel and a multiplier of 1.2. The potential for Chinese police stockpiles to be greatly in excess of this estimate is obvious.

> In the absence of better information, the estimated parameters for the People's Liberation Army, small arms must remain wide.

Police display guns seized from illegal traders in Chengdu, China, January 2005.

© China Photos/Getty Images

Civilian ownership in China is restricted through a licensing system revised in 1996. Although the authorities are legally entitled to examine a licensee's gun collection, there does not appear to be a national requirement for registration of private guns (China, 1996). Consequently, it is unlikely that Chinese officials have accurate figures on the scale of public ownership. Instead there is only a general sense that guns and gun crime are becoming more common (The *Economist,* 2001). Chinese crime statistics do not distinguish firearms crimes. A related indicator is deaths of Chinese police on duty, rising from virtually nothing in the 1970s to roughly 450–500 annually today. A prominent analyst cites this as evidence of a 'skyrocketing' problem (Tanner, 2004). Many of these deaths happen in traffic accidents, but the total should be compared with 45 police deaths by shooting in the United States in 2003 (Anderson, 2004). This does not prove that China is more dangerous than America; it shows only that China is not as peaceful as often assumed.

The only detailed information about Chinese public ownership is from Strike Hard campaigns against illegal gun markets in 1996–2002. According to a statement by the Chinese Foreign Ministry, 2.3 million firearms were seized (SAFER-Net, 2003). In addition, over 30,000 guns originally from PLA arsenals were apprehended (China, 2003). Most of these guns appear to have been confiscated from illegal manufacturers and dealers. Such reports are not a sufficient basis on which to calculate the total dimensions of China's civilian arsenal, but they leave no doubt that it must be at least in the tens of millions.

> While public gun ownership in China is not commonplace, it is not as unusual as commonly assumed.

While public gun ownership in China still is not commonplace, the evidence presented here and in previous editions of the *Small Arms Survey* leads to the conclusion that it is not as unusual as commonly assumed (Small Arms Survey, 2002).

Japan

Not only are guns unusual in Japanese civil society (Box 3.2), but the nation's armed forces are numerically small as well. The only exception to this rule of gun scarcity—and a partial one at that—is the police.

Japan's *Self-Defence Forces* consist of some 239,900 active troops and reserves of around 44,395 (IISS, 2004, p. 176). Japan's armed force levels have changed little in recent decades (IISS, 1980, p. 69; 1985, p. 125; 2000, p. 200). 1990 was probably the year in which Japan's military personnel figures reached their zenith, with around 249,000 active and approximately 48,000 reserves (IISS, 1990, pp. 164–66). If they were armed at the orthodox level of 2.25 firearms per service member, Japan would have a military inventory of around 669,000 small arms. A highly mechanized force, the Japanese military does not appear to plan for massed infantry operations.

Japanese *police* figures show that law enforcement authorities are relatively well-armed. In 1990 there were an estimated 258,800 authorized full-time police personnel in Japan (USDOJ, 1993b). In 2002, 234,000 police personnel were listed, based on a survey of wages of local government employees (JSY, 2005). In the same source, data for 1990 undercut the 1990 figure cited above by around 30,000, so both figures must be treated with some caution. The 2002 figure suggests stockpiles of around 281,000 small arms. However, if we assume that police forces, like militaries, do not necessarily dispose of weapons despite reductions in numbers of personnel, an estimate based on the 1990 figure would suggest around 311,000 stockpiled small arms.

In August 2004, however, the Japanese Ministry of Foreign of Affairs informed the Small Arms Survey that '[t]he total number of small arms possessed by the police force in Japan is about 250,000 as of 31 March, 2004'. The Ministry also reported '[a]s of April 1, 2004, the number of police officers of the Prefecture Police is about 240,000'.[7] These figures suggest Japanese police stockpile somewhat fewer small arms per member than the 1.2 multiplier would suggest.

Democratic People's Republic of Korea

North Korea is effectively closed to research into domestic security issues. No reliable data appears to exist in the public domain concerning police arsenals. Estimates of North Korea's military active and reserve strengths do exist, however, and standard multipliers can be applied to these figures.

North Korean *armed forces* personnel are thought to number between 1.1 million and 1.2 million[8] (Bermudez, 2001, pp. 3–6; IISS, 2004, p. 178). Using a standard multiplier of 2.25 small arms per person, applied to the lower figure, yields just under 2.5 million small arms held by the North Korean armed forces. With reserves estimated at around 4.7 million (IISS, 2004, p. 178), applying the same multiplier gives a combined active–reserve stockpile figure of over 13 million small arms. However, since 'many' of the 3.5 million worker and peasant Red Guard, which comprise many of the reserves, are reportedly unarmed (IISS, 2004, p. 161), they are excluded from this estimate. This generates a combined active–reserve estimate of 4.4 million small arms. On the same assumption, 1995 highs of around 2 million personnel suggest that as many as 4.6 million small arms could be stockpiled today (IISS, 1995, pp. 183–84).

Police forces in North Korea operate under the authority of the Ministry of Public Security. Bermudez (2001, p. 204) estimates that there are around 30,000 staff in administration, civil defence, law enforcement, and security sections of the Ministry. If half of the 30,000 were armed, a 1.2 multiplier would yield a figure of around 18,000 firearms in the hands of police, which is clearly exceptionally low in comparison with other countries in the region. This analysis, however, omits the North Korean intelligence and internal security services, which are undoubtedly large and perform domestic security duties (Bermudez, 2001, p. 7). The IISS (2004, p. 179), on the other hand, estimates Ministry of Public Security paramilitary personnel to total 189,000. It is unclear to what extent these personnel perform duties which would count as police duties in other countries in the region. In view of the degree of uncertainty, these paramilitary forces are included in this chapter's North Korean military force estimates as reserves.

The Small Arms Survey was unable to document the scale of *civilian ownership* in North Korea.

> DPRK military inventories probably hold something between 4 million and 5 million firearms.

Republic of Korea

South Korea makes little or no information available about its small arms stockpiles. However, its police forces provide detailed online information about police numbers and organization.

Armed forces personnel figures are estimated at 687,700 active troops and around 4,500,000 reserves (IISS, 2004, p. 179). Nonetheless, as in the case of North Korea, an estimated 3.5 million civilian defence forces are excluded from the estimate. This leaves approximately 1 million reserves (IISS, 2004, p. 181). At 2.25 small arms per member of the armed forces, the South Korean military would thus control almost 3.8 million small arms for active and reserve forces combined. In 1982 South Korean forces were listed as comprising 601,600 active troops and 1.2 million reserves, excluding 9.5 million paramilitaries for which little information is available (IISS, 1982, p. 89). South Korean force levels, therefore, are estimated to have been at their highest levels in 1982, with some 1.8 million active and reserve personnel and hence around 4.2 million small arms (IISS, 2004, p. 179).

In 2003 there were 92,165 *police officers* in South Korea, a figure which has changed only slightly (an increase of 2,000) in the past decade (KNPA, 2005). At the standard multiplier of 1.2 firearms per officer, the Korean National Police Agency (KNPA) should hold around 111,000 firearms.

Civilian ownership in South Korea cannot be estimated by the Small Arms Survey with available sources of information.

Taiwan

Taiwanese authorities have not revealed their island's total number of *civilian firearms* licences or registrations. But they have become vociferous in their criticism of the island's firearms crime. This was brutally illustrated on 19 March 2004 when President Chen Shui and Vice-President Annette Lu were victims of an assassination attempt, reportedly with an improvised gun (Hong, 2004). Three months later, on 16 June, a gun battle with suspected kidnappers armed with automatic rifles left two police officers dead (Ramzy, 2004). Neither incident was statistically significant, but they persuaded many Taiwanese that they confront a serious problem.

Taiwanese civilian gun ownership laws are strict; the Statute for Self-Defense Related to Firearms stipulates that licences must be renewed every two years (TMI, 2005). However, Taiwanese officials have not revealed the total number of firearms licences or registrations (TMI, 2005). Even so, illegal ownership is a major public issue. A three-month amnesty permitting owners to turn in illegal guns, the fourth in recent years, began on 1 July 2004, followed by a police crackdown on illegal trafficking (Chuang, 2004; Yiu, 2004). According to Interior Minister Su Chia-chuan, in 1989 police seized 9,850 illegal guns. Since then seizures have averaged a little over 1,000 annually, but rose to 1,720 in the first half of 2004 (*China Post,* 2004). This level of confiscation is similar to Japan, where the total number of civilian guns is much better understood.

Taiwan's current *armed forces* are estimated to consist of 290,000 active personnel and 1,657,500 reserves (IISS, 2004, p. 189). Applying the multiplier of 2.25 yields nearly 4.4 million small arms and light weapons in the hands of Taiwan's military. Research suggests that Taiwanese force levels peaked in 1984 at 484,000 active troops and some 1,695,000 reserves (IISS, 1984, pp. 109–10). This suggests a potential present stockpile of around 5 million small arms.

Little information is released in English on the numbers of *police* in Taiwan. The most recently available figures report 75,517 police officers for the year 1990 (USDOJ, 1993c). The multiplier of 1.2 firearms per officer suggests police holdings of small arms in Taiwan of around 91,000. It is unclear whether police forces have changed in number since 1990. In 1999 the Taiwan Provincial Police Administration (TPPA) was taken over by the Taiwan National Police Agency (TNPA, 2005). As the figures cited above include police under both national and provincial administration, reorganization is not thought to have affected numbers of police substantially.

North-east Asia's obscure arsenals

The estimating techniques employed here suggest that north-east Asian military stockpiles amount to between 20 million and 40 million small arms and light weapons (see Table 3.4). Although the data is not good enough to permit concrete comparisons, it appears that the Korean peninsula is the most heavily armed part of this region.

Based on the Small Arms Survey's estimates of other regions, this would suggest that north-east Asian armed forces stockpile more weapons than the militaries of South Asia (around 12 million), Latin America (7 million), and North America (3 million) (Small Arms Survey, 2002, pp. 74, 85, 102; 2004, p. 51).

Regional estimates on police numbers are less complete than those for armed forces. Given that the police forces of North Korea are entirely absent from this analysis and that China, in particular, is likely to field a larger number of armed police than estimated here, a tentative estimate is around 1.8 million police small arms regionally.

The other great enigma for the region is civilian ownership. In most countries of the region it is large enough to be a significant force in social affairs, but not large enough to be readily visible. In the absence of better national reports or public polling, it will be difficult to make more specific civilian estimates.

Table 3.4   Estimated firearms stockpiles in north-east Asian armed forces

Country	Lower parameter (based on current force levels and 2.25 small arms per person)	Upper parameter (based on maximum past force levels and 2.25 small arms per person)
China	6,806,000	25,560,000
Japan	640,000	669,000
N. Korea*	4,356,000	4,574,000
S. Korea**	3,797,325	4,143,600
Taiwan	4,382,000	4,903,000
Totals	**19,981,000**	**39,849,000**

* Excludes some 3.5 million worker/peasant Red Guard. As reported in the IISS (2004, p. 161); 'many units unarmed'.
** It is unclear how many of the 9.5 million paramilitaries listed in the IISS (1982, p. 89) were armed, so these do not appear in the estimate. The 3.5 million Civilian Defence Corps personnel, listed in the IISS (2004, pp. 179-81), are subtracted from reserves of 4.5 million for the same reason.
Note: All figures are rounded. Totals are calculated on original figures and then rounded.
Sources for original armed forces totals: China: (lower) IISS (2004, p. 170), (upper) IISS (1979, pp. 60-61); Japan: (lower) IISS (2004, p. 176), (upper) IISS (1990, pp. 164-66); N. Korea: (lower) IISS (2004, p. 178), (upper) IISS (1995, pp. 183-84); S. Korea: (lower) IISS (2004, p. 179), (upper) IISS (1982, p. 89); Taiwan: (lower) IISS (2004, p. 189), (upper) IISS (1984, pp. 109-10)

Table 3.5   Estimated firearms stockpiles in north-east Asian police forces

Country	Lower parameter (based on current force levels and 1.2 small arms per officer)	Upper parameter (based on maximum past force levels and 1.2 small arms per officer)
China	1,300,000	1,300,000
Japan	281,000 (250,000) *	311,000 (250,000) *
N. Korea	–	–
S. Korea	111,000	111,000
Taiwan	91,000	91,000
Totals	**1,802,000 (1,771,000) ***	**1,832,000 (1,771,000) ***

*In August 2004, the Japanese Ministry of Foreign of Affairs informed the Small Arms Survey that as '[t]he total number of small arms possessed by the police force in Japan is about 250,000 as of 31 March, 2004'. Answers to the questions of the Small Arms Survey National Stockpiles Questionnaire by the Conventional Weapons Division of the Japanese Ministry of Foreign Affairs, August 2004.
Note: All figures are rounded. Totals are calculated from original figures and then rounded.
Sources for original police force totals: China: USDOJ (1993a); Japan: (lower) USDOJ (1993b), (upper) JSY (2005); S. Korea: KNPA (2005); Taiwan: USDOJ (1993c)

This exercise has proved, clearly, that north-east Asia remains far from transparent for assessing small arms stockpiles. However, although the parameters presented here—around 22 million to 42 million small arms in military and police stockpiles—are broad, they clearly illustrate the potential magnitude of north-east Asian small arms holdings.

North-east Asian military and police firearms stockpiles number between 22 million and 42 million.

MIDDLE EAST: RISING CONCERNS AND PERSISTENT UNCERTAINTY

Like north-east Asia, the Middle East presents distinct obstacles to small arms analysis. With few exceptions, official secrecy is a pervasive barrier to informed small arms debate. Only a few countries in the region have released small arms data. Anecdotal press reports, however, testify to rising sensitivity toward the issue, especially aspects like public gun carrying, celebratory firing, and a public sense of greater gun violence. With such concerns in mind, in September 2004 the League of Arab States passed a resolution to coordinate efforts to combat the illicit trade in small arms and light weapons (LAS, 2004). A small number of groups are active in researching small arms problems in Israel, Jordan, Lebanon, Sudan, and Yemen.

Military stockpiles

The Middle East holds approximately 12 million to 16 million firearms

The Middle East hosts the highest defence expenditure as a percentage of gross domestic product (GDP) globally (SIPRI, 2003, p. 303; IISS, 2004). While the end of the cold war, among other factors, has dampened down the arms race in the region, the legacy of decades of military regimes and regional security dynamics is reflected in the Middle East's large conventional armed forces (Feldman and Shapir, 2001, pp. 17, 77).

Egypt, Iran, Israel, Syria, and Turkey, in particular, have very large military personnel numbers. However, other states such as Bahrain and Qatar have small standing armies. This suggests that military small arms stockpiles will differ greatly among Middle Eastern countries. As Table 3.6 illustrates, military small arms stocks in the region could number between 12 million and 16 million. Sub-regionally, nonetheless, there are disparities. The Arabian Peninsula[9] appears to host around 1 million–1.2 million small arms and light weapons, less than one tenth of the combined stocks of the countries to the north and west.

Based on orthodox armament rations, these estimates are far from conclusive. In lieu of reliable totals from regional governments, these figures offer only a general sense of the scale of Middle Eastern military arsenals. Actual national military firearms arsenals could be smaller in some cases, such as Morocco (Box 3.3).

© Laura Boushnak/AFP/Getty Images

Turkish soldiers march during a military parade in Nicosia, Cyprus, July 2003.

Box 3.3   Morocco

While small arms proliferation is serious throughout much of the Middle East, there are important exceptions. Morocco stands out as a country where small arms ownership appears to be rare and gun violence is unusual. The country is not without serious problems, as the Casablanca terrorist attacks of May 2003 revealed (Kalpakian, 2005). Widespread gun ownership and misuse does not appear to be among them, though. What accounts for what is locally known as 'the Moroccan distinction' (Jamal, 2003, p. 107)?

Above all, Morocco does not have a culture that prizes weapons ownership or display. Civilian firearms ownership is permitted for hunting and some ceremonial use. This was not always true. Before French occupation, the country was much like Yemen, sharply divided by tribal and intra-dynastic competition, and well armed. Arriving in 1911, the first French Resident-General of Morocco, Louis-Hubert Lyautey, had to address these problems. His programme of pacification and disarmament of tribesmen continued through the 1930s (Abun-Nasr, 1970, pp. 14-47; 1975, pp. 302-03). One of the earliest priorities of post-independence Morocco was to extend a similar policy to tribal areas in the north and the south-east. The policy was largely successful. There are exceptions, but they now mainly involve the drug trade and smuggling rather than organized violent resistance to the central government.

The rise and collapse of local industry: Unlike many better-armed countries, Morocco lacks a domestic firearms industry. Moroccan traditional gunsmiths produced smooth-bore firearms in the Sus valley and these are still used in the fantasia ceremonies. The French victory in the battle of Islay in 1844 forced the central government to consider modernizing the military and providing for an arms industry. This began in earnest with Sultan Mawlay Hasan (reigned 1873-94), who established munitions factories at Fez and Marrakesh (Abun-Nasr, 1975, pp. 294-95). During the French period Morocco relied on France for arms. Upon independence, the country continued reliance on direct imports (Damis, 1987, p. 148).

Above all, Morocco does not have a culture that prizes weapons ownership or display.

Box 3.3   Morocco (cont.)

Official small arms: Moroccan soldiers are equipped with a variety of Western and Soviet-style weapons. AK-47 types are most common. The state arsenal also includes FAL and M-16 rifles. It is common to see ceremonial units equipped with older Mausers or Enfields, such as at the royal tombs in Rabat. The regular armed forces number roughly 200,000, including about 1,500 troops in the Royal Guard. Regular troops guarding royal palaces and facilities often carry AK-47s without magazines. The Gendarmérie Royale, a force of about 20,000, is unarmed except when guarding government buildings. Its weapons tend to be obsolete, including 1940s vintage sub-machine guns. Many are not functional but are kept only for show.

The National Police and the associated Department of Territorial Security (the secret police, known by its French initials DST) were last reported to include more than 42,000 individuals (El-Sa'aif, 2000/2001, p. 108). It is likely that the number of officers has since increased to perhaps 50,000 police men and women. The Forces Auxiliaires, the national militia of about 30,000, patrols the streets in the company of the police forces, equipped with night-sticks.

Civilian ownership: Game—including deer, ibex, and gazelle—is commonly hunted and eaten in rural areas. Segments of Morocco's elite also enjoy hunting through membership in hunting clubs. These clubs have the licences and the weapons, and access to them is controlled and regulated. Moroccan law prohibits ownership of rifles and handguns and permits only shotguns for hunting, purchased with a licence from local police and gendarmes. Hunting also requires permits and licences issued by the Department of Forestry.

A further, special category of Moroccan firearms is used for ceremonial purposes. These are long, handmade, highly decorated black-powder muskets called *mokahala*—mascara sticks—because of the soot they belch after firing. *Mokahalas* are fired exclusively in traditional *fantasias*. Unlike in other Middle Eastern and North African countries, firearms are not fired in routine celebrations.

Illegal possession and use: The largest class of armed criminals is drug dealers, mostly involved in growing *kif*, a strain of marijuana, and trans-shipment of narcotics to Europe. Certain factors make Morocco a unique case in the drug trade. *Kif* was legal in the country well into the 1960s. The government banned it when thousands of foreigners started to arrive for no other purpose than to consume it. A shift in European policy may eventually enable Morocco to relegalize the product.

To gain insight into the role of firearms in Moroccan crime, 30 days of crime news were examined from the national mass-circulation newspaper *Al Ahdath al Maghribiya* for June 2004. Eight firearms-related incidents were reported for the country during that period; four were related to terrorism and in two the police used firearms. One story mentioned terrorists training with weapons, another

> French colonial policies found armed tribes and left the Moroccan state with a social monopoly on the use of violence.

The climax of a fantasia charge: mokahala in the air. Meknes, Morocco.

reported the seizure of a small terrorist weapons cache. The most unusual story involved a suicide attempt by a policeman after a female fellow-officer ended her relationship with him (*Al Ahdath al Maghribiya*, 2004). Violent crime mostly features bladed weapons or arson (Morocco, 2002, p. 539). These observations suggest one of the lowest rates of civilian ownership in the region, probably less than one for every five or six households, or roughly one for every 20 people.

Why is Morocco not Yemen? Morocco follows the political practices and bureaucratic procedures introduced by the French colonial pattern, still practised to a lesser degree in a few other Arab states like Algeria, Tunisia, and Syria. France found tribes armed with rifles, muskets, and sometimes cannon. It withdrew after having dramatically altered this picture and endowed the state with a social monopoly in the use of violence.

In a country like Morocco, terrorists may threaten the state's control of firearms, but their efforts are unlikely to succeed. As one Moroccan officer put it: 'People understand that without a state, everyone will try to use force to get what they feel is due them, and in those times, everyone loses'.[10] Morocco appears to have the small arms genie under control.

Author: Jack Kalpakian, Al Akhawayn University, Ifrane, Morocco

Table 3.6   Estimated firearms stockpiles in Middle Eastern armed forces

Country	Lower parameter (based on current force levels and 2.25 small arms per person)	Upper parameter (based on maximum past force levels and 2.25 small arms per person)	Sources for original armed forces totals (upper; lower)
Algeria	625,000	720,000	IISS (2004, p. 120; 1985, p. 120)
Bahrain	25,000	25,000	IISS (2004, p. 121; 2003, p. 106)
Egypt	1,935,000	1,935,000	IISS (2004, p. 122)
Iran	2,002,000	2,371,000	IISS (2004, p. 124; 1986, p. 96)
Iraq*	151,000	151,000	Miles (2005)
Israel	1,296,000	1,363,000	IISS (2004, p. 126; 1993, p. 118)
Jordan	305,000	313,000	IISS (2004, p. 127; 1998, p. 131)
Kuwait	88,000	88,000	IISS (2004, p. 128)
Lebanon	162,000	162,000	IISS (2004, p. 129; 2003, p. 114)
Libya	261,000	281,000	IISS (2004, p. 130; 1991, p. 113)
Mauritania	35,000	35,000	IISS (2004, p. 131)
Morocco	779,000	779,000	IISS (2004, p. 132)
Oman	94,000	98,000	IISS (2004, p. 133; 2000, p. 149)
Palestinian Territories	31,000	79,000	IISS (2004, p. 134; 1997, p. 137)
Qatar	28,000	28,000	IISS (2004, p. 134)
Saudi Arabia**	449,000	453,000	IISS (2004, p. 135; 2001, p. 152)
Sudan	236,000	267,000	IISS (2004, p. 246; 1995, p. 257)
Syria	1,464,000	2,414,000	IISS (2004, p. 136; 1995, p. 147)
Tunisia	79,000	95,000	IISS (2004, p. 138; 1987, p. 114)
Turkey	2,010,000	3,947,000	IISS (2004, p. 71; 1990, p. 81)
UAE	114,000	146,000	IISS (2004, p. 138; 2001, p. 149)
Yemen***	240,000	340,000	IISS (2004, p. 139; 1990, pp. 121–22)
Totals	**12,410,000**	**16,092,000**	

*Includes serving or training army, air force, national guard, and coastal defence units (Miles, 2005). Does not include an estimated 4.2 million small arms and light weapons, formerly in the possession of Iraqi military forces, which are now believed to be dispersed throughout Iraqi society (Small Arms Survey, 2004, p. 46).

**Includes 75,000 National Guards in lower and upper parameters.

***Composite of highest active and reserve figures for North and South Yemen prior to unification.

Note: All figures are rounded. Totals are calculated on original figures and then rounded.

Police stockpiles

It is somewhat easier to calculate the scale of Middle Eastern police arsenals than that of military firearms, with enough data available to permit a regional police multiplier to estimate the number of sworn police officers. This figure is not conclusive and must be updated as additional governments make policing figures available.

In the absence of police employment data in the majority of countries in the Middle East, a ratio of police to population is used (Table 3.7) to determine likely police figures, based on five countries for which data is available.

Most Middle Eastern governments treat police numbers and weapons inventories as state secrets, but some have released figures. Others have been the subject of foreign studies arriving at useful, although often dated or imprecise, figures. The cases where police manpower figures are available reveal enormous diversity (Table 3.7). Tunisia appears to be among the most carefully policed countries on Earth; if reports are right, it has one officer for every 73 people.

Table 3.7   Sample police numbers, police/population ratios, and firearms stocks estimates from five Middle Eastern countries

Country	Police officers	Base year	Population	Year (population)	Police/ population ratio	Estimated small arms (1.2 multiplier)
Algeria*	51,000	1993	28,271,000	(1995)	1/554	61,000
Israel	18,600	1994	5,374,000	(1995)	1/289	22,000
Morocco	42,000	2000	29,231,000	(2000)	1/696	50,000
Tunisia	130,000	2002	9,563,000	(2000)	1/74	156,000
Turkey	166,000	2000	68,234,000	(2000)	1/411	199,000
Totals	**407,600**		**140,673,000**		**1/345**	**489,000**

Note: All figures are rounded. Totals are calculated on original figures and then rounded.
* Gendarmérie Nationale and Sûreté Nationale.
Sources: Algeria: Metz (1993); Israel: USDOJ (1993d); Morocco: El-Sa'aif (2000/2001, p. 108); Tunisia: *Economist* (2002); Turkey: UN (2000, p. 461); Population: UNESA (2005)

At the opposite extreme, Sudan has just one police officer for every 1,000 residents, a level more typical of Sub-Saharan Africa. The average for these five countries is one sworn police officer for every 345 national residents.

Table 3.8 applies this figure to the remaining countries in the Middle East and subsequently applies the 2.1 multiplier to deliver an extremely loose police stockpile figure.

Table 3.8   Estimates of police stockpiles of firearms in the remaining 17 Middle Eastern countries

Country	Population (2005)	Police (at 1/345)	Small arms (1.2 multiplier)
Bahrain	727,000	2,000	2,500
Egypt	74,033,000	214,000	257,000
Iran	69,515,000	201,000	241,000
Iraq*	28,807,000	83,000	100,000
Jordan	5,703,000	16,000	20,000
Kuwait	2,687,000	8,000	9,000
Lebanon	3,577,000	10,000	12,000
Libya	5,853,000	17,000	20,000
Mauritania	3,069,000	9,000	11,000
Oman	2,567,000	7,000	9,000
Palestinian Territories	3,702,000	11,000	13,000
Qatar	813,000	2,000	3,000
Saudi Arabia	24,573,000	71,000	85,000
Sudan	36,233,000	105,000	126,000
Syria	19,043,000	55,000	66,000
UAE	4,496,000	13,000	16,000
Yemen	20,975,000	61,000	73,000
Totals	**306,373,000**	**888,000**	**1,066,000**

All figures are rounded. Totals are calculated on original figures and then rounded.
*On the assumption that Iraqi police forces remained more or less intact in the period 2003-04.
Population source: UNESA (2005)

Because virtually all police in the Middle East normally appear to work armed, the orthodox police multiplier of 1.2 small arms per sworn officer has been used. Extrapolated to the other 17 countries of the region, the police forces of the 22 Middle Eastern countries analysed here would host some 1.5 million firearms (Tables 3.7 and 3.8).

This estimate of police firearms stockpiles offers only a starting point for more refined analysis. In addition to the lack of reliable national data, the model misses other internal security and secret police agencies. Nor does the approach take account of the lack of a clear dividing line in a number of Middle Eastern countries between police and military forces, as regimes must often respond to both domestic and international threats to security (David, 1991). The approach is clearest at showing the small relative size of police inventories compared to the armed services, with at least eight to ten times as many firearms.

Box 3.4   Civilian firearms ownership in the Middle East

Of the 22 countries of the region only Israel and Turkey have released official statistics on gun ownership (UN, 1998, pp. 52-53). Although official secrecy shields much from public view, regional observers note a climate of mounting concern. A series of unofficial, Track-2 meetings in Amman in 2001 and 2002 and Cairo in 2004 elicited diverse responses. Officials from several governments were satisfied with the balance between individual rights and national controls. Representatives from some governments—notably Jordan, Sudan, and Yemen—expressed concern that small arms were becoming a factor in regional instability and a threat to public safety. Among outside observers, Middle Eastern gun culture is increasingly seen as a barrier to investment and political development (Widmer and Odibat, 2004, pp. 1-3; Jackman, 2002).

Anecdotal reports do not add up to a complete picture, but news reports leave little doubt that private firearms ownership is common in much of the region and growing. In a permissive environment where firearms ownership is widely seen as a masculine necessity, population and wealth are key determinants to the growth of civilian ownership. The population of the entire region doubled between 1970 and 2000. It is expected to double again by 2050 (PRC, 2004). In Arabic-speaking countries population growth is even faster, and predicted to double between 2000 and 2020 (UNDP, 2002, pp. 35-38). Fuelled by such demographic forces, regional firearms ownership seems likely to grow. More people will desire firearms, and if they can afford them then they are very likely to buy them. Regional economic performance is harder to predict, but it seems unlikely to become a major barrier to continued private small arms buying.

In the absence of official statistics from most Middle East countries, assessment of public stockpile dimensions requires cautious sifting of clues, especially comparison with better-understood cases. The exceptions to this analysis are Iraq and Israel, special cases discussed previously (Small Arms Survey, 2003, pp. 77-78; Small Arms Survey, 2004, pp. 44-50). For insight into the rest of the region, the most useful civilian stockpiles come from Jordan, Lebanon, Morocco, Sudan, Turkey, and Yemen.

The Jordanian figure is based on a semi-official estimate. The country has 126,000 registered firearms, which are believed to constitute some 20 per cent of all firearms in civilian hands, or some 600,000 in all (Al-Fawaz, 2002, p. 91). The Lebanon estimate of 500,000 private guns used here comes from unofficial observers, some of whom prefer a higher figure of 750,000 (Jackman, 2002). In Sudan it is estimated that '25 percent possess small arms and light weapons' and '50 percent of the population in the area has good knowledge on how to use' them (Elobeid, 2002, p. 126). If this means one-quarter of heads of households, it would equal some 1.6 million weapons. The Yemeni estimate of 6 million–9 million private firearms is based on field research by the Small Arms Survey (Miller, 2003). Using these figures for comparison makes it possible to calculate a broader regional estimate (see Table 3.9).

These six examples allow explication of a regional civilian firearms multiplier. This equals an average of 16 civilian-owned firearms per every 100 people (Table 3.9). This is only the average of six relatively well-understood cases; its applicability to the rest of the region is only suggestive. Applied to the region as a whole, though, this allows a crude estimate of civilian firearms throughout the Middle East of approximately 67 million privately owned guns. If a 33 per cent margin of error is allowed to account for wide differences in wealth and gun cultures across the region, the Middle East has anywhere from 45 million to 90 million civilian firearms.

The scale of Middle East firearms stocks revealed in this assessment is tentative and must be considered with caution. Even taken loosely, however, the approach applied here suggests that in the Middle East civilian ownership tends to exceed military and police firearms inventories, probably by a significant margin. The Middle East and north-east Asia may resemble each other as two of the least understood and most opaque parts of the world for small arms policy-making, but they are fundamentally different in other respects. While north-east Asian small arms ownership appears to be dominated by the state, Middle Eastern ownership is probably dominated by civilians. More authoritative and nuanced conclusions must await additional field research, public polling, and official cooperation.

Middle Eastern police forces host around 1.5 million firearms.

Table 3.9   Estimated Civilian Firearms in the Middle East

Country	Population	Rate of firearm ownership	Firearms
Iraq	24,000,000	15/100	8,000,000
Israel*	6,200,000	8/100	503,000
Jordan	6,900,000	9/100	600,000
Lebanon	3,600,000	14/100	500,000
Turkey	67,600,000	12/100	8,000,000
Yemen	18,900,000	37/100	7,000,000
Middle East projected	**420,000,000**	**16/100**	**67,000,000**

Sources: Population statistics: IISS (2003); Iraq: Small Arms Survey (2004, pp. 44–50); Israel: Small Arms Survey (2003, p. 78); Jordan: al-Fawaz (2002); Lebanon: Jackman (2002); Morocco: Box 3.3; Sudan: Elobeid (2002); Turkey: UN (1998, p. 53) (registered guns only); BBC (2003) (unregistered guns); Yemen: Miller (2003)

The Middle East's shadowy stockpiles

Stockpiles of small arms in the military and police forces of the Middle East total some 13 million–17 million weapons. This would suggest that stockpiles in the region are likely to be far smaller than those of north-east Asia. Nonetheless, as the Small Arms Survey (2004, p. 46) notes, perhaps 4.2 million of Iraq's former small arms arsenal are now dispersed among the civilian population.

As is clearly not the case in north-east Asia, perhaps the majority of Iraq's weapons have been removed from state arsenals and are now in the hands of civilians and non-state combatants—which is why they do not appear in Table 3.8. The situation in Iraq is a warning that military and police stockpiles are only as secure as the institutions that control them.

Civilian stockpiles in the Middle East are cautiously estimated at 45 million to 90 million firearms. What is clear, however, from previous studies of select countries is that trends in ownership differ considerably (Small Arms Survey, 2002, pp. 90–94; 2003, pp. 77–80; 2004, pp. 44–50). This suggests that more research, particularly fieldwork, needs to be conducted into firearm ownership in the Middle East before a more accurate regional civilian estimate can be attempted.

CONCLUSION: TRANSPARENT TRUTHS

Whether the theme is the riddles of small arms disarmament and stockpile management, or the dynamics of two poorly-understood regions, this chapter consistently points to the need for better and more comprehensive data on small arms ownership around the world. Time and again, the lack of reliable figures emerges as a barrier to informed debate and effective policy-making. How serious are small arms problems? Which problems should domestic and international attention focus on first? How well do different kinds of disarmament programmes work? All such questions must remain unanswered until there is a much stronger sense of where the guns are and which ones cause the most trouble.

This chapter repeatedly emphasizes the limits of what can be known. But weaknesses should not obscure accomplishments. The differences in the performance of domestic and international disarmament schemes, like the differences between small arms ownership in two major regions, are becoming clearer. Through the incremental work of innumerable researchers and officials generous with their time and energy, a more complete picture of the global distribution of small arms is emerging.

The chapter also emphasizes just how much more remains to be revealed. Stockpile management and control are still slippery and elusive subjects. Except for a handful of countries in the Middle East and north-east Asia, very little systematic data is available on small arms possession in two regions that are home to 25 per cent or more of the world's population. These two regions clearly have a long way to go in improving transparency on small arms issues.

The growing willingness of governments in the Middle East and north-east Asia to discuss stockpile issues is modest compared with achievements elsewhere. Regional action on small arms stockpile management, previously unimaginable in much of the world, now seems more and more likely. Adding the Middle East and north-east Asia to the list of regions with productive dialogues on the subject would leave no part of the world untouched by this trend.

LIST OF ABBREVIATIONS

DDR	Disarmament, demobilization, and reintegration
DST	Département de la Surveillance du Territoire
DTRA	Defense Threat Reduction Agency
GDP	Gross domestic product
IDF	Israeli Defense Forces
KNPA	Korean National Police Agency
KPA	Korean People's Army
KPAF	Korean People's Air Force
KPN	Korean People's Navy
PAP	People's Armed Police
PLA	People's Liberation Army
PP	People's Police
TPPA	Taiwan Provincial Police Administration

ENDNOTES

1 This chapter uses 'Middle East' to refer to the Middle East, North Africa, and selected neighbouring states.

2 Author interview with Centcom personnel, United States Joint Forces Staff College, Norfolk, Virginia, June 2004.

3 Author interview with Centcom personnel, United States Joint Forces Staff College, Norfolk, Virginia, June 2004.

4 In March 2005 Brazil hosted an international meeting on the Regulation of Civilian Ownership and the Use of Small Arms and Light Weapons. The conference was a strong indication of the extent to which both governments and civil societies across the globe recognize the importance of domestic controls on civilian stockpiles.

5 Personal communication from Pablo Dreyfus, 10 December 2003.

6 This figure excludes some 6 million Ordinary Militia, which the IISS (1981, p. 75) claims were generally unarmed.

7 Answers to the questions of the Small Arms Survey National Stockpiles Questionnaire by the Conventional Weapons Division of the Japanese Ministry of Foreign Affairs, August 2004.

8 The figure of 1.2 million is composed of 1,003,00 Korean People's Army (KPA), 60,000 Korean People's Navy (KPN), and 110,000 Korean People's Air Force (KPAF) (Bermudez, 2001, pp. 3–7).

9 The Arabian Peninsula is taken here to include Kuwait, Oman, Qatar, Saudi Arabia, United Arab Emirates, and Yemen.

10 Interview conducted by Professor Jack Kalpakian, Al Akhawayn University, Ifrane, Morocco, with a mid-level military official, International Congress of Military History, Rabat, 1-7 August, 2004.

BIBLIOGRAPHY

Abun-Nasr, Jamil. 1970. *Lyautey in Morocco*. Berkeley: University of California Press.

—. 1975. *A History of the Maghreb*. Cambridge: Cambridge University Press.

Al Ahdath Al Maghribiya (Casablanca). 2004. 'Hawadith wa Qadaya.' Nos. 1953–1983. 31 May–30 June.

Al-Fawaz, Dahir Fahad. 2002. 'The Phenomenon of Light Weapons Proliferation in Jordan.' In Gali Oda Tealakh, Atef Odibat, and Maha Al Shaer, eds. *Small Arms and Light Weapons in the Arab Region*. Amman: The Jordan Institute of Diplomacy, pp. 88–104.

Annenberg Center. 2004. 'Most of Public Wants the Assault Weapons Ban Extended; So Do Half of NRA Households, Annenberg Data Shows.' National Annenberg Election Survey 2004. Philadelphia: The Annenberg Public Policy Center of the University of Pennsylvania. 23 April. Accessed 29 March 2005. <http://www.annenbergpublicpolicycenter.org/naes/2004_03_gun-legislation_4-23_pr.pdf>

Anderson, Curt. 2004. 'Guns, traffic accidents Claimed Most Police Officer Lives in 2003 FBI says'. Associated Press. 8 November. Accessed 1 April 2005. <http://www.csgv.org/news/headlines/11_8_04.cfm>

Australia. 2002. 'The Australian Firearms Buyback: Tally for Number of Firearms Collected and Compensation Paid.' Canberra: Commonwealth Attorney-General's Department.

—. 2003. 'National Handgun Buy-Back Bill 2003.' Bills Digest No. 155, 2002–03. Canberra: Parliament of Australia, Parliament Library. 22 May.

Barton, Frederick and Bathsheba Crocker. 2003. *Post-war Iraq: Are We Ready?* Washington, DC: Center for Strategic and International Studies.

—. 2004. *Progress or Peril? Measuring Iraq's Reconstruction*. Washington, DC: Center for Strategic and International Studies.

BBC (British Broadcasting Corporation). 2003. 'Father seeks tighter gun laws.' BBC News World Edition. London: BBC. 21 August. Accessed 6 April 2005. <http://news.bbc.co.uk/2/hi/uk_news/scotland/3168869.stm>

—. 2004. 'Iraq PM Extends Weapons Amnesty.' BBC News UK Edition. London: BBC. 18 October. Accessed 22 March 2005. <http://news.bbc.co.uk/1/hi/world/middle_east/3752758.stm>

Bermudez, Joseph S. Jr. 2001. *The Armed Forces of North Korea*. London and New York: I. B. Tauris Publishers.

Bourgois, Josephine. 2005. 'Changing Laws, Changing Attitudes: Lessons from Australian Experience.' Background paper prepared for the International Meeting on the Regulation of Civilian Ownership and the Use of Small Arms and Light Weapons. Rio de Janeiro. 16–18 March. Convened by the Centre for Humanitarian Dialogue in collaboration with the Government of Brazil and Sou da Paz.

Centcom. 2003. 'Coalition Establishes Iraq Weapons Policy.' Release number 03-05-87. MacDill Airforce Base, FL: Headquarters United States Central Command. Accessed 29 March 2005. <http://www.globalsecurity.org/wmd/library/news/iraq/2003/05/iraq-030524-centcom03.htm>

Chase, Kenneth. 2003. *Firearms: A Global History to 1700*. Cambridge: Cambridge University Press.

China. 1996. 'Law of the People's Republic of China on the Control of Firearms.' Adopted at the twentieth session of the Standing Committee of the Eighth National People's Congress on 5 July 1996, promulgated by Order No. 72 of the President of the People's Republic of China on July 5, 1996, and effective as of October 1, 1996.

—. 2003. 'National Report of the People's Republic of China on the Implementation of The UN SALW Programme of Action.' Reports submitted to the Department for Disarmament Affairs in 2003. New York: Department for Disarmament Affairs, United Nations. Accessed 26 March 2005. <http://disarmament.un.org:8080/cab/nationalreports/2002/china-e.PDF>

China Post (Taipei). 2004. 'Amnesty Offered for Holders of Arms in Anti-gun Measure.' 19 June.

Chuang, Jimmy. 2004. 'An Amnesty Period for Illegal Firearms Declared by Police.' *Taipei Times*. 19 June, p. 2.

CNN (Cable News Network). 2004. 'Iraq Extends Weapons Amnesty.' New York: Time Warner. 18 October. Accessed 22 March 2005. <http://edition.cnn.com/2004/WORLD/meast/10/18/iraq.amnesty/>

Columbia Daily Tribune (Missouri). 2005. 'Firearms Debate Mellows with Age.' 26 February.

Damis, John. 1987. 'The Western Sahara Dispute.' In William Zartman, ed. *The Political Economy of Morocco*. New York: Praeger, pp. 188–211.

David, Steven. 1991. 'Explaining Third World Alignment.' *World Politics*, Vol. 43, No. 2. January, pp. 233–56.

Diamond, Larry. 2004a. 'Transition to what in Iraq ?' *Middle East Economic Survey*, Vol. 47, No. 22. 31 May. Accessed 30 March 2005. <http://www.mees.com/postedarticles/oped/a47n22d01.htm>

—. 2004b. 'What went wrong in Iraq.' *Foreign Affairs*. Vol. 83, No. 5. September/October. Accessed 30 March 2005. <http://www.foreignaffairs.org/20040901faessay83505/larry-diamond/what-went-wrong-in-iraq.html>

DTRA (Defense Threat Reduction Agency). 2005. 'Small Arms and Light Weapons (SALW).' DTRA Fact Sheets. Fort Belvoir, Virginia: Defense Threat Reduction Agency. Accessed 29 March 2005. <http://www.dtra.mil/press_resources/fact_sheets/display.cfm?fs=salw>

Economist. 2001. 'Guns in China: the Wild East.' 10-16 November, pp. 57–58.

—. 2002. 'Democracy in the Maghreb: Where Voting is a Parlour Game.' 8 June, pp. 37–38.

Eisenstadt, Marnie. 2004. 'Gun Dealers: Ban's Impact Slight.' *The Post-Standard* (Syracuse). 19 September.

Elobeid, Hussein. 2002. 'The Security, Social and Environmental Impacts of Small Arms and Light Weapons Proliferation in Western Sudan (Darfur).' In Gali Oda Tealakh, Atef Odibat, and Maha Al Shaer, eds. *Small Arms and Light Weapons in the Arab Region*. Amman: The Jordan Institute of Diplomacy, pp. 124–27.

El-Sa'aif, Abdullah. 2000/2001. 'The strategic report of Morocco'. Abhath: Revue Des Sciences Sociales. Rabat: The Center of Studies and Research in the Social Sciences. Special Edition. Nos. 53-54.

Feldman, Shai and Yiftah Shapir. 2001. *The Middle East Military Balance 2000-2001*. Cambridge: MIT Press.

Filkins, Dexter. 2004. '9 Iraqi Militias Said to Approve Deal to Disband.' *New York Times*. 8 June, p. A1.

Fisher, Ian. 2004. 'U.S. Gives Leaders in Falluja a Chance to End the Insurgency.' *New York Times*. 20 April, p. A8.

Fong, Tillie. 2004. 'Permits Falling Short.' *Rocky Mountain News* (Denver). 31 May.

Grillot, Suzette, Wolf-Christian Paes, Hans Risser, and Shelly O. Stoneman. 2004. *A Fragile Peace: Guns and Security in Post-conflict Macedonia*. Small Arms Survey Special Report. Geneva: Small Arms Survey. June.

Hauser, Christine. 2004. 'To Get Weapons Away From Iraqis, The Army Sets Up an Arms Bazaar.' *New York Times*. 20 May, p. A14.

Hider, James. 2003. 'Iraqi Gun Runners "Too Professional" to be Caught Out.' *The Times* (London). 18 February.

Hong, Caroline. 2004. 'Election Eve Attack Report Details Bullets, Gun Barrels.' *Taipei Times*. 31 August.

HRW (Human Rights Watch). 2005. 'Rivers and Blood: Guns, Oil and Power in Nigeria's Rivers State.' Briefing paper. New York: Human Rights Watch. February. Accessed 22 March 2005. <http://hrw.org/backgrounder/africa/nigeria0205/>

Hudson, Philip, 2004. 'Victoria Leads Way in Gun Buyback.' *The Age* (Melbourne). 8 August.

ICG, 2004. 'Reconstructing Iraq.' Middle East Report No. 30. Brussels: International Crisis Group. 2 September.

IISS (International Institute for Strategic Studies). 1979. *The Military Balance 1979–1980*. London: Brasseys.

—. 1980. *The Military Balance 1980–1981*. London: Brasseys.

—. 1981. *The Military Balance 1981–1982*. London: Brasseys.

—. 1982. *The Military Balance 1982-1983*. London: Brasseys.

—. 1984. *The Military Balance 1984-1985*. London: Brasseys.

—. 1985. *The Military Balance 1985–1986*. London: Brasseys.

—. 1987. *The Military Balance 1987–1988*. London: Brasseys.

—. 1990. *The Military Balance 1990–1991*. London: Brasseys.

—. 1991. *The Military Balance 1991-1992*. London: Brasseys.

—. 1995. *The Military Balance 1995–1996*. Oxford: Oxford University Press.

—. 1997. *The Military Balance 1997–1998*. Oxford: Oxford University Press.

—. 1998. *The Military Balance 1998–1999*. Oxford: Oxford University Press.

—. 2000. *The Military Balance 2000–2001*. Oxford: Oxford University Press.

—. 2002. *The Military Balance 2002–2003*. Oxford: Oxford University Press.

—. 2003. *The Military Balance 2003–2004*. Oxford: Oxford University Press.

—. 2004. *The Military Balance 2004–2005*. Oxford: Oxford University Press.

Instituto Sou da Paz. 2005. 'Disarmament News.' Year 11, No. 2. Sao Paulo: Insituto Sou da Paz. March.

IRBC (Immigration and Refugee Board, Canada). 2004. 'Country of Origin Research: China: Structure of the Police Force.' CHN42317.E. Ottawa: Research Directorate, Immigration and Refugee Board. 26 January. Accessed 23 March 2005. <http://www.irb-cisr.gc.ca/en/research/ndp/ref/?action=view&doc=chn42317e>

Jackman, David, 2002. 'Traditional Cultural Practices and Small Arms in the Middle East: Problems and Solutions.' Unpublished manuscript. November.

Jamal, Matoky. 2003. 'Various Dimensions of the Small Arms and Light Weapons Phenomenon in Morocco.' In Gali Oda Tealakh, Atef Odibat, and Maha Al Shaer, eds. *Small Arms and Light Weapons Proliferation in the Arab Region: National and Regional Measures*. Amman: The Jordan Institute of Diplomacy, pp. 107–08.

JNPA (Japanese National Police Agency). 2000. 'Number of Gun Shootings and Dead/Injured People in Japan.' Cited in Stop Gun Caravan. Accessed 26 March 2005. <http://www.stopgun.org/english/kenju_English.html>

Jones, Tim. 2004. 'Relaxed Gun Laws Haven't Translated into Demand for Licenses.' *Chicago Tribune*. 20 December.

JSY (Japan Statistical Yearbook). 2005. *Local Government Employees (1980–2002)*. Tokyo: Statistical Research and Training Institute, Ministry of Internal Affairs and Communications. Accessed 23 March 2005. <http://www.stat.go.jp/data/nenkan/pdf/y2401b00.pdf>

Kalpakian, Jack. 2005. 'Building the Human Bomb: The Case of the 16 May 2003 Attacks in Casablanca.' *Studies in Conflict and Terrorism*, Vol. 28, No. 2. March–April, pp. 113–27.

Kirsten, Adele. 2005. *Beyond Post-conflict: Crime, Guns and Reduction Strategies in Post-apartheid South Africa*. Background paper prepared for the International Meeting on the Regulation of Civilian Ownership and the Use of Small Arms and Light Weapons. Rio de Janeiro. 16–18 March 2005. Convened by the Centre for Humanitarian Dialogue in collaboration with the Government of Brazil and Sou da Paz.

KNPA (Korean National Police Agency). 2005. 'General Affairs: Police Workforce Change and Change of Population in Charge by a Single Police Officer.' Police Statistics Cyber National Police Agency. Seoul: Korean National Police Agency. Accessed 23 March 2005. <http://www.npa.go.kr/eng/statistics/staGeneral_03.jsp>

Koper, Christopher. 2004. *An Updated Assessment of the Federal Assault Weapons Ban: Impacts on Gun Markets and Gun Violence, 1994–2003*. Washington, DC: National Institute of Justice. July.

LAS (League of Arab States). 2004. *Resolution (6447) on Arab Coordination to Combat the Illicit Trade in Small Arms and Light Weapons*. Unofficial Translation. Ordinary session 122, session 3. 14 September.

Metz, Helen Chapin. 1993. *Algeria: A Country Study*. Washington, DC: US Government Printing Office. Accessed 24 March 2005. <http://lcweb2.loc.gov/frd/cs/dztoc.html>

Miles, Donna. 2005. 'Troop-Strength Assessment in Iraq Expected This Summer.' Washington, DC: American Forces Press Service, Department of Defense. Accessed 31 March 2005. <http://www.defenselink.mil/news/Mar2005/20050330_369.html>

Miller, Derek. 2003. *Demand, Stockpiles, and Social Controls: Small Arms in Yemen*. Occasional Paper No. 9. Geneva: Small Arms Survey.

Morocco. 2002. 'Statistical Report of Morocco.' Rabat: Directorate of Statistics, Division of Economic Forecasting and Planning, Office of the Prime Minister.

NISRA (Northern Ireland Statistics and Research Agency). 2001. *Demography Profile for Northern Ireland*. 2001 Northern Ireland Census of Population. Belfast: NISRA. Accessed 26 March 2005. <http://www.nicensus2001.gov.uk/nica/browser/profile.jsp?profile=Demography &mainLevel=CountryProfile&mainArea=Northern+Ireland&mainText=&mainTextExplicitMatch=null&compLevel=CountryProfile& compArea=Northern+Ireland&compText=&compTextExplicitMatch=null>

NRA-ILA (National Rifle Association of America, Institute for Legislative Action). 2005. 'Right-to-Carry 2005.' NRA-ILA Fact Sheets. Fairfax: NRA-ILA. Accessed 29 March 2005. <http://www.nraila.org/Issues/FactSheets/Read.aspx?ID=18>

Page, Clarence. 2004. 'Gun Ban that Didn't.' *Washington Times*. 18 September.

PLA (People's Liberation Army). 2004. 'Chapter III: Revolution in Military Affairs with Chinese Characteristics.' *China's National Defense in 2004*. Beijing: PLA Daily. 27 December. Accessed 23 March 2005. <http://english.chinamil.com.cn/special/cnd2004/contents_04.htm>

PRC (Population Resource Center). 2004. 'The Middle East and North Africa.' Population Resource Center. Accessed 4 April 2005. <http://www.prcdc.org/>

Pyadushkin, Maxim, 2003. *Beyond the Kalashnikov: Small Arms Production, Exports, and Stockpiles in the Russian Federation*. Geneva: Small Arms Survey. August.

Ramzy, Austin. 2004. 'Up in Arms: A Rash of Gun Crimes Strikes Taiwan.' *Time Asia* (Hong Kong). 4 August.

SAFER-Net. 2003. 'People's Republic of China.' Regions. 28 July. Accessed 26 March 2005. <http://www.research.ryerson.ca/SAFER-Net/index.html>

Schulman, Mark A. 2004. 'Race Remains Deadlocked After Debates.' SRBI Public Affairs. 16 October. Accessed 29 March 2005. <http://www.srbi.com/time_poll_arc8.html>

Schwartz, Michael. 2005. 'The Taming of Sadr City.' *Asia Times* (Taipei). 11 January. Accessed 29 March 2005. <http://www.atimes.com/atimes/Middle_East/GA12Ak02.html>

Scobell, Andrew. 2003. *China's Use of Military Force: Beyond the Great Wall and the Long March*. Cambridge: Cambridge University Press.

SIPRI (Stockholm International Peace Research Institute). 2003. *SIPRI Yearbook 2003: Armaments, Disarmament and International Security*. Oxford: Oxford University Press.

—. 2004. *SIPRI Yearbook 2004: Armaments, Disarmament and International Security*. Oxford: Oxford University Press.

Small Arms Survey. 2001. *Small Arms Survey 2001: Profiling the Problem*. Oxford: Oxford University Press.

—. 2002. *Small Arms Survey 2002: Counting the Human Cost*. Oxford: Oxford University Press.

—. 2003. *Small Arms Survey 2003: Development Denied*. Oxford: Oxford University Press.

—. 2004. *Small Arms Survey 2004: Rights at Risk*. Oxford: Oxford University Press.

SMPA (Seoul Metropolitan Police Agency). 2005. 'Greetings from the Commissioner: Welcome to the Seoul Metropolitan Police Agency's Home Page.' Seoul: Seoul Metropolitan Police Agency. Accessed 23 March 2005. <http://www.smpa.go.kr/eng/index.htm>

SolPo. 2000. 'The People's Armed Police: The Functions of PAP: A Crippled Police Force.' Posted on ChinaDefense.Com. Accessed 23 March 2005. <http://www.china-defense.com/analysis/pap/pap_4.html>

South Africa. 2001. 'Firearms Control Act.' Act No. 60, 2000. *Government Gazette,* Vol. 430, No. 22214. 10 April. Accessed 29 March 2005. <http://www.info.gov.za/gazette/acts/2000/a60-00.pdf>

Tanner, Murray Scot. 2004. 'China Rethinks Unrest.' *Washington Quarterly,* Vol. 27, No. 3. Summer, pp. 137–56.

TMI (Taiwan Ministry of the Interior). 2005. 'Self-defense Firearms Control: Tightening of Permit Issuance.' Interior Affairs. National Police Administration. Taipei: Ministry of the Interior. Accessed 26 march 2005. <http://www.moi.gov.tw/english/NationalPolice.asp>

TNPA (Taiwan National Police Agency). 2005. 'History.' Taipei: National Police Agency, Ministry of the Interior. Accessed 23 March 2005. <http://www.npa.gov.tw/eg/history.htm>

UN (United Nations). 1998. *United Nations International Study on Firearms Regulation*. New York: United Nations.

—. 2000. *Seventh United Nations Survey of Crime Trends and Operations of Criminal Justice Systems, covering the period 1998–2000.* Vienna: Division for Policy Analysis and Public Affairs, United Nations Office on Drugs and Crime. Accessed 24 March 2005. <http://www.unodc.org/pdf/crime/seventh_survey/7pc.pdf>

UNDP (United Nations Development Programme), 2002. *Arab Human Development Report 2002*. New York: UNDP.

UNESA (United Nations Department of Economic and Social Affairs). 2005. 'World Population Prospects: The 2004 Revision Population Database.' New York: Population Division, United Nations. Accessed 25 March. <http://esa.un.org/unpp>

USDOJ (United States Department of Justice). 1993a. *World Factbook of Criminal Justice Systems: China*. Washington, DC: Office of Justice Programs, US Department of Justice. Accessed 24 March 2005. <http://nicic.org/Misc/URLShell.aspx?SRC=Catalog&REFF=http://nicic.org/Library/019426&ID=019426&TYPE=HTML&URL=http://www.ojp.usdoj.gov/bjs/abstract/wfcj.htm>

—. 1993b. *World Factbook of Criminal Justice Systems: Japan*. Washington, DC: Office of Justice Programs, US Department of Justice. Accessed 24 March 2005. <http://nicic.org/Misc/URLShell.aspx?SRC=Catalog&REFF=http://nicic.org/Library/019426&ID=019426&TYPE=HTML&URL=http://www.ojp.usdoj.gov/bjs/abstract/wfcj.htm>

—. 1993c. *World Factbook of Criminal Justice Systems: Taiwan*. Washington, DC: Office of Justice Programs, US Department of Justice. Accessed 24 March 2005. <http://nicic.org/Misc/URLShell.aspx?SRC=Catalog&REFF=http://nicic.org/Library/019426&ID=019426&TYPE=HTML&URL=http://www.ojp.usdoj.gov/bjs/abstract/wfcj.htm>

—. 1993d. *World Factbook of Criminal Justice Systems: Israel*. Washington, DC: Office of Justice Programs, US Department of Justice. Accessed 24 March 2005. <http://nicic.org/Misc/URLShell.aspx?SRC=Catalog&REFF=http://nicic.org/Library/019426&ID=019426&TYPE=HTML&URL=http://www.ojp.usdoj.gov/bjs/abstract/wfcj.htm>

USDOS (United States Department of State). 2005. 'NATO Project to Destroy Excess Ukrainian Weapons Stocks.' Press Statement. Richard Boucher, spokesman. Washington, DC: US Department of State. 18 February. Accessed 22 March 2005. <http://www.state.gov/r/pa/prs/ps/2005/42472.htm>

Walt, Vivienne. 2004. 'Iraqis Flocking to Sell Arms for Fistful of Cash.' *San Francisco Chronicle*. 24 May.

Widmer, Mireille and Ataf Odibat, 2004. 'Focus on the Middle East and North Africa.' *Small Arms and Human Security Bulletin*. No. 2. February.

Xiancui, Li. 1998. 'Crime and Policing in China.' Seminar presentation by Li Xiancui, Associate Research Fellow, Institute of Public Security, Ministry of Public Security, People's Republic of China; and Visiting Scholar, Justice Studies, Queensland University of Technology. Presented at the Australian Institute of Criminology. Canberra: Australian Institute of Criminology. 7 September. Accessed 23 March 2005. <http://www.aic.gov.au/conferences/occasional/xiancui.html>

Yiu, Cody. 2004. 'Three-Month Firearms Amnesty Starts Today.' *Taipei Times*. 1 July, p. 2.

ACKNOWLEDGEMENTS

Principal author
Aaron Karp

Other contributors
Jack Kalpakian and Keith Krause

Valued at USD 4 billion, the annual authorized trade in small arms and light weapons makes use of harbours such as Singapore's Tanjong Pagar Container Terminal Port.
(© Jonathan Drake/Reuters)

Reaching for the Big Picture:
AN UPDATE ON SMALL ARMS TRANSFERS

4

INTRODUCTION

Following the format established in *Small Arms Survey 2004,* this chapter provides an annual update of the authorized trade[1] in small arms and light weapons. It looks in detail at the major reported exporters and importers, their trading partners, and the types of small arms exchanged. As in previous years, our understanding of the trade remains partial, for several reasons. Data on exports and imports is still limited for certain countries and certain types of small arms; it is at times difficult to interpret, so that many contradictions remain; and there is a time lag in reporting (for many of the calculations in this chapter, we have had to rely on data covering 2002). The Small Arms Trade Transparency Barometer, introduced in *Small Arms Survey 2004,* is therefore an important tool for assessing and promoting transparency. This chapter contains an update of the Barometer, taking into account the evolution of national small arms export reporting in 2004.

The chapter also undertakes a more systematic analysis of the illicit international small arms trade, based on newly collected data on customs seizures of illicit guns. While some quite preliminary conclusions can be drawn from the data, the main finding is that most states make very little information on customs seizures of illicit small arms publicly available. This is all the more surprising as international illicit trafficking has been at the heart of intergovernmental discussions on small arms.

The main findings of the chapter include the following:

- According to available data and estimates, the top small arms exporters (exporting at least USD 100 million of small arms, including parts and ammunition, annually) in 2002—the latest year for which data is available—are the United States, Italy, Brazil, Germany, Belgium, the Russian Federation, and China.
- The top reported small arms importers by value in 2002 were the United States, Cyprus, Saudi Arabia, and South Korea.
- Among the major exporters of small arms and light weapons, the most transparent are the United States, Germany, and the United Kingdom. The least transparent is Israel.
- Improved transparency is particularly needed with respect to end-users of the small arms exported and government-to-government transactions. Moreover, state reporting should distinguish more clearly small arms and light weapons (and their ammunition) from other types of weapons, and reporting should be timelier.
- Customs seizures in European and other industrialized countries during 1999–2003 indicate that the most significant small arms trafficking takes the form of small-scale transfers.
- Handguns are the type of small arm most commonly smuggled to and from these countries.

THE AUTHORIZED GLOBAL SMALL ARMS TRADE: ANNUAL UPDATE

This section provides an update on the authorized global small arms trade. It focuses on the major exporters and importers globally, their trading partners, and the main products exchanged. It includes information not only on small arms and light weapons but also on their parts and accessories[2] and on small arms (as opposed to light weapons) ammunition. The analysis does not include light weapons ammunition because of reporting limitations.[3] The trade in military small arms and light weapons is also most likely underestimated because of limited transparency on the part of many states and unclear reporting formats for certain types of military arms.

The numbers presented here are based on customs data from UN Comtrade, which is the most comprehensive current source of comparable information on the international small arms and light weapons trade (see Box 4.1). Following established practice, to complement the picture of the trade we have used mirror statistics (that is, importers' declarations of their imports are used to calculate exporters' exports, and vice versa). Although in some instances customs data is compared with figures from national arms export reports compiled by individual governments, calculations are based on customs data from UN Comtrade only so as to ensure comparability and to avoid double counting. The calculations on which this section is based are those of the Norwegian Initiative on Small Arms Transfers (NISAT).[4] All figures represent values rather than quantities. It is true that data on quantities of weapons shipped is more concrete and simpler to analyse; but little of it exists at present, either in customs data from UN Comtrade or in national arms export reports.

The documented value of all exports of small arms in 2002 reported in UN Comtrade customs data is approximately USD 2.1 billion. The figure has changed little from that for 2001, though the incomplete nature of the data makes any conclusions regarding growth or decline hazardous. There is therefore no reason to modify our existing estimate of the total value of the authorized trade in small arms, namely, **USD 4 billion** a year. This estimate is based on the assumption that current figures cover only around half the value of the authorized small arms trade. As noted above, this figure includes only limited information on military small arms and light weapons and none on light weapons ammunition due to problems of reporting and transparency. Moreover, the lack of transparency of some of the main producing and exporting countries, such as China and the Russian Federation, further depresses the figure based on UN Comtrade customs data.

The *top exporters* (defined as those countries exporting at least USD 100 million of small arms annually) in 2002 according to customs data and estimates were the United States, Italy, Brazil, Germany, Belgium, the Russian Federation, and China. These are the same countries as in 2001. The *top importers* (defined as those countries importing at least USD 100 million of small arms annually) for 2002 according to customs data were the United States, Cyprus, Saudi Arabia, and South Korea. Here as well, the top positions have remained relatively stable between 2001 and 2002. Many of the top importers of small arms produce few or no small arms of their own, and thus need to source their weapons abroad. The United States, in contrast, with its very large internal market, absorbs a large part of its domestic production (see Small Arms Survey, 2004, pp. 119–21) and at the same time imports large amounts of guns.

General trading patterns have also remained quite stable from 2001 to 2002. Few states have radically shifted suppliers, and a number of them export to and/or import from the same countries in 2002 as in 2001. Western countries trade between themselves to a large extent, although there are some noteworthy exceptions to this pattern. The small arms ammunition trade amounts to a sizeable part of the total trade in small arms and light weapons. This is all the

The small arms ammunition trade amounts to a sizeable part of the total trade in small arms and light weapons.

more striking as the ammunition component of the trade, as noted above, is most likely underestimated given the absence of light weapons ammunition (for a more detailed discussion of ammunition, see Chapter 1).

As always, the data contained in the tables and elsewhere should be interpreted with caution. The exports and imports of less transparent states are most likely underestimated. Our attempts to circumvent this problem for states thought to be particularly important in the global small arms trade clearly cannot solve the problem of a lack of transparency.

Box 4.1   Understanding UN Comtrade customs data

Sources on the authorized trade in major conventional weapons are relatively few and far between. Sources on the small arms trade are even scarcer, as even the specialized media rarely report on small arms transactions due to their comparatively low monetary value and limited strategic importance for most states. Figures on the trade in firearms for the civilian market are seldom mentioned in the press.

National arms export reports at times provides extensive and useful information on small arms exports (see Table 4.3): however, the quantity of reported data varies greatly, and the information given is not always comparable across countries. As noted in previous editions of the *Small Arms Survey* the most comprehensive source of comparable information on the international small arms and light weapons trade is UN Comtrade, or the United Nations Commodity Trade Statistics Database of the UN Department of Economic and Social Affairs/UN Statistics Division.

On a yearly basis, between 120 and 140 countries and areas, which together account for more than 90 per cent of world trade, provide UN Comtrade with comprehensive trade data, detailed by commodity and country.[5] This information is divided into close to 100 chapters of the so-called Harmonized System (HS), which together cover most types of commodities, from live animals to pharmaceutical products. Each individual commodity within a chapter has a special customs code (normally of six digits). 'Arms and ammunition; parts and accessories thereof' form chapter 93 within the HS. A number of commodities within chapter 93 cover different types of small arms, while others do not. Therefore, in its calculations of the yearly trade in small arms and light weapons, NISAT uses some customs codes within chapter 93 but not the chapter as a whole.[6]

Visitors study weapons at a trade fair in Dortmund, Germany, in January 2005. The media rarely mention figures relating to the civilian firearms trade.

© Oliver Stratmann/AFP/Getty Images

The HS is regularly revised. In the most recent revision (HS2002), states provide more fine-grained data on military weapons in particular. While this improves our understanding of the small arms trade, the system is still not perfect, especially with respect to certain types of military weapons, such as mortars, as well as light weapons ammunition. A number of states continue to report using the previous system (HS1996).

Data reported to UN Comtrade is continuously updated. Some states update their trade data several times a year, others yearly. After submission, states can correct the data submitted. This means that it takes quite some time for consolidated data for a large number of countries to become available. Reporting is usually based on customs declarations, but customs data is at times complemented by other sources such as Intrastat declarations (provided by EU countries and recording intra-EU trade), invoices, and enterprise statistics. Just under half of the reporting states use such additional sources (ITC, 2003b).

Although 'compared to most other economic data ... merchandise trade statistics tend to be fairly reliable, as they are by-products of customs control', UN Comtrade statistics are not without shortcomings (ITC, 2003a). One problem that UN Comtrade shares with virtually all types of state reporting is coverage: not all states provide data. Low-income countries (and in particular least developed countries, LDCs) do not report regularly to UN Comtrade (ITC, n.d.), which limits the possibility of gaining a full and accurate picture of the commodity trade, including the small arms trade. Coverage is a more important problem for the small arms trade than for commodity trade generally, as some states that report to UN Comtrade have chosen to conceal some or all of their trade data relating to small arms. For 2002, approximately 105 states and territories provided some information on their trade in small arms to UN Comtrade. Few states provide information on all relevant customs codes; most commonly, the military weapons categories are kept confidential.[7] Even with these limitations, UN Comtrade remains the most complete data source to date.

Box 4.1   Understanding UN Comtrade customs data (cont.)

The most controversial issue is differences between importers' and exporters' reports. This lack of fit also plagues other transparency mechanisms, such as the UN Register of Conventional Arms (Wezeman, 2003, p. 11). Only some of the possible reasons for the discrepancies in UN Comtrade are mentioned here. One reason is exchange rate fluctuations (as a rule, customs authorities record the value of merchandise in local currency). Discrepancies can also stem from differences in coverage of reporting. For example, in some countries coverage includes returned goods (for repairs, refurbishing, and so on). Three out of ten reporting states include transit trade in import and export statistics. About one-third of all states do not include foreign aid in their trade statistics. Fifteen per cent of all states—among them Austria, France, Israel, and the UK—include goods consigned for their armed forces and diplomatic representatives abroad (ITC, 2003b). Some countries may record country of production rather than the exporting country in their statistics. There can also be time lags in registration. Smuggling or unrecorded trade can also lead to discrepancies (because merchandise which is legally exported might not be declared when imported and vice versa), as can under-reporting for tax or other reasons (ITC, 2003a; 2003b; see also Small Arms Survey, 2004, p.116). All this can lead to discrepancies between exporters' and importers' reports.

The International Trade Centre, a joint agency of the United Nations Conference on Trade and Development (UNCTAD) and the World Trade Organization (WTO), attempts to assess the reliability of individual countries' trade statistics by comparing how well each country's data corresponds to the mirror reporting of partner countries (ITC, 2003a). NISAT has replicated this reliability index for the small arms trade, and it is used in all calculations of the trade values made by NISAT.[8]

Small arms exports

As noted, the top exporters of small arms, their parts, and their ammunition by value in 2002 were the United States, Italy, Brazil, Germany, Belgium, the Russian Federation, and China. In 2001 the list was identical, although the order slightly different. Table 4.1 presents top and major exporters (major exporters are defined as those with reported yearly sales of more than USD 10 million). Some countries that were on the list of major exporters for 2001 are now below the threshold for inclusion into Table 4.1. For example, Bulgaria's reported exports were worth USD 2.4 million in 2002, down from USD 17 million in 2001 (based solely on mirror data, as Bulgaria has provided no information to UN Comtrade for either year). This decline can be explained in several ways. It may simply be due to decreased exports. However, Bulgaria may increasingly trade with countries that do not report their small arms imports, such as many developing countries, or it may export more small arms and light weapons in categories that are not captured by UN Comtrade (such as light weapon ammunition). However, it seems likely that any real decrease is temporary, as Bulgaria reportedly signed and/or delivered Kalashnikov rifles to Iraq (with US payment) and India (64,000 rifles) in 2003 and 2004 (Nicholson, 2004; *The Hindu,* 2004; IndiaExpress, Bureau 2004; Center for the Study of Democracy/Saferworld, 2004, p. 26). Romania is a similar case: for 2002, reported imports from Romania fell below USD 10 million (to USD 4.6 million). Romania also does not report its exports to UN Comtrade. However, its most recent national arms export report announces that it exported small arms and light weapons to a value of USD 25.4 million in 2002 (Romania, 2004). This seems to indicate that Romania either trades mainly with other states that do not report to UN Comtrade or that it exports mainly light weapons ammunition and other small arms that are not captured by UN Comtrade.

For 2002 improved data is available on Iran and Singapore, two medium producers on which little export information was previously available (see Small Arms Survey, 2004, pp.101–02). Recorded Iranian exports amount to approximately USD 8.8 million for 2002 (which is just below the threshold for inclusion in Table 4.1). This figure is probably an underestimate, as Iran does not report to UN Comtrade on all categories of small arms and light weapons. Iran's main reported partners include Sudan, Greece, Guinea, Yemen, and Italy. Singapore (also just below the threshold) exported weapons to destinations as varied as Indonesia, Kenya, Botswana, Finland, and the United States.

The exports of Pakistan (another medium producer) remain shrouded in mystery. According to PakistaniDefence.com (2004), the US has expressed an interest in Pakistani small arms for armed forces in Afghanistan and Iraq. Pakistani exports recorded in UN Comtrade are very limited, however, as Pakistan does not report any of its exports. India, although a medium producer of small arms, reports few exports. Since 2001 it has reportedly delivered 26,000 Indian National Small Arms System rifles to Nepal. India subsidized this deal, worth approximately USD 11.7 million, to 70 per cent of its value (India News Online, 2004; Singh Khadka, 2004). The notoriously secretive North Korea reportedly produces small arms, but little is known about its exports.

Visitors look at Pakistani-made infantry weapons at a 2002 defence exhibition in Karachi. Pakistan is a medium-sized producer that does not report on small arms exports.

© Syed Zargham/Getty Images

Two of the three top global producers of small arms, the Russian Federation and China, lack transparency in their small arms exports, which is particularly problematic given their presumed importance in the total small arms trade. The Small Arms Survey therefore seeks information on these two states that goes beyond mirror data. For lack of better information, we maintain the same estimate of Chinese exports (for details, see Small Arms Survey, 2004, ch. 4, Annexe 4.1[9]). This crude estimate for 2001 comes quite close to actual Chinese exports in 1998, the latest year for which complete data is available on China. For the Russian Federation we have not been able to update our information, as Russian authorities had not made new information available at the time that the *Small Arms Survey* went to press. We have noted the 2001 figure in Table 4.1 so as to give the reader a sense of the magnitude of the Russian exports.

As was the case in the 2004 edition of the *Small Arms Survey,* the comparison between customs data and national arms export reports provided in Table 4.1 reveals important discrepancies between the two sources. Clearly, we are far from a full understanding of the authorized trade in small arms.

There are two main reasons for the discrepancies. First, national arms export reports, in contrast to UN Comtrade customs data, often do not include exports of what state authorities categorize as 'civilian' weapons; they typically

There are important discrepancies between customs data and national arms export reports.

focus solely on military or defence products and exclude lethal equipment used by the police or civilians. However, countries that are especially thorough in their small arms and light weapons reporting, such as for example the Czech Republic and Germany, do include civilian as well as military small arms in their national arms export report statistics. As far as transparency is concerned, including exports of both civilian and military small arms, but separating the two where possible, is clearly preferable, not least because much small arms violence occurs in non-war settings and involves 'ordinary' civilians (Small Arms Survey, 2004, ch. 6).

Second, in their export reports countries commonly categorize their national arms exports in accordance with the Wassenaar Arrangement Munitions List (ML), the EU Common Military List (which is based on the Wassenaar List), or some comparable list. Only the ML1 category of the Wassenaar Arrangement list is a 'pure' small arms category, while three other categories are mixed, containing important types of small arms as well as other items.[10] For countries using one of these systems, a conservative counting method is adopted here, recording the artificially low ML1 value in Table 4.1. This value does not capture any light weapons or any small arms ammunition. Hence, while, as noted, UN Comtrade does not permit us to single out light weapons ammunition and certain types of light weapons, the ML system is even more restrictive in this respect. These and other possible reasons for discrepancies are noted in the 'Remarks' column of Table 4.1.[11]

The upshot is that national arms export reports are not fulfilling their full potential as a source of information on the small arms trade. In principle, arms export reports could give much more in the way of details, explanations, and contextual information than pre-formatted customs data (such as that of UN Comtrade); in practice, however, arms export reports are often less useful than UN Comtrade.

Table 4.1   Annual authorized small arms exports for major reported exporters (yearly sales of more than USD 10 million), 2002

Country	USD value customs data (UN Comtrade)*/ Export report° (2002 if not otherwise stated)	Main recipients (listed in order of importance)	Main types of small arms and light weapons exported (listed in order of importance). NB: types refer to UN Comtrade customs codes (see notes)	Remarks
Austria	At least 86 million*	US, Germany, Belgium, Switzerland, Italy*	Pistols/revolvers, ammunition, sporting/hunting rifles, parts/accessories pistols/revolvers, parts/accessories sporting/hunting weapons*	Reports its trade neither in military weapons nor in pistols and revolvers to UN Comtrade. Hence the value of these categories (based on importers' reports) is likely to be underestimated.
Belgium	At least 145 million* EUR 104.0 million (USD 98.4 million)°	Saudi Arabia, Portugal, US, France, Italy*	Ammunition, parts/accessories sporting/hunting weapons, sporting/ hunting rifles, sporting/hunting shotguns*	The discrepancy between customs and arms export report data is difficult to explain. The Comtrade figure could be inflated partly by inclusion of returns of weapons for repairs. It also includes civilian weapons. However, Belgium reports its trade neither in military weapons nor in pistols and revolvers to UN Comtrade. Hence the value for these categories (based on importers' reports) is likely to be underestimated. Export report does not detail recipients of small arms.
Brazil[12]	At least 164 million*	Malaysia, US, Colombia, Germany, Algeria*	Ammunition, pistols/revolvers, sporting/hunting rifles, sporting/ hunting shotguns*	Does not report exports of pistols to UN Comtrade. Hence the value (based on importers' reports) is likely to be underestimated.
Bulgaria	*Medium producer, but little is reported about its exports*			

Table 4.1 **Annual authorized small arms exports for major reported exporters**
(cont.) **(yearly sales of more than USD 10 million), 2002**

Country	USD value customs data (UN Comtrade)*/ Export report° (2002 if not otherwise stated)	Main recipients (listed in order of importance)	Main types of small arms and light weapons exported (listed in order of importance). NB: types refer to UN Comtrade customs codes (see notes)	Remarks
Canada	52 million* CAD 19.4 million (USD 12.4 million)°	US, Australia, Netherlands, Denmark, Norway* Denmark, Norway, Netherlands, Italy, Germany°	Ammunition, sporting/hunting rifles, pistols/revolvers, parts/accessories sporting/hunting weapons, parts/accessories pistols/revolvers*	Customs data and the national report diverge largely because the latter does not take into account exports to the US, which according to the export report are 'estimated to account for over half of Canada's exports of military goods and technology' (Canada, 2004, p.7).
China	At least 22 million* SAS estimate: USD 100 million	US, Philippines, Iran, Sudan, Namibia*	Pistols/revolvers, military weapons, parts/accessories sporting/hunting weapons, sporting/hunting shotguns, sporting/hunting rifles*	Customs data is likely to underestimate actual exports, as China does not report on many of its exports, and hence figures are based on importers' reporting.
Czech Republic	At least 51 million*	US, Germany, France, Israel, Yemen*	Ammunition, pistols/revolvers, sporting/hunting rifles, parts/accessories pistols/revolvers*	Does not report trade in military weapons to UN Comtrade. Hence, the value (based on importers' reports) is likely to be underestimated. Publishes export report that for 2002 contains numbers, not values of small arms transferred, and does not detail recipients of small arms.
Finland	26 million* EUR 2.0 million (USD 1.9 million)°	US, Norway, United Kingdom, Germany, Sweden* Italy, Germany, US, New Zealand, Austria°	Sporting/hunting rifles, ammunition, parts/accessories sporting/hunting weapons, sporting/hunting shotguns*	Customs and export report data diverge probably largely because civilian weapons are excluded from the export report. In the export report it is also difficult fully to distinguish small arms ammunition from other types of ammunition.
France	At least 48 million* EUR 0.4 million (USD 0.4 million)°	Turkey, US, Portugal, Norway, Russia* Switzerland, Belgium, Nigeria°	Military firearms, ammunition, parts/accessories sporting/hunting weapons, sporting/hunting shotguns*	Does not report trade in military weapons and pistols and revolvers to UN Comtrade. Hence the value (based on importers' reports) is likely to be underestimated. Customs and export report data diverge probably largely because small arms ammunition cannot be distinguished from other types of ammunition in the arms export report. In the export report, it is also difficult fully to distinguish small arms and light weapons from other items. Civilian weapons are excluded from the export report.
Germany	At least 159 million*	US, France, Austria, Switzerland, Spain*	Pistols/revolvers, ammunition, sporting/hunting rifles, sporting/hunting shotguns, parts/accessories pistols/revolvers*	Does not report trade in military weapons to UN Comtrade. Hence, the value (based on importers' reports) is likely to be underestimated. Publishes an export report, but it includes information on granted export licences, not actual deliveries of small arms and light weapons, which may be lower.
Israel	At least 22 million*	US, Norway, Mexico, Germany, Poland*	Pistols/revolvers, ammunition, military firearms, parts/accessories pistols/revolvers, parts/accessories sporting/hunting weapons*	Does not report on its small arms trade at all to UN Comtrade. Figures are based on importers' reports. Hence the value is likely to be underestimated.

Table 4.1
(cont.)

Annual authorized small arms exports for major reported exporters (yearly sales of more than USD 10 million), 2002

Country	USD value customs data (UN Comtrade)*/ Export report° (2002 if not otherwise stated)	Main recipients (listed in order of importance)	Main types of small arms and light weapons exported (listed in order of importance). NB: types refer to UN Comtrade customs codes (see notes)	Remarks
Italy	At least 250 million*	US, France, Turkey, Germany, Spain*	Sporting/hunting shotguns, ammunition, pistols/revolvers, sporting/hunting rifles, parts/accessories sporting/hunting weapons*	Does not report trade in military weapons to UN Comtrade. Hence, the value (based on importers' reports) is likely to be underestimated. Publishes an export report, but it includes information on granted licences, not actual deliveries of small arms and light weapons, which may be lower.
Japan	65 million*	US, Belgium, Kenya, Canada, Australia*	Sporting/hunting rifles, parts/accessories sporting/hunting weapons, sporting/hunting shotguns, shotgun barrels*	
Netherlands	20 million*	Saudi Arabia, South Korea, Ireland, Switzerland, US*	Ammunition, military weapons, parts/accessories pistols/revolvers, parts/accessories sporting/hunting weapons*	Some of the recorded exports could be re-exports/transit recorded by the importer. Publishes an export report, but it includes information on granted licences, not actual deliveries of small arms and light weapons, which may be lower.
Norway	45 million* NOK 3.4 million (USD 0.4 million)°	Turkey, Switzerland, Sweden, US, Italy* Denmark, Finland, Italy, Sweden, US°	Ammunition, military weapons, parts/accessories sporting/hunting weapons, rocket/grenade launchers, parts/accessories pistols/revolvers*	Customs and export report data diverge probably largely because small arms ammunition cannot be distinguished from other types of ammunition in the arms export report. In the export report, it is also difficult fully to distinguish small arms and light weapons from other items.
Pakistan	*Medium producer, but little is reported about its exports*			
Portugal	20 million*	Belgium, US, Spain, Germany, Canada*	Sporting/hunting rifles, sporting/hunting shotguns, ammunition, pistols/revolvers*	Publishes an export report, but it does not detail the share of small arms and light weapons of total arms exports.
Romania	25.4 million°	n.a.	n.a.	The Romanian export report details the share of small arms and light weapons exports in total arms exports, but does not indicate the main recipients of the small arms or main types of small arms traded. Romania does not report on its small arms and light weapons trade at all to UN Comtrade, and figures based on importers' reports fall below the threshold.
Russian Federation	At least 41 million* Estimate for 2001 based on official information: no more than 130 million (CAST, 2003, p. 24)	US, Slovakia, Cyprus, South Korea, Lebanon* For 2001: Vietnam, Malaysia, Bhutan, Indonesia, Afghanistan (Northern Alliance), Ethiopia (CAST, 2003, p. 24).	Ammunition, sporting/hunting shotguns, sporting/hunting rifles, military firearms*	Does not report on trade in military weapons and pistols and revolvers to UN Comtrade. Hence the value (based on importers' reports) is likely to be underestimated. This helps explain the large discrepancy between the customs data figure and the figure for 2001 obtained in CAST (2003) through exporting companies.
South Africa	ZAR 151.8 million (USD14.6 million)°	UK, Oman, Colombia, Singapore, Jordan°	n.a.	South Africa does not report customs data to UN Comtrade and figures based on importers' reports fall below the threshold. Civilian weapons are excluded from the export report, which does not indicate main types of small arms traded.

Table 4.1
(cont.)
Annual authorized small arms exports for major reported exporters (yearly sales of more than USD 10 million), 2002

Country	USD value customs data (UN Comtrade)*/ Export report° (2002 if not otherwise stated)	Main recipients (listed in order of importance)	Main types of small arms and light weapons exported (listed in order of importance). NB: types refer to UN Comtrade customs codes (see notes)	Remarks
South Korea	14 million*	US, Australia, Israel, Indonesia, Taiwan*	Ammunition, parts/accessories pistols/revolvers, parts/accessories sporting/hunting weapons, pistols/revolvers, military firearms*	
Spain	At least 47 million* EUR 13.6 million (USD 12.9 million)°	US, Portugal, Turkey, Ghana, France*	Ammunition, sporting/hunting shotguns, pistols/revolvers, parts/accessories sporting/hunting weapons*	Does not report trade in military weapons to UN Comtrade. Hence, the value (based on importers' reports) is likely to be underestimated. The discrepancy between the arms export report figure and the UN Comtrade figure is most likely due to the fact that civilian weapons are excluded from the export report. Export report does not detail recipients of small arms, nor main types of small arms traded.
Sweden	At least 24 million* SEK 6 million (USD 0.6 million)°	Mexico, US, Norway, Denmark, Germany*	Ammunition, military firearms, parts/accessories sporting/hunting weapons, rocket/grenade launchers*	Does not report trade in military weapons to UN Comtrade. Hence, the value (based on importers' reports) is likely to be underestimated. Customs and export report data diverge probably largely because small arms ammunition cannot be distinguished from other types of ammunition in the arms export report. In the export report, it is also difficult fully to distinguish small arms and light weapons from other items. Export report does not detail recipients of small arms.
Switzerland	54 million* CHF 16.3 million (USD 10.5 million)°	Germany, Italy, Singapore, US, Romania* Germany, US, Singapore, Egypt, Finland°	Ammunition, military firearms, pistols/revolvers, parts/accessories sporting/hunting weapons, sporting/hunting rifles*	Customs and export report data diverge probably largely because small arms ammunition cannot be distinguished from other types of ammunition in the arms export report. In the export report, it is also difficult fully to distinguish small arms and light weapons from other items. Civilian weapons are excluded from the export report.
Turkey	30 million*	US, Italy, Germany, unspecified countries, France*	Sporting/hunting shotguns, parts/accessories sporting/hunting weapons, sporting/hunting rifles, ammunition, shotgun barrels*	
UK	92 million*	Unspecified countries, US, Switzerland, Kenya, Canada*	Ammunition, military weapons, military firearms, sporting/hunting shotguns*	Publishes export report, but does not detail the value of small arms and light weapons exports. Instead it provides numbers of small arms and light weapons exported to certain destinations.
US	533 million*	South Korea, Japan, Canada, Turkey, Saudi Arabia*	Ammunition, rocket/grenade launchers, military firearms, pistols/revolvers*	Publishes export report, but it includes mostly information on granted export licences, not actual deliveries of small arms and light weapons, which may be lower.

*UN Comtrade DESA/UNSD, download date: 16 March 2005. Customs codes 9301 (military weapons), 930120 (rocket and grenade launchers etc.). 930190 (military firearms), 9302 (revolvers and pistols), 930320 (sporting and hunting shotguns), 930330 (sporting and hunting rifles), 930510 (parts and accessories of revolvers and pistols), 930521 (shotgun barrels), 930529 (parts and accessories of shotguns or rifles), 930621 (shotgun cartridges), 930630 (small arms ammunition).

NB: 'Ammunition' in the table refers to shotgun cartridges and small arms ammunition combined.

°Export report

Sources: NISAT (2005) (UN Comtrade calculations); Belgium (2003); Canada (2004), Finland (2003); France (2005); Norway (2003); Romania (2004); South Africa (2003); Spain (2003); Sweden (2003); Switzerland (2003).

Small arms imports

The opportunities to compare various sources of information on small arms imports are limited, simply because only one source—customs data—covers a large number of countries. National arms export reports, as their name implies, usually detail only arms exports, and not imports.

There are more changes among major importers than among major small arms exporters between 2001 and 2002.

Unsurprisingly, there are more changes from year to year among major importers (defined as those countries importing small arms worth more than USD 10 million in a given year) than exporters. For military and police weapons in particular, imports depend on procurement decisions, which can vary widely from year to year, in particular for smaller states. For 2002, among the major importers that were absent from the list for 2001 were Bahrain, the Czech Republic, Jordan, Kenya, Malaysia, the Philippines, Poland, and the Russian Federation. In contrast, Argentina, Brazil, Honduras, Lebanon, Taiwan, Thailand, and Venezuela reported importing less in 2002 than in 2001, and no longer appear on the list of major importers.

The top importers—that is, those countries importing small arms worth USD 100 million or more—for 2002 were, in order of importance, the US, Cyprus, Saudi Arabia, and South Korea. As for exporters, the top positions among importers remain relatively stable.

As in previous years, Cyprus is among the top importers. This recurrent peculiarity is a consequence of an opaque transit trade (discussed further in Small Arms Survey, 2003, p. 105; Small Arms Survey, 2004, p. 108). The un-transparent nature of Cypriot trade is underlined by the fact that much of the arms were imported from 'unspecified' countries. Other sources of imports, by value, were the Russian Federation, Italy, Slovakia, and the United Kingdom.

Other possibly large importers on which little data is available are those countries involved in internal or international conflict, such as (in 2002) Afghanistan, Côte d'Ivoire, Indonesia, Liberia, Nepal, the Russian Federation (Chechnya), Sri Lanka, Sudan, and the countries of the Great Lakes region. Imports to the warring parties in these conflicts are undoubtedly illicit in many cases—especially where insurgents are the recipients. As a result, they do not figure in Table 4.2. Transfers to conflict zones are discussed in detail in Chapter 6 (CONFLICT SOURCING).

Table 4.2   Annual authorized small arms imports for major reported importers, 2002

Country	USD value customs data (UN Comtrade)	Main suppliers (top five)	Main types of small arms and light weapons imported. NB: types refer to UN Comtrade customs codes (see notes)	Remarks
Australia	47 million	US, Italy, Canada, unspecified countries, Norway	Ammunition, rocket/grenade launchers, sporting/hunting rifles, pistols/revolvers, sporting/hunting shotguns	
Austria	At least 23 million	Germany, Switzerland, Italy, US, Belgium	Ammunition, parts/accessories sporting/hunting weapons, sporting/hunting rifles, sporting/hunting shotguns	Does not report on its imports of military weapons and pistols/revolvers to UN Comtrade. Hence the value (based on exporters' reports) is possibly underestimated.
Bahrain	At least 23 million	US, Switzerland, UK, Canada, France	Rocket/grenade launchers, ammunition, military firearms, parts/accessories sporting/hunting weapons, sporting/hunting shotguns	Reports on very few imports to UN Comtrade. Hence the value (based on exporters' reports) is probably underestimated.
Belgium	At least 46 million	US, Portugal, Japan, Italy, Germany	Ammunition, sporting/hunting shotguns, sporting/hunting rifles, pistols/revolvers	Does not report on its imports of military weapons and pistols/revolvers to UN Comtrade. Hence the value (based on exporters' reports) is possibly underestimated. Some imports might actually be returns for repairs.

Table 4.2   Annual authorized small arms imports for major reported importers, 2002 (cont.)

Country	USD value customs data (UN Comtrade)	Main suppliers (top five)	Main types of small arms and light weapons imported. NB: types refer to UN Comtrade customs codes (see notes)	Remarks
Canada	59 million	US, Germany, Italy, UK, Japan	Ammunition, parts/accessories sporting/hunting weapons, sporting/hunting rifles, sporting/hunting shotguns	
Colombia	14 million	Brazil, US, Czech Republic, Israel, South Africa	Ammunition, pistols/revolvers, military firearms, rocket/grenade launchers	
Cyprus	448 million	Unspecified countries, Russian Federation, Italy, Slovakia, UK	Military weapons, military firearms, sporting/hunting shotguns, ammunition	
Czech Republic	At least 12 million	Italy, Germany, Austria, US, Hungary	Parts/accessories pistols/revolvers, pistols/revolvers, parts/accessories sporting/hunting weapons, sporting/hunting shotguns, ammunition	Does not report on its imports of military weapons to UN Comtrade. Hence the value (based on exporters' reports) is possibly underestimated.
Denmark	15 million	Germany, Canada, Sweden, UK, Norway	Ammunition, parts/accessories sporting/hunting weapons, sporting/hunting rifles, sporting/hunting shotguns	
Finland	14 million	Italy, Germany, US, Sweden, Singapore	Ammunition, sporting/hunting shotguns, parts/accessories sporting/hunting weapons, sporting/hunting rifles	
France	At least 53 million	Italy, Germany, Belgium, US, Czech Republic	Ammunition, sporting/hunting rifles, sporting/hunting shotguns, parts/accessories sporting/hunting weapons	Does not report on its imports of military weapons and pistols/revolvers to UN Comtrade. Hence the value (based on exporters' reports) is possibly underestimated.
Germany	At least 73 million	Switzerland, US, Italy, Austria, Czech Republic	Ammunition, parts/accessories sporting/hunting weapons, sporting/hunting rifles, sporting/hunting shotguns, pistols/revolvers	Does not report on its imports of military weapons to UN Comtrade. Hence the value (based on exporters' reports) is possibly underestimated.
Greece	At least 16 million	US, Italy, Iran, Spain, Germany	Parts/accessories sporting/hunting weapons, sporting/hunting shotguns, ammunition, rocket/grenade launchers	Does not report on its imports of military weapons and pistols/revolvers to UN Comtrade. Hence the value (based on exporters' reports) is possibly underestimated.
Israel[13]	At least 31 million	US, Czech Republic, South Korea, Spain, Brazil	Parts/accessories pistols/revolvers, ammunition, military firearms, parts/accessories sporting/hunting weapons, rocket/grenade launchers	Does not report any imports to UN Comtrade. Hence the value (based on exporters' reports) is probably underestimated.
Italy	At least 55 million	US, Germany, Switzerland, Belgium, Turkey	Ammunition, rocket/grenade launchers, sporting/hunting rifles, parts/accessories sporting/hunting weapons, pistols/revolvers	Does not report on its imports of military weapons to UN Comtrade. Hence the value (based on exporters' reports) is possibly underestimated.
Japan	77 million	US, Italy, Germany, UK, Australia	Military firearms, ammunition, pistols/revolvers, sporting/hunting shotguns	
Jordan	At least 23 million	US, Switzerland, Canada, Italy, Czech Republic	Military firearms, ammunition, military weapons, pistols/revolvers	Does not report any imports to UN Comtrade. Hence the value (based on exporters' reports) is probably underestimated.
Kenya	11 million	UK, Japan, Singapore, Czech Republic, South Africa	Military weapons, ammunition, pistols/revolvers, sporting/hunting rifles	
Kuwait	At least 18 million	US, Italy, Cyprus, Germany, Poland	Ammunition, military firearms, sporting/hunting shotguns, sporting/hunting rifles	Does not report any imports to UN Comtrade. Hence the value (based on exporters' reports) is probably underestimated.

Table 4.2   Annual authorized small arms imports for major reported importers, 2002 (cont.)

Country	USD value customs data (UN Comtrade)	Main suppliers (top five)	Main types of small arms and light weapons imported. NB: types refer to UN Comtrade customs codes (see notes)	Remarks
Malaysia	72 million	Brazil, US, Switzerland, Czech Republic, Germany	Ammunition, sporting/hunting rifles, military firearms, sporting/hunting shotguns	
Mexico	18 million	Sweden, US, Israel, Belgium, Czech Republic	Military firearms, pistols/revolvers, ammunition, parts/accessories sporting/hunting weapons	
Netherlands	At least 34 million	US, Germany, Canada, Belgium, Norway	Rocket/grenade launchers, ammunition, parts/accessories sporting/hunting weapons, pistols/revolvers	Does not report on its imports of military weapons and pistols/revolvers to UN Comtrade. Hence the value (based on exporters' reports) is possibly underestimated.
Norway	31 million	US, Germany, Israel, Italy, Finland	Ammunition, military firearms, sporting/hunting rifles, sporting/hunting shotguns	
Philippines	12 million	China, US, Brazil, Italy, Austria	Pistols/revolvers, sporting/hunting rifles, ammunition, parts/accessories pistols/revolvers, sporting/hunting shotguns	
Poland	12 million	Germany, Czech Republic, Israel, South Africa, Italy	Ammunition, pistols/revolvers, sporting/hunting shotguns, sporting/hunting rifles	
Portugal	29 million	Belgium, Italy, Spain, France, Germany	Parts/accessories sporting/hunting weapons, sporting/hunting shotguns, shotgun barrels, sporting/hunting rifles, parts/accessories pistols/revolvers	
Russian Federation	At least 12 million	Germany, Italy, Austria, France, Belgium	Sporting/hunting shotguns, sporting/hunting rifles, ammunition, parts/accessories sporting/hunting weapons	Does not report on its imports of military weapons and pistols/revolvers to UN Comtrade. Hence the value (based on exporters' reports) is possibly underestimated.
Saudi Arabia	132 million	Belgium, US, Netherlands, Germany, UK	Ammunition, parts/accessories pistols/revolvers, pistols/revolvers, parts/accessories sporting/hunting weapons	
South Korea	103 million	US, Netherlands, Russian Federation, UK, Italy	Rocket/grenade launchers, ammunition, military firearms, military weapons, parts/accessories pistols/revolvers	
Spain	At least 27 million	Italy, Germany, US, Portugal, Belgium	Sporting/hunting rifles, ammunition, sporting/hunting shotguns, pistols/revolvers	Does not report on its imports of military weapons to UN Comtrade. Hence the value (based on exporters' reports) is possibly underestimated.
Sweden	At least 16 million	Germany, Norway, Finland, US, Italy	Ammunition, sporting/hunting rifles, military weapons, sporting/hunting shotguns, parts/accessories sporting/hunting weapons	Does not report on its imports of military weapons to UN Comtrade. Hence the value (based on exporters' reports) is possibly underestimated.
Switzerland	41 million	UK, Norway, Germany, Austria, Chile	Military firearms, ammunition, pistols/revolvers, sporting/hunting shotguns, sporting/hunting rifles	
Turkey	99 million	US, France, Norway, Italy, Spain	Ammunition, rocket/grenade launchers, military firearms, pistols/revolvers	
United Arab Emirates	At least 10 million	Switzerland, US, UK, Brazil, Italy	Ammunition, military firearms, sporting/hunting shotguns, pistols/revolvers	Does not report any imports to UN Comtrade. Hence the value (based on exporters' reports) is probably underestimated.

Table 4.2   Annual authorized small arms imports for major reported importers, 2002 (cont.)

Country	USD value customs data (UN Comtrade)	Main suppliers (top five)	Main types of small arms and light weapons imported. NB: types refer to UN Comtrade customs codes (see notes)	Remarks
United Kingdom	95 million	Unspecified countries, US, Italy, Germany, Switzerland	Ammunition, military weapons, sporting/hunting shotguns, sporting/hunting rifles, military firearms	
US	571 million	Italy, Brazil, Austria, Japan, Germany	Sporting/hunting shotguns, pistols/revolvers, ammunition, sporting/hunting rifles, parts/accessories sporting/hunting weapons	

Notes: Only countries with reported or estimated yearly imports of more than USD 10 million have been included in the listing.

*UN Comtrade DESA/UNSD, download date: 16 March 2005. Customs codes 9301 (military weapons), 930120 (rocket and grenade launchers, etc.), 930190 (military firearms), 9302 (revolvers and pistols), 930320 (sporting and hunting shotguns), 930330 (sporting and hunting rifles), 930510 (parts and accessories of revolvers and pistols), 930521 (shotgun barrels), 930529 (parts and accessories of shotguns or rifles), 930621 (shotgun cartridges), 930630 (small arms ammunition). NB: 'Ammunition' in the table refers to shotgun cartridges and small arms ammunition combined.

Source: NISAT (2005)

DEVELOPMENTS IN TRANSPARENCY: ANNUAL UPDATE

The most important development in small arms transparency during 2004 arguably concerned the UN Register of Conventional Arms. In 2004, states reported for the first time under the register's newly expanded information exchange (now including some types of light weapons). This section makes a preliminary assessment of this first year of reporting on—at least some—categories of small arms and light weapons.

The section also provides an update of the Small Arms Trade Transparency Barometer—first published in the *Small Arms Survey 2004*—and analyses the strong and weak points of state reporting to date.

The expansion of the UN Register: The beginnings of reporting on light weapons

As noted in the *Small Arms Survey 2004,* several international efforts were made in 2003 to improve transparency in the small arms trade. The goal, not yet achieved, is to bring it up to par with transparency on transfers of major conventional weapons. In December 2003 the Wassenaar Arrangement Participating States agreed to add small arms and light weapons, including MANPADS, to the list of strategic goods on which they exchange information (the information is not made public: this is an intergovernmental transparency device). More or less simultaneously, the UN General Assembly decided to extend the UN Register of Conventional Arms (UN Register) to include artillery pieces equal to or above 75 mm (previously, the threshold was 100 mm), to capture the very common 81 and 82 mm mortars.

A government soldier fires a mortar in Morazan Province, El Salvador. Now that the UN Register has been extended to include artillery pieces equal to or greater than 75 mm, governments should report on their trade in the common 81 and 82 mm mortars.

The missile and launcher category was also extended to include MANPADS. Moreover, a system of voluntary information sharing (which, unlike other parts of state reporting to the UN Register, is not publicly available on the UN Department for Disarmament Affairs, Web site) on all military small arms and light weapons transfers was set up within the UN Register (for further details, see Small Arms Survey, 2004, pp. 115–16). This was the first revision of the Register since its inception in 1992, and it was welcomed in particular by African states, which have found themselves especially vulnerable to reckless small arms transfers (Wezeman, 2003, p. 8).

After one year it is still too early to assess fully the implementation of these measures as well as their influence on small arms transparency. The confidential nature of the Wassenaar Arrangement information exchange prevents any attempt at analysis. However, some preliminary remarks can be made about the UN Register.

As of early 2005, some 115 states had submitted their reports for 2003 to the UN Register of Conventional Arms. Of those states, fewer than one-fifth (about 20 states) reported on their imports, exports, holdings, or procurement through national production of light artillery or MANPADS.[14] For some states, it is difficult to ascertain whether the new categories are incorporated in the reporting, as they give insufficient detail about the weapons on which they report. A few states provided additional information on all military small arms and light weapons transfers. These were Latvia, the Netherlands, Poland, Sweden, and the UK.

> The lack of reporting on light artillery or MANPADS by top exporters and importers is a worrying sign.

The fact that not only European countries but also states such as Israel, Jordan, and Malaysia report on light artillery or MANPADS to the UN Register seems encouraging for the future. However, no African country reported, although, as just noted, African countries lobbied hard for the inclusion of small arms and light weapons in the UN Register. Another cause for concern is the absence of all top exporters of small arms (the United States, Italy, Brazil, Germany, Belgium, the Russian Federation, and China) from the list of reporting countries. Among the top importers, the picture is similarly bleak.

The next few years will show how these short-term trends in reporting translate into more established patterns.

Update on the Small Arms Trade Transparency Barometer

The contradictions and question marks that hang over the exports and imports of small arms show that increasing state transparency in the small arms and light weapons trade is as vital as ever. The Small Arms Trade Transparency Barometer is a tool for comparing states for transparency and for clarifying where progress needs to be made. It assesses the transparency of the major small arms exporting states on a 20-point scale on the basis of the information states publish on their small arms exports in national arms export reports and in customs data as reported to UN Comtrade (see Table 4.3).

Both the 2004 and the 2005 Barometers show that progress is uneven. Most of the major exporters publish at least some of their information in a UN language[15] and make it available on the Internet, thus obtaining high scores under the access category of the Barometer.[16]

As for the *clarity* of the reporting, the picture is more mixed. Here, none of the analysed states gets a full score; indeed, a number of them obtain quite low scores. Countries following the munitions classification system of the Wassenaar Arrangement (or the EU system, which is very similar) in their reporting generally achieve only half or no points on two out of four criteria. That system makes it impossible fully to single out small arms and light weapons and their ammunition from other types of conventional weapons and ammunition (see section on small arms exports, above). Another issue is that few states clarify the origins of the information provided (industry reporting, customs reporting, licensing information, and so on). Without such source information, however, the data becomes less useful, in particular for international comparison. Lastly, none of the analysed countries provides full information on types of end-users of weapons (military, police, other security forces, civilians or civilian retailers, and so forth). Such information is of course crucial, since without it no assessment can be made of the ultimate use of the exported weapons. A few analysed countries provide some information of this kind. France, for example, distinguishes recipients according to branches of the armed forces (navy, army, air force). The Netherlands produces information on end-users of surplus defence equipment sold and on intended end-users of rejected transfer applications under the EU Code of Conduct (Netherlands, 2004, Appendices 4 and 5).

A few countries offer very *comprehensive* data, meaning that the reporting covers government-sourced as well as industry-sourced transactions, exports of civilian as well as military small arms and light weapons, information on parts, and summaries of export laws and regulations as well as international commitments. However, many states are less transparent on their own (government-to-government) transactions than on industry-negotiated deals. A common problem with national arms export reports is that they do not explicitly specify the types of arms and transactions covered, which makes it impossible to assess the comprehensiveness of the reports.

Information on *granted and denied licences* (values/quantities by weapon type and by country and weapon type) is much less common than information on values or quantities of actual deliveries of small arms and light weapons. At times, information on granted and denied licences is limited to the *number* of licenses, and does not include the numbers or value of weapons associated with these licenses (according to weapons type). Information on numbers of licences granted or denied is not awarded any points in the Barometer, as it says little about scale of the proposed transaction. Few countries provide any information on denied licences. Denial information is useful when examining how states apply their arms export laws, in particular if reasons for denials are given. However, it must be remembered that in those countries where industry and export licensing authorities are in constant communication, there are often fewer formal denials (and more 'pre-denials') as industry is well informed about the authorities' views on particular export destinations.[17] Hence, in the Barometer denials are weighted less than granted licences and deliveries.

Many countries offer information on values of *deliveries,* disaggregated both by weapon type and by country and weapon type, thanks to their reporting to UN Comtrade. However, information—in particular complete information— on *numbers* of weapons delivered is much scarcer, as such information is mostly lacking from both UN Comtrade and most national arms export reports. Needless to say, data on quantities of small arms and ammunition shipped is of more use than values, as it is more concrete and simpler to analyse.

It is often impossible to compare a country's granted licences with its actual deliveries, as the format, scope, and underlying definitions of the data are different. So even for many of those countries that provide information on both licences and deliveries, it is next to impossible to see how licences have translated into actual deliveries. Here, too, much still needs to be done to improve transparency.

All this means that no country comes close to full transparency in its small arms trade, and that the states at the top of the Barometer are still quite far from optimally transparent.[18] At the same time, the Barometer shows that no criterion is impossible to fulfil: none of the columns of the barometer is entirely blank. It is thus possible to achieve very high levels of transparency in the small arms trade.

Timeliness of the data provided is not dealt with directly in the Barometer at present. It is worth stressing that there are vast differences in how quickly reporting is made public, both between countries and from one year to the next. Some countries, such as the United Kingdom, now provide arms export data on a quarterly basis (United Kingdom, 2005). France, in contrast, made its arms export report for 2002–03 public only in early 2005.

The Barometer shows on the one hand that no state today comes close to full transparency, and on the other that such transparency is possible.

Table 4.3   Small Arms Trade Transparency Barometer, covering major exporters, based on latest arms export report made publicly available and/or on 2002 customs data from UN Comtrade

Country and source(s) available (E = export report with year of reporting, C = customs data)	Total points (20 points max)	Access (2 points max)	Clarity (4 points max)	Comprehensive- ness (4 points max)	Information on deliveries (4 points max)	Information on licences granted (4 points max)	Information on licences refused (2 points max)
Austria C	6.5	1.5	2	1	2	0	0
Belgium[19] C	6.5	1.5	2	1	2	0	0
Brazil C	7.5	1.5	2	2	2	0	0
Canada[20] E (02) C	12	2	3	3	4	0	0
China[21] C	8.5	1.5	2	1	4	0	0
Czech Republic E (03) C	12.5	2	2.5	3	3	2	0
Finland E (03) C	11	2	2.5	2.5	2	2	0
France[22] E (02-03) C	12.5	2	3.5	3	4	0	0
Germany[23] E (03) C	15.5	2	3	4	2	4	0.5
Israel C	0	0	0	0	0	0	0
Italy E (03) C	12.5	2	3	2.5	3	2	0
Japan C	7.5	1.5	2	2	2	0	0
Netherlands[24] E (03) C	13	2	2.5	3.5	4	1	0
Norway E (03) C	10.5	2	2.5	4	2	0	0
Portugal E (02) C	8	2	2	2	2	0	0
Romania E (02)	5	1.5	1.5	1	1	0	0
Russian Federation C	6.5	1.5	2	1	2	0	0
South Africa E (02)	5	2	1	0	2	0	0
South Korea C	7.5	1.5	2	2	2	0	0
Spain[25] E (03) C	11.5	2	3	3	2.5	1	0
Sweden E (03) C	10.5	2	2	4	2	0.5	0
Switzerland E (04) C	9	2	2.5	2	2	0	0.5
Turkey C	7.5	1.5	2	2	2	0	0
United Kingdom[26] E (03) C	15	2	3	4	4	2	0
United States[27] E (03) C	16	2	3	3	4	4	0

Sources: UN Comtrade DESA/UNSD, download date: 16 March 2005. Customs reporting tabulations from NISAT (2005); Canada (2004); Czech Republic (2004); Finland (2004); France (2005); Germany (2004); Italy (2004); Netherlands (2004); Norway (2004); Portugal (2003); Romania (2004), South Africa (2003); Spain (2004); Sweden (2004); Switzerland (2005); UK (2004); US (2004).

Scoring system
(a) Access *(2 points total):* Information is: available on Internet (half point); available in a UN language (1 point); free of charge (half point);
(b) Clarity *(4 points total):* The reporting includes source information (1 point); small arms and light weapons distinguishable from other types of weapons (1 point); small arms and light weapons ammunition distinguishable from other types of ammunition (1 point); reporting includes information on types of end-users (military, police, other security forces, civilians, civilian retailers) (1 point).
(c) Comprehensiveness *(4 points total):* The reporting covers: government-sourced as well as industry-sourced transactions (1 point); civilian as well as military small arms and light weapons (1 point); information on small arms and light weapons parts (1 point); summaries of export laws and regulations as well as international commitments (1 point).
(d) Information on deliveries *(4 points total):* Data disaggregated by weapons type (value of weapons shipped (1 point), quantity of weapons shipped (1 point)), and by country and weapons type [value of weapons shipped 1 point, quantity of weapons shipped 1 point].
(e) Information on licences granted *(4 points total):* Data disaggregated by weapons type (value of weapons licensed (1 point), quantity of weapons licensed (1 point)), and by country and weapons type [value of weapons licensed 1 point, quantity of weapons licensed 1 point].
(f) Information on licences refused *(2 points total):* Data disaggregated by weapons type [value of licence refused 0.5 points, quantity of weapons under refused licence 0.5 points], and by country and weapons type [value of licence refused 0.5 points, quantity of weapons under refused licence 0.5 points].

NB1: Half the score is granted for a partly fulfilled criterion.
NB2: Under (d), (e), and (f), no points are granted for number of deliveries or number of licences granted or denied, as such figures give little information about the magnitude of the trade.
NB3: Under (d), (e), and (f): 'weapons type' means broader weapons categories (that is, 'small arms' as opposed to 'armoured vehicles' or 'air-to-air mis-siles'), not specific small arms and light weapons types ('assault rifles' as opposed to 'hunting rifles'). The data is disaggregated by weapons type if the share of arms exports of different categories of weapons (small arms and light weapons as opposed to military aircraft, missiles, electronics, and so on) is delineated. The data is disaggregated both by country and by weapon type if the report includes numbers on the quantity or value of weapons of each category transferred to individual recipients (such as, in 2003, X amount of small arms was delivered to country Y).
NB4: The fact that the Barometer is based on two sources—customs data (as reported to UN Comtrade) and national arms export reports—works to the advantage of states that publish data in both forms, since what they do not provide in one form of reporting they might provide in the other. Points achieved from each source of the two sources are added up. However, points are obviously not counted twice (for example, if a country provides both customs data and export reports in a UN language, it gets 1 point for this under access, not more).
NB5: The scores of the 2004 and 2005 Barometers are not directly comparable, due to differences in the application of criteria between the two years.

The Small Arms Trade Transparency Barometer evaluates reporting, but cannot independently verify the veracity of the information given. That is to say, the Barometer assesses the quantity and level of detail of the data made public, but not its accuracy. In 2004, the US Government Accountability Office (GAO) found problems of accuracy with the main US arms export report, the so-called 655 Report. This report claimed that the State Department had approved licenses for the commercial export of Stinger missiles in five instances during fiscal years 2000 and 2002, although US government policy precluded this. It became clear that the reports were incorrect, and they had to be amended. This led GAO to inspect more closely the reliability of the 655 Report. It found 'data reliability problems that raise additional questions about the accuracy and reliability of data in [the report]' (GAO, 2005, p. 2). For example, it is possible to enter only one commodity and one country code into the licensing database (which is the source for 655 Report entries) per license application, regardless of how many commodities and countries appear on an application. As a result, the 655 Report omits the additional commodities or countries listed on some licence applications (GAO, 2005, p. 5). These types of accuracy problems may not be unique to the US. France follows a similar practice: contracts covering matériel from several categories is attributed to the category that is 'the most representative of the contents of the contract' (France 2005, p. 58, our translation). To unearth problems such as these, however, requires access and resources that are usually beyond researchers' means. In contrast, problems of inconsistencies between national export reports and customs data from UN Comtrade are more easily revealed, and are discussed in detail in this chapter's section on small arms exports.

Equally important, because the Barometer focuses on small arms in particular, it cannot be used as a general measure of conventional arms export transparency. Moreover, given that the Barometer includes only those countries that are major exporters of small arms and light weapons (see Table 4.1), it excludes some rather transparent countries. This also necessarily means that the focus is mainly (although not uniquely) on states in Europe and North America, which is where the major exporting countries are found.

The Barometer shows that the most transparent among the major exporting countries are states that publish export reports and report on their customs data to UN Comtrade. At the top of the list are the United States, Germany, and the United Kingdom. At the bottom is Israel, whose transparency has decreased since the 2004 Barometer.

UNDERSTANDING THE INTERNATIONAL ILLICIT TRADE IN SMALL ARMS: FIRST STEPS IN EUROPE

Stemming the international illicit trade[28] in small arms and light weapons is at the heart of the efforts to curb small arms proliferation, at both the international and the regional levels. A first step in systematically assessing the international illicit trade is to examine seizures of illicit small arms crossing national borders. This is one of the few means available to gather internationally comparable data. Border seizures should help elucidate a share of the cross-border black-market transactions.[29] During 2004, the Small Arms Survey thus asked approximately 35 countries considered representative of their respective regions or sub-regions for information on customs seizures of small arms and light weapons. Eight provided information on numbers and types of weapons seized in the five-year period from 1999 to 2003. All countries reporting were from Europe, except for Australia, Canada, and Chile. The following analysis therefore has a mainly European focus, and is necessarily tentative in its conclusions even about that region. It is intended in future years to increase the number of states covered, conditional on state transparency in this respect.

Moreover, the discussion in coming years will be broadened to include police seizures. If we are interested in *international* trafficking it is logical to start with customs seizures; but customs seizures alone give a misleadingly small picture of the illicit trade. A fuller picture of the scope of trafficking (including its international ramifications) would have to include police seizures, which are generally much greater than customs seizures. An (albeit extreme) illustration of the ratio of police to customs seizures is the share of border seizures to total police seizures in Kosovo from mid-2000 to the end of 2002: only 0.8 per cent of small arms seizures by the United Nations Interim Administration Mission in Kosovo (UNMIK) took place along the borders (Khakee and Florquin, 2003, p. 65). Another illustration comes from Bulgaria where, during January 2002–August 2003, customs seized a total of 107 small arms, while the police, during one year (2001), seized 604 small arms (Center for the Study of Democracy/Saferworld, 2004, p. 46). Data on police seizures is also patchy, however. It is important to stress that, while customs and police seizures together should cover the black market fairly well, neither of them captures state-sponsored grey-market transactions. In future such grey-market deals will probably have to be examined on a case-by-case basis.

Officials and police display weapons confiscated in Giessen, Germany.

Table 4.4 suggests that border seizures of small arms were rather low overall in our sample in 1999–2003. The reasons might differ from one state to the next. Swedish customs notes that '[t]here is no information indicating that Sweden is subject to large-scale smuggling of [small arms and light weapons]';[30] the problem of illicit trade in Sweden is of a different nature 'since there is reason to believe that weapons that have been legally imported to Sweden end up in the illegal market'. This might well be true of other countries which, like Sweden, have recorded low numbers of customs seizures. However, such low rates of seizures may in some states reflect the quality of border control. For example, the authorities of Bosnia and Herzegovina have seized few weapons along their borders in recent years. According to a UNDP-sponsored report, this does not mean that levels of trafficking are low; rather, it 'shows the insufficiency of control and confiscation' of small arms and light weapons in particular of the State Border Service (SBS) of Bosnia and Herzegovina (Paes, Risser, and Pietz, 2004, p. 31).

Table 4.4 also shows wide variations in numbers of small arms seized at border posts in Australia, Canada, and the European countries examined. Canada has had the highest absolute and per capita numbers of weapons seized:

in fact, Canada seems to be an exception within this sample of countries. The reason is that a large number of seizures 'were from US travellers carrying firearms purportedly for personal protection' (Canada Border Services Agency, 2004a, p.1). Over 80 per cent of guns were seized at highway border crossings (Canada Border Services Agency, 2004a, p.1)

Table 4.4 **Reported small arms trafficking (total numbers of weapons seized by customs), respondent European and other industrialized states**

Country	1999	2000	2001	2002	2003	Total	Main origin/destination
Australia	n/a	347	622	165	121	1,255 (4 years)	Anecdotal information suggests that the most common country of origin is the US.
Canada	1,336	1,170	1,136	796	1221	5,659	The US is main country of origin, in particular secondary US markets (gun shows, flea markets, private sales).
Germany*	218	117	121	58	63	577	Switzerland is main country of origin, followed by France.
Poland	8	251	44	25	15	346	Slovakia (country of origin of more than 70 per cent of seized guns), Ukraine (country of origin of approximately 8 per cent of guns).
Romania	17	4	14	4	5	44	n/a
Sweden	29	20	22	33	14	118	Increase in weapons from Balkans and, to a lesser extent, the former Soviet Union, especially the Baltic countries.
United Kingdom**	240	641	261	637	280	2,059	n/a
Total						10,059	

Note: Figures cover small arms and light weapons without their ammunition.

*For Germany, only border seizures have been included (German customs can act on a larger part of the national territory than the customs authorities of many other states).

**The UK financial year runs from 1 April to 31 March. Thus, the 1999 entry pertains to information from 1 April 1999 to 31 March 2000.

Sources: **Australia,** correspondence with Bill Ross, Director Assessments and Analysis, Risk Identification and Intelligence Branch, Australian Customs Service; **Canada,** Canada Border Services Agency (2004b); **Germany,** correspondence with Marcel de la Haye, German Ministry of Foreign Affairs, Department for Disarmament and Arms Control, 19 October 2004; **Poland,** correspondence with Robert Kupiecki, Director, Department of Security Policy, Ministry of Foreign Affairs, Poland, 6 August; **Romania,** Correspondence with Radu Horumb, Director, Office for Non-proliferation, Ministry of Foreign Affairs, 22 September 2004; **Sweden** Correspondence with Mats Barregren, Special Advisor, Head Office of Swedish Customs, 28 September 2004; **United Kingdom,** correspondence with Barbara Bernard, Restrictions and Sanctions Team, HM Customs & Excise, 28 June and 19 July 2004.

Trafficked small arms sometimes have surprising origins. Swedish reports of increases in illicit gun trade from the Balkans, and to a lesser extent the former Soviet Union, are in line with commonly held assumptions. That the United States is the main source of non-commercial attempted illegal imports of guns seized by the Australian customs (predominantly shipped in postal parcels) during 1999–2003 is perhaps less expected, especially as Australia is much closer geographically to trafficking hubs in South-east Asia. Likewise, although Poland extensively upgraded its borders with the Russian Federation (Kaliningrad), Belarus, and Ukraine before it became a member of the European Union (EU) in 2004 (Poland Ministry of the Interior and Administration, 2000), most of the small arms that Polish customs seized came from a fellow EU applicant, Slovakia. In 1999–2003, Germany seized more guns on its borders with France and Switzerland than on its better-controlled frontiers with the Czech Republic and Poland.[31]

This is probably because customs cooperation is more developed between countries such as Poland and Slovakia, and between Germany, France, and Switzerland, than between those countries and their eastern neighbours (Busch 1998).

Trafficking of handguns has been more prevalent than that of other types of small arms. A comparison between Tables 4.4 and 4.5 shows that, overall, approximately 60 per cent of all reported seizures of firearms were handguns, ranging from approximately 45 per cent in Australia and Germany to almost 80 per cent in Romania.

Table 4.5   Reported international handgun trafficking (numbers of handguns seized by customs), respondent European and Anglo-Saxon industrialized states

Country	1999	2000	2001	2002	2003	Total
Australia	n/a	170	232	97	55	554
Canada	1,025	874	826	590	454	3,769
Germany	73	85	37	30	31	256
Poland	1	195	17	4	5	225
Romania	15	4	9	3	4	35
Sweden	22	10	20	21	6	79
United Kingdom*	83	417	167	305	127	1,099
Total:						6,017

Note: Figures do not include air or gas pistols.

* The UK financial year runs from 1 April to 31 March. Thus, the 1999 entry pertains to information from 1 April 1999 to 31 March 2000.

Sources: **Australia,** correspondence with Bill Ross, Director Assessments and Analysis, Risk Identification and Intelligence Branch, Australian Customs Service; **Canada,** Canada Border Services Agency (2004b); **Germany,** correspondence with Marcel de la Haye, German Ministry of Foreign Affairs, Department for Disarmament and Arms Control, 19 October 2004; **Poland,** correspondence with Robert Kupiecki, Director, Department of Security Policy, Ministry of Foreign Affairs, Poland, 6 August; **Romania,** Correspondence with Radu Horumba, Director, Office for Non-proliferation, Ministry of Foreign Affairs, 22 September 2004; **Sweden** Correspondence with Mats Barregren, Special Advisor, Head Office of Swedish Customs, 28 September 2004; **United Kingdom,** correspondence with Barbara Bernard, Restrictions and Sanctions Team, HM Customs & Excise, 28 June and 19 July 2004.

According to our limited sample, cross-border trafficking has mostly involved small quantities, often only one gun per seizure. This could be because the international illicit trade in small arms to European countries mostly services criminals' demand for guns, and they smuggle the guns over the borders themselves. It also suggests that the profits from trafficking small arms are low. Swedish customs notes that 'Almost all seizures have been made on one person, linked to a criminal or to a criminal organization, carrying one or two weapons. During the last five years 118 weapons have been seized on 96 occasions, which gives an average of 1.2 weapon per occasion.'[32] The Canadian customs figures show a large number of small seizures and a very small number of large ones; the Canadian authorities note that, 'quantity seizures of firearms (i.e. three or more pieces) are uncommon' (Canada Border Services Agency, 2004a, p. 1). Here, the link to other types of criminal activities is weaker, as Americans who are unaware of Canadian laws carry many of the guns over the border. Over the five-year period covered, only one large seizure was reported, of 497 semi-automatic carbines smuggled from the Russian Federation in a maritime container and seized at the Port of Montreal (Canada Border Services Agency, 2004a, p. 2). A detailed study comes to a similar conclusion about the Netherlands (Spapens and Bruinsma, 2004, ch. 6). The data thus offers a first, imperfect indication of the relative importance of small-scale trafficking into Europe, Australia, and Canada.

CONCLUSION

This chapter attempts to reach an accurate picture of recent trends in the trade in small arms and light weapons, including ammunition and parts. From 2001 to 2002 (the latest year for which data is available), that trade was relatively stable, in terms of both values exported and trading patterns. The major importers and exporters were, with few variations, the same in 2002 as in 2001. There were some fluctuations among major importers, presumably as some countries finalized major procurements and others started procuring small arms and light weapons for their military and police forces. The tables of major exporters and importers show that Western countries often trade between themselves, but also that there are notable exceptions to this pattern. Non-Western exporters often export to a variety of recipient states. The tables also indicate the importance of small arms ammunition transfers in the overall small arms and light weapons trade.

The chapter provides an update of the Small Arms Trade Transparency Barometer. The Barometer is based on information made publicly available by exporting states in the form of national arms export reports and customs data (as reported to UN Comtrade). Generally, improved transparency on small arms exports is essential for a better understanding of the small arms trade. A fundamental requirement is that state reporting clearly singles out small arms and light weapons, as well as their ammunition and parts, from other types of weapons. Moreover, increased transparency is needed in respect of end-users and government-to-government transactions. Reporting could also be timelier.

Lastly, the chapter sets out to examine more systematically certain segments of the illicit trade in small arms. This first attempt at a more systematic analysis focuses on customs seizures, and in view of the limited data available is geographically concentrated on Europe and a few other countries. Although some preliminary conclusions can be drawn—for example, about the importance of the small-scale illicit trade and trafficking in handguns across borders—the main finding is that states have very little publicly available information on customs seizures of illicit small arms. This is all the more surprising given that international illicit trafficking is at the heart of intergovernmental efforts to tackle the small arms problem.

LIST OF ABBREVIATIONS

CAD	Canadian dollar
CHF	Swiss franc
DDA	United Nations Department for Disarmament Affairs
EU	European Union
EUR	Euro
GAO	US Government Accountability Office
HS	Harmonized system
LDCs	Least developed countries
ML	Munitions List of the Wassenaar Arrangement
NISAT	Norwegian Initiative on Small Arms Transfers
NOK	Norwegian krone
RPG	Rocket-propelled grenade launcher
SAR	Special Administrative Region
SBS	State Border Service (Bosnia and Herzegovina)
SEK	Swedish krona
UNCTAD	United Nations Conference on Trade and Development
UNMIK	United Nations Interim Administration Mission in Kosovo
USD	United States dollar
WTO	World Trade Organisation
ZAR	South African rand

ENDNOTES

[1] In this chapter, 'trade' refers to international trade, that is, imports and exports, as opposed to intra-state (domestic) transfers.

[2] Weapon parts are at the heart of a growing controversy in which some experts claim that control over them is less rigorous than over finished weapons (see for example Control Arms, 2004).

[3] Light weapons ammunition is reported in customs data in a category which also comprises ammunition for large conventional weapons.

[4] For more details on calculation methods, see Marsh (forthcoming).

[5] Customs unions, such as those between Lichtenstein and Switzerland and between Monaco and France, report jointly to UN Comtrade. In contrast, a handful of individual states are divided into several customs territories that report separately, mostly because of the legacy of colonialism (for example, China-Macao Special Administrative Region (SAR) and China-Hong Kong SAR). However, these are exceptions, and hence hardly affect our understanding of the global small arms trade.

[6] For the exact codes used, see the notes to Tables 4.1 and 4.2.

[7] Hence our assumption that the trade in military small arms and light weapons is underestimated.

[8] For further details, see Marsh (forthcoming).

[9] The annexe can be accessed on the Small Arms Survey Web site, at <http://www.smallarmssurvey.org/Yearbook%202004/04%20Transfers%20Annexes%20(Web).pdf>

[10] These are: ML2 (guns, howitzers, cannons, mortars, anti-tank weapons, projectile launchers, military flame-throwers, recoilless rifles, and so forth, of a caliber larger than 12.7mm); ML3 (ammunition for ML1, ML2, and ML12—ML 12 comprising high-velocity kinetic energy weapon systems and related equipment), and ML 4 (bombs, torpedoes, rockets, grenades, missiles, and so forth). As none of these categories provides for caliber upper limits, they mix small arms and light weapons with larger weapons and ammunition (for further details, see Wassenaar Arrangement, 2004).

[11] See also Small Arms Survey (2004, p. 101) for other possible explanations for divergences in reporting.

[12] In 2002, Brazil reported a total of USD 117.6m in arms exports to Malaysia. The anomalous size of these reported transactions, along with corroborating press reports of a sale of an advanced missile system to the Malaysian government, suggest that many of these exports were not small arms. Consequently, we have not included them in our calculations. Brazil may record its firearm exports in a somewhat unorthodox way, filing its pistols and revolvers exports under the customs category 'other sporting, hunting or target shooting rifles'. If this is correct, as some preliminary research by Dreyfus and Lessing (2003) seems to suggest, the above figures overestimate the actual trade.

[13] An illustration of the difficulty in interpreting customs data is the report by Norway of shipments of weapons to Israel of a value of over NOK 6m (USD 0.8m) in 2002 (which, if correct, would have made Norway one of the top five reported exporters to that country). This report created a predictable stir in Norway, a country that has been closely involved in the Middle East peace process. In the end, it became clear that the figure referred to weapons that Norway had returned to Israel after they had been used in training exercises in Norway (Hoffmann, 2003). In a similar case, the Austrian Ministry of Foreign Affairs in 2002 issued a licence for the temporary export of parts, which after 'outward processing' were all reimported into Austria (correspondence with Andrea Ikic-Böhm, Head of export control unit, 11 January 2005)

[14] Holdings and procurement are referred to in the UN Register reporting as 'Background information'.

[15] Arabic, Chinese, English, French, Russian, or Spanish.

[16] However, some states, such as Italy and Portugal, obtain this maximum score because they provide customs data to UN Comtrade, which is in English: their national arms exports reports are available only in Italian and Portuguese, respectively.

[17] The role of denials in interpreting the application of strategic export laws should not be overstated. As noted by Björn Hagelin of SIPRI (to whom I am indebted for pointing this out), in most states arms deliveries are still officially regarded as exceptions to the general rule (which is to ban exports of defence products), and hence need government licenses. Rather than reporting on denials, which, in principle, is the 'normal' decision, governments should report, in each individual case, on the reasons why a delivery has been accepted.

[18] For a critique of the UK export report, see Isbister and Kirkham (2005). A similar critique of the German report is published yearly by the Gemeinsame Konferenz Kirche und Entwicklung (GKKE, Joint Conference Church and Development).

[19] Belgium has not published any national arms export report since 2002, because export control was regionalized in September 2003 (for details, see Wallonia, 2004, pp.3-12). This means that each Belgian region in principle reports separately on its arms exports. Reporting periods, statistics provided, etc. varied for the first quarterly reports of Wallonia and Flanders (since then, only Flanders has published additional information). Moreover, Brussels, the third region, has not so far published any export report. On the basis of these diverging reporting practices, it is impossible to evaluate Belgian transparency. The score is therefore based on customs data submissions only.

[20] Canada receives a full score on deliveries, as it is among the few countries that provide information on numbers of small arms transferred to UN Comtrade.

[21] China receives a full score on deliveries, as it is among the few countries that provide information on numbers of small arms transferred to UN Comtrade. This makes the Chinese total score larger than would otherwise be warranted.

[22] France obtains a full 4 points on deliveries, although it should be stressed that deliveries of quantities (as opposed to values) are provided for a four-year period, rather than yearly (France, 2005, p. 67). France gives details of orders ['prises de commande'], which are defined as 'contracts signed and entered into force through a first down-payment' (France, 2005, p. 54, our translation). Orders are not equivalent to licences, and therefore, no points are given in the columns pertaining to licences granted and denied.

[23] Germany provides more detailed information on licences granted and denied for main trading partners and so-called 'third countries', i.e. countries outside the circle of EU, NATO, and NATO-equivalent countries (Australia, Japan, New Zealand, and Switzerland). It has been awarded full points on the relevant criteria nevertheless.

[24] The Netherlands provides unusual—and useful—information on denials, including, as noted in the text, regarding intended end-user. However, it does not provide information regarding the numbers or value of weapons associated with these denied licences, and therefore gets a zero score on licences refused (it does get points for its information on end-users in the 'clarity' section). The Netherlands receives a full score on deliveries, as it is among the few countries that provide information on numbers of small arms transferred to UN Comtrade.

[25] Spain makes public its report on small arms and light weapons exports to the OSCE as an annex to its arms export report. The report contains information both on licences granted (volumes by country and weapon type) and actual deliveries (also volumes by country and weapon type). It covers only the OSCE states, and thus a very limited number of transactions. It is therefore granted only part of the points on licences and deliveries. Other states make their OSCE reports public, but separately from the arms export reports. These are not taken into account in the Barometer.

[26] The United Kingdom provides numbers of small arms licensed for export per country, but not for all types of licences. It has been awarded 2 points on granted licences nevertheless.

[27] The US receives a full score on deliveries, as it is among the few countries that provide information on numbers of small arms transferred to UN Comtrade.

[28] In this chapter, the terms 'illegal' or 'illicit' trade, 'trafficking', and 'smuggling' are used interchangeably.

[29] Black-market transactions are defined as transactions made without official government consent or control. Presumably, such transactions as a rule run the risk of being intercepted by customs authorities. In contrast, customs authorities will not normally be able to disrupt illicit grey-market transfers, whereby governments or their agents transfer weapons by exploiting loopholes or circumvent national or international laws and regulations.

[30] Correspondence with Mats Barregren, Special Advisor, Head Office of Swedish Customs, 28 September 2004.

[31] On the issue of German border control density, see Andreas (2000, p. 118).

[32] Correspondence with Mats Barregren, Special Advisor, Head Office of Swedish Customs, 28 September 2004.

BIBLIOGRAPHY

Andreas, Peter. 2000. *Border Games: Policing the US-Mexico Divide*. Ithaca and London: Cornell University

Australia. Department of Defence. 2003. *Annual Report: Exports of Defence and Strategic Goods from Australia 2001/2002*. Canberra: Defence Trade Control and Compliance, Industry Division. February. Accessed in March 2005.
<http://www.smallarmssurvey.org/resources/Export%20Reports/Australia2001-2002.pdf>

Belgium. 2003. *Rapport du Gouvernement au Parlement sur l'application de la loi du 5 août 1991 relative à l'importation, à l'exportation et au transit d'armes, de munitions et de matériel devant servir spécialement à un usage militaire, et de la technologie y afférente. Du 1er janvier au 31 décembre 2002*. Brussels. July.

Busch, Heiner. 1998. 'Anschluß ans Europa der Polizeien: Die Schweiz und Schengen.' *Bürgerrechte & Polizei/CILIP* 59 (1/98). Accessed in March 2005. <http://www.cilip.de/ausgabe/59/anschlus.htm>

Canada. 2004. *Exports of Military Goods from Canada: Annual Report 2002*. Ottawa: Department of Foreign Affairs and International Trade/Export Controls Division of the Export and Import Controls Bureau. December. Accessed in March 2005.
<http://www.dfait-maeci.gc.ca/trade/eicb/military/miliexport02-en.asp>

Canada Border Services Agency. 2004a. 'Firearms' Obtained through correspondence with Michael Crichton, Manager, Intelligence Analysis Section, Customs Contraband, Intelligence and Investigations, Canada. 10 August 2004.

—. 2004b. Selected Commodities Seizure Reports from the *Integrated Customs Enforcement System*. Obtained through correspondence with Michael Crichton, Manager, Intelligence Analysis Section, Customs Contraband, Intelligence and Investigations, Canada. 10 August 2004.

CAST (Center for Analysis of Strategies and Technologies). 2003. *Russia's Exports of SALW*. Background paper. Geneva: Small Arms Survey.

Center for the Study of Democracy/Saferworld. 2004. *Weapons Under Scrutiny: Implementing Arms Export Controls and Combating Small Arms Proliferation in Bulgaria*. Sofia: Center for the Study of Democracy/Saferworld. Accessed in March 2005.
<http://www.csd.bg/fileSrc.php?id=405>

Czech Republic. 2004. *Export Controls in the Czech Republic in 2003: Controls of Transfers of Military Equipment, Production, Export and Import of Small Arms and Light Weapons*. Prague: Ministry of Foreign Affairs.

Control Arms. 2004. *Lock Stock and Barrel: How British Arms Components Add up to Deadly Weapons*. London: Amnesty International, IANSA, and Oxfam. February. Accessed in March 2005. <http://www.controlarms.org/documents/lock_stock_barrel.pdf >

Dreyfus, Pablo and Bejamin Lessing. 2003. 'Production and Exports of Small Arms and Light Weapons and Ammunition in South America and Mexico.' Background paper (unpublished). Geneva: Small Arms Survey.

Finland. 2003. *Annual Report According to the EU Code of Conduct on Arms Exports: National Report of Finland for 2002*. Helsinki: Ministry of Defence.

—. 2004. *Annual Report According to the EU Code of Conduct on Arms Exports: National Report of Finland for 2003*. Helsinki: Ministry of Defence.

France. 2005. *Rapport au Parlement sur les exportations d'armement de la France en 2002 et 2003*. Paris: Ministry of Defence. Accessed in March 2005. <http://www.defense.gouv.fr/sites/defense/actualites_et_dossiers/rapport_sur_les_exportations_darmement_en_2002_et_2003>

GAO (Government Accountability Office). 2005. 'State Department Needs to Resolve Data Reliability Problems that Led to Inaccurate Reporting to Congress on Foreign Arms Sales.' Washington, DC: GAO. 28 January. Accessed in March 2005.
<http://www.gao.gov/new.items/d05156r.pdf>

Germany. 2004. *Bericht der Bundesregierung über ihre Exportpolitik für konventionelle Rüstungsgüter im Jahre 2003 (Rüstungs-exportbericht 2003)*. Berlin: Bundestag. December

The Hindu (Madras). 2004. 'Home Ministry Rebuts Charges in AK-47 Purchase.' 4 April.

Hoffmann, Kristin. 2003. 'Sendte våpen til Israel etter øvelse i Norge.' *Nationen* (Oslo). 21 June. Accessed in January 2005.
<http://www.nationen.no/incoming/article696286.ece>

India Express Bureau. 2004. 'Cong Accuses Home Ministry of Importing "Inferior" AK-47 Rifles.' 4 April. Accessed in March 2005.
<http://www.indiaexpress.com/news/national/20040404-1.html>

India News Online. 2004. 'Controversy over Indian Rifles for Nepal.' 2 August. Accessed in March 2005.
<http://news.indiamart.com/news-analysis/controversy-over-ind-6919.html>

Isbister, Roy and Elizabeth Kirkham. 2005. *An Independent Audit of the UK Government Reports on Strategic Export Controls for 2003 and the First Half of 2004*. London: Saferworld. January. Accessed in March 2005.
<http://www.saferworld.co.uk/publications/Audit%202003and4/1%20Audit%20Prelims.pdf>

Italy. 2004. *Relazione sulle operazioni autorizzate e svolte per il controllo dell'esportazione, importazione e transito dei materiali di armamento nonche´ dell'esportazione e del transito dei prodotti ad alta tecnologia (anno 2003)*. Rome: Camera dei deputati.

ITC (International Trade Centre). 2003a. *Reliability of Trade Statistics: Indicators of Consistency between Trade Figures Reported by Countries and their Corresponding Mirror Estimates, Explanatory Notes, 2001 Data*. Geneva: UNCTAD/WTO/International Trade Centre Market Analysis Section. Accessed in March 2005. <http://www.intracen.org/countries/structural03/reliability.pdf>

—. 2003b. 'International Merchandise Trade Statistics National Compilation and Reporting Practices.' Geneva: UNCTAD/WTO. Accessed in March 2005. <http://unstats.un.org/unsd/comtrade/mr/rfReportersList.aspx> go to 'Trade Compilation'.

—. n.d. 'Technical notes on trade data.' Geneva: UNCTAD/WTO. Accessed in March 2005.
<http://www.intracen.org/countries/metadata00/technote.htm>

Khakee, Anna and Nicolas Florquin. 2003. *Kosovo and the Gun: A Baseline Assessment of Small Arms and Light Weapons in Kosovo*. Small Arms Survey Special Report. Geneva: Small Arms Survey and UNDP. June. Accessed March 2005.
<http://www.smallarmssurvey.org/SReports/Special%20Report%20Kosovo.pdf>

Marsh, Nicolas. forthcoming. 'Agglomerating Comtrade Customs Data' NISAT Background paper. Oslo: NISAT

Nicholson, Alex. 2004. 'Cheap Imports Outgun Kalashnikov Sales.' Associated Press. 28 July.

NISAT (Norwegian Initiative on Small Arms Transfers). 2005. *Calculations from the NISAT Database on Authorized Small Arms Transfers*. Background paper. Geneva: Small Arms Survey.

Netherlands. 2004. *The Netherlands Arms Export Policy in 2003*. The Hague: Ministry of Economic Affairs and Ministry of Foreign Affairs.
<http://www.antenna.nl/amokmar/pdf/ArmsExports2003.pdf>

Norway. 2003. *Eksporten av forsvarsmateriell i 2002*. Oslo: Ministry of Foreign Affairs. Accessed in March 2005.
<http://odin.dep.no/ud/norsk/publ/stmeld/032001-040026/index-hov006-b-n-a.html>

—. 2004. *Eksport av forsvarsmateriell fra Norge i 2003, eksportkontroll og internasjonalt ikke-spredningssamarbeid*. Oslo: Ministry of Foreign Affairs.

Paes, Wolf-Christian, Hans Risser, and Tobias Pietz. 2004. *Small Arms and Light Weapons Survey (SAS) Bosnia and Herzegovina*. Bonn/Sarajevo: BICC/UNDP. <http://www.seesac.org/reports/SALW%20Survey%20BiH.pdf>

PakistaniDefence.com. 2004. 'US May Buy Small Arms from Pakistan to Support its Iraq and Afghan Operations.' 19 July. Accessed in March 2005. <http://www.pakistanidefence.com/news/MonthlyNewsArchive/2004/July2004.htm>

Poland. Ministry of the Interior and Administration. 2000. *Strategy of Integrated Border Management*. Warsaw: Department of European Integration and International Cooperation (Ministry of the Interior).

Portugal. 2004. Anuário Estatístico da Defesa Nacional–2002. Lisbon: Ministry of Defence. Accessed April 2005
<http://www.mdn.gov.pt/Publicacoes/anuario2002.htm>

Romania. 2004. *Raport Privind Controlul Exporturilor de arme in anul 2002*. Bucharest: National Agency for Export Control. Accessed in March 2005. <www.ancex.ro>

Singh Khadka, Navin. 2004. 'Indian Handshake: After Years of Decline, Indian Development Assistance to Nepal is Increasing Again.' *Nepali Times* (Kathmandu). 13–19 August. Accessed in March 2005. <http://www.nepalitimes.com/issue209/economy.htm>

Small Arms Survey. 2002. *Small Arms Survey 2002: Counting the Human Cost*. Oxford: Oxford University Press.

—. 2003. *Small Arms Survey 2003: Development Denied*. Oxford: Oxford University Press.

—. 2004. *Small Arms Survey 2004: Rights at Risk*. Oxford: Oxford University Press.

South Africa. 2003. *South African Export Statistics for Conventional Arms 2000-2002*. Pretoria: Directorate of Conventional Arms Control.
<http://www.mil.za/SecretaryforDefence/ConventionalArmsControl/NCACC2002/000102p.pdf>

Spain. Ministry of Industry, Tourism and Commerce. 2003. *Informe sobre las estadísticas españolas de exportación de material de defensa y de doble uso (2002)*. Madrid: Subdirección General de Comercio Exterior de Material de Defensa y de Doble Uso.

—. 2004. *Informe sobre las estadísticas españolas de exportación de material de defensa y de doble uso (2003)*. Madrid: Subdirección General de Comercio Exterior de Material de Defensa y de Doble Uso.

Spapens, A.C. and M.Y. Bruinsma. 2004. *Illegale vuurwapens in Nederland: smokkel en handel*. Tilburg: IVA.

Sweden. 2003. *Report on Sweden's Export Control Policy and Exports of Military Equipment in 2002*. Stockholm: Ministry of Foreign Affairs. 13 March.

—. 2004. *Strategic Export Controls in 2003–Military Equipment and Dual-Use Goods*. Stockholm: Ministry of Foreign Affairs. March. Accessed in March 2005. <http://www.regeringen.se/content/1/c6/01/23/26/679300c4.pdf>

Switzerland. 2003. *Ausfuhr von Kriegsmaterial im Jahr 2002*. Berne: Staatssekretariat für Wirtschaft (SECO).

—. 2005. *Ausfuhr von Kriegsmaterial im Jahr 2004*. Berne: Staatssekretariat für Wirtschaft (SECO).

UN Comtrade. 2004. United Nations Commodity Trade Statistics database, Department of Economic and Social Affairs/Statistics Division. Accessed April 2005. <http://unstats.un.org/unsd/comtrade/>

UNGA (United Nations General Assembly). 2001. *Protocol against the Illicit Manufacturing of and Trafficking in Firearms, Their Parts and Components and Ammunition, supplementing the United Nations Convention against Transnational Organized Crime ('UN Firearms Protocol').* Adopted 31 May. Reproduced in UN document A/RES/55/255 of 8 June. Accessed April 2005. <http://www.undcp.org/pdf/crime/a_res_55/255e.pdf>

United Kingdom. 2004. *United Kingdom Strategic Export Controls Annual Report 2003.* London: Foreign and Commonwealth Office.

—. 2005. *Strategic Export Controls: Quarterly Report, July-September 2004.* London: Foreign and Commonwealth Office. Accessed in March 2005. <http://www.fco.gov.uk/Files/kfile/strategicexportcontrolsjulsep2004.pdf>

United States. 2004. *Fiscal Year 2003 "Section 655" Report.* Washington, DC: United States Department of State/United States Department of Defense.

Wallonia. 2004. 'Rapport au parlement wallon sur l'application de la loi du 05 août 1991, modifiée par les lois du 25 et du 26 mars 2003 relatives à l'importation, à l'exportation et au transit d'armes, de munitions et de materiel devant servir spécialement à un usage militaire, et de la technologie y afferente, du 1er septembre 2003 au 31 décembre 2003.'

Wassenaar Arrangement. 2004. Munitions List. <http://www.wassenaar.org/list/WA-LIST%20(04)%201%20ML.doc>

Wezeman, Siemon T. 2003. *The Future of the United Nations Register of Conventional Arms.* SIPRI Policy Paper No. 4. Stockholm: SIPRI. August. <http://editors.sipri.se/pubs/UNROCA.pdf>

ACKNOWLEDGEMENTS

Principal author
Anna Khakee

Other contributors
Nicolas Marsh, NISAT, Tamar Gabelnick, Elli Kytömäki, Stéphanie Pézard, and Ruxandra Stoicescu

Taliban soldiers with FIM-92 'Stinger' MANPADS encircle a hijacked Indian Airlines plane as negotiators discuss hijacker demands. Kandahar, Afghanistan, December 1999.
(© B.K. Bangash/AP Photo)

Locking onto Target:
LIGHT WEAPONS CONTROL MEASURES

5

INTRODUCTION

Throughout 2004, man-portable air defence systems (MANPADS) remained high on the list of international arms control priorities. The sustained threat MANPADS posed to civilian aircraft, coupled with their evident utility to insurgents in such places as Chechnya and Iraq, continued to drive multilateral efforts to bring them under stricter control—often under the rubric of the broader 'war on terror'.

MANPADS are a particular type of light weapon. While this chapter has something to say about light weapons as a whole, it focuses on international efforts to control the transfer of MANPADS. Among its major conclusions are the following:

- Small arms measures of a general nature tend to cover all or most light weapons.
- The Wassenaar Arrangement and the Organization for Security and Co-operation in Europe (OSCE) have led international efforts to curb MANPADS proliferation through the development of especially stringent control measures.
- The transfer control systems needed to support implementation of the Wassenaar–OSCE MANPADS principles are in place in key exporting states.
- These same systems can be used strictly to control the transfer of a broader range of small arms and light weapons.

This chapter begins with a review of international measures: first, those that apply to a broad range of small arms and light weapons, then those that specifically target the transfer of MANPADS. The last part of the chapter shifts the focus to the national level and enquires whether important exporting countries have in place the laws and regulations necessary for the effective implementation of the new MANPADS measures. As the normative framework needed to address the MANPADS problem takes shape at the international level, the key challenges increasingly reside at the national level—with the national implementation of the new international standards.

GENERAL SMALL ARMS INSTRUMENTS

International efforts to control small arms and light weapons often appear preoccupied with firearms—basically the 'small arms' side of the broader 'small arms and light weapons' classification. Yet, as this section demonstrates, existing small arms instruments of a general nature tend, by and large, to cover light weapons as well as small arms.

This section examines several important international instruments to see whether they cover light weapons—including ammunition for light weapons—as well as small arms. These instruments are all general in nature in the sense that they cover no specific type of small arm or light weapon, but rather apply to several categories of small arms and light weapons at once. This assessment is conducted with reference to the definition of 'small arms and light weapons' contained in the 1997 *Report of the Panel of Governmental Experts on Small Arms* (UNGA, 1997).

In the words of the 1997 UN Panel, 'Broadly speaking ... light weapons are those [weapons] designed for use by several persons serving as a crew' (para. 25).[1] They include:

- heavy machine-guns;
- hand-held under-barrel and mounted grenade launchers;
- portable anti-aircraft guns;
- portable anti-tank guns and recoilless rifles;
- portable launchers of anti-tank missile and rocket systems;
- portable launchers of anti-aircraft missile systems; and
- mortars of calibres of less than 100 mm (para. 26(b)).

The 1997 Panel also included light weapons-related ammunition and explosives in its definition:

- shells and missiles for light weapons;
- mobile containers with missiles or shells for single-action anti-aircraft and anti-tank systems; and
- anti-personnel and anti-tank hand grenades (para. 26(c)).

We will see that even those instruments that ostensibly focus on 'firearms', such as the *SADC Firearms Protocol* (SADC, 2001), apply to a much broader range of small arms and light weapons than their titles would suggest. This section is limited to determining the kinds of small arms and light weapons these general instruments cover. As, in most cases, the contents of these instruments have been analysed in previous editions of the *Survey*, this question is not addressed here.[2]

Regional instruments

Two instruments adopted by the Organization of American States (OAS)[3] in 1997–98 led international efforts to come to grips with the small arms problem. The first of these, the *Inter-American Convention against the Illicit Manufacturing of and Trafficking in Firearms, Ammunition, Explosives, and Other Related Materials,* covers the full range of small arms and light weapons, including their ammunition (OAS, 1997, art. I, paras. 3–4).

Even the so-called 'firearms instruments' tend to apply to a broad range of small arms and light weapons.

The same cannot be said, however, for the *Convention's* companion instrument, the *Model Regulations for the Control of the International Movement of Firearms, Their Parts and Components and Ammunition* (OAS, 1998). The definition the *Model Regulations* use for 'firearm' in paragraph 1.3 ('any barreled weapon which will ... expel a bullet or projectile by the action of an explosive') encompasses all small arms, but limits coverage of light weapons in two ways. First, the weapon must have a barrel. This excludes those 'light weapons', such as MANPADS, that meet the terms of the 1997 UN definition, but employ a tube or rail as opposed to a barrel.[4] Second, the weapon must 'expel' the projectile. This excludes those light weapons that use self-propelled projectiles, such as rockets or missiles. In these cases, the weapon does not 'expel' (drive out) the projectile as required by the definition. In essence, only those light weapons that use cartridge-based ammunition qualify as 'firearms' under the *Model Regulations* definition. These include: heavy machine-guns, hand-held under-barrel and mounted grenade launchers that fire spin-stabilized grenades, portable anti-aircraft guns, portable anti-tank guns, and mortars of calibres of less than 100 mm.

Table 5.1   General small arms instruments: substantive scope

Regional instruments	Weapons / ammunition coverage		
	small arms	light weapons	ammunition
OAS Convention (OAS, 1997)	All small arms	All light weapons	For all small arms and light weapons
OAS Model Regulations (OAS, 1998)	All small arms	Light weapons that use cartridge-based ammunition	For all small arms; for light weapons that use cartridge-based ammunition
EU Code of Conduct (EU, 1998; 2003)	Most small arms	All light weapons	For most small arms; for all light weapons
West African Moratorium (ECOWAS, 1998; 1999)	All small arms	All light weapons except portable anti-aircraft missile systems	For all small arms; for all light weapons except portable anti-aircraft missile systems
OSCE Document (OSCE, 2000)	Small arms 'made or modified to military specifications for use as lethal instruments of war'	Light weapons that can be carried by one or more persons	Does not cover ammunition
OAU Bamako Declaration (OAU, 2000)	All small arms	All light weapons	For all small arms and light weapons
SADC Firearms Protocol (SADC, 2001)	All small arms	All light weapons	For all small arms and light weapons
Pacific Islands Forum model legislation (Pacific Islands Forum, 2003)	All small arms	Light weapons that use cartridge-based ammunition	For all small arms; for light weapons that use cartridge-based ammunition
Nairobi Protocol (Nairobi Protocol, 2004)	All small arms	All light weapons	For all small arms; unclear whether light weapons ammunition is covered
Global instruments			
UN Firearms Protocol (UNGA, 2001b)	All small arms	Light weapons using cartridge-based ammunition that can be moved or carried by a single person	For all small arms; for light weapons using cartridge-based ammunition that can be moved or carried by a single person
UN Programme of Action (UNGA, 2001c)	All small arms	All light weapons	Unclear whether ammunition is covered
Wassenaar Arrangement Initial Elements (WA, 2004; 2003b)	Most small arms	All light weapons	For most small arms; for all light weapons
Wassenaar Arrangement Best Practice Guidelines (WA, 2002)	Most small arms	All light weapons	Do not appear to cover ammunition

Notes: This table indicates whether, in principle, the instruments it lists cover small arms, light weapons, and their ammunition. It does not consider to what extent these instruments, through their operative provisions, actually regulate these weapons/ammunition. For additional information on the scope of multilateral instruments with respect to small arms ammunition, see Chapter 1 (AMMUNITION).

Additional source: McDonald (2005)

The scope of the *European Union Code of Conduct on Arms Exports* is broad, covering a wide range of conventional arms, including most small arms, all light weapons, and their ammunition (EU, 1998; 2003).[5] By contrast, portable anti-aircraft missile systems seem to be excluded from the West African Moratorium as they are not mentioned in the follow-up instrument (*Code of Conduct*) that defines the Moratorium's scope of application. No reason for this exclusion is apparent. The Moratorium covers all other light weapons, as well as the full range of small arms, including their ammunition (ECOWAS, 1998; 1999, arts. 2–3, Annex I).[6]

The *OSCE Document on Small Arms and Light Weapons,* adopted by the OSCE[7] in November 2000, applies to military-style small arms as well as light weapons that are 'man-portable'. This appears to mean that the *Document* covers only those light weapons that can be carried by one or more persons—excluding those that are 'portable', pursuant to the 1997 UN Panel definition, in the sense that they can be carried only by a pack animal or light vehicle (see UNGA, 1997, para. 27(a)). The *OSCE Document* does not cover ammunition (OSCE, 2000, pream. para. 3).

As the *Bamako Declaration,* adopted by the Organization of African Unity (now African Union)[8] in December 2000, contains no definition of small arms or light weapons, one would assume that the 1997 UN definition applies. The *Bamako Declaration* was designed, in part, to consolidate an African common position for the July 2001 UN Small Arms Conference. In addition, the *Bamako Declaration* applies to ammunition as and where it so indicates (OAU, 2000).

The period following the July 2001 UN Small Arms Conference saw the adoption of several additional regional instruments. In most cases, however, their roots lay in processes initiated before the 2001 Conference.[9] The legally binding *SADC Firearms Protocol,* adopted in August 2001 and in force since November 2004, is broad in scope. It defines the term 'firearm' to include all the light weapons (as well as small arms) enumerated in the 1997 UN Panel report. The *SADC Protocol* also covers ammunition for both light weapons and small arms (SADC, 2001, art. 1.2).[10]

The model weapons control legislation, endorsed by Pacific Islands Forum[11] leaders at their August 2003 Summit, focuses on firearms and other weapons that can be imported, held, or used by civilians. Its definitions of 'firearm', 'weapon', and 'ammunition' are quite broad, however, and encompass those light weapons, such as heavy machine-guns, that use cartridge-based ammunition. The model legislation also covers ammunition for these light weapons and all small arms (Pacific Islands Forum, 2003, sec. 1.4).[12]

The *Nairobi Protocol,* adopted in April 2004, covers all small arms and light weapons, along with ammunition for small arms (Nairobi Protocol, 2004, art. 1; McDonald, 2005). As is the case with many small arms instruments, the mention of ammunition in the definitions section does not yield much substance in the operational section; none of the *Protocol's* operative provisions mentions ammunition (AMMUNITION).

> One should read the UN Programme of Action as covering small arms and light weapons as these are defined in the 1997 UN Panel report.

Global instruments

In April 2005 the *UN Firearms Protocol* remained the only legally binding small arms measure to be negotiated at the global level. After a slow start, the pace of ratifications picked up considerably and, by late April, the *Protocol* had secured the 40 ratifications needed for its entry into force.[13] The *Protocol* covers all small arms, but applies to only a narrow range of light weapons—specifically, those using cartridge-based ammunition that can be moved or carried by one person. Light weapons satisfying these conditions include hand-held under-barrel grenade launchers that fire spin-stabilized grenades and light mortars with a calibre of well under 100 mm. The *Protocol* applies to ammunition as and where it so indicates.[14]

Despite attempts to include a definition in earlier drafts, the final *UN Programme of Action,* agreed in July 2001, contains no definition of the 'small arms and light weapons' that appear in its title (UNGA, 2001c). Yet, in the absence of any intention expressed to the contrary, one should read the *Programme* as covering light weapons (as well as small arms) as these are defined in the 1997 UN Panel report. The *Programme of Action* is a UN initiative. The 1997 Panel definition has been followed by other UN expert bodies. Moreover, the *UN Programme* refers to the 1997 Panel report, though not to its section on definitions (UNGA, 2001c, note to para. I.22(c)). While the word 'ammunition' does not feature in any of the commitments states undertook in the *Programme of Action,* in some areas it may be relevant (for example, para. II.19 on surplus destruction). Several states have, in fact, provided information on ammunition in reporting on their implementation of the *Programme* (see Kytömäki and Yankey-Wayne, 2004).

As of February 2005 negotiations were continuing, under UN auspices, on an international instrument to trace illicit small arms and light weapons. While the draft text under consideration at that time covered light weapons, it contained no substantive commitments on ammunition.

In addition to its recent initiatives on MANPADS, reviewed in the next section, the Wassenaar Arrangement[15] has measures in place that apply to the broader spectrum of small arms and light weapons. Most of the world's important arms exporting countries are Wassenaar members. Under the Wassenaar Arrangement *Initial Elements,* Participating States agree to control all items set forth in the Wassenaar Arrangement *Munitions List* 'with the objective of preventing unauthorised transfers or re-transfers of those items.' The *Munitions List* covers most small arms, all light weapons, and their ammunition (WA, 2004, *Initial Elements,* sec. III; 2003b). In December 2002, Wassenaar Participating States agreed to a more detailed set of *Best Practice Guidelines for Exports of Small Arms and Light Weapons (SALW).* As the *Guidelines* mention ammunition only in relation to tracing, it appears they do not otherwise apply to ammunition (WA, 2002, para. II.2.d).

MANPADS INSTRUMENTS

In the past few years, often as part of the broader 'war on terror', states around the word have increasingly shifted their attention to a specific type of light weapon: MANPADS. The 2004 edition of the *Small Arms Survey* reported on initial international efforts to curb MANPADS proliferation (Small Arms Survey, 2004, pp. 90–94). This chapter updates that analysis, focusing in particular on the new standards developed by the Wassenaar Arrangement and the OSCE.

The Wassenaar–OSCE MANPADS principles

At US prompting, the Wassenaar Arrangement took up the MANPADS issue in the late 1990s. Initial agreement was reached in December 2000 on *Elements for Export Controls of Man-Portable Air Defense Systems (MANPADS).* These set limits on and prescribed criteria for government licensing of MANPADS exports (WA, 2000).

The 2000 *Elements* were revised and expanded at the December 2003 Wassenaar Plenary Meeting. The 2003 *Elements* are broad in scope, covering not only complete weapons systems but also components and spare parts, ammunition (i.e. missiles), licensed production, and MANPADS-related training and assistance (WA, 2003a, sec. 1). Under the 2003 *Elements,* MANPADS transfers must be individually licensed (sec. 2.2). States must take a range of criteria into account before authorizing their export, with particular emphasis on stockpile security and accountability in recipient countries (secs.

Nicaraguan soldiers with SA-7 MANPADS in July 2004.

© Esteban Felix/AP Photo

2.6–2.9). MANPADS may not be exported to non-state actors that are not acting on behalf of their government (sec. 2.1). Nor may they be re-exported without the prior consent of the exporting government (sec. 2.8).

In addition, the 2003 *MANPADS Elements* oblige Wassenaar Participating States to report their MANPADS transfers to other Wassenaar members (sec. 2.5). They are also required to share information about potential recipient governments that fail to meet the Wassenaar MANPADS standards and 'non-state entities that are or may be attempting to acquire MANPADS' (secs. 2.11–2.12).

Many of these provisions are presented in greater detail in the section below dealing with national transfer controls. For the moment, it is sufficient to note that the Wassenaar MANPADS standards define the high-water mark of current international efforts to curb MANPADS proliferation.

The OSCE has followed the lead of the Wassenaar Arrangement, adopting, in May 2004, the *OSCE Principles for Export Controls of Man-Portable Air Defence Systems (MANPADS)* (OSCE, 2004). These apply, almost word for word, the 2003 *Wassenaar MANPADS Elements* to the OSCE Region. Approximately one-half of all OSCE participating states, including all Western European countries, Canada, the Russian Federation, and the US, are also part of the Wassenaar Arrangement. The OSCE, however, encompasses many states from Eastern Europe and Central Asia that are not part of Wassenaar.

The *OSCE Document on Small Arms and Light Weapons* (OSCE, 2000) already covers MANPADS, but, as noted above, the Wassenaar–OSCE MANPADS principles impose exceptionally strict controls over their export and retransfer. In May 2004, OSCE states also undertook 'to incorporate these principles into their national practices, policies and/or regulations' and to report MANPADS transfers using the information exchange provisions of the *OSCE Document* (OSCE, 2004, secs. 4–5).

> The Wassenaar MANPADS standards define the high-water mark of current international efforts to curb MANPADS proliferation.

Other MANPADS initiatives

Many other regional organizations besides the OSCE have given MANPADS priority attention. Russian pressure led the Commonwealth of Independent States (CIS)[16] to agree to exchange information on MANPADS purchases and sales in September 2003 (CIS, 2003). Among the Asian-Pacific organizations, Asia-Pacific Economic Cooperation (APEC)[17] has been most active on the MANPADS issue to date. In Bangkok in October 2003, APEC leaders committed themselves to:

- adopt strict domestic export controls on MANPADS;
- secure stockpiles;
- take domestic action to regulate production, transfer, and brokering;
- ban transfers to non-state end-users; and
- exchange information in support of these efforts (APEC, 2003).

Both the Association of Southeast Asian Nations (ASEAN) and the ASEAN Regional Forum have acknowledged the importance of the MANPADS issue in various statements and declarations, but they have not gone as far as APEC in committing to specific, concrete measures. APEC's membership is broad, comprising many of the countries of the Pacific Rim, including China, Japan, the Russian Federation, and the United States; it does not, however, include all ASEAN countries. Cambodia, Laos, and Myanmar are all members of ASEAN but not of APEC.

At the international level, in late 2003 the United Nations General Assembly[18] decided to include MANPADS in the United Nations Register of Conventional Arms, along with artillery systems of 75 mm calibre and above (UNGA, 2003a;

2003b). The General Assembly again took up the MANPADS issue in late 2004, adopting Resolution 59/90, which calls upon states 'to combat and prevent the illicit transfer of man-portable air defence systems and unauthorized access to and use of such weapons' (UNGA, 2004, para. 2). The General Assembly also 'encourages Member States … to ensure that such weapons are exported only to Governments or agents authorized by a Government' (para. 5). The Resolution notes 'the importance of information exchange and transparency' in the legal MANPADS trade (last pream. para.) and stresses the need for 'effective and comprehensive national controls on the production, stockpiling, transfer and brokering' of these weapons (para. 3). While important, General Assembly Resolution 59/90 falls short of the much more constraining and specific language found in the Wassenaar–OSCE MANPADS principles.

The International Civil Aviation Organization (ICAO)[19] has stepped up its efforts to strengthen civil aviation security worldwide in the post-September 11 period, identifying MANPADS as a major threat (ICAO, 2004a, para. 2.1). An earlier ICAO resolution on MANPADS, adopted in the autumn of 1998 (ICAO, 1998), was revised and expanded in 2004. In Resolution A35-11, adopted at the ICAO Assembly's 35th session in the autumn of 2004, the Assembly urges Contracting States 'to exercise strict and effective controls on the import, export, transfer or retransfer, as well as storage of MANPADS' (ICAO, 2004c, para. 1). The Assembly also urges Contracting States that are not members of the Wassenaar Arrangement to implement nonetheless the *Wassenaar MANPADS Elements* (para. 5). In addition, the ICAO Assembly calls upon Contracting States 'to ensure the destruction of non-authorized MANPADS in their territory, as soon as possible' (para. 3) and cooperate in international efforts aimed at implementing cost-effective MANPADS countermeasures (para. 2). In Resolution A35-9 concerning 'acts of unlawful interference' against international civil aviation, the Assembly directs the ICAO Council to collaborate with the G8 'and other relevant groups of States' for these purposes (ICAO, 2004b, Appendix H, para. 2).

The G8[20] took up the MANPADS issue at its 2003 Summit in Evian, France. G8 leaders called upon all countries 'to strengthen control of their Manpads stockpiles' (G8, 2003, sec. 1.4), while committing themselves to a series of measures in the areas of production, transfer controls, brokering, and stockpile management designed 'to prevent the acquisition of Manpads by terrorists' (sec. 1.6). They undertook, in particular, '[t]o ban transfers of Manpads to non-state end-users' (sec. 1.6).

At their 2004 Summit, G8 Leaders adopted a 'Secure and Facilitated International Travel Initiative' (SAFTI) (G8, 2004), which set out some additional steps to counter the MANPADS threat, among them:

- accelerating efforts to destroy excess and/or obsolete MANPADS and providing assistance for this where needed (para. 8);
- further strengthening controls on the transfer of MANPADS production technology (para. 10); and
- developing a methodology for assessing airport vulnerability to the MANPADS threat, along with effective countermeasures, while taking into account an ICAO study on this issue (para. 12).

G8 Leaders also agreed to '[w]ork toward expedited adoption of the updated 2003 Wassenaar "Elements for Export Controls on MANPADS" as an international standard' (para. 9). This strong statement of support was bracketed by the OSCE's adoption of these same principles in May 2004 and their endorsement by ICAO in the autumn of 2004. The Wassenaar–OSCE MANPADS principles were not, however, mentioned by the UN General Assembly in the MANPADS Resolution that it adopted at the end of 2004.[21]

ICAO has identified MANPADS as a major threat to civil aviation in the post-September 11 period.

NATIONAL CONTROL OF MANPADS TRANSFERS

International measures invariably rely for their effectiveness on national implementation. International organizations do not mark weapons, license exports, or manage stockpiles. National measures to control MANPADS proliferation are wide-ranging and include efforts to improve stockpile management and retrieve older weapons that could be misused. This section is devoted to a specific but crucial part of this broader picture, namely, controlling the transfer of MANPADS. We begin by considering the extent to which the transfer control systems of five key states—all members of the Wassenaar Arrangement and OSCE—meet the requirements of the Wassenaar–OSCE MANPADS principles. We then consider the situation in two important arms-exporting countries that are not members of these organizations.

MANPADS controls in five key states[22]

The five states selected for this study are Bulgaria, Germany, the Russian Federation, the United Kingdom, and the United States. All these countries are significant arms exporters. All of them produce, or have very recently produced,[23] MANPADS. The Russian Federation, the UK, and the US have also authorized MANPADS transfers in recent years (Small Arms Survey, 2004, p. 87). All five states are members of the Wassenaar Arrangement and the OSCE.

Officials confer prior to the opening of the 9th Wassenaar Arrangement Plenary in Vienna, December 2003. The meeting resulted in the adoption of important new standards for the control of MANPADS exports.

In reviewing the transfer control systems of these five states, we take the various Wassenaar–OSCE MANPADS principles in turn. First, however, it is worth noting that the systems we examine do not single out MANPADS for special treatment. Nor do they normally differentiate between light weapons and military-style small arms (Anders, 2004).

Among the five states, Germany is the exception in this respect. It distinguishes between weapons, including military small arms and light weapons, it classifies as 'defence material' (*Rüstungsgüter*) and other arms it terms 'weapons of war' (*Kriegswaffen*). 'War weapons' are in fact a subcategory of 'defence material'. They include automatic and semi-automatic rifles, automatic pistols, machine guns, and portable missile or grenade launchers (Germany, 1998, part B, secs. I, V–VI). Small arms falling under the rubric of (other) 'defence material' are hand-held smooth-bore firearms with a calibre of less than 20 mm and other handheld firearms with a calibre of 12.7 mm or less that are not covered by the list of war weapons. For example, semi-automatic pistols and shotguns are considered 'defence material', not 'war weapons' (Germany, 2004a, part I, sec. A.0001).

German controls over the transfer of 'war weapons' are stricter than those that apply to (other) 'defence material'. These differences are described in more detail below in the sections dealing with retransfer and restrictions regarding certain destinations. One should note, however, that, although the other four countries do not distinguish among different small arms or light weapons categories in their transfer controls legislation, they may need to make such distinctions in their transfer licensing procedures. Where they are bound by the Wassenaar–OSCE principles, states that have previously applied certain controls only 'as required' now have to apply these to all MANPADS transfer applications. For example, the British system provides for restrictions on arms retransfers, but does not require them in every case. Under the Wassenaar–OSCE principles, it must now automatically impose these on any export of UK-origin MANPADS (see below).

Scope of controls

The Wassenaar–OSCE MANPADS principles cover surface-to-air missile systems that can be carried, operated, and fired by one or more individuals. Their scope is broad and includes not only the complete systems but also 'components, spare parts, models, training systems, and simulators' (WA, 2003a, secs. 1.1–1.2; OSCE, 2004, secs. 1.1–1.2). The term 'component' encompasses ammunition (missiles) for MANPADS.[24]

The range of controlled small arms, light weapons, and related services is broad in the five countries under review.

The Wassenaar–OSCE principles apply to licensed production. They also govern a wide range of activities associated with the acquisition and use of MANPADS, including transfers of know-how and training (sec. 1.2). As indicated in the *Small Arms Survey 2004*, MANPADS are not easy to operate. Proper training can make the difference between a near miss and a successful strike (Small Arms Survey, 2004, p. 85).

Although the Wassenaar–OSCE MANPADS standards have a much wider scope than most other multilateral small arms instruments, the range of controlled small arms, light weapons, and related services is in fact broad in the five countries under review. Transfer controls in all five states cover, in addition to small arms and light weapons, their ammunition, spare parts, and components. These countries also control the provision of technical assistance related to the development, production, and use of controlled goods, as well as the transfer of technology (Anders, 2004).

Export criteria

In authorizing MANPADS exports, Wassenaar and OSCE states must take into account:

- the potential for diversion or misuse in the recipient country;
- the recipient government's ability and willingness to protect against unauthorized retransfers, loss, theft, and diversion; and
- the adequacy and effectiveness of the recipient government's physical security arrangements (WA, 2003a, sec. 2.7; OSCE, 2004, sec. 2.5)

These criteria for the export of MANPADS are consistent with criteria for licensing exports of all types of small arms and light weapons found in other multilateral instruments, including the *UN Programme of Action* (UNGA, 2001c, para. II.11), the *OSCE Document on Small Arms and Light Weapons* (OSCE, 2000, para. III.A.2.), and the *European Union Code of Conduct on Arms Exports* (EU, 1998, criterion 7).

National regulatory frameworks tend not to specify in any detail the counter-proliferation concerns states should take into account when authorizing the export of MANPADS or other small arms or light weapons. Among the five countries under review, only the UK explicitly stipulates, in national policy guidelines derived from the *EU Code of Conduct,* that licensing decisions must take into account any risk that exported equipment 'will be diverted within the buyer country or re-exported under undesirable conditions' (UK, 2000, criterion 7). Other EU states, including Germany, make a general reference to the export licensing criteria of the *EU Code of Conduct* (Germany, 2000, sec. I, para. 1). In all these cases, the *Code* criteria are politically—not legally—binding. Only exceptionally, as in the case of Belgium, have EU states incorporated one or more *EU Code* provisions in legally binding national legislation. Bulgaria, an EU candidate country, has also politically committed itself to the *Code* criteria (EU, 2004, p. 2).

In any case, as a matter of practice, all five states assess the risk for potential diversion prior to authorizing the export of small arms and light weapons. An assessment of the potential risk of diversion may also be seen as implicit in national requirements for end-use documentation (see below).

License types

The Wassenaar–OSCE principles also prohibit 'general' or 'open' licences for MANPADS exports (WA, 2003a, sec. 2.2; OSCE, 2004, sec. 2.2). This is exceptional among multilateral small arms instruments. The five states under review broadly adhere to this requirement. Legislation in the Russian Federation (Pyadushkin, 2003, p. 21) and Bulgaria (Bulgaria, 2002a, art. 5.2) specifies that any export of small arms or light weapons, including MANPADS, must be made on the basis of an individual licence. In contrast, British, German, and US legislation allows global or general licences, as well as individual licences, for small arms and light weapons exports. For example, in the US the Directorate of Defense Trade Controls may in certain cases issue comprehensive export authorizations that allow multiple shipments and re-exports to approved end-users (US, 2004, paras. 123.1, 126.14). Nevertheless, since general licences in Germany, the UK, and the US are granted only in exceptional circumstances, such as government-to-government co-production agreements, it appears that, at least in practice, they broadly meet the Wassenaar–OSCE standard.

Controls on retransfers

The Wassenaar–OSCE MANPADS principles also stipulate that recipients of MANPADS exports must guarantee in advance not to re-export these weapons except with the prior consent of the exporting government (WA, 2003a, sec. 2.8; OSCE, 2004, sec. 2.6). Again, this requirement breaks new ground at the multilateral level. Both the *OSCE Document on Small Arms and Light Weapons* and the *UN Programme of Action* merely urge prior notification before retransfer (OSCE, 2000, para. III.B.5; UNGA, 2001c, para. II.13).

> The Wassenaar–OSCE controls on the retransfer of MANPADS break new ground at the multilateral level.

In general, the five states under review require prior authorization of MANPADS retransfers. Moreover, this requirement usually applies to other small arms or light weapons exports. Any retransfer of US-origin small arms or light weapons is subject to the prior written approval of US authorities (US, 2004, para. 123.9.a–b). Bulgaria and the Russian Federation, at the licensing stage, require prospective recipients of small arms and light weapons or their governments to sign an agreement stipulating that the imported weapons will not be retransferred without the prior consent (usually written) of the exporting state (Bulgaria, 2002a, para. 15.1; Russian Federation, 2000, paras. 5–6).[25]

German retransfer controls vary as a function of weapon type. German law stipulates that the country approve any retransfer of German 'war weapons' (which include MANPADS), technology for 'war weapons', and goods derived from this technology. Although the relevant regulations do not spell this out, in practice such approval means the prior written authorization of the German government, in conformity with the Wassenaar–OSCE MANPADS principles.[26] Germany waives this requirement only if 'defence material' (not included in the category of 'war weapons') or goods derived from technology for such 'defence material' are retransferred to most EU member states,[27] Australia, Canada, Japan, New Zealand, Norway, Switzerland, or the United States (Germany, 2000, sec. 4.3; 2002, appendices 2 and 4). France would therefore need to obtain prior German authorization if it wanted to retransfer German sub-machine guns to Japan, but would not need such authorization if it wished to retransfer German revolvers or shotguns to Japan.

The UK system also differs from the others reviewed here. British end-use undertakings do not normally stipulate that prior consent must be obtained for any retransfer. The UK instead assesses the risk of diversion at the licensing stage. If it decides there is an unacceptable risk that the intended recipient will not comply with end-user-undertakings, it will not authorize the export (UK, 2003a, p. 12).[28] Under the new Wassenaar–OSCE rules, however, the UK must automatically restrict the retransfer of any MANPADS it authorizes for export.

Restrictions on non-governmental end-users

The Wassenaar–OSCE MANPADS principles also stipulate that MANPADS are to be exported 'only to foreign governments or to agents specifically authorised to act on behalf of a government after presentation of an official EUC [end-user certificate] certified by the Government of the receiving country' (WA, 2003a, sec. 2.1; see OSCE, 2004, sec. 2.1). As noted earlier, this restriction of permissible MANPADS recipients is found in other multilateral instruments dealing with these weapons, such as the 2003 *G8 Action Plan* (G8, 2003, sec. 1.6).

Somewhat surprisingly, this principle was rarely spelled out in the national arms export laws or regulations reviewed for this study. One exception is the United Kingdom, which in November 2003 issued an official statement indicating that any future 'license application for the export of MANPADS to any non-governmental body will be considered in the light of the G8 Action Plan' (UK, 2003b, p. 495).

Though explicit bans are few and far between, licensing authorities generally request prior identification of end-users, making it possible, on a case-by-case basis, to prohibit transfers to particular non-state actors. In Bulgaria, for example, prospective exporters must provide, as part of their licence application, the importing country's written confirmation that the importer has the right to import the weapons it is requesting (Bulgaria, 2002b, art. 22.1.5). The Russian Federation also requires the country of import to issue an end-user undertaking before authorizing weapons exports (Russian Federation, 2000, para. 5). Such declarations—implying that the government of the recipient country is aware of and has authorized the requested transfer—may also be required, on a case-by-case basis, in Germany (2004b, para. 17.2), the UK (2004), and the US (2004, para. 123.1).[29]

Restrictions on certain destinations

Although they are not included in the Wassenaar–OSCE MANPADS principles, states normally impose restrictions on the export of arms to certain destinations. The transfer control systems of the five countries reviewed here all incorporate the principle that arms exports that are inconsistent with their international obligations will not be authorized. Typical applications of this principle include end-users or destinations under embargo by regional or international organizations.

In addition, states often restrict weapons transfers to destinations they identify as being of particular concern. The United States, for example, does not normally authorize the export of small arms or light

© Banaras Khan/AFP/Getty Images

Pakistani tribesmen hold rocket-propelled grenade launchers in Dera Bugti, 650 kilometers south-west of Islamabad, following lethal clashes between local tribesmen and Pakistani security forces. March 2005.

weapons to countries such as Cuba, Iran, North Korea, and Syria (US, 2004, para. 126.1.a). Exports to sub-Saharan Africa are also subject to special restrictions (US, 2003a, sec. 2773). Countries may also ease transfer controls with respect to certain destinations. The governments of Germany, the UK, and the US may grant open export licences in relation to countries with which they cooperate in military production projects.[30] Bulgarian law exempts certain states from the requirement for end-use certificates (Bulgaria, 2002a, art. 4.3).

Where restrictions or exceptions apply to specific destinations, these typically cover the export of all arms. As noted earlier, national transfer control systems do not normally differentiate among small arms and light weapons categories for transfer licensing purposes. Germany is the exception. Here, too, it distinguishes between 'war weapons' and (other) 'defence material'. Though exceptions are possible, 'war weapons', such as assault rifles and sub-machine guns, are normally exported only to NATO, EU, and 'NATO-equated' states.[31] In contrast, the export of small arms classified as (other) 'defence material', such as revolvers and shotguns, may be authorized to any destination (Germany, 2000, sec. III).

Delivery verification

The Wassenaar–OSCE MANPADS principles also require exporting governments to satisfy themselves that recipient states are willing and able to provide for the secure storage, handling, transportation, and use of MANPADS material, including the disposal or destruction of excess stocks. National practices offering evidence of this include the '[w]ritten verification of receipt of MANPADS shipments' (WA, 2003a, sec. 2.9; OSCE, 2004, sec. 2.7). While not actually obliging recipient governments to submit written delivery verifications,[32] the Wassenaar–OSCE principles are among the only multilateral small arms instruments that explicitly refer to and underline the importance of this control measure.[33]

Only two of the five states reviewed here require delivery verification for MANPADS exports. Bulgaria requires delivery verification for any export of small arms or light weapons (Bulgaria, 2002b, arts. 22.1.6 and 24). It may also oblige exporters, in their foreign trade contracts, to allow Bulgarian authorities or their agents to confirm delivery through physical inspections (Bulgaria, 2002a, art. 17.7).

The United States requires mandatory delivery checks for all transfers of MANPADS under government-to-government agreements. These are arranged by Security Assistance Organizations based at US embassies in recipient countries (US, 2003b, point C8.3.3.4, p. 276). The US Directorate of Defense Trade Controls can also require, if considered necessary, an import certificate or delivery verification document for the transfer of other arms. Such a certificate has to be issued by the competent authorities in the importing country and serves to confirm that the importer complied with relevant rules in the recipient state (US, 2004, para. 123.14.b).

In the three other states there is no systematic requirement for written delivery verification. Nevertheless, licensing authorities can seek such documentation if they consider it necessary for a particular export of small arms or light weapons.

> The Wassenaar–OSCE principles are among the only multilateral small arms instruments that explicitly underline the importance of delivery verification.

Post-delivery controls by recipient governments

Other security measures recipient governments are encouraged to adopt under the Wassenaar–OSCE MANPADS principles include:

- maintenance of written records of inventories;
- storage conditions satisfying 'the highest standards of security and access control';
- separation of principal MANPADS components, subject to certain exceptions; and

- limiting access to hardware and related classified information to those with 'an established need to know' (WA, 2003a, sec. 2.9; OSCE, 2004, sec. 2.7).

The Wassenaar–OSCE principles also require recipient states to guarantee 'to inform promptly the exporting government of any instance of compromise, unauthorised use, loss, or theft of any MANPADS material' (WA, 2003a, sec. 2.8; see OSCE, 2004, sec. 2.6).

Other multilateral small arms instruments address this issue in general terms when they do so at all. For example, under the *Nairobi Protocol,* 'States Parties undertake to ... establish and maintain complete national inventories of small arms and light weapons held by security forces and other state bodies' (Nairobi Protocol, 2004, art. 6.a).

At the national level, transfer control regulations do not normally make small arms or light weapons exports conditional on the existence, in the recipient state, of specific physical security measures. Among the countries reviewed here, the only exception to this rule is the United States. Under the Golden Sentry programme, governments that import US defence articles of particular concern must agree to certain US-stipulated control measures. For example, recipients of US-origin MANPADS must conduct monthly checks of their MANPADS stocks and submit these records to Security Assistance Organizations based at US embassies in the recipient country.[34]

End-use monitoring by exporting governments

Although the Wassenaar–OSCE MANPADS principles lay down a series of end-user undertakings, as with other multilateral small arms instruments they make no provision for monitoring by the exporting government of compliance with these undertakings.

The United States has more stringent provisions for end-use monitoring than any other country reviewed here, although these apply only to weapons of prime concern. Specifically, US export legislation requires 'end-use verification of ... defense articles and defense services that are particularly vulnerable to diversion or other misuse, or ... whose diversion or other misuse could have significant consequences' (US, 2003a, sec. 2785). For example, under the Blue Lantern programme, applying to commercial exports of US defence articles, US authorities undertook some

© Simon Walker/AP Photo

A US Marine fires a Javelin anti-tank missile at a building near Umm Qasr, Iraq, during military operations aimed at toppling Saddam Hussein's regime. March 2003.

400 checks in 2003, many of which concerned firearms recipients in the western hemisphere suspected of involvement in criminal activities. Several of these checks resulted in the launching of investigations into possible violations of end-user undertakings (US, 2003c, pp. 1–2, 4). This programme is complemented by the Golden Sentry programme, mentioned above, which applies to defence articles of particular concern that are exported under US security assistance programmes with foreign governments. Controls under Golden Sentry include annual cross-checks by Security Assistance Organizations of inventories listing weapons' serial numbers, based on information transferred to them by US export authorities, with inventories submitted to them by the end-user (US, 2003b, point C8.3.3.5, p. 276).

The four other countries that were part of the study do not conduct systematic post-export monitoring—whether in relation to MANPADS or other small arms and light weapons. Government authorities in those states may nevertheless request access to weapons they have licensed for export to verify that end-user undertakings have been complied with. The United Kingdom undertakes post-export monitoring on a case by case basis 'where considered to be of added benefit' (UK, 2003a, p. 12).

MANPADS controls in Brazil and South Africa[35]

Neither Brazil nor South Africa produces MANPADS, but both countries produce light weapons and both host defence industries that produce high-tech weaponry (Jones and Cutshaw, 2004). As the *Small Arms Survey 2005* indicates, Brazil and South Africa each have the capacity to produce sophisticated, guided light weapons, such as MANPADS (PRODUCERS). Both countries, in other words, could soon join the ranks of MANPADS producers.[36]

Applicable norms

As of February 2005, neither Brazil nor South Africa was a member of the Wassenaar Arrangement or the OSCE. Neither country, therefore, was bound by the Wassenaar–OSCE MANPADS principles, although it appeared this would soon change in the case of South Africa. In December 2004 the Government of South Africa decided to apply for Wassenaar membership (South Africa, 2004). The country had been aligning its arms transfer polices with those of the Wassenaar Arrangement for several years prior to this.

Both Brazil and South Africa could soon join the ranks of MANPADS producers.

Both countries are legally or politically bound by a range of other regional and global measures relating to small arms and light weapons in general and MANPADS more specifically. In terms of general small arms and light weapons measures, South Africa is bound by the Africa-wide *Bamako Declaration* and the *SADC Firearms Protocol*, now in force. Brazil is a party to the 1997 OAS Convention. It has also signed, but not ratified, the *UN Firearms Protocol*. South Africa has signed *and* ratified the *UN Protocol*, so will be legally bound by this instrument as soon as it enters into force. Both Brazil and South Africa have also committed themselves to the range of measures found in the *UN Programme of Action*.

Concerning MANPADS, both ICAO Resolution A35-11 and UN General Assembly Resolution 59/90 apply to Brazil and South Africa. While neither set of standards is anywhere near as stringent as those adopted by the Wassenaar Arrangement and OSCE, ICAO Resolution A35-11 specifically urges those ICAO Contracting States that are not Wassenaar members to implement the 2003 *Wassenaar MANPADS Elements* (ICAO, 2004c, para. 5).

Brazil

Research conducted for the Small Arms Survey in the autumn of 2004 was unable to confirm that Brazil's transfer controls system fulfills key Wassenaar–OSCE MANPADS standards (Anders, 2005).[37] On the positive side of the ledger, Brazilian controls on light weapons, their ammunition and components, and related services are comprehensive, in line with the Wassenaar–OSCE MANPADS standards (Brazil, 1995, art. 1, paras. 1.I, 2; 2001, Annex I; 2000, art. 16). Moreover, in support of their licence applications Brazilian exporters are usually asked to submit documentation that identifies end-users and end-uses, and confirms that the transfer, if not expressly authorized by recipient country authorities, is at least permitted under their laws (Brazil, 1995, art. 3, paras. 1–2; Brazil, 2000, art. 178).

This research was, however, unable to confirm that the Brazilian transfer controls system satisfies several other Wassenaar–OSCE requirements. For example, it is unclear whether recipients of Brazilian light weapons are barred from retransferring them without prior Brazilian government consent. Moreover, the legislation examined for this study makes no reference to post-export controls, including delivery verification certificates and other counter-proliferation mechanisms (Anders, 2005). These gaps may simply derive from a failure to make key information public—as opposed to insufficiencies in Brazilian legislation or practice. This 'information gap', however, is such that the extent to which Brazil's transfer controls system meets the Wassenaar–OSCE MANPADS standards is very much an open question.

South Africa

South African legislation appears to meet the requirements of the Wassenaar–OSCE MANPADS principles (Anders, 2005). Moreover, in at least one respect it exceeds them. The scope of South African export controls is quite broad, covering, in addition to light weapons, their ammunition and components, related technology, and services (South Africa, 2002, art. 1.vi, xxix).[38] Licensing decisions must take into account the conventional arms control system of the recipient country and its record of compliance with end-user undertakings (art. 15(i)).

The government of the importing country must undertake not to retransfer South African arms to any other country without the prior approval of the South African government (art. 16(a)). A person authorized by the importing state must also issue an end-user certificate identifying the end-user, undertaking not to retransfer the weapons without South African approval, and promising to furnish a delivery verification certificate as proof of import (art. 17). The obligation to provide a delivery verification certificate, applicable to all light weapons transfers, in fact exceeds the Wassenaar–OSCE standards, which only recommend this measure.

> South African legislation appears to meet the requirements of the Wassenaar–OSCE MANPADS principles.

CONCLUSION

In its first sections, the chapter reviewed a broad range of multilateral instruments that apply to light weapons. Existing small arms measures targeting no specific type of small arm or light weapon tend to cover all or most light weapons as this term was defined by the 1997 UN Small Arms Panel (UNGA, 1997, paras. 26–27). Coverage of ammunition for light weapons is, however, much less extensive.

This relatively broad coverage of light weapons (the weapons themselves) is somewhat surprising as several of the instruments reviewed in this chapter—as reflected in their titles and use of terms—focus on 'firearms', an expression not normally associated with light weapons. Except for the *UN Firearms Protocol,* these 'firearms instruments' nevertheless apply to a wide range of light weapons. At the same time, two instruments that one would assume cover all light weapons—again on the basis of their titles and use of terms—in fact do not, although these omissions are partial.

It is beyond the scope of this study to analyse the content of these various measures. Previous editions of the *Small Arms Survey* provide much of this information. It is sufficient to note here that, taken as a whole, these instruments yield a relatively broad, and in some cases dense, web of regulation that applies to light weapons as well as small arms.

More recent measures aim at MANPADS, a particular type of light weapon. MANPADS control measures have been high on the agenda of regional and international organizations in recent years, especially since 2003. The Wassenaar Arrangement and OSCE have led the way in developing and adopting stringent new standards, although these are not yet universally accepted. While important normative work remains unfinished, especially at the global level, the principal challenge is now shifting from the development of these norms to their concrete implementation at the national level.

As ever, the key to implementation lies with states. International instruments are effective only where translated into law and practice at the national level. This chapter took an initial step towards evaluating national-level implementation with an in-depth review of the transfer control systems of five key exporting countries, all members of the Wassenaar Arrangement and OSCE. In all five countries, the chapter found that those systems provide the basis for full implementation of the Wassenaar–OSCE MANPADS principles. In at least one instance, they appear to exceed these standards—specifically, the US in the area of end-use monitoring.

The chapter did not, however, examine actual implementation. Although the five states have the systems in place that would allow them to meet the Wassenaar–OSCE requirements, further research is needed to ascertain whether they do so in practice. It is also worth noting that these same systems also allow for strict control over the broader range of light weapons (and most small arms). The basic elements of national transfer control systems are the same for all these weapons. At their heart lie licensing procedures that assess and minimize risk, including risk of diversion, in advance of any export.

Although many of the most important arms exporting states in the Wassenaar Arrangement and OSCE have systems in place that allow them to meet the Wassenaar–OSCE MANPADS requirements, the same cannot be assumed of the broader Wassenaar and OSCE memberships, let alone the non-Wassenaar/OSCE world. The last section of the chapter made a brief foray into this wider world.

The transfer control systems of the two non-Wassenaar/OSCE states reviewed in the previous section do not give us a broad picture of the extent to which states around the world, including non-Wassenaar/OSCE members, meet the Wassenaar–OSCE MANPADS requirements. Yet at least two findings probably resonate beyond the two cases. A lack of transparency precluded an evaluation of critical aspects of one country's transfer control system, while a second state—now moving towards Wassenaar membership—satisfied all of the Wassenaar–OSCE MANPADS standards.

Work continues on determining whether states around the world have the control systems that will enable them to fulfil the many commitments they have made in relation to light weapons in recent years. We know that the regulatory framework needed to implement the Wassenaar–OSCE MANPADS principles—among the most stringent of all light weapons measures—is in place in key exporting states. Yet the broader legislative picture is unclear, and—most crucially—it remains to be seen whether law is being matched with practice.

LIST OF ABBREVIATIONS

APEC	Asia-Pacific Economic Cooperation
ASEAN	Association of Southeast Asian Nations
CIS	Commonwealth of Independent States
ECOWAS	Economic Community of West African States
EU	European Union
ICAO	International Civil Aviation Organization
MANPADS	Man-portable air defence system
NATO	North Atlantic Treaty Organisation
OAS	Organization of American States
OSCE	Organization for Security and Co-operation in Europe
SADC	Southern African Development Community
WA	Wassenaar Arrangement on Export Controls for Conventional Arms and Dual-Use Goods and Technologies

ENDNOTES

1 Although most light weapons are indeed designed for use by more than one person, many are in fact designed for use by a single person. The product of political compromise, the 1997 UN Panel Report did not provide an exact definition of light weapons (or small arms). It served, rather, to map out in general terms a range of weapons that, until the mid-1990s, had been largely ignored by the international community.

2 For a more detailed analysis of the scope of these instruments, see McDonald (2005). For more information on their contents, see Small Arms Survey (2001, ch. 7; 2002, ch. 6; 2003, ch. 7).

3 For current OAS membership, see <http://www.oas.org/>

4 In containing the expansion of gases on combustion, a barrel helps impart kinetic energy to a projectile. This results in the phenomenon of recoil transmitted to both weapon and shooter when a barrelled weapon is fired. For this reason, barrels are composed of hard steel alloys. By contrast, launch tubes, such as those used in MANPADS, may guide the projectile's initial direction but do not help drive it forward. The actual thrust comes from the projectile itself. Because a launch tube is open at both ends, little energy is imparted to the tube and consequently to the shooter. Launch tubes are usually made of fibreglass or plastic composites.

5 For current EU membership, see <http://europa.eu.int/abc/governments/index_en.htm>

6 For current ECOWAS membership, see <http://www.ecowas.int/>

7 For current OSCE membership, see <http://www.osce.org/>

8 For current African Union membership, see <http://www.africa-union.org/>

9 See Small Arms Survey (2001, ch. 7).

10 For current SADC membership, see <http://www.sadc.int/index.php>

11 For current Pacific Islands Forum membership, see <http://www.forumsec.org.fj/>

12 Correspondence with Pacific Islands Forum Secretariat, 15 November 2004.

13 The UN Firearms Protocol will enter into force in July 2005, 90 days after the deposit of the 40th instrument of ratification (UNGA, 2001b, art. 18(1)). For the latest information on Protocol signatures and ratifications, see <http://www.unodc.org/unodc/crime_cicp_signatures_firearms.html>

14 The *Protocol's* use of the word 'portable' in defining the term 'firearm' is meant to restrict its scope to 'firearms that could be moved or carried by one person without mechanical or other assistance' (UNGA, 2001b, art. 3(a); 2001a, para. 3). This excludes those light weapons that fit the 1997 UN Panel definition, but can be carried only by two or more persons, a pack animal, or a light vehicle. A further limitation on the *Protocol's* scope arises from its use of the words 'barrelled' and 'expel' in defining 'firearm'. As in the case of the *OAS Model Regulations,* discussed above, these two criteria effectively restrict the *Protocol's* coverage of light weapons to those using cartridge-based ammunition.

15 For current Wassenaar Arrangement membership, see <http://www.wassenaar.org/welcomepage.html>

16 For current CIS membership, see <http://www.cisstat.com/eng/cis.htm>

17 For current APEC membership, see <http://www.apec.org/apec.html>

18 For current UN membership, see <http://www.un.org/members/index.html>

19 For current ICAO membership, see <http://www.icao.int/>

20 For current G8 membership, see <http://www.g7.utoronto.ca/>

21 General Assembly Resolution 59/90 merely 'Urges Member States to support current international, regional and national efforts to combat and prevent the illicit transfer of man-portable air defence systems and unauthorized access to and use of such weapons' (UNGA, 2004, para. 2).

22 This section is based on Anders (2004).

23 Germany ended its (US-licensed) production of Stinger MANPADS systems in late 2004 (EADS, 2004).

24 The intention to include missiles in the *Elements* emerges quite clearly in a later section, which, in referring to the 'principal components' of MANPADS, lists 'the gripstock and the missile in a launch tube' (WA, 2003a, sec. 2.9; OSCE, 2004, sec. 2.7).

25 Bulgarian law also regulates the retransfer of foreign weapons from Bulgarian territory. When submitting their permit application, prospective re-exporters must include the authorization of the state from which the weapons were imported; Bulgaria (2002b, art. 22.3.1).

26 Telephone interview with German arms export official, 16 February 2005.

27 As of 1 March 2005, Germany did not extend this waiver in relation to the following EU states: Cyprus, Estonia, Latvia, Lithuania, Malta, Slovakia, and Slovenia. E-mail correspondence with German arms export official, 2 March 2005.

28 Although these do not normally include retransfer restrictions, UK licensing authorities do require end-user undertakings. These may stipulate that, for example, weapons may not be used to violate human rights or be employed in particular regions and areas. Telephone interview with British arms export official, 8 October 2004.

29 In the case of the US, these documents must, at a minimum, identify the recipient and end-user of US-exported defence articles.

30 Germany and the UK, for example, operate a global project licensing scheme under the *Framework Agreement* (France et al., 2000), while US rules permit 'global project authorizations' for government-to-government cooperative projects with Australia, Japan, Sweden, or NATO member countries. US (2004, para. 126.14.3.i).

31 Australia, Japan, New Zealand, and Switzerland.

32 If a recipient government has measures in place 'that will achieve comparable levels of protection and accountability', no delivery verification would be necessary (WA, 2003a, sec. 2.9; OSCE, 2004, sec. 2.7).

33 For another example, see Nairobi Protocol (2004, art. 10.d).

34 See US (2003b, point C8.3.3.5, p. 276).

35 This section is based on Anders (2005).

36 Brazil has yet to produce any type of guided light weapon, but the country's well-developed defence industry and continuing interest in purchasing high-tech infantry weaponry suggests it may not be long before it seeks self-sufficiency in MANPADS (Campbell, 2003). South Africa already manufactures guided anti-tank missile systems, in addition to various larger guided-weapon systems. Moreover, it has entered the market for integrated or 'networked' air defence, involving very short-range air defence systems (VSHORAD), making MANPADS production a logical next step (Denel, 2005a; 2005b).

37 This research could not confirm compliance (or non-compliance) with these standards on the basis of publicly available information. Follow-up enquiries with Brazilian government officials were unsuccessful in resolving these questions.

38 Note that, while South Africa distinguishes among different categories of weapons in order to facilitate the processing of and reporting on export licences, all weapons categories are subject to the same transfer control standards and procedures.

BIBLIOGRAPHY

Anders, Holger. 2004. *Disaggregating SALW Export Controls: Variations and Points of Convergence between Controls on Light Weapons and Military Small Arms.* Background paper. Geneva: Small Arms Survey.

—. 2005. *Export Controls on Light Weapons and Small Arms: The Cases of Brazil and South Africa.* Background paper. Geneva: Small Arms Survey.

APEC (Asia-Pacific Economic Cooperation). 2003. *Bangkok Declaration on Partnership for the Future.* Bangkok. 21 October. Accessed April 2005. <http://www.apec.org/apec/leaders__declarations/2003.html>

Brazil. 1995. *Lei No. 9.112.* 10 October. Published in *Diario Oficial da Uniao,* of 11 October.

—. 2000. *Decreto No 3.665.* 20 November. Published in *Diario Oficial da Uniao* of 21 November.

—. 2001. *Portaria Interministerial MCT/MD nº 631.* 13 November. Published in *Diario Oficial da Uniao* of 16 November.

Bulgaria. 2002a. *Law on the Control of Foreign Trade Activity in Arms and Dual-Use Goods and Technologies.* Entered into force on 3 September. Reprinted in Gounev, Philip et al., eds. 2004. *Weapons under Scrutiny: Implementing Arms Export Controls and Combating Small Arms Proliferation in Bulgaria.* Report by the Center for the Study of Democracy (CSD) and Saferworld. London: Saferworld. April, Appendix 5.

—. 2002b. *Regulation on the Implementation of the Law on the Control of Foreign Trade Activity in Arms and Dual-Use Goods and Technologies.* Decree No. 274 of 29 November. Reprinted in Gounev, Philip et al., eds. 2004. *Weapons under Scrutiny: Implementing Arms Export Controls and Combating Small Arms Proliferation in Bulgaria.* Report by the Center for the Study of Democracy (CSD) and Saferworld. London: Saferworld. April, Appendix 6.

Campbell, Keith. 2003. 'Brazil Interest in SA Missile Technology.' *Engineering News.* Garden View, South Africa: Creamer Media (Pty) Ltd. 13 June. Accessed 21 February 2005. <http://www.engineeringnews.co.za/eng/news/today/?show=36732>

CIS (Commonwealth of Independent States). 2003. *Agreement on Control Measures against International Transfer of Man-portable Anti-aircraft Missile Systems of 'Igla' and 'Strela' Type in the Member States of the Commonwealth of Independent States.* Yalta. 19 September (unofficial translation of the Russian original).

Denel (Denel Aerospace Group). 2005a. Corporate Web site. Pretoria: Denel (Pty) Ltd. Accessed 21 February 2005. <http://www.denel.co.za/Aerospace.asp>

—. 2005b. 'Sable: Ground Based Air Defence System (GBADS).' Pretoria: Denel (Pty) Ltd. Accessed 21 February 2005. <http://www.denel.co.za/Aerospace/Sable_GBADS.pdf>

EADS (European Aeronautic Defence and Space Company). 2004. 'Erfolgreiches Stinger-Losabnahmeschießen in der Türkei.' EADS N.V. Schiphol Rijk, the Netherlands. 9 November. Accessed 3 March 2005. <http://www.eads.net/frame/lang/de/1024/content/OF00000000400003/1/55/33105551.html>

ECOWAS (Economic Community of West African States). 1998. *Declaration of a Moratorium on Importation, Exportation and Manufacture of Light Weapons in West Africa.* Abuja. 31 October. Accessed April 2005. <http://www.iss.co.za/AF/RegOrg/unity_to_union/ECOWAS.html>

—. 1999. *Code of Conduct for the Implementation of the Moratorium on the Importation, Exportation and Manufacture of Light Weapons.* Lomé. 10 December. Reproduced in Jacqueline Seck, ed. 2000. *West Africa Small Arms Moratorium: High-level Consultations on the Modalities for the Implementation of PCASED.* Geneva/Lomé: UNIDIR/UNRCPDA, pp. 53–62.

EU (European Union). 1998. *European Union Code of Conduct on Arms Exports.* 8 June. Reproduced in UN document A/CONF.192/PC/3 of 13 March 2000. Accessed April 2005. <http://www.smallarmssurvey.org/resources/reg_docs.htm>

—. 2003. *Common Military List of the European Union.* 17 November. Reproduced in *Official Journal of the European Union,* No. 2003/C 314/01. 23 December.

—. 2004. *Sixth Annual Report According to Operative Provision 8 of the European Union Code of Conduct on Arms Exports.* EU Document 13816/04 of 11 November.

France et al. 2000. *Framework Agreement between The French Republic, The Federal Republic of Germany, The Italian Republic, The Kingdom of Spain, The Kingdom of Sweden, and The United Kingdom of Great Britain and Northern Ireland concerning Measures to Facilitate the Restructuring and Operation of the European Defence Industry.* Adopted at Farnborough, UK, 27 July. Entered into force on 18 April 2001. Accessed April 2005. <http://projects.sipri.se/expcon/loi/indrest02.htm>

G8. 2003. *Enhance Transport Security and Control of Man-Portable Air Defence Systems (MANPADS): A G8 Action Plan.* Evian Summit, 1–3 June. Accessed April 2005. <http://www.g8.fr/evian/english/>

—. 2004. *G8 Secure and Facilitated International Travel Initiative (SAFTI).* Sea Island Summit, 8–10 June. Accessed April 2005. <http://www.g8usa.gov/d_060904f.htm>

Germany. 1998. *Kriegswaffenliste,* 26 February. Accessed April 2005. <http://www.ausfuhrkontrolle.info/vorschriften/kriegswaffenkontrolle/kriegswaffenliste.pdf>

—. 2000. *Politische Grundsätze der Bundesregierung für den Export von Kriegswaffen und sonstigen Rüstungsgütern.* 19 January. Accessed April 2005. <http://www.auswaertiges-amt.de/www/de/infoservice/download/pdf/friedenspolitik/abruestung/politischegrundsaetze.pdf>

—. 2002. *Formularmuster zu Endverbleibserklärungen.* Published 10 April. Accessed April 2005. <http://www.ausfuhrkontrolle.info/formulare/pdf/eve_muster.pdf>

—. 2004a. *Ausfuhrliste: Abschnitt A, Liste für Waffen, Munition und Rüstungsgüter.* 1 June. Accessed April 2005. <http://www.ausfuhrkontrolle.info/vorschriften/ausfuhrliste/abs_a.pdf>

—. 2004b. *Außenwirtschaftsverordnung,* 10 October. Accessed April 2005. <http://www.ausfuhrkontrolle.info/vorschriften/awg_awv/awv_auszug.pdf>

ICAO (International Civil Aviation Organization). Assembly. 1998. *MANPADS Export Control.* Resolution A32-23. Adopted at the Assembly's 32nd session, September–October 1998. Accessed April 2005. <http://www.icao.int/icao/en/res/9790_en.pdf>

—. 2004a. *Threat to Civil Aviation Posed by Man-Portable Air Defence Systems (MANPADS).* Working Paper. Assembly: 35th Session. A35-WP/50 EX/16 of 28 July. Accessed April 2005. <http://www.icao.int/icao/en/assembl/a35/wp/wp050_en.pdf>

—. 2004b. *Consolidated Statement of Continuing ICAO Policies Related to the Safeguarding of International Civil Aviation against Acts of Unlawful Interference.* Resolution A35-9. Adopted at the Assembly's 35th session, September–October 2004. Accessed April 2005. <http://www.icao.int/icao/en/assembl/a35/a35_res_prov_en.pdf>

—. 2004c. *Threat to Civil Aviation Posed by Man-Portable Air Defence Systems (MANPADS).* Resolution A35-11. Adopted at the Assembly's 35th session, September–October 2004. Accessed April 2005. <http://www.icao.int/icao/en/assembl/a35/a35_res_prov_en.pdf>

Jones, Richard and Charles Cutshaw. 2004. *Jane's Infantry Weapons 2004-2005.* Coulsdon, Jane's Information Group.

Kytömäki, Elli and Valerie Yankey-Wayne. 2004. *Implementing the United Nations Programme of Action on Small Arms and Light Weapons: Analysis of the Reports Submitted by States in 2003.* Geneva: United Nations Institute for Disarmament Research.

McDonald, Glenn. 2005. *Small Arms Instruments of a General Nature: Applicability to Small Arms, Light Weapons, and Their Ammunition.* Background paper. Geneva: Small Arms Survey.

Nairobi Protocol. 2004. *Nairobi Protocol for the Prevention, Control and Reduction of Small Arms and Light Weapons in the Great Lakes Region and the Horn of Africa ('Nairobi Protocol').* Adopted in Nairobi, Kenya, 21 April. Accessed April 2005. <http://www.saferafrica.org/DocumentsCentre/NAIROBI-Protocol.asp>

OAS (Organization of American States). 1997. *Inter-American Convention against the Illicit Manufacturing of and Trafficking in Firearms, Ammunition, Explosives, and Other Related Materials ('Inter-American Convention').* Adopted in Washington, DC, on 14 November. Entered into force on 1 July 1998. Reproduced in UN document A/53/78 of 9 March 1998. Accessed April 2005. <http://www.oas.org/juridico/english/treaties/a-63.html>

—. 1998. *Model Regulations for the Control of the International Movement of Firearms, Their Parts and Components and Ammunition ('Model Regulations').* 2 June. AG/RES. 1543 (XXVIII – O/98). Accessed April 2005. <http://www.cicad.oas.org/Desarrollo_Juridico/ENG/ModelRegulations.asp>

OAU (Organization of African Unity). 2000. *Bamako Declaration on an African Common Position on the Illicit Proliferation, Circulation and Trafficking of Small Arms and Light Weapons.* Bamako, 1 December. SALW/Decl. (I). Accessed April 2005. <http://www.smallarmssurvey.org/resources/reg_docs.htm>

OSCE (Organization for Security and Co-operation in Europe). Forum for Security Co-operation. 2000. *OSCE Document on Small Arms and Light Weapons.* 24 November. FSC.DOC/1/00. Accessed April 2005. <http://www.osce.org/docs/english/fsc/2000/decisions/fscew231.htm>

—. 2004. *OSCE Principles for Export Controls of Man-Portable Air Defence Systems (MANPADS).* Decision No. 3/04. FSC.DEC/3/04 of 26 May. <http://www.osce.org/documents/fsc/2004/05/2965_en.pdf>

Pacific Islands Forum. 2003. *Weapons Control Bill.* Auckland. 16 August. Obtained from the Pacific Islands Forum Secretariat.

Pyadushkin, Maxim with Maria Haug, and Anna Matveeva. 2003. *Beyond the Kalashnikov: Small Arms Production, Exports, and Stockpiles in the Russian Federation.* Occasional Paper No. 10. Geneva: Small Arms Survey. August.

Russian Federation. 2000. *Statute on the Procedures for Implementing the Russian Federation's Military-Technical Cooperation with Foreign States.* Approved by Presidential Decree No. 1953 of 1 December. Accessed April 2005. <http://projects.sipri.se/expcon/natexpcon/Russia/stat_19533.htm>

SADC (Southern African Development Community). 2001. *Protocol on the Control of Firearms, Ammunition and Other Related Materials in the Southern African Development Community (SADC) Region ('SADC Firearms Protocol').* Adopted in Blantyre, Malawi, on 14 August. Entered into force on 8 November 2004. Accessed April 2005. <http://www.smallarmssurvey.org/resources/reg_docs.htm>

Small Arms Survey. 2001. *Small Arms Survey 2001: Profiling the Problem.* Oxford: Oxford University Press.

—. 2002. *Small Arms Survey 2002: Counting the Human Cost.* Oxford: Oxford University Press.

—. 2003. *Small Arms Survey 2003: Development Denied.* Oxford: Oxford University Press.

—. 2004. *Small Arms Survey 2004: Rights at Risk.* Oxford: Oxford University Press.

South Africa. 2002. *National Conventional Arms Control Act, 2002.* Act No. 41 of 2002. Approved 12 February 2003. Published in *Government Gazette,* Vol. 452, No. 24575 of 20 February 2003. Accessed April 2005. <http://www.info.gov.za/gazette/acts/2002/a41-02.pdf>

—. Government Communication and Information System (GCIS). 2004. Cabinet Statement. 1 December. Accessed April 2005. <http://www.gcis.gov.za/media/cabinet/041201.htm>

UK (United Kingdom). 2000. *Consolidated EU and National Arms Export Licensing Criteria.* 26 October. Accessed April 2005. <http://www.fco.gov.uk/servlet/Front?pagename=OpenMarket/Xcelerate/ShowPage&c=Page&cid=1014918697565>

—. 2003a. *UK Implementation and Support for the UN Programme of Action on SALW.* July 2003. Accessed April 2005. <http://disarmament2.un.org/cab/nationalreports/2002/uk.pdf>

—. 2003b. *Ministerial Statement on Man-portable Air Defence Systems (MANPADS) given by the Minister for Europe, Dr Denis MacShane.* 18 November. Reproduced in UK, *Strategic Export Controls: Annual Report 2003,* Annex G, p. 495. London: UK. June 2004.

—. 2004. *End-User Undertakings: Guidance for Form EUU01.* Published June 2004. Accessed April 2005. <http://www.dti.gov.uk/export.control/applying/euuguidance.htm>

UNGA (United Nations General Assembly). 1997. *Report of the Panel of Governmental Experts on Small Arms.* A/52/298 of 27 August.

—. 2001a. *Interpretative Notes for the Official Records ('Travaux préparatoires') of the Negotiation of the Protocol against the Illicit Manufacturing of and Trafficking in Firearms, Their Parts and Components and Ammunition, Supplementing the United Nations Convention against Transnational Organized Crime.* Reproduced in UN document A/55/383/Add.3 of 21 March.

—. 2001b. *Protocol against the Illicit Manufacturing of and Trafficking in Firearms, Their Parts and Components and Ammunition, Supplementing the United Nations Convention against Transnational Organized Crime ('UN Firearms Protocol').* Adopted 31 May. Reproduced in UN document A/RES/55/255 of 8 June. Accessed April 2005. <http://www.undcp.org/pdf/crime/a_res_55/255e.pdf>

—. 2001c. *Programme of Action to Prevent, Combat and Eradicate the Illicit Trade in Small Arms and Light Weapons in All Its Aspects ('UN Programme of Action').* 20 July. Reproduced in UN document A/CONF.192/15. Accessed April 2005. <http://www.smallarmssurvey.org/resources/2001_un_conf.htm>

—. 2003a. *Report on the Continuing Operation of the United Nations Register of Conventional Arms and Its Further Development.* UN document A/58/274 of 13 August.

—. 2003b. *Transparency in Armaments.* Resolution 58/54 of 8 December. Reproduced in UN document A/RES/58/54 of 10 December.

—. 2004. *Prevention of the Illicit Transfer and Unauthorized Access to and Use of Man-Portable Air Defence Systems.* Resolution 59/90 of 3 December. Reproduced in UN document A/RES/59/90 of 17 December.

US (United States). 2003a. *Arms Export Control Act, United States Code, Title 22: Foreign Relations and Intercourse.* Chapter 39: Arms Export Control. Amended 1 June. Accessed April 2005. <http://pmdtc.org/aeca.htm>

—. 2003b. *Security Assistance Management Manual.* DoD 5105.38-M. Chapter 8: End-Use Monitoring (EUM). 3 October. Accessed April 2005. <http://www.dsca.osd.mil/samm/>

—. 2003c. *End-Use Monitoring of Defense Articles and Defense Services: Commercial Exports.* Report for Fiscal Year 2003. Accessed April 2005. <http://www.pmdtc.org/docs/End_Use_FY2003.pdf>

—. 2004. *International Traffic in Arms Regulations (ITAR).* Revised 1 April. Accessed April 2005. <http://pmdtc.org/reference.htm#ITAR>

WA (Wassenaar Arrangement on Export Controls for Conventional Arms and Dual-Use Goods and Technologies). 2000. *Elements for Export Controls of Man-Portable Air Defense Systems (MANPADS).* Accessed April 2005. <http://www.wassenaar.org/docs/oth_manpads.pdf>

—. 2002. *Best Practice Guidelines for Exports of Small Arms and Light Weapons (SALW).* 12 December. Accessed April 2005. <http://www.wassenaar.org/docs/best_practice_salw.htm>

—. 2003a. *Elements for Export Controls of Man-Portable Air Defence Systems (MANPADS).* 12 December. Accessed April 2005. <http://www.wassenaar.org/2003Plenary/MANPADS_2003.htm>

—. 2003b. *Munitions List.* 12 December. Accessed April 2005. <http://www.wassenaar.org/list/wa-listTableOfContents.htm>

—. 2004. *Guidelines and Procedures, including the Initial Elements (as amended and updated in December 2003 and July 2004).* July. Accessed April 2005. <http://www.wassenaar.org/2003Plenary/initial_elements2003.htm>

ACKNOWLEDGEMENTS

Principal author

Glenn McDonald

Other contributors

Holger Anders, James Bevan, Anne-Kathrin Glatz, Sarah Meek, and Ruxandra Stoicescu

SHOOTING

An introduction to guns in contemporary art

Contemporary artists have generated a wide-ranging body of work in which small arms feature prominently. Using a variety of media and approaches—whether paint, video, photography, sculpture, or mixed-media techniques—these artists consider the role of guns in areas as diverse as the media, video games, arms production, the arms trade, and politics. This brief overview presents a selection of their work.

Andy Warhol, *Gun*, 1981-82
Synthetic polymer paint and silkscreen ink on canvas

GALLERY

Guns and the media

In *Gun* (1981–82), **Andy Warhol** represented a firearm using the same celebrated format that established figures such as Marilyn Monroe, Elvis, and Elizabeth Taylor as icons. Ever ahead of his generation, Warhol branded the gun a symbol of popular culture, drawing attention to the plastic quality of the weapon. Today throughout the world, film stars, rappers, and other role models continue to actively promote that image as a symbol of power and sex appeal.

To what extent has the ubiquitous nature of gun imagery contributed to the trivialization of small arms? A video installation by the Belgian artist **Francis Alÿs** offers an answer to that question. In *Re-enactments* (2002), the artist is filmed walking through the streets of Mexico City with a loaded Beretta in his hand. Nearly five minutes elapse before the police see and arrest him. Strikingly, none of the pedestrians notice the firearm, their attention captivated by the filming camera. Alÿs then asks the police officers for permission to re-enact the armed stroll and the arrest. The second video is thus

identical to the first, except that it is staged. By showing these two documents side-by-side, Alÿs is asking viewers to recognize the power of the spectacle in contemporary society: even police officers are willing to allow an armed man to walk the streets for the sake of filmmaking. The work implicitly calls into question the authenticity of 'reality TV', and notably of crime and police shows.

Today, public television networks and channels such as CNN and Sky News compete to show the most explicit images of breaking news stories. In the manner of reality TV, they actively broadcast real gun violence, including kidnap videos showing hostages surrounded by gunmen as well as actual executions. Yet in a culture where fictional gun violence is commonplace, has the spectator become numb to reality?

Francis Alÿs, *Re-enactments*, 2000
Still of video installation

Courtesy of Galerie Peter Kilchmann, Zurich

143

Swiss artist **Christoph Draeger** considers this problem in his 2002 installation *Black September.* The title of this work refers to the Palestinian terrorist group that abducted and killed 11 members of the Israeli team at the Munich Olympics in September 1972. The installation re-creates the room

Christoph Draeger, *Black September*, 2002
Single channel video on DVD, 13 min

Courtesy of müllerdechiara

where the hostages where held, replete with the television on which the armed hostage-takers were able to follow the highly publicized manoeuvres of the Munich police. In an adjacent space, Draeger projects a film that re-enacts the missing events as they may have taken place in the room. The film—made with surveillance and amateur video cameras—thus presents the missing 'footage'. The viewer is consequently faced with a dual reality: real video documents are complemented by fictional film. Similarly, the room is faithfully recreated, yet it is no more than a reconstruction. In Draeger's work, fact and fiction converge to create a new reality.

Wang Du, *Parade*, 2000
Courtesy of the artist

Not unlike television and film, newspapers, magazines, and Internet sites contribute liberally to the proliferation of gun imagery. Chinese artist **Wang Du** selected images of the Chinese army from magazines and newspapers for his 2000 sculpture installation *Parade*. He reproduced each image in the form of a monumental sculpture, transforming the one-dimensional original into a three-dimensional object while retaining the photographic perspective. By assembling these new forms to create a giant, euphoric 'parade', Du highlights the artifice of images designed to promote militant patriotism. The military parade, traditionally a sober and disciplined display of armed forces, here assumes the air of a Hollywood-style performance, glorifying guns, youth, and nationalism.

Gun play

A number of contemporary artists have responded to the presence of guns in video games, particularly the increasingly realistic, ultra-violent 'shoot'em-ups'. The heroes of some of these games have risen to the rank of cultural icons: both Lara Croft and Resident Evil have been turned into blockbuster Hollywood films and the animated heroine of the game *Bloodrayne* was featured in the October 2004 issue of *Playboy* magazine. In the moral and physical safety of their own homes, the users of these entertainment systems can play at shooting and killing with guaranteed impunity.

The Dutch–Swiss artist **Yan Duyvendak** analyses the social implications of these games in his 2004 performance *You're Dead*. Dressed as a soldier and armed with an automatic rifle, the artist carries out and simultaneously narrates a sequence of manoeuvres that correspond to a video game projected onto a screen behind him. What initially seems like the simple impersonation of a video game character takes on complexity when the artist enacts the same sequence as a player and finally as a soldier in battle. Three levels of engagement become apparent: the character programmed to carry out orders, the player who delights in the excitement of bloody combat, and the soldier who fears for his life. The repeated narration conveys different meanings in each sequence. By passing imperceptibly from one role to the next, the artist compels the viewer to question society's acceptance of gun violence in the video game format and to reflect on the significance of the familiar phrase, 'You're dead'.

Courtesy of the artist

Yan Duyvendak, *You're Dead*, 2004

Along similar lines, the Swedish artists **Tobias Bernstrup** and **Palle Torsson** consider a player's willingness to adapt to the ethics of video game culture. For their project *Museum Meltdown* (1996–99), they customized the game *Half-Life* to simulate the interior of three contemporary art institutions.[1] The games invite the visitor to engage in a frenzied shoot-out in which survival depends on killing monsters and government troops. Players are free to destroy artwork as they move from one room to the next. *Museum Meltdown* thus brings the violence of contemporary culture into the heart of the art institution, traditionally a haven for the conservation of art. The visitor-turned-player is forced to face the destructive instincts present in us all.

Tobias Bernstrup and Palle Torsson, *Museum Meltdown*, Moderna Museet, Stockholm, 1999 (modification of the computer game *Half-Life*)

© 2002 Tobias Bernstrup. Courtesy of Andréhn-schiptjenko

---

[1] Arken Museum for Modern Art, Copenhagen, Denmark, 1996; Contemporary Art Center, Vilnius, Lithuania, 1997; Moderna Museet, Stockholm, Sweden, 1999.

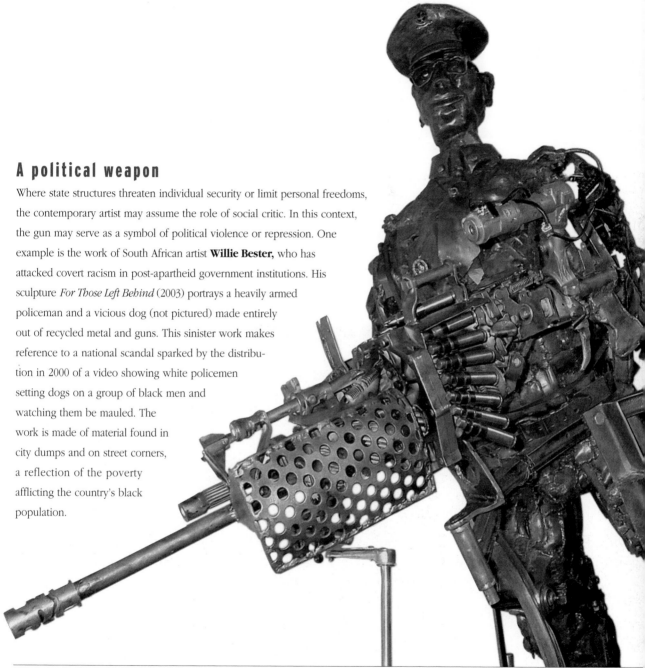

A political weapon

Where state structures threaten individual security or limit personal freedoms, the contemporary artist may assume the role of social critic. In this context, the gun may serve as a symbol of political violence or repression. One example is the work of South African artist **Willie Bester,** who has attacked covert racism in post-apartheid government institutions. His sculpture *For Those Left Behind* (2003) portrays a heavily armed policeman and a vicious dog (not pictured) made entirely out of recycled metal and guns. This sinister work makes reference to a national scandal sparked by the distribution in 2000 of a video showing white policemen setting dogs on a group of black men and watching them be mauled. The work is made of material found in city dumps and on street corners, a reflection of the poverty afflicting the country's black population.

Willie Bester, *For Those Left Behind*, 2003 (detail)
Courtesy of the artist and 34 Long

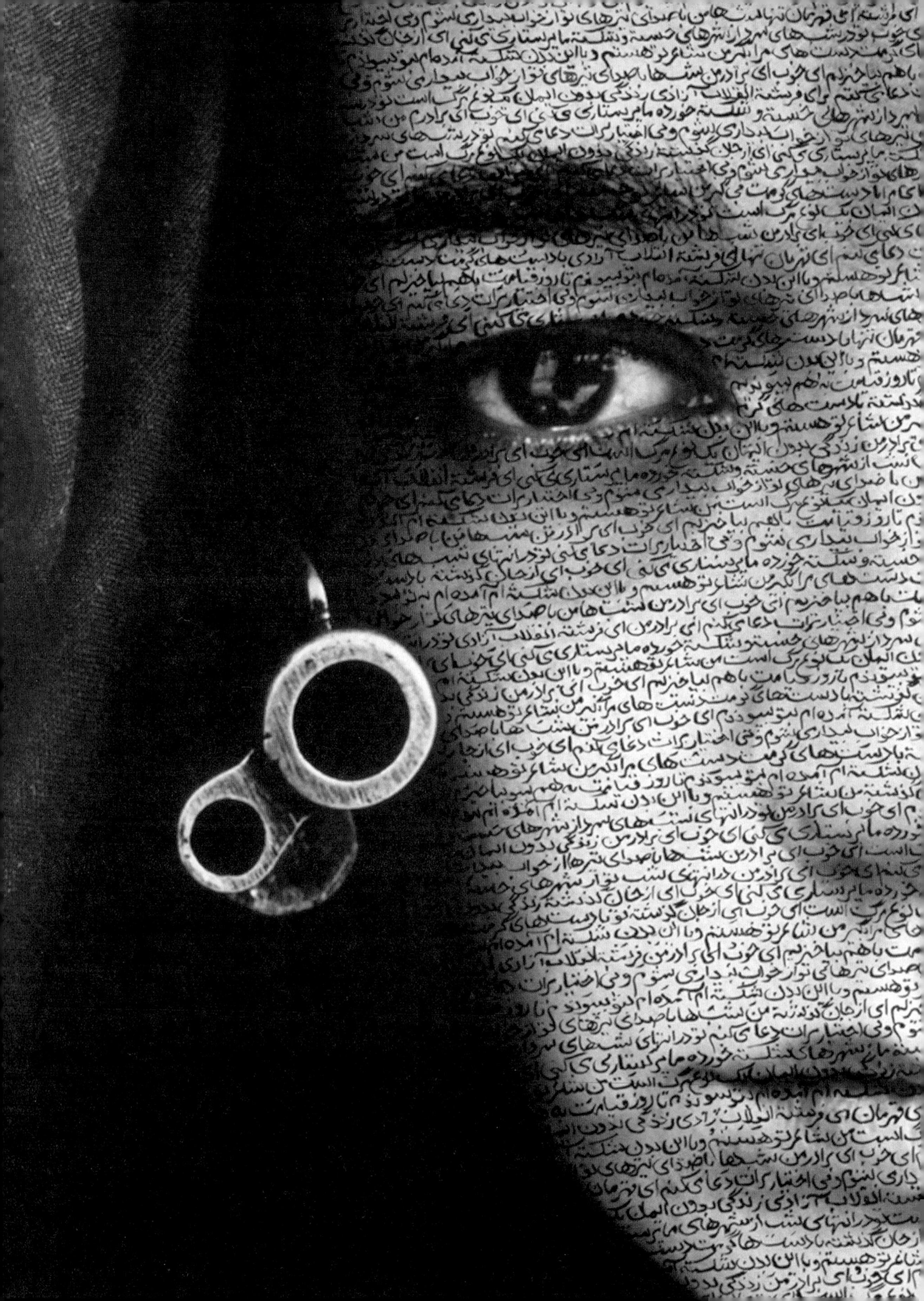

Iranian artist Shirin Neshat uses the gun as a symbol of rebellion and repression in her photographic work, which forms a complex portrait of women in contemporary Iran. 'Speechless' (1996) shows a young Muslim woman, her face painted with text from the Koran in the style of traditional henna body decoration. Her headscarf lifts from her cheek to reveal the tip of a gun barrel aimed at the viewer. On one level the image speaks of the importance of martyrdom in Islamic society—religious acts from which women are traditionally excluded, but to which some aspire. Yet it also suggests the oppression Muslim women are subjected to under strict religious law. This woman is literally masked by the veil and the religious texts on her face. The gun at her head is not controlled by her. The viewer must ask: who is controlling the gun?

Political powers engaged in the arms trade are at the core of Irish artist **Malachi Farrell**'s 2003 installation, *Nothing Domestic*. In a colourful marketplace of gun-laden stalls, countries proffer small arms for sale. An intricate mechanical system unites the vendors via the guns on display, which have been programmed to move in unison to music broadcast on loudspeakers. The arms trade thus becomes an international ballet in which all parties move to the same beat. The absurdity of the dancing guns comments on the global weapons trade, in which states with conflicting political agendas continue to make arms deals.

Malachi Farrell, *Nothing Domestic*, 2003 (detail)
Installation and sound, variable dimensions

Shirin Neshat, 'Speechless', 1996
C print (photo by Larry Barns)
19 cm x 86 cm
© Shirin Neshat, 1996
Courtesy of Gladstone Gallery, New York

Victims and survivors

Complementing the literal representations of guns in contemporary art presented above are works concerned with the effects and ramifications of gun violence. In response to the high levels of gun fatalities in the United States, a number of US artists

have focused on the loss of life and grief of loved ones. In 1990, Cuban-born artist **Félix González-Torres** began work on *Untitled (Death by Gun)*, a nine-inch stack of paper on which he printed photographs of 460 individuals killed by gunshots during the week of 1–7 May 1989. Captions on each photograph provide details about the victims and the circumstances of their deaths. The artist designed the stack so that visitors may take the sheets to keep or pass on to friends; depleted sheets are then reprinted and replaced. This memorial may thus circulate indefinitely.

Félix González-Torres, *Untitled (Death by Gun)*, 1990, nine-inch stack of photolithographs, offset printed in black, sheet: 113 cm x 82.5 cm

In *Shroud: Mothers' Voices* (1992), another US artist, **Bradley McCallum,** concentrates on the mothers of gunshot victims. In this installation, white, shroud-like sheets hang from the ceiling of the exhibition space; each sheet features silk rubbings from photographs of the mothers of local gun victims. Accompanying videotaped interviews feature the same women talking about the children they lost and the people they blame for their deaths. Through this piece, McCallum gives a voice to the families of the victims of gun violence.

Bradley McCallum, *Shroud: Mothers' Voices,* 1992
Silk with photo images, text, and video interviews

Courtesy of the artist

In the work of the German-born Jewish artist **Ruth Liberman,** the target of the gunshot is not a human life, but the written word. The artist aims to obliterate the power of words in documents that underpin political oppression and violence. She focuses on written forms that can have a direct impact on human life: decrees, orders, lists, warnings, and condemnations. For her 2001 triptych *Shot,* Liberman asked a marksman to shoot the German word for 'burden', *Bürde.* By shooting certain German words that she singles out as anti-Semitic or associated with the Holocaust, Liberman is simultaneously destroying the power of these words to communicate and calling attention to the role language plays in violence.

Ruth Liberman, *Shot,* 1992
Iris print on paper, 76 cm x 51 cm
Courtesy of the artist

rnha

Bürq

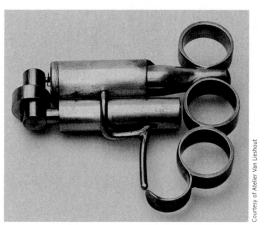

Atelier Van Lieshout, *Pistolet poignée américaine*, 1995
Steel and stainless steel; L: 12 cm, W: 11 cm, H: 2 cm
Courtesy of Atelier Van Lieshout

Legal boundaries

In contrast to artists who focus on gun violence, the following artists develop themes related to arms production. The Dutch **Atelier Van Lieshout** produced some of the most intriguing, and no doubt controversial, examples of this type of work. Between 1995 and 1998, this multidisciplinary artist collective fabricated a series of firearms as artwork, including machine guns and the *Pistolet poignée américaine*. This manufacture formed part of a larger project through which the group aimed to create an autonomous free state. Although the arms were never conceived for use and are not operational, the project highlights the facility with which gun- and bomb-making instructions may be accessed on line and in libraries.

The limits between art and gun possession are also tested in the work of Danish artist **Jens Haaning.** In his piece *Sawn-off* (1993)—a sawn-off shotgun with real ammunition in a plastic bag—the artist explores the border between what is acceptable in the context of an art exhibition and what is acceptable in daily life. Similarly, for *Weapon Production* (1995), Haaning recruited immigrants to manufacture street weapons over a two-week period in a Copenhagen workshop; the space was then opened to the public.

Jens Haaning, *Sawn-off*, 1993
Sawn-off shotgun with ammunition in plastic bag

Taking the flirtation with legal boundaries to the limit is French artist **Philippe Meste.** In his work *Military Surveillance Post* (1994), the artist placed a 'military base' consisting of sand bags and guarded by armed men in the middle of a flea market in Marseille. Meste's use of guns serves not as an anti-military gesture, but rather as a vehicle for the criticism of Western insecurity. The artist utilizes the very tools of security forces to produce anxiety, calling into question the security concerns of highly protected societies. In an even more radical work, Meste attacked the flagship of the French navy, the aircraft carrier *Foch*, with flare rockets launched from a boat in the harbour of Toulon (*L'attaque du Port de Toulon*, or *Attack on Toulon Harbour*, 1993). His attack posed no threat to the sophisticated warship.

Philippe Meste, *Military surveillance post* (Poste militaire), 30 October 1994
Black and white print, 80 cm x 120 cm
Courtesy of Jousse Entreprise, Paris

An object of beauty

What defines the relationship of gunowners to their weapons? In his series *Friendly Fire*, German photographer **Peter Tillessen** steps into gun collectors' homes to capture them with their weapons. Yet the images do not reveal the owners' faces; their anonymity may well reflect a lack of social acceptance of gun collection today. The weapons themselves display a streamlined design and functional simplicity not unlike those of the apartment furnishings. The viewer must get a sense of the owner's relationship to the gun from the body language rather than a facial expression. The gun conveys an extraordinary sense of power and violence within these ordinary settings.

Courtesy of the artist

Peter Tillessen, *Friendly Fire*, 2003
C-print, 40 cm x 50 cm

British artist **Cornelia Parker** considers the gun as a purely formal concept in her 1995 sculpture *Embryo Firearms*. She presents the gun at its earliest stage of production, at the point where its form becomes recognizable. As yet, the object is no more than a piece of metal, yet it already functions as a powerful symbol. By revealing the gun in its nascent form, the artist underlines the fact that deadly weapons are merely pieces of metal. It is man who forges the metal, perfects the mechanisms, and uses the resulting weapon.

Cornelia Parker, *Embryo Firearms*, 1995
Colts 45 at the first production stage
48.6 cm x 33.3 cm x 6.1 cm

With thanks to Colts Manufacturing Company LLC, Hartford, Connecticut
Courtesy of Galerie Guy Bärtschi, Geneva

In our sights

The diversity of ideas and issues explored by this small selection of international contemporary artists demonstrates that small arms continue to be a major concern throughout the world. As long as the gun continues to function as a symbol and weapon—a dual role it is not likely to shed in the near future—artists are sure to reflect on its impact, conveying messages that may help gauge a variety of social responses to the use, abuse, and proliferation of small arms worldwide.

Concept and research: Tania Inowlocki

Text: Katie Kennedy

Special thanks go out to Georges Armaos, Jean-Paul Felley, Nicoletta Forni, Anne Guillemet, Olivier Kaeser, Richard Klein, Emile LeBrun, Sèdjro Mensah, Marie-josé Ourtilane, and Yann Saletes.

An armed Tuareg man attends a meeting of regional Tuareg, Songhai, and other leaders to discuss peace and disarmament. (© Crispin Hughes/Panos Pictures)

Sourcing the Tools of War:
SMALL ARMS SUPPLIES TO CONFLICT ZONES

INTRODUCTION

International illicit arms transfers to conflict and war zones often display features characteristic of newsworthy stories.[1] They tend to involve shady, greedy dealers and financiers with Hollywood-type lifestyles; suspicious means of transport, with airplane registrations being changed mid-flight and jets sometimes touching down on tarmac in the middle of the jungle; and disturbingly ruthless recipients. Some cases embroil politicians and other public figures. No wonder, then, that the media are particularly eager to cover this aspect of the small arms problem.

Given the intense political debates about whether to supply arms and ammunition to areas of conflict, researchers and analysts also devote substantial attention to this issue. The dynamics at work here are complex: states are pitted against religious and human rights groups; exporter states confront states that refuse to authorize particular deals; peace activists denounce gun manufacturers; and so on. Many NGOs, some intergovernmental organizations, and certain governments have reported on transfers of arms—including small arms and light weapons[2]—to various conflict zones, some of them under arms embargo. These reports provide invaluable insight into individual transfers of weapons as well as transfer patterns to particular conflict zones. Much of the writing concentrates on large international transfers to conflict regions—such as those involving many hundreds of weapons or millions of rounds of ammunition.[3]

Today this focus is also partly reflected by the international agenda, which endorses measures to control brokering, improve end-user documentation and controls, and reinforce and extend international arms embargoes. These measures are primarily directed against large illicit shipments of small arms.

This chapter focuses instead on the role of the many different sources of supply in a selected number of recent or current internal conflicts in Africa, the Americas, and Central Asia and the Caucasus. It underscores that sources are varied, and that the focus on large international arms transfers should not obscure the need to study other sources of supply, particularly from a regulatory perspective.

The main conclusions of the chapter are the following:

- As a conflict continues, small arms procurement patterns of governments and of insurgents often become more sophisticated, diverse, and entrenched.
- Transfers to conflict zones include an important 'ant trade', a small but steady trickle of weapons that can produce large accumulations over time.
- Through corruption, theft, free distribution, and sales, government stockpiles constitute an important source of small arms in virtually all conflict zones. In some conflicts, they are the dominant source for all combatants.
- Since the 1990s, economic motives—including greed—have been highlighted as key factors in the arms trade. Even in the post-cold war era, however, political affiliations and loyalties remain important in elucidating small arms transfer patterns.[4]

- In long-standing conflicts whose parties have financial resources at their disposal, local production can be an important source of supply. While rare, this can also apply to insurgents.

- In order to stem the flow of small arms to conflict areas, issues such as border control and corruption must be added to the international agenda.

COMPARING ARMS SOURCING

This chapter compares the sources of small arms used in six recent and current internal conflicts on three continents: Colombia and Haiti in the Americas; Liberia and Mali in West Africa; and Tajikistan and Georgia in Central Asia and the Caucasus. These six internal conflicts differ in terms of origin, duration, existence of an arms embargo,[5] the number of casualties, refugees, internally displaced persons (IDPs), and other categories of victims, and the number of combatants and belligerent groups. By virtue of these variations, the case studies present a wide range of conflict scenarios. Yet since the conflicts are roughly contemporaneous—covering the early 1990s to the present—they allow for meaningful comparisons. Moreover, pair cases represent countries with relative geographical proximity or likeness, so that they could be expected to tap into similar international trafficking networks, even if conflict scenarios are dissimilar. The sample thus allows for some general—albeit tentative—conclusions on the nature of the sourcing of tools of war.

Different sources complement one another and can change throughout a conflict.

This analysis illustrates the complexity of small arms sourcing, the complementary character of different sources, and the changing nature of sourcing throughout a conflict. It considers the various means by which small arms find their way to conflict areas: domestic production (government-authorized or illicit); theft, leakage, sale, and other outflows of weaponry from existing (mostly state) stockpiles; and transfers from abroad (large- and small-scale legal trade, illicit ant trade, or large-scale trafficking). Through its six case studies—and acknowledging the difficult nature of accessing accurate information in this field—this chapter makes a step towards painting a general picture of weapons sourcing to conflict zones.[6]

From insurgent production to international state support: Colombia and Haiti

At the start of 2005, the Colombian armed conflict and the troubles in Haiti were probably the most serious cases of discord in the Western Hemisphere. Patterns of weapons sourcing in the two cases have been rather distinct, not least because of the varying degree of organization of the warring factions, and important differences in resources. In Colombia, domestic production of small arms (both state-controlled and illicit production), state stockpiles, international authorized trade, and international illicit deals (small-scale and the 'classic' larger transactions involving brokers and forged documentation) have played a part in arming combatants. This case exemplifies how weapon sources can be diversified as a conflict wears on, and as fighters become wealthier. In contrast, small arms sources in Haiti have been less varied. The weapons held by the Haitian government, as well as by the different armed groups active in the country, have consisted mostly of bladed weapons and small arms, many of which have reportedly come from the abolished Haitian Army (IISS, 2004). Despite these differences, however, some similarities exist. One is the role of the ant trade; a second is the part inadvertently played by the United States, which has become a source country of illicit guns shipped by members of the Colombian and Haitian diasporas, among others.

Colombia

This section focuses specifically on the main reported sources of small arms in the 1999–2003 period of the Colombian conflict. Colombia has been plagued by internal conflict for many decades. Since the war began, parties' motivations have shifted, and since the 1980s, the drug trade has helped fuel the conflict. The conflict involves state forces, two guerrilla organizations—the Revolutionary Armed Forces of Colombia (Fuerzas Armadas Revolucionarias de Colombia, FARC) and the National Liberation Army (Ejército de Liberación Nacional, ELN)—as well as various paramilitary groups, organized under the umbrella of the United Self-Defence Forces of Colombia (Autodefensas Unidas de Colombia, AUC).

Domestic production has been one important source of small arms in this conflict. Government-authorized small arms production is concentrated in the factories of the state-owned Industria Militar (INDUMIL), which are run by the Ministry of Defence. The company supplies weapons to the Colombian military and police. Between 1994 and 2003, INDUMIL produced approximately 37,500 Galil assault rifles under licence from Israel.[7] It also manufactures a large variety of revolvers, grenades, and small arms ammunition.[8] The Colombian leadership plans to make the country self-sufficient in small arms and ammunition (Dreyfus and Lessing, 2003). In 2002, INDUMIL announced that it was to double its annual production of Galil rifles and associated ammunition (Bourne, 2004, p. 235).

Between 1999 and 2003, however, Colombia still imported a wide range of small arms. As the only legal importer of small arms, INDUMIL receives all imports. The company then sells some of the imported guns (mainly hunting rifles, pistols, revolvers, and shotguns) to civilians. INDUMIL officials claim that because of strict control and registration mechanisms, the bulk of legal civilian trade consists of sales to private security companies (Dreyfus and Lessing, 2003).[9] Thus, it seems that authorized imports of small arms most often end up in the Colombian security sector writ large.

Colombia's largest reported small arms suppliers in 1999–2003 were (in order of significance): the United States (chiefly military weapons, including large quantities of machine guns, ammunition, and parts and accessories for military weapons);[10] Israel (primarily military weapons and their parts and accessories);[11] Brazil (principally ammunition);[12] South Africa (mostly military weapons);[13] the Czech Republic (predominantly pistols);[14] and Italy (mainly pistols).[15] The United States reportedly accounted for approximately one-half of all Colombian small arms imports;[16] it exported a large amount of small arms under the framework of the International Narcotics Control Program (Plan Colombia). US small arms exports to Colombia are thus part of a much larger programme of military assistance and training offered by the United States as part of its 'war on drugs'.[17]

While the Colombian government obtains its small arms from domestic production and government-authorized imports, the insurgent groups and paramilitaries have relied on other sources. In most cases, the sources of small arms available to the AUC and its opponents are similar, but there are some differences. The AUC has unofficially received weapons from army units in Colombia, which has not been the case for the FARC and the ELN (Kurth Cronin, 2004, p. 107). Colombian military and police stockpiles have nevertheless been a key source of small arms for the FARC and the ELN. They have either captured weapons in assaults and skirmishes or purchased them from corrupt officers (Jaramillo, 1999, p. 205). The local black market has been a second source (Jaramillo, 1999, p. 205). In addition, some small arms have reportedly been extracted directly from INDUMIL factories, procured from workers, or through theft from storage facilities (Cragin and Hoffman, 2003, p. 45).

The FARC's illicit small arms production is unique in terms of its scale and the sophistication of the products and manufacturing methods.

In the past decade, insurgent and paramilitary sourcing has changed quite radically, in particular for the FARC. First, as a result of its involvement in the drug economy, the FARC has been able to create a comparatively large-scale, illicit small arms industry, producing sub-machine guns and light weapons such as mortars and hand and mortar grenades (Dreyfus and Lessing, 2003). The group's production differs from much of the illicit, or so-called craft, production conducted elsewhere in the world due to its large volume as well as the sophistication of its products and the manufacturing methods. The FARC reportedly uses front companies to buy machinery and raw materials on the national and international markets; the group copies weapon and ammunition models from hardware designs produced by INDUMIL or foreign companies.[18] Neither the AUC nor the ELN has comparable production capabilities.

Second, with the end of the cold war, large amounts of small arms became available on the wider Latin American illicit markets; in the 1980s, the Soviet Union and the United States had shipped some of these weapons—many of which originated in the former Soviet bloc—to El Salvador, Honduras, and Nicaragua (bound for governments or insurgents).[19] A study published by the RAND Corporation in 2003 asserts that 'thousands, or even tens of thousands, of weapons' shipped by the United States to Central America at various times 'likely remain in caches throughout [the region]' (Cragin and Hoffman, 2003, p. 12). A much-publicized case of a transfer involving cold war-era weapons was the November 2001 shipment of 3,000 Nicaraguan-sourced AK-47s and five million rounds of ammunition to the AUC using forged documentation from Panama (OAS, 2003). Approximately one-third of all small arms trafficked into Colombia between 1998 and mid-2001 was reportedly sourced in El Salvador, Honduras, Nicaragua, Panama, and, to a lesser degree, Costa Rica (Cragin and Hoffman, 2003, p. 21). Not all of this trafficking was in cold war weaponry, however: newer small arms originated in the Caribbean, Mexico, and the United States (Cragin and Hoffman, 2003, p. 23).

A police director inspects a box of mortars seized from paramilitary groups in northern Colombia in July 2000. The arsenal comprised automatic guns, mortars, machine guns, and almost 100 grenades.

© Luis Acosta/AFP/Getty Images

The FARC's burgeoning amounts of cash (stemming from its increasing involvement in the drug trade) permitted it to purchase more small arms abroad, from Central America and a number of other sources.[20] The AUC has a relatively long history of buying small arms on the international illicit market. The group's money is obtained through its participation in the drug economy as well as from 'protection' services supplied to large landowners to end kidnappings by the FARC and the ELN (Cragin and Hoffman, 2003, p. 7).

Besides Central America, the insurgents and paramilitaries have reportedly enjoyed access to other sources of illicit small arms. Several US indictments of traffickers, often of Colombian origin, provide an initial indication of illicit trafficking links between Colombia and the United States (AP, 2004a; 2004c; Seper, 2004; Grech, 2000). Oftentimes, such trafficking allegedly involves transiting through Central American countries (Colombia, Policía Nacional, 2001). All three of Colombia's main armed groups have been engaged in trafficking from the United States (Jaramillo, 1999, p. 207). The AUC, for instance, has reportedly used intermediaries to purchase weapons in US states with liberal gun regulations and export them illegally (Jaramillo, 1999, p. 207).

Illicit small arms have also come from Brazil, Ecuador, Paraguay, Peru, Venezuela, and other South American countries (AI, 2003, pp. 25–27; Cragin and Hoffman, 2003, pp. 28—32; Bourne, 2004, p. 165). Colombian intelligence sources reveal that FARC forces operating in the south of the country during the 1990s frequently purchased Brazilian-made ammunition and pistols in Paraguay: the weapons were then transported on illegal flights from the Triple Border Area between Argentina, Brazil, and Paraguay. Such trafficking has declined of late because of the stricter import and sale controls implemented by Paraguay in 2000 and 2002.[21]

It is sometimes difficult to determine whether a shipment is trafficked without state involvement or actually sponsored by the state. In particular, it is unclear whether alleged Venezuelan transfers to the FARC were state-sponsored or whether they were facilitated by lax stockpile management and security within the Venezuelan Armed Forces.[22] A 2004 study by the International Crisis Group reports that elements of the Ecuadorian military have allegedly been involved in arms trafficking to Colombia, especially to the FARC (ICG, 2004, p. 13).

> It is sometimes difficult to determine whether a shipment is trafficked without state involvement or actually sponsored by the state.

Over time, a number of large transfers of illicit small arms destined for the FARC, the ELN, or the AUC have come to light. The above-mentioned Nicaragua–Panama–AUC shipment is one; another is the 1999 shipment of 10,000 AK-47s to the FARC, implicating former Peruvian President Alberto Fujimori and the head of the Peruvian intelligence service, Vladimiro Montesinos.[23] At least from 1998 to 2001, however, the bulk of the trafficking apparently consisted of 'ant trade' transactions, with small arms constantly trickling into Colombia by land, sea, and air via hundreds of routes. This approach 'preclude[s] the need for forged end-user certificates, sophisticated cover-ups, or any other methods typically used by state-sponsored traffickers or criminal syndicates' (Cragin and Hoffman, 2003, p. xviii). Air trafficking, for example, has relied mainly on small single-engine charter planes carrying not more than a few hundred assault rifles without ammunition (Cragin and Hoffman, 2003, p. 38).

The Colombian example demonstrates how diverse the sources of small arms to a conflict zone can be. They include domestic production, leakages from stockpiles (including those of factories), and most of the various forms of legal and illicit trade. In the Haitian case, the circumstances are rather different.

Haiti

The past few years have seen Haiti teetering between civil unrest and full-fledged civil war. In February 2004, street battles broke out between the groups supporting President Jean-Bertrand Aristide on the one side, and those opposing him on the other. Aristide's forced resignation and expatriation soon followed.

Haiti's numerous armed groups procured some of their guns directly from the Haitian Army (Forces Armées d'Haïti, or FADH), which unlawfully overthrew Aristide in 1991 following his victory in the country's first-ever democratic elections. Soon after a US-led multinational force restored him to power in 1994, Aristide abolished the FADH. Yet before disbanding, the

Supporters of exiled leader Jean-Bertrand Aristide brandish guns during a protest in Port-au-Prince in March 2004.

© Eliana Aponte/Reuters

FADH distributed an assortment of weapons to supporting militias, and many soldiers and police officers deserted, allegedly taking at least their handguns with them (Arthur, 2002, pp. 1, 3).

The informal militias were not systematically disarmed although the UN-sponsored multinational force deployed on Haitian soil between 1994 and 1997 had a disarmament mandate (Stotzky, 1997, p. 160). The force seized heavy weapons from the FADH and confiscated small arms found in caches or carried in public, but militia members could keep their guns if they did not display them openly (Bailey et al., 1998, p. 229). During a gun buy-back scheme, which ran from September 1994 to March 1995, the United States purchased 3,389 weapons[24]; official US information sources reported that many of these were old and unserviceable (US GAO, 2000, pp. 21–22). The gun buy-back initiative allegedly only helped people to rearm with better guns, as they were provided with the necessary funds (Stohl, 2004); US commanders labelled it a 'dismal failure' (US GAO, 2000, p. 22).

Despite the efforts of the US authorities to stem the trade, a steady trickle of illicit small arms has flowed from the United States to Haiti.

The failed attempt to disarm the militias in the mid-1990s was widely criticized. It raised concerns among Haitians and international observers with the UN and the Organization of American States (OAS) that anti-democratic forces could use the weaponry they had been able to keep to overthrow the elected government once again (Stotzky, 1997, p. 160; Stohl, 2004).

In 1991 the United States placed an embargo on the export of defence articles and defence services to Haiti.[25] Despite US authorities' efforts to stem the remaining trade, a steady trickle of illicit small arms has flowed from the United States to its southern neighbour (CCI, 2004, p. 3). Florida—with its relatively liberal gun laws[26]—is reportedly the source of many of the guns that are smuggled into Haiti from the United States (Stohl, 2004; Bergman and Granados, 2004). From 2001 to 2003, 25 per cent of the gun-smuggling cases handled by the Miami office of the Bureau of Alcohol, Tobacco, Firearms and Explosives (ATF) involved firearms bound for Haiti, making the island the top destination for guns illegally exported from south Florida. To a lesser extent, guns are also smuggled from other parts of the United States. Members of the Haitian diaspora were allegedly at the centre of a significant number of gun-smuggling cases (Bergman and de Granados, 2004).

ATF agents have reported that the flow of smuggled small arms to Haiti has been constant, but that there have been peaks during periods of political unrest. The profits derived from smuggling guns from one of the richest countries in the world to one of the poorest have allegedly been high, although reports of black-market prices are notoriously difficult to verify. Smuggling has been organized, but on a small scale. Once 'straw purchasers' (front buyers) procure small arms from individual gun dealers in the United States, other individuals transport them to Haiti. The weapons may be hidden inside electronic equipment or other kinds of innocuous merchandise (Bergman and de Granados, 2004).

The Dominican Republic shares a notoriously porous land border with Haiti. One report states that '[e]vidence does point to a flow of weapons to Haitian rebels from the Dominican Republic in the lead-up to the [2004] unrest'.[27] No detailed information is currently available, however, on the scale and modalities of the alleged trafficking between the Dominican Republic and Haiti. During the crisis, insurgents also allegedly received small arms made in the former Eastern bloc (AK-47 assault rifles and PKM machine guns) and sourced in Central and South America (CCI, 2004, p. 3). Again, few details are available on this alleged trafficking.

One of the very few reported authorized international arms transfers involved South Africa. The government reportedly approved the arms licence without delay, anticipating that the 5,000 pieces of ammunition, 200 smoke grenades, and 200 bullet-proof vests would fortify Aristide's police units during the 2004 crisis. Yet the consignment did not reach Haiti's shores in time to assist the embattled president. Rather, it was returned to South Africa after a stopover in Jamaica (BBC Worldwide Monitoring, 2004; *Business Day*, 2004).

The brief case studies of Colombia and Haiti show that the ant trade can be important in the illicit flow of guns into zones of conflict. They also reveal that the principal regional power, the United States, has at times played a significant role in providing authorized small arms; moreover, it has been an inadvertent source of illicit shipments organized by members of the respective diasporas and others. Finally, leakage from military stockpiles has been a problem in both countries. In other respects, the two nations are very different, with Colombian production having no equivalent in Haiti, and legal and illicit trade in small arms being incomparably larger and more sophisticated in Colombia.

International shipments versus internal stockpiles: Mali and Liberia

The Malian and Liberian conflicts are dissimilar in terms of scale, duration, and intensity. Weapons procurement patterns also differ significantly. In Liberia, important international shipments of small arms to both government and insurgent forces appear to have been motivated by the prospect of political and financial gain. In contrast, pre-existing stocks of small arms were of paramount importance in Mali and sourcing was not influenced by the development of arms markets in the former Soviet Union and Central and Eastern Europe from the early 1990s onwards. The opposite was true of Liberia. Liberian arms sourcing patterns are often perceived as typical of the West African region.[28] The Malian case reveals, however, that the picture is not uniform.

Mali [29]

In simple terms, the Tuareg–Arab insurgency in northern Mali (1990–96) stemmed from long-standing separatist aims among the nomadic Tuareg and Arabs. These aspirations were fuelled by the government's marginalization of northern Mali and the repression of its people. Initially one single movement, the insurgents quickly split into several groups based on tribal and clan affiliations. Primarily, these were:

- the Popular Movement of Azawad (Mouvement Populaire de Libération de l'Azawad, MPLA),
- the Popular Front for the Liberation of Azawad (Front Populaire de Libération de l'Azawad, FPLA),
- the Revolutionary Alliance for the Liberation of Azawad (Armée Révolutionnaire de Libération de l'Azawad, ARLA), and
- the Arabic Islamic Front of Azawad (Front Islamique Arabe de l'Azawad, FIAA). All of these acted under the loose umbrella of the Movement of Azawad United Fronts (Mouvements et Fronts Unis de l'Azawad, MFUA).[30]
- Aside from the Malian Army, the main group fighting this coalition was the Ganda Koy Patriotic Movement (Mouvement Patriotique de Ganda Koy, MPGK), a militia composed of sedentary peoples.

At the outset of the insurgency, Malian armed groups relied almost exclusively on weapons captured in combat or looted from state armouries.

Despite the weapons losses suffered by the Malian Army in the course of the conflict, there are no reports confirming Mali's acquisition of new small arms during this period (Heyman, 2000, pp. 461–62). While such procurement cannot be ruled out, it appears that the Malian military relied to a great extent on arms the country acquired from the Soviet Union and states of the Warsaw Treaty Organization in the 1970s and 1980s (Heyman, 2000, p. 460); the army also seems to have used stocks remaining from the French colonial era.

At the outset of the insurgency, Malian groups had few arms. The MPLA is even said to have launched the insurgency with a single AK-47 (Humphreys and ag Mohamed, 2003, p. 3). Many of the attacks on the government during the first six months of the conflict were aimed specifically at seizing weapons and ammunition, as well as petrol, cars, and food (Lecocq, 2002, p. 232). In the first assault on a government post in Tideremen on 28 June 1990, MPLA fighters seized a dozen assault rifles; in a subsequent attack in Ménaka, they managed to procure around 500 weapons, including 124 assault rifles (Humphreys and ag Mohamed, 2003, p. 3). The rebels' arsenal was thus largely built out of existing army stocks. The MPGK also relied to a great extent on army stockpiles, as a number of its fighters were former Malian soldiers, including deserters who took their weapons with them (Poulton and ag Youssouf, 1998, p. 71; Keita, 1998, p. 20; Baqué, 1995). Some soldiers also sold their guns to MPGK combatants during the rebellion.

Table 6.1 lists various old models of small arms (including remnants of the colonial period) in the hands of Malian insurgent groups and the MPGK. That their arsenals comprised Chinese and Soviet armaments supports the assumption that many of these weapons were seized from the Malian Army.[31] Since these models could be easily obtained in the wider West African sub-region, some may have been smuggled into Mali from neighbouring countries.

Table 6.1 highlights the overall scarcity of modern small arms, and also illustrates how long small arms can remain in circulation. German Second World War-era guns, for instance, were being used 50 years after they were manufactured. During the fighting, light weapons, and especially light weapon ammunition, were particularly scarce.[32]

Table 6.1   Reported small arms and light weapons used by Malian armed groups during the rebellion (1990-96), sourced mainly from Malian state stockpiles

Small arms (country of manufacture, years of production or service)	
Revolvers	Arminius Model 10 (Germany, 1895-1945), Astra 357 Police (Spain, 1980-), Manurhin MR73 (France, 1973-), Nagant: Russian Model 1895 (Belgium and Russia/USSR, 1895-1950)
Pistols	Astra A-50 (Spain, 1960-), Beretta Model 1931 (Italy, 1931-45), Beretta Model 1934 (Italy, 1934-45), Beretta M 951 (Italy, 1953-82), Browning 1903 (Belgium, 1903-), Browning 1910 (Belgium, 1910-), Browning High Power Model 1935 (Belgium, 1935-), MAB PA-15 (France, 1975-90), Makarov (USSR/Russian Federation, 1952-), Sauer M38H (Germany, 1938-45), Stechkin (USSR, 1951-75), Tokarev (USSR/Russian Federation, 1930-)
Rifles and carbines	Mannlicher-Carcano TS (Italy, 1891-1918), MAS M1e 1936 (France, 1936-55), Mauser Karabiner 98k (Germany, 1935-45), Mosin-Nagant rifle (Russia/USSR, 1892-1950)
Assault rifles	Chinese-type 68 rifle (China, 1970-), FN Cal (Belgium, 1966-75), FN FNC (Belgium, 1979-), FN Minimi (Belgium, 1982-), Heckler & Koch G3 (Germany, 1964-), Kalashnikov AK-47 (Romania and USSR/Russian Federation, 1947-) and Type 56 (China, 1958-), Simonov SKS (USSR/Russian Federation, 1946-)
Light machine guns	12.7 mm Gepard M2 (Hungary, 1994-), PK (USSR/Russian Federation, 1964-), RPK (USSR/Russian Federation, 1955-), 7.62 mm RPD (USSR/Russian Federation, 1962-)
Light weapons (country of manufacture, years of production or service)	
Heavy machine guns	DShK (USSR, 1938-80), Type 77 (China, 1980-)
Portable anti-tank guns*	RPG-7
Mortars*	60 mm and 81/82 mm

* Note: For portable anti-tank guns and mortars, ex-combatants did not provide data to help determine the country of manufacture or years of production or service. This lack of information reflects the scarcity and relative unimportance of these weapon types during the rebellion, to which the ex-combatants attested during focus group discussions.

Source: Small Arms Survey focus group discussions with former unit commanders of the MPGK and the MFUA, Bamako, 2-3 September 2004; country and dates of production and service from Hogg (2002)

Reports have indicated that illicit workshops in Mali produce 'craft' hunting rifles, shotguns, and pistols;[33] nevertheless, Malian armed groups appear to have relied solely on industrially produced weapons.

International sourcing of small arms to Malian armed groups was limited to the diaspora in neighbouring countries and to some smaller-scale cross-border purchases. Malian armed groups, by and large, did not receive material military support from foreign governments. While some Tuareg fighters had received training and weapons from Libya in the 1980s, such backing had ceased by the time of the rebellion (Keita, 2002, p. 9; Lecocq, 2004, pp. 312–13).

The significance of diaspora support is difficult to assess, but it is likely to have been only of secondary importance when compared to seizures and purchases from the army. The Songhoy diaspora in Ghana and Nigeria reportedly provided arms and money to the MPGK (Keita, 1998, p. 20). Members of the diaspora apparently paid individual 'transporters' to carry and deliver weapons to the MPGK in Gao.

As for purchases made abroad, Tuareg and Arab groups dispatched special expeditions to buy small arms on the illicit market in Mauritania. The arms were transported using caravans of camels and donkeys or, when available, 4x4 vehicles. These trafficking networks were relatively insignificant and limited to traditional smuggling routes in the early stages of the rebellion. Over the years, they were expanded to other countries in the region (including states in the Mano River Union basin); some remain active today and contribute to continued small arms proliferation in the north of the country. While Chadian, Mauritanian, and Nigerian black markets were the main source of illegal weapons for Malian armed groups in the early 1990s, the illicit arms supply had become more diverse by 1996, with weapons seemingly originating in several of West Africa's conflict hot spots.

> International sourcing of small arms to Malian armed groups was limited to the diaspora in neighbouring countries and to some smaller-scale cross-border purchases

Liberia

Liberia has witnessed internal war for much of the past decade; this section focuses on the most recent outbreak of fighting in 2000–03. In 2000, three years after the country's devastating eight-year civil war had come to an end, Liberia again found itself embroiled in armed conflict. President Charles Taylor, erstwhile leader of the National Patriotic Front for Liberia, or NPFL, faced challenges from two new rebel groups: the Liberians United for Reconciliation and Democracy (LURD) and the Movement for Democracy in Liberia (MODEL). The Armed Forces of Liberia (AFL) and various paramilitary and militia groups fared poorly against the rebels and, by June 2003, the capital, Monrovia, was under siege. In August 2003, Taylor handed over power to Vice-President Moses Blah and went into exile in Nigeria. Within days, peace negotiations took place in Accra, Ghana, and warring parties signed the Comprehensive Peace Agreement.

During the conflict, both rebels and government forces relied extensively on light weapons. Combat would quite systematically begin with a bombardment involving rocket-propelled grenades (RPGs), followed by small arms fire (Brabazon, 2003, p. 9). AFL and pro-government groups mainly used light and medium machine guns, Chinese-made AK-47s, and RPGs (Global Witness, 2003, p. 24). The two insurgent groups possessed a wide variety of small arms and light weapons, from AK-47 assault rifles and M-16 rifles to DSHK 12.7 mm heavy machine guns and SA-7 surface-to-air missiles.[34]

A 13-year-old boy flaunts his machine-gun and helmet in Monrovia, Liberia.

© Joel Robine/AFP/Getty Images

In Liberia, a significant proportion of the warring parties' very diverse arsenal—particularly ammunition—was obtained from foreign sources.

The insurgents seized a number of small arms from Liberian government forces, including FN FAL rifles, AKM assault rifles, and RPO-type grenade launchers (Brabazon, 2003, p. 9). The group also possessed at least nine SA-7 surface-to-air missiles, which it claimed to have captured from a government-backed armed group (Brabazon, 2003, p. 9).

Yet evidence points to a strong reliance on foreign sources. Investigative reports suggest that a significant proportion of the warring parties' very diverse arsenal—particularly ammunition—was obtained from foreign sources, regional and international. These transfers took place despite the UN Security Council arms embargo that covered the country's entire territory—and hence all parties to the conflict (UNSC, 1992; 2001b).

As illustrated in Table 6.2, investigative reports allege that the Liberian government benefited from several large international small arms shipments in 2000–03. Most likely, these transfers only represent the tip of the iceberg. Brokers based as far away as Hong Kong and mainland China reportedly facilitated the transfer of Chinese-made weapons to Liberia's largest logging company, the Oriental Timber Company, which was under President Taylor's control (Global Witness, 2003, p. 19). Regionally, Burkina Faso and Libya have served as transshipment points for arms exported to the Liberian government (Global Witness, 2003, p. 22; UNSC, 2000, paras. 203–04; 2003b, paras. 95–97).

Table 6.2   Selected reported small arms transfers to the Liberian government, 2000–03

Date	Content	Origin, transit, and broker	Source
July 2000	113 tons of 7.62 mm cartridges	Origin: Ukraine Transit: Côte d'Ivoire	*Financial Times,* 2002; Lallemand, 2002, p. 3; BBC News, 2001b
1 June 2002	1,000 automatic rifles (7.62 x 39 mm), 498,960 cartridges (7.62 x 39 mm M67), 2,000 hand grenades (M75)*	Origin: Serbia, transferred using a false Nigerian end-user certificate Broker: Belgrade-based company	UNSC, 2003a, paras. 69–70, Table 1
7 June 2002	1,000 automatic rifles (7.62 x 39 mm, M67), 1,260,000 cartridges (7.62 x 39 mm, M67), 2,496 hand grenades (M75)*	Additional shipment, part of 1 June 2002 deal	UNSC, 2003a, paras. 69–70, Table 1
29 June 2002	1,500 automatic rifles (7.62 x 39 mm), 2,165,500 cartridges (7.62 x 39 mm)*	Additional shipment, part of the 1 June 2002 deal	UNSC, 2003a, paras. 69–70, Table 1
5 July 2002	180,000 rounds of ammunition (7.62 mm for M84), 15,200 rounds of ammunition (9 mm NATO), 75,000 rounds of ammunition (7.62 mm), 100 missile launchers (RB M57), 60 automatic pistols (M84, 7.65 mm), 20 pistols (CZ99, 9 mm), 10 Black Arrow long-range rifles (M93, 12.7 mm), 5 machine guns (M84, 7.62 mm)*	Additional shipment, part of the 1 June 2002 deal	UNSC, 2003a, paras. 69–70, Table 1; AFP, 2002
23 August 2002	100 missile launchers (RB M57), 2,000 mines for RB M57, 75 machine guns (M84, 7.62 mm), 2,800 automatic rifles (7.62 x 54 mm), 27 pistols (CZ99, 9 mm), 92,400 rounds of ammunition (7.62 x 54 mm), 526,000 rounds of ammunition (7.62 x 39 mm), 19,000 rounds of ammunition (9 mm), 6,000 rounds of ammunition (7.65 mm), 9 hunting rifles*	Additional shipment, part of the 1 June 2002 deal	UNSC, 2003a, paras. 69–70, Table 1
25 August 2002	152 missile launchers, 1,000 mines for RB M57, 5,200 rounds of ammunition for the Black Arrow long-range rifle (M93, 12.7 mm), 183,600 rounds of ammunition, (7.62 x 54 mm), 999,180 rounds of ammunition (7.62 x 39 mm), 2 sets of rubber pipelines, 3 propellers, 1 rotor head, 17 pistol holders*	Additional shipment, part of 1 June 2002 deal	UNSC, 2003a, paras. 69–70, Table 1
6–7 August 2003	Between 20 and 40 tonnes of small arms and ammunition	Origin: Serbia Transit: Libya Broker: Belgrade-based company	UNSC, 2003b, paras. 95–97
November 2003	60 mm mortars, 149 boxes of mortar ammunition, 67 boxes of RPGs, 299 boxes of AK-47 assault rifles, 699,000 rounds of ammunition	n/a	Arms Control Association, 2003, p. 3

*Note: Based on a list provided by the Government of Liberia (UNSC, 2003a; paras. 69–70, Table 1).
Source: Kytömäki (2004)

Information on the small arms sources of the insurgents is more difficult to acquire. Nevertheless, LURD and MODEL appear to have received substantial quantities of small arms from some of the regional powers that opposed President Taylor's regime. The Guinean Armed Forces purportedly provided LURD with weapons, ammunition, and logistical and medical support.[35] Some of the 81 mm mortar rounds that LURD combatants used in the June–July 2003 attacks on Monrovia were reportedly shipped from Iran to Guinea and then smuggled to LURD (HRW, 2003a, pp. 18–25). LURD has also allegedly used mortar ammunition made in the United Arab Emirates, which is likely to have somehow 'leaked' from Guinean stockpiles (HRW, 2003a, pp. 18, 25). Weapons were apparently transported in trucks or carried across the border by forcibly recruited civilians (HRW, 2002b, p. 10).

MODEL, meanwhile, reportedly received small arms and uniforms from Côte d'Ivoire (ICG, 2003c, pp. 10–11). This should not come as a surprise, since a number of MODEL combatants were former members of Lima, a group of Liberian mercenaries who fought alongside Ivorian government troops against Côte d'Ivoire's rebel groups.[36]

The comparison between the disparate conflicts in Liberia and Mali shows how the level of reliance on foreign weapon sources can vary vastly within a sub-region. For Malian armed groups, which lacked financial and natural resources and foreign backing, seizures from state stockpiles were the key source of small arms. The Malian state relied mainly on stocks accumulated before the rebellion. For the Liberian insurgents, state stockpiles were of secondary importance. Because of the considerable diamond and timber resources in their possession, as well as foreign political and military backing, Liberian insurgents were in a position to organize and purchase important consignments of small arms from abroad. The same was true for the Liberian government.

> The comparison between Liberia and Mali shows how the level of reliance on foreign weapon sources can vary vastly within a sub-region.

The comparison also reveals that time can be a significant factor in weapons procurement. As a conflict continues, insurgents are often increasingly able to diversify their sources away from mere stockpile seizures. President Taylor's forces and the rebels had already fought for seven years when conflict erupted again in 2000, and hence they could rely on pre-established trafficking networks. This was not the case for Malian groups, which had to start from scratch. As the Malian rebellion wore on, however, insurgent and militia groups also developed increasingly sophisticated trafficking methods, although through different channels and not on the same scale as in Liberia.

The importance of military stockpiles: Tajikistan and Georgia

The Tajik and Georgian civil wars both erupted after the break-up of the Soviet Union. Small arms were important in both conflicts, although government forces in the two countries had access to larger weapons as well. Small arms acquisition patterns in the two cases have some strong similarities. For example, former Soviet stockpiles of small arms were of paramount importance in both conflicts, while domestic production was of little significance. A noteworthy difference is that international supplies played a much greater part in Tajikistan than in Georgia.

Tajikistan [37]

On gaining independence from the Soviet Union in 1991, Tajikistan quickly descended into civil war as a result of regional and political rivalries. The war lasted from 1992 to 1997, with the most intense fighting in 1992–93. The main groups engaged in combat were the Popular Front (Tajik government forces) and the United Tajik Opposition. The war, although relatively short, was ferocious, leading to 60,000–100,000 deaths, 80,000 refugees, and 600,000 IDPs (ICG, 2001, p. i).

In Tajikistan, both external and internal sources of small arms were significant. While the government and the opposition essentially utilized the same internal suppliers (although to differing degrees), external suppliers were more varied.

Fighters in Tajikistan got their small arms from two internal sources: former Soviet military forces based in the country (more often than not siding with Tajik government troops) and local law enforcement units. These two sources were particularly important at the early stages of the conflict (Pirseyedi, 2000, pp. 46–47).

At independence, two branches of the Soviet Armed Forces were represented in the Tajik Soviet Socialist Republic. The first branch comprised five regiments of the 201st Motor Rifle Division (MRD). The second branch consisted of the Soviet border forces serving in Tajikistan—some 8,000 personnel in total—in four commands along the Tajik–Afghan border. The 201st MRD regiments, except the one based in the area of Kulyab, were reportedly sources of supply for both government and opposition factions during the war, with individual officers informally selling small arms or engaging in barter (Pirseyedi, 2000, p. 47).[38] Government fighters and, to a greater extent, opposition forces also stole weapons from the Russian Armed Forces (Pirseyedi, 2000, p. 47). Given that the five regiments possessed more than 15,000 assault rifles, machine guns, and other types of small arms, it is possible that both sides procured (through leakage) as many as several thousand small arms from the 201st MRD.

In contrast, there are few accounts of ex-Soviet border forces selling guns on a large scale, possibly because they were occasionally attacked by the warring parties and thus needed the weapons to defend themselves. An exception seems to have been the border force detachments in the area of Kalaikum, which interviewees and focus group participants frequently identified as a key source of firearms. These detachments were stationed near the Vayho Valley, which later became the opposition's headquarters. Supplies were most probably limited to a few hundred guns.

A Tajik soldier holds his gun and bandolier in December 1992.

© Malcolm Linton/Getty Images

Local law enforcement structures served as further internal sources of guns. These included the Civil Defence, the state security agency (KGB), the Ministry of the Interior (known as the MVD), and the Presidential Guard—comprising about 20,000–30,000 officers in all. At the outset, mainly government forces used their stockpiles. As tensions intensified, the law enforcement structures split, and some officers opted to side with the opposition, bringing with them weapons at their disposal.[39] Opposition forces also reportedly raided some KGB and MVD stations in Dushanbe and Khatlon.[40]

In addition, high schools and universities were in possession of about 1,800 guns for *voennaya podgotovka* (compulsory military training).[41] The *voennkomat* (military draft commission), with offices across Tajikistan, also had some limited stocks. Both sides were quick to seize weapons from these sources.

While both the Tajik government and opposition forces were able to acquire weapons from Soviet military units and from local law enforcement structures, they had different external suppliers. Uzbekistan sided with the government, and its support 'included significant numbers of small arms and ammunition' (Pirseyedi, 2000, p. 53).

Both the Tajik government and the opposition forces acquired weapons from Soviet military units and local law enforcement structures, but they had different external suppliers.

Uzbekistan also encouraged the Afghan warlord Rashid Dostum, an ethnic Uzbek, to help in providing arms (Pirseyedi, 2000, p. 54). In rare cases, government commanders travelled to Afghanistan to purchase weapons.[42]

For the Tajik opposition, Afghanistan represented the main external source of small arms. During the war, thousands of members of the Tajik opposition were based in the country. Along with other fighters, they bought, or swapped weapons within Afghanistan.[43] The money for the weapons apparently came from Pakistan as well as sources in Middle Eastern countries such as Saudi Arabia (Pirseyedi, 2000, p. 54).[44] Another important source of funds was drug trafficking. In 1995, opposition commander Alesha Gorbun reportedly defended the activity, noting that revenue from drug sales was used to buy food, and that 'we ... need money for buying weapons in order to defend ourselves' (*Literaturnaya Gazeta,* 1995, p. 12). External sourcing of small arms, it seems, involved a mixture of large and small shipments.

Georgia [45]

In contrast to Tajikistan, government armed units and insurgent groups depended more exclusively on internally sourced small arms in the three intertwined conflicts that shook Georgia between 1989 and 1993: the South Ossetian conflict, the Abkhaz conflict, and the Georgian civil war. As the Small Arms Survey has already published extensively on Georgia, only a short summary regarding weapons sourcing during the conflict is provided here.

The bulk of weapons in the hands of all of the warring parties in Georgia came from internal holdings, mainly from the substantial ex-Soviet military presence on Georgian territory. In the early phases of the conflict (between 1989 and 1991), however, few small arms and light weapons were leaked from Soviet military stockpiles. Instead, the main sources were non-military in nature, namely police and postal guards, the so-called Voluntary Society of Supporters for the Air Force and Navy (which normally provided military training to civilians), and communist youth organizations. Quantities were small: tens, rather than hundreds or thousands, of guns. Another significant source during this period was personal holdings such as Second World War Mosin rifles.

Armed men aim into a square in Tbilisi, Georgia, in December 1991.

In 1991–93, in contrast, weapons from Soviet stockpiles became widely available, due to the political, economic, and social consequences of the collapse of the Soviet Union. Armed groups seized some weapons, but many were sold, and thousands of Soviet small arms were handed out for free by disintegrating Russian military structures. As a result, an estimated 40,000 small arms and light weapons rapidly found their way into the hands of the various militias.

During the conflict period, there were only two widely reported cases of external procurement: a shipment from Romania of around 1,000 AK-47 assault rifles; and smaller consignments of assault rifles and pistols from the Czech Republic (Darchiashvili, 2003, p. 93).

This brief comparison reveals that former Soviet stockpiles were a crucial small arms source for all parties in the Georgian and Tajik conflicts. All possible types of leakage occurred: theft, seizure, sales, and handouts. In general, handouts were politically motivated. In the Tajik conflict, weapons from other states in the region were also of significance, especially for the opposition; in the Georgian civil war as a whole, this was not the case.

> During the Georgian conflict period, there were only two reported—and relatively small— shipments of small arms from abroad.

CONCLUSION

This chapter has examined the full range of sources of small arms in a sample of conflicts in the Americas, Africa, and Central Asia and the Caucasus. It recognizes the importance of large international transfers in weapons sourcing to many war zones; at the same time, however, it reinforces lesser-known research findings regarding the role of production, government stockpiles, and the so-called ant trade in the fuelling conflict. The chapter thereby emphasizes that the focus on large international deals needs to be put into perspective.

In developing a more comprehensive approach to conflict sourcing, the role of politics must not be overlooked. Small arms proliferation is essentially a political issue—as the politically motivated leakages from military stockpiles and state-sponsored transfers in the above case studies demonstrate. In such instances, political solutions to the conflicts themselves are key to resolving the small arms problem.

The case studies indicate that government stockpiles are an important source of weapons in many war zones, through corruption, theft, seizure, distribution, and sales. In some conflicts, they are even the main source of small arms for all combatants. As a result, decisions regarding small arms exports may take on new weight, given that the weapons of a country that is stable today may be used in a conflict a few years hence.

The Colombian, Haitian, and, to some extent, Malian and Tajik case studies show that the ant trade can be a non-negligible, although elusive, source of small arms. As pointed out in the case of Colombia, in the long run, persistent smaller shipments of small arms can be more significant in terms of volume than occasional large-scale trafficking of guns. Where the ant trade is important, policy responses become more complicated. In addition to controlling brokering, streamlining end-user certificates, and establishing arms embargoes, an effective policy also needs to tackle corruption and make the control of border regions and of the border itself more effective.

A related lesson comes from the Colombian, Haitian, and Malian case studies, which provide some preliminary indications that diasporas play a poorly understood role in gun smuggling. Analysts have stressed the overall importance of diasporas in supporting insurgencies, but more research is required to shed light on their precise role in transferring guns.[46]

This study also concludes that there are often important differences between countries within the same subregion. Liberia and Mali are both members of the Economic Community of West African States, yet their sourcing of the tools of war could hardly be more different. These findings suggest that geographical proximity does not necessarily imply that countries are tapping into similar international trafficking networks. Natural and other resources, foreign political backing, and local histories can overshadow the geographic factor. To combat the proliferation and misuse of small arms, therefore, policies must be tailored to individual states. While regional approaches are useful, their limitations must also be clearly understood.

Lastly, where conflicts become more drawn-out, insurgents are often able to diversify their sources of small arms. This development may take place alongside the growth of a supporting war economy, as noted in the cases of Colombia, Liberia, and Tajikistan. Tackling conflicts early is crucial to preventing weapons procurement patterns from becoming increasingly sophisticated and entrenched—and thus central to efforts to minimize human suffering and material loss.

LIST OF ABBREVIATIONS

AFL	Armed Forces of Liberia
ATF	Bureau of Alcohol, Tobacco, Firearms, and Explosives (United States)
AUC	Autodefensas Unidas de Colombia
ELN	Ejército de Liberación Nacional
FADH	Forces Armées d'Haïti (Haitian Army)
FARC	Fuerzas Armadas Revolucionarias de Colombia
IDPs	Internally displaced persons
INDUMIL	Industria Militar (Colombia)
LURD	Liberians United for Reconciliation and Democracy
MFUA	Mouvements et Fronts Unis de l'Azawad (Mali)
MODEL	Movement for Democracy in Liberia
MPGK	Mouvement Patriotique de Ganda Koy (Mali)
MPLA	Mouvement Populaire de Libération de l'Azawad (Mali)
MRD	Motorized Rifle Division
MVD	Ministry of the Interior (Russian Federation)
OAS	Organization of American States
RPGs	Rocket-propelled grenades
ZAR	South African rand

ENDNOTES

1 This chapter uses the terms trafficking, illegal and illicit trade, and smuggling interchangeably.

2 This chapter uses the terms 'small arms', 'small arms and light weapons', 'guns', and 'weapons' interchangeably. The system of categorization is taken to include small arms ammunition, although it should be noted that information on ammunition is scarce, and more research on this subject is needed.

3 For a similar analysis of current literature, see Bourne (2004).

4 See also Small Arms Survey (2002, pp. 129–30).

5 Imposed by the European Union (EU), the UN, or the United States.

6 In order to focus on the aspect of weapons sourcing, the chapter provides minimal details relating to the conflicts in general.

7 For further details, see Small Arms Survey (2004, p. 23).

8 For further details, see Dreyfus and Lessing (2003).

9 Civilians outside the private security sector tend to rely more on unregistered than legally owned firearms. Some figures indicate that more than two-thirds of all civilian firearms are held illegally. These are bought cheaply on the domestic black market (Cragin and Hoffman, 2003, p. 18).

10 The information on the United States is based on US customs reporting, US national arms export reports, and Colombian import reports to the UN Commodity Trade Statistics Database (UN Comtrade). Source: Norwegian Initiative on Small Arms Transfers (NISAT) database of authorized transfers of small arms and light weapons.

11 The information on Israel is based on Colombian import reports to UN Comtrade (2004), as Israel does not provide UN Comtrade with data on its arms exports.

12 The information on Brazil is based primarily on Brazilian export reporting to UN Comtrade (2004).

13 The information on South Africa is based primarily on Colombian import reporting, as South Africa does not provide UN Comtrade with data on its arms exports. In its 2003 national arms export report, however, South Africa does detail exports to Colombia, amounting to a total of ZAR 53 million (USD 6 million) over a three-year period (2000–02). The South African report only specifies that the transfers were of any type of 'infantry hand-held and portable assault weapons and associated ammunition of a calibre smaller than 12.7mm' (Government of South Africa, 2003). Colombian import data and South African export figures correspond fairly well.

14 The information on the Czech Republic is based primarily on Czech export reporting to UN Comtrade (2004).

15 The information on Italy is based primarily on Italian export reporting to UN Comtrade. There are important discrepancies between Italian and Colombian reporting, with the Colombian authorities detailing substantial imports of parts and accessories for military weapons, which are not recorded in Italian data (UN Comtrade, 2004). Both the Colombians and the Italians registered revolvers and pistols.

16 Based on reporting by exporters, the US share of the total small arms trade in 1999–2003 was approximately 52 per cent. Based on Colombian reports of its small arms imports, its share was close to 54 per cent (UN Comtrade, 2004).

17 For further details, see Amnesty International (2003, pp. 19–24); Isacson et al. (2004); ICG (2002a; 2004).

18 For more on FARC production, see Dreyfus and Lessing (2003).

19 For a discussion of cold war weapons transfers, see Small Arms Survey (2001, Box 5.2, p. 169).

20 As noted by AUC leader Carlos Castaño: 'While I bought a hundred or two hundred rifles in the arms market, the FARC would get one thousand or two thousand' (cited in Molina, 2001, p. 205). Translation from the Spanish: Lisa Misol, Human Rights Watch.

21 Interviews by Pablo Dreyfus with Colombian and Brazilian law enforcement officials (July 2003, Bogota, and August 2004, Bogota, respectively).

22 See Amnesty International (2003, p. 26); Bourne (2004, p. 166; fn. 94, p. 189); Cragin and Hoffman (2003, pp. 28–29); ICG (2004, p. 13).

23 See AP (2004b); Forero (2004); Amnesty International (2003, p. 27); Small Arms Survey (2001, Box 5.7, p. 187); Faiola (2000).

24 This figure is significantly lower than the oft-cited 13,000 weapons (Bailey et al., 1998, p. 229; Muggah, 2005; Stohl, 2004).

25 For information on the US embargo and its 1994 amendment, see the Directorate of Defense Trade Controls of the US Department of States at <http://pmdtc.org/country.htm>. The UN Security Council embargo was in place from 1993–94, and the broader sanctions of the OAS from 1991–94. For a detailed account of these sanctions, see Gibbons (1999).

26 Florida has no one-handgun-per-month limit on gun purchases or state restrictions on the sale or possession of military-style semi-automatic assault weapons. Nor does the state require licences or permits to buy a gun (Brady Campaign, 2005).

27 Stohl (2004), see also Mlade (2004). On the porous nature of this border, see Arthur (2002, p. 7).

28 For instance, there are important similarities between Liberia and Sierra Leone, not only with regard to small arms flows, but also smuggling networks, routes, and actors. Parties involved in the Sierra Leonean civil war benefited from numerous international shipments; see Berman (2000, pp. 3–13).

29 Unless noted otherwise, this section is based on Small Arms Survey focus group discussions with former unit commanders of the MPGK and the MFUA, Bamako, Mali, 2–3 September 2004.

30 Azawad is the name of the home country of the Tuareg.

31 This claim was made during Small Arms Survey focus group discussions with former unit commanders of the MPGK and the MFUA, Bamako, 2–3 September 2004.

32 The shortage of weapons and ammunition forced Malian armed groups to keep methodical accounts; each base had a person responsible for distributing and counting weapons. Combatants were given different weapons and amounts of ammunition depending on their type of operation. When they ran out of ammunition, armed groups set their rifles to single-shot mode and undertook specific missions to seize more from army barracks and posts. They also systematically recuperated the weapons and ammunition of those who fell during the fighting.

33 For an overview of 'craft' production in Mali, see Nimaga (2003) and Kante (2004).

34 Brabazon (2003, pp. 8–9); UNSC (2003a, paras. 109, 112); HRW (2003a, pp. 23–25); Global Witness (2003, pp. 24–25).

35 See UNSC (2001, paras. 174–78; 2003a, para. 68; 2003b, para. 105); ICG (2002, p. 11); HRW (2002a, p. 10; 2003a, pp. 18–25).

36 Confidential written correspondence with a Western diplomat based in West Africa, May 2004.

37 Except where other secondary sources are explicitly cited, this section is based on field research undertaken in 2004 by Stina Torjesen and Neil MacFarlane for the Small Arms Survey (Torjesen, Wille, and MacFarlane, forthcoming, Annexe 4).

38 One eyewitness claims that guns were sold off the back of trucks in the centre of Dushanbe in 1992. Interview no. 92, Dushanbe, 30 March 2004; interview no. 134, Dushanbe, 11 August 2004.

39 Interview no. 75, Dushanbe, 24 February 2004.

40 Interview no. 132, Dushanbe, 17 July 2004.

41 Interview no. 90, Dushanbe, 18 March 2004.

42 One former high-ranking law enforcement officer who fought on the government side claims that he bought 30 grenade launchers for USD 2,000 in Afghanistan in 1991. Interview no. 154, Dushanbe, 25 July 2004.

43 There was a demand for hunting weapons in Afghanistan; one rifle could thus be swapped for two AK-47s. Interview no. 111, Dushanbe, 25 August 2004.

[44] Interview no. 84, Dushanbe, 26 March 2004.

[45] For a more detailed assessment of small arms in Georgia, see previous Small Arms Survey publications: Demetriou (2002) and Small Arms Survey (2003, ch. 6). Unless otherwise stated, this brief case study is based on these earlier publications.

[46] Diasporas are likely among the most important sponsors of insurgent movements: '[m]igrant communities have sent money, arms, and recruits back to their home countries, which have proven pivotal in sustaining insurgent campaigns' (Byman et al., 2001, p. 41).

BIBLIOGRAPHY

AFP (Agence France Presse). 2002. 'Yugoslav Minister Confirms Illegal Arms Shipment to Liberia.' 1 November. Accessed February 2005.
<http://www.setimes.com/cocoon/setimes/xhtml/en_GB/document/setimes/newsbriefs/2002/11/021103-IVAN-001>

AI (Amnesty International). 2001. 'Sierra Leone: a bloody trade.' AI Index: ACT 31/002/2001. June. Accessed February 2005.
<http://web.amnesty.org/web/ttt.nsf/june2001/sierra_leone>

—. 2003. *Colombia: flow of arms contributes to increased human rights violations.* MSP Action Circular. AI Index: AMR 23/010/2003. 8 August.

AP (Associated Press). 2004a. 'Colombian Charged in Florida with Buying Guns.' 20 August.

—. 2004b. 'Peru Ex-Spy Master Arms Trial Suspended Until Feb. 5.' 29 January.

—. 2004c. 'Broken Toilet Foils Gun-Smuggling Plot.' 22 August.

Arms Control Association. 2003. 'Illegal Arms Found in Liberia.' *Arms Control Today.* December. Accessed February 2005.
< http://www.armscontrol.org/act/2003_12/newsbriefs.asp>

Arthur, Charles. 2002. *Small Arms and Disarmament in Haiti.* Background Paper. Geneva: Small Arms Survey. July

Bailey, Michael, Robert Maguire, and J. O'Neil G. Pouliot. 1998. 'Haiti: Military–Police Partnership for Public Security.' In Robert B. Oakley, Michael J. Dziedzic, and Eliot M. Goldber, eds. *Policing the New World Disorder: Peace Operations and Public Security.* Washington, DC: Institute for National Strategic Studies, National Defense University. Accessed April 2005.
<http://www.ndu.edu/inss/books/Books%20-%201998/Policing%20the%20New%20World%20Disorder%20-%20May%2098/cont.html>

Baqué, Philippe. 1995. 'Dérapages de la répression, nouvel enlisement des espoirs de paix dans le conflit Touareg au Mali.' *Le Monde Diplomatique.* April.

BBC News. 2001a. 'Fighting in northern Liberia.' 6 March. Accessed February 2005. <http://news.bbc.co.uk/1/hi/world/europe/1205372.stm>

—. 2001b. 'Liberia illegally importing arms.' 5 November. Accessed February 2005. <http://news.bbc.co.uk/1/hi/world/africa/1639623.stm>

BBC Worldwide Monitoring. 2004. 'South Africa: Opposition DA calls for transparency in deals with Haiti.' 1 March.

Business Day. 2004. 'DA Demands Details on Haiti "Arms Fiasco".' 8 March.

Bergman, Jake and Oriana Zill de Granados. 2004. 'Guns Smuggled from South Florida Arming Haitians.' *Sun-Sentinel* (Florida). 6 March.

Berman, Eric. 2000. *Re-Armament in Sierra Leone: One Year After the Lomé Peace Agreement.* Occasional Paper No. 1. Geneva: Small Arms Survey. December.

Bourne, Michael. 2004. *An Examination of Small Arms Proliferation and Areas of Conflict.* Unpublished Ph.D. thesis, University of Bradford, Department of Peace Studies.

Brabazon, James. 2003. *Liberia, Liberians United for Reconciliation and Democracy (LURD).* Briefing Paper No. 1. London: Royal Institute of International Affairs, Non State Armed Actors project. February.

Brady Campaign. 2005. State Gun Laws Org. Accessed March 2005. <http://www.bradycampaign.org/legislation/state/viewstate.php?st=fl>

Byman, Daniel et al. 2001. *Trends in Outside Support for Insurgent Movements.* Santa Monica, CA: RAND Corporation.

CCI (Cadre de Coopération Interimaire). 2004. *Securité, police et désarmement: rapport final.* Groupe thématique sécurité et gouvernance politique. 22 June. Accessed January 2005. <http://haiticci.undg.org/index.cfm?Module=doc&Page=Document&Type=default&CategoryID=322>

Colombia. Policía Nacional. 2001. 'Apreciación de situación sobre armas cortas en Colombia.' Bogota: Policía Nacional, Dirección General. January.

Cragin, Kim and Bruce Hoffman. 2003. *Arms Trafficking and Colombia.* Santa Monica, CA: RAND Corporation.

Darchiashvili, David. 2003. 'Georgia: A Hostage to Arms.' In Anna Matveeva and Duncan Hiscock, eds. *The Caucasus: Armed and Divided.* London: Saferworld. April, pp. 69–103.

Demetriou, Spyros. 2002. *Politics from the Barrel of a Gun: Small Arms Proliferation and Conflict in the Republic of Georgia (1989–2001).* Occasional Paper No. 6. Geneva: Small Arms Survey.

Dreyfus, Pablo and Benjamin Lessing. 2003. 'Production and Exports of Small Arms and Light Weapons and Ammunition in South America and Mexico.' Background paper (unpublished). Geneva: Small Arms Survey.

Faiola, Anthony. 2000. 'How Fujimori's Grip on Power Slipped in Arms Scandal.' *International Herald Tribune.* 25 September.

Financial Times. 2002. 'The African connection: missiles to Liberia.' 21 October. Accessed February 2005.
<http://www.nisat.org/west%20africa/news%20from%20the%20region/MAIN%20NEWS%20PAGE/Liberia/1999-03-13%20The%20African%20connection%20-%20missiles%20to%20Liberia%20.html >

Forero, Juan. 2004. 'Former Peru Spy Chief Stands Trial for Colombia Weapons Deal.' *The New York Times*. 21 January.

Gibbons, Elizabeth D. 1999. *Sanctions in Haiti: Human Rights and Democracy under Assault*. Westport, CT, and London: Praeger.

Global Witness. 2003. *The Usual Suspects: Liberia's Weapons and Mercenaries in Côte d'Ivoire and Sierra Leone*. London: Global Witness. March.

Government of South Africa. 2003. *South African Export Statistics for Conventional Arms 2000–2002*. Accessed February 2005. <http://www.mil.za/SecretaryforDefence/ConventionalArmsControl/NCACC2002/000102p.pdf>

Grech, Daniel A. 2000. 'Feds Find Weapons Bound for Colombia in Hialeah.' *Miami Herald*. 21 December.

Heyman, Charles, ed. 2000. *Jane's World Armies*, Issue Eight. Southampton: Hobbs The Printers Ltd. December.

Hogg, Ian. 2002. *Jane's Guns Recognition Guide*. Glasgow: HarperCollins Publishers.

HRW (Human Rights Watch). 2002a. *Back to the Brink: War Crimes by Liberian Government and Rebels. A Call for Greater International Attention to Liberia and the Sub Region*. Vol. 14, No. 4 (A). New York: HRW. May.

—. 2002b. *Liberian Refugees in Guinea: Refoulement, Militarization of Camps, and Other Protection Concerns*. Vol. 14, No. 8 (A). New York: HRW. November.

—. 2003a. *Weapons Sanctions, Military Supplies, and Human Suffering: Illegal Arms Flows to Liberia and the June–July 2003 Shelling of Monrovia*. Briefing Paper. New York: HRW. 3 November.

—. 2003b. *The O'odua People's Congress: Fighting Violence with Violence*. Vol. 15, No. 4. New York: HRW. February.

Humphreys, Macartan and Habaye ag Mohamed. 2003. *Senegal and Mali*. Paper presented at the World Bank and International Peace Research Institute, Oslo (PRIO) Civil Conflict Workshop. Oslo, Norway, June 2001. Accessed February 2005. <http://www.columbia.edu/~mh2245/papers1/sen_mali.pdf>

ICG (International Crisis Group). 2001. *Tajikistan: An Uncertain Peace*. Asia Report No. 30. Osh and Brussels: ICG. 24 December.

—. 2002a. *Colombia's Elusive Quest for Peace*. Latin America Report No. 1. Quito and Brussels: ICG. 26 March.

—. 2002b. *Liberia: The Key to Ending Regional Instability*. Africa Report No. 43. Freetown and Brussels: ICG. 24 April.

—. 2003a. *Colombia and its Neighbours: The Tentacles of Instability*. Latin America Report No. 3. Quito and Brussels: ICG. 8 April.

—. 2003b. *Tackling Liberia: The Eye of the Regional Storm*. Africa Report No. 62. Freetown and Brussels: ICG. 30 April.

—. 2003c. *Liberia: Security Challenges*. Africa Report No. 71. Freetown and Brussels: ICG. 3 November.

—. 2003d. *Guinée: incertitudes autour d'une fin de règne*. Africa Report No. 74. Freetown and Brussels: ICG. 19 December, p. 18.

—. 2004. *Colombia's Borders: The Weak Link in Uribe's Security Policy*. Latin America Report No. 9. Quito and Brussels: ICG. 23 September.

IISS (International Institute for Strategic Studies). 2004. *Armed Conflict Database*. Accessed April 2005. <http://www.iiss.org/showpage.php?pageID=25>

Isacson, Adam, Joy Olson, and Lisa Haugaard. 2004. *Blurring the Lines: Trends in US Military Programs with Latin America*. Washington, DC: Latin America Working Group Education Fund, Center for International Policy, and the Washington Office on Latin America. September.

Jaramillo, Daniel Garcia-Peña. 1999. 'Links Between Drugs and Arms in Colombia.' In Jayantha Dhanapala et al., eds. *Small Arms Control: Old Weapons, New Issues*. Geneva: United Nations Institute for Disarmament Research (UNIDIR), pp. 201–07.

Kante, Mamadou Sekouba. 2004. *De la fabrication locale d'armes au Mali: a travers la prolifération des armes légères*. FOSDA Monograph No. 8. Accra: La Fondation Pour la Sécurité et le Développement en Afrique (FOSDA). January.

Keita, Kalika. 1998. *Conflict and Conflict Insurgency in the Sahel: The Tuareg Insurgency in Mali*. Carlisle, PA: US Army War College, Strategic Studies Institute. 1 May.

Keita, Modibo. 2002. *La résolution du conflit Touareg au Mali et au Niger*. Groupe de recherche sur les interventions de paix dans les conflits intra–étatiques (GRIPCI). Montreal: GRIPCI. July. Accessed February 2005. <http://www.dandurand.uqam.ca/download/pdf/etudes/keita/200207-10.pdf>

Kivimäki, Timo. 2003. *Mali: Integrated Approach to Security in Northern Mali*. Helsinki and Copenhagen: CTS Conflict Transformation Service. <http://www.conflicttransform.org/>

Kurth Cronin, Audrey. 2004. *Foreign Terrorist Organizations*. Washington, DC: United States Congressional Research Service (CRS). 6 February.

Kytömäki, Elli. 2004. *International arms transfers to Liberia, 1999–2003*. Background Paper. Geneva: Small Arms Survey. November.

Lallemand, Alain. 2002. 'Drugs, Diamonds and Deadly Cargoes.' In Phillip van Niekerk, ed. *Making A Killing: The Business of War*. Washington, DC: Center for Public Integrity. 18 November 2002. Accessed February 2005. <http://www.publicintegrity.org/bow/report.aspx?aid=156>

Lecocq, Baz. 2002. 'That desert is our country.' *Tuareg rebellions and competing nationalisms in contemporary Mali (1946–1996)*. Ph.D. thesis, University of Amsterdam. November.

Lecocq, Baz. 2004. 'Mali.' In Szajkowski, Bogdan, ed. 2004. *Revolutionary and dissident movements of the world*. 4th (edn.) London: John Harper Publishing, pp. 312–13.

Literaturnaya Gazeta (Moscow). 1995. 'Trafficker Outlines Tajikistan's Drug Transit Operations.' No. 4. 25 January, p. 12.

Mlade, Nicole. 2004. 'Disarmament in Haiti.' Center for American Progress. 27 October. Accessed March 2005. <http://www.americanprogress.org/site/pp.asp?c=biJRJ8OVF&b=233693>

Molina, Mauricio Aranguren. 2001. *Mi Confesión: Carlos Castaño revela sus secretos*. Bogota: Editorial La Oveja Negra.

Muggah, Robert. *Securing Haiti's Transition: Reviewing Human Insecurity and the Prospects for Disarmament, Demobilization, and Reintegration*. Occasional Paper. Geneva : Small Arms Survey. April.

Nimaga, Mahamadou. 2003. *Etude sur la problématique des armes légères au Mali: Cas de Bamako-Gao et Nioro du Sahel*. Unpublished paper commissioned by Oxfam. London: OXFAM. March.

NISAT (Norwegian Initiative on Small Arms Transfers). 2004. *NISAT database of authorised transfers of small arms and light weapons*. <http://www.nisat.org>

OAS (Organization of American States). 2003. *Report of the General Secretariat of the Organization of American States on the Diversion of Nicaraguan Arms to the United Defense Forces of Colombia*. OEA/Ser.G CP/doc.3687/03 of 6 June.

Pirseyedi, Bobi. 2000. *The Small Arms Problem in Central Asia: Features and Implications*. Geneva: United Nations Institute for Disarmament Research (UNIDIR).

Poulton, Robin-Edward and Ibrahim ag Youssouf. 1998. *A Peace of Timbuktu: Democratic Governance, Development and African Peacemaking*. Geneva: United Nations Institute for Disarmament Research (UNIDIR). March 1998.

RFI (Radio France Internationale). 2001. 'Israeli said supplying arms to Sierra Leonean, Liberian rebels arrested in Italy.' 21 June. Accessed February 2005. <http://www.nisat.org/blackmarket/europe/Western%20Europe/italy/2001.06.21-Israeli%20supplying%20arms%20to%20Sierra%20Leonean%20and%20Liberian%20rebels%20arrested%20in%20Italy.html>

Seper, Jerry. 2004. 'Colombian Indicted in Guns Case.' *Washington Times*. 19 August, p. 11.

Small Arms Survey. *Small Arms Survey 2001: Profiling the Problem*. Oxford: Oxford University Press.

—. 2002. *Small Arms Survey 2002: Counting the Human Cost*. Oxford: Oxford University Press.

—. 2003. *Small Arms Survey 2003: Development Denied*. Oxford: Oxford University Press.

—. 2004. *Small Arms Survey 2004: Rights at Risk*. Oxford: Oxford University Press.

Stohl, Rachel. 2004. 'Haiti's Big Threat: Small Arms.' *Christian Science Monitor*. 23 March. Accessed February 2005. <http://www.cdi.org/program/document.cfm?DocumentID=2141>

Stotzky, Irwin P. 1997. *Silencing the Guns in Haiti: The Promise of Deliberative Democracy*. Chicago, IL, and London: University of Chicago Press.

Szajkowski, Bogdan, ed. 2004. *Revolutionary and dissident movements of the world*, 4th (edn.) London: John Harper Publishing.

Torjesen, Stina, Christina Wille, and Neil MacFarlane. 2005. 'Tajikistan's Road to Stability: Reduction in Small Arms and Light Weapons Proliferation and Remaining Challenges.' Geneva: Small Arms Survey. Forthcoming.

UN Comtrade, UN Department of Economic and Social Affairs and the UN Statistics Division. 2004. *United Nations Commodity Trade Statistics database*. Accessed April 2005. <http://unstats.un.org/unsd/comtrade/>

UNSC (United Nations Security Council). 1992. Resolution 788, adopted on 19 November. S/RES/788 (1992).

—. 2000. *Report of the Panel of Experts appointed pursuant to Security Council resolution 1306 (2000) paragraph 19, in relation to Sierra Leone*. S/2000/1195. 14 December.

—. 2001a. *Report of the Panel of Experts concerning Liberia*. S/2001/1015. 26 October.

—. 2001b. Resolution 1343, adopted on 7 March. S/RES/1343 (2001).

—. 2002. *Report of the Panel of Experts concerning Liberia*. S/2002/470. 19 April.

—. 2003a. *Report of the Panel of Experts concerning Liberia*. S/2003/498. 24 April.

—. 2003b. *Report of the Panel of Experts concerning Liberia*. S/2003/937. 28 October.

—. 2004. *Report of the Panel of Experts pursuant to paragraph 22 of Security Council resolution 1521 concerning Liberia*. S/2004/396. 1 June.

US GAO (United States Government Accounting Office). 2000. *Conventional Arms Transfers: U.S. Efforts to Control the Availability of Small Arms and Light Weapons*. GAO/NSIAD-00-141 of 18 July.

ACKNOWLEDGEMENTS

Principal authors
Anna Khakee with Nicolas Florquin

Other contributors
Stina Torjesen, Silvia Cattaneo, Pablo Dreyfus, Rachel Stohl, and Ruxandra Stoicescu

A child stands against
a wall riddled with
bullet holes, the legacy
of Angola's 26-year
civil war. Kuito, Angola,
March 2000.
(© Ami Vitale/Panos Pictures)

Violent Exchanges:
THE USE OF SMALL ARMS IN CONFLICT

7

INTRODUCTION

Throughout history, people engaged in armed conflict have employed many tools of violence, from rocks and sticks to rifles and guided missiles. These armaments have been used to kill, wound, and destroy physical infrastructure, but not with equal effect.

What factors affect people's choice of weaponry and targets? Many variables have a bearing on how small arms and light weapons are used, both within an armed conflict zone and within ostensibly peaceful societies. The answer to the question, therefore, may be as complex as the causes of violent conflict itself. Past studies have highlighted various dynamics, including: the development of gun cultures (Khakee and Florquin, 2003); the presence or absence of social and legal codes to control the use of weapons (Miller, 2003); 'arms racing' among rival groups (Cook and Ludwig, 2003); and links between violence and masculine identity (Cukier, Kooistra, and Anto, 2002).

This chapter does not look in detail at these elements, but instead analyses the broad *facilitating factors* that may encourage or discourage the use of different types of weapons in contemporary armed conflicts. It offers a framework for answering the following question: what are the primary factors that enable or limit the use of weapons? The aim is to provide policy-makers with a checklist of variables with the potential to contribute to the most destructive or indiscriminate forms of weapons use, as a starting point for thinking about how such use might be restricted.

While many subtle social phenomena interact to determine when, if, and how weapons are employed in a particular context, this chapter examines the main influences on the use of weapons with respect to:

- the types of weapons available to armed groups (state and non-state); and
- the kinds of goals espoused by each group.

The first category considers, for instance, potentially strong *material* controls on where weapons can be used and for what purpose. Essential here are *availability factors,* such as the size, weight, and capacity of the weapons, the climatic, topographical, and infrastructural issues that condition their movement, and procurement costs.

The second category takes account of social constraints or shared understanding of acceptable limits to the scale of armed violence. These are *organizational factors*.

The chapter concludes that, by assessing various combinations of availability and organizational factors, one can acquire a better appreciation of an organized group's capacity to engage in armed violence, and of its potential targets. Improved understanding may reveal a number of avenues for limiting the most destructive consequences of armed conflict.

The chapter finds that there are potentially strong 'choke points' that can be exploited to ameliorate the worst instances of weapons use:

- Target the most destructive weapons first, particularly in disarmament, demobilization, and reintegration (DDR) programmes.
- Control more effectively the production and transfer of cheap light weapons to conflict-prone regions.
- Enhance stockpile controls to prevent rapid access to the most destructive varieties of weapons.
- Increase efforts to reduce general local and regional proliferation, as the weapons most readily available are those that are most likely to be used.
- Analyse group goals, command and control, and access to resources thoroughly before introducing restrictive measures.

Methodological considerations

An evaluation of any conflict essentially requires that one look at a number of sub-conflicts, in which the use of weapons varies daily. This is not a new observation. In the early 19th century, Clausewitz (1997, p. 204) wrote: 'our wars are made up of a number of great and small simultaneous or consecutive combats, and this severance of the activity into so many separate actions is owing to the great multiplicity of the relations out of which war arises with us'.

To understand weapons use, it is preferable, therefore, to distinguish between 'type of war' and 'type of warfare' (Kalyvas, 2003, p. 7). Rather than viewing a particular conflict as a 'resource war', a 'low-intensity conflict', or a 'post-modern' or 'new' war, this chapter thus adopts a narrower focus (Kaldor, 1999; Klare, 2002). It concentrates on the particular 'contexts' in which weapons are employed.

The 'context' is the point at which weapons are used to kill, to threaten, to destroy physical infrastructure, or otherwise to facilitate depredation. It signifies the place of convergence between the aims of armed individuals and their opponents. Furthermore, it is the point in space and time at which the negativities of armed violence are most attributable to weapons use.[1]

To analyse meticulously any one context in which weapons are used, a number of other factors must also be taken into consideration. These include: the profile of the actors and their ideologies; their organizational structure; their social basis, military culture, and leadership strategies; the resources they can draw on and the climatic and geographical conditions that influence their operations; domestic or international circumstances; and the specific internal and technological dynamics of the conflict (Kalyvas, 2003, p. 4). Clearly, only some can be addressed here.

The use of weapons in any armed conflict is constrained at any one time by how groups are armed and how they interact with their opponents and the local populace. This is true of clashes between rival gangs in a metropolis such as Los Angeles, or Rio de Janeiro, but it is also true of factional battles in Afghanistan or Sierra Leone, and large-scale military interventions in Chechnya and Iraq.

This study, therefore, views weapons use as the nexus of:

The use of weapons in any armed conflict is constrained by how groups are armed and how they interact with their opponents and the local populace.

- *availability factors*—the physical and supply-side variables that determine, for instance, the type and destructive qualities of weapons available to combatants; and
- *organizational factors*—the elements that influence if, and how, groups of individuals use these weapons.

The chapter is based on three broad assumptions:

- The type of weapon employed in an armed conflict imposes certain fundamental restrictions on how it is used and to what end.
- The physical environment and the organization of armed actors dictate the ease with which groups can acquire certain kinds of weapons.
- The principal variables that determine how armed groups subsequently utilize these weapons are their organizational structures and their operational objectives.

This chapter concentrates on groups that are organized, armed, and use force to achieve their aims, and 'articulate a political or economic agenda rather than private goals' (Capie, 2004, p. 4). The definition does not discriminate between state and non-state armed groups. As recent events in Chechnya, Iraq, and Nepal have demonstrated, the state–non-state dichotomy is problematic for assessing the use and abuse of small arms and light weapons.[2] Furthermore, it is clear that the most established non-state armed groups are better organized, frequently have access to more sources of funds, and are at least as motivated as the armed forces of some developing countries. As Policzer (2002, pp. 3–4) observes:

> Contrary to the dichotomy it predicts, there is a great deal of *overlap* between states and non-state armed groups. In some cases, non-state armed groups look and behave like would-be states, with administrations that provide services to populations under their de facto control. In other cases, de jure states ... [and their armed forces] ... are such only in name, having dismantled their bureaucracies (or failed to build them in the first place), and operating as a series of loosely connected networks.

Sketching availability and organizational factors

Table 7.1 presents a selection of broad inputs that may condition the use of weapons in an armed conflict. Subsequent sections examine these factors, outline their implications for understanding weapons use in an armed conflict, and comment on the affect that they have on control measures.

Table 7.1   Small arms use: Availability and organizational factors

Factor	Description	Examples
Availability	Material controls on the destructive potential of armed violence, which regulate the type of weapons available to combatants and their harmful effects	Weapon design and firepower Size and weight Local proliferation Group resources
Organizational	Social controls on the targeting of violence and limits to the employment of violence to achieve goals	Group structure Organizational objectives Acceptable means of fulfilling aims Conformity to organizational goals Monitoring the behaviour of group members Command and control of members

MATERIAL CONTROLS ON THE DESTRUCTIVE POTENTIAL OF ARMED VIOLENCE

Weapon design and firepower

Understanding of use is often based on an appraisal of consequences, such as categories of individuals targeted and the number of people killed or wounded. The type of weapon used has a considerable bearing on both of these outcomes. While some weapons offer a high degree of precision, others are designed to claim life across large areas and thus provide fewer opportunities to discriminate between intended and unintended targets.

Effects range from the impact of a single bullet fired from a rudimentary craft-produced weapon to the explosive blast following the detonation of a mortar or anti-tank projectile, expelling fragments of metal up to a distance of tens of metres. The likelihood of death, injury, and destruction of infrastructure is great. As the World Health Organization (WHO) (2002, p. 222) notes, 'the level of weapons technology does not necessarily affect the risk of a conflict, but it does determine the scale of any conflict and the amount of destruction that will take place'.

Combatants do not always select the most suitable weapon for a particular purpose. Availability usually informs the decision. Well-funded armed bodies, including the security forces of developed states, use an assortment of specialized weapons, such as sniper rifles for targeted killings or precision-guided munitions. Groups with fewer resources use a variety of the most easily available weapons.

For both sets of actors, the main consideration is not always to minimize casualties, but rather, to employ force most effectively. Key here is 'the concentration of strength against weakness' (Liddell Hart, 1974, p. 334). Combatants prefer superior and reliable firepower.[3]

Box 7.1 Goals and means: death and destruction in Monrovia, Liberia

In July 2003, the Liberian capital of Monrovia came under indiscriminate mortar fire. While initial reports focused attention on extensive shelling by the Liberians United for Reconciliation and Democracy (LURD) rebel group, it has since emerged that Liberian government troops were also involved in the bombardment.[4] The case study below concentrates solely on LURD, however, exploring the reasons behind its radical shift in weapons use.

For LURD, a series of assaults in 2003—culminating in the July attack—represented a major escalation in the use of weapons. In the past, small-scale attacks by LURD on government forces had involved small arms and rocket-propelled grenades (RPGs). The attack on Monrovia was far larger in terms of scale and level of destruction.

This change is attributable to a concatenation of two sets of factors. First, LURD's goal, to remove President Charles Taylor from power, became more pressing as a ceasefire appeared imminent. Second, it sought, and was able to acquire and employ, more destructive weaponry than it had previously had access to.

In 2003, Brabazon (2003, p. 8) made the following comments about how LURD was organized in 2002:

> While LURD do not bear any comparison with a trained African army, their apparent respect for (and dependency on) the civilian population, combined with a strong *esprit de corps* and a degree of basic military training, certainly elevates them above the level of other regional insurgents, specifically the RUF [Revolutionary United Front].

His observations draw attention to two interrelated variables. First, that LURD was a relatively cohesive fighting unit with established command-and-control structures. It was composed primarily of former United Liberation Movement for Democracy in Liberia (ULIMO) fighters. Around 90 per cent of its command structure was made up of former ULIMO commanders, and at least 60 per cent of its troops had a ULIMO background (Brabazon, 2003, p. 7). These soldiers were united in their opposition to President Taylor.

Second, such an established command structure suggests that the group had the potential to control the actions of its fighters vis-à-vis the civilian population. As Brabazon (2003, p. 7) notes, although LURD did not always respect civilians, it did so when senior commanders were around.

Senior commanders were present, though, in Monrovia. They organized the acquisition of mortars, and sanctioned their use. Such action can hardly be characterized as showing respect for the civilian population.

Box 7.1   Goals and means: death and destruction in Monrovia, Liberia (cont.)

The fighting had severe ramifications for the civilian population. According to Human Rights Watch, people were living in structures covered by plastic sheets, which were completely vulnerable to shrapnel from exploding mortar shells. In a US embassy annex occupied by sheltering civilians, for example, '[o]ver twenty-five people died immediately and more than fifty were wounded ... when two mortar rounds fell within the compound' (HRW, 2003, p. 11). The United Nations High Commissioner for Human Rights put the casualty toll from mortar fire in July at 'several hundreds, possibly thousands' (UN, 2003b, para. 3).

The decline in civilian fortunes in 2003 was not attributable to any change in approach to the control of LURD fighters. Nor was it connected to any radical rethinking of goals. Rather, it was due to a reordering of priorities by the rebel group.

The past experiences of former ULIMO commanders in LURD arguably influenced decision-making. ULIMO had suffered a number of setbacks as a result of the August 1996 ceasefire and the 1997 elections, which consolidated President Taylor's hold on power. In 2003, LURD was on the brink of achieving its principal aim, the removal of President Taylor, but it risked losing all in a ceasefire similar to that of 1996.

LURD's main objective in 2003 thus shifted to preventing President Taylor from either holding elections or gaining any territory in advance of peace talks (ICG, 2003a, p. 6). Hence, the unrestrained assault on Monrovia.

The sudden availability of mortars was arguably no accident. As the International Crisis Group (ICG) notes, the declining health of one of LURD's key backers, President Lansana Conté of Guinea, spurred the group into taking maximum advantage of Guinean military assistance (ICG, 2003a, p. 6) (TRANSFERS).

In short, events dictated that it was vital to procure more firepower. An all-out attack was launched on Monrovia because LURD feared that it might be its last chance to remove President Taylor from office. Consequently, when LURD commenced its bombardment of the capital, the welfare of the civilian population was low on its list of concerns.

The case study shows how certain factors were of particular importance in yielding large-scale loss of life in Monrovia. Chief among them were LURD's ability to acquire and field mortars (an availability factor) and the indiscriminate way that it used them (an organizational factor).

The aftermath of the bombardment of Monrovia: civilians killed in the annexe of the US embassy in June 2003.

© Pewee Flomoku/Associated Press

As LURD's assault on Monrovia in July 2003 clearly illustrates, the most serious effects of weapons use stem from the employment of explosive light weapons, such as mortars and RPGs, in areas of high population density. Nonetheless, similar side effects are also observable in situations involving small arms.

Haiti is a case in point. Haitian police officers have been issued with automatic rifles due to the absence of weapons with less firepower. The use of automatic weapons by police is also commonplace in cities such as Bogotá, Colombia, and Rio de Janeiro. In all instances, high-velocity ammunition can penetrate walls, doors, and vehicles, killing or maiming bystanders (AI, 2004; Guyler Delva, 2004; Small Arms Survey, 2004a, pp. 213–43).

Changes in weapons availability affect the trajectory of an armed confrontation. In the Solomon Islands, in early 2000, looting of automatic weapons from police stocks altered the shape of the conflict. Previously, fighting largely involved single-shot weapons that were laborious to reload; subsequently, a single combatant could fire around 30 rounds in a matter of seconds (Small Arms Survey, 2004a, p. 292).

A similar, but more destructive trend was evident in Georgia (Abkhazia and South Ossetia) in 1991–93. Initially (1989–91), limited supplies of small arms, such as pistols and assault rifles, restricted the scope of military action and the number of casualties. Once heavy weapons became available, however, following the opening of Russian military depots in 1991, the intensity of the conflict increased dramatically (Box 7.2). Social violence turned into large-scale warfare, marked by loss of life, destruction of infrastructure, and population displacement (Demetriou, 2002, pp. 9–10, 26–28).

Box 7.2	Weapons availability and effects: Abkhazia and South Ossetia, 1989-93			
Phase	Dates	Weapons	Operations	Effects
1	1989-91	Largely reliant on hunting rifles as well as pistols and rifles stolen from police stations	Small-scale hit-and-run retaliatory operations conducted by small groups of men	Kidnappings, isolated killings, and forced displacement, resulting in some 100-200 deaths. Additional small-scale displacement due to the destruction of a few villages
2	1991-93	Large quantities of small arms and light weapons, including assault rifles, anti-tank weapons, and mortars, plus some heavier weapons	Sieges (of towns) and large-scale military action involving significant numbers of organized and equipped troops. Action aimed at acquiring territory	Massive amount of damage to infrastructure, and the destruction of hundreds of villages and towns. At least 9,000 people killed and more than 300,000 displaced

Source: Demetriou (2002, pp. 25-29)

In the cases outlined above, while combatants were responsible for selecting their targets, the effects of using such weapons were often beyond the control of the user.

The choice of weapon is not *always* constrained, therefore, by consideration of the consequences associated with its use, but it is always constrained by its physical attributes. In all situations, the type of weapon limits how it is employed and the impact that it has on the armed conflict.

Controls on firepower

The ramifications of firepower can be managed by controlling the production of certain weapons and the transfer and stockpiling of these items.

Concerns about general small arms proliferation often overshadow the need to target the most destructive weapons first. Supply-side initiatives should concentrate initially on weapons with the greatest potential to cause massive and rapid loss of life and infrastructural devastation, such as mortars, RPGs, and grenade launchers.

Producers of cheap and highly destructive armaments clearly profit from demand for such weapons in an armed conflict zone. Of note are light weapons such as the RPG-7. Not only is it cheap, manufactured widely, and employed by numerous state and non-state armed groups, but producers are attempting to increase the appeal of this 'old favourite' by enhancing its destructive capabilities. Less well-funded states appear to be the main targets of this marketing drive, many of which are prone to armed conflict (Small Arms Survey, 2004a, p. 36). As a number of the companies implicated are based in Western Europe or in states that are hoping to join the European Union (EU), policy-makers appear to be in a position to prevent such a move (Small Arms Survey, 2004a, pp. 35–36).

Proliferation worries, however, should not mask the fact that many states employ weapons for domestic security purposes, and will continue to do so. Put simply, if armed entities, such as police and paramilitary forces, do not have access to weapons that are suitable for the task at hand, they are likely to use military armaments that place the local populace at greater risk (AI, 2004, p. 28). Moreover, policing by soldiers (the cheap option) in states such as Afghanistan allows financial savings to be made at the expense of an increased threat to lives.

Hence, responsible measures to combat the effects of small arms and light weapons must be based on a nuanced appraisal of the types of weapons that need to be controlled most urgently and their effects.

> Supply-side initiatives should concentrate on weapons with the greatest potential to cause massive and rapid loss of life and infrastructural devastation.

Size and weight of small arms

Small arms and light weapons come in all shapes and sizes, from pistols that are small and light enough to be carried in a pocket to heavy machine guns and grenade launchers that can weigh 100 kilograms or more. These factors, in conjunction with climate and terrain, condition the availability of weapons for any particular user.

Size and weight place constraints on the movement of weapons, which can only be overcome through expenditure on transportation. All groups are affected, but those that suffer most are usually small, resource-poor entities. In contrast, logistical capacity facilitates an increase in the size of weapons used by a group, as well as a change in type and capability. For instance, state armed forces and non-state groups such as the Liberation Tigers of Tamil Eelam (LTTE) have the logistical capacity to move and employ heavy weapons, including large artillery pieces. Resource-poor groups are often restricted to using only small arms.[5]

Effective use often depends on the ability to transfer war materials across all kinds of terrain (Muggah and Bevan, 2004; Yousaf and Adkin, 2001). This is evidenced by arms supplied to mujahideen fighters via mountain passes (from Pakistan's Northwest Frontier Province) during the Afghan–Russian conflict of the 1980s. It is also clear in the trade in weapons between Bougainville and the Solomon Islands in the late 1990s and after the turn of the millennium. When natural features make it easy to move weapons, groups need to invest fewer resources to obtain the items they desire.

The portability of weapons has considerable implications for research and policy-making. At the very least, it provides a rough guide to the type of weaponry that combatants are likely to look to acquire in a given context. This is important information for those trying to discern the types of weapons being transferred to a conflict zone and their potential effects.

Local proliferation

If groups are not in possession of weapons 'suitable' for a task, they have two options: to desist from certain types of violent activity; or to procure those armaments that are most easily available. Local weapons are the easiest to acquire.

Sourcing weapons locally does not mean that groups are able to obtain the most appropriate hardware. Thus, as a medieval serf might have brought a pitchfork into battle, so hunters, for instance, may enter a war with (frequently antiquated) hunting rifles. Locally stockpiled small arms and light weapons will play, therefore, a crucial role in determining the form of an armed conflict.

Masked combatants of the Popular Revolutionary Army (EPR) carry an assortment of the most easily available weapons, including a stick, in Mexico, September 1996.

In the Solomon Islands, the use of home-made guns severely restricted the number of sustained armed exchanges. It was only after military weapons were seized from state armouries that weapons use escalated in terms of scale and impact (Capie, 2003; Small Arms Survey, 2004a). Similarly, rebels in northern Mali were at first ill equipped to engage in protracted hostilities. Violence escalated following the capture of large quantities of military weapons from government forces (Lecocq, 2002, p. 231).

Locally stockpiled small arms and light weapons play a crucial role in determining the form of an armed conflict.

The repercussions for stockpile security are clear. The types of weapons held in a particular geographical area, whether in the hands of the local populace, or in the arsenals of state security forces, are liable to affect the shape of a conflict considerably should one break out.

The continuation of efforts to secure stockpiles in regions of the world where social tensions make armed conflict more likely is essential to condition the use of violence should conflict erupt. This focus, however, needs to be qualitative as well as quantitative. The kinds of weapons stockpiled are at least as important as numbers.

Group resources and the acquisition spiral

Organizational capacity largely determines a group's ability to acquire, move, and use certain types of weaponry. There is a strong link between the resources available to a group and the potential impact that it can have on an opponent and the local populace. Knowing what resources armed actors have available to them is fundamental to understanding how to control the use of weapons.

In a study of 74 post-cold war insurgencies, one publication found evidence to suggest that state support played a major part in the perpetuation of 44 of them. It also intimated, however, that diaspora assistance may be becoming more of a factor in armed conflict (Byman et. al., 2001, p. xv).[6] The second Tamasheq rebellion in northern Mali (1990–96), for instance, witnessed intermittent and minor external support. The small arms and light weapons purchased were bought with funds from 'les grandes partenaires', expatriates with capital and sympathetic to the group's objectives. The phenomenon is perhaps best illustrated by larger groups, though, such as Hezbollah in Lebanon, the LTTE in Sri Lanka, and the Revolutionary Armed Forces of Colombia (Fuerzas Armadas Revolucionarias de Colombia, FARC). These organizations have used extensive networks to procure advanced weaponry, including man-portable air defence systems (MANPADS), from suppliers situated far from the immediate locality (Small Arms Survey, 2004a, pp. 88–89).

In extreme cases, where foreign backing is absent and natural resources are scarce, human capital may be mobilized as a resource in its own right. For example, the National Resistance Army (NRA) in Uganda appealed to ethnic, religious, or spiritual sentiment, in the early 1980s, in order to attract relatively large numbers of recruits. Subsequently, these combatants were tasked with capturing arms from opponents (Weinstein, 2004, pp. 3–4).

Weapons alter the resource–acquisition equation significantly, by enabling groups to seize more and better armaments. In areas where there is a poorly defended opposition, groups are able to strengthen their arsenals considerably. The Malian Mouvement Populaire de Libération de l'Azawad serves as a good example of this acquisition spiral. It apparently began its campaign with a single Kalashnikov rifle. In a succession of attacks, it was able to seize close to 500 weapons. In each case, the quantity captured was greater than before, as the increased stocks allowed more effective assaults to be launched (Humphreys and ag Mohamed, 2003, p. 3).

In simple terms, this means that a group's military effectiveness is enhanced. As some analysts have noted, though, the success of combatants may also lead to a cumulative rise in the level of external support. That is, military gains result in greater interest in the cause, additional finance, and more and better weapons—the acquisition spiral—further strengthening a group's capacity to engage in violence (Byman et. al., 2001, p. 55; Yousaf and Adkin, 2001).

Group resources have considerable implications for steps taken to ameliorate armed conflict. Factors such as an embargo on a state (UN and the Democratic Republic of Congo (DRC)) or the labelling of a group as a terrorist organization (United States and Hezbollah) may impede access by belligerents to small arms and light weapons. These factors are countered, however, by other variables, including support from a neighbouring government (Rwanda and the DRC), state support for a group (Syria and Hezbollah), or the backing of a diaspora (LTTE). Far more research needs to be conducted on the linkages between state and non-state armed entities if an accurate picture is to be painted of the inputs that influence weapons use.

Resource flows, whether of a commercial nature, or connected to the political ambitions of a state or a diaspora, also have the capacity to change qualitatively the degree of violence in an armed conflict by affecting the types of weapons available to disputants. This observation has consequences for analyses carried out before, during, and after a conflict.

In the first instance, the prevalence of small arms and light weapons in a particular region must be viewed as potentially facilitating the acquisition of such armaments in *all* regions. Availability of resources simply enhances the ability of potential combatants to procure small arms and light weapons.

In the second instance, the continued flow of resources to groups has severe ramifications for DDR and peacebuilding programmes. In Afghanistan, for example, there are clear, if indirect, connections between control over the sale of opium and the capacity of warlords to resupply themselves with the types and quantities of weapons that they require (COFR, 2003).

The prevalence of small arms and light weapons in a particular region must be viewed as potentially facilitating the acquisition of such armaments in all regions.

SOCIAL CONTROLS AND THE TARGETING OF ARMED VIOLENCE

So far this chapter has concerned itself primarily with physical factors related to the types of weapons that an armed group can field and their effects. These variables, though, yield little insight into how the use of small arms and light weapons is targeted. This requires an understanding of social controls on weapons use (Table 7.1).

The following sections present a broad overview of how individuals break into armed factions, which have extremely different goals and hence use small arms and light weapons in very different ways. The focus is then narrowed so that an explanation can be offered on how the social composition of these groups facilitates or hinders the development of oversight mechanisms that can control the use of weapons.

Group structure and weapons use

What differentiates the use of small arms and light weapons by groups from individual acts of sporadic violence is that clear patterns can be identified in how the former utilize weapons. Individuals in groups ensure that their behaviour stays within certain parameters and is acceptable to other group members. By doing so, they are relieved of constantly having to evaluate potential courses of action to the extreme. Rather, they follow a rough blueprint (or set of standard operating procedures), which defines acceptable and unacceptable forms of behaviour (Allison, 1971; Steinbruner, 1974). Group behaviour remains relatively stable over time.

Armed individuals share commonalities not shared with unarmed individuals. As one former combatant in Mali pointed out, 'with a weapon, one is automatically isolated from the world'.[7] He admitted that this is because of not only mistrust on the part of the unarmed populace, but also because of the armed combatant's fear that his or her weapon could be stolen and the situation reversed. Weapons redefine perceptions of 'self' and the 'other'. A core motivation of group members is, therefore, to stay 'in the club'.

> As one former combatant in Mali pointed out, 'with a weapon, one is automatically isolated from the world'.

To remain members, individuals relinquish some independent interests (Simon, 1997). In the case of armed groups, an individual may be required to follow codified rules or, in extreme situations, may have to observe a tacit agreement not to steal from or kill other group members for personal gain.[8] These regulations are in place to ensure that a group functions smoothly and that its goals are fulfilled. They can extend from the most fundamental conventions aimed at guaranteeing continued group cohesion, such as those mentioned above, to rules that have a bearing on the efficiency with which a group conducts a campaign of armed violence. The latter may include prohibitions on shooting or stealing from members of friendly civilian populations or principles designed to conserve ammunition supplies. The threat of sanction, ranging from removing individuals from operational duties, to humiliation or ostracism, to death (in the extreme), reinforces such regulations.[9]

To acquire a deep understanding of how weapons are used, one must appreciate the underlying social circumstances of prospective group members and why they are attracted to a particular entity, how their aims shape its broad objectives, and how violence is used to achieve the latter. To comprehend in simple terms how a group is likely to behave, one need only assess, however, its core goals.

The following section addresses initially the impact of recruitment on the formulation of group objectives and subsequent targeting of small arms and light weapons use. Next, it analyses how the social composition of groups affects the development of command-and-control structures and how these mechanisms condition the use of small arms and light weapons, in accordance with the aims of the organization.

Formulation of group goals, command and control, and the use of small arms and light weapons

While war may mask a vast assortment of odious activities, from theft and rape to the taking of personal revenge in the heat of battle, the actions of armed groups are clearly purposive. One can even go as far, therefore, as to characterize conflicts according to the behaviour of the belligerents. For example, one might perceive the conflict in Liberia as one primarily fought for reasons of predation and resource extraction rather than the satisfaction of political aims. Similarly, with regard to Palestinian armed groups, although smuggling and profiteering are undoubtedly among the activities conducted by some entities, the main goal is to establish an independent state. In both instances, the cause or objective defines how armed violence is targeted. A Liberian group may target a village; a Palestinian group may target Israeli police or military units or civilians. In either case, violence so directed may contravene international norms, and some may consider it excessive and indiscriminate. For the groups involved, however, it is normal, legitimate, and/or necessary.

Why are small arms and light weapons employed in such different ways? Why, in some situations, is armed violence targeted expressly at civilian populations, and, in others, at armed forces, institutions, and supporters of a political order? One reason is that the motivations of individuals differ in their immediacy, which is reflected in the composition of groups. The gains from membership of an armed group may be instant, such as a sense of solidarity with other armed individuals, and the ability to plunder more effectively, or they may be more long term in nature. The latter may include better political representation for a particular group of people, repellence of invaders, or secession from a state.

At the outset of an armed conflict, as Kalyvas argues, the use of small arms, and indeed all forms of violence, is often multi-directional and not focused on achieving a particular long-term objective. Myriad acts of violence are often perpetrated against neighbours, as sides have yet to become polarized to the extent that parties to a conflict are clearly identifiable; individuals violently abuse suspected enemies (Kalyvas, 2003, pp. 12–13). It is not necessarily that traditional grievances resurface and crystallize into a campaign of armed violence, but more that, using high levels of instability and hostility as cover, individuals often employ weapons to settle old scores or to satisfy greed-based desires.

In an environment marked by high instability, the ability of individuals to unite in groups has an obvious bearing on the identification of subsequent targets of armed violence. Where leadership and individual will are present, and the possibilities for a forward-looking project are clear, it is likely that cohesive groups will emerge and direct the use of weapons towards, among other things, engaging state security forces (or, conversely, protecting a nation). This is not to say that massacres and atrocities perpetrated against civilians necessarily subside—in fact, there is every chance that they will increase—but rather that combatants adhere to groups espousing lucid aims and often receive training in the use of weapons. Hence, small arms are, for the most part, used tactically and violence is usually highly directed. Where prevailing social conditions do not facilitate such developments, there is a strong incentive for groups to form solely with the intention of gaining from the status quo. These groups employ small arms predominantly to extract resources and to plunder, or indeed to secure any other kind of immediate social or spiritual benefit.

The text above provides some idea of the broad goals that groups espouse. But how do these groups differ in terms of their command-and-control structures, and what are the implications for the daily use of weapons? How can objectives serve as a broad metric for gauging the likely targets of armed hostility?

The structure of armed groups is diverse, ranging from the long-established, highly organized hierarchies common to traditional armies, to entities in which it is hard to discern any kind of system of organization whatsoever. Yet,

At the onset of armed conflict, using high levels of instability and hostility as cover, weapons are used to settle old scores or to satisfy greed-based desires.

as Bowyer Bell (1998, p. 103) stresses, all armed groups in practice must have some type of formal configuration to control to some extent the operational direction of their activities.

Debatably, two key factors determine why group structures differ. First is the ability of commanders to exert influence over armed individuals (and, on the contrary, the willingness of these individuals to relinquish some personal freedoms and to accept the authority of commanders). Second is the capacity of commanders to oversee how group members use their weapons.

While the leaders of a group largely determine the degree of control exercised over members, command and control relies greatly on the willingness of recruits to respect leadership.[10] Arguably, command and control is as much about charisma, of which all leaders have at least a trace, and the level of consensus leading to consent, as it is about feeling compelled due to the threat of punishment (Bowyer Bell, 1998, p. 103).

Young LTTE recruits listen to lectures at a jungle training camp in the Sri Lankan village Vakarai in August 1996.

Organizational goals must comprise credible promises to deliver benefits to group members (Cyert and March, 1963; March and Simon, 1958; Simon, 1997). Only groups able to make credible promises to deliver future benefits, rather than immediate gains, can attract highly committed individuals (Weinstein, 2004, p. 15). Such individuals are more likely to use weapons to satisfy the aims of a progressive project than to employ them for personal gain.[11] As Weinstein notes, in contrast to short-term, gain-seeking groups, it is often far easier for commanders of groups comprising long-term, gain-seeking individuals to exercise control because the latter are less likely to put personal benefit before the satisfaction of group objectives (Weinstein, 2004, p. 32).[12]

A second (closely linked) command-and-control issue is the level of oversight that commanders are willing and able to exercise over group members. Policzer (2002, pp. 8–15) has constructed a comprehensive framework for analysing the structure of a group, based on the quality and quantity of information that leaders acquire about the activities of recruits. His approach focuses on the ability of leaders to receive information and to monitor whether the performance of subordinates is consistent with the goals of the group (Table 7.2). The central hypothesis is that 'organizations that are good information processors are likely to exercise coercion radically different from those that are not' (Policzer, 2002, p. 8). Leaders either monitor the actions of subordinates directly, or through an intermediary within the group, and/or they rely on external sources of information on the activities of group members.

In the latter case, leaders must consider a variety of channels, such as human rights groups and the regional and international media. The relative attention that the leadership devotes to each of these channels alters its ability to monitor the activities of subordinates.

Table 7.2   Types of monitoring within armed groups

Type of monitoring	Source of information	Examples
Internal monitoring	Information generated within the group	Direct monitoring by a leader Monitoring through an intermediary Combination of the two
External monitoring	Information from external sources	Monitoring the immediate populace Monitoring the regional and international media Combination of the two

Note: Table based on ideas proposed by Policzer (2002).

For the study of armed groups, the approach is of great value. While the leadership may often make the decision whether or not to use weapons, different organizational structures control its ability to articulate objectives, be they of an aggressive or benevolent nature.

Table 7.3   Strong and weak monitoring

	High internal monitoring	Low internal monitoring
High external monitoring	Highly organized armed groups frequently with strong international connections, such as the British Armed Forces, Hezbollah, or the LTTE	Organized armed groups within which oversight is intentionally opaque, such as right-wing militias in Colombia and perhaps some private security outfits in Afghanistan
Low external monitoring	Organized armed groups with few linkages to the external environment, such as rebel entities in northern Mali or drug factions in Rio de Janeiro	Armed groups with little in the way of a formal system of organization and few external connections, such as armed elements in Sierra Leone or the Solomon Islands

Note: Table derived from the work of Policzer (2002).

The following sections present two forms of organization—short- and long-term gain-seeking groups—and illustrate how various combinations of membership and leadership strategies affect weapons use. They concentrate on variables that influence the kind of person recruited, his or her objectives, and the degree of accord between the objectives of groups and those of their members.

Box 7.3   From long-term to short-term goals: UNITA's slide from mass mobilization to resource extraction

Since its emergence almost 40 years ago, the National Union for the Total Independence of Angola (União Nacional para a Independência Total de Angola, UNITA) has transformed from a group employing violence for ideological purposes to one using it to further material gains. Although these two concepts are hard to disentangle, a distinct change is nonetheless observable in the goals of UNITA and in the way in which it engages in armed violence.

Jonas Savimbi formed UNITA in 1966 during the struggle against colonial Portugal. It drew support largely from the Ovimbundu people, comprising nearly 40 per cent of the Angolan population. The Ovimbundu enjoyed little political representation within the larger Popular Movement for the Liberation of Angola (Movimento Popular de Libertação de Angola, MPLA).

Seeking national liberation, UNITA could be seen initially as a group promoting long-term goals on behalf of a large section of Angolan society. Describing Savimbi during the early years, Burke (1984, p. 17) notes:

He long concentrated on raising the political consciousness of the peasantry, an important lesson learned from Mao. He established food cooperatives and developed village self-defense units. He also established an elaborate governmental framework in which regional elected councils made their views known through a political commissar to the 35 member central committee whose members were to be chosen every four years at a congress.

> **Box 7.3 From long-term to short-term goals: UNITA's slide from mass mobilization to resource extraction (cont.)**
>
> Of the three main non-state armed groups involved in the colonial era struggle (1966-74), UNITA relied least on external support, depending primarily on political rather than military means to extend its control (Burke, 1984, p. 17). UNITA could not for long describe itself, however, as a movement characterized by widespread ethnic or ideological mobilization.
>
> In the late 1960s and early 1970s, UNITA received military aid and backing from the apartheid Government of South Africa, from the United States, and indirectly from North Atlantic Treaty Organisation (NATO) countries in Western Europe (Johnson and Martin, 1988, pp. 102-106). Military aid continued to flow after the departure of the Portuguese (1975), as the conflict between UNITA and the communist-leaning MPLA deepened. By the late 1970s, and throughout the 1980s, UNITA essentially derived revenues from participating in one of Africa's most protracted proxy conflicts.
>
> As UNITA sought to demonstrate to the outside world its strength vis-à-vis the MPLA government, acts of terrorism came to form a core component of its armed strategy, including kidnapping and hijacking (Burke, 1984, p. 53).
>
> In May 1991, Portugal, the Soviet Union, and the United States brokered the Bicesse Peace Accord, and a ceasefire was implemented to halt the 16-year conflict (ICG, 2003b, p. 2). The agreement signified a turning point with regard to UNITA's goals. From the early 1980s, Savimbi had indicated a willingness to share power with the MPLA if Cuban and Soviet forces left the country (Burke, 1984, p. 56). The peace deal arguably robbed UNITA of a significant portion of its *raison d'être*.
>
> UNITA rejected the results of the September 1992 elections, which the UN deemed free and fair, and resumed fighting in October 1992. The UN Security Council imposed sanctions in 1993. Resolution 864 forbade the sale and supply of weapons and petroleum or petroleum products to UNITA (Fowler and Angell, 2001, pp. 191-92).
>
> In response, UNITA stepped up its transfers of diamonds and other resources for weapons. It offered Congo-Brazzaville and Zaire (now the Republic of Congo and the DRC) natural resources, including diamonds, in return for military and political support (Prendergast, 1999, p. 3). The conflict escalated dramatically; violence was perpetrated primarily to acquire natural resources. As Cleary (1999, p. 146) points out, 'more Angolans died as a result of war in the two years between 1992 and November 1994 than in the sixteen years of conflict before 1991'.
>
> Fighting subsided somewhat in the years immediately following the signing of the 1994 Lusaka Protocol. By 1997, though, the accord had broken down completely.
>
> When the government of Zairian President Mobutu Sese Seko collapsed in April 1997, UNITA lost its most important backer.
>
> The UN imposed further sanctions later in 1997 (Resolution 1127), and in 1998 (Resolution 1173), which included prohibitions on representation abroad and travel and on the sale or export of diamonds by UNITA. Nevertheless, as one ICG report states, 'by mid-1998, freshly rearmed and demanding significant amendments to the Protocol, [UNITA] resumed a low-intensity war' (ICG, 2003b, p. 3).
>
> Given President Mobutu's demise, how was UNITA able to rearm? Prendergast asserts that the organization sought and found assistance and shelter in Burkina Faso and Togo, largely in return for access to natural resources. He notes: 'the fuel for UNITA's resupply efforts during this decade has been diamonds, replacing the aid UNITA received from the United States and apartheid South Africa during the Cold War' (Prendergast, 1999, p. 3). The group took advantage of an extensive network of regional brokers in order to exchange natural resources for arms.
>
> Following Savimbi's death in February 2002, the conflict came to a formal end on 4 April 2002, with the signing of the Luena Accords.
>
> In 2003, the ICG reported that many UNITA units had taken to banditry and organized criminal action due to the collapse of the command structure in the year prior to Savimbi's death (ICG, 2003b, p. 6). The fact that many top UNITA commanders have been offered political positions in the capital, Luanda, and have been supplied with welfare has further encouraged disloyalty among rank-and-file recruits who have been left with nothing. In sum, the long-term goal-seeking group of the 1960s has turned into a short-term goal-seeking group made up of those UNITA members with just a rifle to their name.

Groups may seek pillage or the control of resources, or the social and economic benefits of war may simply outweigh those of peace.

Short-term gain-seeking groups

Groups looking to make short-term gains may include those whose objectives are to pillage or to gain control of resources, such as diamond mines and forests. Alternatively, they may be engaged in an armed conflict simply because the social and economic benefits of war outweigh those of peace. The use of small arms and light weapons varies depending on the particular short-term aim. These groups attract recruits who often care little about the ramifications of violence for the proximate populace. Hence, at first glance, small arms and light weapons use may appear random.

In relation to a number of groups, such as those in Liberia, torture, theft, rape, and mass killing by armed combatants cannot be viewed as part of a systematic political project, or as the result of agreement on goals among a large number of people (Ellis, 1999). In such cases, the use of small arms and light weapons is largely ad hoc, military-style coordination is notably absent, and violence is multi-directional. Fighters with President Taylor's National Patriotic Front of Liberia (NPFL) lived hand-to-mouth and relied on killing, pillaging, or rape to satisfy immediate desires. Weapons were used more to facilitate looting, rape, and other forms of predation, therefore, than to achieve military objectives.

The same is true of conflicts in neighbouring Côte d'Ivoire and Sierra Leone. Weapons have been used, for example, to threaten local people and to extort and kill at will for various reasons. Only infrequently, are fighters persuaded or coerced into launching large-scale assaults on government troops to procure or defend territory.

Once installed in a region, fighters endowed with small arms and light weapons can plunder and kill without having to engage in combat as an element of a long-term political project (Clapham, 1998).

Box 7.4   Group objectives and cycles of armed violence

Violence begets violence. While the presence of armed individuals has the potential to raise insecurity in a region, autocatalytic cycles of armed violence seem to be triggered by how groups appear to act with respect to the people around them.

Former combatants in Mali reported that, while there was always mistrust of armed individuals, if the families and communities of group members accorded the group's objective legitimacy, there was a degree of consensus that it was necessary for members to be armed. If, however, the group was seen to be engaging in action contrary to the aims of local communities, such as banditry, the reverse was true. In North Kivu, DRC, fieldwork conducted between 2002 and 2004 revealed that Mayi-Mayi groups, once perceived as 'brave and fearless fighters' (qualities often attributed to supernatural powers) in the struggle against President Mobutu's regime, held diminished status. The research noted a deep change in local perceptions. People now recognize that the fighters are not invincible and attribute their loss of status to their thieving, banditry, and abuse of the local populace. The outcome is a situation in which local condemnation aggravates the anti-social behaviour of combatants. In turn, this leads to the perpetration of increased acts of violence by the populace against them, resulting in pervasive armed violence in society (Jourdan, 2004, pp. 157-76).

Short-term gains also manifest themselves in ways less related to economic benefit. In some regions, such as North Kivu, DRC, membership of an armed group offers an opportunity for immediate social mobility, representing 'an attempt to accede to material, and above all, symbolic aspects of modernity' (Jourdan, 2004, p. 157). In such instances, not only do combatants use small arms and light weapons to steal for a living, but also they often utilize them in an attempt to invert the social order to their own perceived advantage (Jourdan, 2004, pp. 162–63). Examining the Somali National Movement (SNM), Compagnon (1998, p. 80) remarks:

> The original well-trained militias had been decimated in the heavy fighting … and were replaced by contingents drawn from all [clan] lineage segments. Many of these new combatants came from ravaged towns, and had lost their closest relatives in the war. Most of them had no formal education, because the school system had been disrupted since as early as 1984, and the majority had been unemployed before they became guerrillas. Warfare became a way of life, and the automatic rifle a means of a living.

In such cases, acts of armed violence are often directed at members of older generations, particularly elderly persons who represent the traditional hierarchy. Alternatively, they focus on the procurement of items that symbolize modernity, such as sunglasses, designer clothes, and radios (Ellis, 1999).

Similar patterns are observable vis-à-vis violence committed by state-sponsored armed groups. Members of government-armed militias and paramilitaries, frequently from poor backgrounds and lacking any long-term commitment to a cause, have used weapons to facilitate the predation of the general populace. Mostly, these groups consist of short-term gain-seeking individuals. As Dasgupta (2003, pp. 9–11) argues, the fact that paramilitary units, such as the United Self-Defence Forces of Colombia (Autodefensas Unidas de Colombia, AUC), are often a transitory feature of a state's security apparatus means that group members will regularly attempt to gain access to resources other than those provided by the state.

The high prevalence of short-term gain-seeking individuals has notable implications for the type of command and control instituted within a group. Groups that attract such individuals, for example, the NPFL, are often hard to control and commanders have little incentive or ability to introduce a solid organizational structure. Minimal internal and external

© Reuters

Child combatants hold their weapons on the streets of Monrovia in April 1996.

monitoring produces a situation in which the leader is unlikely to have any real knowledge about the activities of subordinates, or to exercise any degree of control over their actions. There are few restrictions on weapons and most individuals are armed and able to use them with impunity against persons outside of the group.[13]

In contrast to longer-term goal-seeking groups, the command-and-control structures of lesser-organized entities are often more opaque and spheres of authority regularly overlap. Consequently, should a commander wish to control the use of weapons, authority is so fragmented as to render it difficult. A case in point is the Revolutionary United Front (RUF) in Sierra Leone. Despite attempts by senior officials to unite the group, the RUF remained essentially a 'bandit organization solely driven by the survivalist needs of its predominantly uneducated and alienated battle front and battle group commanders' (Abdullah and Muana, 1998, pp. 191–92).

Even in groups in which commanders exercise considerable oversight, and command and control are robust, these processes do not necessarily extend to all combatants. For the purpose of military expediency, commanders often employ small groups of combatants that are peripheral to the group proper. The reasons for this are that they enhance the size of the overall force that a group can field, or they know the area of operations well. Routinely, these combatants are no more than freebooters and show little allegiance to a particular cause. Some commanders admit to having little control over how they use their weapons.[14]

This is a not simply a feature of small, non-state armed groups. Events in Afghanistan demonstrate that armed actors often attach themselves to larger groups for a number of reasons. The armed vigilantism of Jonathan Keith Idema in Kabul is illustrative (Burnett, 2004; *Washington Post,* 2004). Peripheral groups of individuals may be tolerated, because they are useful, or they may be encouraged to participate, so that denials of actions are afforded more credibility. Yet, in both instances, control over how weapons are used is necessarily weaker than with armed groups proper. In extreme situations, such as that of the DRC, quantities of weapons were distributed among militias, without mechanisms in place to record the identity of the recipients (Capie, 2004, p. 9).

Similar situations are apparent when command and control is deliberately vague to ensure deniability for supreme leaders. Often this is the case within the ranks of paramilitaries, constabulary forces, and militia groups that are 'extensions of the centralized authority of national militaries', such as the (Hutu) Interahamwe in Rwanda (Dasgupta, 2004, p. 1). Members of these groups receive a degree of direction on targeting a particular enemy, yet their consequent actions are not coordinated and the leadership usually denies them.

Box 7.5   Structures of control: the drug trade in Rio de Janeiro

Armed violence associated with the drug trade in Rio de Janeiro has received worldwide media attention. Four factions currently dominate Brazil's drug market.[15] While they display little in the way of a formal structure, seemingly 'independent' actors—*donos do tráfico*—and their subordinates act within a framework of loose beneficial alliances. The structure is organized around mutual support—common goals, which encompass mutually desirable objectives for profitable gain and territorial advancement (Dowdney, 2003, p. 43). It is also regulated, however, by extreme violence. In this system, armed violence is far from random; it is tightly controlled.

Each *dono* controls one or several *favelas* and organizes the trade in cocaine and marijuana in these communities, distributes weapons to employees, and maintains diplomatic relations with other *donos* from the same faction (Dowdney, 2003, p. 47).

No *dono* faction has a leader per se, but certain individuals amass power and respect through their leadership skills. Many of these powerful *donos* are in prison, yet they are able to monitor activities in their territories using cellular phones or nominated *donos* on the outside.

Donos have created 'a control system based on violence or the threat of violence whereby traffickers receive community protection in exchange for offering what the state has traditionally failed to provide: the maintenance of social order, support, economic stimulation and provision of leisure activities' (Dowdney, 2003, pp. 53-54).

Recruitment into this system benefits considerably from a distinct lack of options. It is voluntary, simply because entering the drug trade is often 'the best alternative' (Dowdney, 2003, p. 130). This is the case particularly for children and adolescents.

Members may begin their career as *olheiros* or lookouts, progress to become drug sellers, and possibly end up overseeing other members. They may also become *soldados:* permanently armed members of the faction responsible for maintaining order and defence.

Throughout their career, group members and local residents are subject to a system of oversight, orders, rules, and sanctions. Importantly, attaining and preserving group objectives are at the heart of the system. Drugs must be paid for, no one can speak to the police, and territory has to be defended. Petty crimes that, for example, might endanger this system of control or exacerbate tensions with rival factions are punished (Dowdney, 2003, pp. 139-47). Punishment depends on the crime and ranges from expulsion to beatings, and even execution. A serious offence is judged not on social mores, but on its implications for the continued functioning of the system of control—a crime is something that jeopardizes the system. As one 17-year-old replied in response to a question about what would happen if he did not follow the orders of his boss: '[d]epends what he asks ... If it's to kill someone, I have to do it. If I don't kill then it's my life at risk' (Dowdney, 2003, p. 149).

Understanding how faction members use weapons requires that one appreciate the principal goals of the system and the acceptable and unacceptable activities that take place within it.

Note: Box based on research presented in Dowdney (2003). Children of the Drug Trade provides a comprehensive analysis of organized armed violence in Rio de Janeiro. Thanks to the author for his valuable input.
Source: Demetriou (2002, pp. 25-29)

Long-term gain-seeking groups

In contrast, groups that attract recruits looking to secure long-term benefits differ considerably from those composed largely of short-term gain-seeking individuals. Such groups hope to acquire a place in the political system, or employ violence to achieve goals intended to be collectively progressive. The use of weapons differs greatly as a consequence. First, group members are likely to refrain from engaging in violence that might jeopardize these aims. Second, because of collectively progressive goals, commanders are often in a better social position to sanction members who deviate from them. While this is obviously not true at all times, a number of cases are illustrative.

Groups such as Hamas, Hezbollah, and the LTTE comprise members that, for the most part, are committed to a long-term political project. Violence is, therefore, more targeted than with short-term gain-seeking groups such as the NPFL. Hamas, for instance, regularly uses weapons against Israeli troops and citizens. Combatants, though, either refrain from targeting large numbers of popular supporters of Hamas, or are sanctioned if they do. The use of weapons for predation, as in Liberia or Sierra Leone, is clearly not an issue here.

Groups such as the NRA in Uganda displayed similar tendencies before coming to power. Members and leaders shared common principles and objectives when in opposition to the government of President Milton Obote, which were easily reinforced by formalized training in the aims and ideology of the movement. As Clapham (1998, p. 10) argues, the NRA was thus far more effective militarily than groups such as the NPFL, because its troops were less inclined to engage in banditry and other acts of depredation. Furthermore, such activities did not reduce the willingness of members to confront government forces.

Often these groups are highly structured, with distinct hierarchies and clear command-and-control channels. Consequently, leaders are often able to monitor closely the actions of their members. With respect to the Tamasheq rebellion in northern Mali, for example, former Malian Army commanders modelled a number of armed groups along military lines. These groups appeared highly coordinated and leaders were not only knowledgeable about the actions of members on the ground, but also were able to direct them. As a result, such armed groups usually carry out highly targeted killings, and use violence to fulfil outwardly progressive objectives. These aims take precedence over the longing for personal revenge, and the momentary wish to pillage or take advantage of a woman's body.

The extent to which these groups are structured is best illustrated by controls over the distribution of weapons. In Mali, there was a prevailing view that, while combatants controlled their weapons (most had one for personal defence), armament in general was the concern of the commander. In some cases, on joining the group, an individual's weapon became group property. As for arms procured by the group, or captured from the enemy, there was no doubt that these were group property. Subsequent distribution was determined by the type of mission that the user was about to undertake. The serial number and the user's name were noted, and weapons not in employment remained under the supervision of the *chargé des armes*. Once issued, strict controls came into effect concerning the utilization of ammunition.[16]

Within long-term goal-seeking groups, the prospect of controlling the use of weapons against civilian populations is better than in short-term, gain-seeking groups. Key factors in this regard are the frequent need to obtain political support from local populations and effective command-and-control structures. As Clapham notes of the NRA (in Uganda) and the closely related Rwandan Patriotic Front (RPF), overall training and discipline levels, while improving the fighting performance of a unit, were accompanied by an ability to enforce stringent levels of discipline. '[I]ndividuals responsible for rape or murder of civilians were publicly executed' (Clapham, 1998, p. 10).

There is a further element to consider in assessing the command-and-control structures of long-term goal-seeking groups. Very often these groups not only depend on outside support from states and diasporas, but they are frequently highly aware that their supporters, or potential supporters, will monitor their use of weapons. Where there is strong internal and external monitoring, the constraints on the actions of leaders are much greater (Policzer, 2002, pp. 9–10). This does not mean that such groups are necessarily mindful of, or even knowledgeable about, international norms on conduct in armed conflict. Moderation in the use of arms is, however, certainly more of a preoccupation of long-term goal-seeking groups than of those with short-term and often criminal orientations and few international social linkages.

In the Tamasheq rebellion in Mali, knowledge of international norms among former commanders was fragmentary. Leaders reported that they were aware that it was illegal to shoot at parachutists in the air.[17] Most stressed, though, that killings of civilians were punished because groups required popular support. It is this phenomenon of 'self-policing' that most distinguishes long- from short-term, gain-seeking groups.

In these cases, however, attempts to minimize or sanction the misuse of weapons are frequently hindered by the fact that groups lack the necessary structural capacity (Capie, 2004). In other instances, as with modern militaries, combat objectives take precedence over the effects of using small arms and light weapons against non-combatants.

Sierra Leonean 'Kamajor' civil defence militia fighters train in capturing RUF rebels in east Freetown, May 2000.

© Yannis Behrakis/Reuters

197

Box 7.6   Command and control in the Uganda National Rescue Front: an example of tactical considerations outweighing human rights concerns

In 2004, the Center for Conflict Resolution (CECORE) and the Small Arms Survey held interviews with, and carried out a brief survey of, 20 former members of the Uganda National Rescue Front (UNRF). All ranks were represented, from private to major-general. Among the key findings was that controls over weapons were designed not to prevent abuse of non-combatants, but, instead, to maintain the group's fighting potential.

There was complete agreement that all weapons were the property of the group, rather than of the individual. Importantly, as with groups interviewed in Bamako, Mali, in September 2004, not all individuals were armed. In fact, the UNRF, like its Malian counterparts, was structured along military lines. All combatants reported that there were clear lines of command. With slight variations, furthermore, all were able to describe how the group was split into six or seven hierarchical divisions—from platoon to division. Combatants stated that tactical need dictated how the system functioned. Hence, the task at hand determined how the group's limited stock of weapons (there were always fewer armaments than group members) was distributed. Some combatants said that this worked much like a shift system: those given a particular assignment were issued with weapons that previously had been in the hands of colleagues. Only a private described how weapons were kept in storage and had to be signed for and distributed by the 'technician'. Apparently, members were not allowed to take weapons home.

According to former UNRF combatants, outside support was lacking and thus the group had to capture all of the weapons that it needed from government forces. The type of mission influenced its selection. As with groups in Mali, the UNRF employed as much heavy firepower as possible.

The system, while seemingly rudimentary, suggests considerable command and control. It is important to stress, nonetheless, that command and control over the use of weapons may curtail certain actions, but have no bearing on others. When asked whether it was prohibited to use weapons in particular situations, the vast majority of respondents said yes, but not for reasons connected to human rights considerations. Largely, the reasons were tactical, such as not making enemies aware of the presence of the group by shooting. Only four interviewees mentioned the presence of civilians as a factor in a decision not to use weapons. Worryingly, members of the highest ranks were not among them. Of the four, only one recalled specific instances in which weapons use was absolutely forbidden, including in health centres and the market place.

The harshest punishments for contravening orders appear to have been imposed for any form of behaviour that had the potential to diminish the group's ability to fight. Penalties such as digging latrines were handed out for general disobedience, while penalties such as disarmament and solitary confinement were imposed for using group-owned weapons and ammunition to shoot animals. The most severe punishment, death, was reserved for defilement or theft of a weapon belonging to the group. No reports exist of penalties being imposed by commanders for breaches of international norms on conduct in armed conflict.

Policy implications of a focus on group goals and the use of weapons

The rules and expectations that allow a group to organize and function include a stable set of commonly agreed group objectives. These objectives indicate the type of behaviour that a group is likely to encourage, tolerate, or discourage, including weapons use. An analysis of broad group goals thus provides a reliable means of predicting likely targets and the extent of a campaign of armed violence. It also highlights areas where measures designed to address the negative ramifications of armed violence may or may not be successful.

In order to create incentives for fighters to relinquish small arms and light weapons, for instance, it is essential to understand the rewards for peace in the context of the rewards for war. For groups comprising long-term gain-seeking individuals, there is arguably more chance that combatants will avoid small arms and light weapons use that could alienate the local populace, and that they will be willing to relinquish arms to secure the benefits of peace. In contrast, groups made up of primarily short-term gain-seeking individuals are usually focused on taking advantage of immediate benefits offered by a conflict. The way those combatants use weapons will often antagonize large sections of the local population, further distance combatants from the rest of society, and may ensure that the rewards of peace do not outweigh those of war. The likelihood of disarmament is lessened, as reintegration offers little in the way of social or material gain.

Often groups with weak or fragmented command-and-control structures are unable to commit to agreements and pledge with any surety that their members will adhere to their provisions. In relation to the Movement of Democratic Forces in the Casamance (Mouvement des Forces Démocratiques de Casamance, MFDC) in Senegal, economically, the Sadio faction appears to benefit more from conflict than does the rest of the group. As a result, the group's political wing makes commitments on behalf of the military branch and always without a mechanism to ensure compliance (Humphreys and ag Mohamed, 2003, pp. 16–17). In contrast, with respect to a number of groups engaged in the Tamasheq rebellion in northern Mali, former commanders claimed that they surrendered all of the weapons in their possession. None of the weapons held by individuals and groups outside of their control, however, were returned.[18] In arms reduction programmes, therefore, it is essential to target groups with minimal structures or those that are most likely to split into small, armed clusters of plunder-seeking individuals. The reason is that these groups, lacking clear command-and-control structures, are frequently the most uncontrollable in a post-conflict environment and present the greatest threats to local livelihoods. Moreover, these groups, such as the Cobra militia in the Republic of Congo, often retain far more weapons than other groups. Often this is due to extreme lack of organizational coherence and highly individualistic approaches to weapons ownership (Demetriou, Muggah, and Biddle, 2002, p. 18).

It is not just non-state armed groups, though, that demonstrate how weak or fragmented command and control can impact negatively on the use of weapons. Recent events in Afghanistan and Iraq clearly testify to the fact that, when state armed forces and police are overstretched, private armed security groups, paramilitaries, and poorly trained recruits are regularly utilized with little oversight. In Iraq, lack of monitoring was a key variable in the Abu Ghraib prisoner abuse scandal.

An understanding of organizational factors and the use of weapons thus has relevance for all instances in which armed entities (state and non-state) use violence to achieve particular objectives. To date, little attention has been devoted to organizational factors in specific reference to small arms and light weapons. The basic workings of authority differ little among groups, regardless of their structure. Hence, much can be learned from analyses of command-and-control structures in the groups that researchers have access to, such as Western militaries, and the findings can be applied to all types of armed group.

> Violence is never random, but purposive.

CONCLUSION

While the above approach omits many important and nuanced factors that result in weapons use differing from one context to another, it does so with a clear purpose in mind.

It is easy to believe that the use of small arms and light weapons involves an unfathomable mass of issues. Such a view may prevent certain fundamental variables from being appreciated and basic controls from being implemented that can rapidly alleviate the negative consequences of small arms and light weapons use. This study has attempted, therefore, to present some primary constraints on small arms and light weapons use in armed conflict.

Before investigating more complex phenomena, one needs to ask some simple questions about an armed conflict. For example: will reducing proliferation in the immediate vicinity curb the use of weapons by a group or will it be able to acquire them from elsewhere? Would the supply of some types of weapons alter the conflict dramatically, and, if so, who might provide them? Will a short-term gain-seeking group respond positively to a DDR programme? Would an embargo be the most appropriate or efficient means of ending violent conflict in a country already saturated with arms? Would stopping all weapons flows to a country make police forces reliant on existing stocks of unsuitable military armaments?

Several potential 'choke points' exist that might serve to alleviate the use of weapons. The most notable are efforts to reduce availability. This is particularly true of the most destructive forms of light weapons, such as mortars, RPGs, and grenade launchers.

The manufacture of cheap and powerful weapons, especially explosive varieties of light weapons, is clearly aimed at resource-poor states, which are frequently the most prone to conflict. Both production and trade in these armaments need to be more heavily regulated.

Stockpiled weapons are often insecure and their release can have drastic consequences in terms of increased loss of life and damage to infrastructure. Again, these negativities are potentially made greater by the firepower of stockpiled weapons. Better security is a must and destruction is the safest option for weapons not in use.

The same rationale is applicable to efforts to disarm former combatants. The simple fact is that readily available weapons are the ones most likely to be used in an armed conflict. Targeting the most destructive weapons in the immediate locality, or at the regional level, may control the rapid escalation of a future conflict.

At the organizational level, understanding social controls on the use of weapons by armed groups and their linkages with external actors and resource sources is essential to comprehending the potential effect of measures implemented. Violence is never random, but purposive. Addressing the effects of armed violence requires that one appreciate the social logic of a particular group and its relations with friends, foes, and the environment.

Group goals can offer great insight into whether and how a particular armed entity will respond to changes in the availability of weapons. This information is of critical importance for measures such as sanctions and for arms reduction programmes. Restricting local availability may have a strong impact on small, resource-poor, criminal groups, which may not have the capacity to source weapons far afield. Controlling the use of weapons by resource-rich or well-connected armed groups necessitates greater understanding of resource flow complexities and international connections.

Initiatives focused solely on resources, however, are insufficient. Groups that promise their members that they will fulfil long-term and comprehensive goals are able to mobilize human capital for a campaign of armed violence even though they lack significant material and financial resources. Efforts to tackle the use of weapons must extend deep into the politics of an armed struggle if they are ultimately to be successful. Nonetheless, simple controls on availability are crucial.

Finally, attempts to control the use of weapons by an armed group require understanding of its capacity to act in coordination. The ability of commanders to commit to peace processes and DDR programmes is of paramount importance. Fighters that escape oversight and are only weakly bound to command-and-control structures can engage in armed violence irrespective of commitments made at higher levels. Their use of weapons to satisfy personal ambitions is a fundamental obstacle to reducing fears of predation, which feature heavily in post-conflict societies across the globe.

LIST OF ABBREVIATIONS

AUC	Autodefensas Unidas de Colombia
CECORE	Center for Conflict Resolution
DDR	Disarmament, demobilization, and reintegration

DRC	Democratic Republic of Congo
EU	European Union
FARC	Fuerzas Armadas Revolucionarias de Colombia
ICG	International Crisis Group
LURD	Liberians United for Reconciliation and Democracy
LTTE	Liberation Tigers of Tamil Eelam
MANPADS	Man-portable air defence systems
MFDC	Mouvement des Forces Démocratiques de Casamance
MPLA	Movimento Popular de Libertação de Angola
NPFL	National Patriotic Front of Liberia
NRA	National Resistance Army (Uganda)
RPF	Rwandan Patriotic Front
RPG	Rocket-propelled grenade (launcher)
RUF	Revolutionary United Front (Sierra Leone)
SNM	Somali National Movement
ULIMO	United Liberation Movement for Democracy in Liberia
UN	United Nations
UNITA	União Nacional para a Independência Total de Angola
UNRF	Uganda National Rescue Front
WHO	World Health Organization

ENDNOTES

1   This is an important point in research on small arms and light weapons. When a weapon is fired and a target is hit, or where a person is coerced into doing something against his or her will, one can say with some surety that the weapon generates an effect. The assertion becomes weaker the further from the 'scene' of the violence one goes. One could claim, for instance, that small arms and light weapons have a strong impact on development. Yet, one cannot say with any certainty that, given a conflict replete with many kinds of armaments, and characterized by drought, famine, and other sources of insecurity, small arms and light weapons are responsible for factor X.

2   State and non-state groups differ in many ways, but they do not differ greatly with respect to the varieties of weapons that are potentially available to them and their basic behavioural processes. The latter include the articulation of goals, habitual conformity by group members, the threat of sanction to ensure compliance with objectives, and oversight mechanisms. If the two factors do have different impacts on the groups concerned, they are arguably a function of scale.

3   Participatory research involving former combatants, Mali, September 2004 (Small Arms Survey, 2004b).

4   Interview conducted by Ryan Nichols, Small Arms Survey consultant, with General Seyea Sheriff, a former LURD force commander in Monrovia, Monrovia, 1 March 2005; interviews conducted by Ryan Nichols, Small Arms Survey consultant, with an official of the National Commission for Disarmament, Demobilization, Rehabilitation and Reintegration and two local informed observers, Monrovia, 2 March

2005; correspondence with Lisa Misol, Human Rights Watch researcher, 10 March 2005.

5   Participatory research involving former combatants, Mali, September 2004 (Small Arms Survey, 2004b).

6   This is largely because, unlike states, diasporas are more reliable in providing funding and are less likely to seek to exert control over a movement (Byman et. al., 2001, p. xv).

7   Participatory research involving former combatants, Mali, September 2004 (Small Arms Survey, 2004b).

8   No organization, though, permits outright domination of individuals and all members enjoy at least some freedom of action. In sociological terms, 'return' is always a part of the equation (Simmel, 1971). A certain amount of personal freedom relinquished by the individual to the group may be 'returned' in a number of ways. For instance, through the provision of a salary and social welfare, through the furtherance of political ambitions, or, in the extreme, through the ability to shoot, rape, and pillage at will. Nonetheless, groups differ considerably with respect to articulation of goals and tolerated forms of behaviour and the degree to which sanctions are applied.

9   Participatory research involving former combatants, Mali, September 2004 (Small Arms Survey, 2004b).

10 This chapter views leadership as a crucial factor in the articulation and implementation of group goals, but it does not see it as the crucial factor. The norms, rules, and habits that define an individual's perception of 'correct' behaviour are equally attributable to relations

with 'regular' group members, as they are to interaction with group leaders. Nonetheless, group leaders enjoy a higher degree of decision-making autonomy than do most group members. Hence, one would expect decisions to be made and executed with some degree of freedom and in accordance with broad organizational objectives. The oversight mechanisms that they institute and their latent capacity to sanction make them an important variable in evaluating conformity to group goals.

[11] A focus on greed as a motive for armed conflict often masks more fundamental phenomena, such as hopelessness and a commitment to justness through a cause that offers a way out of poverty and a means of empowerment (Ballentine and Sherman, 2003; Agbonifo, 2004). Goals may be articulated in a number of ways and incentives may be *financial, cultural,* or *spiritual.* In a professional army, for instance, economic rewards may be prevalent, but combatants also claim to fight for reasons of loyalty to friends and defence of a country. In non-state groups, a similar mixture of aims and motivations prevails. Identification with a particular class, language, or ethnic group, which may be communicated through reference to historical factors (constructed or not) or rituals (swearing dedication to a certain cause), may reinforce these goals (Humphreys and ag Mohamed, 2003; Stewart, 2002).

[12] Modern Western-style militaries have a combination of short- and long-term motivations with respect to gain. Soldiers are paid a reg-ular salary to meet immediate needs, but they are also conditioned through training (and by a long history designed to increase loyalty to 'king and country') and are controlled within a very tight organizational structure.

[13] Not all members of armed groups are necessarily armed. Members perform functions other than combat-related duties. In better-organized groups, these tasks include record-keeping, controlling armouries, and managing finances. In all groups, they include cooking or even hunting and farming. Nor do armament levels remain stable. As with all consumable resources, stockpiles of arms and ammunition fluctuate according to rates of supply and consumption. At times, therefore, such actors may be armed; at other times, they may be unarmed or without ammunition.

[14] Participatory research involving former combatants, Mali, September 2004 (Small Arms Survey, 2004b).

[15] *Comando Vermelho, Terceiro Comando, Amigos dos Amigos,* and *Terceiro Comando Puro.*

[16] Participatory research involving former combatants, Mali, September 2004 (Small Arms Survey, 2004b).

[17] Participatory research involving former combatants, Mali, September 2004 (Small Arms Survey, 2004b).

[18] Participatory research involving former combatants, Mali, September 2004 (Small Arms Survey, 2004b).

BIBLIOGRAPHY

Abdullah, Ibrahim and Patrick Muana. 1998. 'The Revolutionary United Front of Sierra Leone.' In Christopher Clapham, ed. *African Guerrillas.* Oxford: James Currey, pp. 172–93.

Agbonifo, John. 2004. 'Beyond Greed and Grievance: Negotiating Political Settlement and Peace in Africa.' *Peace, Conflict and Development,* Issue 4 (April), pp. 1–14.

AI (Amnesty International). 2004. 'Guns and Police: Standards to Prevent Misuse.' AI Index ACT 30/001/2004. New York: Amnesty International. 23 February. Accessed 28 March 2005. <http://web.amnesty.org/library/pdf/ACT300012004ENGLISH/$File/ACT3000104.pdf>

Allison, Graham. 1971. *Essence of Decision: Explaining the Cuban Missile Crisis.* Boston, MA: Little, Brown and Company.

Ballentine, Karen and Jake Sherman, eds. 2003. *The Political Economy of Armed Conflict: Beyond Greed and Grievance.* London: Lynne Rienner.

Bowyer Bell, John. 1998. *The Dynamics of the Armed Struggle.* London: Frank Cass.

Brabazon, James. 2003. *Liberia, Liberians United for Reconciliation and Democracy (LURD).* Briefing Paper No. 1. London: Royal Institute of International Affairs, Armed Non-State Actors project. February.

Burke, Robert. 1984. 'UNITA—A Case Study In Modern Insurgency.' Quantico: Marine Corps Command and Staff College. 2 April.

Burnett, Victoria. 2004. 'Alleged Vigilante in Kabul Says He Had US Support. *Boston Globe.* 22 August. Accessed 27 March 2005. <http://www.boston.com/news/world/articles/2004/08/22/alleged_vigilante_in_kabul_says_he_had_us_support?mode=PF>

Byman, Daniel et al. 2001. *Trends in Outside Support for Insurgent Movements.* Santa Monica, CA: RAND Corporation.

Campbell, Bruce and Arthur Brenner, eds. 2000. *Death Squads in Global Perspective: Murder with Deniability.* New York: St Martin's Press.

Capie, David. 2003. *Under the Gun: The Small Arms Challenge in the Pacific.* Wellington, New Zealand: Victoria University Press.

—. 2004. *Armed Groups, Weapons Availability and Misuse: An Overview of the Issues and Options for Action.* Background paper for a meeting organized by the Centre for Humanitarian Dialogue, in advance of the sixth meeting of the Human Security Network. Bamako, Mali. 25 May.

Capie, David and Pablo Policzer. 2004. *Keeping the Promise of Protection: Holding Armed Groups to the Same Standard as States.* A policy brief commissioned for the UN Secretary-General's High Level Panel on Threats, Challenges and Change. Vancouver: University of British Columbia, Armed Groups Project. 15 January.

Clapham, Christopher, ed. 1998. *African Guerrillas.* Oxford: James Currey.

Clausewitz, Carl von. 1997. *On War. Book IV: The Combat.* Translated by J.J. Graham. Ware: Wordsworth Editions.

Cleary, Sean. 1999. 'Angola: A case study of private military involvement.' In Jakkie Cilliers and Peggy Mason, eds. *Peace, Profit or Plunder? The Privatisation of Security in War-torn African Societies.* Pretoria: Institute for Security Studies, pp. 141–74.

COFR (Council on Foreign Relations). 2003. *Afghanistan: Are We Losing the Peace?* Chairmen's report on the work of an independent task force co-sponsored by the COFR and the Asia Society. Accessed 22 November 2004. <http://www.asiasociety.org/policy_business/afghanistan061703.pdf>

Collier, Paul. 2000. 'Rebellion as a Quasi-Criminal Activity.' *Journal of Conflict Resolution,* 44(6), pp. 839–53.

Compagnon, Daniel. 1998. 'Somali Armed Movements.' In Christopher Clapham, ed. *African Guerrillas.* Oxford: James Currey, pp. 73–90.

Cook, Phillip and Jens Ludwig. 2003. *Does Gun Prevalence Affect Teen Gun Carrying After All?* Working Paper Series SAN03-04. Durham, NC: Terry Sanford Institute of Public Policy, Duke University. 15 August.

Cukier, Wendy, Alison Kooistra, and Mark Anto. 2002. 'Gendered Perspectives on Small Arms Proliferation and Misuse: Effects and Policies.' In Vanessa Farr and Kiflemariam Gebre-Wold, eds. *Gender Perspectives on Small Arms and Light Weapons: Regional and International Concerns.* Brief 24. Bonn: Bonn International Center for Conversion, pp. 25–39.

Cyert, Richard M. and James G. March. 1963. *A Behavioral Theory of the Firm.* Englewood Cliffs, NJ: Prentice Hall.

Dasgupta, Sunil. 2003. *Understanding Paramilitary Growth: Agency Relations in Military Organization.* Draft paper for presentation at a conference entitled 'Curbing human rights violations by non-state armed groups'. 13–15 November. Vancouver: University of British Columbia Armed Groups Project.

—. 2004. *Paramilitaries and Small Arms.* Unpublished research paper. Washington, DC: Brookings Institution.

Demetriou, Spyros. 2002. *Politics From the Barrel of a Gun: Small Arms Proliferation and Conflict in the Republic of Georgia (1989–2001).* Occasional Paper No. 6. Geneva: Small Arms Survey. November.

Demetriou, Spyros, Robert Muggah, and Ian Biddle. 2002. *Small Arms Availability, Trade and Impacts in the Republic of Congo.* Special Report. Geneva: Small Arms Survey. April.

Dowdney, Luke. 2003. *Children of the Drug Trade: A Case Study of Armed Violence in Rio de Janeiro*. Rio de Janeiro: Viveiros de Castro E.

Ellis, Stephen. 1998. 'Liberia's Warlord Insurgency.' In Christopher Clapham, ed. *African Guerrillas*. Oxford: James Currey, pp. 155–71.

—. 1999. *The Mask of Anarchy: The Destruction of Liberia and the Religious Dimension of an African Civil War*. New York: New York University Press.

Fowler, Robert and David Angell. 2001. 'Case Study: Angola Sanctions.' In Rob McRae and Don Hubert, eds. *Human Security and the New Diplomacy: Protecting People, Promoting Peace*. Montreal: McGill-Queen's University Press, pp 190–98.

Guyler Delva, Joseph. 2004. 'New bloodshed erupts as Haiti police, gangs clash.' Reuters AlertNet Foundation. 19 November. Accessed 28 March 2005. <http://www.globalexchange.org/tours/haiti/2714.html>

HRW (Human Rights Watch). 2003. *Weapons Sanctions, Military Supplies, and Human Suffering: Illegal Arms Flows to Liberia and the June–July Shelling of Monrovia*. Briefing Paper. New York: HRW. 3 November.

Humphreys, Macartan and Habaye ag Mohamed. 2003. *Senegal and Mali*. Paper presented at the 'Civil Conflict Workshop' organized by the World Bank and the International Peace Research Institute, Oslo (PRIO). Accessed 22 February 2005. <http://www.columbia.edu/~mh2245/papers1/sen_mali.pdf>

ICG (International Crisis Group). 2003a. *Tackling Liberia: The Eye of the Regional Storm*. Africa Report No. 62. Freetown and Brussels: ICG. Accessed 23 February 2005. <http://www.icg.org//library/documents/report_archive/A400960_30042003.pdf>

—. 2003b. *Dealing with Savimbi's Ghost: The Security and Humanitarian Challenges in Angola*. Africa Report No. 58. Luanda and Brussels: ICG.

ICHRP (International Council on Human Rights Policy). 1999. *Ends and Means: Human Rights Approaches to Armed Groups*. Geneva: ICHRP.

Johnson, Phyllis and David Martin, eds. 1988. *Frontline South Africa: Destructive Engagement*. New York: Four Walls, Eight Windows.

Jourdan, Luca. 2004. 'Being at War, Being Young: Violence and Youth in North Kivu.' In Koen Vlassenroot and Timothy Raeymaekers, eds. *Conflict and Social Transformation in Eastern DR Congo*. Gent: Academia Press, pp. 157–76.

Kaldor, Mary. 1999. *New and Old Wars: Organized Violence in a Global Era*. Stanford, CA: Stanford University Press.

Kalyvas, Stathis. 2003. *The Sociology of Civil Wars: Warfare and Armed Groups*. New Haven, CT: Department of Political Science, Yale University. 4 November.

Kapuściński, Ryszard. 1987. *Another Day of Life*. Translated by William Brand and Katarzyna Mroczkowska-Brand. London: Penguin.

Khakee, Anna and Nicolas Florquin. 2003. *Kosovo and the Gun: A Baseline Assessment of Small Arms and Light Weapons in Kosovo*. Special Report. Geneva: Small Arms Survey. June.

Klare, Michael. 2002. *Resource Wars: The New Landscape of Global Conflict*. New York: Henry Holt and Company.

Lecocq, Baz. 2002. 'That Desert is Our Country.' *Tuareg Rebellions and Competing Nationalisms in Contemporary Mali (1946–1996)*. Doctoral thesis. Amsterdam: University of Amsterdam. November.

Liddell Hart, Basil. 1974. *Strategy: The Indirect Approach*, 2nd rev. edn. New York: Signet Books.

March, James G. and Herbert A. Simon. 1958. *Organizations*. New York: John Wiley and Sons.

Mazali, Rena. 2004. *A Serious Gun Habit: Israeli's desensitization to a growing public presence of small arms*. Background paper. Geneva: Small Arms Survey.

Miller, Derek. 2003. *Demand, Stockpiles, and Social Controls: Small Arms in Yemen*. Occasional Paper No. 9. Geneva: Small Arms Survey. May.

Muggah, Robert and James Bevan. 2004. *Reconsidering Small Arms in the Solomon Islands*. Background paper. Geneva: Small Arms Survey.

Policzer, Pablo. 2002. *Human Rights and Armed Groups: Toward a New Policy Architecture*. Geneva: Geneva Call. July. Accessed 22 February 2005. <http://www.genevacall.org/resources/testi-referencematerials/testi-otherdocuments/jul02(ppoliczer).pdf>

Prendergast, John. 1999. *Angola's Deadly War: Dealing with Savimbi's Hell on Earth*. Special Report. Washington, DC: United States Institute of Peace.

Ron, James. 2000. 'Territoriality and Plausible Deniability: Serbian Paramilitaries in the Bosnian War.' In Bruce Campbell and Arthur Brenner, eds. *Death Squads in Global Perspective: Murder with Deniability*. New York: St Martin's Press, pp. 287–312.

Simmel. 1971. *On Individuality and Social Forms*. Donald Levine, ed. Chicago, IL: University of Chicago Press.

Simon, Herbert. 1997. *Administrative Behavior: A Study of the Decision-Making Processes In Administrative Organizations*, 4th edn. New York: The Free Press.

Small Arms Survey. 2004a. *Small Arms Survey 2004: Rights at Risk*. Oxford: Oxford University Press.

—. 2004b. *Atelier Anciens Combattants*. Background paper. Bamako: Small Arms Survey. 2–3 September.

Steinbruner, John. 1974. *The Cybernetic Theory of Decision: New Dimensions of Political Analysis*. Princeton, NJ: Princeton University Press.

Stewart, Frances. 2002. 'Horizontal Inequalities as a Source of Conflict.' In David Malone and Osler Hampson, eds. *From Reaction to Conflict Prevention: Opportunities for the UN System*. London: Lynne Rienner, pp. 105–36.

UN (United Nations). 2001. *The role of diamonds in fuelling conflict: breaking the link between the illicit transaction of rough diamonds and armed conflict as a contribution to prevention and settlement of conflicts*. Resolution adopted by the General Assembly. A/RES/55/56 of 29 January.

—. 2003a. *Letter dated 24 April 2003 from the Chairman of the Security Council Committee established pursuant to resolution 1343 (2001) concerning Liberia addressed to the President of the Security Council*. S/2003/498 of 24 April.

—. 2003b. *Report of the United Nations High Commissioner for Human Rights and Follow-up to the World Conference on Human Rights. Situation of human rights and fundamental freedoms in Liberia*. E/CN.4/2004/5 of 12 August.

—. 2003c. *Letter dated 28 October 2003 from the Chairman of the Security Council Committee established pursuant to resolution 1343 (2001) concerning Liberia addressed to the President of the Security Council*. S/2003/937 of 28 October.

Washington Post. 2004. 'Alleged Vigilantes Show Footage Of Afghan Operations.' 24 August, p. A10.

Weinstein, Jeremy. 2002. *The Structure of Rebel Organizations: Implications for Post-Conflict Reconstruction*. Dissemination Notes No. 4. Washington, DC: World Bank, Social Development Department. June.

—. 2004. *Resources and the Information Problem in Rebel Recruitment*. Stanford, CA: Center for Global Development and Stanford University. October.

WHO (World Health Organization). 2002. *Global Report on Violence and Health*. Geneva: WHO.

Yousaf, Mohammad and Mark Adkin. 2001. *Afghanistan the Bear Trap: The Defeat of a Superpower*. Havertown, PA: Casemate.

ACKNOWLEDGEMENTS

Principal author
James Bevan

Other contributors
Eric Berman, David Capie, Luke Dowdney, Nicolas Florquin, Sahar Hasan, Keith Krause, Emile LeBrun, Glenn McDonald, Lisa Misol, Pablo Policzer, Stella Sabiti, Alex Vines, and Christina Wille

The Albanian flag waves
behind the tip of a gun held
by a KLA fighter during
a ceremony in Likosane,
Kosovo, in February 1999.
(© Ami Vitale/Getty Images)

'Gun Culture' in Kosovo:
QUESTIONING THE ORIGINS OF CONFLICT

8

'GUN CULTURE' AND CONFLICT: A SPURIOUS RELATIONSHIP?

The notion of 'gun culture' occasionally surfaces in the debate on small arms, particularly in connection with the issue of armed conflict. Although it lacks an established definition, the term is commonly used to denote a particular set of 'reasons' for the presence and use of small arms in a given society—reasons that go beyond the 'economic' or 'utilitarian' needs of individuals and the dynamics of local or international markets. In this sense, 'gun culture' is used to indicate a given society's set of values, norms—both social and legal—and meanings that render the presence of firearms and their possession by private individuals acceptable and legitimate. For example, small arms possession among civilians—usually of firearms—can be seen as a symbol of status, of masculinity, or else, as a source of security where state structures are unable, or unwilling, to provide it.

The media and other observers sometimes treat 'gun culture' as the very 'cause' of armed conflict. Some of their accounts present it as the main reason behind the widespread proliferation of small arms in a given society; in turn, this proliferation is blamed for the outburst of violence in areas that experience various forms of political instability.[1] In other reports, this three-step relationship is collapsed into a two-stage process in which 'gun culture' contributes directly to armed conflict.[2] In the latter, 'gun culture' is equated with a 'culture of violence', which can be defined as 'a system of formal or informal social norms and values which accept violence as a possible, normatively acceptable, and a potentially required form of behaviour and relationship between individuals' (Martín-Baró, 1983, p. 127).

'Gun culture' has also been identified as the main reason for the failure of post-conflict recovery programmes.[3] This approach has produced some simplistic, if not patronizing, conclusions. For example, referring to the difficulties encountered by NATO's Kosovo Force (KFOR) in post-conflict demilitarization efforts, one commentator stated that '[t]he easy availability of weapons in Kosovo means that not just ethnic tensions, but everything from bar fights to business disputes is solved with a gun' (Farnam, 2003). A local observer echoed these words:

> In this part of the world, there is a strong belief in customary law which means an eye for an eye.... It is commendable that KFOR is trying to collect weapons, but it is an impossible task. ... In our lifetime the rule of law has never achieved anything, only guns have provided a measure of justice. So you stick to your gun (Farnam, 2003).

While they may appear to substantiate that 'gun culture' can be conducive to armed conflict, these statements are the product of untested assumptions rather than systematic research. This chapter aims to shed light on this relationship between 'gun culture' and armed conflict by investigating the links between ethnic Albanian 'gun culture' and Kosovo's descent into civil war during the 1990s. The chapter also presents brief discussions of four other cases—those of El Salvador, Georgia, Kyrgyzstan, and Tajikistan—which reinforce the conclusions of the main case study.[4]

The key conclusions of this chapter are the following:

- 'Gun cultures' do not automatically translate into armed conflict. If the relationship between the former and the latter is to be seriously investigated, the interplay between social attitudes to the presence of guns and economic, political, as well as historical processes and experiences must be taken into account.
- Broad references to 'gun culture' may have little meaning, given that different social groups often relate to firearms in distinct ways, with significant variations appearing along gender, class, age, and 'ethnic' lines. In this sense, speaking of 'national gun cultures' is a gross oversimplification.
- Social attitudes to guns may change over time, so that it is not possible to speak of a stable permissive (or restrictive) gun culture. Like other cultural features, 'gun culture' is not a given, but the product of social and political interaction. As such, it may constantly evolve and be renegotiated by members of a given community.

The following sections provide a historical overview of ethnic Albanian attitudes towards firearms in Kosovo.[5] They are an attempt to show that, contrary to common assumptions, being accustomed to the presence of small arms and deciding to use them to achieve political goals are two very distinct things; the former does not necessarily lead to the latter.

The case of Kosovo is particularly interesting for at least two reasons. First, 'gun culture' among Kosovo Albanians has often been portrayed as a key—if not *the* key—factor behind the armed conflict as well as post-conflict instability. Second, Kosovo is a paradigmatic example for the whole Balkan region, whose 'gun culture' is often cited to explain 'atavistic violence'. Such simplistic assumptions have often provided explanations where others were not available; in the case of Kosovo they have shifted the focus of public opinion away from the international community's decision not to completely disarm the Kosovo Liberation Army (KLA, or UÇK in Albanian), as discussed below.

SMALL ARMS AND GUN CULTURE AMONG KOSOVO ALBANIANS

Introduction

Foreign observers often portray Kosovo as having a strong 'gun culture'.[6] 'Gun culture', in turn, has been described as a key factor behind the Kosovo conflict during the 1990s, when growing numbers of ethnic Albanians took up arms against representatives of the oppressive Federal Republic of Yugoslavia (FRY). A number of subsequent accounts have also presented 'gun culture' as a fundamental reason behind the security and stability problems afflicting the province during the post-conflict period.[7]

These views are challenged by the fact that the Kosovo Albanian response to increased Serb repression was peaceful during the first half of the 1990s. Indeed, as detailed below, a concerted effort was made to end vendettas (so as to unite ethnic Albanians among themselves) and to respond to repression using peaceful means. In the latter half of the 1990s, however, the KLA and its militaristic, gun-based approach gained ground in the province.

Today, Kosovo is saturated with guns in private possession (Khakee and Florquin, 2003, pp. 11–26; Mustafa and Xharra, 2003). UN amnesties and control and collection programmes have been 'unable to make a dent in the numbers of illegal weapons still in circulation'.[8] Nevertheless, doubts have grown concerning the weight placed on ethnic Albanian 'gun culture' as an explanation for this situation.[9]

During the 1990s, both the militant and the pacifist resistance movements made cultural references to Albanian customary law—usually subsumed under the Ottoman term *kanun*—to promote solidarity among fellow ethnic Albanians. This tradition endorses private gun possession based on the need—whether real or perceived—for self-regulation in securing survival, regulating conflict, and achieving justice and dignity in an insecure environment. At the same time, however, it has continually served the advancement of power and prestige of particular interest groups.

Both the militant and the pacifist sides successfully appropriated and used cultural references to kanun; yet it was the latter's failure to garner international support against the persecution of the Kosovo Albanian majority that tipped the scale in favour of the 'side for war', which was rooted in the rural zone and the diaspora (Kraja, 2003, p. 163).

Within the province, this shift from unarmed to armed resistance reflected that traditionalist rural norms gained ground over those affiliated with the urban middle class. Today, these traditionalist norms still affect attitudes among Kosovo's ethnic Albanians.[10]

Box 8.1   Culture, violence, and small arms in El Salvador

In 2003 the United Nations Development Programme (UNDP) published the study *Armas de fuego y violencia* (Firearms and violence) in El Salvador. The section on arms and the 'culture of violence' deals with social attitudes towards the acquisition and use of firearms in the country, and their possible relationship to small arms proliferation among civilians. The study concludes that although cultural variables are complex and occasionally difficult to pin down, they may shed light on the presence of weapons in a given society. Contrary to mainstream assumptions, however, the report submits that the proliferation of weapons in Salvadoran society is neither recent, nor exclusively tied to the 12-year civil war that ended in 1992 (p. 125). Rather, the study asserts, it is linked to a long-established social system that legitimates violence as a means of interaction. In this sense, the study explicitly refers to a 'culture of violence'.

In order to assess social attitudes to violence in general, and to firearms in particular, UNDP conducted surveys in three focus areas. The first evaluates citizens' willingness to acquire and hold firearms. The second concerns attitudes towards firearms and violence, such as whether firearms are seen as tools of self-defence, means to ensure respect, or a right, and whether preferences for firearms correspond with approval for the use of violence. The third focuses on factors that could favour the existence of a 'culture of violence' and insecurity, including victimization and fear. UNDP surveyed 2,434 respondents who were selected from different municipalities nationwide, both rural and urban. They also spanned different social, age, and gender groups.[11]

The results suggest that, in terms of their relationship with weapons, Salvadorans are essentially divided along gender, age, and urban/rural lines, with men and young people from rural areas having a higher propensity to acquire and use firearms (p. 132). In particular, young men are likely to buy firearms if they live in rural areas and have been direct victims of violence, or if they feel insecure because of a violent environment or because they have heard frequent gunshots (p. 157).

Most of those who acquire guns claim to do it for self-protection or for the protection of their families. In this sense, firearms are defined as instruments of defence, rather than as means of aggression (p. 133). Nevertheless, researchers have also registered the perception of firearms as instruments used to secure respect, a view more commonly encountered in areas where the rate of gun possession is high (p. 133). This notion implies that weapons may provide a form of status to people who lack other distinctions, such as higher education or an advantageous socio-economic position. The research also found that 18 per cent of the surveyed population perceives the possession of firearms as a right.

The general picture emerging from this study points to a 'culture of violence' that rests on value systems that accept and legitimate the use of violence in particular circumstances, including adultery and self-protection (p. 137). Firearm acquisition by private individuals, then, seems to rest on this 'culture of violence', so that the presence and circulation of firearms in Salvadoran society is endorsed by social attitudes legitimating the use of violence and aggression as a way to guarantee security.

In broad terms, this study indicates that 'gun cultures' are not always at the root of 'cultures of violence', but that the latter can indeed underpin the former. Moreover, the report confirms that the application of the term 'gun culture' to a national context is likely to be simplistic or inaccurate.

Source: UNDP (2003)

Pro-Kosovo demonstrators shout slogans around a mock coffin during a rally across from the White House in Washington, DC, in April 1999.

As this case study shows, there are limits to understanding the behaviour of a particular society on the basis of simple dichotomies such as 'strong/weak gun culture'. Indeed, even a deep-rooted appreciation for the presence of guns does not automatically translate into violent behaviour in conflict situations. If anything, the relationship can be reversed: 'cultures of violence' may themselves underpin the development of permissive gun cultures (see Box 8.1).

In the case of Kosovo, traditional constructs of social behaviour, such as kanun and *besa* (see below), can be used by different groups with different aims, each with significant implications for the society's position on whether to take up arms. It follows that notions of cultural approach to firearms cannot serve as the only explanation for a group or society's adoption of militaristic attitudes; rather, these cultural components must be studied within a wider historical, economic, and political context.

Historical-cultural roots of 'gun culture'

Classic sources on northern Albania and Kosovo suggest that 'gun culture' not only has deep historical roots in peasant and pastoral life in the mountain villages, but that it was also shaped by Ottoman rule and the associated methods used to recruit soldiers.[12]

Firstly, as was the case in all mountain-dwelling Balkan societies, shepherds used guns to protect themselves against wild beasts and flock raiders (Coon, 1950, p. 10; Hasluck, 1954, pp. 204–05). Secondly, the Ottoman style of 'indirect rule' fostered the development of the local customary laws known as kanun.[13] These laws were based on the principle of self-regulation (including self-protection) and secured the availability of military resources—in terms of people and equipment—from local societies at the fringes of the empire.

From the mid-14th century, the Ottomans were recruiting 'slave soldiers', known as *janissaries* (Turkish for 'new soldiers'), from Balkan Christian families through a forced levy called *devshirme* (Keegan, 1994, pp. 214, 346). In the following centuries, many ethnic Albanian janissaries—especially those who converted to Islam—reportedly climbed high on the Ottoman military career ladder. Sons of impoverished Albanian peasant families also joined the Ottoman fighting forces as semi-regular mercenaries or served in mercenary troops (*levend*), often in conflict with the central power, such as when paid to support the interests of a governor. They routinely sent remittances to their extended families at home (Hahn, 1854, p. 63; Faroqhi, 1995, pp. 68–69). Throughout the Empire, the Albanian mercenaries became known as *Arnavuts* (Turkish for 'the Albanians') or *Arnauts* (Malcolm, 1998, pp. 150–02). They had to bring their own weapons, as was common in the Ottoman Empire (Faroqhi, 1995, p. 68); this 'investment' must have appeared worthwhile, given that 'Albanians who served with the Ottoman forces returned with luxurious items such as gold, silver-inlaid arms and magnificent Arab horses' (Vickers, 1998, p. 26). Only towards the end of Ottoman rule in the early 20th century did the 'Turkish government' systematically arm some Albanian Muslim clans in order to fight Christian groups (Durham, 1909, p. 121).[14]

From the 17th century on, for purposes of military recruitment, the Ottomans introduced a political order of representation based on territorial units called *bajrak* (from the Turkish for 'a military standard or banner'). The purpose of the bajrak was to 'single out local leaders who could supply fighting men ... and who would gain status and privilege in return' (Malcolm, 1998, p. 16). The basis of the bajrak system was territorial rather than tribal. As a consequence, a large clan's region could be split into several bajraks, each run by its own *bajraktar*, a medium-sized clan might form one bajrak, while several smaller clans could be combined into a single bajrak. In Kosovo, 'because of the geographical dispersal of the clans, the bajrak became an important unit, and the bajraktars wielded great local power as administrators, military leaders and settlers of disputes' (Malcolm, 1998, p. 16).

Janissaries with their weapons. Recruited by the Ottomans, many ethnic Albanian janissaries climbed high on the military career ladder.

© Albanians, mercenaries in the Ottoman army, published by Lemercier, 1857 (lithograph), Preziosi, Amadeo (1816–82)/ Private Collection, The Stapleton Collection/www.bridgeman.co.uk

Those bajraks directly subjected to Ottoman military conscription ensured that of two neighbouring 'houses', one supplied a soldier, the other his equipment (Peinsipp, 1985, pp. 29n).[15] Other sources, however, suggest that every 'house' had to provide both the soldier and his equipment (see Box 8.2). Starting from the 17th century, this equipment comprised firearms introduced by English, Dutch, French, and Swiss gun experts, who were hired by the Ottoman army to modernize its armoury (Keegan, 1994, p. 346). At the same time, the clandestine production of firearms prospered, mainly to meet demands of the irregular mercenary troops; weapons thus became relatively easily available for everyone (Faroqhi, 1995, p. 69; Inalcık, 1974). One observer notes for the 'Gheg country':[16] 'Gunsmiths in the market towns found the mountaineers eager to obtain the new weapons with which they could not only defend their home valleys from invaders, but also work off their local grudges' (Coon, 1950, p. 44).

Box 8.2 'Rituals of war'

When [a bajraktar] learned that war was imminent and troops were required, he had immediately to inform the tribe in the first instance by firing eight shots in quick succession into the air, and in the second by sending out the official runner called *kasnec* with news and a statement of how many men were wanted. One from each house was the usual number. The muster was soon complete, for it was thought shameful to hang back or to hide at home and no time was wasted hunting for deserters. When all had gathered, the march began. Two tribesmen in some cases, and in others four, led off singing. Next came a man closely connected with the bajraktar, preferably his eldest son, carrying the flag. The rank and file followed, firing constantly into the air to show their joy at the call to arms. Any sign of depression at leaving their homes would have been thought disgraceful and unmanly. ... No equipment was issued to bajraktars or 'soldiers'; each brought his own rifle and pistols and came in his ordinary clothes. Nor was any military training given them. Their value as soldiers depended upon the rifle practice which they had had at home. It was usually sufficient to make them all good shots. After a few months the war ended and they came home again, still in their peasant clothes and again firing into the air for joy (Hasluck, 1954, p. 119).

In the mid-19th century, an Austrian consul found that, in northern Albania (and Kosovo), 'everyone walks with arms ... most boys above 12 years of age carry rifles'[17] (Hahn, 1854, p. 92). This situation remained largely unchanged at the turn of the 20th century, towards the end of Ottoman rule (Durham, 1909). In 1908, 1910, and 1912 a number of 'ill-starred official attempts to disarm the population' and to enforce military conscription and taxation spurred popular revolts (Malcolm, 1998, pp. 18, 244, 249). In 1910, the Young Turk government sent armies to quell revolts and disarm the population: in the Albanian Highlands the programme collected 147,525 guns (Malcolm, 1998, p. 242). This event arguably prompted the large-scale arms contraband to replenish regional stocks and supply the so-called Kosovo Albanian *kaçak* movement (from Turkish for 'outlaw'), an insurgence tradition with which many KLA fighters subsequently identified themselves during the 1990s (Malcolm, 1998, p. 242).

In 1911, the kaçaks included approximately 5,000 rebel fighters, including about 100 clan chiefs and bajraktars (Malcolm, 1998, p. 242). From late 1912, with Serb forces replacing Ottoman rule in Kosovo, the movement became increasingly political. Indeed, 'the anti-Albanian policies of the [Serbian] government and local authorities ... were a powerful stimulus to the rebellion' (Malcolm, 1998, p. 273). In late 1918, the kaçaks comprised up to 2,000 core fighters and 100,000 affiliates (Vickers, 1998, p. 100). They directed themselves against the newly formed Kingdom of the Serbs, Croats, and Slovenes and its colonization programmes in Kosovo. From its inception, the kaçak movement singled out and killed not only Serbs, but also Albanian civilians who cooperated with the authorities (Malcolm, 1998, pp. 273, 278). Its members typically hailed from and fought in traditional, rural places such as the Drenica valley, which saw continuous revolts during the early 1920s, or the area around Peja/Peč and other villages in northern and western Kosovo (Malcolm, 1998, pp. 272–73; Vickers, 1998, pp. 99–100).

Serb authorities reacted to the fighters 'by rounding up many extended families of up to fifty members and detaining them all together on pain of death until their "outlaw" relatives surrendered' (Vickers, 1998, p. 101). Arresting and interning the wives of the kaçak leaders proved particularly successful war techniques, as these moves challenged codes of honour (Malcolm, 1998, p. 247). Furthermore, confiscations of private land as part of continuing colonization programmes in the 1920s and 1930s targeted 'mainly the holdings of outlaws' (Bogdanovic, 1995). It should come as little surprise that the KLA movement of the 1990s originated in the same villages in which violent oppression of the kaçaks and atrocities against civilians form a fundamental part of family histories.[18]

During the Second World War, when Nazi Germany and its allies occupied Yugoslavia, Kosovo was under Italian command, which favoured the Albanian population. For example, Italian occupiers

> encourage[d] the establishment of Albanian schools and media and [gave] Kosovo Albanians the right to
> bear arms. Kosovo Albanians [took] revenge on Slavs, harassing and driving out Slavic families ... (Mertus,
> 1999, p. 287).

Yet Kosovo 'emerged from the war into the new Federal Yugoslavia under siege and with its alienated Albanian population regarded, as in 1918, as a threat to the new state' (Vickers, 1998, p. 143). As the 'initial imbalance of power set up an oscillating dynamic of reaction and counter-reaction' (Malcolm, 1998, p. 314), violent oppression repeatedly produced armed resistance. Appeals to kanun and its traditions were used to buttress the armed reaction to Serb repression. Yet reference to the same traditions equally enforced a sense of ethnic identity and solidarity among the Kosovo Albanians who backed the peaceful resistance of the 1990s. Cultural knowledge thus served as a repository for responses to the same waves of repression; these reactions could be either armed or unarmed, militant or peaceful.

Kanun, *besa*, and private gun possession in rural Kosovo

Kosovo Albanian customary law, the kanun, used to be orally transmitted in proverbs and sayings. It is proscriptive rather than ethnographically descriptive, and village councils interpreted and changed its shape in decision-making processes regarding social and political conflict over time (Hasluck, 1954). In Kosovo, as in most of the north Albanian mountain regions, the only significant kanun 'is the most famous of them all: the Kanun of Lek Dukagjin' (Malcolm 1998, p. 17).[19] The Kanun regulated all aspects of social interaction and many of its features are still relevant today. It defined the gendered social roles of everyday family and village life and it established the conduct and procedures of inter-family rituals, such as hospitality (*miqesisa*), feuding (*gjakmarrje*), reconciliation (*besë-lidhje*), and the creation of social solidarity or trust (*besa*). It was based on the concepts of 'honour' (*ndera*, juxtaposed with 'shame', *marre*) and on the centrality and high symbolic content of firearm possession as the means to defend family integrity and reputation. The Kanun presupposed an insecure environment where non-related 'others' could only be categorized as either loyal 'friends' (*miqe*), or treacherous (*pabesë*, 'without besa' or *tradhtare*) or potential 'enemies' (*armiqte*).[20]

> A boy became a man when he received his first gun.

In this society, built on communitarian principles—where collective family or tribal interests overrode individual aspirations—a gun was a man's only private possession (Gjeçov, 1933, p. 9, para. 24/3; Hasluck, 1954, p. 60). As soon as he was deemed able to handle a gun, a boy or young man would receive one from his father or the head of the extended family.[21] This rite of passage transformed a child into a 'person'—an 'honourable man' entitled to land rights and liable to become involved in blood feuds. Without a gun, a man was seen as a woman (Cozzi, 1912, p. 625), as women—who were not supposed to become subjects of blood feuds—customarily lacked the right to inherit land or own guns.[22] A father's most effective punishment of his son for acting against family interests would be to take away his gun for a week or two (Gjeçov, 1933, p. 8, para 20/10b). This symbolism in sayings and rituals, which made the weapon appear as a 'numinous being', underlined the intense relationship of a man to his personal gun (Reiter 1987, p. 155). Interviews with villagers suggest that boys traditionally received their guns at the age of 16; more recently, however, a young man would be regarded as 'equal' to the other adult men of the family only after his return from Yugoslav military service.[23] As in many other societies (see Box 8.3), the possession of firearms has thus come to represent manhood, creating a gendered split in the social attitudes towards small arms possession.

Box 8.3   Guns and masculinity

The interpretation of firearms as symbols of masculinity is a feature common to many societies, both traditional and industrialized. As an Oxfam and Amnesty report highlights, '[c]onventional notions of masculinity ascribe the role of protector and defender to men, and in many cultures this role has become symbolized by the possession of a gun' (Oxfam and AI, 2003, p. 47). This conclusion is supported by the fact that gun possession is primarily a male phenomenon in countries as diverse as the United States, Canada, Kosovo, and Israel (Oxfam and AI, 2003, p. 47; Ben Nun, 2004, p. 35).

Yet the link between firearms and notions of masculinity can be even more explicit. In Lebanon, for example, in the region of Baalbek, people still welcome the birth of a boy by announcing, 'We have increased by one gun' (AFSC and RHSC, 2002, p. 3). With reference to Afghanistan, a BBC observer noted that 'carrying a gun is a passport to adult society for most men' (Morris, 2003). Similarly, a correspondent in northern Iraq reported: 'It is unusual to meet an adult Kurdish man who does not own at least one firearm' (O'Loughlin, 2003). More generally, firearms are commonly considered an integral part of 'manhood' in Middle Eastern countries (AFSC and RHSC, 2002, p. 3).

Historically, an Albanian man would refer to his gun as 'his bride' or 'his loyal companion'; he would also claim to be 'married to his weapon' and that 'his bride had to call out for him', for example by discharging in joy upon arrival at a destination or in anger when killing another man (Peinsipp, 1985, pp. 228, 230). After successful blood revenge, a man's 'rifle could be hung up' and 'go to sleep' (Hasluck, 1954, p. 220).[24] A 'discharged rifle' was a term used in Kanun rhetoric as a synonym for a completed killing.[25] A man could transfer a cartridge to symbolize a threat to kill, a transfer of a feuding duty, or proof of a successful killing in a feud, especially if the bullet was deliberately left at the site of the shooting for the community to recognize that an insulted honour had been cleansed (Hasluck, 1954, pp. 212–13, 217, 221, 228–29).[26] Furthermore, it was expected that the gun of a man killed in a feud would be properly placed by his head, so as to avoid the risk of a heightened blood debt in the next round. Indeed, theft of a gun, particularly in such circumstances, counted as either one half or one full 'blood'—equalling a woman or a man, respectively—depending on the region (Hasluck, 1954, p. 229). The Kanun of Lekë Dukagjin specified that a murderer who stole the weapon of his victim would owe 'two bloods' and would be considered 'black-faced' (Gjeçov, 1933, p. 81, para. 847). Along the same lines, a man whose gun was stolen was expected to kill the offender, even if this prompted a feud, as symbolic emasculation through gun theft was considered an insult to a man's honour. In such a case the thief, but not the avenger, would face community expulsion and fines (Hasluck, 1954, pp. 205, 208, 244; Gjeçov, 1933, p. 89, para. 952).

While taking gun possession by men for granted, the kanun sought to regulate related potential risks. A guest's weapon was always taken from him in the house as a matter of both welcome and precaution; it would be hung on a hook that was especially designed for that purpose (Gjeçov, 1933, p. 65, paras. 614—15). Men who dared raise their weapons at village or tribal assemblies risked being shot for endangering public security; clear prescriptions defined how to handle guns in such situations, such as cradling the weapon in one's lap (Hasluck, 1954, p. 151). Provisions also established the consequences of accidental killings, which—in the absence of the concept of mitigating circumstances—inevitably led to someone 'owing blood'. For instance, if a guest's gun fell from the hook and accidentally discharged, killing a member of the host family, the related responsibility fell on the host if the hook had given way, but on the guest if the strap had broken (Gejçov, 1933, p. 89, paras. 946, 948).

The kanun's clear prescriptions defined how to handle guns in various situations.

Unsurprisingly, observers have recognized gun possession as an integral part of the ethnic Albanian 'jury system'; one commentator notes that in the early 20th century, men would still foreswear their possession 'joyfully in the modern court, especially if this saved a friend or relative or concealed their possession of a rifle; this weapon being their chief treasure, they would deny "500 times" on oath that they had it' (Hasluck, 1954, p. 194).

Context, continuities, and change

Within communist Yugoslavia, Kosovo's rural kanun traditions were 'modernized' in many respects, and transformed in ways adapted to the 'modern' requirements of life in Yugoslavia.

Following the so-called Cominform conflict in 1948, when political relations between the Socialist Federal Republic of Yugoslavia and Albania severely deteriorated, Kosovo's ethnic Albanians came under general suspicion of secessionist interests.[27] Under the infamous minister of the interior Alexander Rankovic, they faced a terror regime marked by frequent abuse and purges by the Yugoslav secret police, a situation that significantly contributed to ethnic polarization in Kosovo. From this time on, the province appears to have been effectively emptied of a substantial number of privately held guns, which some feared could allow an armed uprising.

> One sign of this approach in the mid-1950s was a growing obsession with hunting for weapons among the Kosovo Albanians; whole villages would be cordoned off and the menfolk interrogated or beaten. So

severe was the treatment of those who failed to hand over a gun that many Albanians would prudently buy a weapon in order to have something to surrender (Malcolm, 1998, p. 321).

Despite these measures, nationalist Serbs continued to suspect ethnic Albanians of private gun possession. Kosovo was not alone in seeing its traditions of gun possession challenged by a centralized regime. During the Soviet period, Georgia, Kyrgyzstan, and Tajikistan faced similar strategies (see Box 8.4). In all these cases, the interaction between new and old social norms produced changes in the prevalent 'gun culture', indicating that the latter, like any social construct, is far from a permanent or rigid feature of a given community.

Box 8.4   Changing 'gun cultures' in Georgia, Kyrgyzstan, and Tajikistan[28]

'Gun culture' is often treated as a monolithic or homogeneous phenomenon. This conceptual simplification overshadows two important elements. On the one hand, as suggested by all cases treated in this chapter, 'gun cultures' often display significant degrees of variation across social groups in a given society. On the other, they may change over time, as members of a community reshape their content and meaning. These two features are evidenced in the following brief comparison of Georgia, Kyrgyzstan, and Tajikistan.

Prior to their inclusion in the Soviet Union, Georgia, Kyrgyzstan, and Tajikistan each had specific sets of attitudes and values with respect to weapons possession and use. In both Kyrgyzstan and Tajikistan, weapons possession was not widespread, but rather linked to specific social strata or activities (for example, aristocracy or hunting). In pre-Soviet Georgia, which saw persistent conflict, small arms were initially luxurious and costly goods, mainly possessed by the nobility. With the introduction of revolvers in the 19th century, civilian gun possession became more common. In addition, in Georgia, as in Tajikistan, small arms were regarded as a symbol of masculinity.

With the imposition of Soviet rule, all three societies were subjected to a restrictive gun control regime that required civilian guns to be registered and issued permits mostly to hunters. Illegal possession was extremely rare. By and large, authorities removed guns from civilian life, except in some rural areas and among hunters. By the 1950s, cold war rivalry with Western countries prompted the Soviet leadership to enhance the combat readiness of armed forces and of the general population. Soviet life became highly militarized: a large percentage of the population worked within the armed forces; young men served as conscripts in the army for three years; and teenagers learned basic military skills, including weapons handling, in schools and universities. This approach familiarized citizens in all three countries with weapons use, while authorities strove to glorify soldiers and military excellence. At the same time, weapons were largely associated with the military sphere and the defence of the Soviet Union against a potential Western attack. Yet guns were no longer part of civilian life.

All three societies seem to have adapted and enforced the norm by which civilian weapons possession was inappropriate; carrying and using weapons outside the context of hunting or defence became socially unacceptable, as well as legally punishable. Georgians, however, appear to have adopted these practices half-heartedly, and the traditionally positive attitude towards small arms allegedly remained intact, particularly among young men.

As the Soviet Union collapsed, and as independent republics emerged in 1991, small arms issues came to the fore in all three societies—especially in Georgia and Tajikistan. Despite the shared legacy of the Soviet rule, however, the three populations evince different attitudes towards guns. In Kyrgyzstan, where the political transition to independence was largely peaceful, general attitudes towards guns remain much the same as during Soviet times. Kyrgyz civilians often stress that weapons are dangerous and should not be handled carelessly. In addition, there is strong popular support for the continuation of the strict Soviet gun regime, which limited civilian weapons possession to hunting guns. Civilians reportedly express dissatisfaction over the inability of law enforcement to reduce crime, including illegal weapons possession, to the low levels that were enjoyed during the Soviet times.

In both Georgia and Tajikistan, the transition to independence was marked by conflict, as well as by significant small arms proliferation. Since the 1997 national peace accord, Tajikistan has remained relatively stable. In most areas and social groups, firearms are associated with the civil war and thus have negative connotations. In the capital, Dushanbe, members of the economic elite—some of whom continue to operate in the shadow and drug economies—discourage carrying guns openly for the same reasons (even if they possess weapons for personal protection). In some of the previous opposition areas, however, certain groups continue to feel threatened and seem to be more ready to endorse gun possession among fellow community members.

> **Box 8.4   Changing 'gun cultures' in Georgia, Kyrgyzstan, and Tajikistan (cont.)**
>
> In Georgia, large-scale fighting ended in 1994, but serious tensions connected to its breakaway regions of Abkhazia and South Ossetia have since continued. The 'Rose Revolution' of 2003, which installed President Mikhail Saakashvili, has not resulted in a political solution for either region. Georgians exhibit tacit acceptance of civilian arms possession for security reasons, in particular in areas with minority populations. Nevertheless, significant differences also exist across social groups. People living in urban areas show relatively little interest in or endorsement of civilian gun possession and use; the opposite is true of more traditional individuals in rural and mountainous areas.
>
> As the brief cases of Georgia, Kyrgyzstan, and Tajikistan demonstrate, gun cultures need not be homogeneous across social groups, nor stable over time. In each of these states, the 'gun culture' that is present today is the result of the interplay of traditional and contemporary conceptualizations of small arms with specific political, historical, and economic processes. The three countries under review may have shared a common social and legal gun control system during their decades as Soviet republics, but today they display individual 'gun cultures' nevertheless.

After Rankovic's fall in 1966, the political situation for Albanians in Kosovo improved. Liberalism and decentralization across Yugoslavia led to the 1974 constitution, which granted Kosovo autonomous status as a province of Yugoslavia. Since then, various kanun traditions have visibly dissolved, even in the most traditional villages. Anthropologist Berit Backer noted of the late 1970s:

> The rule [kanun] is still there. If asked, people will say that a primary duty of a man is to kill the murderer of a brother, son, or father.... But nobody does so anymore. Courts, judges, police and prisons have taken over the handling of crimes. People know the traditions and their rules, but on the level of social interaction they do not practise them all anymore... The possibility that 'Albanianness' can be re-codified and expressed in terms of participation in modern institutions and social settings produced by industrial society has been accepted as an alternative (Backer, 1983, p. 174).[29]

Some customs, however, have not subsided as readily. Feuding, for example, has not entirely disappeared in Kosovo, and 'innumerable small-scale feuds' continued into the 1990s in the remoter villages (Malcolm, 1998, p. 20; Reineck, 1991, p. 202). For the period from the mid-1960s to the late 1980s, scholars have suggested that conflicts over land—possibly exacerbated by the fact that 'the judicial means of regulating property and land sales have been ineffective'—resulted in a rising number of blood feuds, particularly in the south-western parts of Kosovo (Duijzings, 2000, p. 126–27). At the same time, many families stayed intact, particularly rural extended ones; nevertheless, the wider patrilineal clan structures and customary village authorities yielded power and significance to Communist Party structures. Some patriarchal customs were able to survive in defiance of Yugoslav legislation; for instance, daughters remained barred from inheriting land and other immovable property (Reineck, 1991, pp. 51–53; Rrapi, 2003, pp. 131–32). To this day, traditional village rituals—including celebratory fire—remain alive in Kosovo across the ethnic dividing lines, with men shooting in the air to express joy during festive occasions such as weddings or New Year (Khakee and Florquin, 2003, p. 33).[30]

Kosovo Albanians say that hunting guns—if they were available—were used during such celebrations.[31] These had to be registered, but in remote villages some people kept hunting guns without being aware of the need to register them. In many households, old pistols, called *kobura*, were kept for use on these occasions.[32]

In early 1981, one year after the death of Marshal Tito and amidst serious economic deterioration in Yugoslavia, ethnic Albanian student demonstrations 'proved to be the clarion call of a new phase, in which Belgrade authorities returned to the repressive style associated with Rankovic, resulting in escalating Serb–Albanian tensions in the province' (Ramet, 2002, p. 6). During the 1980s, the tensions continued to heat up, culminating in Slobodan Milosevic's visit to Kosovo where, on 24 April 1987, he assured local Serbs that 'no one shall dare to beat you'. In 1988 the autonomous status of Kosovo came under more insistent attack and popular ethnic Albanian political leaders were replaced. Kosovo Albanians responded with spontaneous yet peaceful protests in defence of the local party leadership. Three thousand workers of the Trepça mines swore solidarity in the name of the traditional concept of besa, went on strike, and peacefully marched to Pristina 'in defence of Yugoslavia and the constitution of 1974' (Clark, 2000, pp. 47–48). They were eventually joined by about 100,000 additional demonstrators. In 1989, Belgrade changed the constitution, effectively ending Kosovo's status of autonomy. Albanians were dismissed from all state employment and political representation.

In the midst of these political developments, which increasingly moved towards ethnic differentiation and discrimination, Kosovo Albanians sought 'refuge in their past' (Reineck, 1991); they withdrew into the private realm of the extended families (Rrapi, 2003). From that time on, strong revitalization processes of traditional kanun-type practices and structures began in rural communities. Anthropologist Janet Reineck observes that '[i]deological conservatism in rural Kosova had deepened as Albanians responded to mounting ethnic and economic marginalization. Albanians seized upon tradition in order to reinforce their personal and collective dignity, in the face of a demeaned status in Yugoslavia' (Reineck, 1993).

After the end of the war in June 1999, ethnic Albanians published biographies, interviews, and other original KLA sources that had previously been confined to the informal realm of illegality and 'parallelism'.[33] These materials reveal that individual actors and clans began to step up clandestine arms smuggling activities during the early 1990s, shortly after the autonomous status of Kosovo had been withdrawn.

The arms were explicitly acquired for distribution among the population. Until 1998, however, most ethnic Albanians in Kosovo wanted neither war nor arms (Judah, 2000, p. 129). Some gunrunners used the arms themselves in attacks on Serb police stations. These activists hailed mainly from villages in the Drenica valley and the Rrafsh i Dukagjinit plateau[34]; later they would gain fame as founders, leaders, and 'martyrs' of the KLA.[35] While those who identified themselves with the anti-Serb resistance and the 'liberation fight' saw their activities as honourable and legitimate, their targets predictably viewed them as criminal or terrorist.

> Until 1998, most ethnic Albanians in Kosovo wanted neither war nor arms.

The biography of KLA commander Ramush Haradinaj reports that the money used to buy weapons for the local resistance was raised mainly among the diaspora groups, where enthusiasm for war was much higher than at home (Hockenos, 2003, p. 249).[36] Individual families, friends, and private ethnic Albanian sponsors sometimes contributed 'an enormous sum' (Hamzaj, 2000, pp. 28, 31). The People's Movement of (the Republic of) Kosovo (LPRK, later LPK) in Switzerland, for example, began to raise funds under difficult circumstances in 1991; with the public emergence of the KLA in 1997, however, their efforts began to bear substantially more fruit (Kola, 2003, pp. 320–01; Hockenos, 2003, pp. 244–49).[37]

Whereas this informal, militant approach found no wider approval in Kosovo during the early 1990s, ethnic Albanians were able to construct a more peaceful 'parallel system' to the official Belgrade-run structures thanks to massive diaspora contributions as well as local funding. Indeed, in July 1990 the ethnic Albanian delegates gathered outside the closed parliament building and declared *Kosova Republik,* the 'Republic of Kosovo'. Not until Yugoslavia began to unravel and war raged in Slovenia and Croatia did the officially dismissed ethnic Albanian deputies pass a *Resolution on the Independence and Sovereignty of Kosovo*. This claim to independence, made public on 22 September 1991, was soon endorsed by an underground referendum, in which 'virtually the whole Albanian population' participated and '99.87 per cent [of the voters] favoured independence' (Clark, 2000, pp. 82, 117). With little interference from the Serb side, which continued to occupy the formal sector, the informal Albanian parallel state system developed to include a parallel government and parallel provisions for finance, education, and social and health care, among other services; logistically, both the old Communist Party structures and local traditional kinship organization that still prevailed in rural communities were utilized for distributing aid (La Cava et al., 2000, pp. 32–33).

Ideologically, 'non-violence' became the official line of this parallel government, which Ibrahim Rugova was elected to head in May 1992 (Clark, 2000, p. 67). Employing tactics of civil resistance in the face of Serb violent repression, this strategy served as a powerful tool in constructing an implicitly superior—because 'moderate'—ethnic Albanian identity (Clark, 2000, pp. 66–69; Maliqi, 1998, p. 98–105). Non-violence and 'endurance' were also pragmatic responses to the imbalance of arms and power between Kosovo's Serbs and ethnic Albanians. In 1992, Rugova himself announced:

> We would have no chance of resisting the army. In fact, the Serbs only wait for a pretext to attack the Albanian population and wipe it out. We believe that it is better to do nothing and stay alive than to be massacred (Judah, 2001, p. 21).[38]

'Non-violence' became the official line of Ibrahim Rugova's parallel government.

The 'official' ideology of non-militant resistance helped 'to validate the self-worth of Kosovo Albanians at a time when they were being vilified' (Clark, 2000, p. 68). Yet it also aimed at the 'closing of ranks' and thus produced a process of 'defensive homogenization', which involved promoting nationalism through traditionalism and resulted in a comparatively narrow view of non-violence (Maliqi, 1998, pp. 21, 101–04, 135; Clark, 2000, p. 69).[39] This outlook was evident in the mass ceremonies of 'binding besa', which were held throughout Kosovo between 1990 (the 'Year of Reconciliation') and 1992. The initiative involved the entire province in a tradition that had hitherto been practiced at the personal or local level only. It attempted to invert prevalent honour codes by 'shaming' revenge seekers as anti-nationalist, anti-democratic, anti-European, and anti-modern (Clark, 2000, pp. 61–62).

Until late 1991, Pristina University folk culture professor Anton Çetta ran this exceptional reconciliation initiative, which involved about 500 students, many of

Ethnic Albanian leader Ibrahim Rugova in May 1996. He and other pacifist activists distanced themselves from the attacks on Serbs, for which a then little-known KLA took responsibility.

© Srdjan Ilic/AP Photo

whom gave up a full term, as well as various urban intellectuals and clergy across the province. Participants visited—and revisited—families engaged in a feud; in addition, radio and television broadcast appeals for 'magnanimous pardons' in line with the teachings of the kanun. The project set up councils to promote the goal of reconciliation. In this way, it reimported selected kanun structures of authority into villages where these had already been lost. In 1998, the Gjilan Community Council to Avoid Negative Phenomena reported that 'it had settled 541 of the 778 disputes brought before it in the past six years' (Clark, 2000, p. 62). All in all, the campaign managed to resolve about 1,000 feuds between 1990 and 1992, with only a few remaining unsolved (Clark, 2000, p. 63).

Among Kosovo Albanians, such binding besa was undertaken in the name of 'national solidarity' and 'unity' in the face of Serbian repression. The process made reference to ethnic Albanian tradition as well as historical precedents. In the numerous mass ceremonies, onlookers served as witnesses as forgiving families gave their besa 'in the name of the people, youth and the flag' (Clark, 2000, p. 62). The largest such public gathering took place on 1 May 1990 in the village of Verrat e Llukës near Deçan/Dečani. At least 100,000 people—other estimates reach 500,000—gathered on this day, a former communist holiday and one that continues to be celebrated as labour day in some countries.[40] From the end of August 1990, Serb authorities banned such large events and also staged some violent police interventions. Nevertheless:

> the campaign proceeded, but now by holding smaller ceremonies, for instance behind the walls of family compounds. These were all arranged by word of mouth and secretly, often with participants pretending that they were going to a wedding (Clark, 2000, p. 63).

During the first half of the 1990s, the appropriation of tradition by the 'official' parallel leadership of Kosovo aimed to protect civilians. Clandestine preparations for war, such as the training of Kosovo Albanians in Albania, 'seem to have been part of a contingency plan, in case of a Serbian military attack on Kosovo, to withdraw to the borders and fight to defend the population until the promised international military intervention arrived' (Clark, 2000, p. 65; Hockenos, 2003, p. 191).

On the political front, the core of Rugova's authority rested on hopes that he would prevent all-out war with high civilian costs by internationalizing the Kosovo Albanian plight, thereby questioning the legitimacy of Serb rule over Kosovo (Clark, 2000; Judah, 2000, ch. 3; Malcolm, 1998, p. 348). He was to bring about international intervention or external political involvement, 'ranging from diplomatic mediation to the setting up of a UN Trusteeship over Kosovo' (Malcolm, 1998, p. 348). For this purpose, he paid numerous visits to foreign capitals, but he 'achieved little beyond some resolutions by bodies such as the United Nations or the European Parliament' (Malcolm, 1998, p. 348). The strongest blow to Rugova's previously unchallengeable legitimacy, however, was the Dayton Peace Agreement, which was reached in Dayton, Ohio, in November 1995 and effectively ended the war in Bosnia. For international diplomatic reasons, Dayton contained no significant reference to Kosovo.[41] Furthermore, the fact that the Republika Srpska was granted relative autonomy within Bosnia and Herzegovina while the non-violent struggle for a Republic of Kosovo fell on deaf ears led some Kosovo Albanians to conclude that violence was the only remaining recourse (Judah, 2000, p. 120–26; Vickers, 1998, pp. 287–89).

Advent of the KLA

KLA soldiers sing upon returning from the front lines in March 1999, about 50 km east of Pristina.

After Dayton, political friction intensified, Rugova lost trust within the parallel government, and attacks on Serb police increased in the countryside (Judah, 2000, p. 131). These armed initiatives were long organized 'mostly at a level of personal or family connections' (Kola, 2003, p. 319); the village militant groups relied on members of the diaspora in Switzerland, Germany, and the United States to supply them with arms and support their military training in Albania (Kraja, 2003, p. 163; Hockenos 2003, chs. 8–11).[42]

In August 1993—two years before the Dayton agreement—local traditionalist militants met in Drenica and formally united with radical political diaspora representatives to found the KLA.[43] Yet the group was far from becoming a mass movement. In 1993, it only counted about 30 fighters, a number that increased to roughly 90 in the following years (Pushkolli, 2001, p. 250). In 1997, when the KLA 'officially' came out in public, it was composed of about 150 active members who operated clandestinely in Kosovo (Judah, 2000, p. 118). 'The KLA remained fragile and small and, despite launching several attacks in the course of 1997, it was [still] virtually confined to the fringes of Rugova's politics' (Kola, 2003, p. 330).

A first important shift occurred in 1997, when neighbouring Albania descended into anarchy and civil war after the collapse of the so-called pyramid schemes that eradicated many Albanians' life savings. These events, in conjunction with widespread armed violence and criminality, led citizens in Albania to attack and loot the well-stocked armouries throughout the country—a legacy of former dictator Enver Hoxha's obsessive militarization programmes. The population armed itself thoroughly, partly for defence purposes and partly to obtain potentially valuable commodities for free and 'in exchange' for their lost savings. As a result, an abundance of small arms suddenly became easily available to the previously troubled Kosovo gunrunners and soon-to-be KLA fighters.[44]

© David Brauchli/Getty Images

In biographical documents, KLA leaders—many of these previous gunrunners—subsequently described their relief at finally being able to acquire enough weapons for combat in Kosovo.[45] They profited from the disintegration of Albanian state power and rule of law in terms of supplies as well logistics, as borders had become more porous when Albania plunged into civil war and customs officers left their posts unmanned (Vickers, 1998, p. 311). Moreover, the boundaries between conflict and crime blurred as the KLA sought to import contraband weapons from the United States, Western Europe, Albania, and the FRY (Hockenos 2003, p. 252); the European Union and the United Nations placed arms embargoes on the FRY in 1991, and political sanctions applied from early 1998 until September 2001. Some commentators have suggested that KLA arms smuggling and military training were to a large extent funded through several activists' 'proximity to the criminal underworld, including drug trafficking' (Hockenos, 2003, p. 252).[46] In 1998, for example, Agim Gashi, a Kosovo exile pursuing the high life in Milan, achieved notoriety when he was arrested together with 124 other international drug traffickers. He allegedly bought large quantities of weapons for the KLA (Roslin, 1999).

Yet popular support for the militant approach did not grow strong until early 1998, when the Serb forces orchestrated massacres, notably of the Jashari clan in Prekaz. In the aftermath of these killings, the KLA drew masses of potential fighters at a speed that took even its core leaders by surprise (Judah, 2000, pp. 140–01).

> The rudimentary KLA structures soon found themselves overwhelmed. From northern Albania the few men already in place began to dispatch arms and uniforms over the border, the sleepers that Thaçi[47] and his group had recruited over the past few years 'awoke' and village elders, especially in Drenica, decreed that now was the time to fight the Serbs. Village militias also began to form and, whether they were KLA or not, they soon began to call themselves KLA…. Still, it was also increasingly clear that the KLA was beginning to establish some sort of control (Judah, 2000, pp. 141, 147).

While the first attempts to take up arms had failed in the early 1990s, the KLA succeeded in emerging from the 1998–99 war as the 'most successful guerrilla organisation of modern times' (Judah, 2000, p. 110). Unlike Rugova and his supporters, the KLA had achieved the internationalization of the Kosovo conflict. In official post-war Kosovo-Albanian historiography, Adem Jashari has been celebrated as the epic KLA leader who brought in NATO through his sacrifice, which cost the lives of 53 family and clan members, including women and children (Abdyli, 2000, p. 25).

Just as the non-militant movement had previously done, the KLA referred to the kanun to produce internal solidarity and compliance with the cause of 'national liberation'. This step was a relatively logical one, given that the most prominent KLA leaders hailed from traditional, rural extended families in Drenica and the south-western, rural parts of Kosovo; these men including those celebrated today as the KLA's first martyrs, such as Adem Jashari, and those who led the militant movement on the ground after returning home from years spent in the diaspora, such as Hashim Thaçi, Rramush Haradinaj, and Azem Syla.[48] The corresponding worldview recognizes a person who has 'the will' to use a gun as a 'man' (*burr*), and a person who exhibits the readiness to sacrifice his own life as a 'hero' (*trim*) of potentially epic dimensions.[49]

In particular, the KLA used the kanun concept of besa. Firstly, all recruits of the KLA had to swear an oath of allegiance to the cause (Judah, 2000, p. 99), which justified violence against those defined as 'traitors', 'spies', and 'collaborators'. Indeed, KLA communiqués—clandestinely published even before the process of escalation in 1998 and with increasing intensity after 1995—explicitly advised that these should be killed.[50] In the same way, post-war biographies

The militant worldview saw a person with 'the will' to use a gun as a 'man'.

of the most famous KLA commanders confirm that, from early on, violence was systematically used to target not only Serb policemen but also ethnic Albanians who were identified as 'collaborators' and 'traitors'.[51] The Albanian national anthem, frequently used by the KLA during the war at the sites of massacres, is still sung at ceremonies of the Kosovo Protection Corps (KPC).[52] The anthem overtly celebrates weapons, national solidarity, and violence against 'traitors' in the context of the core concept of besa (see Box 8.5).

Box 8.5 The national anthem of Albania

Around the flag we all unite
With one desire and one goal
That all those who will give their oath
Have bound the besa for salvation.

War those only will evade
Who are born as traitors.
A man, however, will not fright,
But die, but die as a martyr.

The arms we hold in our hands
Defend the fatherland in any country
We will not give up our rights
Here enemies (*armiqte* 'non-friends') have no place.

For the Lord Himself has spoken
That nations vanish from the earth.
But Albania will live on,
For you, for you we fight.[53]

Today, the pilgrimage centre at the site of the Jashari massacre in Prekaz in the Drenica valley sells many booklets, one of which—published by the local municipality—offers an 'official', albeit mythologizing, description of Jashari. In stressing the kanun notions of loyalty, besa, and 'friends', it refers to him as one 'among the first' who 'gathered many of his most loyal friends around himself coming from all over Albanian lands deciding to take up arms against the Serbian police' (Halimi and Shala, 2000, p. 9). Another passage reads:

> Raised in a tower house (kulla) where heroes were
> theme of the day together with the century-old battles
> for liberation, he grew to adore heroes. And he never
> parted from his gun. Even as a young man he had said
> and anticipated that he would be dying by gun alone!
> (Halimi and Shala, 2000, p. 14)

These texts reflect a selective approach to cultural allusions, revealing an unabashedly militant orientation.

Guns in Kosovo today

On the whole, today's Kosovo remains awash with guns. In addition to the registered weapons held by official local and international security institutions, an estimated 330,000 to 460,000 are held by civilians, with a stronger

Commemorating the four-year anniversary of the killing of KLA leader Adem Jashari (represented as a sculpture) are his brother Rifat Jashari (centre) and former co-fighters Bajram Rexhepi (right) and Hashim Thaçi (left) in March 2002 in Pristina.

concentration in the rural centres as well as among men over 18 years of age (Khakee and Florquin, 2003, p. viii). Yet the UN Interim Administration Mission in Kosovo (UNMIK) reregulated possession of hunting guns and requires a registration card that is valid for two years.[54] Celebratory fire at weddings and New Year festivities is usually tolerated, as long as it has not involved participation of members of the Kosovo Police Service or the KPC (Khakee and Florquin, 2003, p. 33). In 2003, well before major inter-ethnic violence erupted again in March 2004, the vast majority of surveyed southern Balkan people, including a majority of Kosovo Albanians, said they recognized the 'presence of weapons as a threat to society'.[55] Yet an estimated 60 to 70 per cent of households in Kosovo continued to hold on to weapons regardless of the legal framework (Khakee and Florquin, 2003, p. 17).

This fact has long been linked to the unsolved question of Kosovo's political status (Saferworld, 2002); the general perception among Kosovo Albanians is that independence has yet to be achieved and that the conflict is still in need of closure (Mustafa and Xharra, 2003). At the same time, trust in the capacity of the UN post-war governance structure has decreased in recent years and remains very low (ICG, 2005, p. 4, fn. 22). Alarmingly, 'both ethnic Albanian and ethnic Serb children and youth claim to rely primarily on themselves and on weapons to ensure their security' and crime is widely seen as the major threat to security (Khakee and Florquin, 2003, pp. ix, 33).

Former KLA fighters have claimed that they hold on to their guns because the political future of Kosovo continues to be in a limbo (Heinemann-Grüder and Paes, 2002, pp. 29–31). This presence of small arms in Kosovo has been partly ascribed to KFOR's inadequate efforts to disarm the KLA.[56] In September 1999 only 10,000 guns were surrendered, even though the KLA claimed to have some 20,000 fighters, including volunteers (Heinemann-Grüder and Paes, 2001, pp. 19–21). Importantly, these results reflected KFOR's decision not to pursue the demilitarization too energetically more than the latter's unshakable attachment to firearms. As KFOR officials later admitted, 'The complete disarmament of KLA combatants was not seen as a priority during the first year of the protectorate, as "the KLA was not considered to be a problem at that time"' (Heinemann-Grüder and Paes, 2001, p. 19).

After the end of NATO's military intervention in June 1999 Albanian 'gun smugglers [used] the same routes as for other types of trafficking', though the gunrunning appears to have been limited in comparison to other illegal trade (Khakee and Florquin, 2003, p. 2). A 'substantial part of ex-KLA weaponry, 7,800–9,800 weapons', may have served some other ethnic Albanian insurgence movements: the UÇPMB in southern Serbia in 2000; the National Liberation Army in the former Yugoslav Republic of Macedonia (FYROM) and southern Serbia in 2001; and the clandestine Albanian National Army in Kosovo in 2001 (Khakee and Florquin, 2003, p. 15). By 2003, however, cross-border trafficking of small arms had by and large petered out (Quin et al., 2003).[57]

© Kael Alford/Newsmakers/Getty Images

KFOR troops survey the contents of a secret KLA bunker found in June 2000 during a weapons search in Kosovo's Drenica valley.

Meanwhile, the ongoing active commemoration of the war—notably the frequent KLA memorial tributes—helps to reinforce the habit of civilian gun possession. These events often replaced or transformed former Serb symbols, such as statues or buildings erected during the 1990s, which communicated to ethnic Albanians, 'this is not your place'.[58] Today, '[p]ictures of armed people in schools around Kosovo, as well as posters and statues of former KLA fighters with weapons, have created a [new] kind of gun culture'.[59] Despite the KLA's ideological references to kanun as a marker of proactive self-regulation, however, it is not traditional, rural 'gun culture', or the 'family gun', which explains most of the illegal gun possession among Kosovo Albanians today (Saferworld, 2002). Today, urban youth stress the significance of self-defence and self-defence weapons as sources of security (Khakee and Florquin, 2003, p. 10). There is 'particularly among urban youths … a growing number of automatic military style weapons' associated with criminality and new gang-land activity (Saferworld, 2002). Among young and old, civilians and KLA activists, weapons are held 'for personal and collective security' (Saferworld, 2002), a perception difficult to separate from, on the one hand, fears of crime and, on the other, the political situation and aspirations.

A framed KLA poster with the title *Pushka e parë e lirisë* (The first gun of freedom) shows three fighters who lost their lives.

CONCLUSION

The current features of Kosovo's 'gun culture' are strongly linked to the recent war and the fact that initially isolated militant groups from mainly rural areas were able to gain legitimacy and momentum in a national and international political context. These militant groups actively tied their cause to Albanian history and elements of kanun culture, of which they offered a militant interpretation that would resonate in parts of Kosovo Albanian society, particularly in rural areas. The same historical and cultural references, however, had been used by other Kosovo Albanian political figures to legitimate phases of pacification and reconciliation. The fact that most KLA leaders and much nationalist post-war Kosovo Albanian literature explicitly identified the KLA ideals, leaders, and tactics with the local *kaçak* traditions and customary codes of self-regulation was thus clearly part of a particular politics of (self-)representation and identity construction. Violent opposition to violent ethnic persecution, in other words, was not the inevitable consequence of a culture used to the presence of arms.

This case study calls into question the assumption that 'gun cultures' are at the roots of 'cultures of violence'; in other words, communities that are accustomed to the presence of small arms are not necessarily willing to consider violence as a legitimate means of achieving their goals. Contrary to common assumptions about conflict in Kosovo, and in other regions more generally, this study suggests that the reasons for conflict should be sought in the interplay between cultural factors and the political context as well as social and historical determinants, rather than simply being ascribed to 'strong gun cultures'.

Via the brief discussions on El Salvador, Georgia, Kyrgyzstan, and Tajikistan, this study also highlights how the treatment of 'gun cultures' as monolithic and homogeneous is simplistic and often inaccurate. Within any social context, 'gun cultures' may indeed vary according to age, gender, status, and other factors; furthermore, they may change over time. In this sense, reference to 'national' or 'stable' 'gun cultures' can hardly capture the particular interpretations of the presence and possession of guns in any given society.

LIST OF ABBREVIATIONS

FARK	Forcat Armatosur e Republikes se Kosoves (Armed Forces of Kosova Republic)
FRY	Federal Republic of Yugoslavia
FYROM	Former Yugoslav Republic of Macedonia
KFOR	Kosovo Force (NATO)
KLA	Kosovo Liberation Army
KPC	Kosovo Protection Corps
LDK	Democratic League of Kosovo
PPK	Parliamentary Party of Kosovo
UÇK	Ushtria Çlirimtare e Kosovës (Kosovo Liberation Army)
UNDP	United Nations Development Programme
UNMIK	United Nations Interim Administration Mission in Kosovo

ENDNOTES

1 See, for example, Regg Cohn (2001); Roy (2005); Stohl (2003); Ibrahimi (2004).

2 See, for example, IWPR (2003); Peric Zimonjic (2004); Tola Winjobi (2004).

3 See, for example, Gray (1999); Henley (2003); *Jane's Defence Weekly* (2001); and Morris (2003).

4 The references to El Salvador are based on a UNDP study conducted in 2003. In Georgia, Kyrgyzstan, and Tajikistan, the Small Arms Survey conducted field research. The related results were published in: MacFarlane and Torjesen (2004); Demetriou (2002); and Torjesen, Wille, and MacFarlane (2005). Available on the Small Arms Survey Web site: <http://www.smallarmssurvey.org/publications.htm>

5 While references to a deep-rooted 'gun culture' have been made in connection to both Kosovo Serbs and Albanians (Saferworld, 2002), this report is based on field research that is focused on the notion of 'gun culture' among Kosovo Albanians only. Research on the relationship between 'gun culture', the presence of small arms, and armed violence would benefit from a comparison of 'gun cultures' among ethnic Albanians and Serbs in the province, as well as among ethnic Albanian across the Balkans.

6 See, for example, Gray (1999); IWPR (2003); Singh (2001); Zimonjic (2004).

7 See, for example, Farnam (2003). The post-conflict period began with the establishment of a UN peacekeeping force—the UN Interim Administration Mission in Kosovo (UNMIK)—in June 1999, following the NATO intervention.

8 Marie-France Desjardins, Programme Manager of the UNDP Illicit Small Arms Control Project, quoted in Quin et al. (2003).

9 See, for example, Saferworld (2002): 'Gun-culture, often presented by the media as the main reason for the proliferation of weapons, is exaggerated and unlikely to be the main destabilizing factor in Serbia and Kosovo.'

10 Note, for example, sociologist Gjergji Rrapi's description of adolescent peasant boys, raised primarily among kinship groups of men within typically extended family structures in the 1990s, who denigrated urban boys as raised in nuclear families 'by their mothers only' and saw them as lacking the experience of 'humanity' and masculine, 'heroic' qualities of a 'proper man' (Rrapi, 2003, p. 108).

11 For more information, see the surveys conducted by the Instituto Universitario de Opinión Pública Universidad Centroamericana 'José Simeón Cañas', San Salvador, September 2001. Available at <http://www.violenciaelsalvador.org.sv/documentos/otros/encuesta_armas_fuego.pdf>.

12 The First Ottoman garrisons established themselves in Kosovo alongside late medieval Serbian rule after the battle of Kosovo in 1389. Ottoman rule consolidated by the mid-15th century in Kosovo. It ended after Albanian uprisings with the First Balkan War (1912–13), when the Serbian army occupied Kosovo and northern Albania. See Malcolm (1998, chs. 4–6, 13).

13 The term derives from the Greek word for 'stick' or 'rule' and entered the Ottoman-Turkish language via Arabic.

14 Similarly, the Montenegrin government armed Catholic Albanians in 1911 while the Serb government armed Albanians in 1912 for the fight against the Ottoman Turks (Malcolm, 1998, pp. 243, 250).

15 The words for 'house'—*ship, oda,* or *kulla*—all signify 'an extended family living under one roof'.

16 'Gheg' is an Albanian dialectological distinction that has often been used to denote cultural unity of northern Albanians with Kosovo Albanians. To this day, many social and cultural patterns, kinship groups, and rituals remain identical in northern Albania and Kosovo. International sources from before the London Conference in 1913, when the national boundaries were established, rarely separated these regions. For example, 'Northern Albania' for Durham (1909, map) includes parts of today's Montenegro and of Kosovo reaching up to Peja/Peč and Mitrovica. Coon (1950, p. 4) finds 'mountain Gheg country, newly divide into 3 provinces without regard to tribal boundaries' of Macedonia, Kosovo, and northern Albania.

17 Author's translation from the German.

18 Ethnographic research result of informal interviews with KLA veterans from Drenica and participant observation in KLA commemoration rituals, Stephanie Schwandner-Sievers, February–March 2005.

19 The most acclaimed source on this kanun is Leonard Fox's translation of Shtjefën Gjeçov's ethnographic collection of 1933 (see Gjeçov, 1989). An Albanian Catholic priest, Gjeçov advocated the drafting of national Albanian law (anticipating an Albanian nation state which would include Kosovo) and a more influential role for the Catholic Church among Albanians. Annotations should be read alongside his text, as they help contextualize his assertions and comment on the authenticity of the sayings he collected. See Malcolm (1998, p. 17, fn. 38).

20 For details on the regulative capacities of kanun traditions, see Schwandner-Sievers (1999).

21 See Gjeçov (1933, p. 8, para 21/8; p. 22, para 60/b) and Hasluck (1954, p. 37). The age at which a boy is ready to receive a gun is open to interpretation. Durham (1909, p. 155) mentions that children in specific north Albanian clans could become victims in feuding after the first haircut (at toddler age). Gjeçov's kanun assigns 'adulthood'—normally seen as the point at which a boy/man may receive a gun—to boys at the age of 15 (Gjeçov, 1933, p. 26, para. 95). An ethnic Albanian respondent from Pristina suggested that nowadays, a boy becomes a man at the age of 18; he also stated that a man would have the right to reject the weapon. In so doing, he would never be a legitimate target of feuding; at the same time, however, he would never be considered a 'full man' (informal ethnographic interview, 56-year-old man from Prizren region, Pristina, 16 May 2004).

22 Limited evidence suggests, however, that women could renounce their female sexuality and, as 'sworn virgins', assume many elements of a male social role (Young, 2000).

23 Ethnographic field interview with 45-year-old man, Prizren region, 20 February 2005.

24 These reports refer to the district of Dibër and other northern parts of Albania.

25 See, for example, Gjeçov (1933, p. 68, para. 666).

26 Such symbolism can still be observed in some contemporary cases of Albanian transnational crime (Schwandner-Sievers, 2005, p. 325).

27 Stalin expelled Tito's Yugoslavia from the Cominform in 1948, while, at the same time, Albania's Enver Hoxha tightened relations with Moscow.

28 This box is based on field research conducted by the Small Arms Survey in the three countries (see Endnote 4 for a list of resulting publications); Nizharadze (2004); and interviews conducted by Stina Torjesen with: Alymbekov Narynbek, Ph.D. candidate in historical sciences, Bishkek American University–Central Asia, Kyrgyzstan, August 2004; Anvar Mokeev, doctor of historical sciences and ethnographer, Bishkek Manas University, Kyrgyzstan, August 2004; Sajar Tajimatov, vice dean, Osh State University, Kyrgyzstan, August 2004; Shonsar Shoismatulloev, director AFKOR Research Institute, Dushanbe, Tajikistan, September 2004; and Shukhrob Mirsaidov, deputy head, Department of Criminal Investigation, Ministry of the Interior, Dushanbe, Tajikistan, February 2004.

29 See also Backer (1983, pp. 161–74).

30 In the villages, the birth of a boy can also be a reason for such celebration.

31 In 1989, the Yugoslav federal police estimated that there were about 400,000 illegal weapons in Kosovo, including 150,000 long-barreled ones, in addition to 65,540 registered ones. For more information, see Milan Gorjanc, *Small Arms and Light Weapons and National Security,* unpublished conference paper, 27 January 2000, quoted in BICC (2002, pp. 127–28).

[52] Oral history interview with a 53-year-old Kosovo Albanian man, London, October 2004 (interviewed as part of wider ethnographic research by Stephanie Schwandner-Sievers). After the Warsaw Pact invasion of Czechoslovakia in 1968, Tito aimed to arm the workers of all Yugoslav republics and autonomous provinces in Territorial Defence Units independent of the Yugoslav National Army (JNA) as a means to pre-empt foreign invasions. Weapons were held at municipal, local, and okrug levels. The developments of the 1990s disenfranchised the Kosovo Albanians from official access to this national defence system and its arms (Hoare, 2003, pp. 18–19).

[53] For more on 'parallelism'—the parallel system of ethnic Albanian 'civic resistance' outside the official Yugoslav state structures in Kosovo—see Clark (2000).

[54] Rrafsh i Dukagjinit is the Albanian term for the western part of Kosovo, which Serbs call Metohija.

[55] For biographical examples, see Mehmetaj (2001) on Adrian Krasniqi from Drenica who, today, is celebrated as the first 'martyr' of the KLA because he was killed as the first fighter 'in uniform' during an attack on a Serb police station in 1997 (Judah, 2000, p. 128). See also Hamzaj (2000) on KLA commander Ramush Haradinaj.

[56] Ramush Haradinaj, who lost his brother during gunrunning operations across the Albania–Kosovo border in 1997, resigned as prime minister of Kosovo after the United Nations war crimes tribunal in The Hague indicted him in March 2005.

[57] In the early 1990s, a number of weapons were smuggled from the United States via Albania under pretence of organizing hunting club expeditions (Sullivan, 2004, pp. 216–17).

[38] See also Judah (2000, p. 114). Evidence that emerged after the 1999 conflict shows that the 'pacifist' parallel government, led by the 'ministry of defence' in exile under Bujar Bukoshi, secretly engaged in building a Kosovo Albanian army and police force. The 'official' army of the parallel state, the Armed Forces of Kosova Republic (FARK), recruited Kosovo Albanian officers who had previously worked for the Yugoslav army or police. The FARK was thus able to benefit from continuous contacts with—and arms supplies from—the Croat military (Hockenos, 2003, chs. 8–11; Kola, 2004, ch. 8). During and after the Kosovo war, however, it was the 'unofficial' KLA that played a determining role, integrating part of the FARK forces while persecuting the rest as rivals and 'traitors' (Schwandner-Sievers and Duijzings, 2004).

[39] The observers cited critically compare Ghandi's 'open' ideals of pacifism with the 'closed' character of non-violence based on homogenization processes and traditionalist nationalism in Kosovo during the early 1990s.

[40] Traditional kanun reconciliation usually takes place on religious holidays.

[41] Dayton discussions concluded that the case of Kosovo was an internal affair in which two issues needed to be addressed: the human rights situation and the question of provincial autonomy. Neither independence nor the right of self-determination were discussed as options for the province, disillusioning Kosovo Albanians who had expected an international reward for their suffering and peaceful resistance (Judah, 2000, p. 125; Kola, 2003, pp. 313–14).

[42] These splinter groups—called 'Enverist' for their affinity and contacts with neighbouring Albania's Communist dictator Enver Hoxha in the early 1980s—had individually agitated for armed resistance; some founded the radical LPK party (Judah, 2000, pp. 102–20).

[43] There was an internal split, however, as not all saw a need for long-term preparations to build a proper army before risking outright war. Despite insufficient weapon supplies, those in favour of an immediate continuation of attacks split from the LPK to form the National Movement for the Liberation of Kosovo, or LKÇK; this group subsequently assumed responsibility for many attacks against perceived 'traitors' (or 'collaborators') as well as Serb police. (Judah, 2000, p. 115).

[44] 'According to government estimates, more than half a million weapons—semi-automatic guns, 3.5 million hand grenades and 1.25 million land mines—fell into the hands of the civilian population' in Albania (Jorgensen, 1999). Other estimates put the number as high as 650,000 firearms; however, not all of these were semi-automatic rifles (BICC, 2002, p. 130–31). For details on the impact of these events on the KLA arsenal, see Heinemann-Grüder and Paes (2001, p. 13)

[45] See, for example, Hamzaj (2000, pp. 23, 27, 32–33).

[46] For a selection of critical, though sometimes biased, English-language reports on the topic of the KLA and crime, see Chossudovsky (1999), <http://www.srpska-mreza.com/sirius/KLA-Drugs.html> and <http://www.srpska-mreza.com/sirius/Albania-KLA-Crime.html>.

[47] Hashim Thaçi, political KLA leader and representative at peace negotiations in Rambouillet in February 1999, today heads the oppositional PPK party.

[48] According to Ramush Haradinaj, many urban Kosovo Albanians referred to these fighters in somewhat derogatory terms as 'people from the mountains' (Hamzaj, 2000, p. 100).

[49] Stephanie Schwandner-Sievers, results of ethnographic fieldwork and interviews with KLA veteran fighters in Pristina and villages of Drenica, February–March 2005.

[50] See, for example, Communiqués no. 13 (June 1995), no. 21 (14 July 1996), no. 27 (27 October 1997); furthermore, see Communiqués no. 43 (2 March 1998) and unnumbered (29 August 1998), all published in Elshani (1998, pp. 32, 71, 104–05).

[51] For example, killing 'Albanian speaking collaborators' was described in 1991 as objective of Adrian Krasniqi, the first KLA fighter who died in uniform in 1997. See Mehmetaj (2001, p. 18).

[52] In January 2000, the former KLA was officially transformed into the KPC, a civilian agency tasked with providing emergency response and reconstruction services in Kosovo. The KPC is limited to 200 registered weapons for guarding facilities as well as some celebratory weapons. Suspicion that the KPC has informal access to weapons continues to this day (Khakee and Florquin, 2003, p. 12). Fore UNMIK details on the KPC, see <http://www.unmikonline.org/1styear/kpcorps.htm>.

[53] Author's translation from the Albanian. Available at <http://groups.msn.com/Kosovaweb/poeziprkosovn.msnw> (accessed October 2004).

[54] By May 2003, more than 20,000 guns had been registered in accordance with UN Regulation N. 2001/7 On the Authorisation of Possession of Weapons in Kosovo. If UNMIK Police determine that an individual is 'facing serious threats,' that person may acquire a Weapon Authorization Card. More significantly, hunters or recreational shooters were encouraged to register their hunting and recreational weapons at their local police station and acquire a Weapon Registration Card. About 9,000 hunters are formally organized in hunting associations under the umbrella of the Hunters' Federation of Kosova (Khakee and Florquin, 2003, p. 34 and fn. 95).

[55] UNDP representative Alain Lapon suggests that 80 per cent of the southern Balkan population espouse such critical attitudes (quoted in Zimonjic, 2004). For Kosovo Albanians see Khakee and Florquin (2003, pp. 9, 32–33).

[56] KFOR assisted UNMIK in demilitarizing the KLA, a process stipulated by UN Security Council resolution 1244. See the resolution at <http://daccess-ods.un.org/TMP/3323410.html>.

[57] Quin (2003) cites the police chief in Kukës, northern Albania. Military training was clandestinely conducted around Kukës, and in times of crisis weapons were stored in neighbouring Kosovo and FYROM.

[58] See also Clark (2002, p. 6).

[59] See the statement by independent Pristina sociologist Blerim Latifi, quoted in IWPR (2003).

BIBLIOGRAPHY

Abdyli, Ramiz. 2000. 'Adem Jashari (1955–1998).' *Kosova: Historical/Political Review.* Prishtina/Tirana: The Institute of History. Vol. 8, pp. 21–25.

AFSC and RHSC (American Friends Service Committee and the Regional Human Security Center at the Jordan Institute of Diplomacy). 2002. 'Traditional Cultural Practices and Small Arms in the Middle East: Problems and Solutions.' Workshop report. Amman, Jordan. November. Accessed March 2005. <http://www.geneva.quno.info/pdf/amman_seminar_report.pdf>

Backer, Berit. 1983. 'Behind the Stone Walls.' *Culture Populaire Albanaise.* Vol. 3, No. 3, pp. 161–74.

Ben Nun, Gilad. 2004. *Brutalizing Human Relations: The Impact of Small Arms upon Israeli Society.* Background paper. Geneva: Small Arms Survey.

BICC (Bonn International Center for Conversion). 2002. 'Armed and Dangerous: The Proliferation of Small Arms and Light Weapons in the Balkans.' *Conversion Survey 2002.* Bonn: Nomos.

Bogdanovic, Dimitrije. 1995. 'The Kosovo Question Past and Present.' *Serbian Academy of Sciences and Arts Monographs,* Vol. DLXVI, Presidium No. 2. Accessed April 2005. <http://www.snd-us.com/history/bogdanovicD-kosovo_question.htm>

La Cava, Glora et al. 2000. *Conflict and Change in Kosovo: Impact on Institutions and Society.* Washington, DC: World Bank.

Chossudovsky, Michel. 1999. 'Kosovo "Freedom Fighters" Financed by Organised Crime.' New York: Global Security Forum. April. Accessed March 2005. <http://www.globalpolicy.org/security/issues/kosovo23.htm>

Clark, Howard. 2000. *Civil Resistance in Kosovo.* London: Pluto Press.

—. 2002. *Kosovo: Work in Progress: Closing the Cycle of Violence.* Centre for the Study of Forgiveness and Reconciliation. Coventry University. January. Accessed November 2004. <http://legacywww.coventry.ac.uk/legacy/acad/isl/forgive/images/kosovo.pdf>

Coon, Charleton. 1950. *The Mountains of Giants: A Racial and Cultural Study of North Albanian Mountains' Ghegs.* Cambridge, MA: Peabody Museum.

Cozzi, D. Ernesto. 1912. 'La donna albanese: con speciale riguardo al diritto consuetudinario delle Montagne di Scutari'. *Anthropos,* Vol. 7, pp. 309–35, 617–26.

Demetriou, Spiros. 2002. *Politics from the Barrel of a Gun: Small Arms Proliferation and Conflict in the Republic of Georgia (1998–2001).* Small Arms Survey Occasional Paper No. 6. Geneva: Small Arms Survey. November.

Duijzings, Ger. 2000. *Religion and the Politics of Identity in Kosovo.* London: Hurst.

Durham, Edith. 1909. *High Albania.* London: Edward Arnold.

Elshani, Gafurr. 1998. 'Ushtria Çlirimtare e Kosovës: Dokumente dhe artikuj (KLA: documents and articles).' 2nd edn. Pristina: Zëri i Kosovës.

Farnam, Arie. 2003. 'Gun culture stymies the UN in Kosovo.' *Christian Science Monitor.* 26 September. Accessed March 2005. <http://www.csmonitor.com/2003/0926/p08s01-woeu.html>

Faroqhi, Suraiya. 1995. *Kultur und Alltag im Osmanischen Reich: Vom Mittelalter bis zum Anfang des 20. Jahrhunderts.* Munich: Beck.

Gjeçov, Shtjefën. 1933. *Kanuni i Lekë Dukagjinit.* Lezha, Albania: Kuvendi. Facsimile reprint 2001.

—. 1989. *Kanuni i Lekë Dukagjinit–The Code of Lekë Dukagjini.* Albanian text with parallel English translation by Leonard Fox. New York: Gjonlekaj.

Gray, Andrew. 1999. 'Hidden KLA arms not troubling KFOR.' Reuters. 23 September. Accessed April 2005. <http://agitprop.org.au/stopnato/19990924kla.php>

Hahn, Georg von. 1854. *Albanesische Studien.* Vol. 1. Jena: Friedrich Mauke.

Halimi, Emin and Ajnishahe Shala. 2000. *The Jasharis: The Story of a Resistance.* Skenderaj: Municipal Board, Rilindja.

Hamzaj, Bardh. 2000. 'A narrative about war and freedom (dialogue with the commander Ramush Haradinaj).' Pristina: Zëri.

Hasluck, Margaret. 1954. *The Unwritten Law in Albania.* Cambridge: Cambridge University Press.

Heinemann-Grüder, Andreas and Wolf-Christian Paes. 2001. *Wag the Dog: The Mobilization and Demobilization of the Kosovo Liberation Army.* Bonn: BICC.

Henley, Paul. 2003. 'Albania's Gun Culture Proves Hard to Shift.' BBC News Online. 15 January. Accessed March 2005. <http://news.bbc.co.uk/1/hi/world/europe/2660853.stm>

Hoare, Marko Attila. 2003. *How Bosnia Armed.* London: Saqi.

Hockenos, Paul. 2003. *Homeland calling: exile patriotism and the Balkan Wars.* Ithaca and London: Cornell University Press.

Ibrahimi, Sayed Yaqub. 2004. 'Afghan Gun Culture Costs Lives.' Institute for War and Peace Reporting. 25 November. Accessed March 2005. <http://www.iwpr.net/index.pl?archive/arr/arr_200411_149_2_eng.txt>

ICG (International Crisis Group). 2005. *Kosovo: Toward Final Status.* Europe Report 161, 24 January.

Inalcık, Halil. 1974. 'The Socio-Political Effects of the Diffusion of Fire-Armscheck spelling in the Middle East.' In Bela Király, ed. *War, Technology and Society in the Middle East.* London and Oxford: Oxford University Press, pp. 195–217.

IWPR (Institute on War and Peace Reporting). 2003. 'Arms Amnesty Debate: Radio Television Kosova (RTK).' Report on televised debate. Pristina: IWPR. 8 December. Accessed November 2004. <http://www.iwpr.net/index.pl?local_balkans/kos/events/balkans_lt_arms_081203_eng.html>

Jane's Defence Weekly. 2001. 'How Many Weapons in Macedonia?' 25 August.

Jorgensen, Lotte. 1999. *Giving up Arms for Progress.* Gramsh, Albania: UNDP. Accessed March 2005. <http://www.undp.org/dpa/choices/december99/arms.htm>

Judah, Tim. 2000. *Kosovo: War and Revenge.* New Haven and London: Yale University Press.

—. 2001. 'The Growing Pains of the Kosovo Liberation Army'. In Michael Waller et al., eds. *Kosovo: The Politics of Delusion.* London and Portland: Frank Cass, pp. 20–24.

Keegan, John. 1994. *A History of Warfare.* London: Pimlico.

Khakee, Anna and Nicolas Florquin. 2003. *Kosovo and the Gun: A Baseline Assessment of Small Arms and Light Weapons in Kosovo.* Special Report. Geneva: UNDP and Small Arms Survey.

Kola, Paulin. 2003. *The Search for Greater Albania.* London: Hurst.

Kraja, Mehmet. 2003. *Mirupafshim në një luftë tjetër* (Farewell for another war). Pristina: Rozafa.

MacFarlane, Neil S. and Stina Torjesen. 2004. *Kyrgyzstan: A Small Arms Anomaly in Central Asia?* Small Arms Survey Occasional Paper No. 12. Geneva: Small Arms Survey. February.

Malcolm, Noel. 1998. *Kosovo: A Short History.* London: Macmillan.

Maliqi, Shkëlzen. *Kosova: Separate Worlds.* Pristina: Dukagjini PH.

Martín-Baró, Ignacio. 1983. *Acción e ideología: Psicología social desde Centroamerica.* San Salvador: UCA Editores.

Mehmetaj, Faton. 2001. Mehmetaj. *Adrian Krasniqi-Rexha: Një jetë e një vdekje për atëdhe* (Adrian Krasniqi-Rexha: A life and a death for the fatherland). Gjakova: Zgjimi.

Mertus, Julie A. 1999. *Kosovo: How Myths and Truths Started a War.* Berkeley: University of California Press.

Morris, Kylie. 2003. 'Afghanistan's Gun Culture Challenge.' BBC News Online. 22 February. Accessed March 2005. <http://news.bbc.co.uk/1/hi/world/south_asia/2788167.stm>

Mustafa, Artan and Jeta Xharra. 2003. 'Kosovo Gun Amnesty Setback.' Balkan Crisis Report 464. Pristina: Institute for War and Peace Reporting. 16 October.

Nizharadze, George. 2004. *Gun Culture in Georgia*. Background paper. Geneva: Small Arms Survey. September.

O'Loughlin, Ed. 2003. 'Business Booming for Town's Gun Traders.' *Sydney Morning Herald Online*. 26 April. Subscription access. <http://www.smh.com.au/articles/2003/04/25/1050777410838.html?oneclick=true>

Oxfam and AI (Amnesty International). 2003. *Shattered Lives: The Case for Tough International Arms Control*. Hackney: Colibri Press Ltd. Accessed April 2005. <http://www.controlarms.org/downloads/shattered_lives.htm>

Oxford Albanian–English Dictionary. 1999. Oxford: Oxford University Press.

Peinsipp, Walther. 1985. *Das Volk der Shkypetaren*. Vienna: Boehlau.

Peric Zimonjic, Vesna. 2004. 'Balkans: Millions of Illegal Guns Threaten Peace.' Inter Press Service. 14 January. Accessed March 2005. <http://www.ipsnews.net/africa/interna.asp?idnews=21913>

Pushkolli, Fehmi. 2001. *Zabir Pajaziti: Hero i Kombit* (Zahir Pajaziti: National hero), Pristina: UÇK–Zona Operative e Llapit.

Quin, David et al. 2003. 'Albania, Kosovo and Macedonia: Armed to the Teeth'. Balkan Crisis Report 470. Skopje, Pristina, and Tirana: Institute for War and Peace Reporting and Saferworld.

Ramet, Sabrina. 2002. *Balkan Babel: The Disintegration of Yugoslavia from the Death of Tito to the Fall of Milosevic*. 4th edition. Boulder, CO: Westview.

Regg Cohn, Martin. 2001. 'Kalashnikov Culture: Talking Tough on Guns in Pakistan.' *Toronto Star*. 11 April. Accessed March 2005. <http://www.worldpress.org/cover1.htm>

Reineck, Janet. 1991. *The Past as Refuge: Gender, Migration, and Ideology Among the Kosova Albanians*. Unpublished Ph.D. dissertation. Berkeley: University of California.

—. 1993. 'Seizing the Past, Forging the Present: Changing Visions of Self and Nation among the Kosova Albanians.' *Anthropology of East Europe Review*. Vol. 11, Nos. 1–2.

Reiter, Norbert. 1987. 'Jene Welten: Beschrieben nach ostbalkanslavischer und albanischer Volksprosa'. *Zeitschrift für Balkanologie,* Vol. 23, No. 2, pp. 151–70.

Roslin, Alex. 1999. 'The Kosovo connection: the KLA and the heroin craze of the 90s.' Accessed April 2005. <http://agitprop.org.au/stopnato/20000126drugsrosli.php>

Roy, Saswati. 2005. 'Daily Living with Terror.' *Peace News*. Accessed March 2005. <http://www.peacenews.info/issues/2452/245225.html>

Rrapi, Gjergji. 2003. *Die albanische Großfamilie im Kosovo*. Vienna: Boehlau.

Saferworld. 2002. '"Gun Culture" exaggerated in Federal Republic of Yugoslavia.' London. May. Accessed March 2005. <http://www.saferworld.org.uk/media/pr020702.htm>

Schwandner-Sievers, Stephanie. 1999. 'Humiliation and Reconciliation in Northern Albania: The Logics of Feuding in Symbolic and Diachronic Perspectives.' In Georg Elwert et al., eds. *Dynamics of Violence: Processes of Escalation and De-escalation of Violent Group Conflicts*. Berlin: Duncker & Humblot, pp. 133–52.

—. 2005. '"Culture" in Court: Albanian Migrants and the Anthropologist as Expert Witness.' In Sarah Pink, ed. *The Applications of Anthropology*. Oxford and New York: Berghahn. Forthcoming.

Schwandner-Sievers, Stephanie and Ger Duijzings. 2004. *A War within a War*. Anthropological background report. 31 May. The Hague: International Criminal Tribunal for the former Yugoslavia. Court exhibit.

Singh, Neeraj. 2001. 'Kosovo Must Choose Between Prosperity and Violence.' Pristina: UNMIK Police. Accessed March 2005. <http://www.unmikonline.org/civpol/articles/MustChoose.htm>

Stohl, Rachel. 2003. 'War ends but Iraq battle over small arms just begins.' *Christian Science Monitor*. 28 May. Accessed March 2005. <http://www.csmonitor.com/2003/0528/p11s02-coop.html>

Sullivan, Stacy. 2004. *Be not afraid for you have sons in America: how a Brooklyn roofer helped lure the U.S. into the Kosovo war*. New York: St. Martin's Press.

Tola Winjobi, David. 2004. 'Gun Culture and Stakeholders' Role.' Address presented during the Inauguration Ceremony of the Nigeria Action Network on Small Arms in Abuja, Nigeria, 17 November. Accessed March 2005. <http://www.iansa.org/regions/wafrica/gun_culture.htm

Torjesen, Stina, Christina Wille, and Neil MacFarlane. 2005. 'Tajikistan's Road to Stability: Reduction in Small Arms and Light Weapons Proliferation and Remaining Challenges.' Geneva: Small Arms Survey. Forthcoming.

UNDP (United Nations Development Programme). 2003. Armas de Fuego y Violencia, San Salvador: UNDP.

Vickers, Miranda. 1998. *Between Serb and Albanian: A Short History of Kosovo*. London: Hurst.

Young, Antonia. 2000. *Women Who Become Men: Albanian Sworn Virgins*. Oxford and New York: Berg.

Zimonjic, Vesna. 2004. 'Balkans: Millions of Illegal Guns Threaten Peace.' Inter Press Service. 14 January. Accessed March 2005. <http://www.ipsnews.net/africa/interna.asp?idnews=21913>

ACKNOWLEDGEMENTS

Principal authors
Stephanie Schwandner-Sievers with Silvia Cattaneo

Other contributors
Anna Khakee, Neil MacFarlane, David Mutimer, Wolf-Christian Paes, Michael Pugh, Ruxandra Stoicescu, and Stina Torjesen

A forensic team unearths human remains and clothing at a mass grave near the eastern town of Miljevina, Bosnia, in August 2004. (© Danilo Krstanović/Reuters)

Behind the Numbers:
SMALL ARMS AND CONFLICT DEATHS

9

INTRODUCTION

The steady stream of media reports from the battle zones of Iraq has kept the world regularly informed about at least one aspect of the conflict: the numbers of US and UK servicemen and women being killed. Between March 2003 and April 2005, more than 1,700 had died, and more than 11,000 had been wounded (Iraq Coalition Casualty Count, 2005; Antiwar.com, 2005). One obvious question follows directly from these statistics: how many Iraqis have died in the conflict? In April 2005, the public database Iraqi Body Count, basing its information on media accounts, estimated that there had been between 17,000 and 19,000 Iraqi military and civilian deaths (IBC, 2005).

In late October 2004, however, the British medical journal *The Lancet* published results from an epidemiological survey conducted in Iraq estimating that perhaps 100,000 or more excess deaths had occurred in Iraq since the invasion in March 2003 (Roberts et al., 2004), compared to a similar period before the invasion. Of these 100,000 estimated excess deaths, about 40 per cent—an estimated 39,000 deaths—may be the direct result of combat or armed violence.[1]

The large disparity between these estimates and those presented in previous reports raises important questions about how conflict deaths are measured and reported, not just for individual conflicts, but for global aggregate measures of armed conflict deaths. This chapter surveys the range of estimation techniques—from media report datasets to focused case studies—that are used to arrive at conflict death figures, and discusses the advantages and disadvantages of different methodologies. It clarifies the distinction between direct and indirect conflict deaths, highlights the tendency of certain methodologies to underestimate the number of deaths, and points to ways to improve these figures in future research.

Our ability to estimate more accurately total numbers of conflict deaths is not simply an academic preoccupation—it has important political implications. Official reports of conflict deaths supplied by parties involved in conflicts are often deliberately misleading, whether to minimize or exaggerate casualties for public attention, to cover up atrocities, to maintain the appearance of military superiority, or for a host of other reasons. In the case of Bosnia, for example, conflict death estimates disseminated locally and internationally seem to have been arbitrarily inflated in an attempt to hasten Western intervention (see below).

In addition to reviewing information provided by various global datasets based primarily on media reports, this chapter discusses the results of detailed and careful research studies undertaken during or after particular conflicts—including in Guatemala, Peru, the Democratic Republic of the Congo (DRC), Kosovo, Iraq, Afghanistan, and Sudan—in order to draw reasonable inferences and highlight key findings. The overall goal of the chapter is to present, in clear language for the non-specialist audience, the strengths and weaknesses of different approaches to counting conflict deaths, in order to cut through the confusion that often surrounds this debate. Although further data collection, research, and analysis will be required to improve estimates of conflict dead, recent advances in research methodologies now make it possible to derive more reliable estimates of how many people die in armed conflicts around the world. This chapter reviews the evidence and concludes:

- Most recent global estimates of direct conflict deaths underreport the extent and magnitude of the human death toll, mainly because they depend on incomplete media reports.
- The total number of *direct conflict deaths* is likely to be between two to four times higher than currently reported. The number of direct conflict deaths for 2003 is possibly between 80,000 and 108,000.
- A complete assessment of the human toll from armed conflict must include not only the direct deaths from combat or armed violence, but also the *indirect conflict deaths*. The total number of conflict deaths in both categories in some recent conflicts such as DRC has been many times higher than the number of direct conflict deaths.
- Small arms and light weapons are responsible for the majority—between 60 and 90 per cent, depending on the conflict—of direct conflict deaths. They also play a clear, but unquantifiable, role in causing the indirect deaths from conflict.
- Annual global estimates of conflict deaths are difficult to generate due to dramatic variations in the intensity of individual conflicts over time. More empirical research on specific conflicts, of the type highlighted in this chapter, is required.

This chapter begins by presenting the definitions and key concepts needed to understand the contradictory information on armed conflict deaths. It then introduces the sources, datasets, and methodologies typically used to derive estimates of armed conflict deaths. It explains why the only global, and thus widely cited, datasets or sources underestimate the death toll by comparing different sources of information and offers a judgement on the likely degree to which conflict deaths have been underestimated. Recognizing that significant statistical uncertainties remain, the chapter presents an estimate for the global number of conflict deaths in 2003. It then discusses the specific role of small arms in direct conflict deaths and describes the current state of knowledge on indirect conflict deaths.

Together with the chapter in the 2004 *Small Arms Survey* on criminal or non-conflict violent deaths from small arms, this chapter provides a more complete vision of the overall death toll arising from the use of small arms and light weapons.

CONFLICT, ARMED VIOLENCE, AND DEATH: SOME DEFINITIONAL AND CONCEPTUAL ISSUES

The phenomenon of violent conflict is complex and politically fraught. Labels such as 'war' and 'armed conflict' have specific legal and political meanings (for example, concerning the application of international humanitarian law, or the responsibilities of states party to a conflict), and imply a distinct phenomenon with a clear beginning and end. In reality, however, contemporary conflicts often blur the line between war and other forms of armed violence (Kaldor, 1999, p. 2; Holsti, 1996). For people suffering from high levels of armed violence, to whom definitional debates are hardly relevant, it can be difficult to determine when a 'war' begins or ends, or to distinguish armed conflict from other forms of collective violence (POST-CONFLICT). The way in which terms such as 'war', 'armed conflict', and 'conflict death' are used, however, does have implications for which conclusions can be drawn. It is thus essential to clarify how these terms are used and what they mean.

Definitions of conflict tend to focus on four particular attributes of conflict: *parties, purposes, consequences,* and *geography.*

Parties. The first feature identifying armed conflict is the nature of the parties involved in the violence. The most important actor is the state, and—following Max Weber's definition of the state as an entity enjoying a monopoly over the legal use of force—many classifications have only counted those wars or armed conflicts in which at least one state is directly involved. Today, however, a wide range of non-state parties is included in different definitions, complicating the task of counting conflicts.[2]

Purposes. Many definitions explicitly or implicitly distinguish between war or armed conflict and other phenomena according to their different *purposes* (Holsti, 1996, pp. 1–18). This attribute is particularly important beyond the realm of traditional war between states, namely in the thicket of civil wars and inter-communal conflicts. Some scholars have attempted to distinguish between 'greed' (economic) and 'grievance' (ideological or political) conflicts (Collier and Hoeffler, 2004).[3] Others have focused on the phenomenon of warlord violence, where the line between armed conflict and large-scale criminal violence becomes blurred (Reno, 1998; DeMars, 2000).

Consequences. One of the first features by which wars were classified was their level of mortality. The best-known definition based on mortality is the Correlates of War Project (CoW), which initially established the standard of 1,000 battle deaths as a threshold for 'war' (between states). This figure has near-iconic status in research that aims to analyse systematically different features of violent conflict (Geller and Singer, 1998, p. 27, n. 16; Small and Singer, 1982, p. 55). Although this mortality-based definition of armed conflict appears to put the human consequences at the centre of the analysis, in fact, the CoW project was mainly concerned with determining the proximate and underlying *causes* of inter-state wars, not their consequences. Today, however, our concern is with a greater range of conflicts in which death and injury are widespread, even if the threshold of 1,000 battle deaths is not crossed.[4]

Geography. Some definitions are based on the geographic scope of violence. Most often, a distinction has been made between international (cross-border) and civil or internal armed conflicts. This distinction was traditionally important for the involvement of the international community (which shied away from internal or civil conflicts), the determination of refugee status (versus that of internally displaced persons) or the application of international humanitarian law. This feature has become less relevant, however, since many conflicts are intra-state.

Most research organizations combine a number of these attributes in their definition of conflict. The definition guiding the Uppsala Conflict Data Program (UCDP),[5] for example, combines three of the four elements described above: 'An armed conflict is a contested incompatibility which concerns government and/or territory where the use of armed force between two parties, of which at least one is the government of a state, results in at least 25 battle-related deaths' (UCDP, 2005).

The lower death threshold attempts to include a wider range of conflicts than the CoW database. The definition, however, also specifies that at least one of the parties involved must be a state, and limits armed conflict to those disputes whose purpose is 'government and/or territory'. Crucially, it did *not* originally count those conflicts in which the government was not one of the armed combatants. The UCDP attempted to address this omission by recently creating separate databases that cover *non-state conflict* (conflict between two groups, neither of which is the state), and *one-sided violence* by states or organized groups against civilians (such as massacres and genocide). This approach, however, complicates the data collection and creates an assessment problem, since the most complete data so far only covers the period since 2002.[6]

The relation of small arms and light weapons to conflict is complex and varied. People are killed by small arms-related violence during conflict, in post-conflict phases, and in 'peace time'. When seen through the lens of the small arms debate, delineations between 'conflict' and 'not-conflict' become problematic. For this reason, the Small Arms Survey uses a collective violence definition developed by the World Health Organization (WHO).

> The instrumental use of [armed] violence by people who identify themselves as members of a group—
> whether this group is transitory or has a more permanent identity—against another group or set of indi-
> viduals, in order to achieve political, economic or social objectives (Krug et al., 2002, p. 215).

WHO is concerned with the effects of violence on public health, effects that occur in all conflict irrespective of the size or state involvement. The WHO definition is principally concerned with parties and purpose, although it leaves these categories as open as possible. For the purpose of small arms research we have added the word 'armed' to the definition.

This broad conception of armed conflict has several advantages. It includes fighting between non-state groups and captures genocidal violence, whether perpetrated by a state or not, even if the victims are unarmed. It also identifies armed conflict as a category of collective violence, rather than a *sui generis* phenomenon. By employing this definition, this chapter is able to connect its analysis of armed conflict to that of other violent practices, not all of which are armed and not all of which are collective. The definition locates armed conflict against the broader tapestry of violent exchanges, and, by not drawing sharp and arbitrary lines around it, more accurately reflects the variety and fluidity of contemporary armed violence involving small arms.

Within this definition, it is important to distinguish between *direct conflict deaths,* which occur as a direct consequence of fighting, often due to bodily trauma caused by weapons or ordnance, and *indirect conflict deaths,* which arise from the indirect consequences of armed violence, through such phenomena as death from illness, disease, or starvation that would not have occurred in the absence of the conflict. Indirect conflict deaths are most closely associated with the displacement of civilian populations in violent conflict zones. The sum of direct and indirect deaths can be considered to be excess mortality due to violent conflict: the additional mortality in a population beyond the level that would normally be expected in the absence of conflict. For reasons of convenience, this chapter may refer to excess mortality as 'conflict deaths'. Available evidence suggests that the ratio between direct and indirect deaths varies greatly between different violent conflicts, depending on the nature of the fighting (urban versus rural, fighting between conventional forces versus asymmetric warfare), the deliberate terrorization or targeting of civilians, access to health care facilities, and other factors.

The ratio between direct and indirect deaths varies greatly between different violent conflicts.

The datasets and sources discussed below concentrate on direct conflict deaths. They do not estimate how many direct deaths were caused by small arms and light weapons. Using epidemiological surveys, public health specialists have attempted to capture both direct and indirect conflict deaths, although often with imperfect or imprecise data.

COUNTING CONFLICT DEATHS: MULTIPLE SOURCES, DIFFERENT METHODS, WIDELY VARYING NUMBERS

A complete dataset on people killed in conflict—directly or indirectly—does not exist. All published figures are estimates based on incomplete information. Available information also often comes from a narrow range of sources, from which datasets are then constructed based on various criteria.

This section introduces the sources and methods currently used by researchers and describes how these sources are used to build datasets. For all of these sources and datasets, it examines what is not captured, either by definition or by 'real world' data collection limitations, and draws conclusions about their ability to estimate accurately the number of deaths in armed conflict. Then it briefly describes the most common research methods used to examine particular conflicts; it discusses their utility not only for estimating conflict dead, but also for distinguishing between direct and indirect deaths.

A UN peacekeeper takes notes at a mass grave in Gatumba, Burundi, in August 2004.

Official reports and statistics

Official statements disseminated by warring parties are often the first reports available on the number of conflict deaths. But first does not imply most accurate. While an imprimatur can lend these statements a degree of authority, in practice they should be interpreted cautiously. Not only are official estimates based on incomplete information, but they are also often intended to mislead. As Monty Marshall of the University of Maryland has argued: 'counts are often purely speculative and always political' (Marshall, 2001, p. 3).

Even when relatively open to transparency, military officials often have no way of knowing the true extent of battlefield and civilian casualties. They are rarely present at the violent events and generally do not have data that would allow them to make a complete estimate of the numbers of dead. Knowledge of enemy losses is likely to be particularly limited. In situations of intense fighting, officials usually have more pressing concerns than establishing an accurate count of the number of dead. Systematic mortality surveillance systems also generally break down in times of war, if they ever existed (Hofmann et al., 2004, p. 19; Mathers et al., 2005, p. 172).

Examples of politically motivated misdirection about conflict casualties are numerous. Traditionally, this was called propaganda; the modern word is spin. From Vietnam to Bosnia, Afghanistan, and Iraq, the technique is still in routine use in modern warfare (see Box 9.1). Misdirection is not limited to the warring parties, however. NGOs and advocacy organizations can also exaggerate or underestimate conflict deaths for their own purposes, or they may simply get the facts wrong because of limited access to information.

Box 9.1   Bosnia's conflict dead

In 1995, when UN Member States were debating the strategy for ending the violence in Bosnia and Herzegovina, it became routine to refer to 200,000 people killed in the conflict. In 1997, a US State Department report stated that 250,000 had been killed (US DOS, 1997).

These figures appear to have emerged in 1992 from a number of sources as politically motivated *projections*. In September 1992, a leaked CIA report stated that 150,000 deaths were expected if the West did not intervene in the conflict. The special envoy of the UN High Commissioner for Refugees, José María Mendiluce, apparently predicted 400,000 deaths. In December 1992, Bosnian Foreign Minister Haris Silajdzic told journalists that 128,444 persons had died, including Bosnians, Croats, and Serbs loyal to the Bosnian government. This precise figure seemed to imply that the dead had been counted to the last person. In reality it appears to have been derived by adding the list of 17,466 confirmed dead to an estimated additional 111,000 missing. In June 1993, the Bosnian Deputy Minister for Information, Senada Kreso, told journalists that 200,000 had died.

In 1995, the former Yugoslavia desk officer of the US State Department, George Kenney, suggested that a more realistic estimate of fatalities might be in the range of 25,000 to 60,000. He asserted that Bosnia's foreign minister 'understood the benefit of apparent slaughter' implied by combining missing and killed persons in the same figure. Kenney argued that these figures resonated well against the backdrop of pictures of skeletal Muslim men in Serbian prison camps, and that they were instrumental in garnering political support in the West and much-needed financial donations from the Muslim world. Although the figures he suggested appear to be closer to the truth, it should be noted that they, too, were politically motivated: Kenney was opposed to US intervention in the war.

Beginning in 1996, some research organizations had settled on lower figures. The Uppsala Conflict Data Program, publishing its results in the yearbook of the Stockholm International Peace Research Institute, estimates that the conflict in Bosnia and Herzegovina caused 25,000-55,000 battle-related deaths (SIPRI, 1996, p. 24). The 2002 *Annual Report* of the International Committee of the Red Cross (ICRC) states that the human remains of 15,500 persons had been found since 1992 (ICRC, 2002, p. 236). Not all had been identified. By December 2002 the ICRC had received 20,860 tracing requests for missing persons and had been able to close some 3,385 files (ICRC, 2002, p. 237). The ICRC expects that very few of the missing will be found alive, but points out that not all dead will have been reported missing.

These lower figures on Bosnia's conflict dead should not detract from the devastation wreaked on the communities that were affected by it. They do, however, illustrate the political sensitivity and inaccuracy of early casualty figures that were produced by officials within a particular political context.

Source: Kenney (1995), unless otherwise noted

'Casualty agnosticism' involves avoiding making casualty estimates.

When deliberate misdirection is not used, 'casualty agnosticism' is sometimes employed (Conetta, 2004, p. 28). This practice involves avoiding making casualty estimates. For example, the US administration has stated that estimates of non-US casualties from fighting in Iraq and Afghanistan in the past three years are either not available or not important to assessing campaign success (Conetta, 2004, p. 30). Observers believe, however, that more data is available than has been admitted publicly, and that the main motive is to avoid engaging in discussions that are likely to generate opposition to the conflict in Western and Muslim states. In public interviews, however, US Pentagon officials have acknowledged that they do record non-US deaths, to the extent that when Iraqi civilians appear to have been wrongfully killed, investigations are conducted and financial compensation is paid (The Memory Hole, 2004).

The 1990–91 US–Iraq conflict (Operation Desert Storm) provides an example of how casualty figures may be employed for political aims both during and after a conflict. In 1991, the US Defense Intelligence Agency (DIA) estimated with an error factor of 50 per cent that 100,000 Iraqi soldiers had been killed and 300,000 wounded. In 1993, former DIA analyst John Heidenrich estimated that as few as 1,500 Iraqi soldiers had been killed and around 3,000 wounded on the basis of interviews with Iraqi prisoners of war and numbers of bodies found (Heidenrich, 1993; *Jane's Defence Weekly*, 1993). Carl Conetta states that there were between 20,000 and 26,000 military fatalities in the war (Conetta, 2003, p. 39). It seems that the original number was an overestimate designed in part to demoralize Iraqis based on 'wildly exaggerated claims of casualties' (Bakshi, 1999). One interpretation suggests that a lower number of deaths would 'add strength to claims that the coalition campaign had some success in discriminating between military equipment and military personnel' (Roberts, 1993, p. 171).

Mortality statistics

In many countries, state authorities systematically record deaths and code them according to cause of death. Under its Statistical Information System (WHOSIS), WHO collects death registration data from more than 100 participating states. Some of this data can be used to monitor mortality levels and changes in mortality that might be caused by violent conflict. In many cases, however, data collection systems cease to function during conflict, if they ever functioned before. According to an assessment by WHO, only 64 countries submitted data that was considered complete in 2003 and coverage was minimal in sub-Saharan Africa, where deaths from violent conflict are concentrated. Death data in conjunction with censuses are possible sources for evaluating mortality levels, but this has not been fully explored (Mathers et al., 2005, p. 15).

Independent media reports

Media reports provide another perspective on armed conflict violence—and sometimes a more accurate one—than that provided by government sources. But they, too, must be considered with caution. Media reports are most valuable when they are the product of direct investigation by independent journalists on the ground.

Four factors impede the ability of journalists to gather accurate information. The first is formal restrictions placed on where journalists may travel, and with whom they may speak. Since independent reporting can contradict official government reports—and thus upset carefully managed public relations wars—such restrictions are common.

Secondly, the high levels of personal risk involved mean that reporters often do not have direct access to combat zones. Parties in conflict may also be able to effectively exclude journalists through force or coercion, and the deliberate targeting of journalists. In 2003–04, for example, 93 journalists and 17 media assistants were killed, and more than 2,500 were attacked or threatened, most of them in violent conflict zones (Reporters without Borders, 2005, p. 2).

Thirdly, even when journalists are reporting directly on conflict violence, their

A journalist examines an exhumed mass grave in May 2003. The site was thought to contain up to 600 Kuwaiti prisoners of war executed in 1991 in Habbaniya, north-west of Baghdad, Iraq.

© Roberto Schmidt/ AFP/Getty Images

Box 9.2   Death in Darfur

Between 345,000 and 385,000 people are estimated to have died in Darfur since February 2003. Although figures are uncertain, between 60,000 and 240,000 of these deaths may have been direct conflict deaths. Using different data but broadly similar techniques, other analysts have estimated the total death toll at between 380,000 and 400,000 (Reeves, 2005a; CIJ, 2005).

Two epidemiological studies (WHO/EPIET, 2004; Depoortere et al., 2004) and a series of other reports (Reeves, 2004) provide a first assessment of what the possible death toll in Darfur could be. The first epidemiological survey was carried out by Medécins sans frontières (MSF) from April to June 2004 (Depoortere et al., 2004); the second by the European Programme for Intervention Epidemiology Training and the WHO between June and August 2004 (WHO/EPIET, 2004, p. 2). The two surveys covered sample populations of between 17,000 and 20,000 people in north and west Darfur. Many uncertainties remain and the total death toll will only be known once a more extensive survey of the population in Darfur can be done.

Both surveys found shockingly high mortality rates of similar proportions. The WHO survey found that mortality rates[7] averaged 7.3 deaths per 1,000 people per month (WHO/EPIET, 2004);[8] the MSF survey reported 8 deaths per 1,000 people per month (Depoortere at al., 2004).[9] The mortality rate varied between the two areas. WHO observed the lowest mortality in north Darfur: 4 per 1,000 people died every month (WHO/EPIET, 2004, p. 10). The highest rate was documented by MSF in El Geneina refugee camp, where 17 people died per 1,000 per month (Depoortere et al. 2004, p. 1318). In the absence of conflict the crude mortality rate would be about 1.5 deaths per thousand per month.

Table 9.1 uses these results to estimate excess mortality per month among the whole population of Darfur affected by the conflict (est. 2.2 million). A key assumption, but one that accords well with evidence for the intensity of the conflict and the humanitarian crisis (Reeves, 2005b), is that monthly mortality has remained constant over the course of the conflict, or that the periods studied are close to the median monthly mortality. Estimates can thus be derived for the total death toll for the period from February 2003, when the conflict began, until the end of 2004.

The survey data also makes it possible to distinguish violent deaths (direct conflict deaths) and excess mortality (direct and indirect conflict deaths). Although the range of indirect deaths between the two studies is relatively narrow, the estimates of direct conflict deaths differ significantly. In the WHO study, only 17 per cent of all deaths were attributable to violence compared to more than 60 per cent among the people surveyed by the MSF study.

Table 9.1   Extrapolations from mortality: possible death toll in Darfur, February 2003–April 2005

	Excess deaths per month in all of Darfur	Violent deaths per month in all of Darfur	Excess deaths in all of Darfur in 2004 (12 months)	Violent deaths in all of Darfur in 2004 (12 months)	Excess deaths, February 2003–April 2005	Violent deaths, February 2003–April 2005
WHO[1]	12,795[2]	2,224[3]	153,540[4]	26,688[5]	345,465[6]	60,048[7]
MSF[8]	14,300[9]	8,800[10]	171,600[11]	105,600[12]	386,100[13]	237,600[14]

Sources and notes:

1   WHO/EPIET (2004).

2   Based on the calculation that the excess mortality rate of 5.8 per 1,000 per month (documented mortality rate of 7.3 per 1,000 per month – the expected mortality of 1.5 per 1,000 per month) * 2.2 million people * 1,000 would mean 12,795 excess deaths per month.

3   Based on the calculation that the violent death rate of 1.01 per 1,000 per month [(42 recorded violent deaths * 1,000) / (sample population of 20,776 * recall period of 2 months)] * 2.2 million people * 1,000 would mean 2,224 violent deaths per month.

4   Monthly excess death toll times 12 (12,795 * 12).

5   Monthly violent death toll times 12 (2,224 * 12).

6   Monthly excess death toll times 27 (February 2003 to April 2005 = 27 months) (12,795 * 27).

7   Monthly violent death toll times 27 (2,224 * 27).

8   Depoortere et al. (2004).

9   Based on the calculation that the average excess mortality rate of 6.5 per 1,000 per month (average documented mortality rate of 8 per 1,000 per month – the expected mortality of 1.5 per 1,000 per month) * 2.2 million people *1,000 would mean 14,300 excess deaths per month.

10 Based on the calculation that the average violent death rate of 4.0 per 1,000 per month [(330 recorded violent deaths * 1,000) / (sample population of 17,519 * average recall period of 4.7 months)] * 2.2 million people * 1,000 would mean 8,800 violent deaths per month.

11 Monthly excess death toll times 12 (14,300 * 12).

12 Monthly violent death toll times 12 (8,800 * 12).

13 Monthly excess death toll times 27 (February 2003 to April 2005 = 27 months) (14,300 * 27).

14 Monthly violent death toll times 27 (8,800 * 27).

Box 9.2   Death in Darfur (cont.)

This disparity is probably due to one major difference between the two studies: the WHO study only documented deaths that occurred within the area under review, while the MSF study asked people about deaths that occurred before they reached the refugee camps. The MSF study found that the crude mortality and, in particular, violent deaths were extremely high during the 'village and flight' periods. Once the internally displaced people had arrived in the camps, the mortality rate decreased five- to eightfold and the proportion of violent deaths reached similar levels to those recorded by the WHO study (13 per cent). The implication is that the MSF study estimate is closer to the real picture of direct conflict deaths. Both studies, however, highlight the catastrophic death toll in Darfur, and the crucial importance of the rapid provision of humanitarian relief.

Despite being based on a snapshot of mortality in a few accessible locations over a short period of time (between two and four months), these findings are consistent with the estimates from other independent studies (CIJ, 2005; Reeves, 2004; 2005a). The levels of mortality recorded may not be representative of the entire duration of the conflict, nor are the surveyed areas necessarily representative of the broader region. The situation in refugee camps, on which the surveys focused, may differ from that of Darfur in general. It will not be possible to refine these estimates until surveyors have wider access to Darfur's population.

information often comes from second-hand sources such as local officials, eyewitnesses, medical personnel, and other individuals close to the conflict. The reliability and comprehensiveness of this information is seldom complete.

Finally, the more physically remote a conflict area is, the harder it is for journalists to reach and report on it, as the case of Guatemala demonstrates (see below). So although in some cases media reporting can generate overestimates—such as when reporting the impressions of soldiers fresh from combat (Conetta, 2003, p. 5)—the more common problem with media accounts is likely to be underreporting.

> The most common problem with media accounts is likely to be underreporting.

Even journalists reporting from 'heavily covered' wars suffer from these problems of access. In the case of Afghanistan since 2001, early reports in the Western media estimated civilian deaths resulting from aerial bombardments at 1,000–1,300 (Conetta, 2002a, p. 7). Subsequent surveys of affected communities on the ground established that 5,576 people had died from bombardments, shootings, landmines, unexploded ordnance, and other violence during a nine-month period—more than four times the number reported in the press (Benini and Moulton, 2004, p. 411). A large number of these casualties, it turned out, were victims of the parallel war fought by the Northern Alliance that received much less attention in the Western media than did US military actions.

Similar discrepancies appear to have been evident in the estimates of Iraqi conflict deaths. Media-based estimates of Iraqi military and civilian deaths since military action began in 2003 stood at more than 10,000 by September 2004, and by March 2005 had reached more than 15,000 (IBC, 2005). But this number may underestimate the real death toll from violent means by as much as four times, if extrapolations based on the above-cited figure of 100,000 deaths estimated by Roberts et al. are correct (see below).

The accuracy of media reports ultimately depends on how they were derived. Journalists with first-hand experience of specific conflict incidents are likely to produce more accurate assessments than media statements that are themselves based on official or NGO reports. This inconsistency in accuracy comes to light when different types of media reports are aggregated within a single database. A recent example concerns the situation in Darfur, Sudan. Numerous reports state that 50,000 people have died in this conflict (BBC, 2004b; 2004c), but this figure appears to be based on a misinterpretation and misrepresentation of epidemiological data.[10] It seems to refer only to the few months specifically covered by a WHO study and to include only indirect (non-violent) deaths in camps for refugees or displaced persons (Reeves, 2004; CIJ, 2005). The actual figures, as noted in Box 9.2, are probably many times higher.

For these reasons, media reports must be used carefully and intelligently to avoid turning misleading figures into accepted truths. It should also be recognized that there will almost always be an element of underreporting of conflict incidents in the media, and it is important not to accept incomplete media-based counts as definitive. Broader estimates (such as databases) based on media reports must also be evaluated for the extent to which the media is likely to underreport in any specific conflict, in particular as the fighting becomes particularly intense or if it is located in inaccessible areas. Such media accounts can be supplemented with field research, which helps to provide a more complete picture.

Datasets

Datasets provide longitudinal data on deaths in different conflicts based on a mix of the above sources. The longest time-series dataset is the CoW project, which for some variables have data going back to 1816 (CoW, 2005). Since the early 1990s, a number of different data collection projects have also collected conflict data. Most tended to generate estimates of total numbers of deaths for the entire length of a conflict, and usually divided it by the number of years to obtain an annual average for each conflict.[11] They were thus unable to produce precise annual estimates that took account of variations in the intensity of individual conflicts. The total estimates for each conflict included in these datasets were usually based on figures suggested by governments, NGOs, or others and were thus highly susceptible to imprecision and distortion. In particular, uncritical reporting of incorrect official data probably occurred. For estimates of conflicts in the non-Western and non-industrialized world, the lack of multiple sources is also problematic. Finally, these estimates also often did not necessarily or systematically distinguish between direct and indirect conflict deaths, due to the nature of their sources.

The use of Internet search engines has helped researchers to construct more accurate annual figures as they are based on counts of incidents in a specific year (see Box 9.3). The datasets discussed in this chapter make extensive use of new technologies for data collection. They are the Armed Conflict Database of the International Institute for Strategic Studies (IISS, 2005); the Armed Conflicts Report of Project Ploughshares (Project Ploughshares, 2005); and

---

Box 9.3   Conflict death datasets: who counts what?

In recent years, Internet search engines have made it possible for conflict datasets to collect data by monitoring news reports from around the world on a continuous basis (King and Lowe, 2003). All three of the datasets discussed in this chapter—the Armed Conflict Database of the International Institute for Strategic Studies (IISS, 2005), the *Armed Conflicts Report* of Project Ploughshares (Project Ploughshares, 2005), and the Uppsala Conflict Data Project (UCDP, 2005; Mack et al., 2005)—make use of this technology to some degree. The results are estimates on the numbers of conflict dead in a particular conflict over a specific period of time, usually one year.

There are, however, differences in the way these projects collect and present their data. IISS employs research assistants who monitor news stories on a weekly basis. UCDP and Project Ploughshares tend to collect all stories in Internet research engines at particular points in the year when they are compiling their reports, thus perhaps missing more ephemeral sources that may disappear from the Internet (e.g. radio transcripts). UCDP and Project Ploughshares count conflict victims by calendar year, whereas IISS starts its year on 1 August of the previous year (2004 thus covers 1 August 2003 to 31 July 2004).

The projects also use slightly varying definitions. UCDP uses a collective violence definition and distinguishes between three different types of conflict: (i) inter- and intra-state conflicts, (ii) non-state conflicts, and (iii) 'one-sided violence' of unilateral force against the civilian population. IISS counts military and civilian lives lost as a direct result of an armed conflict, and distinguishes between (i) international armed border and territorial conflict, involving governments in armed conflict over sovereignty and territory, (ii) internal armed conflict that takes place between government forces and organized groups that control sufficient territory to sustain concerted military operations, and (iii) terrorism, including attacks involving one or more factions in significant armed opposition to a state. Violence directly attributable to state-sponsored human rights violations is not included in this definition. Project Ploughshares collects all data related to armed conflict.

the UCDP (UCDP, 2005; Mack et al., 2005), which collects data for the *Human Security Report* (HSR). These datasets or sources generate annual numbers of conflict dead (or numbers for specific conflicts without global totals, in the case of Project Ploughshares), making it possible to examine trends and changes in particular conflicts over time. These newer databases are able to base many of their entries on individual reported incidents and are thus more fact-based than their precursors.

Estimation techniques

What other tools—in addition to datasets and the official government information and media reports from which they are constructed—are available to estimate conflict deaths? Broadly speaking, there are three types of estimation techniques: violence clustering surveys, multiple system estimation, and epidemiological surveys. These techniques are not mutually exclusive and can in some cases be combined to provide a more precise estimate of conflict deaths, mainly by triangulating different sources of information, or by establishing a matrix of information from which more robust conclusions can be drawn.

Violence clustering surveys

This technique to establish numbers of direct conflict deaths is based on the observation that conflict tends not to be spread equally across a region, but clustered in particular areas. It uses a two-step process. Analysts first determine which areas of a country experienced high levels of violence, through media reports, key informant interviews, and

> Violence clustering surveys, capture–recapture, and epidemiological surveys are the three main estimation techniques.

Map 9.1   Districts with victims from direct violence during Operation Enduring Freedom

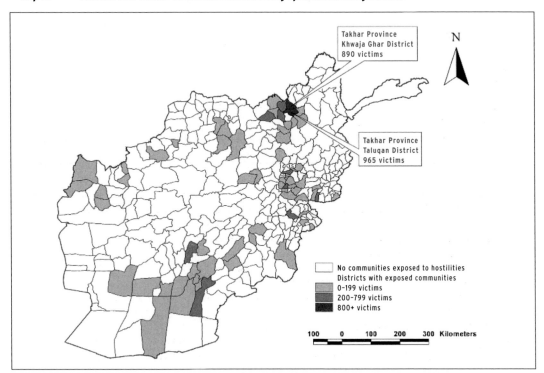

Takhar Province
Khwaja Ghar District
890 victims

Takhar Province
Taluqan District
965 victims

N

No communities exposed to hostilities
Districts with exposed communities
0–199 victims
200–799 victims
800+ victims

100   0   100   200   300 Kilometers

Source: Benini and Moulton (2004, Figure 3, p. 419)

239

field visits to areas thought to have been affected by combat. In the second phase, analysts carry out surveys in the areas where hostilities took place to estimate either mortality rates or total conflict deaths. Estimates are then extrapolated to the affected population, rather than for the entire population of the country.

This methodology has been widely used in surveys on landmines but has only recently been applied in Afghanistan to other kinds of weapons used in war (Benini and Moulton, 2004). It represents a promising method for estimating how many people were killed by different weapon types. Map 9.1 reproduces violence clusters in the Afghanistan study. It shows that violence tends to cluster rather than to be spread evenly across a territory. Studies that do not take these clusters into consideration in the selection of sample areas may over- or under-sample incidents of violence.[12]

Multiple system estimation (capture-recapture)

Multiple system estimation (MSE), a technique also known as 'capture–recapture', was developed in environmental science, biology, and other natural sciences, and has been used to estimate, or measure changes in, wildlife populations.

When applied to conflict deaths, MSE techniques take individual body counts as the starting point for a total conflict deaths estimate. The methodology compensates for inevitable undercounts due to lack of reports, unwillingness of families to cooperate, and human error. The technique uses available incomplete lists of the dead that are derived from different sources (such as victim interviews, police reports, morgue or hospital data, media reports that include names). Arriving at the total number of conflict dead involves calculating the frequency with which names appear on more than one list. The frequency provides an indication of the comprehensiveness of each individual list. The total number of conflict dead is then extrapolated on this basis. MSE assumes that any (dead) individual has an equal chance of appearing on any of the lists.

This method has been used to estimate the conflict dead in Kosovo (1999), in Guatemala (1960–96), and in Peru (1980–2000), and has demonstrated that early media-based numbers of conflict deaths were significant underestimates. It is particularly useful for estimating conflict deaths in protracted fighting in areas from where few reports reach the international community.[13] Yet it does require at least two sources with lists of names to be available.

Epidemiological surveys

In recent years, the tools of epidemiology—developed to monitor the occurrence of mortality and morbidity (injury or illness) in specific populations—have been increasingly applied to the study of interpersonal and collective violence. In principle, this approach uses the same techniques employed in studies on the incidence of disease in a specific population.

Epidemiological studies can be used to collect data on all types of death that occur in a particular population, allowing researchers to distinguish between direct and indirect conflict deaths. Analysts are thus able to construct a better picture of the relationship between direct and indirect conflict deaths, although the total estimates of direct deaths are usually subject to greater uncertainty than overall mortality.[14]

Epidemiological studies of conflict violence have been conducted in DRC, Burundi, Republic of the Congo, Sierra Leone, Darfur (Sudan), Kosovo, and Iraq.[15] Because surveys generate first-hand information about affected households, they can produce the most reliable estimates of the recent conflict death toll for the civilian population in the affected area; however, they do not capture groups that do not belong to the remaining community (e.g. combatants who came from an outside area) or groups that may have fled or have been completely eliminated. Epidemiological surveys can be carried out during phases of violent conflict, but resulting access problems may produce greater risks of under- or over-reporting direct deaths.

Because they must generate their own data through individual and/or household surveys, epidemiological studies are often resource-intensive, costly, and time-consuming. One concern with survey data is that the results can be affected by inappropriate sample design or by enumerators of poor quality. In addition, basic information—such as expected mortality rates and total population figures—seldom available, which makes extrapolations from the survey results to the total population more unreliable.

Combined estimation techniques

Ultimately, many of these methods are best used in combination in order to triangulate different estimates and arrive at a more robust estimate of conflict deaths in a particular case. Epidemiological studies can be conducted as part of violence cluster surveys. Capture–recapture studies can be used to improve estimates in datasets when incident or name lists are available. Individual entries in datasets can be corrected or improved on the basis of more detailed field studies. Table 9.2 illustrates the use of triangulation to derive an estimate of the death toll for the 1998–99 war in Kosovo.

> Basic information—such as expected mortality rates and total population figures—is seldom available.

COUNTING DIRECT DEATHS: UNDERREPORTING IN RECENT CONFLICTS

As noted above, datasets have an inherent tendency to underreport conflict deaths as they rely heavily on media reports. But by what margin do they underestimate these deaths—by a few percentage points or by several times the original estimate? In examining several recent conflicts, this section compares different sources to establish whether a plausible correction factor can be derived for direct conflict deaths in order to arrive at a more complete picture.

First, in an examination of conflicts in Kosovo, Guatemala, Peru, Iraq, and DRC, this section compares figures from media-based datasets with those provided by estimation techniques discussed above.

Kosovo

Table 9.2 shows estimates of conflict deaths in Kosovo in 1998–99 and compares four different studies, which used a variety of estimation techniques, with three media-based datasets. The estimation techniques produce consistently higher estimates than the media-based datasets (except in the case of the high estimate quoted by Project Ploughshares).

These figures illustrate two things. First, the estimation techniques tend to converge on a number of direct conflict deaths between 8,000 and 12,000 depending on the period covered. Second, the figures quoted in the UCDP and IISS databases closely reflect documented body counts (UNGA/UNSC, 2001, p. 33). While they closely match the number of exhumed corpses, they do not provide the full picture of the scale of direct conflict deaths. They appear to underestimate the total number of direct conflict deaths by between two and five times. Project Ploughshares, by contrast, provided a range that included as its lowest figure the exhumed bodies and as the highest the estimate produced by the US Centers for Disease Control and Prevention (Spiegel and Salama, 2000, pp. 2204, 2206).

Table 9.2   Estimated deaths in Kosovo by different sources

Source	Method	Estimated number of conflict deaths	Time period for survey
American Association for the Advancement of Science (AAAS) and American Bar Association (ABA)[1]	Multiple system estimation (MSE)	10,500	20 March–12 June 1999
Centers for Disease Control and Prevention (CDC)[2]	Epidemiological survey	12,000	February 1998–June 1999
International Criminal Tribunal for the Former Yugoslavia (ICTY)[3]	Estimates based on reports and exhumations	4,000 (bodies exhumed); 5,000-12,000 (estimated deaths)	Entire conflict
Physicians for Human Rights[4]	Epidemiological survey	8,000-9,269	May 1998–May 1999
IISS[5]	Media reports	3,000	1 August 1997–31 July 1999
UCDP[6]	Media reports	2,000-5,000 battle deaths	1998–99, but 'no detailed sources on the number of deaths could be found' (UCDP, 2005)
Project Ploughshares[7]	Media reports	4,000-12,000	n/a

Sources and notes:

1   ABA/AAAS (2000, pp. 1, 7). This estimate, based on 3,353 interviews conducted by several NGOs among ethnic Albanians who had fled Kosovo after March 1999, combines information from several lists using MSE.

2   Spiegel and Salama (2000, pp. 2204, 2206). Based on a two-stage health cluster survey among Kosovo's ethnic Albanian population in September 1999 that collected retrospective mortality data, including cause of death, for the period February 1998 to June 1999. War-related trauma was defined as any death occurring as a direct result of an injury sustained during the conflict, including arbitrary killings by gunfire, or by burning or collapsing buildings and other structures. The estimated total death toll was 18,800, which included a total of 6,800 indirect deaths.

3   BBC (1999), UNIS (1999), and UNGA/UNSC (2001, p. 33). In 1999, ICTY based its estimates on the exhumation of 2,108 bodies from about one-third of the reported grave sites and 11, 334 reported deaths. When forensic work ended in 2000, about 4,000 bodies had been exhumed.

4   Iacopino et al. (2001, p. 2016), PHR (1999), figure of 9,269 cited in ABA/AAAS (2000, p. 9).

5   IISS (2005).

6   UCDP (2005).

7   Project Ploughshares (2004).

Guatemala and Peru

The 36 years of violent conflict in Guatemala from 1960 to 1996 are estimated to have resulted in 119,300–145,000 direct conflict deaths. This figure is based on the first comprehensive MSE (capture–recapture) study of conflict deaths, which was conducted for the Guatemalan Commission for Historical Clarification (Ball, 1999; 2003; Ball, Kobrak, and Spirer, 1999).

During the peak of the violence between 1980 and 1983, the press 'missed the story' as it gradually stopped reporting on rural atrocities at a time when massacres were growing in frequency. As early as 1978, when mass killings became deliberate state policy, the reporting fell to zero. Reporters were evidently too afraid to venture into the countryside, or feared retaliation from the government for their interest. The fuller picture did not emerge until long after the conflict, when testimonies were systematically gathered from rural people. Figure 9.1, derived from the data used for the MSE study, clearly reflects the gap in media coverage, with the black line indicating the number of killings reported in the press, and the solid line the estimated number of killings reconstructed from documentary and interview sources using capture–recapture techniques.

In contrast to the MSE estimates, the UCDP dataset refers to at least 45,500 persons killed between 1967 and 1989 (UCDP, 2005).[16] While this figure corresponds roughly to documented numbers, an application of the MSE technique indicates that the real death toll, including undocumented cases, must be around three times higher.[17]

A similar MSE study for Peru estimated that the number of direct conflict deaths in the period 1980–2000 was 69,280, with a range of 61,007–77,552 (Ball et al., 2003, p. 2). This study established that more than half of the conflict dead had not been recorded by name in press or other accounts.[18] The UCDP database records more than 28,000 battle deaths for the period from 1980–1999, suggesting undercounting by at least a factor of two.

Mayan Indians carry the coffins of the victims of a 1982 massacre in a remote village south-east of Guatemala City in June 2003. The bodies of people slain during Guatemala's 36-year civil war have been exhumed from at least six mass grave sites.

© Rodrigo Abd/AP Photos

Figure 9.1   Guatemala: per cent of killings and disappearances occurring in rural areas, by year and by source, 1960-1995

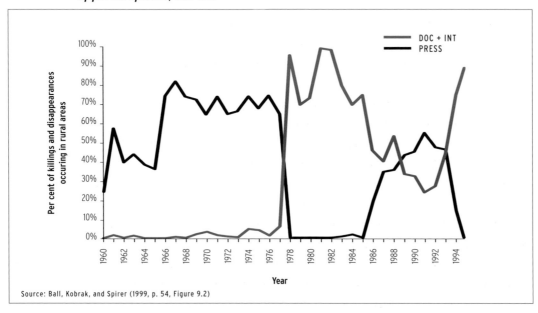

Source: Ball, Kobrak, and Spirer (1999, p. 54, Figure 9.2)

Afghanistan

Under Operation Enduring Freedom in Afghanistan, the most intense fighting lasted 12 weeks, from October to December 2001. Triangulation of different sources (see Table 9.3) suggests that more than 9,000 people died in Afghanistan during this period. This estimate is based on a detailed investigation of media reports of individual clashes, and a violence cluster survey of 600 local affected communities (Conetta, 2002a, pp. 4, 6; Benini and Moulton, 2004, p. 411). For the same period the estimates put forward by UCDP and Project Ploughshares are two to ten times lower.

Table 9.3   Conflict deaths in Operation Enduring Freedom, Afghanistan

Individuals killed	Source	Time period	Deaths
US troop losses[1] (direct conflict deaths among combatants)	Official statements	'autumn 2001 to spring 2002'	54
Afghan militia allied with the US[2] (direct conflict deaths among combatants)	Media-based	October 2001-January 2002	600
Taliban troops[3] (direct conflict deaths among combatants)	Media-based	October 2001-January 2002	3,000-4,000
Afghan civilians direct conflict deaths[4]	Violence cluster survey	September 2001-June 2002	5,576
Subtotal:			**9,000-10,000**
Afghan civilians[5] (indirect conflict deaths)	Unspecified mortality surveys in IDP camps in Afghanistan	15 September 2001-14 January 2002	8,000-18,000
Total:			**17,000-28,000**
Civilians, Taliban and al Qaeda fighters, US troop losses	IISS[6]	August 2001-July 2002	4,000
Battle-related deaths	UCDP[7]	2001	more than 1,000
Civilians, Taliban and al Qaeda fighters	(Project Ploughshares)[8]	2001-02	1,500-5,000

Sources and notes:

1   IISS (2005). Text on 2002; 42 of the 54 died in 'non-hostile' circumstances often involving friendly fire.

2   Conetta (2002a, p. 6).

3   Conetta (2002a, p. 4). This number is based on the total of estimates for major battles.

4   Benini and Moulton (2004, p. 411). During the period under review, September 2001-June 2002, 1,582 died from landmines and unexploded ordnance (UXO) and 3,994 died of bombardments, shooting, and other violence.

5   Conetta (2002a, p. 36). Based on mortality information from 10 IDP camps inside Afghanistan where the mortality rate was found to be between 1.5 to 4 per 1,000 per month. It has been assumed that mortality rates may have been higher outside the camps, where the population received less humanitarian assistance. It is possible that the proposed figure of 8,000 to 18,000 includes direct conflict deaths (of 3,200+).

6   IISS (2005).

7   UCDP (2005).

8   Project Ploughshares (2004).

Iraq

As discussed above, there are substantial differences in estimates of conflict deaths in Iraq between datasets based on media reports (10,000–15,000 deaths) and a recently conducted epidemiological survey (39,000 deaths). When comparing equivalent time periods (see Table 9.4), it is apparent that the dataset estimates are lower than the survey estimates by a factor of 1.9. The survey results have to be interpreted with caution, but they do provide strong evidence of underreporting in the media.[19] On average the media missed every second incident. It is likely that the underreporting was more marked during the periods of high intensity fighting when the media were unable to cover the high number of incidents, in particular because of the dangerous working conditions.

Table 9.4   Estimates for Iraqi civilian deaths

Database	Time period	Conflict deaths estimates from media sources	Extrapolation from epidemiological study[5]	Factor of difference
IISS	August 2002–July 2003	10,000[1]	11,880[6]	1.2
IISS	August 2003–July 2004	15,000[2]	27,180[7]	1.8
UCDP	January–December 2003	8,494[3]	22,080[8]	2.6
Project Ploughshares	January 2003–December 2003	10,000–15,000[4]	22,080[8]	1.5–2.2

Sources and notes:
1 IISS (2005).
2 IISS (2005).
3 Mack et al. (2005).
4 Project Ploughshares (2004).
5 Roberts et al. (2004, p. 1860). Figures are based on the extrapolated total violent deaths in Iraq, excluding Fallujah. The formula applied here is the following: number of violent deaths/1,000 population/month = (number of recorded violent deaths * 1,000) / (sample population * recall period). Numbers were rounded after calculation. One violent death in the sample population of 7,438 during the 14.6 months of the pre-invasion Iraq is equivalent to 0.009 violent deaths per 1,000 per month. Thirteen violent deaths[20] in the sample population of 7,868 during the 17.8 months of the post-invasion period are equivalent to 0.09 violent deaths per 1,000 per month. If this finding is applied to the total population of Iraq (24.4 million), there will have been 225 violent deaths per month in the pre-invasion period (1 January 2002 to 18 March 2003) and 2,265 violent deaths during the post-invasion period (19 March 2003 to 16 September 2004).
6 Roberts et al. (2004, p. 1857). Based on comment 5 above (7.5 * 225 + 4.5 * 2,265 = 11,880).
7 Roberts et al. (2004, p. 1857). Based on comment 5 above (12 * 2,265 = 27,180).
8 Roberts et al. (2004, p. 1857). Based on comment 5 above (2.5 * 225 + 9.5 * 2,265 = 22,080).

Eastern DRC

The example from the eastern part of DRC is particularly instructive because the International Rescue Committee (IRC) conducted four different epidemiological surveys in the area between 2000 and 2003, thereby allowing an analysis of changes over time. The survey results indicate a large number of direct and indirect conflict deaths: perhaps more than 3.8 million direct and indirect conflict deaths as a result of the fighting, the large majority due to treatable and preventable diseases (IRC, 2004a, p. iii).

Table 9.5 compares the findings from the surveys with the data presented by IISS, UCDP, and Project Ploughshares. For the most intense periods of fighting, in particular for 2000 and 2001, the IISS numbers are about five times lower than those of the epidemiological surveys. The epidemiological surveys referred to in the table indicate that more than 190,000 people were direct victims of conflict in 2000 and 2001, while the IISS database records only 40,000 conflict deaths for that two-year period. The two other databases quote numbers that are too low (2,700 for UCDP and 1,200 for Project Ploughshares) to be considered realistic. The sources acknowledge, however, that the intensity of the conflict and difficulties of access meant that 'information on battle-related deaths was sporadic in 2001 and therefore the reliability is low' (UCDP, 2005) or that 'an estimate [...] was made difficult by the remoteness of the conflict' (Project Ploughshares, 2004).

The data from the epidemiological surveys also shows a sharp decline in direct conflict deaths from about 88,000 in 2001 to about 5,500 and 4,600 in 2002 and 2003, respectively. IISS also recorded a sharp decline for the same years, from 30,000 to 6,000 or fewer. The data presented by UCDP and Project Ploughshares appears to have become more reliable as the conflict intensity diminished.[21] The two latter sources, however, still produce estimates that are about 50 per cent lower than the epidemiological studies estimates (see Box 9.2).

Table 9.5   Comparison of conflict death figures for DRC, 2000–03

Year	Epidemiological survey			IISS	UCDP	Project Ploughshares
	Total conflict dead (direct and indirect)	Indirect	Direct	Direct	Battle-related deaths	Direct
2000	924,000[1]	824,000	103,000	30,000	2,500[5]	1,200
2001	937,500[2]	849,000	88,000	10,000	200[6]	– ('thousands')[8]
2002	343,000[3]	337,500	5,500	6,000	4,061[7]	1,000–4,000[9]
2003	286,000[4]	281,000	4,900	4,000	2,154	4,000[10]
Total (2000–03)[11]	**2,490,500**	**2,291,500**	**201,400**	**50,000**	**8,915**	**n/a**

Sources and notes:

1 IRC (2000, p. 1). This report covers the period January 1999–April 2000 and quotes a figure of 77,000 deaths per month. Direct conflict deaths were reported to be 11.1 per cent of total deaths in 2000 (IRC, 2003b, p. 6).

2 IRC (2001a, p. 3). Based on 2.5 million deaths over 32 months, or 78,125 deaths per month. In 2001, the reported percentage of direct conflict deaths was 9.4 (IRC, 2003b, p. 6).

3 IRC (2003b, pp. 6, 13). In 2002, with a decline in fighting, the proportion of direct deaths also declined to 1.6 per cent of the total.

4 IRC (2004a, p. 11). Based on 500,000 deaths in 16 months, or more than 31,000 excess deaths per month, of which 77 per cent were in eastern DRC. The proportion of direct deaths in eastern DRC remained at 1.7 per cent (IRC, 2004a, p. 17, Figure 5).

5 'The figure indicates an absolute minimum. The real death toll could be significantly higher' (UCDP, 2005).

6 'Information on battle-related deaths in DRC was sporadic in 2001 and therefore the reliability of this number is low' (UCDP, 2005).

7 UCDP figures for 2002–2003 from the forthcoming *Human Security Report* (Mack et al., 2005).

8 'An estimate of conflict deaths for 2001 was made difficult by the remoteness of the conflict and the limited media coverage' (Project Ploughshares, 2004).

9 'Independent media reports suggested that over 1,000 people died as a direct result of the conflict with a US State Department report citing over 4,000 ' (Project Ploughshares, 2004).

10 'A US State Department report suggests that over 4,000 civilians died as a direct result of the conflict in 2003. However, due to the remoteness of some of the fighting the real figure may be significantly higher' (Project Ploughshares, 2004).

11 This total does not include prior conflict deaths in 1998–99, which are included in the IRC estimate of 3.8 million total conflict dead (IRC, 2004a, p. iii).

Pulling the numbers together

The cases discussed above all suggest that while the data incorporated into the databases is well researched and based on documented cases, they underreport direct conflict deaths because media reports miss a considerable share of incidents. The degree of underreporting appears to depend on the intensity and remoteness of the conflict, increasing as conflict becomes more intense and more remote. A precise estimate on the extent of underreporting would require classification of conflicts according to intensity, remoteness, and attention paid by the international community, as well as the application of different factors for the expected level of underreporting for different categories. This approach requires further detailed case studies. For now, it is only possible to establish a rough estimate of the extent of underreporting at the global level based on the few studies documented above.

Table 9.6 lists the totals for direct conflict deaths offered by the three main datasets. Even here, significant variation exists—IISS numbers are 50–80 per cent higher than the lowest figures presented.

The above comparisons of estimates for Kosovo, Guatemala, Peru, Afghanistan, Iraq, and DRC suggest that media-based dataset reports underestimate direct conflict deaths by a factor of two to four.[23] This estimate is relatively conservative, and in cases such as DRC in 2000 and 2001, the extent of underreporting was probably greater. Table 9.7

Table 9.6   Dataset estimates of global direct conflict deaths, 2002 and 2003

Dataset	2002	2003
HSR[1]	27,000	27,000
Project Ploughshares[2]	25,303	43,490
IISS[3]	51,000	40,000

Sources:

1   HSR lists 'best' low and high estimates in its database. 'Best' estimates have been offered here: the ranges were 23,274-46,145 (2002) and 25,977-47,398 (2003). These totals include peacekeepers, civilians, and humanitarian aid workers killed in direct conflict. Figures based in part on data collected by UCDP for the 2005 *Human Security Report* (Mack et al., 2005; UCDP, 2005).

2   Project Ploughshares publishes a range of the estimated number of conflict deaths for individual conflicts (Project Ploughshares, 2004). Individual conflict estimates have been added together to provide the totals in this table. For 2002 they are 23,780 to 26,825. For the table above the midpoint of 25,303 has been chosen. For 2003 they are 39,875 to 47,105. For the table above the midpoint of 43,490 has been chosen. Project Ploughshares does not itself provide annual conflict death figures because they believe it to be 'next to impossible' to provide an accurate number.[22]

3   The IISS database continuously monitors newspaper reports (IISS, 2005). Its annual totals will thus continue to change (the database is updated every three months).

presents estimates of annual conflict deaths in 2003 that have been revised using correction factors of 2–4. Applying the highest and lowest numbers on the table yields a total of between 54,000 and 172,000 direct conflict deaths in 2003. A different approach—one that assumes that the lowest database figure calls for the greatest correction, and vice-versa—produces a range of 80,000–108,000 direct conflict deaths in 2003.[24]

Table 9.7   Correcting dataset underestimates of global direct conflict deaths, 2003

Media-based data source estimate		Low correction factor (2)	High correction factor (4)	Mid-point
UCDP	27,000	54,000	108,000	81,000
Ploughshares	43,000	86,000	172,000	129,000
IISS	40,000	80,000	160,000	120,000

Although these figures are higher than those of the most widely cited datasets, they are lower than estimates provided by WHO. WHO has published estimates for the period from 1999 to 2002, ranging from a high of 269,000 (1999) to a low of 172,000 (2002). WHO also works with publicly available datasets and sources, and adjusts for underreporting based on conflict intensity (Mathers, 2005). Unfortunately, no total is available for 2003 to compare with the above-cited adjusted estimate. No details are available about how WHO determines its conflict intensity adjustment factors, making a thorough evaluation of its findings difficult. WHO figures do suggest, however, that the number of direct conflict deaths could be higher than the revised estimate reported above.

> For many conflicts, the degree of underreporting exceeds the range of two to four.

These figures are extremely tentative and result from an attempt to bring to bear information from detailed research on a few specific conflicts on the entire range of contemporary conflicts. In view of this imprecision, this chapter deliberately applies relatively conservative correction factors. Yet for many conflicts, the degree of underreporting exceeds the range of two to four (for example, DRC in 2001 or perhaps Darfur in 2003–04). If the initial findings regarding the possible death toll in Darfur (see Box 9.2) are found to be accurate, between 20,000 and 90,000 deaths may have to be added to the total death count for Darfur alone.[25]

Nevertheless, it is clear that although datasets provide useful information, it is essential to complement these sources with detailed research from the field using survey and estimation techniques.

Since the annual number of direct conflict deaths is considerably larger than media-based datasets indicate, two other questions emerge. What proportion of total conflict death is attributable to small arms and light weapons? And what can be said about the total number of indirect conflict deaths?

SMALL ARMS AND CONFLICT DEATHS

It is widely claimed that small arms are the most commonly used weapons in armed conflict, and that they are responsible for the majority of direct conflict deaths. Yet there is little concrete evidence to support this assertion. This section examines the available evidence in order to quantify better the role that small arms play in conflict deaths.

None of the existing datasets systematically distinguishes deaths by weapon type. The IISS database does include information on weapon types used in conflicts, but it does not provide information about the frequency with which weapons are used. One important conclusion can be made, however: small arms and light weapons have been used in every single conflict recorded by IISS; no other weapon category is as ubiquitous.

In the absence of a comprehensive dataset distinguishing weapon type, this section turns again to a closer analysis of individual conflicts to separate small arms conflict deaths from deaths by other causes. Doing so provides an estimate that between 60 and 90 per cent of direct conflict deaths—depending on the nature of the fighting—are caused by small arms and light weapons.

IISS monitored reports from eight conflicts in Asia, Africa, South America, and the Caucasus on a daily basis for four months (June to October 2004) and entered the number of incidents and reports, including weapons involved, into a database. The results are reported in Table 9.8. The data collection encountered all the underreporting difficulties associated with media reporting discussed above, especially in the cases of Nepal, Colombia, Ivory Coast, and Uganda, as well as the problem of state misrepresentation of data in Chechnya, Algeria, and Nepal.[26] In the absence of any evidence suggesting that the use of any particular weapon would be systematically over- or underreported, however, these difficulties do not appear to affect the analysis of the weapons type used.

In many cases, the type of weapon used was not explicitly indicated, but researchers were able to classify deaths based on available information concerning the nature of the incident and on knowledge of weapons availability, arsenals, and use in the country in question.[27] As Table 9.8 indicates, in the absence of specific information to the contrary, IISS researchers were able to classify the majority of incidents as small arms-related, with a high degree of confidence.[28] In all conflicts, however, it was difficult to make any distinction between small arms and light weapons use.

This data, while still tentative, indicates that small arms and light weapons together account for the majority of direct conflict deaths in these conflicts. Of the 1,364 recorded conflict deaths with specified causes in the eight conflicts, 1,225 could be attributed to small arms and light weapons—somewhat less than 90 per cent of specified cases. The significant number of unspecified cases makes it impossible to provide a precise estimate of the percentage of all conflict deaths caused by small arms. Yet even if none of the unspecified deaths were caused by small arms—a highly unlikely scenario—they would still account for more than 60 per cent of all direct conflict deaths.

Table 9.8   Cause of combat death in selected conflicts for the period from June to October 2004

Conflict	Total deaths counted	Deaths that could not be classified by weapon used	Deaths where weapon used could classified	Breakdown of classified deaths				
				Bladed	Small arms	Light weapons	Small arms and light weapons devices (IED)*	Improvised explosive
Aceh	194	0	194	1	178	15	193	0
Algeria	132	0	132	2	115	4	119	11
Burundi	244	0	244	0	244	0	244	0
Colombia	180	107	73	0	13	35	48	25
Ivory Coast	27	26	1	0	1	0	1	0
Nepal	274	1	273	0	234	0	234	39
Russia/Chechnya	558	343	215	0	153	12	165	50
Uganda	233	1	232	11	221	0	221	0
Total	**1,842**	**478**	**1,364**	**14**	**1,159**	**66**	**1,225**	**125**

*Note: IED include explosives, car bombs, and suicide bombers.
Source: IISS (2004)

Another finding emerges clearly from a review of these eight conflicts: although small arms are an important feature of all of them, their use in relation to other weapon types is highly variable even within the same conflict. In Iraq, a survey found that all civilians killed by non-coalition forces were killed by a firearm, while only five per cent of civilians killed by coalition forces were killed by use of a gun, while a large proportion died from bombardments (Lafta et al., 2005). Iraqi combatants, in contrast, died more frequently in direct combat—and thus from small arms—than from air attacks (Conetta, 2003, p. 37). The factors that affect the prevalence of use of different weapons is an important area of further study, but likely influences are the intensity of fighting, the availability of different weapons types, the nature of combatants (state armies or non-state actors), and tactics (whether there is a policy of targeting civilians, for example). For these reasons, it seems inappropriate to construct a global 'average' of the number or percentage of conflict deaths that are attributable to small arms. Such an average conceals the large variation found between different conflicts.

> The use of small arms in relation to other weapon types is highly variable.

Further, such accounting necessarily omits the other ways that small arms contribute to direct conflict deaths—such as when they are not used to kill but to empower those who handle them. In the 1994 Rwandan genocide, small arms were used to round up and forcibly hold civilians, who were then killed primarily with blades (machetes). That the guns were instrumental in those killings is clear, for without them, the coercion necessary to detain large numbers of people would not have been possible.[29]

This example demonstrates the complexity of trying to unpack the use of small arms and light weapons in conflict. It is equally challenging to come to firm conclusions about indirect deaths, as shown below.

Box 9.4   Operation Iraqi Freedom: UK and US combat deaths

Media outlets reported regularly on the number of US and UK servicemen and women killed in Iraq in 2003-04, based on daily central command statements. These reports, which are publicly available, often described the context of each death, including how the victim was killed. Examples of typical reports include: 'died when he came under small arms fire while conducting combat operations in Falluja' or 'killed when a car bomb detonated near his convoy in Baghdad' (CNN, 2004). The Small Arms Survey conducted a detailed survey of these reports for the six-month period of 20 March to 15 October 2003.[30]

Injured US Marines lie on stretchers after an offensive in Fallujah, Iraq, in November 2004.

This data shows that casualty reports are less detailed during more intensive phases of conflict,[31] which is consistent with the hypothesis that reporting in general declines in quality as fighting intensifies. During the heaviest period of fighting, most reports stop providing weapon type and become vague (e.g. 'died as a result of enemy action'). This trend is highlighted through a comparison of the causes of death in combat between the most intensive period, from 20 March to 30 April 2003, and the months that followed the official end of the combat, from 1 May to 15 October 2003. During the first period, in which about half of all combat-related deaths occurred (109 of 220), the cause of death was specified in only 17 per cent of the reports. As hostilities became less frequent after the combat was declared over on 1 May 2003, reporting improved and cause of death was specified in more than 80 per cent of all reviewed cases.[32]

While the data are not specific enough to estimate the prevalence of small arms-related deaths for the first period, the survey indicated that between 20 March and 15 October 2003, small arms were the single most deadly type of weapon group for US and UK soldiers in Iraq, resulting in 55 per cent of all specified combat deaths.

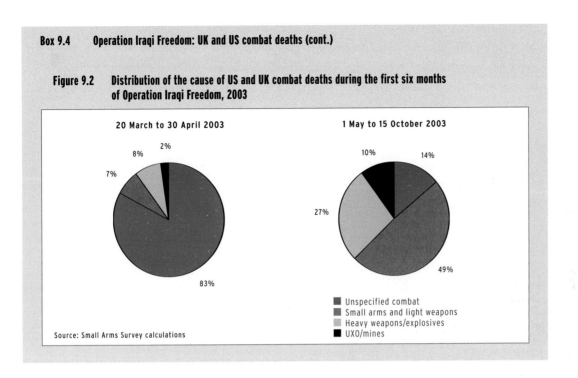

Box 9.4   Operation Iraqi Freedom: UK and US combat deaths (cont.)

Figure 9.2   Distribution of the cause of US and UK combat deaths during the first six months of Operation Iraqi Freedom, 2003

20 March to 30 April 2003

2%
8%
7%
83%

1 May to 15 October 2003

10%
14%
27%
49%

■ Unspecified combat
■ Small arms and light weapons
■ Heavy weapons/explosives
■ UXO/mines

Source: Small Arms Survey calculations

COUNTING INDIRECT CONFLICT DEATHS

Detailed demographic and epidemiological studies can be used to calculate the number of direct combat deaths. But their primary goal is usually to assess the indirect deaths or excess mortality that results from violent conflict or other forms of social disruption, such as migration, genocide, or natural disasters.[33] These indirect deaths are 'caused' in a narrow sense by specific factors, such as higher infant and maternal mortality triggered by a lack of basic health care, or widespread disease mortality resulting from malnutrition, starvation, and limited access to clean water. But in a broader, counterfactual sense, these deaths would not have occurred in the absence of violent conflict, and hence the conflict itself is a cause of these indirect deaths.

That small arms play a leading role in indirect conflict deaths is also certain. But how are they—or any other tool of war—implicated in indirect conflict mortality? Undoubtedly, the widespread proliferation and misuse of small arms during and after conflict reduces the ability of governments, NGOs, and aid agencies to maintain or restore essential services, in addition to establishing a semblance of law and order (Beasley, Buchanan, and Muggah, 2003; Small Arms Survey, 2002, pp. 155–201). Two-thirds of humanitarian aid workers surveyed in a large-scale survey (of 17 humanitarian agencies in more than 90 countries) reported that at least 25 per cent or more of their target population of vulnerable groups were inaccessible due to the perceived availability of small arms and light weapons (Muggah and Buchanan, 2005). The continued suppression of these services due to small arms-related insecurity must therefore be considered a factor in the resulting preventable deaths.

Small arms proliferation and misuse also continues to be a significant cause of direct deaths in post-conflict settings, where violence levels can linger at elevated levels after the fighting has stopped (POST-CONFLICT).

Quantifying the number of indirect conflict deaths and their relationship to direct deaths in violent conflicts is difficult. A limited amount of data based on epidemiological surveys exists for central and West Africa, Iraq, Sudan, Kosovo, and Cambodia. These studies, using a variety of methods, have generated population figures and crude mortality rates (CMR) for populations affected by conflicts in those regions.[34] By comparing these rates to region-wide

Table 9.9 Excess mortality in selected recent violent conflicts

	Expected CMR (deaths per 1,000 people per month)	Documented CMR	Excess CMR	Ratio of 'documented to expected' CMR
Kosovo, 1998-99[1]	0.31[16]	0.72[1]	0.41	2.3
Iraq[2]	0.4[17]	1.0[2]	0.6	2.5
Eastern DRC, January 1999-May 2000	1.3-1.5	5.2[3]	3.7-3.9	3.5-4.0
Eastern DRC, 2001	1.3-1.5	5.4[4]	3.9-4.1	3.6-4.2
Eastern DRC, 2002	1.3-1.5	3.5[5]	2.0-2.2	2.3-2.7
Eastern DRC, 2003-04	1.3-1.5	2.3[6]	0.8-1.0	1.5-1.8
Burundi, Bujumbura Province, 2001	1.3-1.5	3.6[7]	2.1-2.3	2.4-2.8
Burundi, Bujumbura Province, 2002-03	1.3-1.5	3.6[8]	2.1-2.3	2.4-2.8
Burundi, Muyinga Province, 2002	1.3-1.5	3.4[9]	1.9-2.1	2.3-2.6
Burundi, Makamba Province, 2001-02	1.3-1.5	2.0[10]	0.5-0.7	1.3-1.5
Congo-Brazzaville, Pool Region, 2003	1.3-1.5	2.9[11]	1.4-1.6	1.9-2.2
Sierra Leone, Kenema District, 2001	1.3-1.5	3.7[12]	2.2-2.4	2.5-2.8
Sudan, North Darfur, 2004	1.3-1.5	4.4[13]	2.9-3.1	2.9-3.4
Sudan, West Darfur, 2004	1.3-1.5	8.9[14]	7.4-7.6	5.9-6.9
Sudan, Kalma Camp South Darfur, 2004	1.3-1.5	11.4[15]	9.9-10.1	7.6-8.8

Sources and notes:
1 Spiegel and Salama (2000, p. 2204).
2 Roberts et al. (2004, pp. 1857, 1860). Based on the calculation that 142 recorded deaths (including Fallujah) / by the sample population of 7,868 / by the recall period of 17.8 months (19 March 2003 to mid-September 2004) *1000 = 1.0.
3 IRC (2000, pp. 1, 6). Based on the calculation that 606 recorded deaths (p. 1) / by the sample population of 7,339 (p. 1) / by the recall period of 16 months (January 1999 to May 2000 pp. 1, 6) * 1000 = 5.2.
4 IRC (2003b, p. 12). The CMR here refers to the period August 1999 to April 2001.
5 IRC (2003b, p. 12).
6 IRC (2004a, p. 10).
7 IRC (2002a, p. 1).
8 IRC (2003a, p. 3).
9 IRC (2002b, p. 2).
10 IRC (2002c, p. 1).
11 IRC (2004b, p. 3).
12 IRC (2001b, p. 3).
13 WHO/EPIET (2004. p. 10). Based on the calculation that 82 recorded deaths / by the sample population of 9,274 / by the recall period of 2 months (15 June to 15 August 2004) *1000 = 4.4.
14 WHO/EPIET (2004. p. 16). Based on the calculation that 142 recorded deaths / by the sample population of 7.996 / by the recall period 2 months (15 June to 15 August 2004) *1000 = 8.9.
15 WHO/EPIET (2004. p. 22). Based on the calculation that 80 recorded deaths / by the sample population of 3.506 / by the recall period of 2 months (15 June to 15 August 2004)*1000 = 11.4.
16 Spiegel and Salama (2000, p. 2205).
17 Roberts et al. (2004, pp .1857, 1860). Based on the calculation that 46 recorded deaths in pre-invasion Iraq / by the sample population of 7,438 / by recall period of 14.6 months (January 2002 to 18 March 2003) *1000 = 0.4.

average crude mortality rates, or to pre-conflict data for the same area (when available), analysts can estimate excess mortality due to violent conflict.[35] CMR is often expressed in terms of deaths per 1,000 population per month. For acute emergencies, it can be calculated as deaths per 10,000 population per day.

CMR are usually higher during violent conflict than during peacetime, but there is considerable variation in the excess mortality in different conflicts. Table 9.9 provides a range of observed CMR for recent conflicts, or conflict years. In sub-Saharan Africa the CMR for populations not affected by violent conflict is estimated to be 1.3–1.5 deaths per 1,000 per month.[36] The observed CMR in violent conflict zones, however, has ranged from 2.0 (Burundi, Makamba Province, in 2001–02) to 11.4 (in the Kalma refugee camp in South Darfur in 2004). The median observation is a CMR of 3.6 deaths per thousand population per month, or more than double the crude mortality rate for areas not affected by violent conflict.

A useful comparative indicator of the severity of a conflict or a humanitarian crisis is the ratio of 'documented to expected' CMR. During the conflict in Kosovo in 1998–99, the crude mortality rate was 2.3 times greater than rates prior to conflict; in Iraq 2.5 times the prior rate. In the African cases, excess mortality ranged from 1.5 to 8.8 times the expected mortality rate. The highest rates were found in eastern DRC in 1999–2001, and in parts of Sudan in 2004. These numbers highlight the generalized impact that violent conflict has on an entire population, especially vulnerable groups, far beyond just the direct combatant deaths.

Table 9.10   Ratio of direct to indirect conflict deaths in selected recent violent conflicts

	Direct deaths as a percentage of excess deaths	Indirect deaths as a percentage of excess deaths
Kosovo, 1998-99	100.0[1]	0.0
Iraq, post-2003 invasion	84.9	15.1
Cambodia, 1975-79	50.0	50.0
Eastern DRC, 2000	16.5	83.5
Eastern DRC, 2001	12.2	87.8
Eastern DRC, 2002	2.7	97.3
Eastern DRC, 2003-04	5.2	94.8
Congo-Brazzaville, Pool Region, 2003	18.2	81.8
Burundi, Bujumbura Province, 2001	19.7	80.3
Burundi,Bujumbura Province, 2002	40.5	59.5
Burundi, Muyinga Province, 2002	3.4	96.6
Burundi, Makamba Province, 2002	22.7	77.3
Sierra Leone, Kenema District, 2001	5.0	95.0
Sudan, West Darfur, 2004	14.4	85.6
Sudan, North Darfur, 2004	29.6	70.4
Sudan, Kalma Camp, South Darfur, 2004	11.6	88.4
Zalingei, Darfur, 2004	62.8	37.2
Murnei, Darfur, 2004	87.0	13.0
Niertiti, Darfur, 2004	38.5	61.5
El Geneina, Darfur, 2004	10.5	89.5
Median, sub-Saharan Africa	**23.6**	**76.4**

Sources: See Appendix 9.1.

Note:

1 In Kosovo, the number of violent deaths recorded in the sample population actually exceeded the number of calculated excess deaths (both direct and indirect) in the conflict. This may be a statistical artefact due to the small numbers used to calculate ratios, but it also reflects the fact that intentional injury was a cause of death in Kosovo even before the most intense phase of the conflict measured here. Some direct deaths may therefore have been included in the number of expected deaths for the population.

The final piece of the conflict death puzzle is the relationship between direct and indirect conflict deaths. By examining what we know about excess mortality and direct deaths in specific conflicts, we can begin to shed light on this question. Available evidence shows a wide disparity in the proportion of direct and indirect deaths in any given conflict. Based on information from a limited number of conflicts, summarized in Table 9.10, the two extremes seem to be represented by the Kosovo and Iraq conflicts on one hand, and sub-Saharan conflicts on the other. In Iraq, almost 85 per cent of conflict deaths can be directly attributed to armed violence, and in Kosovo all the reported excess deaths are from violence. In sub-Saharan Africa, by contrast, a median figure of 23 per cent of total deaths are direct conflict deaths—the vast majority result from a higher incidence of disease.

Why is there such a great disparity between different conflicts regarding the proportion of direct and indirect deaths? Although this is a new area of inquiry, two hypotheses can be suggested:

Pre-existing health care systems, disease patterns, and the extent of humanitarian response explain differences in ratios. As noted by Spiegel and Salama (2000, p. 2207), infectious diseases commonly associated with malnutrition are the largest cause of mortality during conflicts in less-developed countries. This may explain the observed differ-

> There is a large disparity between different conflicts regarding the proportion of direct and indirect deaths.

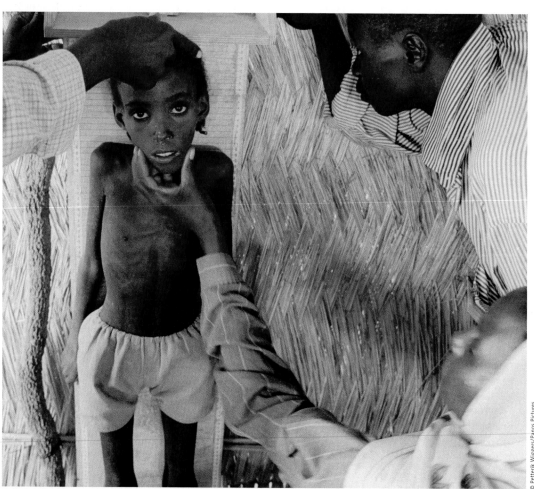

Medical staff examine an eight-year-old girl who is suffering from malnourishment in a Sudanese IDP camp in June 2004. The girl and her family fled their village after Janjaweed Arab militants burnt it down.

© Petterik Wiggers/Panos Pictures

ences between sub-Saharan Africa and Kosovo and Iraq. Both Kosovo's and Iraq's health care systems were better developed before the conflict than those of the sub-Saharan countries presented here. In addition, the period of widespread violence in Kosovo was comparatively short, and the humanitarian response of the international community was more vigorous and covered a greater share of the population than has been the case for most of the populations affected by conflicts in sub-Saharan Africa. The relatively small share of indirect deaths in Iraq compared to African countries may also reflect the nature and relatively concentrated levels of violence in Iraq.[37]

Direct and indirect crude mortality rates change over the duration of the conflict and during the post-conflict phase. It appears that when violence breaks out, direct mortality rates increase rapidly as people are killed; they are followed by an increase in indirect mortality rates. As conflict subsides and violence is brought under control, direct mortality rates decline rapidly. Indirect mortality rates also decline, but somewhat more slowly, and they remain elevated for an unspecified time (Ghobarah, Huth, and Russett, 2001). There is a limited amount of data to demonstrate this point, but the three surveys carried out in DRC between 2000 and 2003 support this hypothesis, showing how the lingering effects of violent conflict are manifest in high levels of excess mortality—indirect deaths—even after the violence has ebbed. Figure 9.3 charts how, in the eastern part of DRC, both direct and indirect death rates have declined since 2000, but direct death rates have fallen much more significantly (approaching zero in 2003) than indirect death rates, which remain worryingly high. Subsequent outbreaks of violence in 2003–04 suggest that mortality rates may have climbed again.

Figure 9.3   Decline in indirect and direct deaths in DRC based on IRC studies

	2000	2001	2002	2003
indirect	824,000	849,000	337,500	281,400
direct	103,000	88,000	5,500	4,600

Sources and notes:
2000: IRC (2000, p. 1). This reports covers the period January 1999-April 2000 and quotes a figure of 77,000 deaths per month as the total death toll. Direct deaths were reported to be 11.1 per cent of the total deaths in 2000 (IRC, 2003b, p. 6).
2001: IRC (2001a, p. 3). Based on 2.5 million deaths over 32 months, or 78,125 deaths per month. In 2001, the reported percentage of direct conflict deaths was 9.4 (IRC, 2003b, p. 6).
2002: IRC (2003b, pp. 6, 13). In 2002, with a decline in fighting, the proportion of direct deaths also declined to 1.6 per cent of the total.
2003: IRC (2004a, p. 11). Based on 500,000 deaths in 16 months, or more than 31,000 excess deaths per month, of which 77 per cent were in eastern DRC. The proportion of direct deaths in eastern DRC remained at 1.7 per cent (IRC, 2004a, p. 17, Figure 5).

The persistence of high levels of indirect conflict deaths after the end of the violent phase of a conflict is an important problem for policy-makers concerned with humanitarian aid and reconstruction. It is often far more time-consuming to restore health infrastructure, services, and security than to negotiate a ceasefire, or even demobilize combatants. States that have been weakened by long-term violent conflicts generally lack the resources and capacity to address these challenges, and progress is not made until long after a conflict has ended (Small Arms Survey, 2003, pp. 125–67). The disruption and increased mortality that persists at the end of a violent conflict needs to be taken seriously into account when planning long-term reconstruction and development programmes.

Assembling the puzzle: global direct and indirect conflict deaths

Without additional information or very general estimates, the figures given above cannot be easily used to construct an overall global estimate of indirect conflict deaths. What is required is some or all of the following information:

- a comprehensive and up-to-date inventory of ongoing conflicts;
- reliable and standardized figures for direct conflict deaths (either raw or adjusted, if necessary, by an appropriate multiplier);
- a good estimate (denominator) of the affected population (which is usually not the total population of a country, but rather of a conflict zone within a country, or spanning an international frontier);
- a baseline pre-conflict expected CMR for the affected population;
- a means of estimating the appropriate ratio of 'documented to expected' CMR, which takes into account such factors as the intensity of the conflict or the coverage and quality of health and other basic services.

Such information is scarce, but a robust model based on existing partial information could be developed. The enormous variations between the ratios of direct and indirect deaths observed in sub-Saharan Africa highlight the need to develop estimation techniques that consider factors of health care provisions in conjunction with conflict intensity. It might be particularly useful in early warning systems, and for alerting the international community to the relative severity of a humanitarian crisis, beyond the impressionistic information conveyed by media accounts or other informants.

Of all the regions affected by armed conflict, sub-Saharan Africa will likely provide the most important indications of how direct and indirect deaths fit together. Not all necessary data points are yet available, however. Among the missing data are CMR estimates for countries not affected by conflict; an average CMR for conflict-affected areas; and accurate population counts for both conflict and post-conflict settings.

But even when this data falls into place, an acceptably precise global count of indirect conflict deaths may remain elusive. Although based only on two recent conflicts, it appears likely that the ratio of indirect to direct deaths is lower in other parts of the world than in sub-Saharan Africa. There are many reasons for this, but one is the ability (or inability) of governments, international organizations, and NGOs to access affected populations and to provide basic services and assistance even during violent conflicts.

It is thus not yet possible to generate an annual global total for conflict deaths. In retrospect, however, the widely circulated estimate of 300,000 annual small arms conflict deaths (Small Arms Survey, 2001) may be too high for recent years. Yet it would be reasonable to assume that overall conflict deaths would reach well beyond 300,000 if indirect deaths were included. Certainly such a figure is within the range suggested by the available evidence and the ratio for sub-Saharan Africa. The true number of conflict dead may of course be higher, but it is not likely to be much lower.

It is important, however, *not* to claim that small arms and light weapons 'caused' all these deaths. As noted above, small arms and light weapons are directly responsible for 60–90 per cent of direct conflict deaths, but they cannot be considered responsible in the same way for indirect deaths—no individual weapon 'causes' an indirect death. Instead, analysts should apply the same counterfactual criterion that is used in epidemiological studies. In the absence of widespread proliferation and misuse of small arms and light weapons, what would be the level of excess mortality (indirect conflict deaths)? It would be much, much lower than has been witnessed in recent wars. From a policy-making perspective, this conclusion is perhaps more important than any statistic.

The distinction between direct and indirect deaths has enormous implications for policy-makers. Knowing the main causes of excess mortality in conflict will help them tailor aid according to the most urgent needs.

For people affected by violent conflict, however, it matters little whether the death of a child or partner was caused by a bullet, or by disease or starvation because the family was forced to flee its home. It is therefore important—as the epidemiological studies stress—to count all deaths from violent conflict, and not simply to focus on those caused by the use of violent means on combatants or civilians.

> Small arms and light weapons are directly responsible for 60–90 per cent of direct conflict deaths.

CONCLUSION

Innovative research and data-gathering in recent years has greatly improved our understanding of how many people are killed in conflict, and how they die. This chapter has provided an overview of different methods of calculating conflict deaths—both for individual conflicts and for global annual estimates. It finds that the datasets based on media accounts—even those that use continuous monitoring technologies—probably underestimate the number of people killed directly in conflict by a factor of between two and four.

More importantly, the evidence is strong that in most conflicts in the developing world, the number of indirect conflict deaths greatly exceeds direct conflict deaths. Many publicly cited estimates do not accurately count those who die indirectly, even though in places such as DRC or Sudan, they greatly outnumber those who die by violent means. A full picture of the human costs—in terms of lives lost—in contemporary conflicts must include indirect as well direct conflict deaths.

Small arms and light weapons are also a big part of the problem; this research suggests that small arms are responsible for 60–90 per cent of direct conflict deaths, and that they play an analogous role in causing indirect conflict deaths.

Going beyond existing knowledge will require not just the refinement of estimation techniques and data collection, but serious field work and studies designed to provide comparative data on the intensity and duration of violent conflicts, on weapons use patterns, and on the reliability of reporting (due to the remoteness of conflict zones or lack of access by the international media). The practical utility and policy relevance of such information is clear, for humanitarian agencies and relief organizations, conflict mediation and resolution efforts, post-conflict disarmament, demobilization, and reintegration programmes, and reconstruction and development efforts.

Data limitations also make it difficult to conclude there has been a recent decline in armed conflict deaths, although the *number* of active armed conflicts seems to have declined (Marshall and Gurr, 2003, p. 12). Improvements in the way media reports are collected and assessed in databases, and greater care in the use of official estimates, may have inadvertently exaggerated the decline in conflict deaths, since many previous figures appear to have included direct and indirect deaths in an indiscriminate way. Today, most data sources only include direct deaths. Further, the apparent decline in conflict deaths may also be only a short-term phenomenon; the overall level of global violence has witnessed periodic spikes and low periods since 1816, but the overall level of conflict mortality per 1,000 people has not varied greatly over the long term (Sarkees, Wayman, and Singer, 2003, p. 66). Despite certain progress in reducing the incidence of inter-state war and in resolving some long-standing conflicts, looming demographic crises and resource scarcities in many parts of the world mean that researchers should not conclude that the era of violent conflict is ending.

Finally, the human impacts of conflict go far beyond direct and indirect mortality. Many of those who survive will bear non-fatal injuries, disability, economic privation, and psychological trauma for the rest of their lives. Thousands will lose a family member, a parent, a friend. Hundreds of thousands will be displaced from their homes and communities for years, possibly forever. Violence does not only destroy lives, but also infrastructure, social capital, and livelihoods. All of these long-term effects warrant greater attention and require better analysis and data from researchers.

APPENDIX 9.1   DIRECT AND INDIRECT CONFLICT MORTALITY RATIOS

	Total Deaths		Direct Deaths		Indirect Deaths	
	Total deaths recorded	Estimated excess deaths in sample population	Recorded in the sample population	% of excess deaths	Estimated indirect deaths among excess deaths	% of excess deaths
Kosovo, 1998-99[1]	105	62	67	108.1	-5	-8.1
Iraq, post-2003 invasion[2]	142	86	73	84.9	13	15.1
Cambodia, 1975-79[3]	n/a	n/a	n/a	50.0	n/a	50.0
Eastern DRC, 2000[4]	606	419	69	16.5	350	83.5
Eastern DRC, 2001[5]	894	690	84	12.2	606	87.8
Eastern DRC, 2002[6]	443	256	7	2.7	249	97.3
Eastern DRC, 2003-04[7]	3174	1044	54	5.2	990	94.8
Congo-Brazzaville, Pool Region, 2003[8]	47	22	4	18.2	18	81.8
Burundi, Bujumbura Province, 2002[9]	214	127	25	19.7	102	80.3
Burundi, Bujumbura Province, 2003[10]	272	163	66	40.5	97	59.5
Burundi, Muyinga Province, 2002[11]	106	59	2	3.4	57	96.6
Burundi, Makamba Province, 2002[12]	84	22	5	22.7	17	77.3
Sierra Leone, Kenema District, 2001[13]	197	119	6	5	113	95
Sudan, West Darfur, 2004[14]	142	118	17	14.4	101	85.6
Sudan, North Darfur, 2004[15]	82	54	16	29.6	38	70.4
Sudan, Kalma Camp, South Darfur, 2004[16]	80	69	8	11.6	61	88.4
Zalingei, Darfur, 2004[17]	100	78	49	62.8	29	37.2
Murnei, Darfur, 2004[18]	322	276	240	87.0	36	13.0

	Total Deaths		Direct Deaths		Indirect Deaths	
	Total deaths recorded	Estimated excess deaths in sample population	Recorded in the sample population	% of excess deaths	Estimated indirect deaths among excess deaths	% of excess deaths
Niertiti, Darfur, 2004[19]	116	78	30	38.5	48	61.5
El Geneina, Darfur, 2004[20]	115	105	11	10.5	94	89.5
Median Sub-Saharan Africa				**23.6**		**76.4**

Sources and notes:

1 Spiegel and Salama (2000, pp. 2205). Based on the calculation that with an expected mortality rate of 0.31 per 1,000 per month, 43 deaths would be expected to occur within the sample population of 8,605 during the recall period of 16 months.

2 Roberts et al. (2004, p. 1860). Based on the calculation that with an expected mortality rate of 0.4 per 1,000 per month, 56 deaths would be expected to occur within the sample population of 7,868 during the recall period of 17.8 months.

3 Data for Cambodia is based on demographic reconstruction and estimates the total number of violent deaths between 1975 and 1979 at 1.1 million, or about half of estimated excess deaths (Heuveline, 2001, p. 125).

4 IRC (2000, pp. 1, 3; 2003b, p. 6). Based on the calculation that with an expected mortality rate of 1.5 per 1,000 per month, 187 deaths would be expected to occur within the sample population of 7,339 during the recall period of 17 months. The total number of deaths of 606 has been taken from IRC (2000, p. 1). The figure of 624 presented in IRC (2003b, p. 6) has not been used here; only the number of violent deaths (69) has been taken into account.

5 IRC (2001a, pp. 8-11; 2003b, p. 6). Based on the calculation that with an expected mortality rate of 1.5 per 1,000 per month, 204 deaths would be expected to occur within the sample population of 11,347 during the recall period of 12 months.

6 IRC (2003b, pp. 5-6). Based on the calculation that with an expected mortality rate of 1.5 per 1,000 per month, 187 deaths would be expected to occur within the sample population of 13,425 during the recall period of 9.3 months.

7 IRC (2004a, pp. 11, 13, 17). Based on the calculation that with an expected mortality rate of 1.5 per 1,000 per month, 2,130 deaths would be expected to occur within the sample population of 88,746 during the recall period of 16 months.

8 IRC (2004b, p. 7). Based on the calculation that with an expected mortality rate of 1.5 per 1,000 per month, 25 deaths would be expected to occur within the sample population of 1,508 during the recall period of 11 months.

9 IRC (2002a, p. 1). Based on the calculation that with an expected mortality rate of 1.5 per 1,000 per month, 87 deaths would be expected to occur within the sample population of 2,822 during the recall period of 20.5 months.

10 IRC (2003a, pp. 3, 17, 18). Based on the calculation that with an expected mortality rate of 1.5 per 1,000 per month, 109 deaths would be expected to occur within the sample population of 3,144 during the recall period of 23.1 months.

11 IRC (2002b, p. 2). Based on the calculation that with an expected mortality rate of 1.5 per 1,000 per month, 47 deaths would be expected to occur within the sample population of 2,068 during the recall period of 15.2 months.

12 IRC (2002c, p. 1). Based on the calculation that with an expected mortality rate of 1.5 per 1,000 per month, 62 deaths would be expected to occur within the sample population of 2,311 during the recall period of 18 months.

13 IRC (2001b, pp. 5, 10). Based on the calculation that with an expected mortality rate of 1.5 per 1,000 per month, 119 deaths would be expected to occur within the sample population of 4,340 during the recall period of 12 months.

14 WHO/EPIET (2004, pp. 16, 17). Based on the calculation that with an expected mortality rate of 1.5 per 1,000 per month, 24 deaths would be expected to occur within the sample population of 7,996 during the recall period of 2 months.

15 WHO/EPIET (2004, pp. 10, 11). Based on the calculation that with an expected mortality rate of 1.5 per 1,000 per month, 28 deaths would be expected to occur within the sample population of 9,274 during the recall period of 2 months.

16 WHO/EPIET (2004. pp. 22, 23). Based on the calculation that with an expected mortality rate of 1.5 per 1,000 per month, 11 deaths would be expected to occur within the sample population of 3,506 during the recall period of 2 months.

17 Depoortere et al. (2004, pp. 1316, 1317, 1318). Based on the calculation that with an expected mortality rate of 1.5 per 1,000 per months, 22 deaths would be expected to occur within the sample population of 2,386 during the recall period of 6.1 months (183 days).

18 Depoortere et al (2004, p. 1316, 1317, 1318). Based on the calculation that with an expected mortality rate of 1.5 per 1,000 per months, 46 deaths would be expected to occur within the sample population of 4,754 during the recall period of 6.4 months (193 days).

19 Depoortere et al. (2004, pp. 1316, 1317, 1318). Based on the calculation that with an expected mortality rate of 1.5 per 1,000 per months, 38 deaths would be expected to occur within the sample population of 5,188 during the recall period of 4.8 months (145 days).

20 Depoortere et al. (2004, pp. 1316, 1317, 1318). Based on the calculation that with an expected mortality rate of 1.5 per 1,000 per months, 10 deaths would be expected to occur within the sample population of 5,191 during the recall period of 1.3 months (39 days).

259

LIST OF ABBREVIATIONS

AAAS	American Association for the Advancement of Science
ABA	American Bar Association
CDC	Centers for Disease Control and Prevention (United States)
CMR	Crude mortality rate
CoW	Correlates of War Project
DIA	Defense Intelligence Agency (United States)
DRC	Democratic Republic of the Congo
HSR	*Human Security Report*
ICRC	International Committee of the Red Cross
ICTY	International Criminal Tribunal for the Former Yugoslavia
IISS	International Institute for Strategic Studies
IRC	International Rescue Committee
MSE	Multiple systems estimate
PHR	Physicians for Human Rights
UCDP	Uppsala Conflict Data Program
UXO	Unexploded ordnance
WHO	World Health Organization
WHOSIS	World Health Organization Statistical Information System

ENDNOTES

[1] The estimate of deaths from violent causes is based on the Small Arms Survey's analysis of raw data collected in this study. The collection of this data was partly sponsored by the Small Arms Survey project.

[2] See, for example, Florquin and Berman (2005).

[3] A critique of this approach is provided by Fearon (2004).

[4] CoW used different battle-death thresholds for inter-state, extra-state, and intra-state wars. Inter-state wars were counted only if they had a minimum of 1,000 battle fatalities among all of the states involved; extra-state wars required an annual average of 1,000 battle deaths; intra-state wars counted civilian as well as military deaths (Small and Singer, 1982, pp. 55–56, 213; Sarkees, 2000, p. 129).

[5] The UCDP database contains specific data for the period since 1989 and less specific data for the period from 1946 to 1989. Since 2002 UCDP has also been collecting data specifically for the forthcoming *Human Security Report* (Mack et al., 2005), and its data was not publicly available at the time of writing (April 2005).

[6] This data will be published in the forthcoming *Human Security Report* (Mack et al., 2005).

[7] The following formula is used: mortality rate = [(the number of deaths in sample) / (the number of living in sample)] / (the recall period) x 1,000.

[8] Based on the calculation that 304 recorded deaths [82 (p. 10) + 142 (p.16) + 80 (p. 22)] / sample population of 20,776 [9,274 (p. 10) + 7,996 (p. 16) + 3,506 (p. 22)] / recall period of 2 months (15 June–15 August.) * 1,000 = 7.3.

[9] Based on the calculation that 653 recorded deaths [100 + 322 + 116 + 115 (p. 1317)] / sample population of 17,519 [2,386 + 4,754 + 5,188 + 5191 (p.1317)] / average recall period of 4.7 months [6.1 (183 days) + 6.4 (193 days) + 4.8 (145 days) + 1.3 (39 days) (p. 1316) / 4] * 1,000 = 8.

[10] The source of this commonly accepted number is unclear but appears to have originated in July 2004 during an interview with the BBC, when a 'major aid agency' that wanted to remain anonymous criticized the UN resolution (BBC, 2004a). Aid agencies and human rights organizations have since quoted this figure (BBC, 2004b; 2004c; 2005a; 2005b).

[11] See, for example, HIIK (2005), VINC (2005), and Marshall (2005).

[12] In Afghanistan, data collection was carried out in 600 affected communities after interviewers had visited 747 communities suspected to have been subjected to air strikes or ground operations. It is 'considered to be close to a full census of the affected communities' (Benini and Moulton, 2004, p. 408). There are some concerns that numbers have been exaggerated by communities, but high correlation of victim counts among neighbouring communities make the authors reasonably certain that the data is reliable (Benini and Moulton, 2004, pp. 407–08).

[13] See Ball, Kobrak, and Spirer (1999), Ball et al. (2003), Laporte (1994), and Ball (2003).

[14] The sample size of epidemiological studies is usually sufficiently large to produce statistically reliable data on crude mortality rates;

however, the sample size is often not sufficiently large to produce a reliable estimate of direct conflict deaths, a sub-group of all deaths measured.

[15] See IRC (2000; 2001a; 2001b; 2002a; 2002b; 2002c; 2003a; 2003b; 2004a; 2004b), WHO/EPIET (2004), Roberts et al. (2004), and Spiegel and Salama (2000).

[16] This figure is found in the UCDP database in the comments concerning battle-related deaths for 1989 (UCDP, 2005).

[17] This theoretical maximum of 50,000 documented deaths in the Guatelmala conflict comes from addng the total number of entries on the three lists, and assuming that individuals do not appear in more than one database. Of course, duplication does occur. A further study documented 37,255 recorded deaths or disappearances (Ball, Kobrak, and Spirer, 1999, p. 8).

[18] The range offered is at the 95 per cent confidence interval. Of the 24,000 recorded reports of people dead or disappeared, 18,397 were specifically name (Ball et al., 2003, pp. 2–3).

[19] The total direct and indirect conflict death toll could be as high as 212,000 if the sample from Fallujah is included in the estimate. Because the study used random clusters based on the assumption that violence was spread equally across of Iraq, it is unclear whether to include estimates from the intensely violent Fallujah cluster. The decision to exclude it from the 100,000 estimate has significant implications not only for the overall figure, but for the direct deaths estimates that we might abstract from it.

[20] The figure of 13 violent deaths comes from a personal communication of the author with Les Roberts, who specified that 7 of the 21 violent deaths listed on p. 1860 were not war-related.

[21] Another possible explanation is that the search engines used for the databases were not as well established in 2000 and 2001, and so produced lower estimates. It is also possible that the epidemiological studies, which did not apply violence clustering techniques, produced inaccuracies (either overestimating in earlier periods or underestimating in 2002–03). The studies themselves do not discuss whether their sample clusters were representative of the violence.

[22] Personal communication.

[23] On average, the underreporting in IISS appears to be 2.6; for UCDP/HSR, the factor is 7.3. See Appendix 9.1.

[24] 43,000 * 2 and 27,000 * 4.

[25] This range is based on the assumption that between 2,224 and 8,880 deaths may have occurred every month since the conflict escalated in February 2003 (*11 months).

[26] The challenges encountered were particular to each conflict. In Nepal, the press tended to account for lives lost due to rebel attacks, but there was limited information on casualties caused by the military and by paramilitaries. In Colombia, many reports concentrated on one casualty, such as a leader of the Fuerzas Armadas Revolucionarias de Colombia (FARC), but failed to mention the deaths of his bodyguards. In Ivory Coast, the reporting was vague and nondescript and at times presented contradictory accounts. In Uganda, the lack of information was seen as the result of attempts to control information flow (IISS, 2004).

[27] For example, the Nepalese counter-insurgency is known to rely primarily on small arms and light weapons, and the Royal Nepalese Army uses heavy weapons and aerial attacks only in exceptional cases.

[28] For Colombia, where weapons use is more complex, such assumptions could not be made. In certain cases, bombs and explosions were recorded, but it was usually not possible to specify small arms fire.

[29] For more information, see Meijer and Verwimp (2005).

[30] The time span for the review was chosen to comprise five equal periods of six weeks, since the first period of Operation Iraqi Freedom—from its start on 20 March to 30 April—was six weeks.

[31] No quantitative measure for the intensity of conflict underlines these conclusions. These descriptions are based on news reports that speak of 'intensive phases' in general terms.

[32] There were 15 unspecified combat deaths of the total 111 counted for the period 1 May to 15 October 2003.

[33] See Reed and Keely (2001), Heuveline (1998; 2001), de Walque (2004), and Verwimp (2004).

[34] CMR can be defined as '[(the number of deaths in sample) / (the number of living in sample + 1/2 deaths in the sample population during the recall period – 1/2 those born during the recall period)] x (1,000) / (the recall period)', and is expressed as 'deaths/1,000 population/month' (IRC, 2003b, p. 3). This chapter follows this usage.

[35] Much of the existing data has been generated by surveys conducted by the IRC in central and West Africa; the CDC also carried out an epidemiological survey in Kosovo in 1999 (Spiegel and Salama, 2000), and WHO and the EPIET surveyed the situation in Darfur, Sudan (WHO/EPIET, 2004). Detailed data and sources are listed in the bibliography and in Appendix 1.

[36] There is no detailed data on crude mortality prior to the conflict. The only reference available is the expected mortality rate for Africa of 1.3 as reported by the UN Population Division (IRC, 2004b, p. 3). The IRC is more conservative by assuming an average expected mortality rate of 1.5 for sub-Saharan Africa (IRC, 2004a, p. iii).

[37] *The Lancet* mortality study on Iraq measured 93 violent deaths per 10,000 in the sample population. That is the fourth highest rate of violence of all countries studied. The highest rate was documented in Kalemie province in DRC (268 per 10,000 in the sample population) followed by Bujumbura Rural in Burundi in 2002 (210 per 10,000 in the sample population), and Moba in Katanga Province in eastern DRC in 2000 (99 per 10,000 in the sample population).

BIBLIOGRAPHY

ABA/AAAS (American Bar Association/American Association for the Advancement of Science). 2000. *Political Killings in Kosova/Kosovo: March–June 1999*. Central and East European Law Initiative (CEELI). Accessed 17 October 2004. <http://shr.aaas.org/kosovo/pk/politicalkillings.pdf>

Antiwar.com. 2005. 'Casualties in Iraq: The Human Cost of Occupation.' Accessed 19 January 2005. <http://www.antiwar.com/casualties/>

Bakshi, G. D. 1999. 'Yugoslavia: Air Strikes Test of the Air War Doctrine.' *Strategic Analysis: A monthly journal of the IDSA*. Vol. 23, No. 5. August 1999. Accessed 17 October 2004. <http://www.ciaonet.org/olj/sa/sa_99bag02.html>

Ball, Patrick. 1999. 'Making the Case: Investigating Large-Scale Human Rights Violations Using Information Systems and Data Analysis.' Report for the Guatemalan Commission for Historical Clarification. Accessed 10 April 2005. <http://shr.aaas.org/mtc/chap11.html>

—. 2003. 'Using Multiple System Estimation to Assess Mass Human Rights Violations: The Cases of Political Killings in Guatemala and Kosovo.' Proceedings of the meetings of the International Statistical Institute, Berlin.

— et al. 2003. *How many Peruvians have died? An estimate of the total number of victims killed or disappeared in the armed internal conflict between 1980 and 2000.* Washington, DC: AAAS. Accessed 17 October 2004.
<http://shr.aaas.org/hrdag/peru/aaas_peru_5.pdf>

— Paul Kobrak, and Herbert F. Spirer. 1999. *State Violence in Guatemala, 1960–1996: A Quantitative Reflection.* Washington, DC: AAAS and International Center for Human Rights Research. Accessed 14 October 2004.
<http://shr.aaas.org/guatemala/ciidh/qr/english/en_qr.pdf>

BBC (British Broadcasting Corporation). 1999. 'Q & A: Counting Kosovo's Dead.' *BBC News.* 12 November. Accessed 14 January 2005.
<http://news.bbc.co.uk/1/hi/world/europe/517168.stm>

—. 2004a. 'UN Sets Deadline for Sudan Action.' 30 July. Accessed 12 April 2005. <http://news.bbc.co.uk/2/hi/africa/3940547.stm>

—. 2004b. 'Deal to Boost Darfur Aid Supplies.' 2 September. Accessed 12 April 2005. <http://news.bbc.co.uk/2/hi/africa/3618450.stm>

—. 2004c. 'UN Attacks Darfur "Fear and Rape."' 25 September. Accessed 12 April 2005. <http://news.bbc.co.uk/2/hi/africa/3690232.stm>

—. 2005a. 'How Many Have Died in Darfur?' 16 February. Accessed 12 April 2005. <http://news.bbc.co.uk/2/hi/africa/4268733.stm>

—. 2005b. 'UN's Darfur Death Estimate Soars.' 14 March. Accessed 12 April 2005. <http://newswww.bbc.net.uk/2/hi/africa/4349063.stm>

Beasley, Ryan, Cate Buchanan, and Robert Muggah. 2003. *In the Line of Fire: Surveying the Perceptions of Humanitarian and Development Personnel of the Impacts of Small Arms and Light Weapons.* Geneva: Small Arms Survey and the Centre for Humanitarian Dialogue. July.

Benini, Aldo A. and Lawrence H. Moulton. 2004. 'Civilian Victims in an Asymmetrical Conflict: Operation Enduring Freedom, Afghanistan.' *Journal of Peace Research,* Vol. 41, No. 4, pp. 403–22.

Capie, David. 2004. 'Armed groups, weapons availability and misuse: an overview of the issues and options for action.' Background paper for meeting organized by the Centre for Humanitarian Dialogue in Bamako, Mali, 25 May 2004. Accessed 2 March 2005.
<http://www.hdcentre.org/datastore/Armed_groups_briefing.pdf>

CIJ (Coalition for International Justice). 2005. 'New Analysis Claims Darfur Deaths Near 400,000.' Washington, DC: CIJ. 21 April.
<http://www.cij.org>

CNN (Cable News Network). 2004. 'Forces: US & Coalition/Casualties.' Accessed 16 November 2004.
<http://cnn.org/SPECIALS/2003/iraq/forces/casualties/2004.11.html>

Collier, Paul and Anke Hoeffler. 2004. 'Greed and Grievance in Civil War.' *Oxford Economic Paper 56,* pp. 563–95. Oxford: Oxford University Press.

Conetta, Carl. 2002a. *Strange Victory: A Critical Appraisal of Operation Enduring Freedom and the Afghanistan War.* Cambridge, MA: Commonwealth Institute Project on Defense Alternatives Research Monograph No. 6. 30 January. Accessed 24 August 2004.
<http://www.comw.org/pda/0201strangevic.pdf>

—. 2002b. *Operation Enduring Freedom: Why a Higher Rate of Civilian Bombing Casualties.* Cambridge, MA: Commonwealth Institute Project on Defense Alternatives Briefing Report No. 11. 18 January, revised 24 January. Accessed 17 January 2005.
<http://www.comw.org/pda/0201oef.html>

—. 2003. *The Wages of War: Iraqi Combatant and Noncombatant Fatalities in the 2003 Conflict.* Cambridge, MA: Commonwealth Institute Project on Defense Alternatives Research Monograph No. 8. 20 October. Accessed 4 March 2005.
<http://www.comw.org/pda/fulltext/0310rm8.pdf>

—. 2004. *Disappearing the Dead: Iraq, Afghanistan, and the Idea of 'New Warfare.'* Cambridge, MA: Commonwealth Institute Project on Defense Alternatives Research Monograph No. 9. 18 February. Accessed 7 March 2005.
<http://www.comw.org/pda/fulltext/0402rm9.pdf>

CoW (Correlates of War). 2005. Project Web page. Urbana, IL: University of Illinois at Urbana-Champaign. Accessed 12 April 2005.
<http://www.correlatesofwar.org/>

DeMars, William. 2000. 'War and Mercy in Africa.' *World Policy Journal.* Vol. 17, No. 2, Summer. Accessed 11 April 2005.
<http://www.worldpolicy.org/journal/demars.html>

Depoortere, Evelyn et al. 2004. 'Violence and mortality in West Darfur, Sudan (2003–04): epidemiological evidence from four surveys.' *The Lancet.* Vol. 364. 9 October, pp. 1315–20. MSF report accessed 18 April 2005.
<http://www.msf.fr/documents/base/2004-10-01-Depoortere.pdf>

Dummett, Mark. 2002. '"Massacre" in DR Congo.' *BBC News World Edition.* 25 May. Accessed 16 March 2005.
<http://news.bbc.co.uk/2/hi/africa/2008359.stm>

Eriksson, Mikael, Peter Wallensteen, and Margareta Sollenberg. 2003. 'Armed Conflict, 1989–2002.' *Journal of Peace Research.* Vol. 40, No. 5, pp. 593–607.

Fearon, James D. 2004. 'Why Do Some Civil Wars Last so Much Longer than Others?' *Journal of Peace Research.* 41 (3), pp. 275–301.

Florquin, Nicolas and Eric G. Berman, eds. *Armed and Aimless: Armed Groups, Guns, and Human Security in the ECOWAS Region.* Geneva: Small Arms Survey.

Garfield, Richard M. and Alfred I. Neugut. 2000. 'The Human Consequences of War.' In Barry S. Levy and Victor W. Sidel, eds. *War and Public Health.* Washington, DC: American Public Health Association, pp. 27–38.

Geller, Daniel and J. David Singer. 1998. *Nations at War: A Scientific Study of International Conflict.* Cambridge: Cambridge University Press.

Gettleman, Jeffrey. 2004. 'For Iraqis in harm's way, $5,000 and "I'm sorry".' *New York Times*. 17 March. Accessed 7 March 2005.
<http://www.nytimes.com/2004/03/17/international/middleeast/17CIVI.html?ex=1081828800&en=aa5e794081465606&ei=5070>

Gilmore, Gerry J. 2001. 'Afghan Civilian Casualty Info Hard to Get, Says Rumsfeld.' US Department of Defense: American Forces Information Service. 4 December. Accessed 14 January 2005. <http://www.pentagon.gov/news/Dec2001/n12042001_200112045.html>

Gleditsch, Nils Peter et al. 2002. 'Armed Conflict 1946–2001: A New Dataset.' *Journal of Peace Research*. Vol. 39, No. 5, pp. 615–37.

Ghobarah, Hazem, Paul Huth, and Bruce Russett. 2001. *Civil wars kill and maim people—long after the shooting stops*. Yale University, Leitner Program in International & Comparative Political Economy. Leitner Working Paper 2001–09. Accessed 16 March 2005. <http://www.yale.edu/leitner/pdf/2001-09.pdf>

Heidenrich, John G. 1993. 'The Gulf War: How many Iraqis died?' *Foreign Policy*. 90, Spring, pp. 108–25.

Heuveline, Patrick. 1998. '"Between One and Three Million in Cambodia": Toward the Demographic Reconstruction of a Decade of Cambodian History (1970–1980).' *Population Studies*. 52 (1), March, pp. 49–65.

—. 2001. 'The Demographic Analysis of Mortality Crises: The Case of Cambodia.' In Holly E. Reed and Charles B. Keely, eds. *Forced Migration and Mortality: A Report of the National Research Council*. Washington, DC: National Academy Press, pp. 102–29.

HIIK (Heidelberger Institut für Internationale Konfliktforschung). 2005. 'KOSIMO (Konflikt-Simulations-Modell).' Accessed 3 March 2005. <http://www.hiik.de/de/kosimo.htm>

Hofmann, Charles-Antoine et al. 2004. *Measuring the impact of humanitarian aid: A review of current practice*. Humanitarian Policy Group Research Report 17. June 2004. Accessed 17 October 2004. <http://www.odi.org.uk/hpg/papers/HPGReport17.pdf >

Holsti, Kalevi Jaakko. 1996. *The State, War, and the State of War*. Cambridge/New York: Cambridge University Press.

Iacopino, Vincent et al. 2001. 'A Population-Based Assessment of Human Rights Abuses Committed against Ethnic Albanian Refugees From Kosovo.' *American Journal of Public Health*. Vol. 91, pp. 2013–18.

IBC (Iraq Body Count). 2005. Accessed 19 January 2005. <http://www.iraqbodycount.net/>

ICRC (International Committee of the Red Cross). 2002. *Annual Report 2002*. Accessed 4 March 2005.
<http://www.icrc.org/Web/Eng/siteeng0.nsf/htmlall/section_annual_report_2002/$File/icrc_ar_02_FULL.pdf>

IISS (International Institute for Strategic Studies). 2004. 'Small Arms Survey–IISS Analysis of Fatalities Caused by Small Arms between 14 June and 14 October 2004.' Background paper (unpublished).

—. 2005. 'The Armed Conflict Database.' Accessed 3 March 2005. <http://www.iiss.org/showpage.php?pageID=25>

Iraq Coalition Casualty Count. 2005. Accessed 19 January 2005. <http://icasualties.org/oif/>

IRC (International Rescue Committee). 2000. 'Mortality in Eastern DRC: Results from Five Mortality Surveys.' Accessed 3 March 2005.
<http://intranet.theirc.org/docs/mortality_I_report.pdf>

—. 2001a. 'Mortality in Eastern Democratic Republic of Congo: Results from Eleven Mortality Surveys.' Accessed 3 March 2005.
<http://intranet.theirc.org/docs/mortII_report.pdf>

—. 2001b. 'Mortality in Kenema District, Sierra Leone: A survey Covering January 2000 to January 2001.' Accessed 3 March 2005.
<http://intranet.theirc.org/docs/sierra_mortality.pdf>

—. 2002a. 'Disability Prevalence Survey. Bujumbura Rural Province, Burundi.'

—. 2002b. 'Disability Prevalence Survey. Muyinga Province, Burundi.'

—. 2002c. 'Disability Prevalence Survey. Makamba Province, Burundi.'

—. 2003a. 'Disability Prevalence Survey. Bujumbura Rural Province, Burundi.'

—. 2003b. 'Mortality in the Democratic Republic of Congo: Results from a Nationwide Survey.' Accessed 3 March 2005.
<http://intranet.theirc.org/docs/drc_mortality_iii_full.pdf>

—. 2004a. *Mortality in the Democratic Republic of Congo: Results from a Nationwide Survey*. Accessed 28 February 2005.
<http://intranet.theirc.org/docs/DRC_MortalitySurvey2004_RB_8Dec04.pdf>

—. 2004b. 'Mortality in the Pool Region: Results of a mortality, immunization, and nutrition survey in Kinkala-Boko Health District, Pool Region, Republic of Congo.' Accessed 28 February 2005.
<http://www.db.idpproject.org/Sites/IdpProjectDb/idpSurvey.nsf/wViewCountries/B0D6765003B80A3FC1256E98002EFF02/$file/Pool+Mortality+Report+-+FINAL.doc>

Jane's Defence Weekly. 1993. 'Report Puts Iraqi Dead at 1500.' Vol. 109/011. 13 March.

Kaldor, Mary. 1999. *New and Old Wars: Organized Violence in a Global Era*. Stanford, CA: Stanford University Press.

Kelly, Jack. 2003a. 'Estimates of deaths in first war still in dispute.' *Pittsburgh Post-Gazette*. 16 February. Accessed 17 October 2004.
<http://www.post-gazette.com/nation/20030216casualty0216p5.asp>

—. 2003b. 'Calculating Casualties.' *Pittsburgh Post-Gazette*. 16 February. Accessed 25 August 2004.
<http://www.post-gazette.com/nation/20030216casualtiesbox0216p9.asp>

Kenney, George. 1995. 'The Bosnian Calculation: How Many Have Died? Not Nearly as Many as Some Would Have You Think.' *The New York Times Magazine*. 23 April, pp. 42–43.

King, Gary and Will Lowe. 2003. 'An automated information extraction tool for international conflict data with performance as good as human coders: a rare events evaluation design.' *International Organization*. 57, Summer, pp. 617–42.

Krug, Etienne G. et al., eds. 2002. W*orld Report on Violence and Health*. Geneva: World Health Organization. Accessed 11 April 2005.
<http://www.who.int/violence_injury_prevention/violence/world_report/en/full_en.pdf>

Lafta, Riyadh et al. 2005. 'Role of Small Arms during the 2003–2004 Conflict in Iraq.' Small Arms Survey publication. Forthcoming.

Laporte, R. E. 1994. 'Assessing the human condition: Capture–recapture techniques.' *British Medical Journal*. Vol. 308, p. 5.

Mack, Andrew, et al. 2005. *The Human Security Report*. Oxford: Oxford University Press. Forthcoming.

Marshall, Monty G. 2001. *Measuring the Social Impact of War*. Accessed 17 October 2004.
<http://www.cidcm.umd.edu/inscr/papers/IPAmgm.pdf>

—. 2005. 'Major Episodes of Political Violence 1946–2004.' Severn, MD: Center for Systemic Peace. 15 January. Accessed 3 March 2005.
<http://members.aol.com/CSPmgm/warlist.htm>

— and Ted Robert Gurr. 2003. *Peace and Conflict 2003: A Global Survey of Armed Conflicts, Self-Determination Movements, and Democracy*. Accessed 14 March 2005. <http://www.cidcm.umd.edu/inscr/PC03web.pdf>

Mathers, Colin D. 2005. 'WHO estimates of deaths due to war.' Unpublished note.

— et al. 2005. 'Counting the dead and what they died from: An assessment of the global status of cause of death data.' *Bulletin of the World Health Organization*. 83 (3), March, pp. 171–77 and appendix.

Meijer, Cécelle and Philip Verwimp. 2005. *Modern and Traditional Weapons in Violent Conflict: Evidence from Rwanda*. Small Arms Survey Occasional Paper. Forthcoming.

Memory Hole, the. 2004. *US Military Keeps Track of Some, If not All, Civilian Casualties in Iraq*. 12 April. Accessed 25 August 2004.
<http://www.thememoryhole.org/war/counting_civilians.htm>

Mueller, John. 2003. 'Policing the Remnants of War.' *Journal of Peace Research*. Vol. 40, No. 5, pp. 507–18.

Muggah, Robert and Cate Buchanan. 2005. *In the Line of Fire: Phase II*. Geneva: Small Arms Survey and Centre for Humanitarian Dialogue.

Murray, C. J. L. et al. 2002. 'Armed conflict as a public health problem.' *British Medical Journal*. Vol. 324. pp. 346–49.

PHR (Physicians for Human Rights). 1999. *War Crimes in Kosovo: A Population-Based Assessment of Human Rights Violations of Kosovar Albanians by Serb Forces*. 15 June. Cambridge, MA: PHR.

Project Ploughshares. 2004. *Armed Conflicts Report 2004*. Accessed 2 March 2005.
<http://www.ploughshares.ca/content/ACR/ACR00/ACR00.html>

—. 2005. *Armed Conflicts Report 2005*. Accessed 3 March 2005. <http://www.ploughshares.ca/content/ACR/acr.html>

Reed, Holly E. and Charles B. Keely, eds. 2001. *Forced Migration and Mortality: A Report of the National Research Council*. Washington, DC: National Academy Press.

Reeves, Eric. 2004. 'Darfur Mortality Update: Current Data for Total Mortality from Violence, Malnutrition, and Disease.' The Hague: Genocide Watch. November 16. Accessed 12 April. <http://www.genocidewatch.org/SudanDARFURMORTALITYUPDATE16nov2004.htm>

—. 2005a. 'Darfur Mortality Update.' 11 March. Accessed April 2005.
<http://www.sudanreeves.org/modules.php?op=modload&name=News&file=article&sid=44&mode=thread&order=0&thold=0d>

—. 2005b. 'Current Security Conditions in Darfur: An Overview.' April 7. Accessed April 2005.
<http://www.sudanreeves.org/modules.php?op=modload&name=News&file=article&sid=48&mode=thread&order=0&thold=0>

Reno, William. 1998. *Warlord Politics and African States*. Boulder: Lynne Rienner.

Reporters without Borders. 2005. *Press Freedom in 2004—The Deadliest Year for a Decade: 53 Journalists Killed*. Reporters without Borders Annual Roundup. Paris: Reporters without Borders. 5 January. Accessed 12 April 2005.
<http://www.rsf.org/IMG/pdf/Bilan_2004_Eng.pdf>

Roberts, Adam. 1993. 'The Laws of War in the 1990–91 Gulf Conflict.' *International Security*. Vol. 18, No. 3. Winter 1993/94, pp. 134–81.

Roberts, Les et al. 2004. 'Mortality before and after the 2003 invasion of Iraq: cluster sample survey.' *The Lancet*. Vol. 364, pp. 1857–64. 20 November. Published online 29 October 2004.

Sarkees, Meredith Reid. 2000. 'The Correlates of War Data on War: An Update to 1997.' *Conflict Management and Peace Science*, 18:1, pp. 123–44.

— Frank Whelon Wayman, and J. David Singer. 2003. 'Inter-State, Intra-State, and Extra-State Wars: A Comprehensive Look at Their Distribution over Time, 1816–1997.' *International Studies Quarterly*. 47, pp. 49–70.

Seybolt, Taylor B. 2001. 'Major Armed Conflicts.' In *SIPRI Yearbook 2001: Armaments, Disarmament and International Security*. Oxford: Oxford University Press, pp. 15–51.

Shesgreen, Deirdre. 2003. 'Pentagon Says it Has No Count of Iraqi Battle Deaths; "It's Not a Useful Figure to Us," Says a Spokesman.' *St. Louis Post-Dispatch*. 9 April. Quoted in Conetta, 2004, p. 41, fn. 117.

SIPRI (Stockholm International Peace Research Institute). *SIPRI Yearbook 1996: Armaments, Disarmament and International Security*. Oxford: Oxford University Press.

Small, Melvin and J. David Singer. 1982. *Resort to Arms: International and Civil War, 1816–1980*. Beverly Hills: Sage.

Small Arms Survey. 2001. *Small Arms Survey 2001: Profiling the Problem*. Oxford: Oxford University Press.

—. 2002. *Small Arms Survey 2002: Counting the Human Cost*. Oxford: Oxford University Press.

—. 2003. *Small Arms Survey 2003: Development Denied*. Oxford: Oxford University Press.

Spiegel, Paul B. and Peter Salama. 2000. 'War and mortality in Kosovo, 1998–1999: an epidemiological testimony'. *The Lancet*. Vol. 355, pp. 2204–09. June 24.

UCDP (Uppsala Conflict Data Program). 2005. Project Web page. Uppsala: Uppsala Universitet, Department of Peace and Conflict Research. Accessed 12 April 2005. <http://www.pcr.uu.se/database/>

UNGA/UNSC (United Nations General Assembly/United Nations Security Council). 2001. Eighth Annual Report of the International Tribunal for the Prosecution of Persons Responsible for Serious Violations of International Humanitarian Law Committed in the Territory of the Former Yugoslavia since 1991. A/56/352–S/2001/865. 17 September. Accessed 18 April 2005.
<http://www.un.org/icty/rappannu-e/2001/AR01e.pdf>

UNIS (United Nations Information Service). 1999. 'Prosecutor for Former Yugoslavia, Rwanda Tribunals Briefs Security Council, Emphasizes Need for Cooperation from States.' UNIS/SC/1155. 11 November. Accessed 14 January 2005.
<http://www.unis.unvienna.org/unis/pressrels/1999/sc1155.html>

US DOD (US Department of Defense). 2001. 'Secretary Rumsfeld Interview with PBS News Hour/Jim Lehrer.' News Transcript. 7 November. Accessed 7 March 2005. <http://www.defenselink.mil/transcripts/2001/t11082001_t1107pbs.html>

US DOS (US Department of State). 1997. Bosnia and Herzegovina Country Report on Human Rights Practices for 1996. Released by the Bureau of Democracy, Human Rights, and Labor. 30 January. Accessed 18 April 2005.
<http://www.state.gov/www/global/human_rights/1996_hrp_report/bosniahe.html>

Verwimp, Philip. 2004 'Death and Survival during the 1994 Genocide in Rwanda.' Population Studies. Vol. 58, no. 2, pp. 233–45.

VINC (Violent, Intrastate Nationalist Conflicts). 2005. VINC Project Home Page. Accessed 3 March 2005.
<http://facstaff.uindy.edu/~bayres/vinc.htm>

de Walque, Damien. 2004. 'The Long-Term Legacy of the Khmer Rouge Period in Cambodia.' World Bank Policy Research Working Paper 3446. Washington, DC: The World Bank Development Research Group. November. Accessed 12 April 2005.
<http://www-wds.worldbank.org/servlet/WDSContentServer/WDSP/IB/2004/12/10/000012009_20041210135851/Rendered/PDF/wps3446.pdf>

White, Matthew. 2005. 'Minor Atrocities of the Twentieth Century.' Accessed 17 October 2004. <http://users.erols.com/mwhite28/warstat6.htm>

WHO/EPIET (World Health Organization/European Programme for Intervention Epidemiology Training). 2004. 'Retrospective Mortality Survey among the Internally Displaced Population, Greater Darfur, Sudan, August 2004.' 15 September. Accessed 3 March 2005.
<http://www.who.int/disasters/repo/14656.pdf>

ACKNOWLEDGEMENTS

Principal author
Christina Wille with Keith Krause

Other contributors
Emile LeBrun, Anne-Kathrin Glatz, Patricia Leidl, and the following IISS researchers, who monitored weapons use in conflict for this chapter: Kartik Bommakanti, Richard Cowley, Christopher Hearne, Dawda Jobarteh, Tracy Richardson, Eugenia Zorbas, and Ivan Zverzhanovski.

'Post-conflict' Iraq: gunmen take aim at coalition soldiers in the center of Basra, southern Iraq, in May 2004, one year after President George W. Bush declared major combat operations over. (© Nabil Al-Jurani/AP Photo)

Managing 'Post-conflict' Zones: 10
DDR AND WEAPONS REDUCTION

INTRODUCTION

> Major combat operations in Iraq have ended. In the battle of Iraq, the United States and our
> allies have prevailed. And now our coalition is engaged in securing and reconstructing that
> country.
>
> —US President George W. Bush, 2 May 2003

The end of war does not necessarily signal a return to security. The introduction of a ceasefire, a peace agreement, or even discrete interventions that seek to disarm warring parties do not guarantee tangible improvements in the safety of either civilians or former combatants. In fact, in 2004, many so-called post-conflict environments presented more direct and indirect threats to civilians than the armed conflicts that preceded them. This raises an important question: what constitutes 'post-conflict'? Does it necessarily begin with a signed peace accord? When does it end? The expression has become so ubiquitous that its very meaning is rarely questioned.

This chapter contends that the post-conflict designation unhelpfully disguises the risks facing many societies emerging from war, as events over the past year in Afghanistan, Iraq, Sudan, and the countries of the Great Lakes Region painfully illustrate. A weary pessimism has now replaced the hubris that once accompanied the signing of a peace deal and the 'transition' to post-conflict reconstruction. Yet there is reason for cautious optimism: the introduction of disarmament, demobilization, and reintegration (DDR) and weapons reduction programmes as part of overall recovery strategies appears to be an important factor in winning the peace.

The post-conflict environment—whether ushered in by a significant reduction in direct mortality, the signing of a peace agreement, the deployment of a peacekeeping force, an arbitrary period of time, or the holding of national elections—is unstable. Too sudden or too slow an influx of relief and reconstruction assistance can trigger a fresh outbreak of armed conflict. Given that tensions may still be simmering and the dividends of 'peace' not equally shared, it is little surprise that almost half of all countries emerging from conflict show a tendency to suffer a relapse within five years of signing a peace agreement (Millennium Project, 2004; Collier et al., 2001). Thus, preventing armed violence from flaring up during the transition is critical to avoiding its escalation into full-fledged war.

Encouragingly, the current preoccupation of donors and multilateral agencies with the promotion of recovery and reconstruction in post-conflict contexts, including support for DDR and weapons reduction, underlines their growing commitment to securing peace. Recurring criticisms of conventional 'post-conflict recovery' packages remain valid: inadequate treatment of the political or structural causes of conflict, insufficient consideration of 'reintegration', delayed disbursement of funds, and the attachment of unrealistic conditions. Nonetheless, there is growing acceptance of the importance of making efforts to decrease the number of small arms and light weapons an integral component of recovery strategies. Since 2000, for example, the UN and the World Bank have launched at least 14 DDR initiatives in post-conflict countries—eight of which were continuing at the end of 2004. Similarly, at least 22 weapons reduction projects were established in post-conflict countries during the same period—and more than 16 were operational in 2004.

Below are the key findings of this chapter:

- In some countries considered 'post-conflict', levels of firearm-related violence are often higher than they were before, or even during, the armed conflict.
- Countries emerging from armed conflict can produce contagion effects with potentially destabilizing ramifications for neighbouring states.
- Multilateral agencies and donors increasingly view DDR and weapons reduction as pivotal pillars of post-conflict recovery.
- There is mounting recognition within the UN of the need to adopt regional and integrated approaches to DDR and weapons reduction.
- Current approaches to DDR and weapons reduction still suffer because of limited political will, confusion over objectives, a disproportionate focus on disarmament selection biases, inadequate financing, and coordination gaps.
- Alarmingly, DDR and weapons reduction continue to substitute for political solutions, the reform of the governance and judicial sectors, and sustainable development.
- Reducing the demand for firearms is a fundamental factor regularly overlooked in the rush to secure peace.

This chapter begins by reviewing the variety of threats confronting civilians in a post-conflict environment. It then turns to a number of concrete interventions designed by international and national actors to alleviate these risks, including DDR and weapons reduction initiatives. Although the 'success' of these endeavours in reducing armed violence in post-conflict contexts is still open to debate, the international donor community continues to pin considerable hope on them.[1] Building on previous work of the Small Arms Survey, the chapter goes on to provide a critical review of DDR and weapons reduction programmes.

SMALL ARMS-RELATED THREATS IN THE POST-CONFLICT PERIOD

It is difficult to gauge definitively the number of direct deaths due to armed conflict, although many have tried (CONFLICT DEATHS).[2] At a minimum, typologies usually distinguish between combatants *fatally injured* in political violence (excluding genocide and massacres) and *excess* civilian deaths. There is also widespread consensus that the proportion of those fatally injured in war is ordinarily less than that of those who have died from secondary or indirect causes. Moreover, public health specialists and epidemiologists are growing increasingly cognisant of the gruesome effects of war that linger in the 'post-conflict' period. While fatal injuries often decline sharply immediately after an armed conflict ends, the fall is less dramatic than previously believed. As the cases of the Democratic Republic of the Congo (DRC) and Iraq show, fatal injuries and excess deaths can remain surprisingly high in the wake of an armed conflict (IRC, 2004; Roberts, 2002; Roberts et al., 2004a; 2004b). A diverse literature exists on the costs of armed conflict.

Direct war-related deaths (and disabilities) range from intentional fatal injuries sustained during pitched battles to 'excess' deaths due to displacement and 'natural' mortality and morbidity associated with and return and resettlement.

While combatants (male and female) are the most obvious casualties, armed conflicts are also a cause of excess mortality and morbidity within the civilian population, largely through the spread of infectious disease, the destruction of assets, the dismantling of livelihoods, and the diversion of scarce resources away from basic services (Muggah and Batchelor, 2002). Legal and humanitarian specialists have repeatedly observed that, in 21st-century armed conflicts, civilians are deliberately targeted, often in direct violation of international humanitarian law (Muggah with Griffiths, 2002; ICRC, 1999).

Analysts have also pointed to the link between internal conflict and regional destabilization. There is basic agreement that most conflicts being waged today are 'internal' or 'intra-state' and involve automatic rifles and heavy machine guns, rocket-propelled grenade launchers, anti-personnel landmines, and mortars (Duffield, 2001; Kaldor, 1999). The threats posed predominantly by men and boys who wield these guns contribute to underdevelopment and have potentially destabilizing ramifications for the surrounding region.[3]

Rethinking post-conflict orthodoxies

A common perception among donors and policy-makers is that when armed conflicts end, safety and security are likely to return. It seems intuitive that death and injury rates, and especially 'collateral damage', will decrease after the shelling stops. Also assumed is that, when normalcy resumes, development and investment will begin anew. The international aid system has, in many ways, adopted wholesale elements of this interpretation.[4] The World Bank, for example, was established with the express purpose of reconstructing war-torn countries, as well as with a view to promoting development elsewhere.[5] Even though this neat interpretation is coming under increasing scrutiny, alternative explanations do not rest comfortably with aid bureaucracies.

It is true that direct deaths often rapidly increase before the signing of a peace agreement, and decline equally dramatically after it is finalized. Yet, as noted above, it is also generally the case that both direct deaths and excess mortality and morbidity remain comparatively high, sometimes at levels higher than before the war (Guha-Sapir and van Panhuis, 2002b; Ghobarah et al., 2004; Pederson, 2002). In reflecting on the 1990–91 Gulf War, Daponte (1993) notes that 'far more persons died from post-war health effects than from direct war effects'.[6] Where wars are exceptionally long and pernicious, these post-conflict excess deaths can rise even further. In Guatemala (see Box 10.1), it is estimated that the number of violent fatalities in the aftermath of the peace agreement have only partially decreased compared to those registered during the 37-year war (Pearce, 1999).[7]

So, are the 'armed conflict' and 'post-conflict' labels of any use if mortality and morbidity rates before and after wars are often indistinguishable? Would it make more sense to describe such countries as 'conflict-affected' (Millennium Project, 2004)? The answer is not as straightforward as one might like to imagine. Certainly, there are normative consequences associated with either label—for instance, international humanitarian law applies during an armed conflict, but not during the post-conflict phase (Small Arms Survey, 2002; Muggah with Griffiths, 2002). Moreover, there are political, economic, legal, and administrative implications associated with whether a country is at, or is emerging from, war. The transition from humanitarian relief to longer-term reconstruction—bridging the controversial 'relief–development gap'—and the assignation of priorities require a coherent determination of whether a country is in the midst of armed conflict.[8] Yet the combination of violent realities and the otherwise non-violent discourse employed by international aid agencies can generate distortions in the identification of both problems and solutions (Macrae, 1999). In the absence of agreement on the objective distinctions between conflict and post-conflict scenarios, analysts have pointed to peace agreements as a conventional indicator of the 'shift' (see Map 10.1).

> After conflicts come to an end, 'direct deaths' and 'excess' mortality and morbidity remain comparatively high— sometimes higher than before the war.

Box 10.1   Firearm-related incidents in Guatemala, 1995–2002

A Guatemalan National Revolutionary Unit guerrilla receives her demobilization papers in May 1997 in the Salcol disarmament camp. Despite these efforts, firearm-related incidents increased after the 1996 peace agreement.

© Reuters

Guatemala endured one of the longest civil wars in Latin American history. It lasted for 37 years, ending with a peace agreement in December 1996. The direct costs were catastrophic: an estimated 140,000–200,000 people were shot and killed, or as many as 5,400 per year (UNDP, 2003). According to reports of the Pan American Health Organization, homicide was the single most common cause of death of men in Guatemala in the early 1980s; most of these homicides related to armed conflict as opposed to crime or accidents (PAHO, 1986). The end of the conflict has not, however, marked a return to stability or peace. In fact, firearm-related deaths have increased since December 1996. Evidence suggests, furthermore, that the wider population has actually experienced a rise in real and perceived insecurity (Moser and Winton, 2002).

Figure 10.1   Number of violent and firearms-related deaths

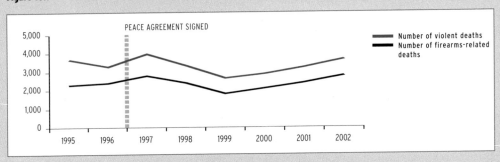

Figure 10.2   Firearm death rate and homicide rate

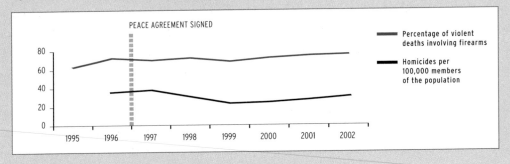

Source: Godnick (2005)

Other transition benchmarks include temporal thresholds and concrete activities on the ground, such as ceasefires, the holding of negotiations, and various weapons reduction, demobilization, and reintegration initiatives.[9]

Map 10.1   Selected conflict and 'post-conflict' zones, 1994-2004*

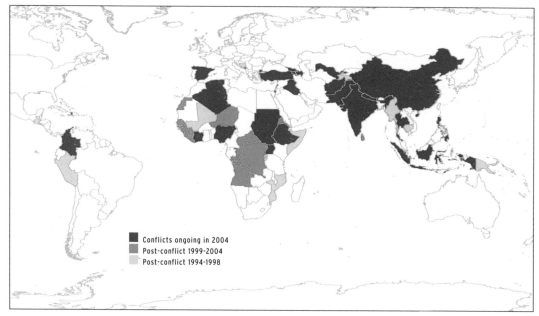

Conflicts ongoing in 2004
Post-conflict 1999-2004
Post-conflict 1994-1998

Sources: IISS (2004); SIPRI (2004); University of Uppsala (2004)

War ends, violence grows?

In what ways do post-conflict conditions differ from the armed conflict circumstances that preceded them? While fatality trends may remain comparable from a *quantitative* standpoint, the dynamics of armed violence can alter *qualitatively* in the post-conflict period. Rather than clashes between combatants, targeted attacks on civilians, and forced displacement leading to excess deaths, the post-conflict environment can witness years of surging rates of violent crime and inter-personal violence.[10] Moreover, the types of armaments used in violence can change, from heavy and light weapons to pistols and revolvers.

As the cases of Kosovo and Nicaragua illustrate, 'substitution effects' are sometimes also registered during the post-conflict period. In part because of the heavy (and enforced) penalties being handed down for possession and use of weapons, acts of violence are increasingly being perpetrated with bladed instruments (see Box 10.2). Additionally, armed violence can move geographically from primarily rural areas to urban centres, as was the case in Guatemala (Moser, 2004).

Research has shown that armed conflicts substantially increase the exposure of civilians, particularly children, youth, and the displaced, to risks that raise the likelihood of mortality and morbidity, including fatal firearm and ordinance injuries (WHO, 2001; Ghobarah et al., 2003; Garfield and Neugut, 1991).[13] Similarly, the civilian population is also disproportionately affected after a war comes to an end. The cases of Afghanistan and Cambodia, which effectively entered post-conflict phases in 2001 and 1991, respectively, are instructive. A survey conducted in Afghanistan

271

Box 10.2   Kosovo: post-war public health effects

Kosovo emerged from conflict in late 1999. It is estimated that, between 1997 and 1999, a combination of shelling and small arms fire claimed the lives of 10,000–13,000 civilians (Khakee and Florquin, 2003). Despite a range of DDR and weapons reduction initiatives in the post-conflict period, it remains a comparatively well-armed society. Flare-ups between Kosovo Albanians and Serbs in Mitrovica in March 2004 indicate that tensions are continuing to fester.

Figure 10.3   Intentional injury profile, Pristina University Hospital, 1999–2002*

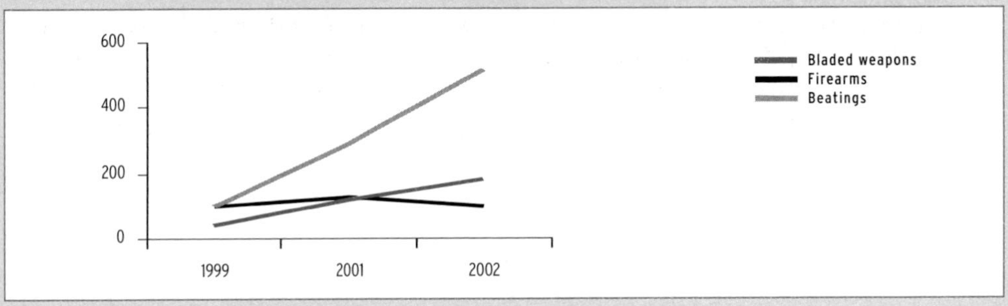

Bladed weapons
Firearms
Beatings

*Note: Data for 1999 reflects injuries tracked in June–December only.
Source: Khakee and Florquin (2003)

Overall levels of armed violence fell precipitously following the intervention of the North Atlantic Treaty Organisation (NATO) beginning in March 1999. Small Arms Survey research finds, however, that certain types of intentional violence seem to have increased over the following years (Khakee and Florquin, 2003). A review of in-patients at Pristina University Hospital (PUH) suggests that, while firearms-related injuries have stabilized, there has been a rise in knife-related injuries, pointing to what is commonly referred to as the 'substitution effect'.[11] This is hardly surprising, since the introduction and enforcement of penalties by NATO's Kosovo Force (KFOR) has indirectly pushed up the relative price of possessing and using firearms.

This data should be treated with caution. Reported firearm injuries at PUH are lower than the total number of firearm-related injuries sustained in Kosovo. While the catchment area of PUH spans the whole of Kosovo, other clinics also reportedly treat acute wounds, including those caused by firearms. Furthermore, ethnic Serbs frequently receive treatment in Mitrovica, indicating a selection bias.[12] There is also evidence that not all firearm-related injuries are treated by public hospitals, particularly those incurred through criminal activities. Moreover, few statistics are available on injuries due to celebratory fire, which occurs regularly (during festivals, weddings, and events to mark the New Year).

(between March 2001 and June 2002) notes that, of the 1,636 individuals treated for injuries due to landmines, grenades, bombs, mortar shells, and cluster munitions from December 2001 onwards, more than *80 per cent* were civilians (Bilukha et al., 2003).[14] A review of injuries in Cambodia conducted by the International Committee of the Red Cross (ICRC) between January 1991 and February 1995 found that weapon injury rates were seasonal and rose in the post-conflict period.[15] Importantly, the ICRC observed that intentional firearm injuries affecting civilians made up by far the largest category of non-combat injuries: almost *60 per cent* of those injured were civilians.

Another reason for excessively high mortality rates in the post-conflict period is that armed violence leads to a reduction in the human and financial resources available for renewed investment in public infrastructure including healthcare systems. Depending on the length and severity of the armed conflict, the public and professional health workforce can be severely depleted.[16] In addition to sharp declines in recurrent expenditures on the quality of and access to public services during a conflict, the restoration of infrastructure (and public confidence) can take years, even decades. Due to the deliberate targeting of public utilities and monitoring and surveillance systems *during* armed

Box 10.3   Disarming the camps: Militarization of refugees and the internally displaced

Armed violence generates vast numbers of refugees and IDPs. In 2004, the United Nations High Commissioner for Refugees (UNHCR) estimated that there were 9.9 million refugees, while the Global IDP Project calculated that there were close to 25 million IDPs.[17] Refugees and IDPs are often unable to return to their home country or original place of residence in the immediate post-conflict period. Many thousands of people may sometimes languish for years in camps and settlements. UNHCR reports that at least 6.2 million refugees in 38 camps are caught up in a 'protracted refugee situation' (UNHCR, 2004). In these circumstances, camps can become 'militarized', and, in turn, constitute a threat to regional and internal stability.

The Small Arms Survey carried out field research in such protracted situations in Africa between July 2004 and January 2005. Based on studies of refugee camps and settlements in Guinea, Rwanda, Tanzania, and Uganda, where UNHCR works to protect refugees and to provide them with critical humanitarian assistance, the research revealed a number of common patterns. First, the political economy of violence in the region conditions the scale and intensity of militarization. Militarization does not take place in a vacuum; it is deeply embedded in historical developments. Second, classic cross-border militarization appears

to have declined in recent years, because of reduced refugee flows, and because of the successful interventions and situation-specific refugee security strategies applied by hosting states and UNHCR.

Worryingly, however, 'internal militarization' seems to have risen, as refugees and IDPs have become increasingly caught up or directly implicated in civil conflicts (Muggah, 2005a). They may be armed, are often recruited into a militia, and will seek to defend their livelihoods. In some countries, it seems that humanitarian agency

Thousands of Sudanese IDPs populate this makeshift camp in Sudan's West Darfur province, captured from a helicopter in September 2004. The threat of 'militarization' in such camps increases with time.

© Ben Curtis/AP Photo

efforts to address refugee insecurity and refugee and IDP militarization—as well as the donor support for these efforts—are only compensating for the failure of asylum and country-of-origin states to meet their responsibilities. Ensuring the civilian and humanitarian character of asylum and protecting civilian populations are, and must remain, primary responsibilities of the state. The 1951 *Convention Relating to the Status of Refugees,* the 1967 *Protocol,* and the 1969 Organization of African Unity *Convention Governing the Specific Aspects of Refugee Problems in Africa* sanction international protection. While there are no comparable instruments for protecting IDPs, various guiding principles have been elaborated.

Clearly, ensuring the civilian and humanitarian character of asylum is a major concern of the international community, especially of UNHCR. In the late 1990s, UNHCR published a conceptual framework document known as the 'ladder of options', outlining levels of refugee insecurity and proposing a range of possible responses to address a given situation effectively. The ladder included an array of 'soft' and 'medium' (practical) options, such as screening borders, community policing, and the deployment of international observers, and 'hard' options, including military intervention when authorized by the UN Security Council. Because the latter has been slow to act on the issue, UNHCR has worked with a number of other actors, such as the UN Department of Peacekeeping Operations (DPKO), to tackle a problem that is ostensibly outside of their remit.[18] Together with host governments (and with the assistance of the international community), UNHCR has also advised on issues such as the repatriation of foreign ex-combatants or 'armed elements' through DDR processes. This is a fairly new area of activity for the agency, however, and achievements and problems need to be evaluated.

conflicts, effective resource planning for public health is regularly undermined in the post-conflict period (Hoeffler and Reynal-Querol, 2003; Levy and Sidel, 1997).

Furthermore, armed violence, particularly violence committed by former soldiers and militia members, can reach epidemic proportions in the shadow of a ceasefire. The *perception* of spiralling intentional violence is also liable to grow, as post-conflict Guatemala amply demonstrates (Moser, 2004; McIlwaine and Moser, 2001). There is also considerable evidence that the assault rifles and light weapons used during the war can resurface and be employed in an uncommon kind of criminality, especially in urban areas. In many cases, former combatants and criminals wielding military-style armaments literally outgun police officers and civilians. Often, these weapons were originally looted from the country's own arsenal.

It is common for organized urban criminality to rise following a conflict. Available data from across the Balkans and Central America indicates that armed criminality and social violence often escalate despite peace agreements (Grillot et al., 2004; Godnick et al., 2003; Braveman et al., 1997); in some cases, these rise above pre-war levels (Guha-Sapir and van Panuis, 2002b). In Uganda and Sierra Leone, the demobilization and reintegration of former combatants appears to have had varying effects in terms of reducing crime. A study tracing demobilized Ugandan soldiers in the 1990s, for example, found that, prior to their disbandment, soldiers without land were responsible for significantly raising district-level crime rates. Statistically, they were 100 times more likely to commit a crime than the average citizen. By contrast, district-level crime rates did not go up after the return of those who had been properly demobilized (Collier, 1994). In the case of Sierra Leone, however, it appears that DDR has had little effect in reducing the stigmatization of returning combatants or promoting non-violence or the dismantling of factions (Humphreys and Weinstein, 2004).

In many cases, these lingering effects of conflict spill across borders, into neighbouring and ostensibly 'peaceful' countries (Millennium Project, 2004; World Bank, 2003a; 2003b). Former soldiers regularly cross international frontiers, contributing to the militarization of refugee and internally displaced person (IDP) camps, often with the tacit support of host governments, as in the Great Lakes Region and West Africa (see Box 10.3). Criminal gangs and militia groups often coalesce into syndicates, in many instances forging cross-border partnerships and subsisting on, among other things, the trade in drugs, contraband, and military-style weapons.

Many of the indirect consequences of violence during the post-conflict period are hidden and thus difficult to discern. The chronic psychological and psychosocial traumas present among displaced populations have been investigated (Barbara, 1997; Sabin et al., 2003). Studies of combatants and civilians indicate that a considerable proportion is exposed to a high incidence of extreme violence involving firearms and other types of armaments, and that a significant number suffer from long-term mental disability (Humphreys and Weinstein, 2004; Butler, 1997; CDC, 1988).[19] Participatory research conducted in post-conflict contexts, including Cambodia, Papua New Guinea (Bougainville), the Solomon Islands, and Sri Lanka, also highlights surprisingly common patterns of insecurity, such as sexual violence,[20] and impacts on physical and social mobility, familial cohesiveness, and access to sustainable livelihoods among soldiers and civilians alike.[21]

Demand for weapons in the post-conflict period

The end of armed conflict does not necessarily signal a reduction in demand for weapons. In fact, where penalties are neither implemented nor enforced, the propensity for civilians and former combatants to acquire weapons can increase. Moreover, there is a sense that, partly because of the continued presence of automatic rifles, grenades, and handguns, arming in self-defence becomes normalized.

In some post-conflict environments, the presence of leftover weapons can increase the chance of a fatal outcome. In El Salvador, for example, between June 2001 and May 2002, some 3,704 persons entered the state public health system with firearm injuries, while 7,592 entered with injuries caused by sharp objects, such as knives and machetes. Whereas pistols and revolvers were responsible for many of the injuries sustained, assault weapons and grenades also figured prominently (Godnick et al., 2003). The availability of small arms and light weapons in situations where the costs of ownership are low and the motivations for acquisition are stable or rising can lead to an escalation in armed violence.

Societies often remain heavily armed, despite the political resolution of a conflict, for numerous reasons. At the macro level, states are frequently over-committed in terms of defence expenditure; concomitantly, they have to maintain large armies. National defence spending in developing countries can rise dramatically during an internal armed conflict—to an average of five per cent of gross domestic product (GDP), as compared to 2.8 per cent during peacetime (World Bank, 2003b). Conversely, it also regularly takes years for defence expenditure to contract to pre-war levels, with implications for infrastructure and healthcare spending, as well as for income-earning potential (Brauer and Dunne, 2004).[22] Moreover, the surfeit of weaponry, some of it looted or poorly managed, often results in it being recycled into the hands of civilians. The real 'price' of weapons may decline—a necessary, but insufficient, factor behind an increase in demand.

Small arms demand, however, can also arise out of perceived horizontal disparities in the post-conflict period. Countries emerging from conflict regularly register sizeable external debts, which can have serious consequences for the collection and allocation of domestic revenues. While various international agencies have established a host of macroeconomic stabilization instruments to ease the transition, socio-economic fault lines often quickly emerge.[23] As economies tend to expand after a period of severe contraction, sharp socio-economic inequalities are not uncommon.[24] The per capita earning power of the middle class and the poor are not uniform during this time (Millennium Project, 2004; Sambanis, 2003). Consequently, widespread disenfranchisement and resentment can fuel inter-personal violence. Thus, individual and collective 'preferences' for weapons can grow in the delicate period after a war ends.

At the micro level, collective and individual demand for weapons can remain high, partly as a result of the continued desire for self-protection, predatory and rent-seeking behaviour, and long-standing or recent socially determined norms on weapons possession (GUN CULTURE). New empirical research on armed groups in the Solomon Islands, Papua New Guinea, and South Africa indicates that demand for firearms—as with most commodities—is ultimately conditioned by high 'preferences', low real and relative 'prices', and the ability to mobilize sufficient monetary or non-monetary 'resources' for procurement.[25]

The 'preference' for weapons can grow in the delicate period following the end of war.

SECURING THE PEACE: DDR AND WEAPONS REDUCTION

Awareness of the risk factors accompanying transition processes is growing. For example, recent evidence warns that there is a positive correlation between the length and intensity of an armed conflict and the relative likelihood of renewed armed violence.[26] Other dangers associated with the latter stages of transition—inadequate and uneven assistance, disproportionate and ineffective targeting, poor growth, and insufficient attention to peace-building,[27] including disarmament—are becoming more established.[28]

Nonetheless, something of a post-conflict orthodoxy has emerged. Diamond captures this view, arguing that efforts to rebuild a shattered, war-torn country should comprise at least four components:

[p]olitical reconstruction of a legitimate and capable state; economic reconstruction, including the rebuilding of the country's physical infrastructure and the creation of rules and institutions that enable a market economy; social reconstruction, including the renewal ... of a civil society and political culture that foster voluntary cooperation and the limitation of state power; and the provision of general security, to establish a safe and orderly environment (Diamond, 2004, p.2).

In post-conflict environments in which the state has crumbled or collapsed, security is the foundation on which all else depends. Without minimum security, people cannot trade, organize, rebuild communities, or participate meaningfully in politics or economic development.

Multilateral donors now regularly advance a number of formulaic security- and development-oriented interventions to secure the peace. The World Bank, for example, has elaborated a series of 'best practices' to assist affected countries, donors, and multilateral agencies in navigating volatile post-conflict settings (World Bank, 2003b; 2003d). It advocates the deployment of international peacekeepers and the introduction of stabilization measures in the earliest stages of the post-conflict period. Subsequent to this comes the gradual phasing in of financial aid over the next five years, particularly when absorptive capacity is 'optimum' for growth. And finally, within a decade, democratic institutions are established. All of these activities are generally subsumed under the mantle of reconstruction and development; alternatively, they are described as a 'security first strategy'. Included in this bundle of initiatives are DDR and weapons reduction, two strands that—while sharing certain attributes and often overlapping—are in fact distinct.

Very generally, DDR is a process introduced after a conflict that primarily focuses on ensuring the reintegration of combatants (from standing armies, police forces, or insurgent factions) into civilian life.[29] While a single doctrine has yet to be produced for DDR, a considerable literature has emerged in recent years, much of it descriptive, theoretical, or distilling so-called best practice and lessons learnt.[30] By contrast, weapons reduction is a generic term encapsulating a diverse cluster of programmes that seek to reduce the number of armaments principally in civilian hands. Essentially filling the lacunae left by DDR, weapons reduction initiatives often fall outside peace deals and tend to adopt a more disparate approach than does DDR. They emphasize everything from legislation and regional border agreements to practical activities designed to remove weapons and reduce incentives for possession. A third process, security sector reform (SSR), transforms institutions of the security sector—including the police, the military, and the judiciary[31]—and compels them to accept greater democratic (civilian) control and increased transparency and accountability (Ball, 2001; 2002; Smith, 2002). A key objective of SSR is to convert defence and police personnel into providers of legitimate security and to install accountable, professional, appropriately sized, and affordable security sectors. Ensuring that the linkages between DDR, weapons reduction, and SSR are robust and well defined is a continuing challenge.[32]

> Multilateral and bilateral development agencies are changing their attitudes towards the security sector.

A developmental approach to DDR and weapons reduction?

Due in part to the chilling realities they confront in post-conflict contexts, multilateral and bilateral development agencies are changing their attitudes towards the security sector. The development community appears to have shed many of its prejudices with respect to the security sector and is slowly grappling with issues such as military reform and practical disarmament. Moreover, it is now widely accepted that persistent personal or human insecurity of the kind often encountered in countries emerging from war can obstruct human development and achievement of the Millennium Development

Goals.[33] Indeed, persistent insecurity caused by small arms, and the itinerant former combatants who use them, can jeopardize sustainable investment, good governance, and, ultimately, socio-economic recovery in the post-conflict environment (UNF, 2004; Millennium Project, 2004; Muggah and Batchelor, 2002). Related to this is the theory that misguided, rapid, or uneven development can itself fuel insecurity and armed violence.[34] In response, the development community now recognizes that it has to face up to the challenges connected with building sustainable human security.

Nevertheless, the operational responses of many agencies and donors remain narrowly conceived. Post-conflict recovery is seldom situated in the context of a country's political economy or existing civil-military relations,[35] and donors instead continue to favour technical and apolitical interventions with short time horizons. Consequently, DDR and weapons reduction are two kinds of intervention regularly advanced to redress insecurity.

A short history of DDR

DDR is a comparatively recent instrument adopted by the development community in the context of post-conflict reconstruction. The term DDR is used here, although acronyms such as DDRR, DDRRR, and DRP have been regularly employed over the past few years (Ginifer et al., 2004; Muggah, 2004a).[36] The optimism of the early 1990s spurred on a renewed international commitment to UN-sponsored peacekeeping missions and reconstruction efforts. Since 1948, the UN has sponsored 59 peacekeeping missions, most of them launched after the end of the cold war. Many of these early peacekeeping missions, from Cambodia to Namibia, were initial test cases for DDR. The conventional approach emphasized disarmament after a ceasefire or peace agreement, as in El Salvador, Mozambique, and Nicaragua, followed by limited reintegration. While no doctrine or minimum standards emerged to guide DDR, it became an important element of peace processes, usually introduced early in the post-conflict period and geared toward neutralizing potential spoilers in the absence of clearly defined peace accords.[37]

> DDR and weapons reduction are two kinds of intervention regularly advanced to redress insecurity.

In 1998, a UN Secretary-General report declared that one of the priorities of post-conflict peace-building was the disarmament and demobilization of ex-combatants and others and their reintegration into productive society (UN, 1998). Various UN Security Council presidential statements issued in 1999 highlighted the importance of successful DDR and underscored that 'disarmament, demobilization and reintegration cannot be seen in isolation, but rather, as a continuous process which is rooted in and feeds into a broader search for peace, stability and development' (UNSC, 1999a). A year later, the Secretary-General submitted a detailed report to the Security Council on the role of UN peacekeeping missions in DDR (UNSC, 2000a).

Within a few years, DDR came to occupy a central position in military–civilian transition operations, pursued by donors of the Organisation for Economic Co-operation and Development (OECD), the UN, the World Bank, affected governments, and myriad agencies and NGOs. In the UN General Assembly and Security Council, the United Nations Department for Disarmament Affairs (UNDDA) and DPKO strongly advocated for disarmament to be made an integral part of peace settlements (Faltas and Chiaro, 2001). Standardized templates for DDR were introduced and best practice articulated by UN divisions, such as DPKO, and predominantly Western think tanks (Kingma, 2000; Berdal, 1996).[38] In rare instances, various types of weapons reduction initiatives were piloted before the implementation of full-scale national disarmament programmes and DDR projects. In others, linkages with development and peace-building were gradually established (Small Arms Survey, 2003, pp. 293–95).

Considering the tremendous amount of energy invested in advocating for DDR and weapons reduction, surprisingly little evidence is available to help determine the effectiveness of such programmes, whether in terms of meeting

Box 10.4   DDR in Sierra Leone: successful reintegration?

Between 1998 and 2002, Sierra Leone's National Commission on DDR registered some 76,000 combatants and collected and destroyed around 42,330 weapons and 1.2 million pieces of ammunition. The programme was supported by a Multi-Donor Trust Fund, valued at USD 31.5 million, as well as by Emergency Recovery Credits and a Post-Conflict Fund grant (Bradley et al., 2002). The intervention is widely heralded as a model initiative in promoting 'reintegration' (CERI, 2004; Mazurana and Carlson, 2004; Bradley et al., 2002).

A 2004 study uses survey data to assess the effectiveness of the DDR process in Sierra Leone (Humphreys and Weinstein, 2004). It identifies some important successes, but also raises questions about its longer-term effectiveness. Conducted in 2003, the study includes a large-scale survey of 200 non-combatants and 1,000 ex-combatants from all Sierra Leonean factions and regions. Its purpose was:

- to evaluate the motivations of those who participated in political violence;
- to collect systematic information on organizational structures and the economic behaviour of the warring parties; and
- to gather representative data on combatants' experiences of the demobilization process and the extent to which they were successfully reintegrated into their communities.

A man pours fuel over guns before burning them at Lungi, Sierra Leone, in January 2002.

© Alistair Thomson/Reuters

In particular, the authors note that the DDR process was implemented in an even-handed way. The research indicates that there was no evidence that any of the various factions were treated preferentially in the design or implementation phases. In a society rife with factional differences, where perceptions of mistreatment could have undermined the peace process, this neutrality is extremely important.

The report points out that non-participants in the DDR process (representing just over ten per cent of the sample) did not fare any worse with regard to reintegration than did participants. Indeed, they were just as likely to be accepted by family members and neighbours; to return to their home communities; to reject factions as major political actors in the post-war period; and to embrace non-violent means of affecting political change. Further, there is some evidence that non-participants resolved problems concerning community acceptance faster than did participants.

The authors stress, however, that the findings must be treated with caution. On the one hand, those who did not participate in DDR may differ in fundamental ways from those who opted to participate. For example, the DDR programme may have taken on the hardest reintegration cases—notably, fighters from the Revolutionary United Front (RUF). On the other hand, it is possible that those who did not take part in the process formally may have derived some of its benefits. Consequently, the effects of DDR would not be reflected so strongly in observed differences between those who did and those who did not participate.

The fact that, on average, those who did participate did not reintegrate more easily than those who did not, could indicate that DDR programmes do not currently play a sufficiently important role in redressing community stigmatization. Rather, success in post-war reintegration has largely been the result of the war coming to an end. The RUF was decisively defeated, the country had grown weary of fighting, and there was broad acceptance of the peace terms.

Ultimately, a randomized controlled evaluation is the only way to appraise systematically the effectiveness of DDR programmes. If implemented in a way that avoids creating inequities, it could generate very precise estimates of the impact of DDR in general, and specific interventions in particular, on the prospects for post-war reintegration.

Source: Humphreys and Weinstein (2004)

their own discrete objectives or contributing to security more generally (see Box 10.4). For example, a 2004 survey of more than a dozen DDR and weapons reduction initiatives observes that none of the interventions could 'claim [to have had] a statistically significant impact on security ... [despite] many observed changes in individual and community perceptions of security' (CICS, 2004). The World Bank also remarks in the case of DDR that 'no statistical analyses of the effects of military integration on the likelihood of war recurrence are available, [although] in several cases military integration [is] associated with a lowered rate of war recurrence' (World Bank, 2003b, p. 149).

Nevertheless, DDR was incorporated into mainstream development thinking soon after the World Bank began to concentrate on the security sector. The World Bank had in fact immersed itself in DDR debates comparatively early on and has been involved in the demobilization and reintegration components of DDR since the late 1980s. Subsequently, it has provided demobilization and reintegration project (DRP) assistance to more than 16 countries (27 projects) for designing and financing interventions. It has frequently done so in close partnership with those UN agencies that typically handle disarmament, weapons destruction, and SSR (Colletta et al., 1996). Indeed, the World Bank was one of the first institutions to develop an analytical capacity in this sector. Furthermore, it 'has broadened its response from a focus on providing financial capital and rebuilding physical infrastructure, to a comprehensive approach also including initiatives to support the demobilization and reintegration of ex-combatants ... an especially vulnerable group in the post-conflict setting' (World Bank, 2003b).[39]

> The World Bank immersed itself in DDR debates comparatively early on.

Yet while it has made a considerable investment in the demobilization and reintegration of both vulnerable groups and combatants, the World Bank has never explicitly addressed the disarmament component of DDR. The main reason for this relates to its mandate. The World Bank's *Operational Manual* states: 'In view of its mandate, the Bank does not engage in peacemaking or peacekeeping, which are the functions of the United Nations and certain regional organizations. It also does not provide direct support for disarming combatants' (World Bank, 2001d). Some insiders assert that this is more a matter of the World Bank not wishing to become involved in issues that could threaten its reputation than a constraint imposed by its mandate.

Weapons reduction: a potted history

Weapons reduction, which has a lengthier history than DDR, is not confined to either conflict or post-conflict situations. Although weapons reduction is today included in development, peace-building, policing, and other sectors, it has its roots in the US crime prevention initiatives of the 1950s. At the time, practical approaches to reducing weapons availability generally entailed buying them back, despite awareness that this was only a short-term solution and encouraged illegal firearms markets. By the 1970s and 1980s, weapons reduction efforts had broadened their focus (beyond arms per se) to encompass the individual agents who possessed them and the permissive regulatory structures that facilitated acquisition. Police and criminology specialists increasingly adopted holistic approaches to weapons reduction, concentrating simultaneously on raising the cost of obtaining firearms via penalties, and providing cash incentives to encourage their relinquishment.

Weapons reduction is, in many ways, a surprising new addition to the development sector's arsenal. Throughout the 1990s, the negative correlation between armed violence and underdevelopment became ever more difficult to ignore (Humphreys, 2002; Stewart and Fitzgerald, 2001). As pervasive weapons use increasingly compromised development interventions, reducing availability was no longer a matter of choice, but of grim necessity. More recently, as some policy circles have sought to establish ties between underdevelopment and terrorism, weapons reduction has become part of a general drive to reduce poverty in the post-conflict period.[40]

As with DDR, weapons reduction lacks a doctrine or clear conceptual basis. In fact, it involves various activities, ranging from the tightening of the regulatory framework for civilian arms possession to public awareness campaigns that concentrate on 'gun cultures'. This approach is fast becoming a core element of post-conflict recovery strategies (Ginifer et al., 2004).

Weapons reduction initiatives are increasingly being linked with DDR. They are frequently introduced as follow-on activities, as in Kosovo, the Republic of Congo, or Sierra Leone (Ginifer et al., 2004). Discrete initiatives in the weapons reduction portfolio, such as 'Flames of Peace' in Mali, Serbia, and Sierra Leone, have also been tagged on to formal DDR. In addition, weapons reduction is now introduced to address gaps in ongoing DDR programmes, particularly in relation to weapons storage and disposal, pubic awareness campaigns, community mobilization, and demand reduction. By engaging civil society groups and stigmatizing weapons ownership, as with the 'Strengthening Mechanisms for Small Arms Control' project of the United Nations Development Programme (UNDP) in El Salvador (2001–03), weapon reduction activities have also opened up the possibility of achieving long-term, sustainable reversals in community criminality and violence.[41]

Weapons reduction can be divided into at least two distinct categories: reduction by command (phase one); and voluntary reduction (phase two).[42] Weapons reduction by command often forms part of a general disarmament strategy during and immediately following peace negotiations—although it can also take place outside of formal agreements. These so-called phase one initiatives are generally administered by peacekeepers and militaries and are organized, centralized, supervised, public, involuntary, and collective (Faltas et al., 2001). Examples are the continuing disarmament efforts of the United Nations Mission in the Democratic Republic of the Congo (MONUC) or the United Nations Stabilization Mission in Haiti (MINUSTAH). Also included in this category are cross-regional initiatives, such as the Southern African Regional Police Chiefs Co-operation Organisation, which has collected thousands of weapons in the region.

Voluntary reduction activities, meanwhile, are often introduced later in the transition process, and are designed to address civilian arms possession. These so-called phase two interventions advance a combination of collective and individual incentives, are decentralized, and are often preceded by various penalties to deter illegal ownership. Examples include 'weapons for development', 'community arms collection for development', 'weapons lotteries', voluntary amnesties, and 'weapon-free zones'. Multilateral and bilateral donors, including UNDP and other development agencies, increasingly favour phase two initiatives (see Annexe 1).

Engineering consent: focusing on incentives

The development community has injected new and dynamic thinking into DDR and weapons reduction interventions. As a result, they are now typically wide-ranging in terms of their parameters and approach.[43] Specifically, development actors have broadened the traditional focus on cash incentives to include a host of other 'carrots' to tempt individuals into relinquishing weapons and to re-engineer the preferences of armed agents. For example, while buy-backs are voluntary and concentrate on influencing an individual's choices, Weapons in Exchange for Development (WED) programmes, while also voluntary, centre on modifying community preferences (Figure 10.4). A concerted attempt to shape perceptions of weapons ownership—through stigmatization and public awareness campaigns—is central to new weapons reduction efforts. By contrast, traditional random stop-and-search interventions are involuntary and primarily target individuals. Community searches, while sometimes coercive, focus on building confidence among residents and are often conducted in tandem with community policing.

Figure 10.4   Weapons reduction incentives

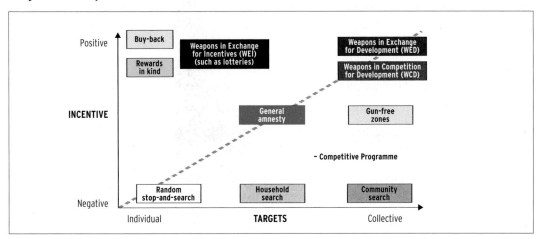

Source: Wilkinson (2004)

Moreover, development actors have underscored that effective and sustainable weapons reduction should nurture local ownership. Over the past five years, UNDP, as well as British and German development cooperation agencies, the European Union (EU), the International Organization for Migration (IOM), and others, have launched weapons reduction projects in more than 45 countries. Yet the extent to which these have successfully contributed to promoting human security, let alone development, remains something of an empirical question.

A number of shifts are taking place in contemporary approaches to DDR and weapons reduction. Although they are still regularly pursued at the national level, there appears to be growing emphasis on regional approaches to DDR and weapons reduction—explicit recognition of the transnational dimensions of arms proliferation and foreign ex-combatants. Good examples are the Multi-Country Demobilization and Reintegration Program in the Great Lakes Region (2002–06) and Operation Rachel involving Mozambique and South Africa (1995–2003) (see Annexe 10.1). In the case of Latin America, there is also growing awareness of the importance of institutionalizing activities through national legislatures in order to ensure their sustainability.

There also appears to be some limited reorientation of focus on the demand for weapons. Recent initiatives in post-conflict Haiti (2004–05) and the Solomon Islands (2003–04), for example, are concentrating as much on collecting weapons as on re-engineering community attitudes toward firearms—through the introduction of 'gun-free spaces' and reconciliation activities (see Box 10.5). Public awareness campaigns and strong messaging have helped to spawn social penalties for arms acquisition and ownership, and can simultaneously raise the price of, and reduce the preference for, firearms. While debates persist over the advantages of individual versus collective incentives for surrendering weapons, acknowledgement of the demand aspects of weapons possession is growing (Muggah and Brauer, 2004; Muggah, 2004d). Greater attention to demand reduction is likely to become an increasingly important feature of DDR and weapons reduction interventions in coming years.

> Recent initiatives in Haiti and the Solomon Islands are concentrating on re-engineering community attitudes towards firearms.

While new and energetic approaches to demand reduction are being introduced in DDR and weapons reduction initiatives, many are still top-down, and are not accountable to the very communities they seek to support. Many agencies continue to adopt *blueprint* methodologies for DDR, devoting insufficient attention to customary norms and practices. As the following section makes clear, a major debate is continuing on the goals and appropriate ways of measuring

Box 10.5 *Konflik i nostap nao ia**: arms reduction in the Solomon Islands

The Solomon Islands is emerging from a brutal episode of violence, colloquially referred to as the 'tensions'. From 1998 to 2003, between 150 and 200 people were fatally injured and between 430 and 460 people were non-fatally injured—a sizeable number considering that the country's population is only 409,000.[44] At the height of the tensions, more than 35,000 Solomon Islanders were displaced throughout the two main islands, Guadalcanal and Malaita. All of this turmoil was caused by an estimated 3,500–5,000 illegal high-powered, manufactured weapons (Nelson and Muggah, 2004).

Figure 10.5 **Frequency of arms and laceration injuries, National Referral Hospital, 1994-2004**

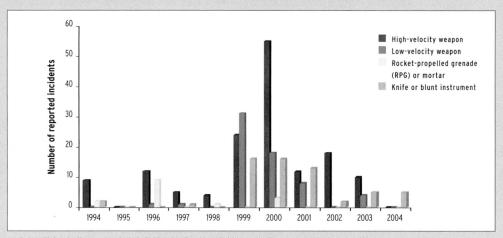

Notes: High-velocity weapons include M-16 and police-issue SL88 assault rifles, and pistols; low-velocity weapons include shotguns, .22 rifles, and home-made armaments.

Source: Nelson and Muggah (2004)

The country entered a post-conflict period following the signing of the Townsville Peace Agreement on 15 October 2000. Despite the accord and the deployment of an international peace monitoring team, fighting continued between the two principal factions, the Isatabu Freedom Movement and the Malaita Eagle Front.

A number of other initiatives were conducted between 2001 and 2003, including the demobilization of more than 2,500 special constables (police reservists) believed to be responsible for much of the armed violence. The National Peace Council also introduced a weapons reduction initiative, the 'weapons-free village' scheme, leading to the return of 67 firearms of varying quality (Muggah, 2003).

Under the Pacific Island Forum's Biketawa Declaration and authorized by International Assistance Bill 200, a 2,250-strong Regional Assistance Mission for Solomon Islands (RAMSI) force was dispatched to the country's capital, Honiara, in July 2003. Operation Helpem Fren was given an 18-month mandate, and was primarily a policing endeavour. From the beginning, it sought to establish security through robust deterrence-based approaches in Honiara in order to enable government, businesses, and communities to operate free of armed intimidation. By the end of 2003, security had been extended to outlying islands.

A memorial dedicated to the prospect of a gun-free Solomon Islands.

the success of DDR and weapons reduction. Indeed, the majority of evaluations to date have concentrated on the number and quality of weapons collected or destroyed and the types of incentives introduced. In addition, most offer anecdotal evidence on whether communities have benefited from a weapons-free environment or the lives of 'bene-ficiaries' and their communities have improved.[46] Few evaluations provide evidence on whether security and safety have changed meaningfully in response to the intervention. The reasons for this lack of information are varied, although they can be partly attributed to a lack of upfront funding for monitoring and analysis.

A critical look at DDR and weapons reduction

In the rush to promote DDR and weapons reduction as integral elements of post-conflict recovery, their many shortcom-ings tend to be glossed over. These limitations are interconnected and often poorly understood. At the outset, it should be recalled that, with regard to DDR, less-developed countries in particular confront a host of difficulties not faced by demobilizing armies in OECD nations and parts of Asia (Colletta et al., 1996).[47] DDR and weapons reduction are espe-cially complex in environments where there is no tradition of transparency and civilian oversight of the military, and where fundamental institutions, such as the police and judiciary, have broken down. Other major weaknesses relate to the dis-proportionate focus on disarmament, at the expense of longer-term activities such as reintegration, and the ambiguous criteria invoked for measuring 'success' or 'failure'. Related to this are the ambiguous 'objectives' often ascribed to DDR and weapons reduction. Moreover, strategies to manage expectations, to ensure effective institutional collaboration, to raise adequate funds, and to create appropriate incentives are often formulated with insufficient advance preparation.

Disarmament bias

Despite the development sector's growing involvement in promoting DDR and weapons reduction, the number of weapons collected continues to serve as a benchmark of the success of an intervention rather than the extent to which it has improved security, much less redressed gender imbalances or advanced poverty reduction.[48] Many donors and governments continue to prioritize the gathering of hardware. This 'disarmament bias' persists, even though there is mounting evidence that absolute numbers of arms collected do not necessarily contribute to improved security, or even to the building of confidence. In addition, even when considerable numbers of arms have been collected, DDR and weapons reduction efforts continue to neglect their safe storage or destruction—a crucial activity in unstable environments where police and military structures are notoriously prone to 'recycling' arms back into the community.

Measuring success

Another major criticism of DDR and weapons reduction pertains to the meaning of 'success' itself. Success is often defined differently because the objectives (and motives) of numerous actors are widely divergent and even contradictory during the post-conflict period. Due in large part to acute political pressure to initiate DDR or weapons reduction rapidly, there is seldom adequate reflection on their short-, medium-, and long-term objectives. For example, many military and government strategists concede that DDR serves a pragmatic and temporary function: collecting weapons and disarming and deterring potential spoilers. They might also agree that DDR should serve a symbolic purpose, such as building confidence between erstwhile combatants and their communities. Development agencies and donors may also, confusingly, see DDR and weapons reduction as either tied to, or substituting for, viable long-term development programmes, and former combatants as a creative and dynamic source of productive labour. Furthermore, in situations where hard choices regularly need to be made, DDR can also seek to lead or replace a genuine political process in the post-conflict period. In resource-scarce environments, where DDR or weapons reduction are the only initiatives on offer, this can result in the setting of dangerous precedents (Muggah, 2004a).

DDR and weapons reduction frequently substitute for 'political' solutions.

Where the precise aims of DDR or weapons reduction efforts are not completely clear, donors and implementers can adopt objectives that far exceed what can realistically be achieved. In Sudan, for example, it is expected that DDR will compensate for decades of underdevelopment. The cases of the Central African Republic, Liberia, the Republic of Congo, and others testify to the limitations of DDR, where goals and benchmarks of success measurements were poorly articulated from the outset (CENTRAL AFRICAN REPUBLIC). While some donors, development agencies, and policymakers may see advantages in keeping their aims as flexible as possible, it is of little surprise that primary stakeholders, combatants, and civilians often treat DDR and weapons reduction initiatives with suspicion, and even contempt.

To complicate matters, ambiguous labelling frequently frustrates DDR and weapons reduction initiatives. There are no clear or generally accepted definitions of what constitutes effective 'disarmament', 'demobilization', or 'reintegration', and there is no consensus on when these processes end or how their effectiveness can be gauged. The conceptual and practical difficulties associated with distinguishing between 'combatants' and 'civilians' are also well known—and are predominant in post-conflict countries such as Afghanistan, Haiti, and Iraq, as well as in the Great Lakes Region of Africa (CERI, 2004; Jensen and Stepputat, 2001; Muggah, 2004a).[49] Sometimes the demobilized include ex-soldiers from a national army and the former rebel fighters with whom they have been at war, as in Angola and Sierra Leone. In other instances, the demobilized are soldiers from two warring national militaries, as with Eritrea and Ethiopia. In Afghanistan and the Republic of Congo, it is difficult, if not impossible, to distinguish between legitimate combatants and civilians. In many cases, the distinction between formal combatants and part-time warriors is glossed over or quietly ignored (CERI, 2004).

Management of expectations

Development actors often overlook a key challenge: the effective management of expectations. If DDR or weapons reduction are undertaken without an effective communications or public awareness strategy, the consequences can be disastrous. DDR pursued in the Philippines and West Africa reveals how the mismanagement of expectations and inadequate preparation for disarmament generated counterproductive, even lethal, outcomes (see Box 10.6). As in

Box 10.6   UN peacekeeping operations: *plus ça change*

More than a decade ago, then UN Secretary-General Boutros Boutros-Ghali pledged that the UN would not make the same mistake in Mozambique as it had in Angola. Disarmament during the second UN Angola Verification Mission (UNAVEM II) had not been meaningfully implemented in the lead-up to the country's 1992 national elections. Recognizing that the election results had not gone his way, the UNITA rebel leader, Jonas Savimbi, plunged the country back into civil war using arms he had never turned in.

Boutros-Ghali made clear that the UN Operation in Mozambique (ONUMOZ), unlike UNAVEM II, would destroy significant quantities of arms and ammunition. Moreover, it would engage the civilian population as well as the protagonists' armed forces. In the end, however, the UN made negligible progress in accounting for arms circulating throughout the country (Berman 1996). Fortunately, the Resistência Nacional Moçambicana (RENAMO) rebel leader, Afonso Dhlakama, in addition to replacing his fatigues with Italian-tailored suits, gracefully accepted electoral defeat. In both cases, the international community failed to take full advantage of an opportunity to address the issue of small arms proliferation decisively.

Despite widespread recognition of the inadequate approaches to weapons collection adopted by UN peace operations, the situation remains dire. In that context, the Report of the Panel on United Nations Peace Operations, the so-called *Brahimi Report*, underscored the importance of ensuring consistent funding for DDR (UNSC, 2000a; paras. 42 and 47). Two years into the 'post-Brahimi era', the UN nevertheless failed to implement the report's recommendations concerning DDR of ex-combatants in DRC when the mandate for MONUC was amended (Durch et al., 2003, p. 28).

In Liberia, however, UNMIL received funds to rehabilitate former combatants as part of the regular assessed peacekeeping budget (Durch et al., 2003), but not in a sustainable manner. The initial funds set aside for the DDR programme were based on an estimate of 38,000 ex-combatants. In the end, however, 107,000 individuals entered the programme and were eligible to receive benefits. Donors are reportedly unwilling to make up the shortfall and the programme has run into problems. Whether the fundamental problem lies with loose eligibility criteria or a gross underestimation of absolute numbers, it is clear that operational and logistical demands exceeded the donor community's store of political and financial will (Berman, 2005).

Former combatants hand over their weapons to the UN in exchange for money during UNMIL's disarmament programme in December 2003. The UN grossly underestimated how many ex-fighters would be eligible for DDR.
Author: Eric G. Berman

Liberia, a reintegration industry has been spawned in Mindanao, Philippines, where international agencies, such as UNDP and the United States Agency for International Development (USAID), continue to support tens of thousands more Moro National Liberation Front ex-combatants and dependents than are believed to exist (Muggah, 2004c). In many cases, combatant numbers are inflated in order to claim benefits. In such scenarios, DDR and weapons reduction may not only turn into 'reward' programmes, but they can also fuel an illegal and transnational weapons market.[50] Local entrepreneurs—themselves often power brokers or former combatants—frequently hijack such initiatives and consolidate a domestic or regional trade in small arms and light weapons. The emergence of black markets in the wake of DDR and weapons reduction projects has been witnessed most recently in, among other places, Guinea, Haiti, Sierra Leone, and the Solomon Islands (Milner, 2004; Nichols, 2004; Muggah, 2005c).

Institutional barriers

The objectives of various stakeholders are often widely divergent in the 'post-conflict' period.

DDR and weapons reduction face considerable institutional challenges. For example, despite the recent theoretical gains made in linking development activities with practical disarmament outlined above, 'turf' battles persist between agencies on the ground. Approaches to organizing and implementing DDR and weapons reduction vary from the assignation of a 'lead agency' to oversee the process in its entirety to an emphasis on better 'coordination' among a range of separate agencies. Alarmingly, a number of development agencies are still reluctant to accept the relevance of programmes to reduce armed violence, particularly where small arms and light weapons are viewed as either external to their mandate or too sensitive an issue. As a result, DDR and weapons reduction are frequently not integrated into Poverty Reduction Strategy Papers and other post-conflict recovery mechanisms.

Financing

Due in part to conflicting interpretations of success, and different objectives and perceptions of the target group, DDR and weapons reduction activities are regularly under-funded. The matter is complicated by a poor appreciation among donors of the various dimensions of DDR and weapons reduction programmes. Another contributing factor is institutional disagreements between development actors over specific roles and responsibilities. Funding for reintegration activities is often deficient from the outset. Instead, resources are directed towards more 'visible' interventions, such as the collection of firearms, as was the case with former combatants with UNITA (União Nacional para a Independência Total de Angola) (Hitchcock, 2004).[51] Alternatively, financing of disarmament is sometimes inadequate due to mandate constraints and organizational reticence to take on 'hard' security issues. In still other cases, funding is simply poorly targeted. Producing a doctrine for, and clarifying the objectives of, DDR and weapons reduction activities would go some way toward resolving many of these problems.

Incentives

Because of these and other lingering disagreements, DDR and weapons reduction initiatives are often difficult to design. A common sticking point concerns whether to keep incentives as broad or as narrow as possible. Whenever DDR is conceived as a means of eliminating spoilers, and the combatant is consequently viewed as an impediment to stability, the programme is structured around reducing the capacity of ex-combatants to contribute to further destabilization. DDR interventions are thus targeted exclusively at high-risk groups and assistance is provided not as a 'reward' but as a clear 'incentive' to lay down weapons. By contrast, if the programme is conceived as an opportunity for longer-term development, then combatants and their dependents are potentially cast as *prima facie* storehouses of human capital. DDR activities are thus designed with incentives built in to encourage their widest possible participation in economic development.

The future of DDR and small arms control

Over the past few years, DDR and weapons reduction initiatives, whether pursued bilaterally or through regional and multilateral organizations, have been tested and refined by both the development and the security sectors (US GAO,

2000; UNDP, 2004a; 2005). There is acknowledgement that DDR and weapons reduction represent something new and must be regarded as actions taking place at the intersection of security and development. Moreover, there appears to be consensus that DDR and weapons reduction cannot be pursued independently of broader structural reforms in the governance and security sectors. Many developed countries, such as Germany and Sweden, have launched comprehensive programmes to review ways of strengthening approaches to DDR and weapons reduction.[52] In some instances, developing countries are experimenting with DDR and weapons reduction without international prodding or donor assistance.

The Panel on United Nations Peace Operations carried out a major review of peacekeeping operations in transitional and post-conflict contexts (UNGA, 2000). Its final product, known as the *Brahimi Report*, warns of deploying troops under the auspices of ambiguous mandates and identifies specific risks of conducting disarmament in such environments. Importantly, it stresses the importance of having clear chains of command, ensuring that adequate funds are made available for DDR in peacekeeping operation budgets, establishing a common doctrine, obtaining funding for reintegration from the assessed budget of the UN, and appreciating the dangers of contrasting objectives (see Box 10.6). In addition to UN mechanisms, smaller coalitions of states and regional organizations, such as the Economic Community of West African States, the EU, and the North Atlantic Treaty Organisation (NATO), have started to ensure coherence in their approach to DDR and weapons reduction (Small Arms Survey, 2003).[53]

The *Brahimi Report* helped produce clear institutional and organizational shifts in relation to DDR and weapons reduction. Bilateral development donors, the World Bank, UNDP, and various other UN agencies and NGOs are increasingly supporting—and even replacing—the traditional security sector as core backers of DDR and weapons reduction. These same actors are also increasingly backing a combination of community police programmes, cross-border initiatives to repatriate foreign ex-combatants, and SSR more generally. UNDP, for example, has set up a global Weapons Collection, Management and Destruction (WCMD) project and provides technical assistance for disarmament.[54] For its part, the World Bank has established a Post-Conflict Unit, which focuses on, among other things, advancing demobilization and reintegration programmes, landmine clearance, community-based rehabilitation, and meeting the special needs of children (World Bank, 2003b). Ensuring coordination between the UN and the World Bank in DDR and weapons reduction remains a major challenge and a massive opportunity.

In the past few years, DDR and weapons reduction have become progressively entrenched in the new post-conflict recovery orthodoxy. The UN Secretary-General's High-level Panel on Threats, Challenges and Change describes disarmament and demobilization as a 'priority for successful peace implementation' in post-conflict contexts (UNGA, 2004).[55] Particular emphasis is placed on ensuring continuous funding for the 'reintegration' aspects of DDR from the assessed budget of the UN. In addition, while core small arms concerns do not figure prominently in the Panel's final recommendations,[56] DDR and weapons reduction continue to enjoy widespread support and have been identified as one of the top priorities for Africa in the New Partnership for Africa's Development, or NEPAD. Importantly, the Millennium Project also draws attention to the importance of collecting and destroying weapons: '[m]uch greater international commitment is needed to collect and destroy weapons in the aftermath of conflict. Too often, collected weapons later come back into circulation' (Millennium Project, 2004, p. 189).

The UN is again revisiting its approach to DDR. Under the leadership of an Inter-Agency Working Group on DDR, it is developing an ambitious set of policy guidelines on DDR in 'post-conflict' environments in order to improve the effectiveness and sustainability of the organization's efforts.[57] These guidelines are to be based on lessons learnt and best practice identified in past and current DDR operations in Africa, Asia, Europe, and Latin America, with a partic-

There appears to be consensus that DDR and weapons reduction cannot be pursued independently of broader structural reforms.

Box 10.7   Reducing Haiti's arms: a legacy of failure

Armed violence reached new heights on the streets of Port-au-Prince in 2004. Between September 2003 and December 2004, at least 700 people were fatally wounded by small arms fire. At least 50 per cent of these deaths, and many hundreds of non-fatal gun injuries, occurred following the departure of President Jean-Bertrand Aristide in February 2004. MINUSTAH was mandated to bring peace and security to the country in April 2004 (UNSC, 2004). By the end of the year, some 6,700 peacekeepers and more than 1,600 civilian police had been dispatched. The disarmament, demobilization, and reintegration of several armed groups—from ex-army combatants to popular political organizations—forms a central plank of the strategy of the UN and the Interim Government of Haiti in the run-up to presidential and legislative elections on 13 November 2005.

It is important to remember that Haiti has been the site of several DDR and weapons reduction initiatives over the past century. Disarmament was attempted as far back as 1915, following the arrival of a US occupation force. International and national actors have launched other small-scale efforts since the early 1980s—mostly coercive endeavours, although some have involved buy-back schemes and voluntary strategies (see Table 10.1). Slightly more than 19,500 weapons have been collected since the mid-1990s, of which 2,435 (fewer than 12.5 per cent) have been destroyed (Muggah, 2005c).

Practical DDR and weapons reduction efforts have been spectacular failures. One of the largest followed from the US-led Operation Uphold Democracy in 1994. A large-scale buy-back initiative was undertaken between September 1994 and March 1995 ostensibly to reduce risks presented to US marines, to promote stability, and to reduce the number of weapons in circulation.[59] The US 10th Mountain Division collected more than 10,000 items, of which 3,684 were reportedly small arms and light weapons. Few weapons were destroyed, and many are believed to be back in the hands of the armed groups in the slums of Port-au-Prince. Some were even recycled into police training programmes administered by the US Department of State. US military commanders described the disarmament programme as a 'dismal failure' in terms of reducing the number of weapons in circulation or achieving a secure and stable environment (US GAO, 2000). Similarly unsuccessful were efforts made by the Organization of American States and the UN in the late 1990s to institutionalize regulations and disarmament through parliamentary action, public awareness campaigns, and attempts to establish national focal points.

Table 10.1   Reported weapon reduction activities, 1995-2004

Operation	Date	Type	Reach	Weapons collected	Weapons destroyed
US military	1994-95	Coercive	National	15,236*	2,088
US military	1995-95	Buy-back	National	3,684**	n/a
Sweeps by Haitian National Police (HNP)	1995	Coercive	National	n/a	n/a
HNP Operations	2002	Coercive	Port-au-Prince	51	n/a
HNP Operation Hurricane	2002	Coercive	National	5	n/a
HNP Operations	2002	Coercive	Port-au-Prince	37	n/a
HNP and Organization of American States	2003	Coercive	National	233	233
UNDP	2003	Voluntary	Port-au-Prince	55	55
Multinational Interim Force (MIF)	2004	Coercive	National	135	39
MINUSTAH	2004	Coercive	National	65	20
Total				**19,501**	**2,435**

Notes: * This figure comprises 7,450 rifles, 2,961 assault rifles, 2,413 handguns, 1,446 sub-machine guns, 604 shotguns, 5 M5 tank artillery, 1 M3A1 tank grease gun, and various others weapons of undetermined origin. Also seized was as an assortment of V150, anti-tank, mortar, howitzer, AAA, RR, B399, and automatic ammunition. ** Some 10,196 'items' were collected; 3,684 were classified as small arms and light weapons (US Army War College, 1996).

Source: Muggah (2005c)

ular focus on guaranteeing context specificity. Moreover, they intend to advance a framework for integrated planning and operations within the UN, thus ensuring that the different competencies and capacities of individual agencies, funds, and programmes can be harnessed to achieve the shared goal (MDDRWG, 2005). Efforts are already underway to develop integrated DDR operations in post-conflict Burundi, Sudan, and Haiti (see Box 10.7). Although DPKO and UNDP have traditionally taken the lead on DDR and weapons reduction, agencies as diverse as IOM, the International Labour Organization, and UNHCR are also increasingly becoming involved.[58]

CONCLUSION

Human security regularly deteriorates in the delicate period after wars are officially declared over. As a result, so-called post-conflict realities rarely bare much resemblance to what is implied by their definition. Rather, death and injury rates often remain comparatively high even after an armed conflict has come to an 'end'. The post-war contagion effects of armed violence can impact on the surrounding region.

Encouragingly, donors and multilateral agencies are today promoting DDR and weapons reduction as core pillars of the transition from armed conflict to peace. The World Bank has backed at least 16 demobilization and reintegration projects since the early 1990s. UNDP has overseen at least 45 weapons reduction initiatives and DDR interventions in more than 30 countries. The development sector has adopted a prominent role in violence reduction among combatants and civilians.

Just as there are many types of armed conflict, however, there are also many kinds of post-conflict contexts. In addition, while the transition from war to peace is influenced by the dynamics of an original armed conflict, the relief, development, and security-oriented strategies introduced in its wake similarly affect its shape. Lessons learnt from past DDR and weapons reduction interventions highlight the importance of articulating clear objectives and specifying clear benchmarks, as well as remaining cognisant of cultural, institutional, and communication barriers. When these are not adequately considered in advance, DDR and weapons reduction endeavours can have only a limited impact.

Despite their popularity among donors, policy-makers, and various multilateral agencies, DDR and weapons reduction frequently target the wrong people. Voluntary schemes that build primarily on rational self-interest and do not take into consideration the local context (such as buy-back programmes without adequate security guarantees) tend to enjoy only limited success and can do more harm than good. By contrast, interventions that endorse normative compliance—by building on existing customary institutions—advance a process that engenders ownership and more sustainable weapons reduction. Such approaches must acquire greater appreciation of the values and standards of particular societies so that appropriate disarmament incentives and deterrents can be elaborated.

For DDR and weapons reduction to be successful in generating security, they must be initiated at the earliest possible moment in the post-conflict period. Integrated and flexible interventions that bring together the combined expertise of multidisciplinary actors are increasingly favoured. It is also evident that 'successful' DDR is usually a discrete intervention with clear timetables, rather than a substitute for full-scale political or developmental reform. 'Joined-up' DDR and weapons reduction interventions, *together* with SSR, are increasingly regarded as fundamental to the positive transformation of the security sector. Ultimately, DDR and weapons reduction must be institutionalized within a normative framework—one that includes SSR.

Concrete and durable achievements are now regularly expected from DDR and weapons reduction. This is the case whether they are construed as interventions designed to reduce the number of firearms in a given post-conflict context, to improve safety, to contribute to community and economic development, or to diminish the prospects of renewed conflict. Their effectiveness in any of these areas remains unknown, however. There is also a persistent danger that DDR and weapons reduction schemes will continue to be viewed exclusively as an 'entitlement' for former soldiers instead of as a mechanism to improve security and development levels in traumatized communities. Unless their objectives become clearer and their capacity to enhance security is irrefutably demonstrated, DDR and weapons reduction may prove to be little more than another flash in the pan.

ANNEXE 10.1

A sample of DDR and weapons reduction initiatives in post-conflict countries, 2000–04

Project name	Countries involved	Primary agency	Project duration	DDR	Weapons reduction
				Regional programmes	
Operation Rachel	Mozambique, South Africa	Police sector and donors	1995–2003		Phase 1 and 2 weapons reduction activities and destruction of arms caches
Multi-Donor Reintegration Programme	Angola, Burundi, the Central African Republic (CAR), Democratic Republic of Congo (DRC), Namibia, Republic of Congo, Rwanda, Uganda, Zimbabwe	World Bank	2002–06	A combination of DDR programmes, including special projects targeting 'vulnerable groups'	
Small Arms Control in Central America	Belize, Costa Rica, El Salvador, Guatemala, Honduras, Nicaragua, Panama	El Salvador office of UNDP	June 2003– May 2004		Pilot initiatives, building of UNDP capacities
Small Arms Control in the Mano River Union	Guinea, Liberia, Sierra Leone	Liberia office of UNDP	September 2004– August 2005		Pilot initiatives, action plans, dialogue
South Eastern Europe Clearinghouse for the Control of Small Arms and Light Weapons (SEESAC)	Albania, Bosnia and Herzegovina, Bulgaria, Croatia, Macedonia, Moldova, Romania, Serbia and Montenegro	Belgrade office of UNDP	March 2002– February 2005		Assistance with implementing the Stability Pact Regional Implementation Plan
Small Arms Collection, Repatriation and Reintegration of DRC Ex-Combatants	DRC, Republic of Congo	IOM	2002	A combination of DDR projects, including interventions targeted at 'children'	
				National programmes	
Sub-Saharan Africa and the Horn of Africa					
Weapons Collection in Angola	Angola	UNDP	2001–02		Voluntary weapons collection activities throughout the country
DDR in Angola	Angola	UNDP	2002–03	DDR activities for UNITA troops	
Insecurity Reduction in the CAR and Reintegration and Community Support Projects	CAR	United Nations Peace-building Office (BONUCA) in the CAR and UNDP	March 2004– February 2007	Community-based DDR—focus on social reintegration of ex-combatants	
Support for Socio-economic Reintegration in the Comoros	Comoros	UNDP and the Government of Comoros	2001–02, 2003–05	Create the framework for economic reintegration of ex-combatants	

A sample of DDR and weapons reduction initiatives in post-conflict countries, 2000–04 (continued)

Project name	Countries involved	Primary agency	Project duration	DDR	Weapons reduction
Community Recovery for DDR in DRC	DRC	UNDP/BCPR	November 2003–October 2006	Recovery of communities to permit them to absorb returning IDPs and ex-combatants	
DDRRP in Liberia	Liberia	Liberia office of UNDP	2004–06	DDR activities for government forces and Liberians United for Reconciliation and Democracy (LURD) and Movement for Democracy in Liberia (MODEL) rebels, including weapons reduction, demobilization, and livelihood assistance	
Collection of illicit small arms and support for development in Niger	Niger	Niger office of UNDP	July 2001–August 2004		Pilot initiative to collect weapons through the National Commission for Control and Collection of Illicit Arms
Reintegration and arms collection in the Republic of Congo	Republic of Congo	IOM and Republic of Congo office of UNDP	May 2000–November 2002	DDR activities, including livelihood assistance and arms collection	
UNAMSIL (United Nations Assistance Mission for Sierra Leone) DDR programme	Sierra Leone	UNAMSIL	2001–02	Demobilization and reintegration of Armed Forces Revolutionary Council (AFRC) and Revolutionary United Front (RUF) fighters and former members of the Sierra Leone Army and the Civil Defence Force (CDF)	
Community Weapons Collection and 'Arms for Development' Programme	Sierra Leone	Sierra Leone office of UNDP	2002–05		Establishment of arms registries, licensing arrangements, and pilot projects to collect weapons
Weapons Control and Reduction Project	Somalia	Somalia office of UNDP	January 2003–March 2004		Support for a National Advisory Council, stockpile management, and community-based weapons control
Puntland Disarmament, Demobilization, and Reintegration Project	Somalia	Somalia office of UNDP and GTZ	January 2003–June 2004	Register militia members, establish armouries for storage, train new police recruits, reintegration programmes	
Asia, Middle East, and the South Pacific					
New Beginnings Project in Afghanistan	Afghanistan	UN	2003–04	DDR activities focusing on ex-combatants and militia groups	
DDR of the Free Aceh Movement (GAM)	Indonesia (Aceh)	Indonesian government	2004	DDR activities being prepared for combatants with the (GAM)	
Weapons seizures and reduction in Iraq	Iraq	Coalition of States	2004		Weapons reduction activities throughout the country, focusing on collection and, in some cases, destruction

A Sample of DDR and weapons reduction initiatives in post-conflict countries, 2000–04 (continued)

Project name	Countries involved	Primary agency	Project duration	DDR	Weapons reduction
Violence Reduction and Peace Consolidation in Papua New Guinea (PNG)	PNG (Bougainville)	UNDP, United Nations Office for Project Services (UNOPS), and the United Nations Political Office in Bougainville (UNPOB)	May 2004–December 2005		Arms reduction pilot projects and building capacity in the PNG government
Demobilisation and Reintegration of Ex-Combatants and Vulnerable Groups	Solomon Islands	Fiji office of UNDP	2000–03	DDR activities with Special Constables and ex-militia members	
Support to the Weapons Free Village Campaign	Solomon Islands	Fiji office of UNDP and National Peace Council	January 2003–December 2004		Community-based weapons reduction and reconciliation projects
Balkans and the Caucasus					
Albania weapons control project	Albania	Albania office of UNDP	February 2002–February 2004		Public awareness, capacity-building, weapons reduction, and development investment
Operation Harvest and assorted small arms projects	Bosnia and Herzegovina	Bosnia and Herzegovina office of UNDP	1999–2005		Baseline assessment, capacity-building, and weapons reduction pilot initiatives, focusing on both ethnic Albanian ex-combatants and civilians
Weapons collection in Croatia	Croatia	Government	2001		Voluntary weapons reduction initiatives targeting civilians
Weapons reduction in Georgia	Georgia	OSCE	2002		Voluntary weapons reduction activities in communities
Illicit Small Arms Project	Kosovo	Kosovo office of UNDP	August 2002–December 2003		Community policing, strengthening regulatory framework, weapons in exchange for development
Operation Essential Harvest	Former Yugoslav Republic of Macedonia (FYROM)	Macedonia office of UNDP	2003–05		Capacity-building for Government of FYROM, safer-community strategies, public awareness, community policing
SEESAC	Serbia and Montenegro	Belgrade office of UNDP	2002–03		Weapons reduction and customs control—focus on civilian disarmament
Small Arms control in Serbia and Montenegro	Serbia and Montenegro	Belgrade office of UNDP	May 2004–June 2005		Capacity-building for the Governments of the Republics of Serbia and Montenegro, surplus weapons destruction
Latin America and the Caribbean					
Strengthening Mechanisms for Small Arms Control	El Salvador	El Salvador office of UNDP	February 2001–December 2003		Strengthening regulatory controls, public awareness, and demand reduction
Support for national disarmament and community-based arms reduction	Haiti	Haiti office of UNDP	May 2003–December 2004		Strengthening regulatory controls and community-based disarmament pilot projects

A sample of DDR and weapons reduction initiatives in post-conflict countries, 2000–04 (continued)

Project name	Countries involved	Primary agency	Project duration	DDR	Weapons reduction
Community-based DDR	Haiti	Haiti office of DPKO and UNDP	2004–06	Community-based DDR and strengthening of regulations	
Strengthening Small Arms Control	Honduras	Honduras office of UNDP	April 2003–December 2004		Capacity-building toward designing a national strategy for disarmament, public awareness, training, and forensics support

Sources: World Bank (2002; 2003a; 2003b); UNDP (2004a; 2004b); Small Arms Survey (2003); MDRP (2005)

LIST OF ABBREVIATIONS

CAR	Central African Republic
CDC	Centers for Disease Control
DDR	Disarmament, Demobilization, and Reintegration
DPKO	UN Department of Peacekeeping Operations
DRC	Democratic Republic of Congo
EU	European Union
GDP	Gross Domestic Product
HNP	Haitian National Police
ICRC	International Committee of the Red Cross
IDP	Internally Displaced Person
IOM	International Organization for Migration
KFOR	Kosovo Force
MINUSTAH	United Nations Stabilization Mission in Haiti
MONUC	United Nations Mission in the Democratic Republic of Congo
NATO	North Atlantic Treaty Organisation
NGO	Non-governmental organization
OECD	Organisation for Economic Co-operation and Development
OSCE	Organisation for Security and Co-operation in Europe
PUH	Pristina University Hospital, Kosovo
RAMSI	Regional Assistance Mission to the Solomon Islands
RUF	Revolutionary United Front, Sierra Leone
SEESAC	South Eastern Europe Clearinghouse for the Control of Small Arms and Light Weapons
SSR	Security sector reform
UNAVEM	United Nations Angola Verification Mission
UNDDA	United Nations Department for Disarmament Affairs

UNDP	United Nations Development Programme
UNHCR	United Nations High Commissioner for Refugees
UNIFEM	United Nations Development Fund for Women
UNITA	União Nacional para a Independência Total de Angola
USAID	United States Agency for International Development
WCMD	Weapons Collection Management and Destruction
WED	Weapons in Exchange for Development
WHO	World Health Organization

ENDNOTES

[1] The World Bank, for instance, claims that 'a structured DDR process, which demobilizes combatants in stages and emphasizes their ability to reintegrate into society, may reduce the risk of ex-combatants turning to violent crime or rejoining rebel groups in order to survive' (2003b, p. 159).

[2] See Lacina and Gleditch (2004). Though often inaccurate, mortality estimates are regularly selected because they are more easily captured than other indicators, particularly those that have to contend with competing definitions and cultural interpretations (Keely et al., 2000). In the post-conflict period, longitudinal research generally focuses on 'excess' mortality or involves direct surveillance of mortality over time. Methods include retrospective probability surveys as well as pre- and post-analysis of census data (Heuveline, 2001).

[3] Ghobarah et al. find that the effects of armed conflicts in contiguous countries are substantial. In their sample, about 75 per cent of states plagued by civil war at home were affected by civil wars in neighbouring states. Of the 83 countries exposed to civil wars in neighbouring states, more than half were embroiled in a civil war at home (Ghobarah et al., 2004).

[4] See, for instance, GTZ (2004) and the Web site of the World Bank's Post-Conflict Unit, <http://www.worldbank.org/essd/essd.nsf/Post-Conflict/home> (accessed February 2005).

[5] The 'reconstruction' dimension quickly disappeared following the introduction of the Marshall Plan after the Second World War. The World Bank then swiftly turned to 'development efforts', particularly in the former colonies of European countries.

[6] Daponte argues that, in fact, '[t]here were relatively few deaths (approximately 56,000 to military personnel and 3,500 to civilians) from direct war effects. Post-war violence accounted for approximately 35,000 deaths. The largest component of deaths in this reconstruction derives from the 111,000 attributable to post-war adverse health effects. Of the total excess deaths in the Iraqi population, approximately 109,000 were ... men, 23,000 ... women, 74,000 ... children' (Daponte, 1993). See the International Physicians for the Prevention of Nuclear War (IPPNW) Web site: <http://www.ippnw.org/MGS/PSRQV3N2Daponte.html> (accessed February 2005).

[7] To put the public health costs in perspective, the World Health Organization (WHO) estimates that some 269,000 people died and 8.44 million years of productive life were lost to death and disability due to the direct and immediate effects of all international and civil wars in 1999 (WHO, 2001, p. 168). By comparison, Ghobarah et al. calculate that as many as 15 million 'excess' lives were lost in 1999 due to death and disability indirectly—because of related diseases in war-affected and neighbouring societies, and the lingering ramifications of war over the previous eight years (Ghobarah et al., 2004).

[8] The World Bank, for example, often introduces a transitional support strategy for short-to-medium-term involvement in a country (up to 24 months). It can only be administered if the 'active conflict' has diminished sufficiently to allow World Bank staff to travel, if there is a reasonable expectation of continued stability, if there are effective counterparts, and if there is evidence of strong international cooperation and the potential for a well-defined role. The World Bank has also established Post-Conflict Progress Indicators to determine whether International Development Association resources can be allocated to eligible countries. These 12 indicators are grouped in three clusters: security and reconciliation; economic recovery; and social inclusion and social development. Countries considered 'post-conflict' according to this rating system include Afghanistan, Angola, Burundi, Côte d'Ivoire, DRC, East Timor, Eritrea, Republic of the Congo, and Sierra Leone. These nine states were eligible for some USD 500 million in Fiscal Year 2004 on top of regular performance-based assistance (World Bank, 1998; 2003b; 2003e).

[9] Together with the World Bank and the UNDP, the GTZ appears to view the 'two-year' period following the end of an armed conflict as a 'transition' or as 'post-conflict' (GTZ, 2004).

[10] See, for instance, World Bank (1998; 2003b) and post-conflict countries reviewed in Small Arms Survey (2004).

[11] As the primary referral hospital for traumatic injuries, the PUH recorded some 98 incidents in 2002. In 2001, there were an estimated 125 reported firearm-related injuries, and more than 100 between June and December 1999, immediately following the conflict (Khakee and Florquin, 2003).

[12] Ethnic Serbs also receive treatment and care at Camp Bondsteel, the US KFOR brigade headquarters in the south-east (Khakee and Florquin, 2003).

[13] The Centers for Disease Control and Prevention (CDC), PAHO, and the WHO have demonstrated this point. Together they have supported the establishment of post-conflict injury surveillance programmes in El Salvador, Honduras, Mozambique, Nicaragua, and Sri Lanka.

[14] An earlier case study by the ICRC, carried out between January and March 1995 (conflict) and between September 1995 and March 1996 (post-conflict), found that the annual incidence of weapon injuries decreased by only 33 per cent between the 'conflict' and 'post-conflict' periods. The ICRC also discovered, however, that mortality rates for weapon injuries increased from 2.5 per cent to 6.1 per cent during the post-conflict period (ICRC, 1999). Despite the decline in overall weapon injuries, therefore, more people died per month from weapon injuries during the post-conflict period.

[15] In a survey of 863 weapon injuries, the ICRC found that injury rates fell while the United Nations Transitional Authority in Cambodia (UNTAC) was in the country (71 firearm injuries per 100,000). Nevertheless, after the force departed, they rose to levels higher

than those registered prior to the conclusion of the peace deal (from 147 per 100,000 to 163 per 100,000) (ICRC, 1999, pp. 33–38).

[16] In East Timor, for instance, before 1999, the health force numbered 3,500—of which 2,632 were Timorese. After the armed conflict, only 31 qualified Timorese doctors and fewer than 23 medical students were prepared to return to work. In Cambodia, in 1975, there were 487 doctors; by 1979, this number had fallen to 43. While massive increases in the size of the health force were reported by the mid-1990s, many employees were not necessarily suited to meet the needs of Cambodian society (Smith, 2003). See also Guha-Sapir and van Panhuis (2002b).

[17] These populations are widely dispersed: some 3.3 million refugees are in Central Asia and the Middle East, 2.8 million are in Africa, 2.4 million are in Europe, more than 600,000 are in the Americas, and more than 800,000 in Asia and the Pacific. IDPs are distributed across at least 52 countries in Africa (12.7 million), Asia and the Pacific (3.6 million), the Americas (3.3 million), Europe (3 million), and the Middle East (2 million). See <www.unhcr.ch> (Accessed March 2005).

[18] The UN High Level Panel on Threats, Challenges and Change has acknowledged that '[p]articularly egregious violations, such as occur when armed groups militarize refugee camps, require emphatic responses from the international community, including from the Security Council acting under Chapter VII of the Charter of the United Nations. Although the Security Council has acknowledged that such militarization is a threat to peace and security, it has not developed the capacity or shown the will to confront the problem' (UNGA, 2004, p. 63).

[19] In a 2004 cohort survey of US soldiers and marines returning from Iraq (1,709) and Afghanistan (1,962), for instance, between 66 and 97 per cent claimed to have been shot at. Furthermore, as many as 95 per cent of respondents were exposed to dead bodies and human remains and as many as 28 per cent claimed responsibility for killing a non-combatant (Hoge et al., 2004).

[20] The CDC, for example, has observed how, in recent years, an increased number of rape and sexual violence cases have been reported in conflict and post-conflict settings—much of the abuse perpetrated at gunpoint. See <http://www.cdc.gov/nceh/ierh/Research&Survey/WarRelated.htm> (accessed March 2005).

[21] For a discussion of participatory research and armed violence, see, for example, Banerjee and Muggah (2002); Moser and Muggah (2003); and LeBrun and Muggah (2005, forthcoming).

[22] Knight et al. find that an additional 2.2 per cent of GDP spent on the military, sustained for seven years (the typical length of an armed conflict), would lead to a permanent loss of about 2 per cent of GDP (Knight et al., 1996).

[23] The World Bank and the International Monetary Fund, for example, have established the Heavily Indebted Poor Countries initiative and the Post-Conflict Unit of the World Bank has instituted small-scale grant and credit provisions for other conflict-affected nations. Pre-arrears arrangements to support early recovery efforts have also been introduced in specific circumstances (World Bank, 2003e).

[24] The World Bank notes that the first post-conflict decade often demonstrates robust macroeconomic progress: average annual per capita growth is around 1.1 per cent faster than normal (World Bank, 2003b, p. 153).

[25] On Papua New Guinea and the Solomon Islands, see Muggah (2004c) and Nelson and Muggah (2004). On South Africa, see Kirsten et al. (2004).

[26] See, for example, the work of Collier and Hoeffler (2002), which shows how a history of armed conflict is a predictor of the onset of conflict. See also World Bank (2003b).

[27] As Tschirgi observes, '[d]espite over ten years of practice, there is no commonly agreed post-conflict peace-building policy or doctrine'. Peacemaking, peacekeeping, and peace-building are viewed as 'instruments in the UN's toolkit to respond to conflicts at the end of the Cold War'. Although peace-building was originally introduced to consolidate peace in 'post-conflict' countries, Tschirgi notes that the concept was expanded in the 1990s to encompass conflict prevention, conflict management, and post-conflict reconstruction (Tschirgi, 2004, p. i).

[28] See, for example, GTZ (2004); World Bank (1998; 2003b); Collier and Hoeffler (2002); Tschirgi (2004).

[29] The World Bank reports, however, that where armed conflicts end with a negotiated settlement, rebel reintegration occurs in about 50 per cent of cases. Without a treaty, reintegration is rarer, taking place in approximately 14 per cent of cases (World Bank, 1998).

[30] Much of this literature continues to analyse DDR in terms of its constituent parts rather than as an overarching concept. See, for example, CERI (2004); Kingma (2000; 2002); GTZ (1996; 2001; 2004); Jensen and Stepputat (2001); Berdal (1996); and Ginifer et al. (2004).

[31] Ball describes the 'security sector' in broader terms, including 'the security forces (military, paramilitary, police), the agencies of government and parliament responsible for oversight of these forces, informal security forces, the judiciary and correction system, private security firms and civil society' (Ball, 2001, p. 47).

[32] The World Bank has assessed the relationship between DDR and SSR in the context of the Great Lakes Region. It notes that the linkage between the two must be made explicit in order for countries to take part in the Multi-Country Demobilization and Reintegration Program (MDRP). The paper underlines the importance of conducting defence reviews, establishing clear benchmarks for the 'appropriate' size of the armed forces and police, absorbing ex-combatants into the military, and earmarking requisite funds—all factors essential in DDR planning. It also claims that 'the window of opportunity for SSR and DDR in many post-conflict countries may be relatively narrow. The timetables for SSR and DDR can be under pressure from the overall peace process' (World Bank, 2003a, p. 4).

[33] See, for example, the report of the Millennium Project (2004, ch. 12), which considers strategies for countries affected by conflict.

[34] This factor is now acknowledged in the *Guidelines on Conflict Prevention*, produced by the Development Assistance Committee of the Organisation for Economic Co-operation and Development (OECD DAC, 2001), and highlighted in the report of the UN Secretary-General's High-level Panel on Threats, Challenges and Change (UNGA, 2004).

[35] See, for example, Cooper et al. (2003); Douma (2001); and Le Billon (2000).

[36] These acronyms refer to Disarmament, Demobilization, Reinsertion, and Reintegration (DDRR); Disarmament, Demobilization, Reinsertion, Rehabilitation, and Reintegration (DDRRR); and Demobilization and Reintegration Programme (DRP).

[37] After demobilizing, combatants often lose their power to bargain with the government. In cases where post-war peace is premised on a voluntary agreement, the drastic change in the parties' relative bargaining capabilities makes the agreement difficult to ensure over time. The government, which retains its military capacities, can renege on its promise after the rebels have disarmed. The government has both the power and the incentive to renegotiate the settlement or to defect from it unilaterally. This is particularly common in situations where an armed conflict had no definitive outcome, but rather, the violence ended with a ceasefire, truce, or negotiated compromise. One way that parties have attempted to protect themselves against violations of a peace deal has been to integrate parts of a rebel force into the national military. See, for example, World Bank (2003b; 2003c).

[38] DPKO has observed that 'disarmament, demobilization and reintegration form a continuum. Demobilization is only possible when there is some kind of disarmament' (DPKO, 1997).

[39] The World Bank identifies two events of the mid-1990s as catalysts for a new approach to conflict and post-conflict situations. The first came in 1994, when the agency was asked to preside over the multi-donor Holst Fund for the West Bank and Gaza Strip. The second came in 1995, when it was asked by the European Commission to plan and coordinate international investment in post-conflict Bosnia and Herzegovina. By the late 1990s, it was active in Afghanistan,

East Timor, the Great Lakes Region of Africa, Kosovo, Rwanda, and Sierra Leone (World Bank, 1998; 2003b).

[40] The US Department of State's recently formed Office of Weapons Removal and Abatement, for example, intends to reduce 'threats to public health and social stability in nations affected by persistent landmines, freely available small arms and light weapons, abandoned ordnance, excess man-portable air defense systems (MANPADS), and poorly secured munitions stockpiles'. It will do so by curbing illicit trafficking and indiscriminate use of small arms and pursuing 'post-conflict cleanup of such weapons'. See <http://www.state.gov/t/pm/wra> (accessed March 2005).

[41] Moreover, in the case of El Salvador, there was explicit recognition that destroying a marginal surplus of weapons was less important than focusing on the political, social, and legal aspects of weapons possession and availability.

[42] For more information, see Small Arms Survey (2002; 2003).

[43] See Faltas and Paes (2004); Small Arms Survey (2003); Faltas et al. (2001); Meek (1998).

[44] At least 50–60 people were fatally injured in 2003 alone. Non-fatal firearm injuries have not been counted, but epidemiological estimates suggest a ratio as high as three non-fatal shootings to each lethal gun injury, or as many as 150–180 wounded. Coupled with the 257 people injured between 1998 and 2002, one arrives at an estimate of at least 400. Armed crime, particularly extortion, kidnapping, and intimidation, eased considerably after the arrival of RAMSI (Muggah, 2003).

[45] Key informants in the Australian Department of Defence anticipated some casualties due to the proliferation of four (still unrecovered) 50mm cannons. The decision not to deploy armoured personnel vehicles was largely based on the possible misuse of these weapons.

[46] There is growing recognition of the need for effective baseline studies and evidence-based approaches. For example, knowledge of distribution, type of weapons, and ownership patterns can inform efforts to provide realistic reintegration support (Kingma, 2002).

[47] In wealthy nations, the return of erstwhile soldiers to civilian life is usually a fairly well-managed and predictable process. In 2003 BICC announced that the number of government soldiers in uniform worldwide declined for the twelfth successive year. There are now an estimated 21 million soldiers: some 10.9 million are in Asia. The only region where the number of soldiers increased was Africa: by 17 per cent between 1997 and 2001 (BICC, 2003, p. 64). DDR initiatives conducted in industrialized nations are often exceptionally well financed and generally undertaken within a framework of appropriate checks and balances.

[48] DDR is often criticized for being 'gender blind'. The United Nations Development Fund for Women (UNIFEM) has repeatedly observed that women ex-combatants, despite the essential roles they play in post-conflict DDR processes, are frequently excluded. Because of the focus on men, the needs of women ex-combatants are often inadequately addressed during the demobilization phase, often resulting in untenable situations of deteriorating health and poverty (UNIFEM, 2004).

[49] A matter of considerable debate is how to determine whether an individual seeking DDR- or weapons reduction-related assistance

is a combatant. In the absence of credible registries and lists, the World Bank claims that such criteria can include: 'self-identification, proven affiliation with a known armed group, and/or proof of military ability, such as weapons handling. Especially for special projects involving irregular forces, particular attention needs to be paid to avoiding the creation of perverse incentives (i.e. individuals or groups arming themselves in order to subsequently benefit from a program of demobilization)' (World Bank, 2003a). But designation of status is often exceedingly difficult in practice.

[50] UNDP has expressed particular concern about the dangers of DDR being perceived as an 'entitlement' for armed elements. For a more detailed discussion, see UNDP (2005).

[51] In other cases, reintegration is often emphasized at the expense of disarmament. In Rwanda, for instance, DDR morphed into a de facto relief operation rather a transitional programme to promote security (World Bank, 2003b).

[52] See, for example, the preliminary findings of the Stockholm Initiative on Disarmament Demobilisation Reintegration, <http://www.sweden. gov.se/sb/d/4890> (accessed March 2005).

[53] At the request of the European Parliament and the European Commission, the United Nations Institute for Disarmament Research (UNIDIR) has initiated a study entitled 'European Action on Small Arms, Light Weapons and Explosive Remnants of War'. The findings will be released at the end of 2005.

[54] In addition to supporting workshops and seminars on arms control and evidence-based policy-making, the WCMD project has produced standard operating procedures and weapons reduction tools for activities involving governments, country offices, NGOs, and other international actors.

[55] The Panel asserts that 'demobilizing combatants is the single most important factor determining the success of peace operations. Without demobilization, civil wars cannot be brought to an end and other critical goals—such as democratization, justice and development—have little chance for success. In case after case, however, demobilization is not accorded priority by funders. When peace operations are deployed, they must be resourced to undertake the demobilization and disarmament of combatants' (UNGA, 2004, p. 61).

[56] See UNGA (2004, p. 36, paras. 95–97).

[57] The Inter-Agency Working Group on DDR includes UNICEF, UNDDA, DPKO, UNIFEM, UNDP, UNHCR, and the United Nations Population Fund (UNFPA).

[58] In 2004, DPKO took the lead on DDR activities in Afghanistan, Burundi, Côte d'Ivoire, Haiti, and Sudan. DDR initiatives launched by DPKO and UNDP are ongoing in Haiti (2004), CAR (2003), Liberia (2003), DRC (2002), Sierra Leone (2002), Solomon Islands (2002), Somalia (2002), Niger (2001), Republic of Congo (2001), and elsewhere.

[59] IOM and USAID also launched a demobilization initiative between 1994 and 1996, which resulted in the demobilization of almost 5,500 former members of the army (Muggah, 2005c).

BIBLIOGRAPHY

Addison, Tony, ed. 2003. *From Conflict to Recovery in Africa.* New York: Oxford University Press.

Anderson, Mary. 1999. *How Aid Can Support Peace—Or War.* Boulder, CO: Lynne Rienner.

Archer, David and Richard Gartner. 1976. 'Violent Acts and Violent Times: A Comparative Approach to Post-War Homicide Rates.' *American Sociological Review,* 41, pp. 937–63.

Ball, Nicole. 2001. 'Transforming Security Sectors: The IMF and World Bank Approaches.' *Conflict, Security and Development,* 1(1), pp. 45–60.

—. 2002. *Dilemmas of Security Sector Reform: Response to 'Security Sector Reform in Developing and Transitional Countries.* Berlin: Berghof Research Centre for Constructive Conflict Management. Accessed December 2004.
<http://www.berghof-handbook.net/articles/ssr_ball.pdf>

Banerjee, Dipankar and Robert Muggah, eds. 2002. *Human Security in South Asia: Participatory Research on Small Arms.* Colombo: Regional Centre for Strategic Studies.

Barbara, Joanna Santa. 1997. 'The Psychological Effects of War on Children.' In Barry S. Levy and Victor W. Sidel, eds. *War and Public Health*. Oxford and New York: Oxford University Press and the American Public Health Association.

Bendana, Alejandro. 1999. *Demobilization and Reintegration in Central America: Peace-building Challenges and Responses*. Managua: Centro de Estudios Internacionales.

Berdal, Mats, 1996. *Disarmament and Demobilization after Civil Wars*. Adelphi Paper No. 303. Oxford: Oxford University Press.

Berman, Eric. 1996. *Managing Arms in Peace Processes: Mozambique*. Geneva: United Nations Institute for Disarmament Research.

—. 2005. 'Field Research on Small Arms and Its Importance for Peace Operations: A Practitioner's View.' In Martin Carment and David Rudner, eds. *Peacekeeping Intelligence: New Players, Extended Boundaries*. London: Routledge Taylor and Francis Group. Forthcoming.

BICC (Bonn International Center for Conversion). 2003. *Conversion Survey 2003: Global Disarmament, Demilitarization and Demobilization*. Baden-Baden: Nomos Verlagsgesellschaft.

Bilukha, Oleg, Muireann Brennan, and Woodruff Bradley. 2003. 'Death and Injury from Landmines and Unexploded Ordnance in Afghanistan.' *The Journal of the American Medical Association (JAMA)*, 290 (5), pp. 650–53.

Bradley, Sean, Philippe Maughan, and Massimo Fuasto. 2002. 'Sierra Leone: Disarmament, Demobilization and Reintegration (DDR).' *World Bank Findings: African Region*, 81. October.

Brauer, Jurgen and Paul Dunne. 2004. *Arms Trade and Economic Development: Theory, Policy, and Cases in Arms Trade Offsets*. London: Routledge.

Braveman, Paula et al. 1997. 'Public Health and War in Central America.' In Barry S. Levy and Victor W. Sidel, eds. *War and Public Health*. Oxford and New York: Oxford University Press and the American Public Health Association.

Butler, Declan. 1997. 'Admission on Gulf War Vaccines Spurs Debate on Medical Records.' *Nature*, 390, pp. 3–4.

Carballo, Manuel. 2001. 'Reflections.' In James Keely and Holly E. Reed, eds. *Forced Migration and Mortality*. Washington, DC: National Academy Press.

Cardozo, Barbara et al. 2003. 'Mental Health, Social Functioning and Feelings of Hatred and Revenge of Kosovar Albanians One Year After the War in Kosovo.' *Journal of Traumatic Stress*, 16(4), pp. 351–60.

CDC (Centers for Disease Control). 1988. 'Health Status of Vietnam Veterans: Psychological Characteristics.' *Journal of the American Medical Association (JAMA)*, 259 (18), pp. 2701–07.

CERI (Centre for International Studies and Research). 2004. *The Politics and Anti-Politics of Contemporary Disarmament, Demobilization and Reintegration Programs*. Paris: CERI.

Chachiua, Martinho. 1999. 'Arms Management Programme: Operations Rachel 1996–1999.' *ISS Monograph Series*, No. 38, June. Accessed 23 March 2005. <http://www.iss.co.za/Pubs/Monographs/No38/TitleAndContents.html>

CICS (Centre for International Cooperation and Security). 2004. 'Assessing and Reviewing the Impact of Small Arms Projects on Arms Availability and Poverty.' Draft Synthesis Report. Bradford: CICS, University of Bradford. July.

Cole, Thomas. 2003. 'Taking Aim at Gun Violence: Tracing Bullets and Guns to Sideline Scofflaw Dealers.' *Journal of the American Medical Association (JAMA)*, 290 (5), p. 583–85.

Colletta, Nat, Markus Kostner, and Ingo Wiederhofer. 1996. *Case Studies in War-to-Peace Transition: the Demobilization and Reintegration of Ex-Combatants in Ethiopia, Namibia and Uganda*. Washington, DC: World Bank. Accessed 23 March 2005. <http://www-wds.world bank.org/servlet/WDSContentServer/WDSP/IB/1996/06/01/000009265_3961214183011/Rendered/PDF/multi_page.pdf>

Collier, Paul. 1994. 'Demobilization and Insecurity: A Study in the Economics of the Transition from War to Peace.' *Journal of International Development*, 6. pp. 343–51.

Collier, Paul and Anke Hoeffler. 2002. *Greed and Grievance in Civil Wars*. Working Paper. Oxford: Centre for the Study of African Economies, Oxford University.

— and Måns Söderbom. 2001. *On the Duration of War*. Oxford: Centre for the Study of African Economies, Oxford University.

Cook, Phil. 2001. 'The Cost and Benefits of Reducing Gun Violence.' *Harvard Health Policy Review*, (2)2, pp. 23–28.

Cooper, Neil, Jonathan Goodhand, and Michael Pugh. 2004. *War Economies in their Regional Context: The Challenges of Transformation*. London: Lynne Rienner.

Cruz, José Miguel and María Antonieta Beltrán. 2000. *Las Armas en El Salvador: Diagnóstico Sobre su Situación y su Impacto*. San Salvador: University Institute for Public Opinion (IUDOP), Central American University.

Cuadra, Elvira. 2004. *El trinomio del fuego*. Managua: Centro de Estudios Internacionales.

Daponte, Beth. 1993. 'A Case Study in Estimating Casualties from War and Its Aftermath: The 1991 Persian Gulf War.' *Medicine and Global Survival*, 3(2). Accessed January 2005. <http://www.ippnw.org/MGS/PSRQV3N2Daponte.html>

De Beers, David. 2002. *An Integrated Approach to Small Arms Management: The EU ASAC Programme on Curbing Small Arms and Light Weapons in Cambodia*. Presentation to the Gesellschaft für Technische Zusammenarbeit (GTZ), Berlin, 19 December.

Demetriou, Spyros, Robert Muggah, and Ian Biddle. 2001. *Small Arms Availability and Trade in the Republic of Congo*. Study prepared by the Small Arms Survey for the International Organization for Migration and United Nations Development Programme. September. Accessed April 2005. <http://www.undp.org/bcpr/smallarms/docs/roc_small_arms_study.pdf>

DFID (Department for International Development). 2003. *Tackling Poverty by Reducing Armed Violence: Recommendations from a Wilton Park Workshop*. London. 14–16 April.

Diamond, Larry. 2004. 'What Went Wrong in Iraq.' *Foreign Affairs*, 9(1). Accessed March 2005. <http://www.foreignaffairs.org/20040901faessay83505/larry-diamond/what-went-wrong-in-iraq.html>

Douma, Pyt. 2001. *Political Economy of Internal Conflict: A Review of Contemporary Trends and Issues*. Conflict Research Unit Working Paper No. 1. Clingendael: Netherlands Institute of International Relations.

Doyle, Martin and Nicholas Sambinis. 2004. *Making War and Building Peace: The United Nations after the Cold War*. New York: St. Martin's Press.

Duffield, Mark. 2001. *Global Governance and the New Wars: The Merging of Development and Security*. London: Zed Books.

Durch, William et al. 2003. *The Brahimi Report and the Future of UN Peace Operations*. Washington, DC: The Henry L. Stimson Center.

ECHA (Executive Committee on Humanitarian Assistance). 2000. 'Harnessing Institutional Capacities in Support of the Disarmament, Demobilisation and Reintegration of Former Combatants.' Paper prepared by ECHA Working Group, New York. 19 July.

Faltas, Sami, Glenn McDonald, and Camilla Waszink. 2001. *Removing Small Arms from Society: A Review of Weapons Reduction and Destruction Programmes*. Occasional Paper No. 2. Geneva: Small Arms Survey.

Faltas, Sami and Joseph Di Chiaro III, eds. 2001. *Managing the Remnants of War: Micro-disarmament as an Element of Peace-building*. Baden-Baden: Nomos Verlagsgesellschaft.

Faltas, Sami and Wolf-Christian Paes. 2004. E*xchanging Guns for Tools*. Brief No. 29. Bonn: BICC.

Garfield, Richard and Alfred Neugut. 1991. 'Epidemiologic Analysis of Warfare: A Historical Review.' *Journal of the American Medical Association (JAMA),* 226 (68), pp. 688–91.

Ghoborah, Hazem, Paul Huth, and Bruce Russett. 2003. 'Civil Wars Kill and Maim People—Long After the Shooting Stops.' *American Political Science Review,* 97, pp. 189–202.

—. 2004. 'The Post-War Public Health Effects of Civil Conflict.' *Social Science and Medicine,* 59, pp. 869–84.

Ginifer, Jeremy, Michael Bourne, and Owen Greene. 2004. *Armed Violence in Small Arms and Light Weapons, Post-Conflict Reconstruction and Disarmament, Demobilisation and Reintegration Initiatives*. Briefing Paper for DFID. Bradford: CICS, University of Bradford.

Ginifer, Jeremy and Christiana Solomon. 2004. *A Review of DDR and Arms Reduction Activities*. Background paper. Geneva: Small Arms Survey.

Godnick, Bill, Robert Muggah, and Camilla Waszink. 2003. *Balas perdidas: el impacto del mal uso de armas pequeñas en Centroamérica*. Geneva and London: Small Arms Survey and the International Action Network on Small Arms (IANSA).

—. 2005. 'Firearm Death and Injury Rates in Central America.' Background Paper. Geneva: Small Arms Survey.

Gomes Porto, João and Imogen Parsons. 2003. *Sustaining the Peace in Angola: An Overview of Current Demobilization, Disarmament and Reintegration*. Bonn: BICC. Paper 27. Accessed 24 March 2005. <http://www.bicc.de/publications/papers/paper27/paper27.pdf>

Grillot, Suzette, Shelly Stoneman, Hans Risser, and Wolf-Christian Paes. 2004. *A Fragile Peace: Guns and Security in Post-conflict Macedonia*. Special Report No. 4. Geneva: Small Arms Survey.

GTZ (Gesellschaft für Technische Zusammenarbeit). 1996. *Concepts and Experiences of Demobilisation and Reintegration of Ex-Combatants: Guidelines and Instruments for Future Programmes*. Division 4334, Emergency and Refugee Aid. Eschborn: GTZ.

—. 2001. *Demobilisation and Reintegration of Ex-Combatants in Post-War and Transition Challenges of External Support*. Eschborn: GTZ.

—. 2003. *Activity Area: Demobilisation and Reintegration of Ex-combatants*. Accessed November 2004. <http://www.wedoit.net/dea/demoblisationandreintegrationofex-combatants.asp>

—. 2004. *Practical Guide to Multilateral Needs Assessments in Post-Conflict Situation: A Joint UNDG, UNDP and World Bank Guide, prepared by GTZ with the support of BMZ*. Washington, DC: World Bank.

Guha-Sapir, Debbie and Willem van Panhuis. 2002a. *Armed Conflict and Public Health: A Report on Knowledge and Knowledge Gaps*. Brussels: Center for Research on the Epidemiology of Disasters.

—. 2002b. *Mortality Risks in Recent Civil Conflicts: a Comparative Analysis*. Brussels: Center for Research on the Epidemiology of Disasters.

Hampson, Fen and Mark Zacher. 2003. *Human Security and International Collaboration: Some Lessons from Public Goods Theory*. Background paper for the Commission on Human Security. Ottawa. Accessed November 2004. <http://www.ksg.harvard.edu>

Hansch, Steve. 2001 'Five Illustrations of Uncertainty: Mortality in Afghanistan, Bosnia, North Korea, Rwanda and Sierra Leone.' In James Keely and Holly E. Reed, eds. *Forced Migration and Mortality*. Washington, DC: National Academy Press.

Heuveline, Paul. 2001. 'The Demographic Analysis of Mortality Crises: the Case of Cambodia: 1970–79.' In James Keely and Holly Reed, eds. *Forced Migration and Mortality*. Washington, DC: National Academy Press.

Hitchcock, Nicky. 2004. *Disarmament, Demobilization and Reintegration: The Case of Angola*. Peacekeeping Note. Durban: African Centre for the Constructive Resolution of Disputes (ACCORD). Issue 1. Accessed 31 March 2005. <http://www.trainingforpeace.org/pubs/accord/ct104pg36.pdf>

Hoeffler, Anke and Marta Reynal-Querol. 2003. *Measuring the Costs of Conflict*. Mimeo. Oxford: University of Oxford.

Hoge, Charles, et al. 2004. 'Combat Duty in Iraq and Afghanistan, Mental Health Problems, and Barriers to Care.' *New England Journal of Medicine,* (351) 1, pp. 13–22.

Humphreys, Macartan. 2002. *Economics and Violent Conflict*. Mimeo. Cambridge, MA: Harvard University.

— and Jeremy Weinstein. 2004. *What the Fighters Say: A Survey of Ex-Combatants in Sierra Leone: June–August 2003*. A survey carried out by Columbia University and Stanford University in partnership with the Post-conflict Reintegration Initiative for Development and Empowerment (PRIDE). Accessed February 2005. <http://www.columbia.edu/~mh2245/SL>

ICRC (International Committee of the Red Cross). 1999. *Arms Availability and the Situation of Civilians in Armed Conflict*. Geneva: ICRC.

IMMAP (Information Management and Mine Action Programs). 2004. *Rapid Humanitarian Assessments: How Rational?* Navigating Post-Conflict Environments. New York: IMMAP.

Instituto de Derechos Humanos de la Universidad de Centroamérica. 1991. 'La Salud en Tiempos d Guerra.' *Estudios Centroamericanos,* 46, pp. 653–71.

IRC (International Rescue Committee). 2004. *Mortality in the Democratic Republic of Congo: Results from a Nationwide Survey*. New York: IRC.

IISS (International Institute of Strategic Studies). 2004. *Armed Conflict Database*. Accessed March 2005. <http://www.iiss.org/showpage.php?pageID=25>

Jensen, Steffen and Finn Stepputat. 2001. *Demobilising Armed Civilians*. Centre for Development Research (CDR) Policy Paper. Copenhagen: CDR.

Kaldor, Mary. 1999. *New and Old Wars: Organized Violence in a Global Era*. Cambridge: Polity Press.

Keely, Charles, Holly Reed, and Ronald Waldman. 2001. 'Understanding Mortality Patterns in Complex Humanitarian Emergencies.' In Charles Keely and Holly Reed, eds. *Forced Migration and Mortality*. Washington, DC: National Academy Press.

Khakee, Anna and Nicolas Florquin. 2003. *Kosovo and the Gun: A Baseline Assessment of Small Arms and Light Weapons in Kosovo*. Special Report. Geneva: Small Arms Survey.

Kingma, Kees, ed. 2000. *Demobilization in Sub-Saharan Africa: the Development and Security Impacts*. Houndmills: Macmillan.

—. 2002. 'Demobilization, Reintegration and Peace-building in Africa.' *International Peacekeeping*, 9(2), pp. 181–201.

Kirsten, Adele et al. 2004. *Islands of Safety in a Sea of Guns: Gun-Free Zones in Fothane, Diepkloof & Khayelitsh*. Background paper. Geneva: Small Arms Survey.

Knight, Michael, Loayza Norman, and Dadvid Villanueva. 1996. 'The Peace Dividend: Military Spending Cuts and Economic Growth.' *IMF Staff Papers,* 43(1), pp. 1–37.

Lacina, Bethany and Neils Gleditsch. 2004. *Measuring War: A Typology and a New Dataset of Battle Deaths*. Oslo: Center for the Study of Civil War.

Le Billon, Philippe. 2000. *The Political Economy of War: What Relief Agencies Need to Know*. Network Paper No. 33. London: Overseas Development Institute.

LeBrun, Emile and Robert Muggah, eds. 2005. *Participatory Research on Armed Violence in the Pacific*. Occasional Paper. Geneva: Small Arms Survey. Forthcoming.

Levy, Barry and Victor Sidel, eds. 1997. *War and Public Health*. Oxford: Oxford University Press.

Macrae, Joanna. 1999. *Aiding peace ... and war: UNHCR, returnee integration, and the relief–development debate*. Working Paper No. 14. Geneva: Centre for Documentation and Research, United Nations High Commissioner for Refugees.

Mazurana, Dyan and Khristopher Calson. 2004. *From Combat to Community: Women and Girls of Sierra Leone*. Washington, DC: Women Waging Peace and the Policy Commission.

McIlwaine, Cathy and Caroline Moser. 2001. 'Violence and Social Capital in Urban Poor Communities: Perspectives from Colombia and Guatemala.' *Journal of International Development* (13), pp. 965–84.

MDDRWG (Multi-Agency Disarmament, Demobilisation and Reintegration Work Group). 2005. *Rationale and Guiding Principles for IDDR*. New York: MDDRWG, UN.

Measure DHS. 2000. *Cambodia Demographic and Health Survey*. Phnom Penh: National Institute of Statistics, Ministry of Planning and Health.

Meek, Sarah. 1998. *Buy or Barter: The History and Prospects of Voluntary Weapons Collection Programmes*. ISS Monograph Series No. 22. Pretoria: Institute for Security Studies (ISS).

Millennium Project. 2004. *Investing in Development: A Practical Plan to Achieve the Millennium Development Goals*. New York: United Nations.

Milner, James. 2004. *The Militarization and Demilitarization of Refugee Camps and Settlements in Guinea: 1999–2004*. Background paper. Geneva: Small Arms Survey.

Moser, Caroline. 2004. *Urban Violence and Insecurity: An Introductory Roadmap*. Environment and Urbanization Brief No. 10. London: International Institute for Environment and Development (IIED).

— and Andy Winton. 2002. *Violence in the Central American Region: Toward an Integrated Framework for Violence Reduction*. Working Paper No. 171. London: Overseas Development Institute (ODI).

Moser-Puangsuwan, Yeshua and Robert Muggah, eds. 2003. *Whose Security Counts? Participatory Research on Armed Violence in Southeast Asia*. Bangkok: Free Press and Nonviolence International.

Muggah, Robert. 2003. *Reconsidering Small Arms in the Solomon Islands*. UNDP Background Paper. Honiara/Geneva: United Nations Development Programme. August.

—. 2004a. 'The Anatomy of Disarmament, Demobilisation and Reintegration in the Republic of Congo.' *Conflict, Security and Development,* 4(1), pp. 21–37.

—. 2004b. *The Prospects for Disarmament, Demobilisation and Reintegration of the Moro Islamic Liberation Front*. Manila. Study commissioned by UNDP and the World Bank. Manila: UNDP.

—. 2004c. *Diagnosing Demand: Motivations and Means of Firearms Acquisition in Papua New Guinea and the Solomon Islands*. Discussion Paper 7 (1). Canberra: State Society and Governance in Melanesia (SSGM) project, Australian National University (ANU).

—. 2005a. *A Crisis Turning Inwards: Refugee and IDP Militarisation in Uganda*. Humanitarian Exchange No. 29. London: Overseas Development Institute (ODI).

—. 2005b. 'No Magic Bullet: A Critical Perspective on DDR and Weapons Reduction in Post-Conflict Contexts'. *Commonwealth Journal of International Affairs,* 94 (379), pp. 237–50. Forthcoming.

—. 2005c. *Securing Haiti's Transition: Prospects for Disarmament, Demobilization and Reintegration*. Occasional Paper 14. Geneva: Small Arms Survey.

— and Peter Batchelor. 2002. *Development Held Hostage: The Socio-Economic Effects of Small Arms and Light Weapons on Human Development*. New York: UNDP.

— and Jurgen Brauer. 2004. 'Diagnosing Demand: An Economic Framework to Assessing the Demand for Small Arms.' Discussion Paper 50. Department of Economics. Durban: University of Kwazulu-Natal..

—, ed. 2005. *Refugee Militarization in Africa*. Geneva: Small Arms Survey and BICC. Forthcoming.

— with Martin Griffiths. 2002. *Reconsidering the Tools of War: the Humanitarian Impacts of Small Arms and Light Weapons*. ODI Network Paper No. 39. London: Overseas Development Institute (ODI).

—. Philippe Maughan, and Christian Bugnion. 2003. *A Joint Independent Evaluation for the European Commission, UNDP and the MDRP Secretariat*. 13 February to 6 March. Accessed 23 March 2005.
<http://www.undp.org/bcpr/smallarms/docs/DDR_evalcongo_e.pdf>

MDRP (Multi-Country Demobilization and Reintegration Program in the greater Great Lakes region). 2005. *Multi-Country Demobilization and Reintegration Program: A regional approach to support the demobilization and reintegration of ex-combatants in the greater Great Lakes region of Africa*. Washington, DC: World Bank. Accessed 23 March 2005. <http://www.mdrp.org/>

—. 2003. 'Guidelines and Procedures for Special Projects for Potential Implementing Partners.' 15 April. Accessed 23 March 2005. <http://www.mdrp.org/special_project_procedures.pdf>

Murray, Christopher and Alan Lopez, eds. 1996. *The Global Burden of Disease*. Cambridge, MA: Harvard University School of Public Health, WHO, and World Bank.

Nelson, Carol and Robert Muggah. 2004. *Disarming the Solomons: An Evaluation of Weapons-Free Villages*. Independent study commissioned by the Small Arms Survey. Geneva: Small Arms Survey.

Nichols, Ryan. 2004. *DDR in Liberia*. Background paper. (unpublished). Geneva: Small Arms Survey.

OECD DAC (Organisation for Economic Co-operation and Development, Development Assistance Committee). 2001. *Guidelines on Helping Prevent Deadly Conflict*. Paris: OECD DAC. Accessed January 2005. <http://www.oecd.org/dataoecd/15/54/1886146.pdf>

Ozanne-Smith, Joan, et al. 2004. 'Firearm-Related Deaths: the Impact of Regulatory Reform.' *Journal of Injury Prevention,* 19, pp. 289–86.

PAHO (Pan American Health Organization). 1986. *Health Conditions in the Americas 1981–1984*. Vol. II. Scientific Publication 500/1986. Washington, DC: PAHO.

Pearce, Jenny. 1999. 'Peace-Building at the Periphery: Lessons from Central America.' *Third World Quarterly,* 20(1), pp. 51–68.

Pedersen, Douglas. 2002. 'Political Violence, Ethnic Conflict and Contemporary Wars: Broad Implications for Health and Well Being.' *Social Science and Medicine,* 55, pp. 175–90.

Roberts, Les. 2002. *Mortality in Eastern DRC: Results from 5 Mortality Surveys*. New York: International Rescue Committee.

—. 2004a. 'Mortality Before and After the 2003 Invasion of Iraq: Cluster Sample Survey.' *The Lancet*. 364, pp. 1857–64. Accessed February 2005. <http://image.thelancet.com/extras/04art10342web.pdf>

—. 2004b. *Small Arms Survey in Iraq*. Background paper. Geneva: Small Arms Survey.

Sabin, Miriam, Barbara Lopes Cardozo, Larry Nackerud, Reinhard Kaiser, and Luis Varese. 2003. 'Guatemalan Refugees Twenty Years Later: Factors Associated with Poor Mental Health Outcomes.' *Journal of the American Medical Association (JAMA),* 290, pp. 635–42.

SaferAfrica. 2003. *Operations Rachel*. Pretoria: SaferAfrica. Accessed 23 March 2005. <http://www.saferafrica.org/DocumentsCentre/Monographs/Rachel/Rachel.pdf>

Sambanis, Nicholas. 2002. 'A Review of Recent Advances and Future Directions in the Literature on Civil War.' *Defence and Peace Economics,* 15, pp. 215–44.

—. 2003. 'Using Case Studies to Expand the Theory of Civil War.' Paper prepared for 'The Political Economy of Civil Wars.' World Bank and Yale University case study project. New Haven: Yale University.

Schiavo-Campo, Salvatore. 2003. *Financing and Aid Management Arrangements in Post-Conflict Situations*. CPR Working Paper 6. Washington, DC: World Bank.

SIPRI (Stockholm International Peace Institute). 2004. *SIPRI Yearbook 2004: Armaments, Disarmament and International Security*. Oxford: Oxford University Press.

Small Arms Survey. *Small Arms Survey 2001: Profiling the Problem*. Oxford: Oxford University Press.

—. 2002. *Small Arms Survey 2002: Counting the Human Cost*. Oxford: Oxford University Press.

—. 2003. *Small Arms Survey 2003: Development Denied*. Oxford: Oxford University Press.

—. 2004. *Small Arms Survey 2004: Rights at Risk*. Oxford: Oxford University Press.

—. and UNIDIR (United Nations Institute for Disarmament Research). 2005. *Listening for a Change! Participatory Evaluations of DDR and Arms Reduction in Mali, Cambodia, and Albania*. Geneva: Small Arms Survey and UNIDIR. Forthcoming.

Smith, Chris. 2001. 'Security-Sector Reform: Development Breakthrough or Institutional Engineering?' *Conflict, Security and Development,* 1(1), pp. 5–19.

Smith, Joyce. 2003. 'Human resources for health: identifying opportunities to provide direction and coherence to inescapable change in a post-conflict environment.' Paper prepared for AusAid Post-Conflict Symposium. Sydney. September.

Stewart, Frances and Valpy Fitzgerald, eds. 2001. *War and Underdevelopment: Volume 1: The Economic and Social Consequences of Conflict*. Oxford: Oxford University Press.

—. Cindy Huang, and Michael Wang. 2001. 'Internal Wars in Developing Countries: An Empirical Overview of Economic and Social Consequences.' In Frances Stewart and Valpy Fitzgerald, eds. 2001.

Tschirgi, Necla. 2004. 'Post-Conflict Peacebuilding Revisited: Achievements, Limitations and Challenges.' Report of the WSP International/IPA Peace-building Forum Conference. October.

UN (United Nations). 1998. *The Causes of Conflict and the Promotion of Durable Peace and Sustainable Development in Africa*. A/RES/53/92.

UNDP (United Nations Development Programme). 2001. *Defining UNDPs Role in Disarmament, Demobilisation and Durable Solutions (D3)*. Mission Report—UNDP/Donor Mission to DRC and the Great Lakes Region. New York: UNDP/Emergency Reponse Division. 6 August–13 September. Accessed 31 March 2005. <http://www.undp.org/bcpr/pubinfo/transitions/2001_10/d3_mission_report.pdf>

—. 2003. *Guatemala: una agenda para el desarrollo humano. Informe sobre el desarrollo humano 2003*. Guatemala City: UNDP.

—. 2004a. *A Compilation of SADU Missions*. Geneva: Bureau for Conflict Prevention and Recovery.

—. 2004b. 'Arms for Development: UNDP Recovery and Peace Building Unit: Sierra Leone.' Progress report.

—. 2005. *Guidelines for Disarmament, Demobilization, and Reintegration*. UNDP practice note. Geneva: Bureau for Conflict Prevention and Recovery. Forthcoming.

UN DPKO (United Nations Department of Peacekeeping Operations). 1997. *Multidisciplinary Peacekeeping: Lessons from Recent Experience*. Accessed January 2005. <http://www.un.org/Depts/dpko/lessons/handbuk.htm>

—. 1999. *Disarmament, Demobilization and Reintegration of Ex-combatants in a Peacekeeping Environment: Principles and Guidelines*. New York: Lessons Learned Unit, DPKO.

UNF (United Nations Foundation). 2004. *Issues Before the UN's High-Level Panel: Small Arms and Light Weapons*. New York: UNF and the Stanley Foundation. 29–30 March.

UNGA (United Nations General Assembly). 2004. *Note by the Secretary-General*. A/59/565 of 2 December. Also referred to as the UN High Level Panel on Threats, Challenges and Change. Accessed March 2005. <http://www.un.org/secureworld/report.pdf>

UNHCR (United Nations High Commissioner for Refugees). 2004. *Protracted Refugee Situations*. EC/54/SC/CRP.14.

UNIFEM (United Nations Development Fund for Women). 2004. *Getting it Right, Doing it Right: Gender and Disarmament, Demobilization and Reintegration*. New York: UNIFEM.

University of Uppsala. 2004. *Uppsala Conflict Database*. Accessed 23 March 2004. <http://www.pcr.uu.se/database>

UNSC (United Nations Security Council). 1999a. *Statement by the President of the Security Council*. S/PRST/1999/21 of 8 July.

—. 1999b. *Statement by the President of the Security Council*. S/PRST/1999/28 of 24 September.

—. 2000a. *Report of the Secretary-General: The Role of United Nations Peacekeeping in Disarmament, Demobilization and Reintegration*. S/2000/101 of 11 February.

—. 2000b. *Report of the Secretary-General: Methods of Destruction of Small Arms, Light Weapons, Ammunition and Explosives*. S/2000/1092 of 15 November.

—. 2004. *Resolution 1529*. S/RES/1542.

UNSG (United Nations Secretary General). 1998. *Report of the Secretary-General on the United Nations Operation in Mozambique (ONU-MOZ)*. S/24892. New York: United Nations. 3 December.

US Army War College. 1996. *United Nations Observer Mission in Haiti (UNMIH): A Working Bibliography*. Accessed March 2005. <http://carlisle-www.army.mil/usacsl/new_site/divisions/pki/military/casestudies/studydocs/unmih.htm>

US GAO (United States General Accounting Office). 2000. *Conventional Arms Transfers: U.S. Efforts to Control the Availability of Small Arms and Light Weapons*. Washington, DC: GAO.

Walter, Barbara. 1997. 'The Critical Barrier to Civil War Settlement.' *International Organization*, 51(3), pp. 335–65.

De Watteville, Nathalie. 2003. 'Demobilization and Reintegration Programs: Addressing Gender Issues.' *World Bank Findings*, 227. June.

Wilkinson, Adrian. 2004. *Integrated SALW Control in SEE*. Presentation to the UNIDIR Weapons for Development Conference, 14–15 September.

World Bank. 1998. *Post-Conflict Reconstruction: the Role of the World Bank*. Washington, DC: World Bank. Accessed 23 March 2005. <http://www-wds.worldbank.org/servlet/WDSContentServer/WDSP/IB/1998/04/01/000009265_3980624143531/Rendered/PDF/multi_page.pdf>

—. 2002. *Greater Great Lakes Regional Strategy for Demobilization and Reintegration*. Report No. 23869-AFR. 25 March. Accessed 23 March 2005. <http://www.mdrp.org/gl_dr_regional_strategy.pdf>

—. 2003a. *Position Paper: Linkages between Disarmament, Demobilization and Reintegration of Ex-Combatants and Security Sector Reform*. MDRP Secretariat Paper. Washington, DC: World Bank and MDRP Secretariat. Accessed 23 March 2005. <http://www.mdrp.org/ssr-paper.pdf>

—. 2003b. *Breaking the Conflict Trap: Civil War and Development Policy*. Washington, DC: World Bank. Accessed 23 March 2005. <http://web.worldbank.org/external/default/WDSContentServer/IW3P/IB/2003/06/30/000094946_0306190405396/Rendered/PDF/multi0page.pdf>

—. 2003d. 'Development Cooperation and Conflict: Operational Policies 2.30.' *World Bank Operational Manual*. Washington, DC: World Bank.

—. 2003e. *World Bank Group Work in Low-Income Countries Under Stress: A Task Force Report*. Washington, DC: World Bank.

WHO (World Health Organization). 2001. *World Report on Violence and Health*. Geneva: WHO.

ACKNOWLEDGEMENTS

Principal author

Robert Muggah

Other contributors

Eric Berman, Jurgen Brauer, Jeremy Ginifer, William Godnick, Iain Hall, Sahar Hasan, Macartan Humphreys, Caroline Moser, Carol Nelson, Ryan Nichols, Les Roberts, Christiana Solomon, Ruxandra Stoicescu, Jeremy Weinstein, and Adrian Wilkinson

CAR loyalist soldiers drive around Bangui in November 2002, shortly after President Ange-Félix Patassé squashed an uprising with the help of fighters called in from Libya and DRC.
(© Christine Nesbitt/AP Photos)

The Central African Republic:
A CASE STUDY OF SMALL ARMS AND CONFLICT

INTRODUCTION

In the past ten years, the Central African Republic (CAR) has hosted four international peacekeeping operations and witnessed conflicts in neighbouring states that have routinely made international headlines. Yet, relatively little literature exists on the country. As will be shown, this study has relevance far beyond the troubled, landlocked nation that is its subject. It challenges many widely held assumptions about security-sector reform (SSR) that have continental and global implications. The study also provides a richer context for acquiring a better understanding of continuing threats to peace and security throughout the region. It underscores how conflicts are interrelated and how progress in one country can harm that of another if proper attention is not paid.[1]

CAR—a country spanning 623,000 square kilometres (somewhat larger than Portugal and Spain combined)—has fared poorly and experienced considerable turmoil since gaining independence from France in 1960. Its 3.9 million citizens are among the poorest people in the world. There have been four coups d'état, the latest on 15 March 2003, when former military Chief of Staff General François Bozizé overthrew President Ange-Félix Patassé (see Table 11.1).

Table 11.1   Central African heads of state, 1960–2005

President	Tenure	Ethnic group	Birthplace/ home town (prefecture)	Position prior to assuming office	Reason for leaving office (date)
David Dacko	1960–65	Ngbaka	Bouchia (Lobaye)	Minister of the Interior, Economy, and Trade*	Coup d'état (31 December 1965)
Jean-Bédel Bokassa	1966–79	Ngbaka	Bobangui (Lobaye)	Chief of staff of the armed forces	Ousted in absence by French troops (21 September 1979)
David Dacko	1979–81	Ngbaka	Bouchia (Lobaye)	Bokassa's personal adviser	Coup d'état (1 September 1981)
André Kolingba	1981–93	Yakoma	Kembé (Basse Kotto)	Chief of staff of the armed forces	Election defeat (19 September 1993)
Ange-Félix Patassé	1993–2003	Sara	Paoua (Ouham-Pendé)	Former prime minister	Coup d'état (15 March 2003)
François Bozizé	2003–	Gbaya	Bossangoa (Ouham)**	Former chief of staff of the armed forces	

Notes:
* CAR enjoyed substantial autonomy prior to independence.
** President Bozizé was born in Mouila, Gabon, but grew up and has his roots in Bossangoa.
Sources: BBC (2005); Sangonet (2005); *Telegraph* (2003); Fundación CIDOB (2001a; 2001b); Kalck (1992)

Still, CAR has been relatively peaceful compared to the majority of its neighbours. Of the five countries that border CAR, only Cameroon can say the same. Chad, the Democratic Republic of the Congo (DRC), the Republic of the Congo, and Sudan have all endured civil wars and insurgencies.

Map 11.1   Central African Republic and its neighbours

Small arms did not figure prominently in the country's misfortune until 1982. It was then, after a failed coup attempt (Kalck, 1992, p. xlii), that non-state actors in CAR began to take receipt of arms from abroad. The change in government in Chad in 1982 also had serious ramifications for CAR, including the movement of armed personnel across the border.

The 1980s and early 1990s witnessed a number of coup attempts, suspected coup attempts, and relatively small-scale violence involving dissatisfied factions and the Forces armées centrafricaines (FACA) (Kalck, 1992, pp. xliv-lv).

The situation, however, deteriorated sharply in 1996, when elements of FACA mutinied, culminating in the looting of the country's largest arms depot at the Kassaï barracks, in the capital, Bangui (McFarlane and Malan, 1998, pp. 49–51).[2]

In 1997, following the overthrow of Zairian President Mobutu Sese Seko, thousands more weapons flooded into CAR. A similar situation ensued two years later, when the Ugandan-backed Mouvement de libération du Congo (MLC), a rebel group led by Jean-Pierre Bemba, defeated the Forces armées congolaises (FAC) of Laurent Desiré Kabila, Mobutu's successor. During 2002 and 2003, still more weapons entered CAR via Chad, which backed General Bozizé's military campaign.[3]

This chapter focuses on events between the years 1996 and 2003 that have affected the state's ability to regulate weapons among civilians and have led to a massive influx of arms into large parts of the country. Together, they have created a clear threat to national security and to law and order.

The chapter comprises four main sections. The first examines small arms availability and distribution with respect to state and non-state actors in CAR. The second looks at small arms flows and trafficking, both direct transfers from states and indirect transfers from states and armed groups. The third assesses the impacts of small arms use and availability. The fourth analyses the various disarmament efforts undertaken in CAR in recent years.

Below are the main findings.

- Armed elements in CAR seriously outgun government forces (with the exception of the presidential guard), which are not prepared to counter them.

- The government, which claims that 50,000 small arms are circulating nationally beyond its control, may be *underestimating* the scale of the problem.

- Long-standing arms stockpile multipliers for the FACA are extremely small. Consequently, past calculations of government small arms holdings throughout Africa may be well below present estimates.

- Peacekeeping operations have not been a significant source of weapons.

- While regional states have supplied weapons to government forces and to rebels seeking to acquire power, the type of hardware has been relatively limited and has not included surface-to-air missiles.

- Non-state actors not only receive *matériel* and other kinds of support from governments, but they can also play a crucial role in aiding recognized state administrations.

- While firearms-related deaths and injuries in CAR may be relatively insignificant compared to other conflict zones in the region, the country suffers greatly from the economic and psychological effects of small arms use and availability.

- Arms recovery programmes in CAR have been poorly designed and badly implemented. In addition, they have been considerably less successful than touted and arguably have undermined national security.

> Most armed elements in CAR seriously outgun government forces.

AVAILABILITY AND DISTRIBUTION OF SMALL ARMS

Central African governments have relied on and supported different services within the armed forces and security sector to varying degrees. For the first 20 years of independence, however, the state more or less effectively—and, at times, ruthlessly—monopolized the coercive use of force.[4] This changed in the early 1980s, with the establishment of the first armed opposition groups.[5]

President Patassé, a Sara from the north, never trusted the army, whose ranks his predecessor, André Kolingba (see Table 11.1), had filled to an unprecedented extent with fellow Yakomas from the south. Instead of trying to reform the institution, he built up the presidential guard at its expense—which largely explains why, in 1996, so many soldiers opted to mutiny. When the presidential guard failed to provide him with the protection he sought, he created a succession of pro-government militias.

Patassé never exercised effective control over the weapons that his regime distributed to such entities. These militias were relatively well armed, many receiving AK-47 (or Chinese Type 56) assault rifles.[6] By contrast, many government soldiers possessed antiquated weapons, such as MAS-36 bolt-action (single-shot) rifles.

Governmental institutions issued with small arms

Forces armées centrafricaines

Attempted coups, mutinies, and politically motivated neglect—as well as selective reward processes—have taken their toll on FACA. After the 1996 mutinies, FACA received little support. President Bozizé, though, has shown interest in reforming and strengthening the institution (Frères d'Armes, 2000, pp. 22–24).

FACA soldiers march in a parade in Bangui, March 2004.

© Desirey Minkoh/AFP/Getty Images

The force has never been very large, and its strength appears to have peaked under President Jean-Bédel Bokassa. By the end of his tenure in September 1979, the armed forces consisted of 7,500 soldiers (Decalo, 1989, p. 165). The subsequent presence of French troops (until 1998) contributed to CAR's security and hence FACA's strength was reduced substantially. By 1996, it had been cut by more than 50 per cent. In 2000, according to then Central African Minister of Defence Jean-Jacques Demafouth, 500 new recruits joined its ranks (Frères d'Armes, 2000, p. 19). Their addition, along with an influx of several hundred presidential guard members, brought the size of FACA to close to 4,000. Approximately 1,250 soldiers, however, reportedly fled to the DRC after Kolingba's unsuccessful coup attempt of May 2001.[7] Another 300 apparently attached themselves to General Bozizé's rebel force in November 2001.

It is difficult to ascertain the quantity and type of weaponry in service with FACA. In October 1963, shortly after independence, the army was lightly armed, possessing 1,017 weapons. All but ten of these items were small arms. The only rifle issued was the MAS-36, comprising nearly two-thirds of firearms in the military's inventory. Light weapons consisted of two 12.7 mm machine guns, four 60 mm mortars, and four 81 mm mortars (SHAT, 1963, p. 38). The introduction of Kalashnikov assault rifles over the years has not changed the bottom line: FACA is a lightly armed force.

Gendarmerie

Rather than complementing the army, the gendarmerie has historically competed with it—and with other government security agencies—for the president's trust and support. Reportedly, there were 1,600 gendarmes in 1970 and some 1,300 in 2000, with plans to increase the size of the force to 1,800 (Frères d'Armes, 2000, p. 34). In June 2002, 200 new recruits (the first since 1994) began a nine-month training course at the gendarmerie school in Kolongo (Frères d'Armes, 2002, p. 40), suggesting that the force has yet to realize its planned strength, or that intentions have changed. According to President Bozizé, there were 1,310 gendarmes in 2003 (CAR, 2003, p. 6). Gendarmes are principally armed with pistols, MAT-49 sub-machine guns, MAS-36 bolt-action rifles, and Kalashnikov assault rifles.[8] Forces loyal to General Bozizé ransacked many of their depots in 2002.

Presidential guard

The force primarily responsible for protecting the president has had many names over the years. Two things have remained fairly constant, however: it has been comparatively well staffed; and it has been relatively well treated. Furthermore, its members are better armed than colleagues serving with other armed services and public security institutions in the country.

Under President Patassé, presidential security personnel, whether in uniform or not, could be identified by the personal firearms they carried. They tended to be outfitted with Kalashnikov assault rifles, AA-52 light machine guns, and rocket-propelled grenade launchers (RPGs).[9]

In 1997, President Patassé undertook to transform the presidential guard into the Force spéciale de défense des institutions républicaines (FORSDIR), a process completed in early 1998 (Bureau of Democracy, Human Rights, and Labor, 1999). At the end of 1999, the strength of FORSDIR was officially put at 642, but Faltas contends that its actual size was closer to 900 (Faltas, 2000, p. 92). In 2000, as part of a package of negotiated reforms, President Patassé changed FORSDIR into the Unité de la Sécurité Présidentielle (USP), and, at least on paper, integrated it into FACA. Although the USP was supposed to report to the chief of staff of the armed forces and ultimately to be accountable to the minister of defence, in reality it continued to report to, and take orders directly from, the president and remained largely autonomous.[10]

Police

Police services in CAR have never enjoyed significant government support. In 1963, for example, the police, which then numbered 315, possessed just 61 firearms: 6 pistols; 40 sub-machine guns; and 15 rifles. All of the latter were bolt-action Mousquetons, first produced in the 19th century (SHAT, 1963, pp. 62–63). Subsequently, police officers were usually armed with French MAS-36s, another bolt-action rifle, but of more recent (Second World War) vintage. Currently, however, they are effectively unarmed. Most police depots were looted during the mutinies and coup attempts of 1996–97 and 2001–02. The key exception is the police unit tasked with combating banditry: the Office central de répression du banditisme (OCRB). Its members used to be armed with MAS-36s, but in December 2003, all 45 of them were issued with a Kalashnikov assault rifle.[11] This was possible because the OCRB is allowed to use some of the armaments that it recovers from criminals (see Arms recovery and disarmament efforts, below).[12] In December 2003, President Bozizé authorized a transfer of 50 Kalashnikovs for the 1,685-strong police force and provided officers with 50 magazines and 1,500 additional cartridges.[13]

> Most police services in CAR are effectively unarmed.

Other

It is more difficult to document the structures and firearms in service with other governmental institutions outside of the armed forces and police. According to French military archives, in 1963 three such public forces possessed armaments: forest guards; hunting guards; and diamond mine district personnel.[14] The first two were armed with MAS-36 rifles, while the third was equipped with pistols (SHAT, 1963, p. 65). Together, they likely did not number more than 100 people, if that. In 2000, the state employed 70 guards to protect its natural resources—no new recruits have been hired since the mid-1980s (Blom and Yamindou, 2001, p. 11). In December 2003, the number stood at 51.[15]

The former state intelligence services—the Centre national de recherche et d'information (CNRI) and the Section d'enquête, de recherche et de documentation (SERD)—with approximately 250 personnel were officially dismantled in 1997. The staff and arms of the CNRI, the larger of the two agencies, were transferred to FORSDIR.[16] It is not believed that the current intelligence service, the Direction générale de la documentation et des enquêtes (DGRE), is particularly large or well armed. SERD, which was to have been dismantled, still exists, however. One informed observer put SERD's strength at 20–50 men and said all carried arms.[17]

Non-governmental armed groups

Mouvement de libération du peuple centrafricain

Many members of President Patassé's political party, the Mouvement de libération du peuple centrafricain (MLPC), were armed. President Patassé and his supporters first received arms after his unsuccessful bid for the presidency in 1981. Some MLPC cadres remained armed even after President Patassé took office in 1993. President Bozizé's government has placed the strength of an armed 'parallel police force' of MLPC members at 820 (CAR, 2003, p. 7). It is unclear whether this is the same as a 'MLPC militia' mentioned by some informed observers. One source put the strength of this group at between 500 and 1,000 in 2003, adding that each member is equipped with an automatic weapon and some perhaps with crew-served armaments and grenade launchers.[18]

CAR President Ange-Félix Patassé is escorted by his guards in Bangui, May 1996.

© Francois Mori/AP Photo

Karakos, Balawas, and Sarawis

Following the mutinies of 1996, President Patassé, who had previously relied primarily on the presidential guard and armed MLPC elements, now felt that these forces were insufficient to guarantee his personal and political survival. He thus established three Bangui-based militias known as the Karakos, Balawas, and Sarawis. These neighbourhood militias would soon grow to encompass some 1,500 individuals in total. They largely comprised unemployed young men whom the president counted among his supporters.

Bangui has eight *arrondissements* (districts), divided into *quartiers* (see Map 11.2).[19] The Karakos militia was based in the Boy-Rabe quartier, where mostly Gbaya reside (Leaba, 2001, p. 172), in the fourth arrondissement. The Balawas militia, comprising chiefly members of the Kaba ethnic group, was based in the Combattant quartier in the eighth arrondissement. The Sarawis militia was concentrated in the Sara quartier, named after the ethnic group residing there in large numbers, in the fifth arrondissement. Sarawis militia members were also present in large numbers in other quartiers of the fifth arrondissement, such as Malimaka, Miskine, Mustapha, and Ngouciment. Each militia was around 500 strong, and armed mostly with Kalashnikovs.[20]

Map 11.2   Bangui *quartiers*

Société centrafricaine de protection et de surveillance

President Patassé subsequently created two more militias. In 1999, he established the Société centrafricaine de protection et de surveillance (SCPS). Headed by his chauffeur, Victor Ndoubabé (the son of a family friend), the SCPS was ostensibly a private security company. While it did engage in commercial activities, it is best seen as a standby militia force tasked with providing security to the president.[21] President Patassé had been under substantial international pressure to reform and scale down significantly the FORSDIR. Indeed, the SCPS would come to count among its number former FORSDIR members (Leaba, 2001, p. 168).

Ndoubabé was killed in the March 2003 coup,[22] and the SCPS ceased to exist as a cohesive unit shortly thereafter. In early 2003, informed observers placed its strength at between 1,000 and 1,500. According to President Bozizé, the number of surviving ex-SCPS guards in November 2003 was 850 (CAR, 2003, p. 7). These guards were armed with Kalashnikovs.[23]

'Abdulaye Miskine'

In 2000, President Patassé established yet another militia known by the name of its leader, 'Abdulaye Miskine'—whose birth name, according to President Patassé, is Martin Koumta Madji. Chad has accused Miskine of being a Chadian insurgent who killed another rebel leader. President Patassé maintained that he was a Central African patriot who Chad had wrongly identified. Leaving aside his contentious background and objectives, there is consensus that, at the time of General Bozizé's October 2002 coup attempt, the militia numbered between 300 and 350.[24] President Patassé armed them with Kalashnikovs.[25] Miskine departed CAR in November 2002,[26] but later returned. With Bozizé's successful coup, it is widely believed that Miskine does not currently have any armed troops under his command.

Self-defence units and vigilante groups

There also is at least one armed 'neighbourhood watch-type' organization in CAR that deserves mention. In 1984, Yaya Ramadan—the village chief of Tiroungoulou, a respected religious leader in the region, and a former mayor of Birao—established a self-defence unit (SDU) in Vakaga prefecture. He recognized the threat that poaching posed to the region's wildlife, as well as to the well-being of his fellow citizens. Ramadan believed that revenues from international hunting represented a potentially lucrative and sustainable source of income.

The SDU, which received government approval, was relatively well armed. Bangui's support was political, not military, in nature, and did not encompass the provision of any weaponry. The militia procured its arms privately (probably from local sources), mostly Kalashnikov assault rifles, but also G-3s, M-14s, and FN-FALs. In August 2003, the group numbered between 250 and 300.[27]

© Olivier Nyirubugara

Central African vigilante group members from Ouham prefecture in north-west CAR, February 2004.

As evidenced by the photograph of the group of armed men from the village of Donzi in Ouham prefecture, other armed neighbourhood watch-type organizations, or vigilante groups, are operating throughout CAR.

Other

Just as Patassé subcontracted his security to a variety of militia, many other functions that were previously the sole responsibility of the state are now being carried out by private companies and ad hoc state-authorized (but foreign funded) concerns. While several private security companies have been established in the past five years in Bangui, with the exception of the SCPS, they are effectively unarmed. A few are equipped with *pistolets d'alarme* (blank-firing pistols).

CAR President François Bozizé salutes troops in Bangui, March 2004.

© Desirey Minkoh/AFP/Getty Images

Recognizing that the state was unable to protect national wildlife, the European Community launched, in 1988, the first of several anti-poaching initiatives (complementing government efforts) that involved the recruitment of armed guards. At the height of the programme in the early 1990s, the European Union was funding 120 armed anti-poaching guards in CAR. By December 2003, there were around half as many.[28] The guards are armed with Kalashnikov rifles and two AA-52 machine guns, which the ministry of defence issued to them. In addition, the teams retain some *matériel* seized from poachers.[29] In 1990, the World Wildlife Fund (WWF) also financed an anti-poaching initiative in CAR. Initially, ten eco-guards were recruited. By June 2003, there were 40. The government furnishes each guard with a MAS-36 rifle. Teams also have access to a couple of automatic rifles.[30]

Stockpiles

The successful coup d'état in CAR on 15 March 2003 has both clarified and obscured the situation regarding the small arms and light weapons holdings of government forces. As already noted, General Bozizé and his supporters raided many police and gendarmerie depots across the countryside after the failed coup of October 2002. Most of the weapons have not been returned, and missing items have not been replaced.

Yet the government has entered into a dialogue with the World Bank in a bid to garner international financial support for SSR. As part of this endeavour, it has recorded the strength of FACA, the gendarmerie, and the police, as well as of various non-state armed groups. The numbers provided are largely believed to be accurate in the case of the state, although it is noteworthy that Bozizé did not provide figures on his presidential guard (which is not believed to be part of the figure he provided for FACA). As for former militias, Bozizé appears to have provided a defensible estimate, although it is possible that he overestimated the size of some groups in an effort to secure additional financing. The government has not offered data, however, on stockpiles of small arms and light weapons.

Historical analysis of inventories can help to shed light on current holdings. Very good information is available on the weapons that were in service with Central African state actors 40 or so years ago. The Government of France kept detailed records of small arms and light weapons in the hands of numerous Central African government services, as well as of their force strengths. Thus, for 1963 it is possible to determine accurate multipliers. They range from a high of 1.60 (the ratio of weapons to forces) for the gendarmerie to a low of 0.19 for the police.[31] Based on subsequent events and available information, the values of current multipliers (except for the presidential guard) are probably in keeping with these figures. The following ratios are used respectively for FACA, the gendarmerie, and the police: 1.25, 1.15, and 0.67. The rationale is that the weapons in service with FACA and the gendarmerie will have been reduced because of President Patassé's policy of marginalization and General Bozizé's looting.

Bozizé's republican guard—or presidential guard—is reportedly well armed. As previously mentioned, the Central African government conspicuously chose not to disclose information on this unit when discussing its security and disarmament needs and plans. Eyewitness reports, however, suggest a ratio of 3.00, which is in keeping with information available on the ex-USP. The strength of the unit is not known, although a figure of 1,000 men is thought to be a conservative estimate.

> Bozizé's presidential guard is reportedly well armed.

Box 11.1   Determining a stockpile multiplier for FACA

It is also possible to calculate a multiplier for FACA in 1996 with some degree of specificity. According to the Government of CAR, in November 1996, at the time of the third army mutiny, 2,389 small arms and 127 light weapons were stored at Kassaï barracks (UNSC, 1997a, para. 22). Demafouth believes that government record-keeping was adequate at the time, and that the figures that it provided to the ad hoc African peacekeeping force known as the Mission interafricaine de surveillance des accords de Bangui (MISAB) were largely accurate. The army's other depot was at Bouar, and contained around 800 weapons, mostly Kalashnikov assault rifles. Very few light weapons were kept at Bouar.[32] Demafouth adds that the strength of FACA was approximately 3,000-3,500 in 1996.[33] This would put the ratio of weapons to soldiers at very close to 1.0. The government, however, took weapons from Kassaï barracks and moved them across town to the presidential guard's armoury at Camp de Roux after the first mutiny in April (McFarlane and Malan, 1998, p. 50). It was not possible to ascertain how many weapons were removed and how many may have been returned. But there is no reason to believe that the ratio of weapons to soldiers would have been higher for the army than it was for the presidential guard at the time (which Demafouth put at around 1.3).[34] Thus, the multiplier for FACA in 1996 would not have been very different from the 1963 multiplier of 1.34.

By the end of 2003, there had not been an appreciable change in the FACA multiplier compared to 1996. President Patassé continued to starve the military of funds and weapons, while aiding the presidential guard and other forces on which he felt he could rely. Although they could not be verified, reports of the army purchasing weapons from MLC rebels point to the dire straits in which the institution found itself. The multiplier certainly would not have increased under Patassé.

After the March 2003 coup, however, Bozizé recovered 1,300 weapons, primarily with the help of the Chadian Army (UN OCHA, 2003a) (and, to a lesser extent, Communauté économique et monétaire de l'Afrique centrale (CEMAC) peacekeepers). It is not known how many of these weapons, if any, were transferred to FACA.

Table 11.2   Estimated small arms stockpiles in CAR, state agencies, and other (former) armed groups

State agencies (data as of September 2003)			Active and recent non-state armed groups (data as of November 2003)			
Service	Estimated strength	Multiplier	Estimated holdings	Group	Estimated strength	Multiplier	Estimated holdings
FACA	4,442	1.25	5,552	Ex-Balawas	510	0.67	342
Gendarmerie	1,310	1.15	1,507	Ex-Sarawis	600	0.67	400
Police	1,600	0.67	1,072	Ex-Karakos	593	0.67	397
Other*	250	1.00	250	Ex-MLPC	820	2.00	1,640
Presidential guard	1,000	3.00	3,000	Ex-USP	1,345	3.00	4,035
				Ex-SCPS	850	2.00	1,700
				Vakaga prefecture SDU	275	1.30	358
Totals			**11,381**	**Totals**			**8,872**

*Includes Intelligence (DGRE and SERD) and anti-poaching units.
Sources: Vakaga prefecture SDU: median of informed estimate (250-300); presidential guard: informed estimate; other: informed estimate; remainder: CAR (2003, pp. 6-7)

The ratios used to determine the stockpiles of non-state groups tend to be higher than those employed for governmental bodies. It is assumed here that each member of the Balawas, Sarawis, and Karakos militias received approximately two weapons for each three people recruited. Members of the MLPC, SCPS, and USP are thought to have had access to arms in excess of their respective strengths. In response to the May 2001 coup attempt, for example, MLPC officials were widely reported to have dispensed weapons, including Kalashnikovs, to party loyalists in Bangui in an effort to apprehend citizens who may have received firearms from Kolingba supporters.[35] More recently, during the March 2003 coup d'état, eyewitnesses claim that thousands of weapons were looted from the home of General Bombayeke, the head of the USP.[36]

Worryingly, these groups are generally armed with weapons of greater firepower and lethality than those in the possession of the state. Certainly, this is true of the gendarmerie and the police: the relatively few armaments that remain in their hands include a large number of MAS-36 bolt-action rifles. As noted above, President Patassé tended to arm his presidential guard and various militias with assault rifles. There are numerous reports of forces loyal to Patassé also having been equipped with light machine guns and RPGs.[37]

Additionally, there is reason to believe that assault rifles are now generally available throughout Central African society. As discussed below (see Arms recovery and disarmament efforts), it is increasingly common for police and anti-poaching guards to recover Kalashnikovs. In the past, they tended to collect and come into contact with rudimentary and antiquated shotguns and hunting rifles.

The government's calculation of the number of weapons in general circulation may *underestimate* the scale of the challenge. According to General Xavier Yangongo, the Chairman of the Commission de la défense et de la sécurité, up to 50,000 illegally-held guns are in general circulation (UN OCHA, 2003d), although he has provided no documentation or analysis to support the assertion. Many people might be inclined to dismiss it, therefore, as little more than a negotiating ploy on behalf of the government to extract resources from the World Bank and the wider international donor community for (yet) another arms collection programme. The number of guns in society, though, could be significantly higher. It is not unreasonable to assume that the six known militias and the SDU in Vakaga prefecture possess around 9,000 firearms in total. If only one person out of every 100 in CAR (with an estimated population of 3.9 million citizens) was armed, this would add another 39,000 firearms to the pool. Anecdotal evidence strongly suggests that large sections of the population are armed and that the ratio of weapons to people is certainly higher than 1:100.

Twenty years ago, small arms proliferation throughout Central African society was not a pressing concern. Indeed, as late as 1979, relatively few arms were in circulation outside of state personnel. When government forces attacked civilians in January and April 1979,[38] citizens fought back with poisoned arrows (Kalck, 1992, p. xxxv). The situation has changed markedly since then. For example, according to an expatriate who lived and worked in Bamingui-Bangoran and Vakaga prefectures for several years, nearly every household in Vakaga is armed, with every person over 30 owning a weapon. These are not craft-production hunting rifles, but commercial firearms. The Kalashnikov is most common, but there are also quite a number of FN-FALs. Far fewer armaments are circulating in Bamingui-Bangoran.[39] Across the country in Sangha-Mbaéré prefecture, more than 60 per cent of the population of the Kouapili district of Salo reportedly possessed at least one firearm in 1998. These weapons, however, tended to be rudimentary, locally produced hunting rifles (Mogba and Freudenberger, 1998, p. 118). Manufactured shotguns are also in plentiful supply. Russian 12-gauge shotguns made by Baikal are so prevalent in that part of the country that locals use the term 'Baikal' to describe all such weapons.[40] Apparently, in the south-east of the country, it is not uncommon for three or four families in a ten-family village to own locally made weapons.[41]

The vast number of weapons that have entered CAR in recent years in ways other than direct state-to-state transfers supports the contention that more than 50,000 weapons are circulating outside of government control. The next section elaborates on this point.

SMALL ARMS FLOWS AND TRAFFICKING

As noted in the first section, successive Central African governments kept their armed forces and police relatively small and poorly armed. It is only in comparison to other entities that a particular service could be described as 'well armed'. With few natural resources with which to barter, and essentially no role in the cold war competition between the superpowers, direct transfers from states have been rather limited. France was the largest supplier of arms and ammunition. Chad and Libya have also provided significant quantities of *matériel*. Support from each of these countries is reviewed below, as is that of China, which is believed to have delivered military equipment, including small arms, in the past ten years. Nations not mentioned above that provided arms during the presidential eras of David Dacko and Jean-Bédel Bokassa include Israel[42] and Romania.[43] It proved very difficult, however, to obtain information on these countries' transfers, given the passage of time and the relatively low level of assistance offered. Of greater significance is that it appears that government-to-government transfers are not as important a source of small arms as are indirect weapons transfers by defeated, demobilized, or 'visiting' armed forces of neighbouring states.

Direct transfers from states
France

Not surprisingly, the colonial power, France, remained CAR's primary military supplier in the years following independence. In 1963, for instance, most weapons in state inventories were French and the few weapons not French-made probably came from France (see Table 11.3).

Table 11.3   Weapons in service with Central African state actors, 1 October 1963

Weapon				Recipient				
Category		Model	Total	Armée de terre	Gendarmerie	Republican guard	Police	Other*
Small arms	Pistols and revolvers	MAC/MAS-1950	419	105	314	-	-	-
		MAB 7.65	30	-	-	-	6	24**
	Sub-machine guns	MAT-49	367	221	126	20	-	-
		MAS-38	30	-	-	-	30	-
		Sten	10	-	-	-	10	-
	Rifles	Mousqueton	338	-	-	323	15***	-
		MAS-36/51	1,630	636	359	555	-	80****
		MAS-49/56	60	-	60	-	-	-
	Light machine guns	FM-24/29	10	-	10	-	-	-
		AA-52	57	45	12	-	-	-
		Bren	14		5	9	-	-
Light weapons	Heavy machine guns	12.7 mm	2	2	-	-	-	-
	Mortars	60 mm	4	4	-	-	-	-
		81 mm	4	4	-	-	-	-
Total			2,975	1,017	886	907	61	104

Notes:
* Other includes the Gardes forestiers with 50 MAS-36s, the Gardes chasse with 30 MAS-36s, and the Personnels des circonscriptions minières de diamant with 24 7.65 mm pistols.
** It is assumed that this is the same MAB pistol as the one used by the police.
*** The 8 mm rifles in service with the police are believed to be the same as the model (Mousqueton) used by the Republican Guard.
**** Grenade-launching MAS-36 rifles are included in the total. The army and the gendarmerie had 58 and 6 of these weapons, respectively.
Source: SHAT (1963, pp. 38, 51, 58, 63, 65)

France remained CAR's primary military patron until 1970, when relations between the two countries sharply deteriorated. Nevertheless, it remained engaged in CAR due to larger political considerations. These considerations, however, changed by the late 1970s. Strategic considerations, and concerns over human rights, drove France to curtail its military assistance and ultimately to orchestrate the overthrow of President Bokassa.[44] After President Bokassa was removed from office, France re-engaged with CAR militarily, shipping several consignments of small arms and light weapons during the early years of the Kolingba presidency (see Table 11.4).

France's military support for CAR during the tenure of President Patassé was largely indirect, via its own troops and then regional peacekeeping missions. Given the president's long-standing open hostility toward France, Paris was not favourably predisposed to the new president. Even so, it was Paris that pushed hard for President Kolingba to hold free and fair democratic elections in September 1993, and it did so with the clear understanding that Patassé would almost certainly emerge victorious. When FACA soldiers mutinied in April 1996, CAR-based French soldiers came to the aid of President Patassé. France backed the January 1997 peace accord and the establishment of MISAB. In 2002, France provided weapon systems and armaments for troops serving with the CEMAC peacekeeping mission. Direct transfers of French military equipment to President Patassé's government, though, were very limited. CAR did receive some matériel, such as vehicles, when France's military base in Bouar formally closed in 1998, but no small arms or light weapons were handed over.[45] According to the French government, the only small arms and light

Table 11.4   Weapons transfers from France to CAR, 1981–2003

Year of transfer	Type of weapon		Shipment value (with rounded USD equivalent****)	Number of weapons
	Category	Manufacturer/model(s)		
1981	Automatic rifles	Manurhin Défense	EUR 228,673 (USD 240,000)	n/a
1981	Anti-tank weapons	LRAC 89 mm*	n/a	50
1983	Anti-tank weapons	LRAC 89 mm	n/a	50
1984	Machine guns	SFM/SFET**	EUR 76,225 (USD 80,000)	n/a
1984	Assault rifles	DAT (now GIAT)***	EUR 2,287 (USD 2,400)	n/a
1985	Assault rifles	DAT (now GIAT)	EUR 30,490 (USD 32,000)	n/a
1986	Assault rifles	DAT (now GIAT)	EUR 22,827 (USD 24,000)	n/a
1994	Spare parts	MAT-49, AA-52, pistols	EUR 15,245 (USD 16,000)	n/a
1995	Spare parts	MAT-49, AA-52, pistols	EUR 6,860 (USD 7,200)	n/a

* Lance Rocket Antichar (LRAC)
** Société française des Munitions de Chasse, de Tir et de Guerre (SFM) / Société française d'Équipement de Tir (SFET)
*** Direction des Armements Terrestres (DAT) ; Groupement Industriel des Armements Terrestres (GIAT)
**** Rounded USD equivalents based on 1 January 2003 exchange rate.
Source: Written correspondence with French Ministry of Defence, 5 September 2003.

weapons transferred to CAR during the ten years President Patassé was in office were spare parts, with the last exchange occurring in 1995 (see Table 11.4).[46]

Libya

President Bokassa turned to Libya for support during the final years of his rule. He visited Tripoli in 1976, where he converted to Islam. Shortly after returning home, he reverted to Catholicism. Perhaps this explains the decision of Libyan President Muammar Qaddafi to assist Central African rebels intent on his overthrow.[47] Regardless, Libya continued to assist President Bokassa militarily up to his demise. Libyan aeroplanes transported stocks of war *matériel* to Bangui in August 1979, and a small number of advance units were put in position to support the president (Decalo, 1989, p. 163). Indeed, Bokassa was in Tripoli at the time of the coup.

Libya also supplied weapons to CAR during the tenure of President Patassé. In 1998, it dispatched two or three transport aircraft filled with armaments, including small arms and light weapons, to CAR, using the airport outside of Ndélé, not the one in Bangui. These items were destined for the USP headed by General Bombayeke,[48] not for General Bozizé, and more broadly for FACA, to which Bombayeke was supposedly subordinate. In May 2001, President Qaddafi supplied additional weapons to aid President Patassé, this time directly to Bangui.

Libya also employed intermediaries. Some of the weapons Chad provided to CAR following the 1996 army mutinies came from Libya.[49] Libya also delivered significant quantities of *matériel* to the MLC in Gbadolite, DRC, in October and November 2002 (in support of President Patassé), when the airport in Bangui was not safe to use.

Lybia assisted President Bokassa militarily up to his demise.

Chad

Chadian support for President Patassé, unlike that of France, involved both troops and small arms. During the 1980s, N'djamena apparently did not transfer any weapons to Bangui, despite having procured huge excess stocks from Libya.[50] Following the 1996 army mutinies in CAR, however, President Patassé received some 500 Kalashnikovs from

Chad.[51] Chad contributed troops during the MISAB operation and the follow-on United Nations Mission in the Central African Republic (MINURCA). A small number of military advisers remained in CAR after MINURCA departed in February 2000.

Unfortunately for President Patassé, Chad also supplied weapons to the rebel outfit trying to overthrow him. According to Major Namboro Kette, cabinet chief of the head of the general staff, General Bozizé received all of his arms from Central African sources.[52] This claim reinforces the steadfast assertion of Chad that it did not extend any support to General Bozizé. There are credible reports, though, that Chad provided logistical assistance as well as *matériel*, including small arms and light weapons.[53] The apparent introduction of anti-personnel landmines by General Bozizé's forces[54] suggests that they did indeed receive outside help, as CAR is not known to have possessed any such devices.[55] It is not possible, however, to prove that Chad supplied these landmines. What is perhaps more important is not what Chad granted to General Bozizé, but what it seemingly did not: surface-to-air missiles (see Box 11.2).

Box 11.2   CAR, CHAD, and surface-to-air missiles

The Government of the United States provided significant levels of *matériel* in the 1980s to the Forces armées du nord (FAN) of Chad led by Hissène Habré. Washington did so because it was concerned about Libyan designs on Chad and President Qaddafi's increasingly close relationship with Habré's political rival, Goukouni Weddeye. Weapons included the Redeye surface-to-air missile (Foltz, 1995, p. 23). After the October 2002 coup attempt in CAR, when Libyan counter-insurgency aircraft were bombarding General Bozizé's forces, there was a real worry in the United States that Chad might furnish General Bozizé with such armaments. Apparently this did not happen.

China

Beijing provided Bangui with various small arms and other military equipment. The possibility of China supplying *matériel* to CAR came up during negotiations in 1997 to re-establish diplomatic relations between the two countries. For CAR, it was impolitic to retain diplomatic relations with Taiwan at a time when it was seeking UN Security Council support for a UN peacekeeping operation to succeed MISAB (given that China could exercise its veto).[56] Relations were re-established in January 1998, two months before the Security Council authorized MINURCA. According to Demafouth, the consignment of *matériel* arrived by road from the Cameroonian port of Douala in 2000. Equipment included small arms and light weapons as well as vehicles.[57]

Indirect transfers from regional armed forces

Chad

Despite the presence of myriad political and military actors in Chad and its long history of warfare since gaining independence in 1960, the armed forces involved in these conflicts were not a significant source of weaponry for CAR in the 1960s and 1970s. Largely this is because southerners dominated the Government of Chad, based in N'djamena, some 500 kilometres north of the border with CAR. While political tensions existed in southern Chad, even within the same ethnic group, the situation was relatively calm compared to that in the north,[58] the inhabitants of which considered themselves to be substantially disenfranchised. After the southern-dominated Chadian government fell in 1979, CAR remained largely unaffected by the Chadian conflict for three more years. The cold war backdrop to the Chadian conflict, however, heightened Western fears of Libyan adventurism. Combined with regional politics, these factors contributed to a huge inflow of *matériel* during this period, including small arms and light weapons,[59] which would later have a profound effect on CAR.

The situation changed dramatically in the second half of 1982. Habré, who seized control of the capital that June, successfully employed a mixture of diplomacy and military might to pacify the threat posed to his fledgling administration by the armed opposition in the south. Nevertheless, many commandos, or Codos, from a military force that was part of a former Government of Chad, refused to join the new national army or lay down their weapons. Disaffected youth aligned themselves with these commandos (Foltz, 1995, pp. 21–22). Academic literature on Chad states that, by 1985–86, there were some 15,000 Codos. Only around 1,500 took advantage of the opportunity to join the armed forces loyal to Habré (Tartter, 1990, pp. 194–95). Many of those who did not join the military turned their attention (and their weapons) to supporting banditry along the roads of CAR and are known as *Zaraguinas* or *coupeurs de routes*. Today, for many Central Africans, the terms Codos and Zaraguinas or coupeurs de routes are interchangeable.

The situation deteriorated in the 1990s, when the Chadian Armed Forces went through a process of significant downsizing as part of a World Bank-initiated SSR programme. More than 25,000 soldiers were demobilized (World Bank, 2003). Despite international reintegration efforts, thousands of people found themselves essentially unemployed without skills or the opportunity to transition successfully into civilian life. Many Central Africans believe the problem with Zaraguinas or coupeurs de routes along CAR's roads escalated sharply as a direct result of weapons and armed personnel crossing from Chad into CAR in search of livelihoods.

More recently, members of the Chadian Armed Forces reportedly sold some of their weapons while transiting CAR after having served in the DRC. (Chadian President Idriss Déby, who seized power from Habré in 1990, contributed some 2,000 troops to assist DRC President Kabila in 1998.) On withdrawing from the DRC in May and June 1999, they spent more than a week in Kaga Bondoro, the capital of Gribingui prefecture, while the Central African authorities met with Chadian officials to try to find a way to assuage the soldiers' pent-up grievances. Paying the troops defused tensions. It is understood, though, that some of the soldiers sold an unknown number of firearms to Central Africans while in CAR.

> Chadian Armed Forces sold an unknown number of firearms to Central Africans while in CAR.

Sudan

The three Central African prefectures that border Sudan are very sparsely populated and government oversight of the area is extremely limited.[60] Thousands of soldiers with the Sudan People's Liberation Army (SPLA) are believed to have crossed into CAR in the 1980s looking for food and security (during periods of drought and Sudanese military offensives). Demafouth noted that, in 1985, perhaps 10,000–15,000 Sudanese sought refuge in CAR. He added that, according to the Central African police commissioner at the time, combatants made up approximately 50 per cent of this number, and estimated that they brought around 5,000 weapons with them. It was not uncommon for SPLA members to trade their weapons.[61]

Democratic Republic of the Congo (formerly Zaire)

In 1997 and 1999, fighting in Zaire, later the DRC, resulted in large numbers of armed men crossing into CAR. The first wave came in the first half of 1997, when members of President Mobutu's presidential guard, police, and gendarmerie and the Forces armées zaïroises (FAZ) retreated across the border to escape Kabila's advancing Alliance des forces démocratiques pour la libération du Congo-Zaïre (AFDL). A similar exodus occurred in 1999, when forces loyal to Kabila fled across the frontier with CAR to evade Bemba's MLC and the Ugandan People's Defense Forces (UPDF).

These troops appear to have brought more than 10,000 weapons into CAR. Conversations with former members of FAC and FAZ who now reside in CAR revealed that they and their compatriots traversed the Ubangui River with numerous types of small arms, but few heavy weapons. Weaponry included a large number of pistols (mostly Belgian 9 mm models), sub-machine guns (largely Israeli Uzis, plus some Egyptian Port Saids), rifles (Belgian FN-FALs, German G-3s, Israeli Galils, US M-16s, and Kalashnikovs manufactured in the Soviet Union and elsewhere), and anti-tank weapons (Soviet RPG-7s). As for crew-served weapons, only 60 mm mortars were taken into CAR, and not in vast quantities. Most of these weapons have not been accounted for. Mutinous FACA soldiers seized many of them; the government also procured thousands.

UN Secretary-General Kofi Annan originally reported that many weapons taken from FAC had been jointly guarded by Congolese and Central African troops (UNSC, 1999a, para. 26). Later, however, he acknowledged 'persistent reports that some of [these] weapons [...] had not been surrendered but clandestinely sold'. He added that 'only a few of the weapons could be recovered' (UNSC, 1999b, para. 38).

Libya provided transport aircraft to fly many Congolese troops back to Kinshasa, but without their weapons (UNSC, 1999b, para. 36). The Central African government admitted keeping 3,328 light arms belonging to FAC in safe storage until the war in the DRC was resolved (UNSC, 2000, para. 26). Of the 3,250 light arms that the Central African government collected from Congolese soldiers via MINURCA, the central authorities destroyed some 500 in 2000. Of the remaining 2,750 or so weapons, Demafouth said that approximately 300 were M-16s, 200 were Galils, and 100 were Uzis. Most of the others were Kalashnikovs.[62]

A fighter in the rebel MLC orders a surbordinate to take a defensive position in Sibut in February 2003, one week after the MLC retook the town from other rebels.

© Rodrique Ngowi/AP Photo

In an unusual move, in June 2001, Bemba dispatched 700 MLC soldiers to protect President Patassé from a coup attempt in CAR. Within a month, the MLC troops had returned to the DRC.[63] When President Patassé's government came under attack again on 25 October 2002, Bemba sent some 2,000 soldiers.[64] This time, they remained behind after the immediate threat of rebellion had subsided. Bemba received considerable weaponry, presumably from Libya, in connection with this undertaking. Several Libyan military transport aircraft landed in Gbadolite, DRC, the site of the MLC's headquarters, between 26 October and 3 November 2002. Bemba denied the UN access to the airport, so it is very difficult to know what exactly was delivered.[65] It is not known how much, if any, of this equipment went directly to the CAR government. In less doubt, though, is that MLC cadres transferred weapons to Central African citizens. Bemba did not provide his troops in CAR with a per diem, food, or lodging.[66] As a result, MLC rebels looted properties and committed gross human rights violations. MLC troops allegedly sold excess small arms to anyone willing to purchase them.[67]

> MLC rebels allegedly sold excess small arms to anyone willing to purchase them.

Republic of the Congo

Geographical, political, and developmental considerations all suggest that relatively few combatants from the internal conflicts in the Republic of the Congo have crossed that nation's border with CAR. The frontier between the two countries along the Dzanga–Sangha Dense Forest Special Reserve is very remote. Eastward, along the southern border of CAR's Lobaye prefecture, the movement of goods and people is comparatively greater. Overall, it appears that the frontier has remained quiet in contrast to CAR's borders with Chad, the DRC, and Sudan.

Although significant numbers of combatants do not appear to have crossed into CAR from the Republic of the Congo, small arms and ammunition circulating in CAR are known to have originated in that state. Richard Carroll of WWF (US) noted that, between 1997 and 1998, there were indications that Kalashnikovs had come across the border with the Republic of the Congo after its six-month civil war ended in October 1997. He cautioned, however, that home-made hunting rifles and old Soviet 12-gauge shotguns—popular with expatriate hunters temporarily based in the country—remain by far the most popular weapons found in the Dzanga–Sangha Dense Forest Special Reserve.[68]

Rwanda

Several thousand Rwandans entered CAR between 1994 and 1997. Relatively few arrived in 1994–96, but the situation changed in 1997, following the emptying of Rwandan refugee and military camps in eastern Zaire after Kabila instigated his rebellion. During the first half of 1997, the United Nations High Commissioner for Refugees (UNHCR) estimated that some 3,000 Rwandans crossed into CAR. Many (more than 1,000) would have been members of the Interahamwe and former members of the Forces armées rwandaises (FAR).[69] The majority of Rwandans entering CAR did not have any weapons. A former Rwandan soldier who entered Bangui from Zongo said that many armed Rwandans (like armed Zairians) sold their weapons while in Zaire or had their firearms confiscated by the Central African authorities.[70] Most Rwandans have since left CAR.[71]

Weapons generated within CAR

Indigenous production

CAR does have a state-run military company, but it does not manufacture arms (Frères d'Armes, 2000, p. 27). Artisans fabricate many weapons, however. It is difficult to obtain information on the number of people involved in such

SMALL ARMS SURVEY 2005

activities. Occasional references in published reports indicate that are mostly, if not only, rudimentary hunting rifles produced. These weapons number in the tens of thousands (Mogba and Freudenberger, 1998, p. 118).

Seizures from government forces

Mutinies have also served as an important domestic source of weaponry. Perhaps the most significant case of seizure and redistribution of weapons occurred in 1996, when Central African soldiers emptied the arms depot at Kassaï barracks. According to the government, more than 2,500 small arms and light weapons were taken. During 2001 and 2002, General Bozizé's forces (while retreating north from the capital toward CAR's border with Chad) captured weapons from gendarme depots, at which police armaments also were kept. After the failed coup attempt of 2002, additional depositories were ransacked.[72]

Weapons lost by African peacekeeping forces

CAR has hosted more distinct armed peacekeeping missions (four since January 1997) than any other country or conflict zone in the past ten years.[73] When one takes into account troop rotations, it is likely that more than 5,000 personnel have entered and left CAR since 1997. The four peacekeeping operations have supplied mutinous soldiers or rampaging citizens with only a few weapons. In June 1997, mutinous troops attacked a Burkinabe squad stationed in N'garagba. The mutineers seized around a dozen personal weapons.[74] During the March 2003 coup, CEMAC lost a pistol, some rifles, and two heavy machine guns, not to mention other non-lethal equipment. The rifles have since been returned.[75] Some believe that the government reclaimed the two 12.7 mm machine guns, but, as of June 2003, it had not handed them back to CEMAC. The pistol has not been reclaimed either.

CEMAC peacekeepers in Bangui prepare to fight armed robbers in northern CAR in July 2003.

© Olivier Nyirubugara

EFFECTS AND IMPACTS OF SMALL ARMS

The paucity of record-keeping and restrictions on travel due to the general level of heightened insecurity over the past few years have made it especially difficult to document the effects of small arms use on Central African society. Direct consequences, such as firearm-related deaths and injuries, are not systematically recorded, and even if they were, the figures would not be particularly revealing for reasons highlighted below. Considerably more is known about the impact that small arms (and light weapons) have had on the country's wildlife. The indirect ramifications of small arms use and availability are profound but even more difficult to document, although significant progress has been made toward understanding the very real socio-economic repercussions of small arms proliferation for CAR (Small

Arms Survey, 2003, pp. 125–67). The few examples of the indirect results of armed robberies and roadblocks, although anecdotal, illustrate the range of effects that small arms have had on Central Africans—95 per cent of whom live on less than one US dollar a day (UN OCHA, 2005).

Death and injury

Medical records suggest that small arms use is not responsible for a large number of casualties in the capital, but these statistics are misleading. Interviews conducted in 2003 with the directors of two of the four main hospitals in Bangui indicate that, even during periods of heightened insecurity and violence, such as coup attempts, very few people were admitted to hospital because of gunshot wounds. For example, fewer than 50 people were admitted to the community hospital following the failed coup of May 2001, and a similar number were admitted after the unsuccessful coup attempt of October 2002—six died of their wounds.[76] These figures likely understate the gravity of the matter. The Director of Hôpital de l'Amitié, Cecile Koyangbanda, states that such statistics are of limited utility in analysing gun-related violence and deaths, as many people bury the dead without taking the body, or reporting the case, to the hospital.[77] The cost of medical care is prohibitive for many Central Africans. Not only are the deceased rarely brought to hospital, but many people with gunshot wounds go untreated.

Many Central Africans with gunshot wounds go untreated.

Anecdotal reports suggest that the incidence of gunshot victims is a significant problem. A doctor who operates an NGO-subsidized clinic—the only such facility in the north-west part of the country to remain open during the insecurity of 2002–03—reports that she regularly sees patients with gunshot wounds, often due to cross-border conflict with armed groups and highway bandits from Chad.[78] In November 2002, at Ngola Market just outside of Bangui, 120 cattle herders (and many more cattle) apparently were killed during a battle between government troops and MLC supporters and General Bozizé's forces (UN OCHA, 2003c).

Poaching

Central Africa's wildlife has also suffered greatly because of firearm use. Poaching has been conducted in CAR for as long as people can remember. It was not deemed to be a significant problem, however, when hunters used traditional devices including spears, traps, home-made rifles, and the occasional commercial shotgun. The introduction of modern assault rifles and machine guns has had devastating consequences. Richard Carroll of WWF, who worked in northern CAR in the 1970s and early 1980s, says that poaching was always a problem in the area. Things changed dramatically, however, around 1982, when there was an influx of assault rifles and the Kalashnikov replaced the more traditional spear.[79] Sudanese poaching parties do not rely only on Kalashnikovs, but also utilize machine guns and RPGs (Lowy, 2002). According to conservationists Allard Blom and Jean Yamindou, the size of the Central African elephant population fell from 50,000 in the 1970s to around 5,000 by the mid-1990s (Blom and Yamindou, 2001, p. 14). When there were no more elephants, Sudanese poachers began to kill large numbers of buffaloes, giraffes, hippopotami, various species of antelopes, and giant elands.[80]

The trade in bush meat is another major factor in CAR's dwindling wildlife.[81] To a lesser extent, animals in the country are hunted for sport and are killed because of religious and mystical beliefs.

Mutinies and coup attempts

Army mutinies and coup attempts result in much more than loss of life and political turmoil. They invariably involve massive displacement of populations, and a slew of other problems that remain long after the situation is reported to be 'calm' and even after those who fled have returned home. This was certainly the case with respect to the three mutinies of 1996 and the ensuing unrest throughout the first half of 1997 in the capital (see Box 11.3). Similar problems, though, manifested themselves following the shorter upheavals associated with the May 2001 and October 2002 coup attempts. For example, Amnesty International (2004) found the practice of rape to be widespread, with hundreds of women sexually assaulted at gunpoint by MLC members as well as by Central African fighters between October 2002 and March 2003. In addition, small arms use has had repercussions for people's livelihoods. The livestock sector, which, according to the Association of Livestock Farmers, is responsible for generating 35 per cent of rural earnings, was especially hard hit. The association estimated that its members lost as much as 50 per cent of their cattle during the fighting of October 2002–March 2003 between pro- and anti-government forces (UN OCHA, 2003c).

Box 11.3   The impact of the 1996 mutinies on the Central African economy and civil society

'The mutinies in the CAR resulted in 70,000 internally displaced persons (IDPs), 130 destroyed industries and businesses, and 3,000 lost jobs resulting from the closing of industries and commercial enterprises. According to sources at the Ministry of Planning and International Cooperation, in 1996, these conflicts increased inflation by 3 percent, decreased per capita income by 3 percent, decreased exports by 16 percent, decreased imports by 23 percent, and decreased state revenues by 33.6 percent. These changes caused a dramatic increase in external debt, a decrease in overall security in the country because of the breakdown of law and order and spread of military weapons, a serious decrease in medical services, and shortages of even basic medical supplies. In a country that already had extremely limited medical services, at least three health centers were destroyed during the mutinies. Funeral services were limited during this time, and people were buried in backyards, causing serious health hazards. Finally, very little schooling occurred during the period (1996 and 1997).

'Embassies and international organizations closed, leading to the suspension or permanent closure of projects, such as those concerned with the AIDS campaign [...], primary health [...], and blood transfusions [...]. The offices of at least 12 donor-financed projects were ransacked or completely destroyed [...]. Of these, some closed down permanently, while others had to start from scratch and relocate to new offices in Bangui once the situation returned to normal.'

Source: Blom and Yamindou (2001, pp. 13–14)

Armed robbery

Criminals routinely use firearms. Several interlocutors spoke of 'five or six' armed robberies committed on an average night in Bangui after the October 2002 coup attempt. The prevalence of armed robbery is believed to be much greater than reported. A sense of futility, more than fear of retaliation, appears to account for why many armed robberies go unreported.[82]

Interestingly, it is perhaps the *fear* of armed robbery and not its *occurrence* that has a stronger impact on the community. Even if statistics showing a decline in the number of armed robberies could be trusted, there is reason to believe that stress related to insecurity in Bangui—specifically the fear of armed robbery—remains widespread throughout the populace. The director of an NGO working in CAR noted that staff members were clearly operating well below their level of ability. He attributed the decline to fear of armed robbery, and noted that events surrounding the coup of March 2003 had exacerbated the situation. People were on edge, not listening, and making careless mistakes.[83]

Roadblocks

Armed highway robbers and roadblocks impede transport throughout the country, causing the price of goods to rise, posing a danger to drivers, and reducing hunting safari tourism, which generates considerable revenues for the state and local communities (see Box 11.4). Besides lamenting the dismal state of repair of the country's roads, the head of a transportation company in CAR detailed the prevalence of roadblocks throughout the country. He said that, on all of the main arteries, there are roadblocks every 20–40 kilometres. At each blockade, his drivers are habitually asked to pay bribes of 500–3,000 CFA Francs (USD 1–6). The people demanding money—often those employed by the state, such as police officers or soldiers—are frequently armed with Kalashnikovs and RPGs. They are more dangerous and unpredictable when they have been drinking. One of the company's drivers was shot while transporting a load for UNHCR in 2003.[84]

Box 11.4   Lost revenues from the downturn in hunting safaris in 2003

By all accounts, safari hunting enthusiasts are not easily dissuaded from pursuing their hobby. Political tensions in the capital often have little bearing on their decisions, as tour operators frequently go to great lengths to ensure the safety of their clients. Private planes and first-class treatment can mitigate or circumvent many of the usual annoyances and inconveniences. But they come at a price: a typical two-week safari costs in excess of USD 20,000 per person.

Revenues generated from safari hunting in CAR are not inconsequential and represent a significant income stream for communities in very remote locations far from Bangui and other major towns and cities. 'Trophy fees'—rates that governments charge to hunters for the animals they kill or injure—can range from a few hundred to several thousand US dollars per animal. Various supplemental charges are based on trophy fees, such as a taxidermy and trackers tax, and a community development tax, each typically a ten per cent surcharge. Additional costs include daily game park and veterinary fees. One should note that this list is far from a complete.

Mechanisms have been put in place to ensure that monies generated from this activity benefit the local communities surrounding the wildlife reserves. These funds finance development projects and pay the salaries of government workers who otherwise would go unremunerated.

In 2003, however, the armed conflict made it very difficult, and sometimes impossible, to resupply the lodges in many of the country's wildlife reserves. The result was a sharp downturn in safari hunting tourism.

ARMS RECOVERY AND DISARMAMENT EFFORTS

Since 1997, there have been numerous initiatives to recover weapons in the Central African Republic. Government forces, such as the police and forest rangers, have recovered hundreds of weapons. Many more weapons have been retrieved through internationally supported programs. The one thing all these initiatives have in common is that relatively few weapons collected have been destroyed.

Relatively few weapons collected in CAR have been destroyed.

Unilateral national initiatives

The OCRB, the police unit in charge of combating banditry, has routinely seized weapons. Before 1996, it used to recover largely pistols and locally crafted hunting rifles. In recent years, however, it has seized rifles, machine guns, and even the occasional mortar. By late December 2003, the OCRB had recovered 51 small arms and 14 grenades.[85] These numbers, which are slightly elevated in comparison to previous years, belie the changing scope of the problem. The police service believes that bandits are more numerous and better armed than before. At the same time, the strength of the OCRB has been substantially reduced. Whereas there were 130 OCRB police officers in February 2003,[86] the number had fallen to 45 by December—with only one vehicle to pursue robbers.[87]

The Government of CAR has recovered thousands of weapons along its international borders at times of heightened alert (using ad hoc patrols and deployments). President Patassé's presidential guard allegedly confiscated weapons from more than 4,000 FAZ troops who crossed into Mobaye in April 1997.[88] In 1999 alone, for instance, President Patassé acknowledged recovering 3,328 weapons from FAC personnel (UNSC, 2000, para. 26). Given the much larger quantities of weapons that are likely to have been transferred across the border, and the disincentive for national authorities to provide a full and accurate account, the true number of armaments seized is likely to be significantly higher.

The weapons were stored at Camp Béal in Bangui. In October 2002, President Patassé's supporters took them to defend the capital following the launch of General Bozizé's coup attempt. The weapons were not returned.[89]

Internationally assisted initiatives
Anti-poaching efforts (1988)

Foreign-funded anti-poaching projects have established various kinds of working relationships with the government vis-à-vis the recovery of small arms and light weapons. For example, the Programme de développement de la région nord (PDRN) operated under an arrangement whereby it kept commercially manufactured weapons that it seized from foreign poachers, but returned any arms collected from Central Africans to the national authorities. Home-made firearms, regardless of ownership, were destroyed. The PDRN's successor, the Programme de développement des zones cynégétiques villageoises (PDZCV), operating under the EU-funded Conservation et utilisation rationnelle des écosystèmes forestiers d'Afrique centrale (ECOFAC) programme, adheres to the same rules.[90]

> Anti-poaching projects have included efforts to recover small arms and light weapons.

Eco-guards in the Ngotto Forest have confiscated more than 200 long-guns and thousands of rounds of ammunition since 1997. Approximately 60 per cent of them are hand-crafted. Factory-produced 12-gauge shotguns include French, Russian, Belgian, and Italian models. German Mauser rifles, including .375 and .458 models, have also been recovered.[91]

MISAB and MINURCA programmes (1997–2000)

In 1997, the CAR government initiated a concerted arms collection programme with international assistance. As part of the agreement concluded between the government and the army mutineers in January 1997, MISAB was to undertake a major arms recovery effort. A small financial incentive was offered to individuals to entice them into relinquishing their weapons with no questions asked. (UNSC, 1997b, paras. 7–10) Inducements ranged between USD 13 for a pistol, sub-machine gun, or rifle and USD 123 for a 120 mm mortar system, assuming that the weapons were in good condition.[92] Smaller sums were offered for *matériel* handed over in a mediocre or poor state. As further encouragement, those who failed to turn in their weapons within a stipulated (short) amount of time were to be pursued through the courts. MISAB's last report to the UN Security Council stated that 1,373 small arms and a little under 118 light weapons were recovered (UNSC, 1998b, para. 14).[93] MISAB also stated that it had collected 464,604 munitions rounds and 26,714 explosives and detonators (UNSC, 1998b, para. 14). It is likely that the final numbers were somewhat higher, given that MISAB continued to patrol Bangui for an additional five weeks before MINURCA replaced it.

Undoubtedly, the recovery of so many arms, along with the equally important political dialogue that took place alongside the initiative, helped to stabilize an explosive situation that had resulted in significant loss of life. Tensions remained high in the capital after the signing of the Bangui Accords in January 1997, and many people died in major flare-ups in late June 1997 (USDOS, 1998).[94] The significance of the recovery programme, however, has been consistently misrepresented. Claims that more than 90 per cent of heavy weapons and more than 50 per cent of light weapons were retrieved during the MISAB operation are routinely made. These percentages, though, are based on a comparison of the total number of weapons recovered and the number seized from Kassaï barracks. Yet this was just one component, albeit an important one, of the disarmament programme. President Patassé's government had every interest in promoting this viewpoint, as it took the pressure off the government of having to account for weapons that it had provided to the militias. MISAB, meanwhile, may have been motivated to highlight an 'uncontested' success when other aspects of the peace accords were not going so well. Whatever the underlying factors, one thing is certain: such a characterization is at best inappropriate and at worst disingenuous. Worryingly, the UN has perpetuated this myth.[95]

The disarmament effort was implemented selectively and not in the spirit of the accords, focusing primarily on the arrondissements that were home to the mutineers. Faltas (2000, p. 90) reports that 'while weapon collection took illegal arms off the streets, it increased the bitterness, frustration and insecurity of the population in the rebels' quarters by disarming the mutineers, but not their adversaries.'

To explain the relatively low rate of recovery of light weapons, MISAB emphasized the ease with which small arms could be transported out of Bangui or successfully hidden. Furthermore, it acknowledged that a demand for these weapons still existed, complicating recovery efforts. It hypothesized that rebels may have hastily discarded an unknown quantity of armaments in the forest or the Ubangui River following encounters with MISAB during the June 1997 armed confrontations. Finally, it reported that some 130 rebels never returned to their barracks and were believed to have absconded with their small arms, many to another country (UNSC, 1997b, para. 13).

No weapons collected during MISAB's tour of duty were destroyed. The arms collected were transferred to the UN mission in April 1998.[96]

Weapons collection continued under MINURCA, but on a limited scale. Although its mandate did not contain an explicit reference to weapons collection (UNSC, 1998c), UN peacekeepers did pursue leads on weapon caches. According to MINURCA Force Commander General Mouhammad Hachim Ratanga, they retrieved weapons from throughout the capital—the force did not concern itself with whether a particular quartier was perceived as pro- or anti-government.[97] According to the UN, MINURCA recovered 128 small arms, 21,724 rounds of ammunition, and 243 explosives between December 1998 and early October 1999 (UNSC, 1999b, para. 38).

Very few of these weapons were destroyed. MINURCA destroyed some obsolete ammunition, and in a public ceremony on 16 July 1999 burnt 158 obsolete small arms (Faltas, 2000, p. 90). A second public ceremony took place on 11 January 2000, during which the remaining 'unserviceable' arms collected by MISAB and MINURCA were destroyed (UNSC, 2000, para. 26). It was not possible to determine the exact number of weapons involved, but Demafouth said that most were MAS-36 bolt-action rifles, plus a few Kalashnikovs.[98] The remainder of the recovered armaments had been transferred to the CAR government the previous week (UNSC, 2000, para. 25). The small number of weapons destroyed suggests that most of those collected were in good condition.

National Programme for Disarmament and Reintegration (2002-03)

In 2002, the CAR government launched a new programme to recover arms and to provide marketable skills. The principal objectives of the National Programme for Disarmament and Reintegration (Programme national de désarmement et de reinsertion, or PNDR) were to recover around 10,000 small arms and light weapons and to offer livelihoods training to 2,000 individuals who opted to participate (UNDP, 2003a, p. 1). Political and military developments in CAR, however, made it difficult to implement the programme as planned. The failed coup attempt of October 2002, the heightened instability that followed in its wake, and the successful coup of March 2003 greatly complicated matters. Despite—or perhaps because of—these challenges, the PNDR was fully funded. In January 2003, USD 1.96 million had been secured from donor countries and the UN. Canada, Germany, Italy, and Norway together contributed more than 55 per cent of the necessary funds, with the United Nations Development Programme (UNDP) covering the shortfall (UNDP, 2003b, p. 10).

The PNDR recovered approximately 1,100 weapons. The data includes so many inconsistencies that it is impossible to determine with any certainty what actually occurred. Reports of the PNDR, UNDP, and the UN Secretary-General contain different figures. Of these three sources, the PNDR, which bears primary responsibility for implementing the project, is considered authoritative as it has the most details. Within the reports of the PNDR, the figures believed to be most accurate come from its detailed accounts of individual weapons recovered. Based on PNDR data, in an early report, the CAR government enumerated 891 small arms and 14 light weapons collected between 23 January and 31 May 2002, supplying serial numbers when possible (CTD, 2002, pp. 2–21). In a May 2003 document, the PNDR similarly listed additional firearms collected since the first destruction ceremony on 15 June 2002 (see below): 135 small arms and 3 light weapons (PNDR, 2003a, sec. VI). Eighty-four weapons collected in Bangassou and Mobaye were not included, as they were to be destroyed on site for security reasons (PNDR, 2003a, secs. IV and VI). The total number, therefore, is 219. Only 59 of these 84 additional weapons are mentioned in the May 2003 document, and not in the same level of detail as the other 135 (PNDR, 2003a, sec. IV). Apparently, 25 of these 84 weapons were transferred to Bangui separately.[99]

Information on ammunition collected under the PNDR is even more difficult to acquire with any confidence. The PNDR reported that it recovered 134,832 rounds of ammunition and 1,444 explosives. In addition, more than 859 magazines were turned in. Other *matériel* received included binoculars, uniforms, and communications equipment (PNDR, 2003a, sec. VI). Part of the confusion arises from the fact that some of the weapons the government seized during the failed coup attempts of May 2001 and October 2002 appear to have been added to PNDR statistics. There is considerable disagreement between the Comité technique de désarmement (CTD) and PNDR officials as to the origin of the weapons stored in the three containers at Camp Béal, in Bangui. Three officials extremely familiar with the programme provided very different accounts of what took place.[100] It does not seem plausible that the PNDR collected 135,000 rounds of ammunition from fewer than 1,000 people. Rather, it seems that most of the ammunition recovered from the two mutinies has been grouped with the weapons recovered by the PNDR, calling into question the programme's record-keeping.

Two hundred and twenty individuals who participated in the project (UN OCHA, 2003d) were selected to receive training.[101] The amount of money that a recipient received for relinquished weapons and ammunition determined eligibility. The minimum was 8,000 CFA Francs (USD 14). The rationale behind this figure was that it would reward those who gave up weapons in good condition. No one who turned in a weapon in an average or poor state would reach this threshold.[102] There is no indication that former combatants—the programme's target audience—received the lion's share of the training.

Instruction was offered in a number of skills over a four-month period. Training began in August 2003 and lasted until December 2003. Skills were provided to those seeking employment as carpenters, electricians, mechanics, and tailors, as well as in other trades and professions (UN OCHA, 2003d). Each trainee received a reintegration package, including tools appropriate for their chosen occupation, valued at up to USD 500 (UN OCHA, 2003d). The project was scheduled to conclude at the end of January 2004.[103]

Two arms destruction ceremonies took place under the PNDR. The first was held on 15 June 2002, during which 705 small arms and 9 light weapons were set ablaze (PNDR, 2003a, sec. I). No ammunition or explosives were destroyed because of the inability of the PNDR to dispose of them safely. A second ceremony was convened on 25 July 2003 (PNDR, 2003b). The PNDR reported that it destroyed 209 small arms and 3 light weapons, as well as 134,352 rounds of ammunition, 1,361 grenades, 27 mortar shells, 54 rockets, and 1 anti-personnel landmine (PNDR, 2003b, p. 3). The PNDR also stated that, during this time, it destroyed 11 additional small arms (eight Kalashnikovs, two MAT-49s, and one MAS-36), 41 canon and mortar shells (eight 107 mm canon shells and 22 60 mm, two 81 mm, and nine 82 mm mortar shells), and 1,582 rounds of 7.5 mm, 7.62 mm, 9 mm, and 12.7 mm ammunition, among other military equipment (PNDR, 2003b, p. 3). For the reasons discussed above, there is cause to question this breakdown. Of the many possible explanations for the discrepancies between the number of weapons reportedly recovered and those subsequently destroyed, the most plausible is that the government would have sought to keep collected *matériel* that was in good working order.

CONCLUSION

Between 1996 and 2003, a series of events significantly transformed Central African society. The government itself has been responsible for some, but over others it had no control. The state's ability to regulate weapons among civilians is essentially non-existent. The massive influx of arms into large parts of the country represents a threat to national security and to law and order.

Regardless of President Bozizé's political skills, the proliferation of small arms throughout CAR will further complicate an already challenging situation. CAR today is a tinderbox, but there is still hope that tensions can be defused. The country has enjoyed a mostly peaceful history—independence from France came without an armed struggle—and small arms were not prevalent among civilians until 1982. Recent years have not been as kind to the country, with a succession of mutinies and coup attempts roiling the nation and conflicts in various neighbouring states spilling across its borders. These developments have contributed to a lack of security in CAR. Zaraguinas roam the roads with seeming impunity outside of the capital and armed robberies occur frequently in Bangui and elsewhere.

Disarmament efforts to date have been largely a waste of money, as evidenced by the recirculation rather than the removal of arms. In some ways, disarmament initiatives exacerbated tensions within the population, because the apparent selectivity with which schemes were implemented hardened differences between groups. Nevertheless, disarmament is still a hugely important endeavour worthy of international support; but the programme must be designed and implemented more competently. Future initiatives ought to target the numerous armed groups that Patassé created, Chadian Zaraguinas, and Bozizé's Liberators. The focus ought to be on collecting assault rifles and light weapons rather than antiquated bolt-action rifles (USE). Weapons and ammunition collected should be destroyed.

It is hoped that the study's findings will aid policy-makers in devising new security-sector reform and disarmament, demobilization, and reintegration programmes, both in CAR and in other places. For the problems that ail the Central African Republic—a weak central government, regional conflicts, the proliferation of small arms and light weapons, to name but a few—are, unfortunately, not unique to CAR.

The state's ability to regulate weapons among civilians is essentially non-existent.

LIST OF ABBREVIATIONS

AFDL	Alliance des forces démocratiques pour la libération du Congo-Zaïre
CAR	Central African Republic
CEMAC	Communauté économique et monétaire de l'Afrique centrale
CNRI	Centre national de recherche et d'information
CTD	Comité technique de désarmement
DGRE	Direction générale de la documentation et des enquêtes
OCRB	L'office central de répression du banditisme
DRC	Democratic Republic of the Congo
ECOFAC	Conservation et utilisation rationnelle des ecosystèmes forestiers d'Afrique centrale
EU	European Union
FAC	Forces armées congolaises
FACA	Forces armées centrafricaines
FAN	Forces armées du nord
FAR	Forces armées rwandaises
FAZ	Forces armées zaïroises
FORSDIR	Force spéciale de défense des institutions républicaines
MINURCA	United Nations Mission in the Central African Republic
MISAB	Mission interafricaine de surveillance des accords de Bangui
MLC	Mouvement de libération du Congo
MLPC	Mouvement de libération du peuple centrafricain
NGO	Non-governmental organization
PDRN	Programme de développement de la région nord
PDZCV	Programme de développement des zones cynégétiques villageoises
PNDR	Programme national de désarmement et de réinsertion
RPG	Rocket-propelled grenade (launcher)
SCPS	Société centrafricaine de protection et de surveillance
SDU	Self-defence unit
SERD	Section d'enquête, de recherche et de documentation
SSR	Security-sector reform
UN	United Nations
UNDP	United Nations Development Programme
UNHCR	United Nations High Commissioner for Refugees
UPDF	Ugandan People's Defense Forces
USP	Unité de la Sécurité Présidentielle
WWF	World Wildlife Fund

ENDNOTES

1 This chapter is a based on a longer manuscript to be published by the Small Arms Survey.

2 Elements of the army mutinied on three separate occasions in 1996: in April, May, and November (McFarlane and Malan, 1998, pp. 49–51).

3 Author interviews with knowledgeable sources, Bangui, June and December 2003.

4 The brutal methods employed by government forces during the Bokassa era may have cowed opponents from taking up arms.

5 One group, the Mouvement centrafricain de libération nationale (MCLN), was created in 1979, but initially received training and equipment outside of CAR. It was quickly uprooted and neutralized after an attack in Bangui in 1981. The Mouvement de libération du peuple centrafricain (MLPC), a CAR-based political party, began to receive arms after the 1981 general election (in which it was not successful in its bid to capture the presidency). See the section on Small arms flows and trafficking in this chapter.

6 The acronym 'AK-47' refers explicitly to the Kalashnikov AK-47. Because the term is often used to refer to a variety of weapons that are derived from the basic AK-47 design, the term 'Kalashnikov' is used here to refer to these derivatives and not a specific model or country of origin.

7 The United Nations High Commissioner for Refugees (UNHCR) reported in 2001 that 1,250 former FACA troops crossed into the DRC after the failed coup (UNHCR, 2001b). Around 80 per cent went to a town some 100 kilometres from Zongo, across the Ubangui River from Bangui. The other 20 per cent or so remained in Congolese villages along the river (UNHCR, 2001a).

8 Author interview with Jean-Jacques Demafouth, former Minister of Defence, Government of CAR, Paris, 3 September 2003.

9 Author interview with Jean-Jacques Demafouth, former Minister of Defence, Government of CAR, Paris, 3 September 2003.

10 Author interview with Jean-Jacques Demafouth, former Minister of Defence, Government of CAR, Geneva, 9 April 2003.

11 Author interview with Ernest Latakpi, general director, Police Administration, Ministry of Interior, Government of CAR, Bangui, 19 December 2003.

12 Author interview with Louis Mazangue, Director, OCRB, Ministry of Interior, Government of CAR, Bangui, 18 February 2003.

13 Author interview with Ernest Latakpi, general director, Police Administration, Ministry of Interior, Government of CAR, Bangui, 27 June 2003.

14 The Gardes forestiers, Gardes chasse, and Personnels des circonscriptions minières de diamant, respectively.

15 Author interview with Michel Bonannée, water and forest engineer, head of mission, Ministry of Water, Forests, Hunting, and Fishing, Government of CAR, Bangui, 17 December 2003.

16 Author interview with Jean-Jacques Demafouth, former Minister of Defence, Government of CAR, Paris, 3 September 2003.

17 Author interview with knowledgeable source by telephone, 5 April 2005.

18 Written correspondence with knowledgeable source, 2003.

19 Most of these smaller neighbourhoods have a historic link to a particular region or ethnic group in the country. There are no laws or physical boundaries (other than streets) separating quartiers, but people have tended to settle among family members and, over time, the ethnic character of these areas has made them distinct. This is so even though inter-marriage is not uncommon. Patrilineal descent is prevalent throughout society.

20 Author interview with Jean-Jacques Demafouth, former Minister of Defence, Government of CAR, Geneva, 8 April 2003.

21 The SCPS provided security for logging companies, diamond mining interests, and those responsible for sensitive deliveries, such as

of money. Author interview with Jean-Jacques Demafouth, former Minister of Defence, Government of CAR, Paris, 3 September 2003.

22 Written correspondence with Olivier Nyirubugara, former IRIN correspondent in Bangui, 31 March 2005.

23 Author interview with Jean-Jacques Demafouth, former Minister of Defence, Government of CAR, Paris, 16 June 2003.

24 Author interviews with knowledgeable sources, Bangui, February and June 2003.

25 Author interview with Jean-Jacques Demafouth, former Minister of Defence, Government of CAR, Paris, 3 September 2003.

26 Under an October 2002 agreement, Bangui and N'djamena committed themselves to ensuring that Bozizé would leave Chad for France and that Miskine would depart CAR for Togo. See UN OCHA, 2002a.

27 Based on an author interview with Olivier Feneteau, Technical Advisor, Zones Cynégétiques Villageoises component, CAR Office, Conservation et utilisation rationnelle des ecosystèmes forestiers d'Afrique centrale (ECOFAC), Paris, 2 September 2003.

28 Author interviews with: Raymond Mbitikon, head, Zones Cynégétiques Villageoises component, CAR Office, ECOFAC, Bangui, 18 December 2003; Gérard Motkin, administrative and financial director, CAR Office, ECOFAC, Bangui, 18 December 2003; and Alain Penelon, head, Ngotto Forest component, CAR Office, ECOFAC, Bangui, 19 December 2003.

29 Written correspondence with Olivier Feneteau, technical advisor, Zones Cynégétiques Villageoises component, CAR Office, ECOFAC, 7 August 2003.

30 Author interview with Richard Carroll, director, Africa and Madagascar Program, World Wildlife Fund (US), 6 August 2003, by telephone.

31 These figures are based on the following ratios: 886:555 and 61:315, respectively. It is assumed that the weapons of French personnel attached to these services were included in the totals (68 French nationals were attached to the gendarmerie and seven to the police). If these French personnel kept their weapons separately, the ratios for the Central African gendarmerie and police would rise to 1.82 and 0.20, respectively. The ratios for the republican guard and the army were nearly identical: 1.35 (907:672) and 1.34 (1,017:761), respectively. The ratio for the republican guard would not change if the two French personnel attached to the service had kept their weapons outside of the state armouries, but if this were true for the 110 French personnel attached to the army, that service's multiplier would rise to 1.56. (SHAT, 1963, pp. 34, 38, 49, 57, 62).

32 Author interview with Jean-Jacques Demafouth, former Minister of Defence, Government of CAR, Paris, 11 December 2003.

33 Interview by Nicolas Florquin with Jean-Jacques Demafouth, former Minster of Defence, Government of CAR, 23 March 2005, by telephone.

34 Author interview with Jean-Jacques Demafouth, former Minster of Defence, Government of CAR, 23 March 2005, by telephone.

35 Author interview with Lucy Jones, former Reuters correspondent, 5 August 2003, by telephone.

36 Written correspondence with Olivier Nyirubugara, former IRIN correspondent in Bangui, 22 March 2005.

37 Author interviews with knowledgeable sources, Bangui, February and June 2003.

38 In January 1979, government troops employed deadly force to suppress protests against President Bokassa's order that students wear school uniform. Some 200 civilians lost their lives. In April 1979, security forces rounded up elementary and high school students, resulting in the massacre of more than 100 young people. President Bokassa is widely believed to have participated in the killings. See O'Toole (1986, pp. 53–54).

39 Author interview with knowledgeable source, Bangui, June 2003.

40 Author interview with Richard Carroll, director, Africa and Madagascar Program, World Wildlife Fund (US), 6 August 2003, by telephone.

41 Interview by Louisa Lombard with knowledgeable source, Bangui, June 2003.

42 Klieman (1985, p. 139) states that Israel is 'regarded' as having provided military assistance to CAR, but offers no further information. Beit-Hallahmi (1987, p. 71) writes that Israel provided arms to the Central African army during the Bokassa regime.

43 Author interview with knowledgeable sources, Bangui, February and June 2003.

44 France was concerned that President Bokassa was prepared to grant Libya a military base in CAR, as well as access to uranium deposits, in exchange for financial and military aid, and that Libyan President Moammar Qaddafi appeared amenable to such a deal. France viewed such a strategic relationship as a threat to its access to uranium deposits in CAR. Moose (1985, p. 81).

45 Author interview with Col. Patrice Sartre, military adviser, Secretary-General of National Defence, Office of the Prime Minister, Paris, 18 June 2003.

46 Allegations of French military support for the failed coup of May 2001 appear to be unfounded. President Patassé accused France publicly of involvement, and displayed weapons that he claimed his forces had retrieved from Kolingba's residence (see, for example, Jones, 2001). France did not refute that the weapons were of French origin, but denied any connection to the coup. It said that the weapons were intended for CAR's gendarmerie. As a former head of state and minister of defence, Kolingba could have stored weapons in his residence, as there was little to no oversight of his actions. Moreover, additional weapons could have been obtained from the area of Mobaye, where Kolingba is from and from where he derives substantial support. 'Proof' offered to date has not supported the claims.

47 Qaddafi offered training in Libya to several hundred members of the MCLN, headed by Rudolphe Iddi Lala. In 1979, Qaddafi sent MCLN cadres to Chad to fight on behalf of his ally, Goukouni Weddeye. Iddi Lala eventually made his way back to CAR, where he orchestrated the July 1981 bombing of a Bangui cinema. The MCLN was rooted out and shortly after the blast ceased to be a coherent force or threat. Author interview with Jean-Jacques Demafouth, former Minister of Defence, Government of CAR, Geneva, 8 April 2003.

48 Author interview with knowledgeable source, Washington, DC, 2003.

49 Author interview with knowledgeable source, Washington, DC, 2003.

50 Some analysts value the *matériel* at more than USD 1 billion (see Foltz, 1995, p. 29). Iraq purportedly benefited most from this windfall. Author interview with William J. Foltz, H.J. Heinz Professor of African Studies and Political Science, Yale University, 25 August 2003, by telephone.

51 Author interview with knowledgeable source, Bangui, February 2003.

52 Author interview with Maj. Namboro Kette, cabinet chief of the head of the general staff, Bangui, 27 June 2003.

53 Author interview with knowledgeable source, Bangui, February 2003.

54 Author interview with knowledgeable source, Bangui, February 2003.

55 Indeed, Bangui denies having used or possessed mines (UN OCHA, 2002b).CAR signed and ratified the Ottawa Convention on the Prohibition of the Use Stockpiling Production and Transfer of Anti-Personnel Mines and on their Destruction on 8 November 2002.

56 CAR would have taken notice of China's lack of enthusiasm for the proposed UN peacekeeping mission in Guatemala. China originally vetoed the resolution—Guatemala maintained diplomatic relations with Taiwan. China subsequently relented and approved the mission, but ensured that it would be small in scale and in existence for a short period.

57 Author interview with Jean-Jacques Demafouth, former Minister of Defence, Government of CAR, Geneva, 9 April 2003.

58 According to Buijtenhuijs (1998, pp. 22–23), in Chad, the 'north' commonly refers to some three-quarters of the country's territory, while the 'south' comprises just the five southern-most prefectures. Citizens' relative adherence to Islam largely influences this definition. The populations of these two regions are roughly equal.

59 For background on the conflict, French and US military support for Habré, and Libyan assistance to Goukouni, the head of a 'transitional' government that ruled Chad from 1979–82, see Lemarchand (1985, pp. 239–56).

60 Only slightly more than 5 per cent of the country's inhabitants live in Haut-Mbomou, Haute-Kotto, and Vakaga prefectures (UN OCHA, 2003b, p. 9). Moreover, Jones (2002) reports, for example, that the citizens of Mboki, a town in Haut-Mbomou prefecture, have not received any mail since 1974.

61 Author interview with Jean-Jacques Demafouth, former Minister of Defence, Government of CAR, Geneva, 8 April 2003.

62 Author interview with Jean-Jacques Demafouth, former Minister of Defence, Government of CAR, Geneva, 8 April 2003.

63 The MLC troops were in CAR fewer than two weeks (UN OCHA, 2001).

64 The number of MLC troops sent to CAR has been reported as high as 3,000. See UN OCHA (2002c).

65 Author interview with peacekeepers, UN Mission in the Democratic Republic of Congo (MONUC), Mbandaka, February 2003.

66 Author interview with Jean-Jacques Demafouth, former Minister of Defence, Government of CAR, Paris, 16 June 2003.

67 Author interview with knowledgeable source, Bangui, June 2003.

68 Author interview with Richard Carroll, Director, Africa and Madagascar Program, World Wildlife Fund (US), 10 June 2003, by telephone.

69 Author interview with UNHCR official, Bangui, February 2003.

70 Author interview with ex-FAR officer, Bangui, December 2003.

71 Author interview with UNHCR official, Bangui, December 2003.

72 Author interview with Maj. Namboro Kette, cabinet chief of the head of the general staff, Bangui, 27 June 2003.

73 Mission interafricaine de surveillance des accords de Bangui (MISAB), 1997–98; La Mission des Nations Unies en République centrafricaine (MINURCA), 1998–2000; Peacekeeping force of the Community of Sahelo-Saharan States (CEN-SAD), 2001–03; Peacekeeping force of the Communauté économique et monétaire de l'Afrique centrale (CEMAC), 2003 to date.

74 Author interview with Lt.-Col. Dominique Kouerey, former Head of Plans, Headquarters, MISAB, Libreville, 22 June 2003.

75 Author interview with Rear-Admiral Martin Mavoungou Bayonne, Force Commander, CEMAC, Bangui, 26 June 2003.

76 Interview by Louisa Lombard with official, community hospital, Bangui, June 2003. Statistics for the March 2003 coup were not available at the time of the interview.

77 Interview by Louisa Lombard with Cecile Koyangbanda, director, community hospital, Bangui, 26 June 2003.

78 Interview by Louisa Lombard with Ione Bertocchi, director, Ngaoundaye Hospital, Bangui, 27 August 2004 (used with the permission of the United Nations Development Programme, Bangui).

79 Author interview with Richard Carroll, director, Africa and Madagascar Program, World Wildlife Fund (US), 10 June 2003, by telephone.

80 Written correspondence with Fred Duckworth, professional hunter, Safaria, 12 September 2003.

81 For all intents and purposes, the distinction between 'poaching' and 'bush-meat trade' is a question of political correctness. The term poaching has a negative connotation, suggesting heartless people who prey on defenceless animals for crass commercial gain. Those trading in bush meat, meanwhile, are often viewed as impoverished, kind-hearted village folk trying to eke out a living. This difference, of course, is lost on the animals.

82 Many victims of criminal activity, including armed robbery, choose not to file a report, as they believe that the police and the state are powerless to do anything about the problem. Interview by Louisa Lombard with knowledgeable source, Bangui, June 2003.

83 Interview by Louisa Lombard with a knowledgeable source, Bangui, June 2003.

84 Interview by Louisa Lombard with Marc-André Cahlik, owner, transportation company, Bangui, 27 June 2003.

85 Author interview with police superintendent Yves-Valentine Gbeyoro, Director, OCRB, Bangui, 19 December 2003.

86 Author interview with Controller General Louis Mazangue, Director, OCRB, Ministry of the Interior, Government of CAR, Bangui, 18 February 2003.

87 Author interview with police superintendent Yves-Valentin Gbeyoro, Director, OCRB, Ministry of the Interior, Government of CAR, Bangui, 27 June 2003.

88 Author interview with Guy Guernas, Associate Protection Officer, UNHCR, Bangui, 14 February 2003.

89 Author interview with Col. Jules Bernard Ouandé, Minister Delegate, head of security and disarmament, Ministry of the Interior, Government of CAR, Bangui, 20 December 2003.

90 Author interview with Olivier Feneteau, Technical Advisor, Zones Cynégétiques Villageoises component, CAR Office, ECOFAC, Paris, 2 September 2003.

91 Author interview with Alain Penelon, head, Ngotto Forest component, CAR Office, ECOFAC, Bangui, 19 December 2003.

92 'Taux de Recompense' courtesy of PNDR, Bangui, February 2003. The figures are based on an average value of the CFA Franc of 609.33 for July, August, and September 1997, the period when the vast majority of weapons were turned in.

93 The figures in the document are supplied as percentages of the weapons seized from Kassaï barracks, provided in previous Security Council documents (UNSC, 1998a, p. 7).

94 A resumption of hostilities in late June resulted in some 500 deaths and 70,000 internally displaced persons (US DOS, 1998).

95 For example, Secretary-General Annan wrote in 2001 that, '[t]o date, 95 per cent of the heavy weapons that have been in circulation since the mutinies of 1996 and 1997 have been recovered, compared with 65 per cent of light weapons' (UNSC, 2001, para. 23).

96 Author interview with General (ret.) Mouhammad Hachim Ratanga, Libreville, 19 June 2003.

97 Author interview with General (ret.) Mouhammad Hachim Ratanga, Libreville, 19 June 2003.

98 Author interview with Jean-Jacques Demafouth, former Minister of Defence, Government of CAR, Geneva, 8 April 2003.

99 Author interview with knowledgeable source, Bangui, December 2003.

100 Author interviews with knowledgeable sources, Bangui. February, June, and December 2003.

101 Author interview with Harouna Dan Malam, Chief Technical Assistant, PNDR, United Nations Office for Project Services (UNOPS), Bangui, 15 December 2003. The PNDR had previously reported that, as of October 2002, 826 individuals had taken part in the programme (UNDP, 2003a, p. 4) The reason for the discrepancy is not clear, but it may be that records were lost during the October 2002 coup attempt.

102 Author interview with Harouna Dan Malam, Chief Technical Assistant, PNDR, UNOPS, Bangui, 15 December 2003.

103 Written correspondence with Fabrice Boussalem, Recovery Specialist, Bureau for Crisis Prevention and Recovery, UNDP, 15 January 2004.

BIBLIOGRAPHY

Amnesty International. 2004. 'Central African Republic: Five Months of War Against Women.' AFR 19/001/2004. 10 November. Accessed 7 April 2005. <http://web.amnesty.org/library/Index/ENGAFR190012004?open&of=ENG-CAF>

BBC (British Broadcasting Corporation). 2005. 'Timeline: Central African Republic.' *BBC News.* 22 March. Accessed 5 April 2005. <http://news.bbc.co.uk/1/hi/world/africa/country_profiles/1067615.stm>

Beit-Hallahmi, Benjamin. 1987. *The Israeli Connection: Who Israel Arms and Why.* New York: Pantheon Books.

Blom, Allard and Jean Yamindou. 2001. 'A Brief History of Armed Conflict and its Impact on Biodiversity in the Central African Republic.' Washington, DC: Biodiversity Support Program.

Buijtenhuijs, Robert. 1998. 'Chad in the age of the warlords.' In David Birmingham and Phyllis M. Martin, eds. *History of Central Africa: the Contemporary Years since 1960.* New York: Addison Wesley Longman, pp. 21–40.

Bureau of Democracy, Human Rights, and Labor. *Central African Republic Country Report on Human Rights Practices for 1998.* Washington, DC: Bureau of Democracy, Human Rights, and Labor, US Department of State. 26 February. Accessed 8 June 2003. <http://www.state.gov/www/global/human_rights/1998_hrp_report/car.html>

CAR (Government of the Central African Republic). 2003. 'Lettre de Politique Générale du Gouvernement en matière de Défense Globale, du processus de Désarmement, de Démobilisation et de Réinsertion (DDR) en particulier.' For the attention of James D. Wolfensohn, President of the World Bank Group. Bangui: Ministère de la Défense Nationale, de la Restructuration de l'Armée et du Désarmement. 5 November.

CTD (Comité technique de désarmement). 2002. 'Situation des armes-munitions-explosifs-matériels militaires et effets divers, ramassés par le CTD (du 23 janvier au 31 mai 2002): Proposées à la destruction.' Bangui: CTD. June.

Decalo, Samuel. 1989. *Psychoses of Power: African Personal Dictatorships.* Boulder, CO: Westview Press.

Faltas, Sami. 2000. 'Mutiny and Disarmament in the Central African Republic.' In Sami Faltas and Joseph Di Chiaro, III, eds. *Managing the Remnants of War: Micro-disarmament as an Element of Peace-building.* Baden-Baden: Nomos, pp. 77–96.

Foltz, William J. 1995. 'Reconstructing the State of Chad.' In I. William Zartman, ed. *Collapsed States: The Disintegration and Restoration of Legitimate Authority.* Boulder, CO: Lynne Rienner, pp. 15–31.

Frères d'Armes. 2000. 'Dossier RCA.' No. 226. Paris. Ministère des Affaires étrangères/Direction de la Coopération Militaire et de Défense, pp. 15–36.

—. 2002. 'Reprise du partenariat gendarmerie en RCA.' No. 237. Paris: Ministère des Affaires étrangères/Direction de la Coopération Militaire et de Défense, p. 40.

Fundación CIDOB (Centro de investigación, docencia, documentación y divulgación de Relaciones Internacionales y Desarrollo). 2001a. 'François Bozizé, República Centroafricana.' Biografías de Líderes Políticos CIDOB. Barcelona. Accessed 4 April 2005. <http://www.cidob.org/bios/castellano/lideres/b-009.htm>

—. 2001b. 'Ange-Félix Patassé, República Centroafricana.' Biografías de Líderes Políticos CIDOB. Barcelona. Accessed 4 April 2005. <http://www.cidob.org/bios/castellano/lideres/p-019.htm>

Jones, Lucy. 2001. 'France accused over CAR coup attempt.' *BBC News Online.* 18 June. Accessed 5 August 2003. <http://news.bbc.co.uk/2/hi/africa/1394392.stm>

—. 2002. 'Sudan's forgotten refugees.' *BBC News Online.* 28 March. Accessed 6 April 2005. <http://news.bbc.co.uk/1/hi/world/africa/1893179.stm>

Kalck, Pierre. 1992. *Historical Dictionary of the Central African Republic,* 2nd ed. Translated by Thomas O'Toole. Metuchen, NJ, and London: Scarecrow Press.

Klieman, Aaron S. 1985. *Israel's Global Reach: Arms Sales as Diplomacy.* Washington, DC: Pergamon–Brassey's Publishers Inc.

Leaba, Oscar (pseudonym). 2001. 'La crise centrafricaine de l'été 2001.' *Politique africaine.* No. 84, pp. 163–75. December.

Lemarchand, René. 1985. 'The Crisis in Chad.' In Gerald J. Bender, James S. Coleman, and Richard S. Sklar, eds. *African Crisis Areas and U.S. Foreign Policy.* Berkeley, CA: University of California Press, pp. 239–56.

Lowy, Joan. 2002. 'Some conservationists fighting back—with guns.' *Scripps Howard News Service.* 17 December. Accessed 11 August 2003. <http://www.knoxstudio.com/shns/story.cfm?pk=GREENWARRIORS-12-17-02&cat=II>

McFarlane, Fiona, and Mark Malan. 1998. 'Crisis and Response in the Central African Republic: A New Trend in African Peacekeeping?' *African Security Review.* Vol. 7, No. 2. pp. 48–58.

Mogba, Zéphirin and Mark Freudenberger. 1998. 'Human Migration in the Protected Zones of Central Africa: The Case of the Dzanga-Sangha Special Reserve.' In Heather E. Eves, Rebecca Hardin, and Stephanie Rupp, eds. *Resource Use in the Trinational Sangha River Region of Equatorial Africa: Histories, Knowledge Forms, and Institutions.* Yale School of Forestry and Environmental Studies, Bulletin Series, No. 102, pp. 59–97.

Moose, George E. 1985. 'French Military Policy in Africa.' In William J. Foltz and Henry S. Bienen, eds. *Arms and the African: Military Influences on Africa's International Relations.* New Haven, CT: Yale University Press, pp. 59–97.

O'Toole, Thomas. 1986. *The Central African Republic: The Continent's Hidden Heart.* Boulder, CO: Westview Press.

PNDR (Programme national de désarmement et de réinsertion). 2003a. 'Dossier de destruction des armes, munitions et accessories militaires.' Bangui: PNDR. May.

—. 2003b. 'Rapport d'évaluation de la deuxième cérémonie d'incinération des armes, munitions et explosifs organisée au PK 55, route de Mbaïki: vendredi 25 juillet 2003.' Bangui: PNDR. September.

Sangonet. 2005. 'Le général François BOZIZE se déclare enfin candidat à la présidentielle 2005.' Actualité Centrafrique de sangonet—spéciale élections 2005. Accessed 5 April 2005. <http://www.sangonet.com/actu-snews/ICAR/Dsp/Boz-Cpt05/Bozize_candidat-pt2005.html>

SHAT (Service Historique d'Armée de terre). 1963. 'Forces Armées—Force Publiques—et Jeunesse Pionnier Nationale de la République Centre-Africaine.' (Coded Secret. Courtesy of Service Historique d'Armée de Terre.) Paris: Ministère de la Défense. 20 October.

Small Arms Survey. 2003. *Small Arms Survey 2003: Development Denied.* Oxford: Oxford University Press.

Tartter, Jean R. 1990. 'National Security.' In Thomas Collelo, ed. *Chad: a Country Study.* Washington, DC: Federal Research Division Library of Congress, pp. 194–95.

Telegraph. 2003. 'David Dacko.' 22 November. Accessed 5 April 2005. <http://www.telegraph.co.uk/news/main.jhtml?xml=/news/2003/11/22/db2203.xml>

UNDP (United Nations Development Programme). 2003a. 'Synthèse du rapport annuel d'activités du P.N.D.R (janvier à décembre 2002)'. Bangui: UNDP. 14 January.

—. 2003b. 'Note sur les activités de désarmement, démobilisation et reconversion (DDR) en République Centrafricaine.' Bangui : UNDP. February.

UNHCR (United Nations High Commissioner for Refugees). 2001a. 'Transfer of former Central African Republic soldiers completed; civilians to be moved to new camp.' *UNHCR News.* 20 November. Accessed 5 April 2005. <http://www.unhcr.ch/cgi-bin/texis/vtx/news/opendoc.htm?tbl=NEWS&id=3bfa7d5c4&page=news>

—. 2001b. 'Central African Republic refugees turn down call from their country's president to return home.' *UNHCR News.* 5 December. Accessed 5 April 2005. <http://www.unhcr.ch/cgi-bin/texis/vtx/news/opendoc.htm?tbl=NEWS&id=3c0e32570&page=news>

UN OCHA (United Nations Office for the Coordination of Humanitarian Affairs). 2001. 'Central African Republic: FLC Leader Arrested after Troops Ran Wild in Bangui.' *IRIN News.* 18 July. Accessed 25 April 2005. <http://www.irinnews.org/print.asp?ReportID=9738>

—. 2002a. 'Great Lakes: Abdoulaye Miskine flown to Togo.' *IRIN News.* 5 November. Accessed 9 September 2003. <http://www.irinnews.org/print.asp?ReportID=30769>

—. 2002b. 'Central African Republic: Mine Clearance Under Way.' *IRIN News.* 12 November. Accessed 26 April 2005. <http://www.irinnews.org/print.asp?ReportID=30874>

—. 2002c. 'Central African Republic: Regional Peace Force Begins Patrolling Bangui Streets.' *IRIN News.* 30 December. Accessed 25 April 2005. <http://www.irinnews.org/print.asp?ReportID=31520>

—. 2003a 'Central African Republic: Chadian troops recover 1,300 firearms in Bangui.' *IRIN News.* 25 March. Accessed 1 April 2005. <http://www.irinnews.org/print.asp?ReportID=33044>

—. 2003b. 'Flash Appeal for Humanitarian Assistance to the Central African Republic.' 8 May. Accessed 6 April 2005.
<http://www.reliefweb.int/appeals/2003/files/car03.pdf>

—. 2003c. 'Focus on the Impact of War on Herdsmen.' *IRIN News*. 26 November. Accessed 8 August 2004.
<http://www.irinnews.org/report.asp?ReportID=38096&SelectRegion=Great_Lakes>

—. 2003d. 'Central African Republic: Special report on the disarmament, demobilization, reintegration of ex-fighters.' 8 December.
Accessed 6 April 2005. <http://www.irinnews.org/S_report.asp?ReportID=38283&SelectRegion=Great_Lakes>

—. 2005. 'Central African Republic: Post-election focus—a country in crisis or recovery?' 18 March. Accessed 8 April 2005.
<http://www.irinnews.org/report.asp?ReportID=46184&SelectRegion=Great_Lakes>

United Nations Security Council (UNSC). 1997. *Letter Dated 16 September 1997 from the Secretary-General Addressed to the President of the Security Council [containing] Enclosure: Third report to the Security Council pursuant to resolution 1125 (1997) concerning the situation in the Central African Republic), 15 September 1997. S/1997/716 of 16 September 1997.*

—. 1997. *Letter Dated 14 October 1997 from the Secretary-General Addressed to the President of the Security Council [containing] Enclosure: Fifth report to the Security Council pursuant to resolution 1125 (1997) concerning the situation in the Central African Republic (13 October 1997). S/1997/795 of 14 October 1997.*

—. 1998a. *Letter Dated 2 January 1998 from the Secretary-General Addressed to the President of the Security Council [containing] Appendix: Second Report to the Security Council pursuant to resolution 1136 (1997) concerning the situation in the Central African Republic (2 January 1998). S/1998/3 of 5 January 1998.*

—. 1998b. *Letter Dated 11 March 1998 from the Secretary-General Addressed to the President of the Security Council [containing] Appendix: Report to the Security Council pursuant to resolution 1152 (1998) concerning the situation in the Central African Republic (10 March 1998). S/1998/221 of 12 March 1998.*

—. 1998c. Resolution 1159, adopted 27 March. S/RES/1159 (1998).

—. 1999a. *Seventh Report of the Secretary-General on the United Nations Mission in the Central African Republic. S/1999/788 of 15 July 1999.*

—. 1999b. *Eighth Report of the Secretary-General on the United Nations Mission in the Central African Republic. S/1999/1038 of 7 October 1999.*

—. 2000. *Ninth Report of the Secretary-General on the United Nations Mission in the Central African Republic (MINURCA). S/2000/24 of 14 January 2000.*

—. 2001. *Report of the Secretary-General on the situation in the Central African Republic and on the activities of the United Nations Peace-building Support Office in the Central African Republic. S/2001/35 of 11 January 2001.* Accessed 7 April 2005.
<http://daccessdds.un.org/doc/UNDOC/GEN/N01/208/40/PDF/N0120840.pdf?OpenElement>

USDOS (United States Department of State). 1998. 'Central African Republic Country Report on Human Rights Practices for 1997.' 30 January.
Accessed 7 April 2005. <http://www.state.gov/www/global/human_rights/1997_hrp_report/car.html>

World Bank. 2003. 'Chad: Demobilization and Reintegration Pilot Program—Structural Adjustment Credit.' New York: World Bank,
Disability Project Directory. Accessed 24 February 2003. <http://wbln0018.worldbank.org/HDNet/hddocs.nsf>

ACKNOWLEDGEMENTS

Principal author
Eric G. Berman

Other contributors
Nicolas Florquin and Louisa Lombard

Index